The New Charismatic Bible

The New Testament

New Dawn Publishing

Randal Cutter, Editor

The New Charismatic Bible, New Testament

Copyright © 2024 Randal Cutter

All rights reserved worldwide.

ISBN: 0990904755

ISBN-13: 978-0-9909047-5-5

The "New Charismatic Bible, the New Testament" text may be quoted in any form (written, visual, electronic or audio), up to and inclusive of two hundred (200) verses without the express written permission of the publisher, providing the verses quoted do not amount to a complete book of the Bible nor do the verses quoted account for twenty-five percent (25%) or more of the total text of the work in which they are quoted. For such uses, notice of copyright must appear on the title or copyright page as follows:

Scripture quotations taken from the New Charismatic Bible, the New Testament Copyright © 2024 by Randal Cutter. Used with permission. All rights reserved worldwide.

When quotations from the New Charismatic Bible, the New Testament text are used by a local church in non- saleable media such as church bulletins, orders of service, posters, overhead transparencies, or similar materials, a complete copyright notice is not required, however the title, "New Charismatic Bible, the New Testament," or its abbreviation, "TNCB," must appear at the end of each quotation.

Permission requests that exceed the above General Use Guidelines must be directed to and approved in writing by New Dawn Publishing, 9955 NW 31st Street, Coral Springs FL 33065, USA.

Cover Logo: salmanbehram © 123rf.com Used with permission under extended license.

Please report typographical errors to: NDP@NewDawn.org

Distributed by: New Dawn Publishing
9955 NW 31st Street
Coral Springs, FL 33065
www.newdawn.org

Books of the New Testament

Matthew	1
Mark	89
Luke	146
John	239
Acts	308
Romans	389
1 Corinthians	426
2 Corinthians	460
Galatians	482
Ephesians	494
Philippians	505
Colossians	513
1 Thessalonians	521
2 Thessalonians	528
1 Timothy	533
2 Timothy	543
Titus	550
Philemon	554
Hebrews	556
James	583
1 Peter	592
2 Peter	602
1 John	608
2 John	617
3 John	619
Jude	621
Revelation	624

Preface

While there are many good Bible translations available to us today, there is certainly a need for one such as this. Those who began to translate the Bible from its original languages into English, for the most part had limited or no experience of the Holy Spirit in their lives. This is not a criticism. The work they did in their translations is amazing, and their understanding has stood the test of time.

However, as the Lord has used their efforts to inform his people, the Holy Spirit has poured out in various and sundry ways throughout history since then. We now have far more experience of the Holy Spirit, and thus better understanding of what is being described in biblical passages about human response to the presence of the Holy Spirit. If we have walked in these experiences, we can better understand those references, and translate them in such a way that recaptures what the readers of the original language intuitively understood.

Two references from the New Testament will help capture the difference in understanding. While most versions translate Mark 3:21 in a way that makes it appear that Jesus' relatives were accusing him and his disciples of being out of their minds, and thus not able to care for themselves. However, the Greek behind that verse uses a word that doesn't speak about state of mind, but of a spiritual experience. In this version, it is translated,

> "When his relatives heard about this, they set out to take control of him; for they agreed that he was overcome by an ecstatic spiritual experience."

The second reference is from Mark 16:8, which describes how the woman left the tomb after the angels told them that Jesus had been raised. It has often been translated in a rather enigmatic way, as if the women were confused and afraid to speak. However, again, the Greek behind the verse uses words that describe an overwhelming spiritual experience, rather than muddled thinking or fear. In this version it is translated,

> "They went out from the tomb and ran away, for trembling and spiritual ecstasy had overwhelmed them. They said nothing to anyone because they were filled with awe."

These are snapshots of how the people of God respond to the presence of the Spirit of God. Because they have not been translated by people who have some understanding of what happens when the Holy Spirit is moving, we have lost the language to express such activities, and thus we often relegate those experiences to the realms of the unknown and the feared.

This translation is intended to begin to remedy that loss. One of its main purposes is to restore to the people of God the language necessary to inform the people of God of how the Spirit moves.

Since this is a translation, it is not creating new concepts. It is simply uncovering the concepts that are already in the original languages, but have been lost because of a lack of familiarity about what has been described.

In this way, the New Charismatic Bible, and this volume, the New Charismatic New Testament, are intended to help the body of Christ recover a culture and language for the times in which we live. These are times when the Holy Spirit is moving in amazing ways, and this version will help us see just how what he is doing today relates to New Testament times.

Introduction

Philosophy of Translation

Whenever one translates a portion of the Bible, it is important to describe the philosophy of translation that is used. This is especially important in an era where new versions of the Bible are being published that call themselves translations, even when they are most definitely anything but a translation. Translations, by definition, give the meaning of the original language, not the meaning of a supposed Aramaic original, or the translator's opinions about a particular text. Translations must translate the plain meaning of the original language.

Translators accomplish this type of translation in two basic ways. The most accurate translations use a word-for-word approach in their methods. The King James Version is an example of this approach. The problem with word-for-word translations is that they are often more difficult to read because of differences between the English language and ancient languages. Of course, word-for-word does not imply that the translation doesn't recognize idioms in the original language. Idioms often must be translated apart from the plain meaning of the original words in order to be understood. Imagine trying to translate such common English idioms as "Cat got your tongue?" or "Let the cat out of the bag" into another language using only the plain words. In one instance, the reader might wince in horror and pain over the idea of a feline attacking the human tongue; in the other the reader might also wince, but this time in horror at the idea that the cat needed to be freed because someone was so cruel as to place a cat in a bag. In order to accurately translate those idioms into another language, the translator must say something like, "Why are you so quiet?" or that someone is "revealing a secret."

Translators have also used a second approach, a thought-for-thought translation. This approach allows the translators to make the version more readable by translating each thought conveyed in the original. While in many instances they are able to achieve this with an almost word-for-word approach, in far more instances they must transition to a thought-for-thought approach in order to maintain a consistent style of readability. As a result, in some instances the thought-for-thought approach can be less accurate, or more open to the translator's theological opinions. This approach also allows the translators to change the gender of the original text. More recent versions of some thought-for-thought versions have changed words such as fathers to parents, or brothers to brothers and sisters. Their rational is simply that the target audience wasn't only the male audience, but included females, so they believe it is legitimate to make such changes. Those of us who much prefer the word-for-word approach become very uncomfortable about an approach that adds or changes the original words in such a drastic fashion. Even with this discomfort, there is no doubt that we have excellent thought-for-thought translations that are reliable and beneficial for those who use them, and we can use them for our devotional reading with a level of confidence.

Of course, there is another category of Bibles often labeled translations, but they are not. They are paraphrases. Paraphrases may work with the original languages, or they may not. Their goal is to capture the original meaning of the text—as they see it—and communicate that in a way that is easily readable. By their very nature they can be useful for devotional reading, but not for serious biblical study.

Of late, we have seen the rise of paraphrases that call themselves translations. Since they do not faithfully translate from the original language, but rather paraphrase it or another version, they should not be called translations. A true translation is a word for word or thought for thought version created from the original languages. Bible students should be aware of the difference.

This translation of the New Testament is a word-for-word translation which attempts to account for almost every word in the Greek text. In some cases, that will be very apparent—note the many times in this translation where a sentence starts out, "Jesus responded and said." In a thought-for-thought translation one would simply translate, "Jesus said." In a word-for-word translation, the reader will see the entire phrase repeated every time it is used because the translator is attempting to account for every word used in the text of the original language.

Another example in this version is the common Greek expression *idou* (ἰδού). It has often been translated as "Behold," or "Lo." Thought-for-thought translations often simply drop this word from the translation. In this word-for-word translation the word *idou* is translated, but it is translated in a variety of different ways that attempts to match the purpose of the word in its context. So the reader will see such words as *significantly*, *notably*, *look*, and other ways of translating it that bring freshness to the text, and contextual faithfulness to the purpose that *idou* plays in the text.

Of course, there are phrases and word uses in the New Testament that are almost impossible to understand in a word-for-word translation. In those cases, the translator has no option but to depend on the thought-for-thought translation method in order to assure readability.

Other Items to Note

This translation has attempted to be as faithful as possible to the Greek text of the Bible. For that reason, the reader will note some changes to the way that certain words are translated. A few examples follow.

The Heavens: While most translations will translate this plural expression as a singular, this version retains the plural whenever it shows up (i.e. The Kingdom of the Heavens). The rationale for this is simple, in 2 Corinthians 12 the apostle Paul speaks of the third heaven. In the minds of those who lived at Paul's time there were three heavenly realms consisting of the realm in which humans live, the realm in which evil spiritual forces reside, and the realm in which God resides. Since this is the case, there is benefit in capturing the difference between the singular and the plural in a translation. It will demonstrate a bit more about what the author was thinking as he used the expression.

Scribal Scholars: While most translations translate the Greek word as "scribes," this translation calls them "scribal scholars" to emphasize how they were viewed in Jesus' day. They did not just copy the Scriptures, they were viewed as scholars in their own right.

Ecstatic Spiritual Experiences: While most translation will simply translate the Greek words behind this expression as "amazed," or "astounded"—and certainly in some instances that is the correct translation—there are also many instances where the word refers to spiritual experiences caused by an outpouring of the Holy Spirit or his power. This translation has footnoted those times to highlight the importance of these expressions.

Weights, Measures, and Monetary Value: When the Bible uses a reference to distance or other measures, or a particular currency, many translations put the equivalent value for our culture right into the text. However, in some cases the Holy Spirit may be highlighting the actual numerical value of the measure or currency to the reader. For that reason, this translation usually gives the actual numerical value of the item in the Greek, along with its Greek name, and what that means for modern readers in the footnote.

Italicized Words in the Body of the Text: In some instances, the context demands an addition of a word or phrase that is not in the text. In those instances, the words are italicized in the body of the text to alert the reader.

MATTHEW

The Genealogy of Jesus

Chapter One

¹The account of the origin of Jesus Christ, son of David, son of Abraham:

²Abraham fathered Isaac, Isaac fathered Jacob, Jacob fathered Judah and his brothers,
³Judah fathered Perez and Zerah by Tamar, Perez fathered Hezron, Hezron fathered Ram,
⁴Ram fathered Amminadab, Amminadab fathered Nahshon, Nahshon fathered Salmon,
⁵Salmon fathered Boaz by Rahab, Boaz fathered Obed by Ruth, Obed fathered Jesse,
⁶and Jesse fathered David the king. David fathered Solomon by the wife of Uriah,
⁷Solomon fathered Rehoboam, Rehoboam fathered Abijah, Abijah fathered Asa,
⁸Asa fathered Jehoshaphat, Jehoshaphat fathered Joram, Joram fathered Uzziah,
⁹Uzziah fathered Jotham, Jotham fathered Ahaz, Ahaz fathered Hezekiah,

¹⁰Hezekiah fathered Manasseh, Manasseh fathered Amon, Amon fathered Josiah,

¹¹Josiah fathered Jeconiah and his brothers at the time they were resettled in Babylon.

¹²After they resettled in Babylon, Jeconiah fathered Shealtiel, Shealtiel fathered Zerubbabel,

¹³Zerubbabel fathered Abihud, Abihud fathered Eliakim, Eliakim fathered Azor,

¹⁴Azor fathered Zadok, Zadok fathered Achim, Achim fathered Eliud,

¹⁵Eliud fathered Eleazar, Eleazar fathered Matthan, Matthan fathered Jacob,

¹⁶Jacob fathered Joseph the husband of Mary, by whom Jesus was born, the one called Christ.

¹⁷So all the generations from Abraham to David are fourteen generations, and from David to the resettlement in Babylon were fourteen generations, and from the resettlement in Babylon to the Christ were fourteen generations.

Joseph Receives Revelation

¹⁸The birth of Jesus Christ happened this way: His mother, Mary, was engaged to Joseph; but before they were intimate, she was found to be carrying a child through the Holy Spirit. ¹⁹Since Joseph, her husband, was a righteous man, and did not wish to expose her publicly, he decided to divorce her privately. ²⁰But when he considered these things, unexpectedly, an angel of the Lord appeared to him in a dream and said, "Joseph, son of David, do not be afraid to accept Mary as your wife. For the child she has conceived is from the Holy Spirit. ²¹She will give birth to a son, and you will give him the name, Jesus; for he will save his people from their sins. ²²All this has taken place to fulfill what was spoken by the Lord through the prophet saying, ²³'Take note! The virgin will be pregnant and will bear a son, and they will call his name Immanuel'[i] " (which means, "God with us").

---

[i] Isaiah 7:14

24When Joseph woke up from his sleep, he did as the angel of the Lord commanded him, and he accepted Mary as his wife. 25But he did not have intimacy with her until after she bore a son; and they called his name Jesus.

The Magi Respond to a Sign

Chapter Two

1After Jesus was born in Bethlehem of Judea, in the days of Herod the king, notably, Magi from the east came to Jerusalem 2asking, "Where is the one who has been born king of the Jews? For we saw his star when it rose,[ii] and we have come to worship him."

3But when Herod the king heard it, he was troubled, and all Jerusalem with him. 4When he had gathered all the chief priests and scribal scholars of the people, he subjected them to an examination about where the Christ would be born. 5Then they explained to him, "In Bethlehem of Judea, for so it is written through the prophet,

> 6" 'And you Bethlehem of the region of Judea,
>   you are by no means the least among the princes of Judea, for from you will come a prince who will shepherd my people, Israel.' "[iii]

7Then, when Herod had secretly summoned the Magi, he ascertained from them the exact time the star started to shine. 8He sent them to Bethlehem and said, "Go and carefully find out about the child. Then, when you have found out, report to me so that I also may come and worship him."

9When they had heard the king, they journeyed on. Suddenly, the star which they had seen when it rose, led them until it stood over the place where the child was. 10When they

---

[ii] Traditionally, "in the east." Also verse 9. Since the sun rises in the east, the expression also came to mean, "east."

[iii] Micah 5:2

saw the star, they rejoiced with overwhelming joy. [11]When they came into the house, they saw the child with Mary his mother, and they fell down and worshiped him. Then they opened their treasures and brought him gifts of gold, incense, and myrrh. [12]Because they were warned in a dream not to return to Herod, they went back to their own country by a different route.

An Angelic Warning

[13]When they had departed, unexpectedly, an angel of the Lord appeared to Joseph in a dream and said, "Get up, take the child and his mother, flee to Egypt, and stay there until I tell you. For Herod is about to seek the child to kill him."

[14]So, when he got up, he took the child and his mother at night, and left for Egypt. [15]He was there until the death of Herod, so that the word given by the Lord through the prophet might be fulfilled that said, "From Egypt I called my son."[i]

[16]Then Herod, when he saw that he had been tricked by the Magi, was very angry. He sent and killed all the male children two years old and under in Bethlehem and in all the region around it, according to the time which he had ascertained from the Magi. [17]Then the word was fulfilled spoken through Jeremiah the prophet:

> [18]"A voice was heard in Ramah, weeping and much mourning, Rachel weeping for her children, and she was not willing to be comforted because they are no more."[ii]

Joseph Responds to a Second Dream

[19]But when Herod had died, note this, an angel of the Lord appeared in a dream to Joseph in Egypt [20]and said, "Get up, take the child and his mother and go to the land of Israel. For the ones seeking the life of the child have died."

---

[i] Hosea 11:1

[ii] Jeremiah 31:15

21Then he got up and took the child and his mother and returned to Israel. 22But when Joseph heard that Archelaus reigned over Judea instead of his father Herod, he was afraid to go there. Then, when he had received direction in a dream, he left for the regions of Galilee. 23When he arrived, he settled in a city called Nazareth. Thus, the word given through the prophets was fulfilled that he would be called a Nazarene.

The Baptizer Steps into His Prophetic Purpose

Chapter Three

1Then in those days John the Baptizer[iii] appeared preaching in the desert of Judea. 2He was proclaiming, "Repent, for the Kingdom of the Heavens has drawn near." 3For this is the one spoken about by Isaiah the prophet when he said,

> "A voice calling out in the desert:
> 'Prepare the way of the Lord.
> Make his path straight.'"[iv]

4John himself had clothing of camel's hair, and a wide leather belt around his waist. His food was locusts and honey from the fields. 5Then Jerusalem, all Judea, and all the country of the Jordan began to go out to him, 6and they were baptized by him in the Jordan River as they confessed their sins.

7But when he observed many of the Pharisees and Sadducees coming to his baptism, he said to them, "You children of venomous snakes, who told you to flee from the punishment[v] to come?

8"So then, produce fruit worthy of repentance. 9Do not think to say among yourselves, 'We have father Abraham.' For I tell you that God is able to raise up children to Abraham from these stones. 10But already the ax is resting on the root of the trees. So,

---

[iii] Traditionally, "Baptist," The word describes action; so "Baptizer" here.

[iv] Isaiah 40:3

[v] Traditionally, "wrath."

every tree that does not bear good fruit is cut down and thrown into the fire.

¹¹"I, for my part, am baptizing you in water for repentance, but one who is coming after me is greater than I am. I am not worthy to carry his sandals. He will baptize you in the Holy Spirit and fire. ¹²His winnowing fork is in his hand, and he will thoroughly clean the grain on his threshing floor. He will gather his wheat into his barn, but he will burn the chaff with unquenchable fire."

The Spirit of God Empowers Jesus at His Baptism

¹³Then Jesus came to the Jordan from Galilee to John to be baptized by him. ¹⁴But John tried to stop him and said, "I am the one who needs to be baptized by you, and you come to me?"

¹⁵But Jesus responded and said to him, "Allow it this time. For it is appropriate for us, in this way, to do everything right." Then he allowed it.

¹⁶After Jesus was baptized, he immediately came up out of the water. Incredibly, the heavens opened for him, and he saw the Spirit of God descending in the form of a dove and land upon him. ¹⁷Even more incredibly, a voice from the heavens said, "This is my cherished Son, in whom I am well pleased."

The Testing of Jesus

Chapter Four

¹Then Jesus was led up by the Spirit into the wilderness to be tempted by the Accuser.[i] ²When he had fasted forty days and nights, he was hungry at the end of it. ³The tempter came and said to him, "Since[ii] you are the Son of God, speak so that these stones become bread."

---

[i] Traditionally, "devil." The name means to slander or accuse. For this reason, this word is most often translated "Accuser" in this Bible version.

[ii] Or, traditionally, "if."

⁴But he answered and said, "It is written, 'Man will not live on bread alone, but upon every word[iii] spoken from the mouth of God.'"

⁵Then the Accuser took him to the holy city and put him on the pinnacle of the temple ⁶and said to him, "Since you are the Son of God, throw yourself down, for it is written,

> " 'He will command his angels concerning you,
>   and they will lift you up in their hands so
>   that you do not strike your foot against a
>   stone.' "[iv]

⁷But Jesus said to him, "Again it is written, 'Do not test the Lord your God.' "[v]

⁸Once more, the Accuser took him away to a very high mountain and showed him all the kingdoms of the earth and their glory. ⁹He said to him, "I will give you all these things if you fall prostrate and worship me."

¹⁰Jesus said to him, "Go away, Satan![vi] For it is written, 'Worship the Lord your God and venerate him alone.' "[vii]

¹¹Then the Accuser left him, and significantly, angels came and began to serve him.

Jesus Begins to Fulfill the Prophetic Scriptures

¹²When Jesus heard that John had been arrested, he withdrew to Galilee. ¹³Since he had left Nazareth, he came and lived in Capernaum by the sea in the regions of Zebulun and Naphtali, ¹⁴in order that what was spoken through Isaiah the prophet might be fulfilled that said,

---

[iii] See Deuteronomy 8:3. The Greek word used here often refers to God's supernatural provision, as the Hebrew does in the Deuteronomy passage.

[iv] Psalm 91:11-12

[v] Deuteronomy 6:16

[vi] The word "Satan" means adversary.

[vii] Deuteronomy 6:13

¹⁵"Land of Zebulon and land of Naphtali, road to the sea across the Jordan, Galilee of the Gentiles—¹⁶the people who reside in darkness have seen a great light; and upon those who inhabit the region and sit in the shadow of death, a light has dawned."[i]

¹⁷From that point, Jesus began to preach and say, "Repent, for the Kingdom of the Heavens has drawn near."

Jesus Begins to Build His Ministry Team

¹⁸While Jesus was walking beside the Sea of Galilee, he saw two brothers, Simon who was called Peter, and Andrew, his brother. They were casting a net into the sea, for they were fishermen. ¹⁹He said to them, "Come follow me, and I will appoint you as fishermen who catch men." ²⁰Then they immediately left their nets and followed him.

²¹When he went on from there, he saw two other brothers, James[ii] son of Zebedee and John, his brother. They were in the boat with their father, Zebedee, mending their nets. He called them ²²and they immediately left the boat and their father and followed him.

Jesus Preaches the Gospel of the Kingdom and Demonstrates It

²³Jesus went through all of Galilee teaching in their synagogues, preaching the good news[iii] of the Kingdom, and healing every disease and every sickness among the people. ²⁴The report about him went out into all of Syria, and they brought everyone who was ill with various diseases and pains, those who were held captive by demons, those who suffered seizures, and the paralyzed; and he healed them. ²⁵Large crowds from Galilee,

---

[i] Isaiah 9:1-2

[ii] Greek text, "Jacob." James is the Anglicized form of Jacob used since the first English translations. Unless it refers to the patriarch Jacob, it is translated as James in this New Testament.

[iii] The Greek word can be translated "Gospel" or "Good News." The word gospel means good news. It is translated both ways in this Bible version.

the Decapolis, Jerusalem, Judea, and the Trans-Jordan followed him.

The Sermon on the Mount and the Beatitudes

Chapter Five

¹When Jesus saw the crowds, he went up a high hill. After he sat down, his disciples drew near to him. ²He opened his mouth and began to teach them saying,

³"Blessed are those who are spiritually poverty-stricken,
>   for theirs is the Kingdom of the Heavens.

⁴"Blessed are those who grieve,
>   for they will be encouraged.

⁵"Blessed are those who are gentle,
>   for they will inherit the earth.

⁶"Blessed are those who hunger and thirst for righteousness,
>   for they will have as much as they want.

⁷"Blessed are those who show mercy,
>   for they themselves will be shown mercy.

⁸"Blessed are those whose hearts are clean,
>   for they will see God.

⁹"Blessed are those who make peace,
>   for they will be named Sons of God.

¹⁰"Blessed are those who have been persecuted on behalf
>   of righteousness, for theirs is the Kingdom of the
>   Heavens.

¹¹"Blessed are you when they criticize you, persecute you, and falsely report every kind of evil against you because of me. ¹²Be glad and rejoice, for your reward is great in the heavens; for in the same way, they persecuted the prophets who came before you.

Matthew 5:13

Living as Salt and Light

¹³"You most certainly are the salt of the earth; but if the salt foolishly loses flavor, how will it become salty again? It is good for nothing except to be thrown out and trampled by men.

¹⁴"You most certainly are the light of the world; a city located on a hill cannot be hidden, ¹⁵nor do they light a lamp and place it under their grain measuring bowl. Rather they place it on a lampstand, and it shines for everyone in the house. ¹⁶In the same way, let your light shine in front of men, so that they see your noble works and glorify your Father who is in the heavens.

The Righteous Standards of the Kingdom

¹⁷"Do not think that I have come to do away with the Law or the Prophets, I have not come to do away with them, but to do them. ¹⁸For I tell you the truth, until the heaven and the earth pass away, not one iota or one stroke[i] will pass away from the Law, until everything has happened. ¹⁹Therefore, whoever does away with one of the least of these commands and teaches men to do the same will be called least in the Kingdom of the Heavens. But whoever does them and teaches them, this one will be called great in the Kingdom of the Heavens. ²⁰Indeed, I tell you that unless your righteousness greatly exceeds the scribal scholars and the Pharisees, you will most certainly not even enter the Kingdom of the Heavens.

The Place Where Murder Starts

²¹"You have heard that it was said to the ancients, 'Do not murder,' and 'Whoever commits murder will be liable to the legal consequence.' ²²But I say to you that everyone who is angry with his brother will be liable to the legal consequence, and whoever says to his brother, 'Rhaka,'[ii] will be liable to the

---

[i] The iota and the stroke are two of the smallest items in the Hebrew alphabet.

[ii] Rhaka was an Aramaic term of bitter contempt for someone.

Sanhedrin, but whoever says, 'Fool,' will be liable to the Gehenna[iii] of fire.

23"Therefore, if you are offering your gift at the altar, and there remember that your brother holds something against you, 24leave your gift there in front of the altar and go first and be reconciled with your brother. Then come and offer your gift.

25"Reach a settlement with your legal adversary quickly while you are with him on the road, lest your legal adversary deliver you to the judge, and the judge deliver you to the court officer, and you are put into prison. 26I tell you the truth, you will most certainly not get out from there until you have repaid the last quadrans.[iv]

The Place Where Adultery Starts

27"You have heard that it was said to the ancients, 'Do not commit adultery.'[v] 28But I say to you that everyone looking at a woman with sexual desire for her has already committed adultery with her in his heart. 29So, if your right eye causes you to stumble into sin, remove it and throw it from you; for it is better for you that you lose one of the parts of your body and not have your whole body thrown into Gehenna. 30Also, if your right hand causes you to stumble into sin, cut it off and throw it from you; for it is better for you that you lose one of the parts of your body and not have your whole body pass into Gehenna.

31"It has been said, 'Whoever divorces his wife must give her a certificate of divorce.'[vi] 32But I say to you that everyone who divorces his wife, except on the grounds of an illicit sexual relationship, forces her into adultery, and whoever marries this divorced woman commits adultery.

[iii] Gehenna refers a valley known as "the valley of the sons of Hinnom." It was a place of child sacrifice and gross impurity. It came to symbolize the place of eternal punishment. Also in verses 29 and 30.

[iv] A small copper coin worth about a 64th of a denarius.

[v] Exodus 20:14; Deuteronomy 5:18

[vi] See Deuteronomy 24:1.

The Place Where Lying Starts

³³"Again, you have heard that it was said to the ancients, 'Do not commit perjury, but fulfill your oaths sworn to the Lord.' ³⁴But I am telling you not to swear at all, neither by heaven, for it is the throne of God, ³⁵nor by the earth, for it is a footstool for his feet, nor to Jerusalem, for it is the city of the great king; ³⁶nor should you swear by your head, for you are not able to make one hair white or black. ³⁷But let your speech be, 'Yes, yes, no, no.' Anything beyond these is from the evil one.

Living as Kingdom People

³⁸"You have heard that it was said, 'An eye for an eye and a tooth for a tooth.' ³⁹But I say to you, do not oppose an evil one, rather, whoever slaps you on the right cheek, also turn the other to him. ⁴⁰Also, the one who desires to bring a judgment against you in order to take your inner garment, give him also your outer garment; ⁴¹whoever wants to press you into service for one mile,[i] go with him two. ⁴²Give to the one who asks you, and do not turn away from the one who wants to borrow from you.

⁴³"You have heard that it was said, 'Love your neighbor and hate your enemy.' ⁴⁴But I say to you, bless those who curse you, do good to those who hate you, love your enemies and pray on behalf of those who mistreat you and persecute you, ⁴⁵so that you might be sons of your Father who is in heaven; for he causes his sun to shine upon the evil people and the good people, and the rain to fall upon the righteous and the unrighteous.

⁴⁶"For if you love the ones who love you, what reward do you have? Do not the tax collectors do this same thing? ⁴⁷And if you greet only your brothers, what is special about what you are doing? Do not the Gentiles[ii] do the same?

---

[i] Roman soldiers were able to force (press) civilians to carry things for them up to a mile.

[ii] Some manuscripts, "tax collectors."

⁴⁸"Therefore, all of you be perfect just as your heavenly Father is perfect.

Keeping Righteous Acts Hidden: Charitable Giving and Prayer
Chapter Six
¹"Watch carefully so that you do not practice your righteous observances in front of men, to be seen by them. If you do, you will not receive a reward from your Father who is in the heavens.

²"Therefore, when you give charitable gifts to the poor, do not have a trumpet blown in front of you, as the hypocrites do in the synagogues and in the streets so that they might be honored by men. I tell you the truth; they have received their reward. ³But when you give charitable gifts to the poor, do not let your left hand know what your right hand is doing ⁴so that your charitable giving might be done in secret. Then your Father, who sees into what is hidden, will pay you back.

⁵"Also, when you pray, do not be like the hypocrites; for they love to take their stand in the synagogues and on the street corners to pray so that they might shine in front of men. I tell you the truth, they have received their reward. ⁶But when you pray, go into your personal room and close the door to pray to your Father who is in a hidden place. Then your Father who sees into what is hidden, will pay you back.

⁷"When you pray, do not babble on and on like the Gentiles, for they think that they will be heard because of their verbosity. ⁸So, do not be like them, for your Father knows what you need before you ask him.

The Prayer Pattern of the Kingdom

⁹"Therefore, you should pray like this:

> "Our Father, the one in the heavens,
>> let your name be honored as holy.
> ¹⁰"Let your Kingdom come,
>> let your will manifest on earth

> as it is manifest in heaven.
> ¹¹"Grant us our daily supply of bread
> for the current day;
> ¹²and release us from our debts,
> as we too have released our debtors;
> ¹³and do not bring us into testing,
> but deliver us from the evil one;
> for the Kingdom is yours, and the power,
> and the glory forever. Amen.

¹⁴"For if you release men from their offenses, your heavenly Father will also release you. ¹⁵But if you do not release men, your Father will not release you from your offenses.

Keeping Righteous Acts Hidden: Fasting

¹⁶"When you fast, do not act dejected like the hypocrites, for when they are fasting, they distort their faces in order that they might shine before men. I tell you the truth, they have received their reward. ¹⁷But when you fast, anoint your head and wash your face ¹⁸so that you do not shine before men, but before your Father who is in a hidden place; and your Father who sees into what is hidden will pay you back.

Developing a Generous Eye

¹⁹"Stop storing up riches for yourself on earth, where moth and insects consume it, and where thieves break in and steal. ²⁰But store up riches for yourself in heaven, where neither moth nor insects consume it, and where thieves do not break in and steal. ²¹For where your wealth is located, your heart will also be located there.

²²"The body's lamp is the eye. Therefore, if the eye is generous, your whole body will shine. ²³But if your eye is greedy,[i] your whole body will be darkness. Therefore, if the light that is in you is dark, how intense the darkness!

---

[i] Or, "jealous."

Matthew 6:34

Serving God Rather than Resources

²⁴"No one is able to serve two masters, for either he will dislike the one and love the other, or he will hold fast to the one and treat the other with contempt. You are not able to serve God and wealth.

Leaving Worry Behind

²⁵"For this reason I tell you, do not worry about your physical needs, what you will eat or what you will drink, or about your body, what you will wear. Isn't physical life more than food, and the body more than clothing? ²⁶Look at the birds in the sky, for they do not plant, harvest, or gather into barns, yet your heavenly Father feeds them; aren't you of greater value than they are?

²⁷"Who from among you is able to add one cubit[ii] to his stature by worrying? ²⁸And why are you worrying about clothing? Examine the wildflowers in the field, how they grow; they do not become weary from work, nor do they spin. ²⁹But I tell you that not even Solomon in all his glory dressed as one of these. ³⁰But if God clothes the grass of the field in this way, which is here today and tomorrow is thrown into the oven, will he not care for you much more, you of little faith!

³¹"So, you do not have to worry, saying, 'What will we eat?' or 'What will we drink?' or 'What will we put on?' ³²For the Gentiles strive after all these things, and your heavenly Father understands that you require all of them; ³³rather seek first the Kingdom of God and his righteousness, and all these things will be added to you. ³⁴So, you do not have to worry about tomorrow, for tomorrow will worry about itself. Each day has adequate difficulty on its own.

[ii] A cubit is about eighteen inches.

Refuse to Criticize Others

Chapter Seven

¹"Do not condemn, so that you might not be condemned; ²for you will be evaluated with the criteria you use to evaluate others, and you will be measured with the criteria you use to measure. ³Why do you see the small chip of wood in the eye of your brother, but you do not notice the beam in your own eye? ⁴Or how can you say to your brother, 'Permit me and I will take the small chip of wood from your eye,' but take note, there is a beam in your eye? ⁵Hypocrite, first take the beam from your eye, and then you will see clearly to take the small chip of wood from your brother's eye.

Protect What God Has Given You

⁶"Do not give that which is holy to dogs, and do not throw your pearls in front of pigs, so that they do not trample them under their feet and turn and rip you to shreds.

Expecting God to Answer Prayer

⁷"Keep asking, and it will be given to you. Keep seeking and you will discover it. Keep knocking and it will be opened to you. ⁸For everyone who keeps asking receives; everyone who keeps seeking finds; and it will be opened to the one who keeps knocking.

Expect God to Answer Prayer with Good Things

⁹"This is how a normal man acts: when his son asks for a loaf of bread, he will not give him a stone, will he? ¹⁰Or if he asks for a fish, he will not give him a snake, will he? ¹¹So, if you who are defective[i] know to give good gifts to your children, how much more will your Father who is in the heavens give good things to those who keep asking him. ¹²Therefore, all the things that you might wish men do for you, you do for them in the same way; for this is the Law and the Prophets.

---

[i] Or, "evil."

Persevering Toward the Path to Life

¹³"Come in through the narrow gate, for wide is the gate and broad is the road leading to ruin, and the ones who are coming in through it are many. ¹⁴The gate is narrow and the road that leads to life is difficult, and the ones finding it are few.

Recognizing God's Servants by Their Fruit

¹⁵"Protect yourselves from false prophets. They come to you dressed like sheep, but inside they are vicious wolves. ¹⁶You will recognize them from their fruits. They do not pick grapes from thorn plants, nor figs from thistles, do they? ¹⁷In the same way, every good tree produces good-looking fruit, and the worthless tree produces unwholesome fruit. ¹⁸A good tree is not able to produce unwholesome fruit, and a worthless tree is unable to produce good-looking fruit. ¹⁹Every tree that does not produce good-looking fruit will be cut down and thrown into the fire. ²⁰Therefore, you will recognize them from their fruits.

²¹"Not everyone who says to me, 'Lord, Lord,' will enter into the Kingdom of the Heavens, but the one who does the will of my Father who is in the heavens *will enter in.* ²²Many will say to me on that day, 'Lord, Lord, we prophesied in your name, didn't we? We drove out demons in your name, didn't we? We did many miracles in your name, didn't we?' ²³Then I will publicly declare to them, 'I was never acquainted with you. Leave me, you who work at lawlessness.'

Building Your Life to Withstand Every Trial

²⁴"Therefore, everyone who listens to these words of mine and makes a habit of them will be like a wise man, who built his house upon the rock. ²⁵The rain came down, the torrents of water came, and the winds blew and struck that house, but it did not fall, for it has been established on the rock. ²⁶But everyone who listens to these words of mine and does not make a habit of them will be like a foolish man who built his house upon the sand. ²⁷The rain came down, the torrents of water came, the

winds blew and struck that house, and it collapsed and was completely destroyed."

28Then, when Jesus finished these words, the crowd was spellbound by his teaching. 29For he was teaching them as one who had authority, and not as their scribal scholars.

Jesus Touches a Leper and Heals Him

Chapter Eight

1When he had come down from the hill, many crowds followed him. 2Surprisingly, a leper came to him and fell prostrate before him. He said, "Lord, if you are willing, you are able to heal me."

3When Jesus stretched out his hand, he touched him and said, "I am willing; be cleansed." Immediately, his leprosy was cleansed away. 4Then Jesus said to him, "See that you tell no one, but go show yourself to the priest, and bring the gift that Moses commanded as a witness to them."

A Demonstration of Great Faith: The Centurion

5When Jesus entered Capernaum, a centurion approached and appealed to him 6saying, "My cherished servant is confined to bed immobilized, and he is being dreadfully tormented."

7Jesus said to him, "I personally will come and heal him."

8But the centurion responded and said, "Lord, I am not worthy that you enter under my roof; but only speak the word, and my cherished servant will be healed. 9For I am also a man who is under someone who commands me, and I have soldiers under me. When I say to this one, 'Go,' he goes, and to another, 'Come,' he comes, or to my servant, 'Do this,' he does it."

10When Jesus heard, he was amazed and said to those who were following, "Truly I tell you, there is no one in Israel in whom I have found such great faith as this. 11I tell you, many will come from the east and the west and feast with Abraham, Isaac, and Jacob in the Kingdom of the Heavens, 12but the sons of the Kingdom will be sent out into the darkness outside. There will be weeping and gnashing of teeth there."

¹³Then Jesus said to the centurion, "Go, as you have believed, let it happen for you." His cherished servant was healed in that hour.

Jesus Demonstrates Authority over Sickness and Disease

¹⁴When Jesus arrived at Peter's house, he saw his mother-in-law incapacitated, suffering with a fever. ¹⁵He touched her hand, and the fever left her. She arose and began to serve him.

¹⁶When evening arrived, they brought him many people who were demonized; he cast out the spirits with a word and healed all those who had any type of illness. ¹⁷He did this to fulfill what was spoken through Isaiah the prophet when he said,

"He himself took our sicknesses and bore our diseases."[i]

The Difficulty of Journeying with Jesus

¹⁸Then, when Jesus saw a crowd around him, he ordered that they cross over to the other side of the sea. ¹⁹A scribal scholar approached him and said, "Teacher, I will follow you wherever you might go."

²⁰Jesus responded to him, "The foxes have dens and the birds of the sky have nests, but the Son of Man does not have a place to lay his head."

²¹Then another of his disciples said to him, "Lord, allow me first to go and bury my father."

²²But Jesus responded to him, "Follow me, and let those who are dead bury their dead."

Jesus Demonstrates Authority over Weather Patterns

²³When he boarded the boat, his disciples followed him. ²⁴Suddenly, a violent storm whipped up the sea, so that the boat was swamped by the billowing waves, but Jesus continued

---

[i] Isaiah 53:4

sleeping. ²⁵His disciples came and woke him crying, "Lord, save us! We are foundering!"

²⁶He responded to them, "You of little faith, why are you acting like cowards?" Then he got up and rebuked the wind and the sea, and an exceptional calm descended on the sea. ²⁷The men were astonished and said, "What sort of man is this, that even the winds and the sea obey him?"

Jesus Demonstrates Authority over the Demonic Realm

²⁸When he arrived on the other side of the lake in the country of the Gadarenes,ⁱ two demonized men came out from the tombs and met him. They were extremely violent, so that no one had the ability to travel on that road. ²⁹They unexpectedly cried out and said, "Why are you harassing us, Son of God? Have you come here to torment us before the set time?"

³⁰There was a herd of many pigs grazing a distance from them. ³¹The demons begged him asking, "If you drive us out, send us into the herd of pigs."

³²He responded to them, "Go." When they went out, they went into the pigs; and suddenly the entire herd rushed headlong down the steep incline into the lake, and they drowned in the waters. ³³Those who were watching over them fled. They went into the city and reported everything, including what had happened to the demonized men. ³⁴Incredibly, the whole city came out to meet Jesus. When they saw him, they pleaded with him to depart from their borders.

Jesus Demonstrates Authority to Forgive

Chapter Nine

¹He embarked in the boat and crossed over and came to his own city. ²Significantly, they brought a paralyzed man to him who was lying upon a stretcher. Jesus recognized their faith and said

---

ⁱ A region where Gentiles lived.

to the one who was paralyzed, "Be confident child, your sins are forgiven you."

3At that point, some of the scribal scholars said within themselves, "This man is blaspheming."ii

4When Jesus recognized their thoughts he said, "Why are you contemplating evil in your hearts? 5For what is easier to say, 'Your sins are forgiven,' or to say, 'Get up and walk.' 6But so that you might know that the Son of Man has authority on the earth to forgive sins"—then he said to the paralyzed man, "Get up, pick up your stretcher, and go to your house." 7Then he got up and went to his house. 8When the crowds saw it, they were filled with fear, and they glorified the God who gave such authority to men.

Jesus Demonstrates His Love for Outcasts

9When Jesus had gone from there, he saw a man sitting at the customs house. He was called Matthew. Jesus said to him, "Follow me!" He arose and followed him.

10Something unusual occurred when Jesus was reclining at a table in Matthew's house.iii Many tax collectors and sinners had come and were dining with Jesus and his disciples. 11When the Pharisees saw it, they began to question his disciples, "Why does your teacher eat with tax collectors and sinners?"

12When Jesus heard, he responded, "The healthy have no need of a doctor, but those who are sick. 13When you leave, learn what this means: 'I desire mercy and not sacrifice.' For I have not come to call the righteous, but sinners to repentance."

Preserving the Old and the New Wineskins

14Then the disciples of John came to him and asked, "Why do we and the Pharisees fast frequently, but your disciples do not fast?"

---

ii Blasphemy is about speaking profanely of sacred things, to slander God, or to speak against him.

iii Or, "the house." It is identified as Matthew's house in Mark 2:15.

[15]Jesus answered them, "The guests at the wedding are not able to mourn as long as the bridegroom is with them, are they? But the days will come when the bridegroom is taken away from them. Then they will fast. [16]No one sews a piece of shrinkable cloth upon an old garment, for the patch will pull away from the garment and the tear will become worse. [17]Nor does anyone put new wine into old inflexible wineskins. But if they do, the wineskins will burst, the wine will pour out, and the wineskins will be ruined. On the contrary, they put new wine into new wineskins, and both are protected."

Jesus Demonstrates Authority over Sickness and Death

[18]While he was explaining these things to them, notably, one of the rulers came and fell prostrate before him. He said, "My daughter has just died, but come and lay your hands on her, and she will live." [19]Jesus arose and, along with his disciples, began to follow him.

[20]Just then a woman who had suffered from bleeding for twelve years approached from behind him and touched a tassel on his garment; [21]for she reasoned within herself, "If only I touch his garment, I will be healed."

[22]But after Jesus turned and saw her, he said, "Be confident, daughter. Your faith has rescued you." The woman was healed from that hour.

[23]Then Jesus came to the ruler's house and saw the flute players and the crowd in turmoil. [24]He began to say, "Move away, for the little girl has not died, but is sleeping." But they laughed at him.

[25]When the crowd had been thrown out, he went in, took her hand, and the little girl was raised up. [26]Then this report went out into the whole of that region.

Jesus Demonstrates Authority over Blindness

²⁷While Jesus was going on from that place, two blind men followed him. They were crying out saying, "Son of David, have mercy on us!"

²⁸When he had gone into the house, the blind men approached him. Jesus said to them, "Do you believe that I am able to do this?"

They said to him, "Yes Lord."

²⁹Then he touched their eyes and said, "Because of your faith, it will happen for you." ³⁰As a result, their eyes were opened, and Jesus strongly warned them saying, "See that you let no one know about this." ³¹But they left and spread it around that entire region.

Jesus Demonstrates Authority over Demonic Maladies

³²Just then, while they were going out, they brought a man to him who was demonized and could not speak. ³³After the demon was driven out, the man who could not speak spoke. The crowds were astounded and said, "Nothing like this has ever happened in Israel."

³⁴But the Pharisees began to say, "By the prince of demons he drives out demons."

Preaching and Demonstrating the Kingdom: More Workers Needed

³⁵Jesus was going around all the cities and villages teaching in their synagogues, preaching the good news of the Kingdom, healing every disease and every sickness among the people. ³⁶When he saw the crowds he was filled with compassion for them, for they were troubled and dejected like sheep that did not have a shepherd. ³⁷Then he said to his disciples, "On one hand, the harvest is great, but on the other, those who are working are small in number. ³⁸Therefore, plead with the Lord of the harvest that he might compel workers to go into his harvest."

The Disciples Sent to Preach and Demonstrate the Kingdom

Chapter Ten

¹Jesus sent for his twelve disciples and gave them authority over unclean spirits, to drive them out, and to heal every disease and sickness.

²These are the twelve apostles' names: First, Simon who is called Peter, and Andrew his brother; then James the son of Zebedee, and John his brother; ³Philip and Bartholomew; Thomas and Matthew the tax collector; James son of Alphaeus and Thaddaeus; ⁴Simon the Zealot[i] and Judas Iscariot, the one who also handed him over to his enemies.

⁵Jesus sent out these twelve giving them instructions and saying, "Do not go on a road to the Gentiles, and do not go into a city of the Samaritans. ⁶But rather go to the lost sheep of the house of Israel. ⁷While you are going, preach saying, 'The Kingdom of the Heavens has drawn near.' ⁸Heal those who are sick, raise the dead, cleanse lepers, and drive out demons. You have received a gift. Give a gift. ⁹Do not procure gold, silver, or copper coins for your money belts, ¹⁰or a travel bag, two shirts, sandals, or a cudgel;[ii] for the worker is worthy of his provision.

¹¹"Whatever city or village you might enter, carefully find out who is worthy in it, and stay there until you leave. ¹²When you are entering his house, greet it; ¹³if the house is worthy, let your peace come upon it; but if it is not worthy, let your peace return to you. ¹⁴Whoever does not welcome you or listens to your words, while you are leaving that house or that city, shake the dust off your feet.

¹⁵"I tell you the truth, it will be more tolerable for the land of Sodom and Gomorrah on the day of judgment than for that city.

---

[i] Or, "Cananian," the Aramaic equivalent of zealot.
[ii] Here and in Luke 9:3 Jesus forbids the "rhabdos." In Mark 6:8 he allows a single rhabdos. The word can mean "staff" or "cudgel" (a staff weapon). Matthew and Luke capture the prohibition against weapons, Mark focuses on the limit to one walking staff.

Jesus Warns of Resistance to Their Message

¹⁶"Pay attention! I am sending you as sheep in the midst of wolves. Therefore, be wise as snakes and innocent as doves. ¹⁷Protect yourself from men, for they will hand you over to governing councils and whip you in their synagogues. ¹⁸They will bring you before governors and kings on account of me, for a witness to them and to the Gentiles. ¹⁹However, when they hand you over to the authorities, do not worry what you will say, or how to say it, for what to say will be given to you in that hour. ²⁰For you will not be the one speaking, but the Spirit of your Father speaking through you.

²¹"Brother will hand over brother to death, and a father his child; children will turn against their parents and condemn them to death. ²²You will be despised by everyone on account of my name, but anyone who endures until the end, this is the one who will be rescued. ²³Nevertheless, when they persecute you in this city, flee to another, for I tell you the truth, you will most certainly not finish going through the cities of Israel before the Son of Man comes.

²⁴"A disciple is not above his teacher, nor a servant above his master. ²⁵It is sufficient for the disciple that he might be like his teacher, and the servant like his master. If they have called the master of the house Beelzebul,[iii] how much more the members of his household.

²⁶"Therefore, do not be afraid of them, for there is nothing that has been concealed that will not be revealed, nor hidden that will not be made known. ²⁷What I tell you in the dark, speak in the light, and what you hear in your ear, shout from the housetops; ²⁸and do not be afraid of those who kill the body, but

---

[iii] Another name for Satan.

are not able to kill the soul.[i] Rather, fear the one who is able to destroy both soul and body in Gehenna.[ii]

The Value of Every Life to the Father

[29]"Are not two sparrows sold for an assarion?[iii] Yet one of them will not fall upon the ground apart from your Father. [30]But even the hairs of your head are all numbered. [31]Therefore, stop being afraid; you are far more valuable than many sparrows.

Critical Choices in Hard Times

[32]"Therefore, anyone who will commit to me before men, I will also commit to him before my Father in the heavens. [33]But anyone who disowns me before men, I will also disown him before my Father in the heavens.

[34]"Do not assume that I have come to bring peace upon the earth. I have not come to bring peace, but a sword. [35]For I have come to 'separate a man from his father, a daughter from her mother, and a bride from her mother-in-law. [36]A man's enemies will be the members of his household.'[iv]

[37]"The one who loves his father or mother more than me is not worthy of me; and the one who loves his son or daughter more than me is not worthy of me. [38]He who does not take up his cross and follow after me, is not worthy of me. [39]The one who gains his life[v] will lose it, and the one who suffers loss to his life for my sake, will gain it.

[40]"The one who receives you receives me, and the one who receives me receives the one who sent me. [41]The one who

---

[i] The soul is the seat of the mind, emotions, and will.

[ii] Gehenna refers to a valley known as "the valley of the sons of Hinnom." It was the place of child sacrifice and gross impurity. It came to symbolize the place of eternal punishment.

[iii] An assarion was about a tenth of a denarius, which was a day's wage for a soldier or day laborer.

[iv] See Micah 7:6.

[v] Or, "soul."

receives a prophet because he is a prophet will receive the wages of a prophet; and the one receiving a righteous man because he is a righteous man will receive the wages of a righteous man. ⁴²In the same way, whoever gives even a cup of cold water to one of these little ones because he is a disciple, I am telling you the truth, he will most certainly not lose his wages."

John the Baptizer's Question About the Christ

Chapter Eleven

¹When Jesus finished instructing his twelve disciples, he departed from there to teach and preach in their cities.

²But when John heard about the works of the Christ while he was in prison, he sent a question through his disciples and asked him, ³"Are you the one who is coming, or shall we wait for another?"

⁴Jesus responded and said to them, "Go report to John what you hear and what you see: ⁵blind people are seeing, lame people are walking about, lepers are being cleansed, deaf people are hearing, dead people are raised to life, and poor people are hearing the proclamation of the good news. ⁶Blessed is the one who does not stumble over me."

Jesus Defends John

⁷Then, while John's disciples were leaving, Jesus began to speak to the crowds about John. "What did you go out into the desert to see? A reed swaying in the wind? ⁸But what did you go out to see? A man who dressed himself in luxurious clothing? Look, those who wear luxurious clothing are in the houses of kings. ⁹But what did you go out to see? A prophet? Yes, I say to you, and more than a prophet. ¹⁰This is the one about whom it is written:

" 'Take note! I am sending my messenger before you, he will prepare the way before you.'[i]

[11]"I am telling you the truth, there has not appeared among those born of women any greater than John the Baptizer, but the least in the Kingdom of the Heavens is greater than he. [12]From the days of John the Baptizer until now the Kingdom of the Heavens has been forcing its way forward, but violent men are trying to overpower it.[ii] [13]For all the prophets and the Law prophesied until John, [14]and if you are willing to accept it, he is Elijah, the one who is to come. [15]The one who has ears, let him understand.

[16]"But to what shall I compare this generation? It is like small children sitting in the marketplaces, who call out to other children [17]and say,

" 'We played the flute for you and you did not dance; we sang a funeral song for you and you did not wail.'

[18]For John came neither eating *normally* nor drinking *wine*, and they say, 'He has a demon.' [19]The Son of Man came eating *normally* and drinking *wine*, and they say, 'Look! A man who eats too much and is a heavy drinker, a friend of tax collectors and sinners.' Yet, wisdom is proven by her achievements."

The Danger of Rejecting the Christ and His Kingdom

[20]Then he began to reprimand the cities in which the most of his miracles were done, because they did not repent.

[21]"Woe to you, Chorazin, woe to you, Bethsaida! For if the miracles that were done in you had been done in Tyre and Sidon, they would have repented long ago in sackcloth and ashes. [22]But I tell you, it will be more bearable for Tyre and

---

[i] Malachi 3:1

[ii] In the context of John's imprisonment, Jesus is referring to those who oppose the advance of the Kingdom. See Luke 16:16 for a more positive perspective of people entering the Kingdom in spite of this opposition.

Sidon on the day of judgment than for you. ²³And you, Capernaum, you will not be exalted to heaven, will you? You will go down to Hades. For if the miracles that were done in you had been done in Sodom, it would have remained until this day. ²⁴But I tell you that it will be more tolerable for Sodom on the day of judgment than for you."

Jesus Celebrates Those Who Receive Him

²⁵On that occasion, Jesus responded and said, "I acknowledge you, Father, Lord of the heaven and the earth, for you have hidden these things from the wise and intelligent and revealed them to the inexperienced. ²⁶Yes, Father, for these things are pleasing before you. ²⁷All things have been handed over to me by my Father, and no one knows the Son except the Father, and no one knows the Father except the Son and the ones to whom he wishes to reveal him.

Jesus Extends an Invitation to Those Who Need Rest

²⁸"Come to me all who are tired and carrying a heavy load, and I will personally give you rest. ²⁹Take my yoke upon you, and learn from me, for I am gentle and humble in heart, and you will find rest for your souls; ³⁰for my yoke is useful and my burden is light."

God's Desire for Mercy from His People

Chapter Twelve

¹At that time, Jesus passed through grain fields on the Sabbath. His disciples started to get hungry and began to pluck the heads of grain and eat them. ²But when the Pharisees noticed, they asked him, "Look closely, why are your disciples doing what it is not lawful to do on the Sabbath?"

³He said to them, "Haven't you read what David did when he and those with him were hungry? ⁴How he went into the house

of God and ate the bread of the offering? It was not lawful for him or those who were with him to eat it, only the priests could. ⁵Or haven't you read in the Law that on the Sabbath the priests in the temple desecrate the Sabbath and are guiltless? ⁶But I tell you that one greater than the temple is here. ⁷If you had known what this means, 'I desire mercy and not sacrifice,'ⁱ you would not have condemned the innocent. ⁸For the Son of Man is Lord of the Sabbath."

Setting a Trap for Jesus

⁹When he departed from there, he went into their synagogue. ¹⁰Significantly, a man was there who had a hand with withering paralysis. So that they might bring charges against him, they inquired of him asking, "Is it lawful to heal on the Sabbath?"

¹¹But he responded to them, "What man is there among you who has one sheep, and if it falls into a cistern on the Sabbath, will he not take hold of it and lift it out? ¹²How much more valuable, then, is a man than a sheep! So, it is lawful to do good things on the Sabbath."

¹³At that point he spoke to the man, "Stretch out your hand." He stretched it out and it was restored as healthy as the other hand. ¹⁴But the Pharisees went out and took counsel against him planning how they might destroy him.

¹⁵Because Jesus knew this, he departed from there. Large crowds followed him and he healed them all. ¹⁶He strongly warned them not to make it known.

¹⁷This was so that the word of Isaiah the prophet might be fulfilled that said,

> ¹⁸"Behold my servant, whom I have chosen, my beloved in whom my soul is well pleased, I will put my Spirit upon him, and he will proclaim justice to the nations.

ⁱ Hosea 6:6

¹⁹"He will not strive or call out, nor will anyone hear his voice in the streets.

²⁰"A broken reed he will not break, and a faintly glowing wick he will not put out, until he leads forth justice to victory, ²¹and the nations will hope in his name."[ii]

The Foolishness of Ascribing Kingdom Power to Satan

²²Then a demonized man who could not see or speak was brought to him, and Jesus healed him, so that the man who could not speak was able to speak and see. ²³All the crowds were beside themselves with ecstatic joy[iii] and began to say, "This man isn't the Son of David, is he?"

²⁴But when the Pharisees heard this, they said, "This man cannot expel demons except with the help of Beelzebul,[iv] the ruler of the demons."

²⁵Jesus knew their thoughts and said to them, "Every kingdom divided against itself will destroy itself, and every city or house divided against itself cannot stand. ²⁶So, if Satan expels Satan, he is divided against himself. Therefore, how can his kingdom stand? ²⁷And if I expel demons by Beelzebul, by whom do your sons expel them? For this reason, they will be your judges. ²⁸But if I expel demons by the Spirit of God, then the Kingdom of God has overtaken you.

²⁹"Or how is anyone able to enter into the house of a strong man and forcefully take his belongings unless he first restrains the strong man? Then he can thoroughly ransack his house.

³⁰"The one who is not with me is against me, and the one who does not gather people together with me, scatters them.

[ii] Isaiah 42:1-4

[iii] "Beside themselves with ecstatic joy" translates a Greek verb used when referring to a spiritual phenomenon or visionary experience in ancient times.

[iv] Another name for Satan. Also verse 27.

Matthew 12:31

The Danger of Ascribing Things of the Spirit to Satan

³¹"For this reason, I tell you that all sin and slander[i] will be forgiven men, but slander against the Spirit will not be forgiven. ³²If someone speaks a word against[ii] the Son of Man, it will be forgiven him. But if someone speaks against the Holy Spirit, it will not be forgiven him, in this age nor the one to come.

The Bad Fruit of the Pharisees

³³"Either make a tree good, and its fruit will be good, or make a tree unwholesome, and its fruit will be unwholesome. For from its fruit a tree will be recognized. ³⁴You children of venomous snakes! How can you speak good things when you are evil? For from that which is abundant in the heart, the mouth speaks. ³⁵The good man sends out good things from his good storehouse, and the evil man sends out evil things from his evil storehouse. ³⁶But I tell you that men will give account for every worthless word that they speak on the day of judgment. ³⁷For by your words you will be acquitted, and by your words you will be found guilty."

A Stubborn Request for more Signs

³⁸Then some of the scribal scholars and Pharisees responded to him and said, "Teacher, we want to see an authenticating sign from you."

³⁹But he responded to them and said, "A wicked and adulterous generation is demanding an authenticating sign, yet an authenticating sign will not be given to it except for the sign of the prophet Jonah. ⁴⁰For just as Jonah was in the belly of the huge sea creature three days and three nights, so also the Son of Man will be in the heart of the earth three days and three nights.

---

[i] Or, "blasphemy." Blasphemy is about speaking profanely of sacred things, to slander God, or to speak against him. Also verse 32.

[ii] Or, "blasphemes."

⁴¹"Men of Nineveh will rise up with this current generation on the day of judgment and condemn it, because they repented at the preaching of Jonah, and be aware, one greater than Jonah is here. ⁴²The Queen of the South will awaken at the judgment with this current generation and condemn it, for she came from the ends of the earth to hear the wisdom of Solomon, and consider this, one greater than Solomon is here.

⁴³"Now whenever an unclean spirit comes out of a man, it travels through barren places seeking rest, but does not find it. ⁴⁴Then it says, 'I will return to my house from which I have come.' When it comes, it discovers that it is vacant, swept clean, and decorated. ⁴⁵So it goes and brings along with it seven other spirits more wicked than it is. When they come, they dwell there, and the last *condition* of that man is worse than the first. So it will be with this evil generation."

Jesus' Family Comes to Take Charge

⁴⁶While he was still speaking to the crowds, unexpectedly, his mother and brothers had stationed themselves outside seeking to speak to him.[iii] ⁴⁷Then someone said to him, "Look, your mother and your brothers have taken a position outside and are seeking to speak to you."

⁴⁸But Jesus responded to the one speaking to him and said, "Who is my mother, and who are my brothers?" ⁴⁹Then he stretched out his hand toward his disciples and said, "See, my mother and my brothers. ⁵⁰For whoever does the will of my Father in the heavens, he is my brother, sister, and mother."

The Parables of the Kingdom

Chapter Thirteen

¹On that day, Jesus went out of the house and was sitting beside the sea. ²So many crowds gathered around him that he stepped

---

[iii] Mark 3:21 makes it clear they had come to take charge of Jesus, whom they believed was overcome by an ecstatic spiritual experience.

into a boat and sat down. The entire multitude stood upon the beach. ³He spoke many things to them in parables.

The Parable of the Planter and the Soils

He said, "Pay close attention! A planter went out to plant seeds. ⁴As he broadcast the seed, some fell beside the path and the birds of the air came and gulped it down. ⁵But other seeds fell upon an area of shallow soil over buried rocks. As a result, the seed sprouted immediately because the soil wasn't deep enough. ⁶When the sun rose, the heat dried the plant and because its roots could not reach deep enough, it withered. ⁷Other seeds fell among thorny plants, and the thorny plants grew up and crowded out the seedlings. ⁸Finally, some fell into rich soil and produced fruit; one a hundred times what was sown, one sixty times, and one thirty times. ⁹The one who has ears, let him understand."

The Mysteries of the Kingdom Reserved for Disciples

¹⁰The disciples approached and asked him, "Why do you speak to them in parables?" ¹¹He responded and said to them, "Because the mysteries of the Kingdom of the Heavens are given to you, but they are not given to them. ¹²For whoever possesses *insight*, *more* will be given to him, and he will have an overabundance; but whoever does not possess it, even what he has will be taken away from him. ¹³For this reason, I speak to them in parables because

> " 'Though they see, they will not see; and though they hear, they will not hear and understand.'[i]

¹⁴The prophecy of Isaiah is fulfilled by them that says,

> " 'You will listen and listen, but will not understand. You will observe and observe, but you will not perceive.
>
> ¹⁵" 'For the heart of this people has grown insensitive; with their ears they hear with

---

[i] Compare Deuteronomy 29:4; Jeremiah 5:21; Ezekiel 12:2.

difficulty, and they have closed their eyes so that they do not see with their eyes, they do not hear with their ears, they do not understand with their hearts, and change so I would heal them.'ⁱⁱ

¹⁶But blessed are your eyes, for they see, and your ears, for they hear.

¹⁷"For I tell you the truth, many prophets and righteous men strongly desired to see what you see, but did not see, and to hear what you hear, but did not hear.

The Parable of the Planter and the Soils Explained

¹⁸"You, therefore, must understand the parable of the planter. ¹⁹Whenever someone hears the message of the Kingdom and does not understand it, the evil one comes and steals the seed that had been broadcast into his heart. This is the seed that was planted by the path. ²⁰The seed that was planted on buried rocks is the person who hears the message, and instantly receives it with joy, ²¹but he does not have root in himself. On the contrary, he is unstable. When tribulation or persecution comes because of the message, he immediately stumbles away from it. ²²The seed that was planted among the thorns is the person who understands the message, but the worries of this age and the deceitful pleasures of wealth choke out the message and it is unfruitful. ²³The seed that was planted on rich soil is the person who hears the message and understands. He indeed yields fruit, and some produce a hundred times what was planted, some sixty, and some thirty."

A Parable of Kingdom Infiltration: The Weeds in the Field

²⁴Jesus set another parable before them saying, "The Kingdom of the Heavens is similar to the *predicament* of a man who planted good seed in his field. ²⁵But while his men were sleeping, the enemy came and replanted weeds in the middle of the wheat and went away. ²⁶When the plants sprouted and produced fruit, then the weeds were revealed also.

ⁱⁱ Isaiah 6:9-10

27"The servants of the estate's owner came and said to him, 'Sir, we planted good seed in your field, didn't we? Then what is the source of these weeds?'

28"He said to them, 'An enemy has done this.' The servants asked him, 'Then do you want us to go and gather them now?'

29"He responded, 'No, so that you do not uproot the wheat along with them as you are gathering the weeds. 30Leave them both to grow together until the harvest, and at the appropriate time during the harvest, I will say to the reapers, "Gather the weeds first, bundle them into sheaves in order to burn them; but collect the wheat into my storehouse."'"

A Parable of the Kingdom's Growth: The Mustard Seed

31Jesus set another parable before them saying, "The Kingdom of the Heavens is similar to a mustard seed, which a man took and planted in his field. 32It is smaller than all the garden seeds, but when it has grown it is greater than all the garden vegetables and becomes a tree. It is so large that the birds of the sky come and nest in its branches."

A Parable of Growing Kingdom Influence: The Yeast

33Jesus spoke another parable to them, "The Kingdom of the Heavens is like yeast, which a woman took and hid in three measures of flour until the time when the entire lump of dough was leavened."

34Jesus spoke all these things to the crowds in parables, and he did not share anything with them without using parables.

35This was so that the word was fulfilled that was spoken through the prophet which said,

> "I will open my mouth in parables, I will speak plainly of things that were hidden since the founding of the world."[i]

---

[i] Psalm 78:2

The Parable of the Weeds in the Field Explained

³⁶Then, when he had left the crowds, he went into the house, and his disciples came to him asking, "Make the parable of the weeds in the field clear to us."

³⁷He responded and said, "The one who plants the good seed is the Son of Man. ³⁸The field is the world, and the good seed— these are the sons of the Kingdom; but weeds are the sons of the evil one. ³⁹The enemy who plants them is the Accuser.[ii] The harvest is the completion of the age, and the reapers are angels.

⁴⁰"Therefore, just as the weeds are gathered and burned in the fire, so it will happen at the completion of the age. ⁴¹The Son of Man will send his angels, and they will gather from his Kingdom all stumbling blocks and those who practice lawlessness. ⁴²They will throw them into the flaming furnace. There will be weeping and gnashing of teeth there. ⁴³Then the righteous will blaze brightly as the sun in the Kingdom of their Father. The one who has ears, let him understand.

Parables of Kingdom Value: The Hidden Treasure and the Pearl

⁴⁴"The Kingdom of the Heavens is similar to a treasure that has been hidden in a field. When a man finds it, he hides it again, and because of his joy he goes and sells everything—as much as he has—and buys that field.

⁴⁵"Again, the Kingdom of the Heavens is similar to a man who is a traveling merchant who is seeking good pearls. ⁴⁶When he found one pearl of great value, he went and sold everything— as much as he had—and bought it.

A Parable of Kingdom Gathering: The Net

⁴⁷"Again, the Kingdom of the Heavens is similar to a large net pulled through the sea that gathers all kinds *of fish*. ⁴⁸When

---

ii Traditionally, "devil." The name means to slander or accuse. For this reason, this word is most often translated "Accuser" in this Bible version.

it was full, they drew it up upon the shore, sat down, and sorted the good fish into containers, but they threw the bad fish out.

49"That is the way it will be at the completion of the age. The angels will go out and separate the evil people from the midst of the righteous, 50and they will throw them into the flaming furnace. There will be weeping and gnashing of teeth there.

51"Have you understood all these things?" They said to him, "Yes."

52Then Jesus said to them, "Therefore every scribal scholar who has been taught about the Kingdom of the Heavens is similar to a man who manages a household. He brings old things and new things out of his storeroom."

Jesus Rejected in His Hometown

53When Jesus had finished these parables, he departed from there. 54When he came to his hometown, he taught them in their synagogue with the result that they were surprised and said, "How did this wisdom and these miracles come to this man? 55Isn't this the carpenter's son? Isn't his mother named Mary, and his brothers named James, Joseph, Simon, and Judas? 56Aren't his sisters with us? Then where did this man get all these things?"

57So, they were scandalized by him. But Jesus said to them, "A prophet is not without honor except in his hometown and in his own house."

58He did not do many miracles there because of their unbelief.

Herod's Concern About a Resurrected John the Baptizer

Chapter Fourteen

¹At that time, Herod the tetrarch heard the report about Jesus. ²He said to his servants, "This is John the Baptizer! He has been raised from among the dead, and that is why miraculous powers are working in him."

³For Herod had arrested John, bound him, and put him in prison because of Herodias, his brother Philip's wife. ⁴For John had begun to declare to him, "It is against the Law for you to have her."

⁵While Herod wished to kill him, he was afraid of the crowd, because they accepted him as a prophet. ⁶But when Herod's birthday celebration was held, the daughter of Herodias danced in their midst and pleased Herod. ⁷So, he announced to her with an oath that he would give her whatever she requested. ⁸Then at the urging of her mother, she said, "Give me the head of John the Baptizer here on a serving tray."

⁹Even though the king was filled with sorrow, he gave an order to grant the request because of his oaths and his dinner guests. ¹⁰He sent the order to the prison and had John beheaded there. ¹¹Then his head was brought on a serving tray and given to the girl, and she carried it to her mother.

¹²When John's disciples came, they took his body and buried him. Then they went and brought the news to Jesus.

Jesus Departs from Herod's Realm

¹³When Jesus heard *about Herod's interest in him*,[i] he departed from there in a boat to an uninhabited place away from the public. But when the crowds heard, they followed him on foot from the cities. ¹⁴When he arrived, he saw many crowds. He had compassion on them and healed their sick.

---

[i] Verse 13 resumes the narrative begun in verses 1 and 2. Verses 3 through 12 are an excursus on why Herod had apprehensions about a resurrected John.

Matthew 14:15

Jesus Multiplies Loaves of Bread and Fish for Five Thousand

¹⁵But when evening drew near, his disciples came to him and said, "This place is uninhabited, and the time *of the evening meal* has already passed. Dismiss the crowds so that they might go to the villages and buy food for themselves."

¹⁶But Jesus responded to them, "They have no need to go, you give them something to eat."

¹⁷They said to him, "We do not have anything here except five loaves of bread and two fish."

¹⁸Then he said, "Bring them here to me."

¹⁹He ordered the crowds to settle down on the grass. He received the five loaves and two fish. When he had looked up into heaven, he said a blessing, broke the bread and gave it to his disciples. The disciples gave it to the crowds. ²⁰They all ate and had as much as they wanted; and they picked up what they did not need—twelve full baskets of broken pieces. ²¹About five thousand men ate, without counting women and children.[i]

A Manifestation of the Kingdom: Walking on Water

²²Jesus immediately forced his disciples to embark in the boat and cross ahead of him until he could dismiss the crowds. ²³When he had dismissed the crowds, he went up the mountain by himself to pray. When evening arrived, he was alone there. ²⁴But the boat was already very distant from the land and was being tossed about by the waves; for there was a contrary wind.

²⁵Then, during the fourth watch[ii] of the night, Jesus came to them walking on the sea. ²⁶When the disciples saw him walking upon the sea, they were terrified and said, "It is a ghost!" Then they cried out in fear.

---

[i] Estimates are that between fifteen and twenty thousand people were present.

[ii] This was between 3 and 6 in the morning.

²⁷Jesus immediately spoke to them and said, "Take courage. It is I. Stop being afraid."

²⁸Peter responded to him and said, "Lord, if it is you, command me to come to you upon the waters."

²⁹Then he said, "Come."

Peter got out of the boat, walked upon the waters, and went to Jesus. ³⁰Then, because Peter saw the strong wind, he was afraid, and he began to sink. He cried out shouting, "Lord, save me."

³¹Jesus immediately stretched out his hand and grabbed him. He said to him, "You of little faith, why did you waver?"

³²When they went up into the boat, the wind abated. ³³Those in the boat worshiped him saying, "You are truly the Son of God!"

A Demonstration of Faith in Jesus' Healing Power

³⁴When they had crossed to the other side, they came to the region of Gennesaret. ³⁵When the men of that place recognized him, they sent word into that entire surrounding region, and they brought all those who were sick to him. ³⁶They pleaded with him that they might simply touch a tassel on his garment. All who touched it were completely healed.

A Hypocritical Focus on External Matters

Chapter Fifteen

¹Then Pharisees and scribal scholars came to Jesus from Jerusalem and said, ²"Why do your disciples set aside the traditions of the elders? For they do not wash their hands when they eat bread."

³But Jesus answered and said to them, "Why also do you set aside God's commands on account of your traditions? ⁴For God said, 'Honor your father and your mother,'[iii] and 'Let the one

---

[iii] Exodus 20:12; Deuteronomy 5:16

who speaks evil of his father or mother die.'[i] ⁵But you say, 'Whoever says to his father or mother, "Whatever you might have benefited from me is a gift *to the temple*," ⁶then he must not financially honor his father or mother.' You invalidate the Word of God on account of your traditions. ⁷Hypocrites! Isaiah beautifully prophesied about you when he said,

> ⁸" 'This people honor me with their lips, but their heart is far distant from me.
> ⁹But they worship me for no purpose, teaching as doctrines the commandments of men.'[ii]"

Impurity from the Heart, Not from External Matters

¹⁰When he called the crowd together, he said to them, "Listen and understand. ¹¹It isn't what goes into the mouth that makes a man impure, but what proceeds from his mouth. This makes a man impure."

¹²Then his disciples came to him and said, "Do you know that when the Pharisees heard this message they stumbled over it?"

¹³But Jesus responded and said, "Every plant that my heavenly Father has not planted will be pulled out by the roots. ¹⁴Leave them, they are blind guides of the blind; and if a blind man guides a blind man, both will fall into the ditch."

¹⁵Then Peter responded and said to him, "Interpret this parable to us."

¹⁶But Jesus said, "You still have no understanding? ¹⁷Don't you understand that anything that goes into the mouth is received by the stomach and then passes out into the latrine? ¹⁸But the heart is the source of the things that come out of the mouth, and these things make a man impure. ¹⁹For evil thoughts, murders, adulteries, illicit sexual relationships, thefts,

---

[i] Exodus 21:17; Leviticus 20:9

[ii] Isaiah 29:13

false testimonies and slanders all come out from the heart. ²⁰These things are what make a man impure; but to eat with unwashed hands does not make a man impure."

A Demonstration of Great Faith: The Canaanite Woman

²¹Jesus went out from there and left for the regions around Tyre and Sidon. ²²At that time, a Canaanite woman from that area came out and was crying out saying, "Have mercy on me, Lord, Son of David. My daughter is badly demonized."

²³But he did not answer her a word. His disciples began appealing to him and suggesting, "Send her away, for she is behind us crying out."

²⁴He responded *to her request* and said, "I have not been sent except to the stray sheep of the house of Israel."

²⁵But she came and fell face down before him and said, "Lord, help me!"

²⁶He responded and said, "It is not right to take the children's bread and throw it to their dogs."

²⁷She said, "Yes Lord, but even their small dogs eat from the tiny bits that fall from their master's table."

²⁸Then Jesus responded and said to her, "O woman, great is your faith! Let it be for you as you wish." Her daughter was healed from that hour.

Demonstrating the Kingdom Through Healing

²⁹Jesus left there and went along the sea of Galilee, and he went up the mountain and was sitting there. ³⁰Many crowds came to him. They had the lame, blind, crippled, those who could not speak, and many others with them; and they laid them at his feet, and he healed them.

³¹As a result, the crowd was stunned and glorified the God of Israel when they saw those who could not speak now speaking, the crippled made whole, the lame walking, and the blind seeing.

Jesus Multiplies Loaves of Bread and Fish for Four Thousand

³²Then Jesus sent for his disciples and said, "I have compassion for the crowd, because they have already been with me for three days, and they have not had anything to eat. I do not want to send them away hungry so that they do not get exhausted along the way."

³³But the disciples said to him, "Where, in this barren place, will we find the bread that is needed so that so large a crowd has enough?"

³⁴Jesus responded to them, "How many loaves do you have?"

They said, "Seven loaves and a few fish."

³⁵Then he directed the crowd to settle down on the ground. ³⁶He took the seven loaves of bread and the fish, gave thanks, broke them, and gave them to the disciples, and the disciples gave them to the crowds. ³⁷Everyone ate and had as much as they wanted, and they picked up seven large basketfuls of what they did not need. ³⁸Four thousand men had eaten, without counting women and children.[i] ³⁹When he dismissed the crowds, he embarked in the boat and went to the region of Magadan.

A Hypocritical Request for more Signs

Chapter Sixteen

¹The Pharisees and Sadducees came to him and tested him. They requested that he show them an authenticating sign from heaven.

²But Jesus responded and said to them, "When it is evening, you say, 'Fair weather is on the way, for the sky is red.' ³And early in the morning, 'There will be stormy weather, for the sky is red and overcast.' Hypocrites! On the one hand, you know how to

---

[i] Estimates are that between twelve thousand and sixteen thousand people were present.

discern the appearance of the sky, but you cannot discern the signs of the times, can you? ⁴A wicked and adulterous generation is demanding an authenticating sign, yet no authenticating sign will be given to it, except for the sign of the prophet Jonah." Then he left them behind and went on his way.

A Demonstration of Little Faith: The Yeast of Unbelief

⁵When the disciples had embarked for the other side *of the lake*, they forgot to bring bread. ⁶Then Jesus said to them, "Be aware of, and be alert for, the yeast of the Pharisees and Sadducees."

⁷The disciples discussed this among themselves saying, "He said this because we did not bring bread."

⁸But Jesus, because he knew this, asked, "You of little faith, why are you discussing that we have no bread? ⁹Do you not yet understand, and don't you remember the five loaves for the five thousand, and how many baskets of leftovers you gathered? ¹⁰Or the seven loaves for the four thousand and how many large baskets we gathered? ¹¹How do you not understand that I did not speak about loaves to you? But be alert for the yeast of the Pharisees and Sadducees."

¹²Then they grasped that he did not tell them to be alert for the yeast in bread, but for the teaching of the Pharisees and Sadducees.

The Christ, the Son of the Living God

¹³When Jesus came to the district of Caesarea Philippi, he began to question his disciples by asking, "Who are men saying that the Son of Man is?"

¹⁴They responded, "Some say John the Baptizer, others Elijah, and still others say Jeremiah or one of the prophets."

¹⁵He asked them, "But who do you say I am?"

¹⁶Then Simon Peter responded and said, "You are the Christ, the Son of the Living God."

¹⁷Jesus responded to him and said, "Blessed are you, Simon son of John,[i] for flesh and blood did not reveal this to you, but my Father who is in the heavens. ¹⁸I also say to you that you are Peter, and upon this rock I will build my church, and the gates of Hades will not prevail against it."

The Keys of the Kingdom Promised to the Church

¹⁹"I will give you the keys of the Kingdom of the Heavens, and whatever you lock[ii] on the earth, it will stay[iii] locked in the heavens, and whatever you unlock on the earth, it will stay unlocked in the heavens."

²⁰Then he strongly warned his disciples that they should tell no one that he was the Christ.

Peter Opposes Jesus' Revelation of Future Suffering

²¹From that point, Jesus began to reveal to his disciples that it was necessary that he go to Jerusalem and suffer many things from the elders, chief priests, and scribal scholars, to be killed, and on the third day be awakened.

²²After Peter had taken him aside, he began to rebuke Jesus and said, "God be merciful to you, Lord. This will never happen to you!"

²³But when Jesus turned, he said to Peter, "Get behind me, Satan! You are a stumbling block to me, for you are not thinking about the things of God, but the things of men."

²⁴Then Jesus said to his disciples, "If anyone wants to come after me, he must deny his own *will*, take up his cross, and follow me. ²⁵For whoever desires to save his soul[iv] will lose it, but whoever suffers loss to his soul for my sake will discover it. ²⁶For

---

[i] Or, "Bar-Jonah," which is Aramaic for "son of John."

[ii] Keys lock and unlock. This could also be translated as bind-loose, prohibit-permit, tie-untie, and the like.

[iii] The tense of the verb stresses an action completed in the past that has lasting results. It will stay locked or unlocked.

[iv] The soul is the seat of the mind, emotions, and will.

what does a man benefit if he captures the whole world, but suffers loss to his soul? Or what will a man give in exchange for his soul? ²⁷For the Son of Man will come in the glory of his Father with his angels, and then he will repay each one according to his actions. ²⁸I am telling you the truth, there are some who are standing here who will by no means taste death until they see the Son of Man coming in his Kingdom."

Jesus' Transfiguration

Chapter Seventeen

¹After six days Jesus took Peter with him, along with James and his brother John, and brought them up a high mountain by themselves. ²He was transfigured[v] in front of them. His face shone just like the sun and his clothes became white as light; ³and suddenly, Moses and Elijah appeared to them speaking with Jesus.

⁴Peter responded and said to Jesus, "Lord, it is good for us to be here. If you desire, I will make three meeting tents here, one for you, one for Moses, and one for Elijah."

⁵At that point, while he was still speaking, a bright cloud enfolded them, and a voice from the cloud was saying, "This is my cherished Son, with whom I am well pleased. Listen to him."

⁶When the disciples heard this, they fell upon their faces and were very much afraid. ⁷Jesus came to them, and when he touched them, he said, "Get up and stop being afraid." ⁸When they raised their eyes, they saw no one except Jesus alone.

⁹While they were coming down the mountain, Jesus gave them clear instructions saying, "Tell no one about the vision until the time the Son of Man rises from the dead."

---

[v] Or, "transformed." The Greek word refers to a change in form.

¹⁰The disciples questioned him and asked, "Why do the scribal scholars say that it is necessary that Elijah come first?"

¹¹Jesus responded and said, "On the one hand, Elijah is coming and will restore all things. ¹²But on the other hand, I tell you that Elijah has already come, but they did not recognize him. Instead, they did what they wanted with him. In the same way, the Son of Man is about to suffer under them." ¹³Then the disciples understood that he was speaking to them about John the Baptizer.

A Demonstration of Little Faith: The Demonized Boy

¹⁴When they had come to the crowd, a man approached him and knelt before him. ¹⁵He said, "Lord, have mercy on my son, for he is disturbed and suffers terribly. For he frequently falls into the fire and into the water. ¹⁶I brought him to your disciples, but they were not able to heal him."

¹⁷Jesus responded and said, "Oh faithless and confused generation! How long will I be with you? How long must I be patient with you? Bring him here to me." ¹⁸Then Jesus rebuked the demon, and it came out from him, and the child was healed from that hour.

¹⁹Then the disciples came to Jesus privately and asked, "Why were we not able to drive it out?"

²⁰He told them, "Because you have little faith. I tell you the truth, if you have faith like a mustard seed, you can say to this mountain, 'Move from here to there,' and it will move. There will be nothing you are unable to do. ²¹In addition, this kind does not leave except by prayer and fasting."

More Revelation on Jesus' Mission and Future

²²As they were coming together in Galilee, he said to them, "The Son of Man is about to be handed over into the hands of men. ²³They will kill him, but on the third day he will be awakened." Then the disciples were painfully grieved.

²⁴When they arrived in Capernaum, those who collected the two-drachma[i] tax came to Peter and asked, "Your teacher pays the two-drachma tax, doesn't he?"

²⁵He answered, "Yes."

When he entered the house, Jesus anticipated his question and asked, "What do you think, Simon? From whom do the kings of the earth collect tribute or the poll tax, from their sons or from strangers?"

²⁶Peter answered him, "From strangers."

Jesus told him, "Therefore, the sons are exempt. ²⁷But in order that we do not cause them to stumble, go to the sea, throw out a hook and take the first fish that comes up. When you open its mouth, you will find a four-drachma coin. When you get that, give it to them for you and me."

True Greatness in the Kingdom

Chapter Eighteen

¹At that time, his disciples approached Jesus and asked, "Who, then, is greatest in the Kingdom of the Heavens?"

²When he had called a small child, he placed the child in the middle of them. ³He said, "I tell you the truth, unless you are changed and become like children, you will never enter into the Kingdom of the Heavens. ⁴Therefore, whoever humbles himself like this little child, he is the greatest in the Kingdom of the Heavens; ⁵and whoever receives one child such as this in my name, receives me.

---

[i] This was the temple tax. A drachma was equivalent to a denarius, which was a day's wage for a soldier or a day laborer.

Matthew 18:6

Protecting the Innocent from Stumbling

⁶"But whoever causes one of these little ones who believe in me to stumble into sin, it would be better for him that a donkey-driven millstone be hung around his neck, and that he be thrown into the open sea.

⁷"Woe to the world because of stumbling blocks, for stumbling blocks must come, but woe to the man through whom stumbling blocks come. ⁸If your hand or your foot causes you to stumble into sin, cut it off and throw it from you. It is better for you to come into life with a disabled arm or crippled leg than to have two hands or two feet and be thrown into the eternal fire. ⁹Also, if your eye causes you to stumble into sin, pull it out and throw it from you. It is better for you to come into life with one eye rather than to have two eyes and be thrown in the Gehenna[i] of fire.

Rescuing Those Who Have Stumbled

¹⁰"See to it that you do not look down on one of these little ones, for I tell you that through all things their angels in the heavens see the face of my Father in the heavens. ¹¹For the Son of Man has come to rescue the one who has been lost.

¹²"What do you think? If some man owns a hundred sheep, and one wanders away from among them, won't he leave the ninety-nine, go to the foothills and seek the one that is wandering? ¹³Then, when he finds it, I tell you the truth, he rejoices over it more than the ninety-nine who did not wander. ¹⁴In just this way, there is no intention in the presence of my Father, who is in the heavens, that even one of these little ones be lost.

---

[i] Gehenna refers to a valley known as "the valley of the sons of Hinnom." It was the place of child sacrifice and gross impurity. It came to symbolize the place of eternal punishment.

Make Every Effort to Restore a Stumbling Brother

¹⁵"But if your brother wrongs you, go expose his wrong between you and him alone. If he should hear you, you have avoided losing your brother. ¹⁶But if he does not hear you, take with you one or two others again, that at the mouth of two or three witnesses every word is verified. ¹⁷Then, if he pays no attention to them, speak to the church; and if he also pays no attention to the church, let him be like a Gentile or a tax collector to you.

¹⁸"I tell you the truth, whatever you lock[ii] on the earth, it will stay[iii] locked in heaven, and whatever you unlock upon the earth, it will stay unlocked in heaven.

¹⁹"Again, I am speaking truth to you, if two from among you agree on earth concerning the whole of a matter, whatever you might ask, it will be brought into existence by my Father in the heavens. ²⁰For where two or three are brought together in my name, there I am in the midst of them."

The Never-Ending Need to Forgive

²¹Then Peter came to him and said, "Lord, how often can my brother sin against me and I must *still* forgive him? Seven times?"

²²Jesus responded, "I tell you not seven times, but seventy-seven times.

²³"For this reason, the Kingdom of the Heavens is like a man, a king, who wanted to settle accounts with his servants. ²⁴When he began to settle accounts, a man who owed him ten thousand talents[iv] was brought before him.

[ii] Keys lock and unlock. This could also be translated as bind-loose, prohibit-permit, tie-untie, and the like.

[iii] The tense of the verb stresses an action completed in the past that has lasting results. It will stay locked or unlocked.

[iv] A talent of silver was about six thousand denarii. Since a denarius was the average daily wage of a soldier or day laborer, each talent was the equivalent of twenty years of wages.

25But because he did not have the ability to repay, his lord ordered him to be sold, along with his wife, his children, and all that he had, to pay him back.

26"Because of this, he fell prostrate before him and said, 'Have patience with me, and I will repay everything to you.' 27Then the lord of that servant felt compassion, released him, and forgave him of the debt.

28"But that servant went out and found one of his fellow servants who owed him a hundred denarii.[i] He grabbed him and began to choke him saying, 'Pay back what you owe me!'

29"Because of this, his fellow servant fell and pleaded with him saying, 'Have patience with me and I will pay you back.' 30But he was unyielding. Instead, he went and threw him into prison until he could repay what he owed.

31"Therefore, when his fellow servants saw what he had done, they were deeply distressed and went and described everything that had happened to their lord.

32"Then his lord summoned him and said to him, 'You malicious servant, I forgave you everything that you owed since you pleaded with me. 33Was it not necessary that you have mercy on your fellow servant just as I had mercy on you?' 34His lord was filled with anger and handed him over to the tormentors until he could pay back all that he owed.

35"In just this way, my heavenly Father will also act toward you if each of you does not forgive his brother from your heart."

Chapter Nineteen

1When Jesus finished these words, he left Galilee and went to the regions of Judea across the Jordan. 2Large crowds followed him, and he healed them there.

---

[i] Since a denarius was the average daily wage of a soldier or day laborer, this was about four months worth of wages.

The Pharisees Test Jesus About Divorce

³Then Pharisees came to him to test him and asked, "Is it right for a man to divorce his wife for any reason?"ⁱⁱ

⁴Then Jesus asked, "Haven't you read that at the beginning the creator made them male and female? ⁵He said,

> " 'For this reason, a man will leave his father and mother and be bonded to his wife, and the two will be one flesh.'ⁱⁱⁱ

⁶So that they are no longer two, but one flesh. Therefore, what God has joined in marriage, let man not divide through divorce."ⁱᵛ

⁷They said to him, "Why then did Moses issue an order to give a certificate of divorce in order to divorce?"ᵛ

⁸He said to them, "Moses permitted you to divorce your wives because of your stubborn hearts, but it was not this way from the beginning. ⁹I am telling you that anyone who divorces his wife for any other reason than an illicit sexual relationship, and marries another woman, commits adultery. The man who marries this divorced woman also commits adultery."

¹⁰The disciples said to him, "If this is the only reason that a man may divorce his wife, there is no advantage to getting married." ¹¹But he said to them, "All men are not able to receive this advice, but those to whom it has been given are able. ¹²For there are asexual men who were born that way from their mother's womb; there are asexual men who were physically altered by men; and there are asexual men who have cut themselves off from physical intimacy for the sake of the

---

ⁱⁱ This was a hotly contested topic among the rabbis of Israel. One school of thought believed that a man could divorce his wife over a burned dinner. A wife had no such recourse.

ⁱⁱⁱ Genesis 2:24

ⁱᵛ The Greek word translated "divorce" was a technical term for divorce.

ᵛ See Deuteronomy 24:1-4.

Kingdom of the Heavens. The one who can receive this advice, let him receive it."

The Priority of Little Ones

¹³Then they brought children to him in order that he might place his hands on them and pray; but his disciples scolded them. ¹⁴But Jesus said, "Allow the children to come to me, and do not hinder them, for the Kingdom of the Heavens consists of such as these."

¹⁵After he placed his hands on them, he left that place.

Wealth as a Potential Impediment to the Kingdom

¹⁶Then, of note, a person came to him and asked, "Teacher, what good must I do in order that I may possess eternal life?"

¹⁷Jesus responded to him, "Why are you asking me about what is good? There is one who is good. But if you want to enter into life, keep the commandments."

¹⁸He asked him, "Which ones?"

Jesus responded, "You shall not commit murder, you shall not commit adultery, you shall not steal, you shall not deliver false testimony, ¹⁹honor your father and mother, and you shall love your neighbor as yourself."

²⁰The young man said to him, "I have kept all these things; what yet do I need?"

²¹Jesus said to him, "If you wish to achieve your goal, go sell the things you possess and give the money to the poor, and you will have treasure in the heavens. Then come follow me."

²²When the young man heard this message, he went away grieving, for he had many possessions.

²³Jesus said to his disciples, "I am telling you the truth, a rich man will enter into the Kingdom of the Heavens with great difficulty."

²⁴"Again, I tell you, it is easier for a camel to pass through the eye of a needle than for a rich man to enter into the Kingdom of God."

²⁵When his disciples heard it, they were very much surprised and said, "Who, then, can be saved?"

²⁶When Jesus considered it, he said to them, "With men this is impossible, but with God all things are possible."

Giving Up All for the Kingdom: A Promise

²⁷Then Peter responded and said to him, "Consider this, we ourselves have left everything and followed you. What then will there be for us?"

²⁸Jesus said to them, "I tell you the truth, that you who have followed me, at the rebirth when the Son of Man sits upon his glorious throne, you also will sit on twelve thrones judging the twelve tribes of Israel; ²⁹and everyone who leaves houses, brothers, sisters, father, mother, children, or fields on account of my name, will receive a hundred times more and will inherit eternal life. ³⁰But many prominent people will be last, and the last will be first."

Guarding Against False Expectation and Greed in the Kingdom

Chapter Twenty

¹"For the Kingdom of the Heavens is like a man who managed a household, who went out in the early morning to hire workers for his vineyard. ²When he had agreed with the workers for a denarius[i] for the day, he sent them into his vineyard.

³"He also went out about the third hour and saw others standing in the marketplace with no work. ⁴He said to those, 'You also go into my vineyard, and I will give you what is right.'

---

[i] A denarius is a day's wage for a soldier or a day laborer. Also in verses 9, 10, 13, and 19.

⁵Then they went. He went out again about the sixth and ninth hour and did the same. ⁶About the eleventh hour he went and found others just standing, and he said to them, 'Why have you been standing here the whole day with no work?'

⁷"They said to him, 'Because no one has hired us.' He said to them, 'You also go into my vineyard, and you will receive what is right.'

⁸"When evening had come, the master of the vineyard said to his supervisor, 'Call the workers and pay them their wage, beginning with the last ones hired until the first.'

⁹"When the ones who were hired about the eleventh hour came, they each received a denarius. ¹⁰When those who were hired first came, they thought that they would receive more; but they also received a denarius each. ¹¹After they received it, they began to grumble against the master of the house ¹²and said, 'These last men worked an hour, but you have made them equal to those of us who have endured the burden of the day and the sun's heat.'

¹³"But he responded to one of them and said, 'Friend, I am not treating you unfairly. Did you not agree with me for a denarius? ¹⁴Take what is yours and go; I want to give these last men the same as you. ¹⁵It is legal for me to do what I wish with what is mine, isn't it? Or is your eye envious because I am good?'

¹⁶"In this way, the last will be first, and the first last. For a great many are invited, but the elect[i] are few in number."

Jesus Points to the Crucifixion

¹⁷While Jesus was going up to Jerusalem, he took the twelve disciples by themselves and spoke to them on the way. ¹⁸"Pay close attention, we are going up to Jerusalem, and the Son of Man will be handed over to the chief priests and scribal scholars,

---

i The term translated "elect" is used over twenty times in the New Testament and most often is a reference to those who are called by God to true faith that perseveres.

and they will condemn him to death. ¹⁹They will deliver him to the Gentiles so that they mock, whip, and crucify him, but on the third day he will be raised again."

A Basic Misunderstanding About the Kingdom

²⁰Then the mother of the sons of Zebedee came to him with her sons, she knelt down and requested a special favor of him.

²¹He asked her, "What do you want?"

She said to him, "Say that these two sons of mine might sit, one on your right and one on your left in your Kingdom."

²²Then Jesus responded and said, "You do not know what you are asking. Are you able to drink the cup that I personally am about to drink, and be baptized in the baptism in which I am baptized?"

They said to him, "We are able."

²³He said to them, "On the one hand, you will drink my cup and be baptized in the baptism in which I am baptized, but the ability to sit on my right and left is not mine to give. It is for those for whom it is prepared by my Father."

²⁴When the ten heard about it, they were angry with the two brothers. ²⁵When Jesus had called them together, he said, "You know that the rulers of the Gentiles exercise dominion over them, and their great men misuse their power over them. ²⁶It will not be this way among you. But whoever wants to be great among you will be your servant, ²⁷and whoever wants to be first among you will by your slave; ²⁸just as the Son of Man has not come to be served, but to serve and to dedicate his life as a redemption payment[ii] for many people."

Jesus Responds to Persistent Faith: Opening Blind Eyes

²⁹While they were leaving Jericho, a large crowd followed after him. ³⁰At that time, there were two blind men sitting at the side

---

[ii] Or, traditionally, "as ransom for many people."

of the road. When they heard that Jesus was passing by, they cried out shouting, "Have mercy on us, Lord, Son of David!" ³¹The crowd rebuked them so that they would be quiet, but they cried out even more shouting, "Have mercy on us, Lord, Son of David!"

³²Then Jesus stood still, called out to them, and said, "What do you desire that I do for you?"

³³They answered him, "Lord, we want our eyes to be opened."

³⁴Because Jesus was moved with compassion, he touched their eyes, and they immediately received their sight; and they followed him.

The King Arrives in Jerusalem

Chapter Twenty-One

¹When they drew near Jerusalem and came to Bethphage on the Mount of Olives, Jesus sent out two disciples ²saying to them, "Go to the village across from you, and right away as you enter it,[i] you will find a donkey tied up and a colt with her. Untie them and lead them to me. ³But if anyone says anything to you, explain that their Lord has need of them. Then they will send the animals at once.

⁴This occurred in order that the word might be fulfilled that was spoken through the prophet,

> ⁵"Say to the daughter of Zion, 'Look, your king is coming to you, gentle and seated on a donkey, upon a colt, the offspring of a donkey.'"[ii]

⁶When the disciples had gone and done just what Jesus instructed them, ⁷they brought the donkey and the colt and placed their garments on them; and he sat upon the garments. ⁸The majority of the crowd spread their garments out in the

---

[i] Or, "you will promptly find a donkey."

[ii] See Isaiah 62:11 and Zechariah 9:9.

road, and others cut branches from trees and were spreading them in the road.

⁹Then the crowds going in front of him, and those coming behind, were crying out,

> "Hosanna to the Son of David, blessed is the one
> who is coming in the name of the Lord;
> hosanna in the highest."[iii]

¹⁰When he had entered into Jerusalem, the entire city was stirred and said, "Who is this man?"

¹¹But the crowds were saying, "This is the prophet Jesus, the one from Nazareth in Galilee."

Jesus Exercises His Authority at the Temple

¹²Jesus went into the temple and threw out all those selling and those buying in the temple. He also overturned the tables of the money changers and the stands of those selling doves. ¹³He said to them, "It is written,

> " 'My house will be called a house of prayer, but
> you have made it a bandits' lair.'[iv] "

¹⁴The blind and the lame came to him in the temple, and he healed them. ¹⁵When the chief priests and the scribal scholars saw the astounding things he had done, and the children shouting in the temple saying, "Hosanna to the Son of David," they became angry. ¹⁶So, they said to him, "Are you hearing what these children are saying?"

But Jesus said to them, "Yes. Have you never read, 'From the mouths of small children and nursing babies you have provided praise?'[v] "

¹⁷After he left them, he went outside the city to Bethany, and lodged there.

[iii] See Psalm 118:25-26.

[iv] See Isaiah 56:7 and Jeremiah 7:11.

[v] Psalm 8:2

Matthew 21:18

A Fig Tree and the Power of Faith

18Early in the morning, while he was going back to the city, he became hungry. 19When he saw one fig tree at the roadside, he went to it, but found nothing on it except leaves—nothing else. So, he said to it, "May there no longer be fruit from you throughout this age;" and the fig tree immediately withered.

20When the disciples noticed it, they were surprised and asked, "How did the fig tree wither so rapidly?"

21Jesus responded and said to them, "I tell you the truth, if you possess faith and do not talk yourself out of it, not only will you do what happened to the fig tree, but you can say to this mountain, 'Be lifted up and be thrown into the sea,' and it will happen. 22Also, all things—as much as you might ask for in prayer—if you believe you will receive."

Jesus' Authority Challenged

23When he arrived at the temple, the chief priests and elders of the people came to him while he was teaching and said, "By what authority are you doing these things, and who gave you this authority?"

24Jesus responded and said to them, "I will also ask you one thing, which if you tell me, I will also tell you by what authority I am doing these things. 25From where did the baptism of John come, from heaven or from men?"

But they discussed it among themselves saying, "If we should say, 'From heaven,' he will say to us, 'So, why didn't you believe him?' 26But if we say, 'From men,' we fear the crowd, because they all esteem John as a prophet."

27So, in response to Jesus, they said, "We do not know."

He said to them, "I also will not tell you by what authority I am doing these things."

The Two Sons: A Parable on Obedience

²⁸"What do you think? A man had two children. He came to the first and said, 'My child, go today and work in the vineyard.'

²⁹"He responded and said, 'I will not.' But later he had a change of heart and went out.

³⁰"He went to his other child and said the same to him. He responded and said, 'I will, sir,' but he did not go out. ³¹Which of the two did the will of his father?"

They answered, "The first one."

Jesus said to them, "I am telling you the truth, the tax collectors and the prostitutes are entering ahead of you into the Kingdom of God. ³²For John came to you by the path of righteousness, but you did not believe him. However, the tax collectors and the prostitutes believed him, but when you saw it, you did not also later repent so that you believed him.

The Parable of the Tenant Farmers

³³"Listen to another parable. There was a man who managed an estate. He planted a vineyard, put a wall around it, cut out a winepress in it, and built a tower. Then he leased it to tenant farmers and went on a journey. ³⁴When harvest drew near, he sent his servants to the tenant farmers to receive his part of the harvest. ³⁵The tenant farmers took hold of his servants, they beat one, they killed another, and stoned a third. ³⁶Again, he sent another group of servants, more numerous than the first group, but the tenant farmers did the same thing to them. ³⁷At last, he sent his son to them saying, 'They will have regard for my son.'

³⁸"But when the tenant farmers saw the son, they said among themselves, 'This is the heir. Come let us kill him and we will obtain his inheritance.' ³⁹They took hold of him, threw him out of the vineyard, and killed him.

⁴⁰"Therefore, when the master of the vineyard comes, what will he do to those tenant farmers?"

⁴¹They said to him, "He will ruthlessly destroy these evil men, and lease the vineyard to other tenant farmers who will pay him his portion of the harvest at the proper time."

⁴²Jesus said to them, "Have you never read in the Scriptures,

> " 'A stone which the builders rejected, this one
>   has become the most essential cornerstone.
>   This turn of events was from the Lord, and it
>   is wonderful in our eyes'[i]?

⁴³"For this reason, I tell you that the Kingdom of God will be taken from you and given to a people who will produce its fruit. ⁴⁴Everyone who falls upon this stone will be shattered, but if it falls on anyone it will grind him into dust."

⁴⁵When the chief priests and Pharisees heard his parable, they knew that he was speaking about them. ⁴⁶So, they were seeking a way to arrest him, though they were afraid of the crowd, since they esteemed him as a prophet.

The Parable of the Wedding Banquet: Filling the Kingdom

Chapter Twenty-Two

¹Jesus responded and spoke again to them in parables saying, ²"The Kingdom of the Heavens is like man who was king, who held a marriage celebration for his son. ³He sent his servants to request the presence of those who had been invited to the marriage celebration, but they were not willing to come.

⁴"Again, he sent other servants instructing, 'Say to those who have been invited, "Listen closely, I have prepared my feast. My bulls and grain-fed animals have been skinned and dressed, and everything is ready. Come to my marriage celebration." ' ⁵But they disregarded the invitation and went away, one to his own estate, and another to his business. ⁶The rest restrained his servants, abused them, and killed them. ⁷But the king was

---

[i] Psalm 118:22-23

furious. He sent his soldiers and killed those murderers and set their city ablaze.

⁸"Then he said to his servants, 'The marriage feast is prepared, but those who were invited were not worthy. ⁹So, go to the entrance roads of the city, and invite as many as you find to my marriage celebration.' ¹⁰Those servants went out to the roads and gathered everyone they could find, both the reprobate and the respectable; and the marriage feast was filled with those invited to dine.

¹¹"But when the king came to see those who were feasting, he saw a man there who was not wearing wedding clothing. ¹²He asked him, 'Friend, how have you entered here without wearing wedding clothing?' But he was silent.

¹³"Then the king said to his servants, 'Tie his hands and feet and throw him outside into the darkness. There will be weeping and gnashing of teeth there.'

¹⁴"For a great many are invited, but the elect[ii] are few in number."

The Pharisees Test Jesus: Paying the Poll Tax

¹⁵Then the Pharisees went and took counsel about how they might trap him with words. ¹⁶So, they sent their disciples along with the Herodians to Jesus saying, "Teacher, we know that you are sincere, that you teach the way of God in truth, and that you are not intimidated by anyone for you do not regard the reputation of men. ¹⁷Therefore, tell us what you think? Is it lawful to pay the poll tax to Caesar or not?"

¹⁸But Jesus knew their evil intent and responded, "Why are you testing me, you hypocrites? ¹⁹Show me the coin used for the tax." They brought him a denarius. ²⁰He asked them, "Whose image is this, and whose inscription?"

²¹They said to him, "Caesar's."

[ii] On the term "elect" see Matthew 20:16 footnote.

In response he said to them, "Therefore give back the things of Caesar to Caesar, and the things of God to God." ²²When they had heard *this*, they were stunned. Then they left him and went away.

The Sadducees Test Jesus: The Marriage Conundrum

²³On that day, Sadducees, who say there is no resurrection, came to him and questioned him ²⁴and asked, "Teacher, Moses said, 'If anyone who does not have children dies, his brother, as his closest relative, should marry his wife and raise up offspring for his brother.'[i] ²⁵Now among us there were seven brothers. The first one married but then died. Since he had no children, he left his wife to his brother. ²⁶The same thing happened to the second and third brothers, all the way down to the seventh brother. ²⁷Then last of all, the woman died. ²⁸Therefore, in the resurrection, whose wife will she be from among the seven brothers? For they all had married her."

²⁹Jesus responded and said to them, "You are deceived because you do not know the Scriptures or the power of God. ³⁰For in the resurrection they neither marry nor are given in marriage, but they are like the angels in heaven. ³¹But concerning the resurrection of the dead, have you not read what was spoken to you by God when he said,

> ³²" 'I am the God of Abraham, and the God of Isaac, and the God of Jacob'[ii]?

He is not the God of the dead, but of the living."

A Test About the Greatest Commandment

³³When the crowds heard this, they were surprised at his teaching. ³⁴But when the Pharisees heard that he had silenced the Sadducees, they gathered together at the same location. ³⁵One from among them, a legal expert, began questioning him to test him: ³⁶"Teacher, which commandment in the Law is greatest?"

---

[i] See Deuteronomy 25:5.

[ii] Exodus 3:6.

37He responded to him, "Love the Lord your God with your whole heart, your whole soul, and with your whole mind.[iii] 38This is the greatest and first commandment. 39But the second is like it: Love your neighbor as yourself.[iv] 40The whole Law, and the Prophets as well, depend on these two commandments."

A Test for the Leaders: Whose Son is Christ?

41Now since the Pharisees were gathered together, Jesus questioned them, 42asking, "What do you think concerning the Christ? Whose son is he?"

They replied to him, "David's."

43He asked them, "So, how does David, by the Spirit, call him Lord? He said,

> 44" 'The Lord said to my lord, "Sit at my right hand, until I put your enemies beneath your feet."'[v]

45If, therefore, David calls him, 'Lord,' how is he his son?"

46No one was able to answer a word to him, and from that day, no one had the courage to question him any longer.

Jesus Condemns the Religious Leaders of Israel

Chapter Twenty-Three

1Then Jesus spoke to the crowds and his disciples 2and said, "The scribal scholars and Pharisees sat down in Moses' seat. 3Therefore, you must do and follow everything they tell you, but do not act like they do; for they speak but do not do. 4They bind together heavy burdens that are hard to carry, and they place them upon men's shoulders, but they themselves do not wish to

---

[iii] See Deuteronomy 6:5.

[iv] Leviticus 19:18

[v] Psalm 110:1

lift their finger to remove them. ⁵They do all their works to be seen by men; for they make their phylacteries[i] large and the tassels on their garments long. ⁶They love the place of honor at the feasts, the most distinguished seats in the synagogues, ⁷the welcome they receive in the markets, and to be addressed as 'Rabbi' by men. ⁸But you, do not be addressed 'Rabbi,' for you have one Teacher, and you all are brothers. ⁹Also, do not address any religious leader[ii] as your father upon the earth, for one is your father, your heavenly Father; ¹⁰and do not be addressed as doctors,[iii] for you have one Instructor, the Christ. ¹¹But the greatest among you will be your servant. ¹²Whoever exalts himself will be humbled, and whoever humbles himself will be exalted.

¹³"Woe to you, scribal scholars and Pharisees, hypocrites! You lock the Kingdom of the Heavens in front of men. For you do not enter yourself, and you do not allow those who are entering to go in.

¹⁴"Woe to you, scribal scholars and Pharisees, hypocrites! You consume widow's houses and pray long prayers as an excuse. Therefore, you will receive greater judgment.

¹⁵"Woe to you, scribal scholars and Pharisees, hypocrites! You traverse sea and dry land to make one proselyte, and when he becomes one, you make him double the son of Gehenna[iv] as you are.

¹⁶"Woe to you, blind leaders, you who say, 'Whoever swears by the temple, it is nothing. But whoever swears by the gold of the temple must keep the oath.' ¹⁷Foolish and blind men! For

---

[i] A box worn by Jewish men containing bits of Scripture. It was a literal application of Deuteronomy 6:8.

[ii] Literally, "do not address anyone as your father" The context, however, is about the religious leaders.

[iii] Or, "teachers." The Latin word "Doctor" means teacher.

[iv] Gehenna refers to a valley known as "the valley of the sons of Hinnom." It was the place of child sacrifice and gross impurity. It came to symbolize the place of eternal punishment.

what is greater, the gold or the temple that consecrates the gold? ¹⁸You also say, 'Whoever swears by the altar, it is nothing. But whoever swears by the offering upon it must keep the oath.' ¹⁹Blind men, for what is greater, the offering or the altar that consecrates the offering? ²⁰Therefore, the one who swears by the altar swears by it and by everything on it. ²¹And the one who swears by the temple swears by it and by the one who inhabits it. ²²And the one who swears by heaven swears by the throne of God and the one who is seated on it.

²³"Woe to you, scribal scholars and Pharisees, hypocrites! You give a tenth of the mint, dill, and cumin, but you forsake the important things of the Law: justice, mercy, and faith. These things are required, but you should also not forsake the other things. ²⁴Blind leaders! You who strain out a gnat while swallowing a camel!

²⁵"Woe to you, scribal scholars and Pharisees, hypocrites! You clean the outside of the cup and the plate, but inside you are full of violent greed and lack self-control. ²⁶Blind Pharisee! First clean the inside of the cup, so that the outside might also be clean.

²⁷"Woe to you, scribal scholars and Pharisees, hypocrites! You are like tombs that have been whitewashed; they look lovely on the outside, but inside they are full of the bones of the dead and all kinds of impurity. ²⁸In this way, you look righteous to men on the outside, but on the inside, you are filled with hypocrisy and lawlessness.

²⁹"Woe to you, scribal scholars and Pharisees, hypocrites! You build the tombs of the prophets and make the graves of the righteous beautiful, ³⁰and you say, 'If we had lived in the days of our fathers, we would not have shared in the blood of the prophets with them.' ³¹So, you give testimony against yourselves that you are the sons of those who murdered the prophets. ³²You then, fill up the measure of your fathers. ³³Snakes, children of venomous serpents, how will you escape from the punishment of Gehenna?

³⁴"For this reason, pay close attention, I am sending prophets, wise men, and scribal scholars to you; you will kill and crucify some of them, whip others in your synagogues, and persecute them from city to city. ³⁵This is so that all the righteous blood shed upon this land[i] will come upon you; from the blood of righteous Abel down to the blood of Zechariah son of Berekiah[ii], whom you murdered between the temple and the altar. ³⁶I am telling you the truth, all these things will come upon this current generation.

³⁷"Jerusalem, Jerusalem, the one who kills the prophets and stones those sent to her; how often I have wanted to gather your children like a hen gathers her chicks under her wings, but you did not want it. ³⁸Be aware, your house is left to you abandoned. ³⁹For I say to you, you will most certainly not see me from now on until you say, 'Blessed is the one who is coming in the name of the Lord.'[iii] "

Looking Ahead to the Destruction of Jerusalem and Beyond

Chapter Twenty-Four

¹When Jesus came out of the temple and was leaving, his disciples approached him and drew his attention to the construction of the temple. ²But Jesus responded and said to them, "You see all these things, don't you? I am telling you the truth, there will most certainly not be one stone left here on another stone; there isn't one that will not be thrown down."

³Then, while he was sitting upon the Mount of Olives, his disciples came to him privately saying, "Tell us, when will these

---

[i] Often translated as "earth," but the word can refer to Israel as the land, and the context here virtually demands that it be translated "this land."

[ii] See Zechariah 1:1.

[iii] Psalm 118:26

things happen, what is the sign of your visitation,[iv] and of the end of the age?"[v]

Jesus Answers a First Question

⁴Then Jesus responded and said to them, "See to it that no one lead you astray. ⁵For many will come opposing my name saying, 'I am the Christ,' and they will deceive many. ⁶At that time, you will begin to hear of wars and reports of wars. Pay attention! Do not be alarmed! For this must happen, but it is not yet the fulfillment[vi] *of my words*. ⁷For first, people group will rise against people group,[vii] and kingdom against kingdom, and famines and earthquakes will occur in a variety of places. ⁸All these things are only the beginning of birth pains.

⁹"Then they will give you over to affliction. They will even kill you. At that time, you will be hated by all the nations on account of my name. ¹⁰Then many will stumble into sin and betray each other, and they will hate each other; ¹¹and many false prophets will be raised up and will deceive many. ¹²Because of the lawlessness that will multiply, the love of many will grow cold, ¹³but the one who endures to the fulfillment *of my words*, this is the one who will be rescued. ¹⁴This good news of the Kingdom will be proclaimed throughout the Roman world[viii] as a testimony to all the nations, and then the fulfillment will come.

[iv] Or, "parousia." Parousia is a technical term that can mean coming, presence, or visitation.

[v] See Matthew 13:39f. The end of the age is the time of the final harvest of unbelievers out of this age. Also see Matthew 28:20, where Jesus promises to be with his people to the end of the age.

[vi] This word (telos) is often translated "end," but is also used to speak of fulfillment of a word or prediction. Here, the context is the fulfillment of Jesus' word about the destruction of the temple. Also verses 13 and 14.

[vii] Or, traditionally, "nation will rise against nation," though his next words about kingdom against kingdom would appear to address the nations.

[viii] Or, "inhabited world," usually referring to the Roman world.

¹⁵"So, when you see the abomination that causes devastation standing in the holy place, the one spoken about through Daniel the prophet,[i] (the one reading this must understand), ¹⁶then let those in Judea flee to the mountains. ¹⁷Anyone upon the housetop must not go down to gather things from his house, ¹⁸and anyone in the field must not return to get his garment. ¹⁹But woe to those who carry *a baby* in the womb, and those who are nursing during those days; ²⁰and pray that your escape does not happen in cold weather or on the Sabbath. ²¹For then there will be a great affliction as has not happened from the beginning of the world until now, nor will it ever happen again. ²²Unless those days were shortened, no one would be rescued. But on account of the elect,[ii] those days will be shortened. ²³Then if someone should say, 'See! Here is the Christ,' or 'He is over here,' do not believe it. ²⁴For false messiahs and false prophets will be raised up, and they will provide great signs and portents in order to deceive, if it were possible, even the elect. ²⁵Pay close attention, I have told you in advance. ²⁶Therefore, if they say to you, 'Listen, he is in the desert,' do not go out; or, 'Take note, he is inside the house,' do not believe it. ²⁷For just as the flash of lightning coming from the east also shines in the west, thus will be the visitation[iii] of the Son of Man. ²⁸Where the dead body is, there the eagles will gather.

²⁹"Then immediately after the affliction of those days the sun will grow dark, and the moon will not provide its light, and the stars will fall from heaven, and the powers of the heavens will tremble.[iv]

---

[i] See Luke 21:21 which appears to refer to the Roman army as a fulfillment of this sign. See also Daniel 9:27.

[ii] The term translated "elect" is used over twenty times in the New Testament and is most often a reference to those who are called by God to true faith that perseveres Also in verses 24, 31, 37, and 39.

[iii] Or, "parousia." Parousia is a technical term that can mean coming, presence, or visitation.

[iv] See Isaiah 13:10; 24:23; and 34:4 for this common Old Testament sign portending judgment against a nation.

³⁰"Then the sign that the Son of Man is in heaven will appear, and then all the tribes of the land will mourn, and they will see the Son of Man coming upon the clouds of heaven with power and great glory. ³¹Then he will send his messengers with the sound of a great trumpet, and they will gather his elect from the four winds from one end of the heavens to the other.

³²"Now learn the parable of the fig tree, when its branches are already soft, and it produces leaves, you know that the summer is near at hand. ³³In just the same way, you also, whenever you see all these things, know that it is near to the door. ³⁴I am telling you the truth; this current generation will most certainly not pass away until all these things happen. ³⁵The heaven and the earth will pass away, but my words will never pass away.

Jesus Answers a Second Question

³⁶"Now concerning[v] your question about the day and hour, no one knows except the Father alone, not even the angels of the heavens nor the Son. ³⁷Just as it was in the days of Noah, so it will also be at the visitation of the Son of Man. ³⁸For like it was in those days before the cataclysm, people were eating and drinking, marrying and giving in marriage until the day Noah entered into the ark; ³⁹and they did not understand until the cataclysm came and took them all. It will be just like that at the visitation of the Son of Man. ⁴⁰Then two men will be in the field, one will be taken, and one will be left. ⁴¹Two women will be grinding grain in the mill, one will be taken, and one will be left.

⁴²"Therefore, watch, because you do not know what day your Lord will come. ⁴³But know this, that if the master of the house had known at what watch of the night the thief was coming, he would have kept watch, and he would not have permitted his

---

[v] Jesus signals that he is moving to the next question using the normal way of doing so, "Now concerning your next question" (peri de). Compare Paul's similar use of this term in 1 Corinthians chapter 7 and following.

house to be burglarized. ⁴⁴For this reason, you also must be ready, because the Son of Man is coming at an hour when you do not believe he will.

⁴⁵"Who, therefore, is the faithful and wise servant, whose lord puts in charge over his household to give everyone their food at the correct time? ⁴⁶Blessed is that servant when his lord comes if he finds him acting in this way. ⁴⁷I am telling you the truth; he will put him in charge of all his possessions. ⁴⁸But if that servant is bad and says in his heart, 'My master is staying away a long time,' ⁴⁹and then begins to abuse his fellow servants, and to eat and drink with the heavy drinkers, ⁵⁰the master of that servant will come on a day he does not expect, and at an hour he does not know. ⁵¹He will cut him to pieces, and assign his portion with the hypocrites, where there will be weeping and gnashing of teeth.

The Importance of Keeping Watch: The Ten Virgins
Chapter Twenty-Five
¹"At that time, the Kingdom of the Heavens will be like ten virgins, who took their lamps and went out to meet the bridegroom. ²But five of them were foolish, and five possessed understanding. ³For the foolish ones took their lamps but did not take oil with them. ⁴However, the understanding ones took oil in containers with their lamps. ⁵When the bridegroom was delayed, they all became sleepy and fell asleep.

⁶"In the middle of the night, a shout went out, 'Pay attention, the bridegroom is here! Come out to meet him.' ⁷Then all those virgins got up and prepared their lamps.

⁸"But the foolish ones said to the understanding ones, 'Give some of your oil to us. Our lamps are going out.'

⁹"But the understanding ones responded saying, 'There will not be enough for you and us. Go rather to the ones who sell oil

and buy some for yourselves.' ¹⁰But when they went out to buy some, the bridegroom came, and the ones who were ready went in with him to the marriage feast; and the door was shut.

¹¹"But later the rest of the virgins came saying, 'Lord, Lord, open the door for us.'

¹²"But answering, he said, 'Truly I say to you, I do not know you.' ¹³Therefore watch, because you do not know the day nor the hour the Son of Man is coming.

The Importance of Being Engaged: Using Opportunities

¹⁴"For it will be like a man traveling away from home. He called his servants and granted them authority over his possessions. ¹⁵To one he gave five talents,ⁱ to another, two, and to another, one; each according to his capability. Then he left on his journey. ¹⁶The one who had received the five talents immediately went and worked with them, and he made another five talents in profit. ¹⁷In like manner, the one who had received two talents made another two talents in profit. ¹⁸But the one who had received one talent went out and dug a hole in the ground and hid his master's silver.

¹⁹"After a long time, the master of those servants came home and settled accounts with them. ²⁰Then the one who had received five talents came and brought the other five talents. He reported, 'Master, you gave me five talents. See I have made another five in profit.'

²¹"His master said to him, 'You have done well, good and faithful servant. You have been consistently faithful with a few things, I will put you in charge of many things. Come experience the joy of your master.'

ⁱ A talent of silver was about six thousand denarii. Since a denarius was the average daily wage of a soldier or day laborer, each talent was the equivalent of twenty years of wages. A talent of gold was worth about thirty times more than this.

²²"Then the one who had received two talents also came. He reported, 'Master, you granted me authority over two talents. See, I have made another two talents in profit.'

²³"His master said to him, 'You have done well, good and faithful servant. You have been consistently faithful with a few things, I will put you in charge of many things. Come experience the joy of your master.'

²⁴"Then the one who received the one talent also came. He reported, 'Master, I knew you, that you are a harsh man, reaping where you did not sow and collecting where you did not invest. ²⁵So I was afraid and went out and hid your talent in the ground. See, here is what is yours.'

²⁶"Then his master responded and said to him, 'You evil and fear-driven servant! You knew that I reap where I have not sown, and collect where I did not invest? ²⁷Then weren't you obligated to invest my silver with the bankers so when I returned I would have received my property with interest? ²⁸Therefore, take the talent from him and give it to the one who has ten talents. ²⁹For everyone who has faithfully worked with my property will be given even more, and he will have an abundance. But the one who has not done so, even what he has will be taken from him. ³⁰Throw the worthless servant into the darkness outside. There will be weeping and gnashing of teeth out there.'

Separating the Wise from the Foolish: The Sheep and Goats[i]

³¹"When the Son of Man comes in his glory, and all the angels with him, he will sit upon his throne of glory. ³²Then all the nations will be gathered in front of him, and he will separate them from each other just as a shepherd separates the sheep from the goats. ³³He will put the sheep on his right, but the goats on his left.

---

[i] This section may be Jesus' answer to a third question about the end of the age (see Matthew 24:3). "The end of the age" is used in Mt. 13:39-40 to speak of sorting believers from unbelievers at the end of the age.

³⁴"Then the King will say to those on his right, 'Come you who are blessed of my Father, inherit the kingdom prepared for you from the founding of the world. ³⁵For I was hungry, and you gave me something to eat; I was thirsty and you gave me a drink; I was not one of you, and you welcomed me with kindness; ³⁶I was naked and you gave me clothes; I was sick, and you cared for me, in prison and you came to me.'

³⁷"Then the righteous will respond and ask him, 'Lord, when did we see you hungry and give you something to eat, or thirsty and give you a drink? ³⁸When did we see that you were not one of us and welcome you with kindness, or naked and give you clothes? ³⁹When did we see you sick or in prison, and come to you?'

⁴⁰"The King responded and said to them, 'I testify to you, as much as you have done it on behalf of one of the least of these my brothers, you have done it for me.'

⁴¹"Then he will say to those on the left, 'Go away from me, you who are cursed, into the eternal fire prepared for the Accuser and his angels. ⁴²For I was hungry, and you did not give me something to eat; I was thirsty and you did not give me a drink; ⁴³I was not one of you, and you did not welcome me with kindness; I was naked and you did not give me clothes; I was sick and in prison and you did not care for me.'

⁴⁴"Then they will respond and ask, 'Lord, when did we see you hungry, thirsty, not one of us, naked, sick, or in prison and not serve you?'

⁴⁵"He will respond to them and say, 'I testify to you, as much as you have not done it on behalf of one of the least of these, you have not done it for me.' ⁴⁶At that time these will depart unto eternal punishment, but the righteous to eternal life."

Passover Draws Near: Jesus' Enemies Plot His Death

Chapter Twenty-Six

¹When Jesus had finished all these explanations, he said to his disciples, ²"You know that in two days, the Passover will start, and the Son of Man will be handed over to be crucified."

³Then the chief priests and the elders of the people gathered together in the courtyard of the high priest, who was called Caiaphas, ⁴and they consulted together so that they might arrest Jesus in a deceptive way and kill him. ⁵But they kept repeating, "Not during the feast, so that there is no outcry among the people."

Jesus Prepared for His Burial

⁶When Jesus was in Bethany at the house of Simon the leper, ⁷a woman who had an alabaster container of very expensive aromatic oil came and poured it over his head while he reclined at the table. ⁸But when the disciples saw it, they were angry and said, "Why has this been wasted? ⁹This aromatic oil could have been sold for a lot of money, and the proceeds given to the poor."

¹⁰But when Jesus noted this, he said, "Why are you giving this woman trouble? For she has done an honorable thing to me. ¹¹You always have the poor with you, but you will not always have me. ¹²When she poured this aromatic oil over my body, she did this to prepare me for burial. ¹³I am telling you the truth, wherever this good news is proclaimed in the whole world, what she has done will be spoken about in her memory."

Judas Seeks a Payday: He Agrees to Betray Jesus

¹⁴Immediately after this,ⁱ one of the twelve, the one called Judas Iscariot, went to the chief priests ¹⁵and said, "What are you willing to give me so that I hand him over to you?" Then they promised him thirty silver coins. ¹⁶From that time on, he kept looking for an appropriate opportunity to hand him over.

ⁱ According to John 12:4-6, Judas had been the one who led the attack over the anointing of Jesus because he was greedy for the money.

Jesus Blocks Judas' Ability to Disrupt the Last Supper

17On the first day of the Feast of Unleavened Bread, the disciples came to Jesus and asked, "Where do you wish that we prepare the Passover for you to eat?"

18He said, "Go into the city until you meet a notable man,[ii] and say to him, 'The teacher says, "My time is near at hand. I am keeping the Passover with my disciples at your place."'" 19The disciples did as Jesus instructed them, and they prepared the Passover.

20When evening had come, Jesus was reclining at the table with his twelve disciples. 21While they were eating, he said, "I am telling you the truth, one from among you will hand me over to my enemies."

22Because they were very distressed, each one began to ask him, "It is certainly not me, Lord, is it?"

23Then he answered and said, "The one who dips his hand with me in the dish, this one will hand me over. 24On the one hand, the Son of Man will go just as it is written concerning him, but woe to that man through whom the Son of Man is handed over. It would be good for that man if he had not been born."

25Then Judas, the one who was handing him over to his enemies, responded and asked, "It is certainly not me, is it, Rabbi?" Jesus said to him, "You yourself have declared it."

Jesus Gives New Meaning to the Passover Meal

26While they were eating, Jesus took a loaf of bread and blessed it. He broke it, and when he had given it to his disciples he said, "Take, eat; this is my body."

[ii] Both Luke 22:10 and Mark 14:13 state that the man was carrying a container of water.

²⁷Then, after he took the cup and gave thanks, he gave it to them and said, "Drink from it, everyone; ²⁸for this is my blood of the new covenant which is being poured out on behalf of many for the forgiveness of sins. ²⁹But I say to you, I will most certainly not drink from this fruit of the vine from now until that day when I drink it with you in a new way in my Father's Kingdom."

Jesus Predicts the Disciples' Failure

³⁰After they sang a hymn, they went out to the Mount of Olives. ³¹Then Jesus said to them, "You will all stumble over me this night, for it is written, 'I will strike the shepherd, and the sheep of the flock will be scattered.'ⁱ ³²But after I am raised, I will go ahead of you into Galilee."

³³Then Peter responded and said to him, "If everyone stumbles over you, I will never stumble over you."

³⁴Jesus said to him, "I am telling you the truth, on this night, before the rooster crows, you will deny that you know me three times."

³⁵Peter said to him, "If I must die with you, I will most certainly never deny knowing you." In a similar way, all the other disciples spoke the same way.

Jesus' Struggle in Gethsemane

³⁶Then Jesus arrived with them at a place called Gethsemane, and he said to his disciples, "Sit here while I go over there to pray." ³⁷He took Peter and the two sons of Zebedee and began to be distressed and troubled. ³⁸Then he said to them, "My soul is very distressed, even to the point of death; remain here and stay awake with me."

³⁹When he had gone a small distance, he fell upon his face praying, and said, "My Father, if it is possible, let this cup pass by me; however, do not do as I desire, but as you desire."

ⁱ Zechariah 13:7

⁴⁰Then he went to his disciples and found them sleeping. He said to Peter, "So you did not have the strength to stay awake with me for one hour? ⁴¹Stay awake and pray, so that you do not enter into temptation; the spirit is certainly ready, but the flesh is weak."

⁴²Again, he went away for the second time and prayed saying, "My Father, if it is not possible to have this cup pass by without drinking it, let your will be done."

⁴³He went again and found them sleeping, for their eyes were heavy. ⁴⁴He left them again and went away and prayed for a third time, saying the same prayer again.

⁴⁵Then he went to his disciples and said to them, "Sleep and take your rest at another time. Look, the hour has drawn near, and the Son of Man is being delivered into the hands of sinners. ⁴⁶Get up! Let us go! See, the one who is handing me over has drawn near."

Jesus Betrayed and Arrested

⁴⁷While he was still speaking, indeed Judas, one of the twelve approached; and there was a large crowd with him armed with swords and clubs sent from the chief priests and elders of the people. ⁴⁸The one who was handing him over to his enemies had given them a sign explaining, "The one I kiss is the one. Arrest him." ⁴⁹He immediately approached Jesus and said, "Greetings, Rabbi," and kissed him.

⁵⁰But Jesus said to him, "Friend, for this greeting you have come?"

Then they came and laid hands on Jesus and arrested him. ⁵¹Unexpectedly, one of those with Jesus reached out his hand and drew his sword. He struck the servant of the high priest and cut off his ear.

⁵²Then Jesus said to him, "Return your sword to its place; for everyone who takes up the sword will suffer loss by the sword. ⁵³Or do you think that I am not able to call upon my Father, and

he will at once provide me with more than twelve legions[i] of angels? ⁵⁴Then how would the Scriptures be fulfilled that say it must happen in this way?"

⁵⁵At that hour, Jesus said to the crowds, "Have you come out with swords and clubs to apprehend me like you would a rebel? I was sitting with you each day in the temple teaching, and you did not arrest me. ⁵⁶But this whole thing has taken place that the Scriptures of the prophets might be fulfilled." Then all his disciples abandoned him and fled.

Jesus Tried and Condemned

⁵⁷Those who had arrested Jesus brought him back to Caiaphas, the high priest, where the scribal scholars and the elders had gathered.

⁵⁸Peter followed him at some distance to the courtyard of the high priest, and when he went in, he was sitting with the officials to see what would happen.

⁵⁹Then the chief priests and the entire Sanhedrin were seeking for false witnesses against Jesus so that they might put him to death. ⁶⁰But they did not find any, though many false witnesses came forward. Finally, two came forward ⁶¹and said, "This man said, 'I am able to destroy the temple of God and rebuild it in three days.'"

⁶²The high priest rose up and asked him, "Will you answer nothing? What are these men testifying against you?" ⁶³But Jesus kept silent.

Then the high priest said to him, "I charge you under oath by the living God that you tell us if you are the Christ, the Son of God."

⁶⁴Jesus said to him, "You yourself have declared it. In addition, I tell you that from this time forward you will see the Son of Man sitting at the right hand of power and coming on the clouds of heaven."

---

[i] A Roman army legion, though its size varied, averaged about 5,000 men.

⁶⁵Then the high priest tore his clothes and said, "He has blasphemed!ⁱⁱ Why do we still have need of witnesses? Look, now you have heard the blasphemy, ⁶⁶what do you think?"

Those who responded said, "He is worthy of death."

⁶⁷At that time, they spat in his face and beat him; but some who slapped him ⁶⁸said, "Prophesy to us, Christ, who struck you?"

Peter's Failure

⁶⁹Peter was sitting outside in the courtyard. One servant girl approached him and said, "You yourself were also with Jesus the Galilean."

⁷⁰But he denied knowing him in front of them all and said, "I do not know what you are saying!"

⁷¹When he had gone out to the entrance, another girl saw him and said to those who were there, "This man was with Jesus of Nazareth."

⁷²Again, he denied knowing him with an oath, "I do not know the man!"

⁷³After a little while, those standing around approached Peter and said, "You are certainly one of them, for even your manner of speaking makes you obvious."

⁷⁴Then he began to call down curses on himself, and to swear, "I do not know the man!"

Immediately, a rooster crowed; ⁷⁵and Peter remembered the word of Jesus which he had spoken, "Before a rooster crows, you will deny that you know me three times." After he went outside, he wept bitterly.

ⁱⁱBlasphemy is about speaking profanely of sacred things, to slander God, or to speak against him.

Jesus Handed over to Pilate

Chapter Twenty-Seven

¹When morning arrived, all the chief priests and the elders of the people took counsel against Jesus in order to put him to death. ²They bound him, led him away, and handed him over to Pilate the governor.

Judas' Death

³Then, when Judas, the one who had handed him over, saw that he was condemned, he regretted his decision and returned the thirty silver coins to the chief priests and elders. ⁴He said, "I have sinned by handing over innocent blood *to you*."

They responded, "What is that to us? You take responsibility for that."

⁵Judas threw the silver coins into the temple and departed. After he left, he went out and hanged himself.

⁶Then the chief priests took the silver coins and said, "It is not right that we put them into the temple treasury, since it is a payment for blood."

⁷When they took counsel together, they bought the potter's field with the silver coins for a burial place for foreigners. ⁸So, that field has been called the Field of Blood to this day. ⁹Then the word *given* through Jeremiah the prophet was fulfilled that said,

> "And they took the thirty silver coins, his estimated value that was set by those from among the sons of Israel. ¹⁰And they gave them for the potter's field, as the Lord directed me."[i]

Jesus' Trial Before Pilate

¹¹Now Jesus was arraigned before the governor; and the governor interrogated him asking, "Are you the king of the Jews?"

---

[i] This prophecy is a compilation of several passages in Jeremiah and in Zechariah 11:12-13.

Jesus replied, "You yourself are saying it."

¹²While he was being charged by the chief priests and elders, he did not answer. ¹³Then Pilate asked him, "Don't you hear how many charges they are bringing?" ¹⁴But he did not give him an answer for even one charge, so that the governor was very bewildered.

¹⁵Now the governor kept a tradition during the feast to release to the crowd one prisoner whom they wanted. ¹⁶At that time, they held a well-known prisoner named Barabbas.[ii] ¹⁷So, when they had gathered, Pilate asked them, "Whom do you wish that I release to you, Barabbas, or Jesus who is called Christ?" ¹⁸For he knew that they had handed him over out of jealousy.

Pilate's Wife Receives a Warning Dream

¹⁹While he was sitting upon his judgement seat, his wife sent *a message* to him that said, "Let nothing transpire between you and that righteous man; for today I have suffered much in a dream about him."

The Religious Leaders Persuade the Crowd

²⁰But the chief priests and the elders persuaded the crowds[iii] to request Barabbas, and to execute Jesus. ²¹The governor responded and asked them, "Of the two, which do you prefer that I release to you?"

They said, "Barabbas."

²²Pilate asked them, "Then what should I do with Jesus, the one called Christ?"

Everyone said, "Let him be crucified!"

²³But he said, "What has he done wrong?"

[ii] Early tradition (and a minor number of Greek manuscripts) identify this man as "Jesus Barabbas" (also in verse 17).

[iii] Since Jesus was arrested overnight in secret, the only bystanders present would have been those interested in clemency for Barabbas, not Jesus.

They shouted all the more, "Let him be crucified!"

²⁴When Pilate saw that he was achieving nothing, but rather that a disturbance was beginning, he took water and washed his hands in front of the crowd and said, "I am innocent of this man's blood. You take the responsibility."

²⁵All the people responded and said, "His blood be on us and our children."

²⁶Then he released Barabbas to them, but he had Jesus whipped severely, and handed him over to be crucified.

The Soldiers Add to Jesus' Suffering

²⁷At that time, the soldiers of the governor took Jesus into the Praetorium[i] and gathered the entire Roman cohort around him. ²⁸They removed his clothing and wrapped a scarlet military cloak around him. ²⁹They also wove a crown from thorny weeds and put it upon his head, and they put a reed in his right hand. Then they knelt before him and mocked him saying, "Greetings, King of the Jews!" ³⁰Then they spat on him and took the reed and struck him on his head. ³¹When they had mocked him, they took off the robe and dressed him in his own clothing and led him out to be crucified.

Jesus is Crucified

³²When they were going out, they found a man from Cyrene by the name of Simon. They pressed him into their service so that he might carry Jesus' crossbeam. ³³When they came to the place called Golgotha, which is called place of the skull, ³⁴they gave him wine mixed with bitter liquid[ii] to drink, but after he tasted it, he did not want to drink it.

³⁵When they crucified him, they divided his clothing by casting lots, so that the word through the prophet might be fulfilled,

---

[i] The Praetorium was the palace of the Roman governor.

[ii] Mark 15:23 identifies the bitter liquid a myrrh.

"They divided my clothing among themselves,
and cast lots for my garment."[iii]

[36]Then, while they were sitting down, they began to keep watch over him there. [37]They also placed the accusation against him above his head. It read, "This is Jesus, the King of the Jews." [38]At the same time, two rebels were crucified with him, one on his right side, and one on his left side. [39]Those who were passing by slandered[iv] him and were shaking their heads. [40]They said, "You are the one who was going to destroy the temple and rebuild it in three days. Save yourself! If you are the Son of God, come down from the cross."

[41]In like manner, the chief priests also were mocking him along with the scribal scholars and elders. They kept on saying, [42]"He saved others and is not able to save himself. He is the king of Israel; let him come down now from the cross and we will believe in him. [43]He relies on God, let God rescue him now if he wants him—for he said, 'I am a Son of God.'" [44]The two rebels who were also crucified with him were also disparaging him with the same insults.

Signs and Portents Around Jesus' Suffering and Death

[45]Darkness came upon all the land from the sixth hour until the ninth hour.[v] [46]Jesus cried out with a loud voice about the ninth hour and said, "Eli, Eli, lama sabachthani?" that is, "My God, My God, why have you abandoned me?"[vi]

[47]Then some who were standing there, after they heard, said, "This man is calling Elijah."

[48]Immediately, one from among them ran over and took a sponge, filled it with sour wine, placed it on a reed, and gave him

---

[iii] Psalm 22:18

[iv] Or, "blasphemed."

[v] From noon to 3:00 PM.

[vi] Psalm 22:1

a drink; ⁴⁹and the rest said, "Allow this!ⁱ Let us see whether Elijah will save him."

⁵⁰Then Jesus, when he again cried out with a loud voice, released his spirit.

⁵¹Just then, the curtain of the temple was split into two pieces from top to bottom, the land was shaken, and the rocks were split. ⁵²The tombs were also opened, and many bodies of the saints who had fallen asleep were raised to life.ⁱⁱ ⁵³They came out from the tombs, and after Jesus' resurrection went into the holy city. They appeared to many people.

⁵⁴When the centurion and those who were with him keeping watch over Jesus, saw the earthquake and the things that had happened, they were very much afraid and kept on saying, "Truly this man was the Son of God."

The Faithful Few Continue to Watch and Serve

⁵⁵There were many women there observing from a distance. They had followed Jesus from Galilee to provide for him. ⁵⁶Among them were Mary Magdalene, Mary the mother of James and Joseph, and the mother of the sons of Zebedee.

⁵⁷When evening had come, a wealthy man from Arimathea arrived. His name was Joseph, and he himself also was a disciple of Jesus. ⁵⁸This man went to Pilate and requested the body of Jesus. Then Pilate ordered that it be given to him. ⁵⁹When Joseph took the body, he wrapped it in a clean linen cloth ⁶⁰and placed it in his own new tomb which he had chiseled in the rock. When he had placed a large stone against the opening of the tomb, he departed. ⁶¹Mary Magdalene was there, and the other Mary. They were sitting near the tomb.

ⁱ In Mark the soldier says, "Allow me to do this." In Matthew, the other soldiers agree with him and speak on behalf of the one giving the drink since the Centurion had to give permission for it to happen.

ⁱⁱ See Romans 3:25. This was a sign that Jesus' death had now paid for their sins also.

Pilate Sets a Guard

⁶²On the next day, the one after the Day of Preparation,[iii] the chief priests and Pharisees came together to Pilate. ⁶³They said, "Sir, we have remembered that while he was still alive that deceiver said, 'I will rise again after three days.' ⁶⁴Therefore, issue an order that the tomb be made secure until the third day, so that his disciples don't come, steal him during the night, and say to the people, 'He was raised from among the dead.' The last deception will be greater than the first one."

⁶⁵Pilate said to them, "Take charge of a guard unit. Go, make it secure as you know how." ⁶⁶Then they went and made the tomb secure, posting the guard and placing a seal upon the stone.

Jesus Rises from the Dead

Chapter Twenty-Eight

¹After the Sabbath, toward sunrise on the first day of the week, Mary Magdalene and the other Mary came to see the tomb.

²Incredibly, a great earthquake shook the area; for an angel of the Lord came down from heaven. When he had come, he rolled away the stone and sat on it. ³His appearance was like lightning, and his clothes were white as snow. ⁴Those who kept watch shook with fear, and became as dead men.

⁵Then the angel responded and said to the women, "Stop being afraid; for I know that you are seeking Jesus, who was crucified. ⁶He is not here, for he was raised to life, just as he said. Come and see the place where he lay. ⁷Now go quickly to tell his disciples, 'He was raised from among the dead,' and 'Know this, he is going ahead of you into Galilee. You will see him there.' See, I have told you."

[iii] The day of Preparation (Friday) was the day one prepared for the Sabbath (Saturday)

⁸They went out from the tomb quickly, with fear and great joy, and ran to bring the news to his disciples. ⁹At that point, while they were going, Jesus met them and said, "Greetings!" They came and clung to his feet and worshiped him. ¹⁰Then Jesus said to them, "Stop being afraid! Go and bring the news to my brothers so that they go into Galilee. There they will see me."

The Guards Recover

¹¹But while they were going, note that some of the guards went into the city and brought the news to the high priests about all the things that had happened. ¹²When they met with the elders and took counsel together, they gave a large amount of silver to the soldiers, telling them, ¹³"Say, 'His disciples came by night and stole him while we were sleeping.' ¹⁴If this is reported to the governor, we will persuade him, and we will keep you safe from any concern." ¹⁵So, they took the silver and did as they were told; and this report has spread among all the Jews, even to this day.

The Disciples Meet Jesus in Galilee: The Great Commission

¹⁶But the eleven disciples went to Galilee to the mountain to which Jesus had directed them. ¹⁷When they saw him, they worshiped him. But some hesitated.[i]

¹⁸Then Jesus came and spoke to them saying, "All authority in heaven and on earth has been granted to me. ¹⁹Therefore, when you go from here, make all nations into disciples, baptizing them in the name of the Father, and of the Son, and of the Holy Spirit, ²⁰teaching them to obey all the things I have commanded you. And know this, I am with you all the days that remain from now until the end of this age. Amen."

---

[i] According to 1 Corinthians 15:6, over five hundred disciples had gathered. The gospels focus on the interaction of Jesus with the twelve, but he had given this command to the wider group of disciples who began to gather together at the mountain in Galilee as Jesus had told them.

MARK

The Baptizer Steps into His Prophetic Purpose

Chapter One

¹The beginning of the Gospel[i] of Jesus Christ, the Son of God.

²Just as it is written in Isaiah the prophet,

> "Behold I am sending my messenger before you,
> who will prepare your journey."[ii]
>
> ³"A voice calling in the desert, 'Prepare the way
> of the Lord. Make his highways straight.'"[iii]

⁴John came baptizing in the desert and preaching a baptism of repentance for the forgiveness of sins. ⁵All the region of Judea, and all those in Jerusalem, went out to him. Confessing their sins, they were baptized by him in the Jordan River. ⁶John was wearing camel hair with a leather belt around his waist. He was eating locusts and honey from the fields. ⁷While he was

---

[i] The Greek word can be translated "Gospel" or "Good News." The word gospel means good news. It is translated both ways in this Bible version.

[ii] Malachi 3:1

[iii] Isaiah 40:3

preaching, he explained, "One greater than I am is coming after me. I am not even worthy to stoop down and loose the thong of his sandals. ⁸I baptize you with water, but he will baptize you in the Holy Spirit."

Jesus Empowered by the Spirit, and Tested by Satan

⁹In those days, it happened that Jesus came from Nazareth of Galilee and was baptized by John in the Jordan. ¹⁰As soon as he came up out of the water, he saw the heavens rent open and the Spirit descending on him like a dove. ¹¹Then a voice came from the heavens, "You are my cherished Son. I am well pleased by you."

¹²Then the Spirit immediately compelled him to go out into the desert. ¹³As a result, he was in the desert forty days being tested by Satan. He was with the wild animals, but the angels were attending to him.

Jesus Begins to Preach the Gospel of the Kingdom

¹⁴Later, after John was arrested, Jesus came into Galilee preaching the good news about God ¹⁵by reporting, "The time is completed, and the Kingdom of God has drawn near. Repent and believe the good news."

Jesus Begins to Build His Ministry Team

¹⁶At another time, while he was going along beside the sea of Galilee, he saw Simon and his brother Andrew casting a net into the sea, for they were fishermen. ¹⁷Then Jesus said to them, "Come after me, and I will make you into fishermen who catch men." ¹⁸At once they dropped their nets and followed him.

¹⁹After he went a little further, he saw James[i] the son of Zebedee and his brother John mending their nets in their boat. ²⁰So he immediately called them. Then, after they left their

---

[i] Greek text, "Jacob." James is the Anglicized form of Jacob used since the first English translations. Unless it refers to the patriarch Jacob, it is translated as James in this New Testament.

father Zebedee in the boat with the hired workers, they followed after him.

Jesus Demonstrates the Kingdom: Authority over a Demon

21 They went into Capernaum, and on the next Sabbath, Jesus went into the synagogue and was teaching there. 22 Those in attendance were overwhelmed by his teaching, for he was teaching them as one who had authority, and not like the scribal scholars. 23 Right at that time, a man who was in their synagogue and had an unclean spirit shouted out 24 demanding, "Why are you bothering us, Jesus of Nazareth? Have you come to destroy us? I know who you are, the Holy One of God."

25 So Jesus rebuked him and said, "Be silent and come out of him!" 26 After it convulsed the man, and cried out with a great cry, the unclean spirit left him.

27 Everyone was so astonished that they questioned each other asking, "What is this? *It is* a new teaching demonstrated with authority. He even commands the unclean spirits, and they obey him." 28 So the report about him promptly went out everywhere into the entire region of Galilee.

Jesus Demonstrates the Kingdom: Healing the Sick and Demonized

29 When they came out of the synagogue, they went directly to the house of Simon and Andrew. James and John accompanied them. 30 But Simon's mother-in-law was lying down with a fever, so they spoke to Jesus about her as soon as he arrived. 31 Then he went to her. He took her by the hand and raised her to her feet. At that moment, the fever left her, and she was able to begin serving them.

32 Then, when evening came, when the sun had set *and the Sabbath ended*, they brought to him everyone who had any type of illness, and those troubled with demons. 33 So the whole city was gathered at the door. 34 At that time, Jesus healed many who had various severe diseases. He also drove many demons out, but he did not permit the demons to speak because they knew him.

Mark 1:35

Jesus' Defines His Purpose to His Disciples

³⁵He rose early the next morning while it was still dark and went out *of the house*. Then he traveled to a deserted place where he spent time praying. ³⁶Simon and those with him searched for him. ³⁷When they found him, they told him, "Everyone is seeking you."

³⁸But Jesus said to them, "Let us go to other cities that have marketplaces, in order that I also might preach there. I have come for this very purpose." ³⁹So he went into all of Galilee preaching in their synagogues and driving demons out.

Jesus Touches a Leper and Heals Him

⁴⁰Then a leper came to him. He pleaded with him on his knees and said, "If you are willing, you are able to heal me."

⁴¹Jesus was filled with compassion, so he extended his hand and touched him. Then he said to him, "I am willing. Be clean!" ⁴²After he said *this*, the leprosy immediately left him, and he was clean. ⁴³Then Jesus bluntly warned him, and immediately sent him away.

⁴⁴He said this to him, "See that you tell nothing about this to anyone, but go show yourself to the priests and make the offering for your cleansing that Moses commanded, as a testimony to them." ⁴⁵But when the man had gone, he began to share what happened openly, and spread the word everywhere, so that Jesus was no longer able to come into a city openly. So, he remained outside in deserted places. In spite of this, people kept coming to him from everywhere.

Jesus Demonstrates Authority to Forgive

Chapter Two

¹Some days after the healing of the leper, when Jesus came again to Capernaum, the word went out that Jesus was home. ²As a result, so many gathered that there was no longer any room *at the house*, not even near the door. Then Jesus spoke the word to them. ³At that

time, four men came to him bringing a paralyzed man whom they were carrying. ⁴Since they were not able to bring him through the crowd, they removed some tiles above where Jesus was speaking. After they were finished breaking it open, they lowered the bed on which the paralytic was lying. ⁵When Jesus saw their faith, he said to the man who was paralyzed, "Son, your sins are pardoned."

⁶But some of the scribal scholars were sitting there and thinking in their hearts, ⁷"What is this man saying? He is blaspheming!ⁱ Who is able to forgive sins except the One God?"

⁸Then immediately, when Jesus perceived in his spirit that they were thinking this way, he said to them, "Why are you thinking these things in your hearts? ⁹What is easier, to say to the paralytic, 'Your sins are pardoned,' or to say, 'Get up, pick up your bed and walk around'? ¹⁰But in order that you might know that the Son of Man possesses authority to pardon sins upon the earth," he said to the paralyzed man, ¹¹"I say to you, 'Get up! Pick up your bed and go home.'" ¹²Then the man got up, picked up his bed immediately, and went out in front of everyone. So, all the people were beside themselves with ecstatic joy,ⁱⁱ and they glorified God by saying, "We have never seen such things!"

Jesus Demonstrates His Love for Outcasts

¹³Jesus went out again beside the sea, and all the people kept coming to him, so he continued teaching them. ¹⁴While he was walking along, he saw Leviⁱⁱⁱ the son of Alphaeus sitting at the tax collection station, and he said to him, "Follow me!" So he stood up and followed him.

¹⁵As it happened, Jesus ended up dining at Levi's house, and many tax collectors and sinners were enjoying a meal with Jesus and his disciples; for many tax collectors and sinners were

---

ⁱ Blasphemy is about speaking profanely of sacred things, to slander God, or to speak against him.

ⁱⁱ "Beside themselves with ecstatic joy" translates a Greek verb used when referring to spiritual ecstatic phenomena in ancient times.

ⁱⁱⁱ Also called Matthew (see Matthew 9:9-13).

already following him. ¹⁶When the scribal scholars who belonged to the *party* of the Pharisees saw that Jesus was eating with sinners and tax collectors, they began questioning his disciples, "Why is he eating with tax collectors and sinners?"

¹⁷When Jesus heard about it, he said to them, "Those who are healthy have no need of a physician, but only those who are ill. I have not come to call righteous people, but sinners."

Preserving the Old and the New Spiritual Forms

¹⁸Then John's disciples and the Pharisees were fasting. So they came and questioned him, "Why do John's disciples and the disciples of the Pharisees fast, but your disciples are not fasting?"

¹⁹So Jesus responded to them, "The guests at a wedding cannot fast while the bridegroom is with them, can they? As long as they have the bridegroom with them, they are not able to fast. ²⁰But the days will come when the bridegroom is taken from them. In that day they will fast."

²¹"No one sews a piece of shrinkable cloth upon an old garment. But if someone does, the old garment's new patch will separate from the main part of the garment, and the tear will become more severe. ²²In the same way, no one puts new wine into old inflexible wineskins. But if someone does, the fermenting wine will break the wineskins, and the wine and the wineskin will be destroyed. On the contrary, new wine must go into new flexible wine skins."

The Son of Man is Lord of the Sabbath

²³At another time, while he was passing by a grain field on the Sabbath, and his disciples began to walk along picking heads of grain, ²⁴the Pharisees questioned him, "Look, why do they do what is not legal to do on the Sabbath?"

²⁵But Jesus said to them, "Have you never read what David did when he had need, when he and those with him were hungry? ²⁶How he went into the house of God during the time of Abiathar the high priest, and he ate the bread of presentation,

which you are not permitted to eat if you are not a priest? And how he also gave it to those with him?"

²⁷Then he said to them, "The Sabbath was created for man, but man was not created for the Sabbath. ²⁸For this reason the Son of Man is also master of the Sabbath."

Setting a Trap for Jesus

Chapter Three

¹Then Jesus went again into the synagogue. A man was there who had a hand with withering paralysis. ²So the Pharisees were watching Jesus to see if he would heal the man on a Sabbath day, because they wanted to accuse him *of violating the Sabbath*. ³Jesus said to the man who had the hand with the withering paralysis, "Stand up in the middle *of the congregation*."

⁴Jesus then questioned them, "Is it lawful to do good on the Sabbath or, instead, to allow evil to occur; to rescue someone's life, or allow him to die?" But they refused to speak. ⁵He looked around at them with exasperation, and was deeply grieved by their hardness of heart. Jesus said to the man, "Extend your hand." The man extended his hand, and it was restored as healthy as his other hand.

⁶When the Pharisees left the meeting, they immediately took counsel with the followers of King Herod about how they might destroy Jesus.

The Crushing Chaos of the Crowds

⁷After that, Jesus traveled with his disciples from there to the sea, and multitudes of people from Galilee followed. Multitudes more also came to him from Judea, ⁸Jerusalem, Idumea, the far side of the Jordan, and the region of Tyre and Sidon, because they heard all that he was doing. ⁹There were so many people that he directed his disciples to make a small boat ready for him, so that the people would not crush him; ¹⁰for he had healed so

many people, that those who still had afflictions would fall against him in order to touch him.

¹¹In addition, whenever unclean spirits saw him, they fell down before him and shrieked, "You are the Son of God!" ¹²In response, he repeatedly reprimanded them so that they would not make him known.

Twelve Apostles to Preach and Demonstrate the Kingdom of God

¹³At another time, Jesus went up a mountain and summoned the ones he himself preferred, and they came to him. ¹⁴Then he selected twelve, whom he also named apostles, in order that they might be with him, that he might send them to preach, ¹⁵and that they might walk in authority to expel demons. ¹⁶So he selected the twelve, and he gave the name Peter to Simon; ¹⁷he also gave the name Boanerges, which means "Sons of Thunder," to James the son of Zebedee, and to his brother John.

¹⁸He also selected Andrew, Philip, Bartholomew, Matthew, Thomas, James son of Alphaeus, Thaddaeus, Simon the Zealot, ¹⁹and Judas Iscariot, who also handed him over to his enemies.

Jesus' Family Sets Out to Take Charge

²⁰Then he came to his house, and again the crowd gathered there. Jesus and his disciples were so busy that they were not even able to eat a bit of bread. ²¹When his relatives heard about this, they set out to take control of him; for they agreed that he was overcome by an ecstatic spiritual experience.[i]

The Foolishness of Ascribing Kingdom Power to Satan

²²Then the scribal scholars who came down from Jerusalem began to say, "He has been possessed by Beelzebul,"[ii] and, "He drives out demons by the leader of the demons."

---

[i] "An ecstatic spiritual experience" translates a Greek verb used when referring to spiritual ecstatic phenomena in ancient times.

[ii] Another name for Satan.

²³After Jesus had summoned the scribal scholars, he spoke to them in parables: "How is Satan able to expel Satan? ²⁴If a kingdom has been divided against itself, that kingdom is not able to stand. ²⁵In the same way, if a house has been divided against itself, that house cannot stand. ²⁶So, if Satan has risen against his own followers, and is divided against them, he cannot stand. On the contrary, his end has come. ²⁷Instead, it is like this: No one is able to enter into the house of a strong man to steal his goods, unless he first restrains the strong man. Only then will he steal from his house."

The Danger of Ascribing Things of the Spirit to Satan

²⁸"I am telling you the truth, all sins will be forgiven the sons of men, even the many slanders by which they have abused others. ²⁹But whoever slanders[iii] the Holy Spirit will never find forgiveness, even *if he lives* to the end of time. Just the opposite, he is guilty of an eternal sin."

³⁰*He said this* because they were saying: "He has an unclean spirit."

Jesus' Family Arrives to Take Charge

³¹Then Jesus' mother and brothers arrived. They stayed outside of the house and sent a message summoning him. ³²A crowd *of disciples* was sitting around him, and they said to him, "Look, your mother and your brothers and sisters are outside asking about you."

³³He responded by asking them, "Who is my mother and my brothers?"

³⁴With that, Jesus looked at those seated in a circle around him and said, "See, my mother and my brothers. ³⁵For whoever does the will of God, this one is my brother, sister, and mother."

[iii] Or, "blasphemes." To blaspheme is about speaking profanely of sacred things, to slander God, or to speak against him.

Mark 4:1

The Parables of the Kingdom

Chapter Four

¹At another time Jesus again began to teach beside the sea, and a rather large crowd surrounded him. So, he boarded a boat and sat in it out on the sea, but the entire crowd stayed on the land next to the sea. ²At that time, he began to teach them many things in parables. He conveyed his teaching like this:

The Parable of the Planter and the Soils

³"Listen closely and consider this: A planter went out to plant seed. ⁴But while he was broadcasting the seed, some fell beside the road, and the birds came and ate the seed. ⁵Then other seed fell upon an area of shallow soil over buried rocks. As a result, the seed sprouted immediately because the soil wasn't deep enough. ⁶When the sun rose, the heat dried the plant, but because its roots could not reach deep enough, it withered. ⁷Yet other seed fell among thorny plants. The thorny plants grew up and crowded out the seedling, and it produced no fruit. ⁸Finally, other seeds fell into rich soil. While they were growing and increasing in size, they kept producing fruit. One yielded thirty times what was sown, one sixty times, and one a hundred times."

⁹Then he began to use the expression, "Whoever has ears to hear, let him understand."

The Mysteries of the Kingdom Reserved for Disciples

¹⁰When he happened to be away from the crowds, those around him—including the twelve—were asking him about the parable. ¹¹He said to them, "The mystery of the Kingdom of God has been given to you, but to those who are outside everything is given in parables. ¹²In order that,

> " 'Seeing they might see and not perceive, and
> hearing they might hear and not understand,
> otherwise they might turn back, and I might
> forgive them.' "[i]

---

[i] Isaiah 6:9

The Parable of the Planter and the Soils Explained

¹³Then he said to them, "Do you not understand this parable? How then will you truly understand any parable? ¹⁴The planter plants the word. ¹⁵But this is what happens to those beside the road where the word is broadcast: whenever these people hear, Satan comes instantly and takes the word that was broadcast into them. ¹⁶This is what happens to the seed broadcast upon the rocky soil: whenever these people hear the word, they immediately receive it with joy, ¹⁷but they have no root in themselves and are only temporary. Later, when trouble or persecution occurs because of the word, they promptly stumble away. ¹⁸This is what happens to the seed broadcast into the thorny plants: these people are the ones who have heard the word, ¹⁹but the concerns of this age and the deceitful pleasures of wealth, as well as lusts over everything else, enter in and crowd out the word. As a result, it becomes unfruitful. ²⁰Finally, the last ones are the seed broadcast upon the rich soil: These people are the ones who hear the word and receive it as true. As a result, they yield fruit, one thirty times what was sown, one sixty times, and one a hundred times."

The Kingdom Revealed

²¹He also was telling them, "You don't bring a lamp into a room in order to place it under a small basket or under your couch, do you? You bring it in order to place it on a lamp stand, don't you?

²²"For the Kingdom[ii] is only hidden in order that it might be revealed; and it is only concealed in order that it might be plainly seen. ²³If anyone has ears to hear, let him understand."

The Importance of Seeking Understanding

²⁴He was also telling them, "Pay attention to what you are hearing. It will be measured out to you with the same standard of measurement you use. To you who understand, even more will be

---

[ii] Or, "it is only hidden," referring to the Kingdom. It is not intended to stay hidden.

added, ²⁵for the one who has, even more will be given to him; but the one who does not have, even what he has will be taken from him."

The Parable of the Kingdom's Growth: The Power of the Seed

²⁶He also said, "The Kingdom of God is very much like a man who broadcasts seed upon the ground. ²⁷Then he may sleep at night, or rise up during the day, but the seed sprouts and grows though the farmer does not understand how. ²⁸The ground yields fruit without further help *from the man;* first the initial green stalk makes an appearance, then the head of the grain forms, then the mature kernels develop at the top. ²⁹When the grain has ripened, the man immediately wields his sickle, because the harvest has come."

A Parable of the Kingdom's Growth: The Mustard Seed

³⁰He also said, "To what shall we compare the Kingdom of God, or by what parable shall we illustrate it? ³¹*We shall compare it to* a seed of a mustard plant. When it is planted in the ground, it is smaller than all the other agricultural seeds. ³²Yet when it is planted, it grows and becomes larger than all the *other* garden plants. It has such large branches that the birds of the sky are able to nest in its shadow."

³³He was speaking the word to them with many such parables, not going beyond their ability to understand. ³⁴He did not speak to them apart from parables; however, he explained everything privately with his own disciples.

Jesus Demonstrates Authority over Weather Patterns

³⁵Later on that day, when evening had come, he said to his disciples, "Let us go across to the other side *of the lake.*" ³⁶Since Jesus was already in the boat, the disciples were able to take him across once they disengaged from the crowd. Other boats also came along with them. ³⁷Just then an exceptional windstorm developed, and the waves were breaking into the boat so that the water began to swamp the boat. ³⁸As for Jesus, he was in the back of the boat with his head upon a cushion, sleeping. His

disciples woke him and said to him, "Teacher, doesn't it bother you that we are about to founder and die?"

³⁹When he woke up, he rebuked the wind, "Be silent!" He also said to the sea, "Restrain yourself!" So, the wind ceased, and an exceptional calm descended on the sea.

⁴⁰Then he asked them, "Why are you acting like cowards? Do you still not have faith?"

⁴¹But they were overwhelmed with fear, and said to each other, "Who can this man possibly be, that even the wind and the sea obey him?"

Jesus Demonstrates Authority over the Demonic Realm

Chapter Five

¹Then they came to the other side of the sea near the region of the Gerasenes.ⁱ ²When he had traveled away from the boat, a man with an unclean spirit came quickly out from the tombs to meet him. ³This man made his shelter among the tombs because it was no longer possible to bind him, even when they used chains. ⁴For he had often been bound with shackles and chains, but he tore the chains apart and smashed the shackles; no one was strong enough to restrain him. ⁵As a result, night and day he continually cried out among the tombs and in the hills, even cutting himself with sharp stones. ⁶When he saw Jesus from a distance away, he ran and threw himself down before him.

⁷He cried out with a deafening shriek, and then he said, "Why are you harassing me, Jesus, Son of the Most High God! I invoke God against you; you may not torture me!" ⁸For Jesus had been commanding him, "You unclean spirit, come out from the man!"

⁹Jesus also asked him, "What is your name?"

ⁱ A region of Gentiles.

Then the man answered him, "My name is Legion,[i] because we are many." ¹⁰He continued to appeal to Jesus with increasing urgency, hoping that he would not send them out of the region.

¹¹But in that place a large heard of pigs was grazing near a hillside. ¹²So the spirits begged him saying, "Send us into the pigs, in order that we might enter them." ¹³Then he permitted them. After the unclean spirits came out, they entered into the pigs, and the herd rushed headlong down the hill into the sea. There were about two thousand of them, and they all drowned in the sea.

¹⁴Those who were feeding the pigs fled, and carried the news into the city and throughout the countryside. As a result, the residents came to see what had happened. ¹⁵So, they approached Jesus, and they saw the man who had been possessed by the legion of demons sitting clothed and in his right mind. Then they were afraid.

¹⁶Those who had been watching, carefully explained what had happened to the demonized man, and also about the pigs. ¹⁷In response, they began to beg him to depart from their territory.

¹⁸But while Jesus was entering the boat, the man who had been demonized begged him that he might stay with him. ¹⁹However, Jesus did not permit him, but said to him, "Go to your home, to your family and friends, and report to them everything the Lord has done for you; and *tell them* that he had mercy on you." ²⁰Then the man went away and began to proclaim in the Decapolis[ii] everything Jesus had done for him, and everyone was filled with wonder.

Jesus Demonstrates Authority over Sickness and Death

²¹After Jesus crossed over in the boat again to the other side, a large crowd gathered together around him. So, he stayed beside the sea.

---

[i] A Roman army legion, though its size varied, averaged about 5,000 men. Also in verse 15.

[ii] A region east of the Sea of Galilee with ten Greek cities.

Mark 5:36

²²It wasn't long before Jairus, one of the officers of the synagogue, arrived. When he saw Jesus, he fell at his feet ²³and begged him earnestly saying, "My young daughter is near death. I beg you to come so that you might lay your hands upon her that she might be healed and live." ²⁴Then Jesus went with him. But the large crowd kept following him, and crushed against him on every side.

²⁵There was a woman behind Jesus who had suffered from an unusual flow of blood for twelve years. ²⁶She had endured much under the care of many physicians and had exhausted all of her savings without receiving any benefit. In fact, she only grew worse. ²⁷When she heard about Jesus, she came up from behind him and touched his clothing. ²⁸For she thought to herself, "Even if I only touch his clothing, I will be delivered." ²⁹Her flow of blood dried up at once, and she felt in her body that she was healed from the affliction.

³⁰At that moment, Jesus stopped and turned to the crowd following him and said, "Who touched my clothes?" For he felt in his body that power had gone out from him.

³¹Then his disciples responded to him, "You see the crowd pressing in all around you, yet you ask, 'Who touched me?'" ³²But he continued to look around to see who had done it.

³³Finally, the woman, shaking with fear, came and fell before him. She knew what had happened to her and revealed the whole truth to him. ³⁴Then he said to her, "Daughter, your faith has rescued you. Go in peace, be whole and leave your affliction behind."

³⁵While he was still speaking, messengers came from the family of the synagogue officer saying, "Your daughter has died. Why continue to trouble the teacher?"

³⁶But Jesus ignored the report and said to the synagogue officer, "Do not fear, only trust."

³⁷At that time, he did not permit anyone to accompany him except Peter, James, and John the brother of James. ³⁸Then they came to the house of the synagogue officer. Jesus saw the uproar, as well as those who were loudly weeping and wailing, ³⁹and he entered the house and said to them, "Why are you so distressed, and why are you weeping? The child has not died, but she is sleeping."

⁴⁰But they began to laugh scornfully at him. When Jesus himself had forced them all to leave the house, he took the child's father and mother and those he brought with him, and he went into where the child was. ⁴¹Jesus held the child's hand, and said to her, "Talitha koumi," which is translated, "Little girl, I say to you, stand up!"

⁴²Immediately the little girl arose and began to walk about, for she was only twelve years old. Those who saw it were instantly beside themselves with ecstatic joy.[i] ⁴³Then Jesus gave them very clear instructions that no one should be told about it. He also suggested that they give her something to eat.

Jesus Rejected in His Hometown

Chapter Six

¹Then Jesus left that area and went to his hometown; his disciples also accompanied him. ²When the Sabbath came, he began to teach in the synagogue, and many of those who listened were overwhelmed with surprise. They began to ask, "Where did this man get these teachings? Where did he receive this wisdom? How are such miracles being done through his hands? ³Isn't this the carpenter, the son of Mary, and the brother of James, Joseph, Judas, and Simon? His sisters are also here among us, aren't they?" So, they were shocked and scandalized by him.

---

[i] Beside themselves with ecstatic joy" translates a Greek noun used when referring to spiritual ecstatic phenomena in ancient times.

⁴Then Jesus said to them, "A prophet is not usually looked down upon except in his hometown, among his own relatives, and in his own house." ⁵As a result, he was not able to do any miracles there, except that he did place his hands on a few sick people and healed them. ⁶He was surprised at their unbelief, so he went instead to the surrounding villages teaching them.

The Disciples Sent to Preach and Demonstrate the Kingdom

⁷Later, he called the twelve and began to send them out two by two. He also gave them authority over unclean spirits. ⁸He also commanded them, "Take nothing on the road except a single walking staff. Do not take any bread, nor a bag for provisions, nor copper coins in your money belts. ⁹Of course, you may wear sandals, but do not wear two shirts."

¹⁰He also said to them, "Remain at the location where you have been welcomed into a home until you depart from that town. ¹¹But the place that does not welcome you, and the people that do not listen to you, shake the dust from under your feet when you leave that town as a witness to them."

¹²Then they went out and preached so that the people might repent. ¹³They also cast out many demons, and they anointed many sick people with oil and healed them.

Herod's Concern About a Resurrected John the Baptizer

¹⁴At that time, King[ii] Herod heard *about Jesus*, for his reputation had become known. Some were also saying, "John the Baptizer[iii] has been raised from the dead, and for this reason miraculous powers are working in him."

¹⁵But others were saying, "It is Elijah." Still others were saying, "*He is* a prophet like one of the Prophets."

¹⁶However, when Herod heard, he said, "*It is* John, whom I beheaded. He has risen from the dead."

[ii] Herod was not a king, but a tetrarch. He had desperately wanted the title. Mark's use of the term may be ironic throughout this section.

[iii] Traditionally, "Baptist," The word describes action; so "Baptizer" here.

Mark 6:17

¹⁷Herod himself had sent men, arrested John, and bound him in prison. *It was all* because of Herodias, the wife of his brother Philip, whom Herod had married. ¹⁸For John had repeatedly said to Herod, "It is against the Law for you to marry your brother's wife." ¹⁹Herodias was furious with John, and wanted to kill him; but was not able *to do so* ²⁰because Herod was afraid of John and was protecting him. He knew John was a righteous and holy man. He listened to him often but was perplexed by him. Yet he enjoyed listening to him.

²¹The perfect time *to make an attempt on John's life* arrived on Herod's birthday, when he put on a banquet for his nobles, military commanders, and the chief men of Galilee. ²²When the daughter of Herodias herself came in and danced, she delighted Herod and those dining at the table with him. The king said to the teenage girl, "Ask me whatever you wish, and I will give it to you." ²³He swore emphatically to her, "Whatever you ask of me, I will give to you, even up to half my kingdom."

²⁴She went out and asked her mother, "What shall I ask?" Her mother said, "*Ask for* the head of John the Baptizer."

²⁵She went to the king quickly and asked urgently, "I want you, without delay, to give me the head of John the Baptizer on a serving tray."

²⁶The king was filled with profound sorrow, but on account of the oaths and those dining at the table, he did not want to reject her request. ²⁷The king immediately sent *a messenger* and commanded the executioner to bring John's head. Then the executioner went and beheaded John in the prison, ²⁸and brought his head upon a serving tray. Herod then gave it to the teenage girl, and the little girl gave it to her mother.

²⁹When John's disciples heard, they came and carried his body away, and placed it in a tomb.

Jesus Departs from Herod's Realm

³⁰*After their mission,* the apostles gathered around Jesus and reported to him everything they had done and taught. ³¹At that time, he said to them, "Come by yourselves to an uninhabited place and rest alone for a little while." *He said this* because so many were coming and going that they could not even find time to eat.

³²Then they went in the boat to an uninhabited place by themselves. ³³But the crowds saw them as they left, and many recognized *them.* People from all the cities ran together on foot to the uninhabited area, and they arrived before Jesus and the disciples. Then they gathered together with him.

³⁴When they arrived, Jesus saw the large crowd and felt compassion for them, because they were like sheep who did not have a shepherd; so, he began to teach them many things.

Jesus Multiplies Loaves of Bread and Fish for Five Thousand

³⁵When many hours had gone by, Jesus' disciples came to him and said, "The place is remote, and many hours have already passed. ³⁶Send the people away so that they can go to the countryside and the surrounding villages and buy something to eat for themselves. For they do not have anything to eat."

³⁷But he responded to them, "You give them something to eat." They asked him, "Shall we go and buy two hundred denarii[i] worth of bread and give it to them to eat?"

³⁸He questioned them, "How many loaves do you have? Go and see." When they found out they said, "Five loaves and two fish."

³⁹Then he commanded them all to sit as if arranged for a banquet in rows upon the green grass. ⁴⁰They sat down in orderly groups of hundreds and fifties. ⁴¹At that point, Jesus took the five loaves and the two fish, and looking up to heaven

---

[i] A denarius is a day's wage for a soldier or a day laborer. Two hundred denarii would be about eight month's wages.

he pronounced a blessing and broke the bread into pieces. Then he gave it to his disciples in order that they might serve it to the people, and he shared the two fish with everyone ⁴²so that they all ate as much as they wanted. ⁴³They also carried away twelve baskets of leftover pieces of bread, along with the fish. ⁴⁴Those who ate the bread numbered about five thousand men.[i]

A Manifestation of the Kingdom: Walking on Water

⁴⁵As soon as the meal was finished, Jesus forced his disciples to get in the boat and journey across the sea to Bethsaida, while he personally sent the crowd away. ⁴⁶After he sent everyone away, he went up a mountain to pray.

⁴⁷By the time the sun had set, the boat was in the middle of the sea while Jesus was alone on the land. ⁴⁸Jesus could see his disciples being painfully tested as they rowed, because the wind was against them. Around the fourth watch of the night, he came near them walking upon the sea; he was intending to pass by them. ⁴⁹When they saw him walking upon the sea, they cried out in terror, thinking he was a phantom.

⁵⁰They all saw him and were trembling with fear. But he quickly responded and said to them, "Take courage, it is I; stop being afraid." ⁵¹He went to them in the boat, and the wind stopped. They were entirely beside themselves, overwhelmed with ecstatic joy,[ii] ⁵²but they did not understand about the loaves; their hearts had become insensitive.

A Display of Faith

⁵³They crossed over and came to shore near Gennesaret, and they anchored *the boat*. ⁵⁴When they disembarked from the boat, the people of the region immediately recognized him, ⁵⁵and they rushed throughout that entire region *spreading the news*. Then

---

[i] Estimates are that between fifteen and twenty thousand people were present.

[ii] "Overwhelmed with ecstatic joy" translates a Greek verb used when referring to spiritual ecstatic phenomena in ancient times.

they began to carry the afflicted around on stretchers wherever they heard that he was.

⁵⁶Wherever he went, whether it was in a village, a city, or in the countryside, the residents would place those who were sick in the marketplace and beg him to let them touch a tassel on his garment. All those who were sick, who touched him, were healed of their illness.

A Hypocritical Focus on External Matters

Chapter Seven

¹At another time the Pharisees and some of the scribal scholars came from Jerusalem and gathered around him. ²When they saw some of Jesus' disciples eating bread with ritually unclean hands, that is, with hands that had not been ritually washed, they complained.

³For the Pharisees and all the Jews do not eat unless they perform a ritual washing of their hands by making a fist,[iii] clinging to the tradition of the elders.

⁴In addition, *when they come* from the marketplace, they do not eat unless they baptize[iv] themselves. They also cling to many other traditions that they have inherited, such as the baptizing of cups, pitchers, copper vessels, and dining couches.

⁵The Pharisees and the scribal scholars questioned Jesus: "Why are your disciples not walking according to the tradition of the elders, but instead eat bread with ritually unclean hands?"

[iii] It is generally believed that the Pharisees made a fist after washing their palms to prevent recontamination. This phrase is usually left untranslated in modern versions.

[iv] The Greek word is baptizo. It is used twice in this verse and once in verse 8.

⁶In response he said to them, "Isaiah prophesied accurately about you hypocrites, as it is written,

> " 'This people honor me with their lips,
> but their heart is far distant from me.
>
> ⁷" 'They worship me with no purpose, teaching as
> doctrines the commandments of men.'[i]

⁸"You have abandoned God's command, and are clinging to the traditions of men *including* the baptizing of pitchers and cups, and the many other things like this that you do."

⁹He also said to them, "You are good at overruling the commands of God in order to keep your traditions. ¹⁰For Moses said, 'Honor your father and mother,'[ii] and, 'Let the one who speaks evil of his father or mother die.'[iii] ¹¹But you say, 'If a man says to father or mother, "Whatever financial support you might have received from me is Corban"' (that is, a gift for the temple treasury,) ¹²you no longer allow him to provide for his father or mother. ¹³You are invalidating the word of God by the traditions which you have handed down; you also do many other things just like this."

Impurity is from the Heart: Declaring All Food Clean

¹⁴When Jesus summoned the crowd again, he said to them, "Everyone, listen to me and understand! ¹⁵There is nothing outside of a man that is able to defile him when it goes into him; but the things coming out of a man are able to defile him. ¹⁶If anyone has ears to hear, let him understand."

¹⁷Later when they went into a house away from the crowd, his disciples questioned him about the parable. ¹⁸He asked them, "Are you so without understanding? Do you not understand that everything that enters a man from the outside is not able to defile him? ¹⁹*It can't defile him* because it does not go into his

---

[i] Isaiah 29:13

[ii] Exodus 20:12; Deuteronomy 5:16

[iii] Exodus 21:17; Leviticus 20:9

heart, but into his stomach, and then goes out of his body into the latrine."

Jesus said this, thus cleansing all foods.

20He also said, "The things that come out of a man defile the man. 21For from within—from the heart of men—evil thoughts arise, also adulteries, illicit sexual relationships, murders, 22thefts, greed, wicked deeds, deceit, unrestrained sensuality, an envious eye, slanders, arrogance, and willful ignorance. 23All these evil things come from within, and they defile a man."

A Demonstration of Great Faith: The Syrophoenician Woman

24Then Jesus left and went into the region of Tyre and Sidon. He arrived at a house but did not want anyone to know. However, he was not able to remain hidden; 25in fact, when a woman whose daughter had an unclean spirit heard about him, she immediately came and fell at his feet. 26But the woman was a Greek who was Syrophoenician by birth. She asked repeatedly that he cast the demon out of her daughter.

27He said to her, "Let the children have as much food as they want first. For it is not healthy to take the children's food and feed it to the house dogs."

28But she responded and said to him, "Yes Lord, but the house dogs eat the scraps of the children *that fall* under the table."

29He said to her, "For this answer, you may go; the demon has gone out of your daughter."

30Then she went to her house and found the child collapsed upon the bed, but the demon had left her.

Jesus Heals a Man from a Greek Region

31Jesus again went out from the region of Tyre, and came through Sidon, and then traveled along the Sea of Galilee to the middle of the region called the Decapolis.[iv]

[iv] A region east of the Sea of Galilee with ten Greek cities.

³²The residents of the region brought a man to him who could not hear, and had difficulty speaking; and they begged Jesus to lay hands on him. ³³Then Jesus took the man from the crowd for privacy, placed his fingers into his ears, and when he spit, he held the man's tongue. ³⁴He looked up to heaven, groaned, and said to him, "Ephphatha," which means, "Open up!"

³⁵Immediately the man's hearing was opened up, the restriction on his tongue was removed, and he began to speak clearly. ³⁶Jesus gave them explicit instructions that they tell no one. But the more he instructed them, the more they spread the news, ³⁷because they were overwhelmed with wonder. They kept saying, "He has done all things well. He even makes the deaf hear and the mute speak."

Jesus Multiplies Loaves of Bread and Fish for Four Thousand

Chapter Eight

¹At that time, a large crowd gathered around Jesus again. Since they did not have anything to eat, he called his disciples together and said to them, ²"I have compassion for the crowd; they have already been with me three days, and they do not have anything to eat. ³If I send them away to their homes without food, they will become faint along the way; some of them have even come from a long distance."

⁴His disciples responded to him, "Where would anyone find bread to feed them here in this barren place?"

⁵He asked them, "How many loaves do you have?"

They told him, "Seven."

⁶So he commanded the crowd to settle down upon the ground. He took the seven loaves of bread, gave thanks, broke them into pieces, and gave the loaves to his disciples for them to distribute. Then they distributed the bread to the crowd. ⁷They also had a few small fish. He blessed them and told his disciples

to also distribute the fish. ⁸The people ate and had as much as they wanted. The disciples picked up seven larger baskets of leftover fragments, ⁹even though there were about four thousand men.ⁱ After this Jesus sent the people home. ¹⁰He immediately embarked in a boat with his disciples and traveled to the region of Dalmanutha.

A Hypocritical Request for more Signs

¹¹Just then the Pharisees came out and began to badger him, testing him by seeking from him an authenticating sign from heaven. ¹²He sighed deeply in his spirit and said, "Why is this generation seeking a sign? I am telling you the truth; no sign will be given to this generation." ¹³He left them, boarded the boat again, and crossed over to the other side.

A Demonstration of Little Faith: The Yeast of Unbelief

¹⁴However, the disciples had forgotten to bring bread, except for one loaf they had with them in the boat. ¹⁵At that time, Jesus gave them clear instructions telling them, "Watch out for the yeast of the Pharisees and the yeast of the Herodians."

¹⁶The disciples concluded among themselves that Jesus said this because they had no bread.

¹⁷He knew their thoughts and said to them, "Why have you concluded that I said this because you did not bring bread? Don't you yet know or understand? Have your hearts become insensitive? ¹⁸You have eyes, but do you not see? You have ears, but do you not hear? Don't you remember ¹⁹when I broke five loaves for the five thousand? How many full baskets of fragments did you pick up?"

They said to him, "Twelve."

²⁰"When I broke seven loaves for the four thousand, how many larger baskets full of fragments did you pick up?"

ⁱ Estimates are that between twelve thousand and sixteen thousand people were present.

They said to him, "Seven."

²¹He asked them, "You do not understand yet, do you?"

Jesus Heals a Blind Man in Two Stages

²²Then they arrived at Bethsaida. The people brought a blind man to Jesus and urged him to touch the man. ²³Jesus took the hand of the blind man and brought him outside of the village. He spit in the man's eyes, laid his hands on him, and asked him, "What do you see?"

²⁴Then his sight returned, and he said, "I see men walking about, to be specific, I am seeing them like they are trees."

²⁵Jesus laid his hands on the man's eyes again, and he saw clearly; his sight was fully restored, and he could see everything distinctly. ²⁶After that Jesus sent the man to his own house saying, "Do not go into the village."

Peter's Confession of Faith: The Christ

²⁷Sometime later Jesus and his disciples went out to the villages of Caesarea Philippi. While they were on the road, he began to question his disciples asking them, "Who do men say that I am?"

²⁸They responded to him saying, "*Some say* John the Baptizer, others *say* Elijah, and others *say* that you are one of the prophets."

²⁹He asked them, "But who do you say I am?"

Peter answered and said to him, "You are the Christ."

³⁰Then he strongly warned them that they should say nothing to anyone about him.

Peter Opposes Jesus' Revelation of the Future

³¹He also began to teach them that it was necessary for the Son of Man to suffer many things; to be rejected by the elders, the chief priests, and the scribal scholars; and to be killed and

raised to life after three days. ³²He spoke this message openly to them, but Peter took him aside and began to rebuke him.

³³But when Jesus turned away *from him* and looked at his disciples, he rebuked Peter and said, "Stay behind me, Satan! You are thinking from the perspective of men, not God."

³⁴After that he called the crowd together with his disciples and said to them, "If anyone desires to follow after me, he must deny his own *will*, take up his cross, and follow me. ³⁵For whoever desires to save his soul[i] will lose it, but whoever loses his soul for my sake, and for the good news, will save it. ³⁶For what benefit is there for a man to gain the whole world and suffer loss to his soul? ³⁷For what can a man give in exchange for his soul?

³⁸"For whoever is ashamed of me and my words in this adulterous and sinful generation, the Son of Man will also be ashamed of him when he comes with his holy angels in the glory of the Father."

Chapter Nine

¹He also said to them, "I am telling you the truth, some of you standing here will certainly not taste death before you see the Kingdom of God established in power."

Jesus' Transfiguration

²Six days later, Jesus took Peter, James, and John and brought them up a high mountain by themselves. Then he was transformed in front of them. ³His garments were gleaming intensely white, in a way that no one who washes or bleaches clothes on earth could possibly do. ⁴At the same time, Elijah appeared to them with Moses, and the two of them were speaking with Jesus.

---

i The soul is the seat of our mind, emotions, and will.

⁵Peter responded *to it all* by saying to Jesus, "Rabbi, It is good for us to be here. I will make three meeting tents, one for you, one for Moses, and one for Elijah." ⁶He said this because he was so frightened that he did not know how to respond.

⁷Just then a cloud came and overshadowed them, and a voice came from the cloud, "This is my cherished Son; listen to him."

⁸Right after that they looked around, but they no longer saw anyone with them except Jesus alone.

The Elijah who was to Come

⁹While they were coming down from the mountain, he gave them clear instructions that they not explain to anyone the details of what they had seen until the Son of Man rose from the dead. ¹⁰They understood the instruction, but they debated among themselves what "to rise from the dead" meant.

¹¹They also questioned him asking, "Why do the scribal scholars say that Elijah must precede the Messiah?"

¹²He responded to them, "Elijah most certainly does come first to restore all things. But why is it written about the Son of Man that he must suffer and be despised and mistreated? ¹³However, I am telling you that Elijah has come, and they did to him what they wished, just as it is written about him."

A Demonstration of Little Faith: The Demonized Boy

¹⁴When he came to the disciples, he saw a large crowd around them and the scribal scholars quizzing them. ¹⁵As soon as everyone in the crowd saw him, they were startled, and ran to welcome him.

¹⁶He asked them, "Why are you quizzing them?"

¹⁷One from the crowd answered him, "Teacher, I brought my son to you because he has a spirit that stops him from speaking. ¹⁸In addition, whenever it overcomes him, it throws him to the ground in convulsions, and he foams at the mouth, grinds his teeth, and becomes so stiff he cannot move. I spoke to your disciples hoping they would cast it out, but they were not able."

¹⁹Then Jesus responded and said to him, "Oh unbelieving generation! How long will I be with you? How long must I be patient with you? Bring the boy to me."

²⁰They brought him to Jesus. When the spirit saw Jesus, it immediately threw him into a convulsion, and he fell down on the ground rolling around and foaming at the mouth.

²¹Jesus asked his father, "How long has something like this been happening to him?"

The man said, "From childhood. ²²Many times it also has thrown him into the fire or waters trying to kill him. But if you are able to do anything, have pity on us and help us."

²³But Jesus said to him, " 'If you are able?' All things are possible for him who believes."

²⁴The father of the child immediately began to cry out and said, "I believe. Help *me* with my lack of faith!"

²⁵When Jesus saw that the crowd was surging toward him, he reproved the unclean spirit and said to it, "I command you, deaf and mute spirit, leave him and no longer enter into him."

²⁶After the demon cried out and threw the boy into severe convulsions, he left. The boy appeared so lifeless, that many said he had died. ²⁷But Jesus grasped his hand and raised him, and he stood up.

²⁸When he went into a house, his disciples came privately and asked him, "Why were we not able to cast it out?"

²⁹He said to them, "This type cannot come out except through prayer and fasting."

More Revelation on Jesus' Mission and Future

³⁰Then he went out and began traveling through Galilee, but he did not want anyone to know, ³¹because he was teaching his disciples. He was explaining to them, "The Son of Man is being delivered into the hands of men; they will kill him, but after his death he will rise again after three days."

32But they did not understand his message, and they were afraid to ask him about it.

True Greatness in the Kingdom

33They came to Capernaum. When he had come into his house, he asked them, "What were you discussing on the road?" 34But they remained silent, for *while they were* on the road, they had been discussing who was most important.

35He sat down, called the twelve, and said to them, "If you want to be first, you will be the last of all and the servant of all."

36He chose a child and set the child in their midst, then he took the child in his arms and said to them, 37"Whoever receives a child such as this one in my name receives me. Whoever receives me does not receive me, but the one who sent me."

Discerning Allies in the Kingdom

38John interrupted him, "Teacher, we saw someone casting out a demon in your name, but we stopped him because he doesn't travel with us."

39Jesus responded, "Do not stop him. It is not possible for someone who does a miracle in my name then to turn quickly and speak evil of me. 40For the one who is not against us is for us. 41For whoever gives you a cup of water to drink because of who you are—because you follow Christ—I am telling you the truth, he will never lose his payment.

Protecting the Innocent from Stumbling

42"However, whoever causes one of these little one who believes in me to stumble into sin, it would be better for him instead if a millstone, the type that a donkey turns, were tied around his neck and he was hurled into the sea. 43If your right hand causes you to stumble into sin, cut it off. It is better for you to enter into life with only one hand than to enter into Gehenna[i]—into the unquenchable fire—with two hands.

⁴⁴" 'Where their worm does not die, and the fire never goes out.'[ii]

⁴⁵"If your foot causes you to stumble into sin, cut it off. It is better for you to enter into life with only one foot, than to enter into Gehenna with two feet.

⁴⁶" 'Where their worm does not die, and the fire never goes out.'

⁴⁷"If your eye causes you to stumble into sin, remove it. It is better for you to enter into the Kingdom of God with only one eye, than to be thrown into Gehenna with two eyes.

⁴⁸" 'Where their worm does not die, and the fire never goes out.'

⁴⁹For everyone *there* will be salted with fire, even as every sacrifice is seasoned with salt.

⁵⁰"Salt is good, but if the salt leeches away, how will you make it salty again? Have salt in yourselves and be at peace with each other."

The Pharisees Test Jesus About Divorce

Chapter Ten

¹Jesus arose and went from there to the territory of Judea and the regions beyond the Jordan. The crowds gathered around him once more, and as he was accustomed, he again began to

---

[i] Gehenna refers a valley known as "the valley of the sons of Hinnom." It was a place of child sacrifice and gross impurity. It came to symbolize the place of eternal punishment. Also in verses 45 and 47.

[ii] See Isaiah 66:24. Also in verses 46 and 48.

Mark 10:2

teach them. ²When the Pharisees arrived, they began to test him by asking him if it was lawful for a man to divorce his wife.[i]

³Jesus responded to them, "What did Moses command you?"

⁴They replied, "Moses permitted the writing of a certificate of divorce so that a man could divorce his wife."[ii]

⁵But Jesus said to them, "He wrote this command for you because of the hardness of your heart. ⁶From the beginning of creation,

> " 'He made them male and female. ⁷Because of this a man will leave his father and his mother and unite with his wife, ⁸And the two will be one flesh.'[iii]

"So they are no longer two, but one flesh. ⁹Therefore, what God has joined in marriage, let man not divide through divorce."[iv]

¹⁰When they were in the house, his disciples again began to question him about this. ¹¹He said to them, "The man who divorces his wife and marries another woman, he himself is committing adultery against her. ¹²In the same way, if a woman abandons[v] her husband and marries another man, she herself is committing adultery."

The Priority of Little Ones

¹³At that time, they began to bring small children to Jesus so that he might hold them. But his disciples scolded them.

---

[i] This was a hotly contested topic among the rabbis of Israel. One school of thought believed that a man could divorce his wife over a small thing like a burned dinner. A wife, however, had no such recourse.

[ii] See Deuteronomy 24:1-4.

[iii] Genesis 2:24

[iv] The Greek word translated "divorce" was a technical term for divorce.

[v] In Jewish law, only a husband could divorce. However, a woman could simply abandon the relationship, stepping into the situation Jesus here mentions.

¹⁴When Jesus saw it, he was displeased and said to the disciples, "Allow the children to come to me, do not stop them; for the Kingdom of God is made up of those who are like these children. ¹⁵I am telling you the truth, except you receive the Kingdom of God like a small child, you will never enter into it." ¹⁶Then he embraced the children, placed his hands on them, and blessed them.

Wealth as a Potential Impediment to the Kingdom

¹⁷Later, while he was going out along the road, one man came running and knelt before him asking him, "Good teacher, what must I do in order that I may inherit eternal life?"

¹⁸Jesus said to him, "Why are you calling me good? There is no one good except the one God. ¹⁹You know the commandments,

> " 'Do not murder, do not commit adultery, do not steal, do not bear false witness, do not cheat, honor your father and mother.'[vi] "

²⁰He responded to Jesus, "Teacher, I have been careful to keep all these things from my youth."

²¹Jesus looked directly at him and felt love for him, so he said to him, "You still need to do one thing. Go and sell everything you own, give it to the poor, and you will possess treasure in heaven. After that, come and follow me." ²²The man was appalled by Jesus' statement, and he went away grieving; for he had much property.

²³Jesus looked around at his disciples and said, "How difficult it is for those who have wealth[vii] to enter into the Kingdom of God."

²⁴His teaching stunned the disciples. In response to that astonishment, Jesus again said to them, "Children, how difficult

---

[vi] See Exodus 20:12-16 and Deuteronomy 5:16-20.

[vii] Or, "possessions." Also in verse 24.

it is for those who trust their wealth to enter into the Kingdom of God. ²⁵It is easier for a camel to go through the eye of a needle than for a wealthy man to enter into the Kingdom of God."

²⁶The disciples were overcome by surprise, saying to each other, "Who is able to be saved?"

²⁷Jesus looked at them, and said, "It is impossible from men's perspective, but not from God's perspective. For all things are possible with God."

Giving Up All for the Kingdom: A Promise

²⁸The Peter began to say to him, "See, we have left everything and have followed you."

²⁹Jesus responded to him, "I am telling you the truth, there is no one who has left house, brothers, sisters, mother, father, children or fields for my sake and the sake of the good news, ³⁰who will not also receive a hundred times more now in this age —houses, brothers, sisters, mothers, children, and fields, together with persecutions—and in the coming age, eternal life. ³¹For many who are first will be last, and the last will be first."

Jesus Points to the Crucifixion

³²At another time, they went up on the road to Jerusalem with Jesus leading the way ahead of them. The disciples were bewildered, but those who were following them were afraid. He again took the twelve to the side, and began to explain to them what was about to happen to him, ³³"Pay close attention! We are going up to Jerusalem, and the Son of Man will be handed over to the chief priest and the scribal scholars. They will condemn him to death, and hand him over to the Gentiles. ³⁴They will mock him, spit on him, whip him, and kill *him*. But after three days he will come back to life."

A Basic Misunderstanding About the Kingdom

³⁵After this, James and John, the sons of Zebedee, approached him petitioning him, "Teacher, we want you to do for us whatever we ask you."

³⁶He responded to them, "What do you wish that I might do for you?"

³⁷They said to him, "Grant to us that one of us might sit on your right hand, and one of us might sit on your left hand in your glory."

³⁸But Jesus said to them, "You do not know what you are asking. Are you able to drink the cup which I personally am drinking, or to be baptized in the baptism with which I myself am baptized?"

³⁹They responded to him, "We are able."

Jesus said to them, "You will drink the cup I personally am drinking, and you will be baptized in the baptism that I myself will be baptized. ⁴⁰But the ability to sit on my right or my left is not mine to give, but it is for those for whom it has been prepared."

⁴¹When the twelve heard, they began to be angry with James and John. ⁴²However, Jesus called them and said to them, "You know that those who are recognized as rulers of the Gentiles reign over them, and their important men exercise authority over them. ⁴³This is not the way you are to do it. Instead, whoever desires to be important among you will be your servant. ⁴⁴Whoever wishes to be first among you will be a slave to everyone. ⁴⁵For even the Son of Man did not come to be served, but to serve and to dedicate his life as a redemption payment[i] for many people."

---

[i] Or, traditionally, "as ransom for many people."

Mark 10:46

Jesus Responds to Persistent Faith: Opening Blind Eyes

⁴⁶At that time they arrived at Jericho. While Jesus, his disciples, and a large crowd were leaving Jericho, Bartimaeus the Son of Timaeus, a blind beggar, was sitting along the road. ⁴⁷When he heard that Jesus the Nazarene was there, he began to cry out and to say, "Jesus, Son of David, have mercy on me!" ⁴⁸Many in the crowd were admonishing him to be quiet. But he cried out even more, "Son of David, have mercy on me!"

⁴⁹Jesus stopped and said, "Call him."

They called the blind man telling him, "Take courage. Get up. He is calling you." ⁵⁰He threw off his cloak, jumped up, and came to Jesus.

⁵¹Jesus responded to him and asked, "What do you wish that I do for you?"

The blind man said to him, "Rabboni,[i] that I might see again."

⁵²Jesus said to him, "Go! Your faith has rescued you." Immediately he was able to see, and he began to follow Jesus on the road.

The King Arrives in Jerusalem

Chapter Eleven

¹When they were approaching Jerusalem by Bethphage and Bethany near the Mount of Olives, Jesus sent two of his disciples ²and instructed them, "Go into the village ahead of you, and as soon as you enter it, you will find a colt that has been tied. No one has ever sat upon it. Untie it and bring it here. ³If someone asks you, 'Why are you doing this?' say, 'The Lord has need of it.' He will immediately send it back here."

---

[i] The word used is "Rabboni," a form of the word "Rabbi," which means "Teacher." However, Rabboni itself is more personal. It means "My Rabbi," (My Teacher).

⁴So, they went and found the colt tied outside next to a door on the street, and they untied it. ⁵Some of those who were standing there asked them, "What are you doing untying the colt?" ⁶But they explained to them just as Jesus had instructed, and they gave the disciples permission.

⁷They brought the colt to Jesus, and they threw their garments upon it, and he sat on it. ⁸Many also spread their clothing on the road, and others cut leaf-filled branches from the trees and were spreading them in the road. ⁹Those who went ahead, and those who followed shouted,

> "Hosanna! Blessed is the one coming in the name of the Lord.
> ¹⁰"Blessed is the coming kingdom of our father David. Hosanna in the highest."[ii]

¹¹Jesus entered Jerusalem, went to the temple, and examined every part of it. Then, because it was already evening, he went out to Bethany with the twelve.

¹²On the next day, after they departed from Bethany, Jesus grew hungry. ¹³When he spotted a fig tree with leaves some distance away, he approached to see what he might find on it. When he arrived at the tree, he did not find anything except leaves, for it was not yet the season for figs. ¹⁴In response, he said to it, "May no one eat fruit from you in this age." His disciples were listening.

Jesus Exercises His Authority at the Temple

¹⁵When they came to Jerusalem, Jesus went to the temple and began to throw out those who were buying and selling in the temple. He also overturned the tables of the moneychangers and the stands of those selling doves. ¹⁶In addition, he did not allow anyone to carry their goods through the temple.

[ii] Psalm 118:25-26

¹⁷He taught them and explained to them, "Is it not written,

> " 'My house will be called a house of prayer for all the nations'[i]?
>> But you have made it a bandits' lair."[ii]

¹⁸When the chief priests and scribal scholars heard, they began to seek how they might destroy him, for they feared him, because the entire crowd was astounded by his teaching.

The Fig Tree and the Power of Faith

¹⁹When evening came, he went out from the city. ²⁰In the morning, when they passed by the fig tree, they saw it was withered from the roots.

²¹Peter remembered and said to Jesus, "Rabbi, look! The fig tree that you cursed has withered away."

²²Jesus responded and said to him, "Have faith in God! ²³I am telling you the truth, whoever says to this mountain, 'Lift yourself off the ground and throw yourself in the sea,' and does not talk himself out of it in his heart, but believes that what he is speaking is happening, for him, it will happen. ²⁴For this reason I am telling you, believe that you are receiving all the things for which you are asking and praying, and for you, it will happen. ²⁵However, whenever you stand praying, forgive if you have anything against anyone, in order that your Father who is in the heavens might forgive your offenses. ²⁶If you do not forgive, neither will your Father who is in the heavens forgive your offenses."

Jesus' Authority Challenged

²⁷They came again to Jerusalem, and while he was walking around in the temple, the chief priests, the scribal scholars, and the elders approached him. ²⁸They asked him, "By what authority are you doing these things?" and, "Who gave you this authority that you do these things?"

---

[i] Isaiah 56:7

[ii] See Jeremiah 7:11.

²⁹In response, Jesus said to them, "I will ask you one question. Give me your answer, and I will tell you by what authority I am doing these things. ³⁰The baptism of John, was it from heaven or from men? Give me your answer."

³¹They discussed it among themselves saying, "If we say that it is from heaven, he will ask, 'Then why didn't you believe him?' ³²But can we say that it is from men?" They were afraid of the crowd, for the people all believed John truly was a prophet.

³³They responded to Jesus and said, "We do not know."

So, Jesus said to them, "Neither will I tell you by what authority I am doing these things."

The Parable of the Tenant Farmers

Chapter Twelve

¹Then he began to speak to them in parables. "A man planted a vineyard. He put a wall around it, dug a vat for the juice of the crushed grapes, and built a watchtower. He leased it to tenant farmers and left for an extended journey. ²He sent a servant to the tenants at harvest time in order that he might receive from the tenants some of the fruit of the vineyard. ³They took the servant, physically mistreated him, and sent him away with nothing. ⁴Again, the owner of the vineyard sent another servant to them, but they hit him over the head and humiliated him. ⁵The owner sent another, but they killed him. He also sent many others; they beat some of them and killed others.

⁶"He had one more he could send, a cherished son. He sent him to them last, saying, 'They will give proper honor to my son.'

⁷"But those tenants said among themselves, 'This is the heir. Come let us kill him, and the inheritance will be ours.' ⁸They took him, killed him, and threw his body out of the vineyard.

⁹"Therefore, what will the owner of the vineyard do? He will come and destroy the tenant farmers and give the vineyard to others.

¹⁰"Haven't you read this Scripture?

> " 'The stone which the builders rejected; this one has become the most essential cornerstone. ¹¹This has come from the Lord, and it is wonderful to our eyes.' "[i]

¹²They began seeking a way to arrest him, but they were afraid of the crowd. For they knew that he spoke this parable against them. They allowed him to continue, and they left him, ¹³but they sent some of the Pharisees and Herodians to him in order to catch him in what he said.

The Pharisees Test Jesus: Paying the Poll Tax

¹⁴When they arrived, they said to him, "Teacher, we know that you are truthful, and are not influenced by anyone. We know this because you pay no attention to status among men, but you teach the way of God according to truth. Is it lawful to pay the poll tax to Caesar or not? Do we pay it or not pay it?"

¹⁵But Jesus recognized their hypocrisy and said to them, "Why are you testing me? Bring me a denarius that I might see it." ¹⁶They brought one. He said to them, "Whose image and inscription is this?"

They responded to him, "Caesar's."

¹⁷Then Jesus said to them, "Give back the things of Caesar to Caesar, and the things of God to God."

They were astonished by him.

The Sadducees Test Jesus: The Marriage Conundrum

¹⁸Then the Sadducees came to him. They teach that there is no resurrection. They began questioning him asking, ¹⁹"Teacher, Moses wrote to us that if someone's brother dies, and leaves a wife but not a child, that his brother should take his wife and raise up offspring for his brother."[ii]

---

[i] Psalm 118:22-23

[ii] See Deuteronomy 25:5.

²⁰"There were seven brothers. The first took a wife but died and left no offspring. ²¹So, the second brother took her, but he died and did not leave offspring. The third brother did likewise. ²²The seven brothers did not leave any offspring; last of all the woman also died. ²³In the resurrection, when they rise again, whose wife will she be? For all seven had been married to her."

²⁴Jesus said to them, "Isn't the reason you are deceived that you do not know the Scriptures or the power of God? ²⁵For when they rise from the dead, they will not marry nor be given in marriage, but they will be like the angels in the heavens. ²⁶But concerning those who are dead, that they will be raised, have you not read in the Bible about Moses and the bush? How God spoke to him saying,

> " 'I am the God of Abraham, and the God of Isaac, and the God of Jacob?'

²⁷He is not the God of dead people, but of those who are alive. You are very deceived."

A Test About the Greatest Commandment

²⁸When one of the scribal scholars came and heard their question, and saw that Jesus responded well to them, he asked Jesus, "What commandment is the greatest of all?"

²⁹Jesus replied, "The first is,

> " 'Hear, Israel, the Lord our God is one Lord. ³⁰Love the Lord your God with your whole heart, with your whole soul, with your whole mind, and with your whole strength.'[iii]

³¹This is the second, 'Love your neighbor as yourself.'[iv] There is not another commandment greater than these."

³²The scribal scholar said to him, "Well done, teacher. You have spoken truthfully that he is one, and there is no other except him. ³³To love him with your whole heart, with your

---

[iii] Deuteronomy 6:4-5

[iv] Leviticus 19:18

whole understanding, with your whole soul, with your whole strength, and to love your neighbor as yourself is greater than all burnt offerings and sacrifices."

34When Jesus saw that he had answered wisely, he said to him, "You are not far from the Kingdom of God." After that, no one dared any longer to question him.

A Test for the Leaders: Whose Son is Christ?

35Sometime after Jesus had answered them, while he was teaching in the temple, he began to ask, "How can the scribal scholars say that the Christ is David's son? 36David himself said by the Holy Spirit:

" 'The Lord said to my Lord, "Sit at my right hand,
until I place your enemies under your feet." ' i

37David himself calls him Lord, then how is he his son?"

The large crowd was listening gladly.

Jesus Condemns the Scribal Scholars

38While he was teaching, he said, "Pay attention to the scribal scholars, the ones who love to walk about in scholarly robes and be recognized in the marketplace. 39They love the special seats in the synagogue, and places of honor at meals. 40They devour the wealth of widows, and to conceal their actions, they pray lengthy prayers. Men like these will receive extreme judgment."

The Greatest Offering

41Later, after he sat down across from the place that people gave their offerings, he saw how the crowd threw copper coins into the offering box, but many wealthy people were putting large amounts into it. 42Then one poor widow came and put in two leptons,ii which is equivalent to a quadrans.

---

i Psalm 110:1

ii A quadrans was a small copper coin worth about a 64th of a denarius— less than two percent of a day's wage for a soldier or a day laborer. Thus, a lepton would be less than one percent of a day's wage.

⁴³He called his disciples together and said to them, "I am telling you the truth, this poor widow put more in the offering box than anyone else who gave an offering. ⁴⁴All the rest gave from their expendable income, but she gave even though she can't make ends meet. She gave everything; all that she had to live on."

Looking Ahead to the Destruction of Jerusalem and Beyond

Chapter Thirteen

¹While Jesus was going out of the temple, one of his disciples said to him, "Teacher, notice the impressive stones and buildings."

²But Jesus responded to him, "Do you see these great buildings? Not even one stone will be left upon another. They will all be pulled down."

³Later, while he was sitting on the Mount of Olives across from the temple, Peter, James, John, and Andrew asked him privately, ⁴"Tell us, when will these things happen, and what sign will there be that all these things are about to be accomplished?"

Jesus Answers a First Question

⁵Then Jesus began to tell them, "Watch that no one deceives you. ⁶Many will come in opposition to my name. They will say, 'I am *the Christ*,' and they will deceive many. ⁷But when you hear of wars and reports of wars, do not be alarmed, it must happen, but it is not yet the fulfillment[iii] of my words. ⁸For people group will rise against people group,[iv] and kingdom against kingdom. There will be earthquakes in place after place. There will also be

---

[iii] This word (telos) is often translated "end," but is also used to speak of fulfillment of a word or prediction. Here, the context is the fulfillment of Jesus' word about the destruction of the temple. Also verse 13.

[iv] Or, traditionally, "nation will rise against nation," though his next words about kingdom against kingdom would appear to address the nations.

famines and political confusion. These things are the beginning of labor pains.

⁹"But you all must pay attention. They will deliver you to governing councils and you will be beaten in synagogues. You will stand before governors and kings on account of me as a witness to them. ¹⁰It is of first importance that the good news must be preached to all the Gentiles. ¹¹Whenever they take you and deliver you to the authorities, do not worry ahead of time about what you will say. On the contrary, speak what is given to you in that hour. For it will not be you speaking, but the Holy Spirit.

¹²"Brother will deliver brother *to the authorities for* death, and a father his child. A child will rise up in rebellion against his parents, and they will put them to death. ¹³You will be hated by everyone on account of my name. But the one who endures to the fulfillment of my words, will be delivered.

¹⁴"So, when you see the abomination that causes desolation[i] standing where it must not be (let the one reading understand), then those who are in Judea must flee to the mountains. ¹⁵Anyone on top of his house must not descend from the roof in order to enter his house to take anything from it. ¹⁶Anyone in the field must not turn back to take his cloak. ¹⁷How terrible it will be for those who are pregnant and those who are nursing children in those days. ¹⁸So, pray in order that it not happen in harsh weather conditions. ¹⁹For those days will be filled with tribulation of a kind that has not occurred from the beginning of the creation, from when God created it, until that moment. Such tribulation will never happen again. ²⁰Unless the Lord shorten the time, no one would survive. But for the sake of the elect,[ii] whom he has chosen, he will shorten that time. ²¹If someone

---

[i] See Luke 21:21 which appears to refer to the Roman army as a fulfillment of this sign. See also Daniel 9:27.

[ii] The term translated "elect" is used over twenty times in the New Testament and is most often a reference to those who are called by God to true faith that perseveres Also in verses 22 and 27.

says to you at that time, 'Look, here is the Christ,' or, 'Look he is there,' do not believe them. ²²For false messiahs and false prophets will arise and perform signs and wonders in order to deceive the elect, if that were possible. ²³But you must pay attention. I have told you all this ahead of time.

²⁴"Then in those days, after that tribulation, the sun will be darkened, and the moon will not give its light. ²⁵The stars will fall from the heaven, and the powers that are in the heavens will tremble.[iii]

²⁶"Then they will see the Son of Man coming in the clouds with much power and glory. ²⁷At that time, he will send his messengers, and they will gather his elect from the four winds, from one end of the earth to the other.

²⁸"Learn from the parable of the fig tree. When its branch is already tender and it puts out leaves, you know that summer is near at hand. ²⁹In the same way also you, when you see these things happening, know that it is near, at the door. ³⁰I am telling you the truth; this current generation will certainly not pass away until all these things have happened. ³¹The heaven and the earth will pass away, but my word will never pass away.

Jesus Answers a Second Question

³²"Now concerning[iv] your question about the day and hour, no one knows, not even the angels in heaven nor the Son, but only the Father. ³³Watch and stay alert, for you do not know when that time will come. ³⁴It will be like a man going on a journey who leaves his house and gives to each of his servants the authority to accomplish his master's work. He then charges the doorkeeper to keep watch.

[iii] See Isaiah 13:10; 24:23; and 34:4 for this common Old Testament sign portending judgment against a nation.

[iv] Jesus signals that he is moving to the next question using the normal way of doing so, "Now concerning your next question" (peri de). Compare Paul's similar use of this term in 1 Corinthians chapter 7 and following.

³⁵"Therefore, keep watch. For you do not know if the Lord of the house will return in the evening, at midnight, before sunrise, or in the morning; ³⁶you do not want him to come unexpectedly and find you sleeping. ³⁷Now what I say to you, I say to all of you, 'Keep watch.'"

Passover Draws Near: Jesus' Enemies Plot His Death

Chapter Fourteen

¹Now the Passover and Unleavened Bread[i] were two days away. The chief priests and the scribal scholars were seeking how they might set a clever trap for Jesus, arrest him, and kill him. ²For they kept insisting, "Not during the feast, or there could be an outcry among the people."

Jesus Prepared for His Burial

³While Jesus was in Bethany, reclining at the table in the house of Simon the Leper, a woman came with an alabaster jar of very expensive aromatic oil made of pure nard. She broke the alabaster jar and poured it out on his head.

⁴But some were murmuring indignantly among themselves, "Why has this aromatic oil been wasted? ⁵For this fragrance could have been sold for over three hundred denarii[ii] and the proceeds given to the poor." Then they began to correct her harshly.

⁶But Jesus said, "Leave her. Why are you causing her grief? What she has done for me is appropriate. ⁷For you will always have the poor living with you, and whenever you wish, you may do well by them. But you will not always have me. ⁸What she

---

[i] The Feast of Unleavened Bread, a seven-day festival observing the Israelites departure from Egypt begins the day after the Passover celebration. The first day of this festival, and the last day, are special sabbath days.

[ii] A denarius is a day's wage for a soldier or a day laborer. Three hundred denarii would be about a year's wages.

could do, she has done. She has anointed my body in preparation for burial ahead of time. ⁹I am telling you the truth, wherever the good news is preached throughout the world, what she has done will also be told in memory of her."

Judas Seeks a Payday: He Agrees to Betray Jesus

¹⁰Then Judas Iscariot,[iii] one of the twelve, went to the chief priests in order to hand Jesus over to them. ¹¹When they heard, they were glad and promised to give silver coins to him. So he began seeking an opportunity to hand him over *to them*.

Jesus Blocks Judas' Ability to Disrupt the Last Supper

¹²On the first day of Unleavened Bread, the day they usually sacrificed the Passover lamb, Jesus' disciples asked him, "Where do you want us to go and prepare in order that you might eat the Passover?"

¹³In response, he sent two of his disciples and said to them, "Go into the city, a man carrying a water jar will meet you. Follow him, ¹⁴and whatever house he enters, say to the owner, 'The teacher says, "Where is my meeting room where I may eat the Passover with my disciples?"' ¹⁵Then he himself will show you a large room on the second floor, it will be furnished and ready. You will prepare for us there."

¹⁶The disciples left him and came into the city. They discovered everything just as he had told them, so they prepared the Passover.

¹⁷When evening arrived, Jesus came with the twelve. ¹⁸While they were eating at the table, Jesus said, "I am telling you the truth: One from among you, one who is eating with me, will hand me over to my enemies."

¹⁹They began to grieve and to say to him one by one, "It isn't me, is it?"

[iii] According to John 12:4-6, Judas had been the one who led the attack over the anointing of Jesus because he was greedy for the money.

²⁰But he said to them, "It is one of the twelve, one who is dipping in the bowl with me. ²¹The Son of Man will go just as it is written concerning him, but woe to that man through whom the Son of Man is handed over to his enemies. It would be better for that man if he had not been born."

Jesus Gives New Meaning to the Passover Meal

²²While they were eating, he took some bread and blessed it. Then he broke it and gave it to them and said, "Take this. It is my body."

²³He also took the cup, gave thanks and gave it to them. They all drank from it. ²⁴He said to them, "This is my blood of the new covenant that is poured out on behalf of many.

²⁵"I am telling you the truth, I will not drink from the fruit of the vine until that day when I drink it afresh in the Kingdom of God."

Jesus Predicts the Disciples' Failure

²⁶After that, they sang a hymn and went out to the Mount of Olives. ²⁷Jesus said to them, "You will all stumble into a trap on this night, for it is written,

> 'I will strike the shepherd, and the sheep will be scattered.'[i]

²⁸But after I have been raised, I will go before you into Galilee."

²⁹Then Peter responded to him, "Even if everyone else stumbles, at least I will not."

³⁰But Jesus said to him, "I am telling you the truth, today, this night, before the rooster crows twice, you yourself will deny knowing me three times."

³¹Peter said emphatically, "Even if I must die with you, I will never deny knowing you." The rest of them repeated the same thing.

---

[i] Zechariah 13:7

Jesus' Struggle in Gethsemane

32They came to the place whose name was Gethsemane, and Jesus said to his disciples, "Sit here while I pray." 33After that, he took Peter, James, and John with him and began to be distressed and filled with anguish. 34He said to them, "My soul is profoundly sorrowful even unto death. Remain here and stay alert."

35He traveled a short distance, fell upon the ground, and began to pray that if it was possible, the hour pass from him. 36But he added, "Abba Father, all things are possible for you. Take this cup away from me. But not what I desire, but what you desire."

37He came and found the them sleeping. So, he said to Peter, "Simon, are you sleeping? Were you not able to stay alert for one hour? 38Stay alert and pray, in order that you do not enter into temptation. The spirit indeed is ready, but the flesh is weak."

39Again, he left and prayed, saying the same words. 40When he came back, he found them sleeping again, for their eyelids were very heavy. They did not know how to respond to him.

41He came the third time and asked them, "Are you still sleeping and resting? Enough of that, the hour has come. Look, the Son of Man is being handed over into the hands of sinners. 42Get up and let us go. See, the one who is handing me over is near."

43At that moment, while Jesus was still speaking, one of the twelve, Judas, arrived. A crowd was with him sent from the chief priests, scribal scholars, and the elders. They carried swords and clubs.

44Now the one who was handing him over had given a signal to them saying, "Whomever I kiss, he is the one. Arrest him, make him secure, and take him away." 45When he came, he immediately went to Jesus and said, "Rabbi," and kissed him. 46Then they arrested him and took him into custody. 47But one who had been standing there drew his sword, struck the servant of the high priest, and cut off his ear.

⁴⁸Jesus responded and said to them, "Have you come with swords and clubs to capture me as if I were a rebel? ⁴⁹Each day I was with you in the temple teaching, and you did not arrest me. But this is happening in order that Scriptures might be fulfilled."

⁵⁰Then the disciples abandoned him, and everyone fled. ⁵¹A certain young man was following him wearing only a linen sheet to cover himself. They seized him, ⁵²but he left the linen sheet and fled from them naked.

Jesus Tried and Condemned

⁵³They led Jesus to the high priest, and all the chief priests gathered, along with the elders and scribal scholars.

⁵⁴Peter followed him from a distance into the courtyard of the high priest. He sat with his officials and warmed himself at the fire.

⁵⁵Meanwhile, the chief priests and the whole Sanhedrin were seeking testimony against Jesus in order to put him to death, but they could not find any. ⁵⁶For many people were bearing false witness against him, but their testimony did not agree.

⁵⁷Then some arose giving false testimony against him saying, ⁵⁸"We heard him saying, 'I will destroy this temple made by hands, and after three days I will build another not made by hands.'" ⁵⁹Even then, their testimony did not agree.

⁶⁰Then the high priest stood up in their midst and questioned Jesus asking, "Aren't you going to answer? What are these men testifying against you?" ⁶¹But he remained silent and did not answer a thing.

Again, the high priest questioned him and asked, "Are you the Christ, the son of the blessed one?"

⁶²Then Jesus said, "I am, and you will see the Son of Man sitting on the right hand of power and coming with the clouds of heaven."

⁶³Then the high priest tore his inner garment and said, "What more do we need of witnesses? ⁶⁴You have heard the

blasphemy.[i] What is your decision?" They all condemned him as worthy of death.

⁶⁵Some of them began to spit on him, and to cover his face and strike him repeatedly saying to him, "Prophesy!" The officials also struck him with open-handed blows as they took him away.

Peter's Failure

⁶⁶While Peter was below in the courtyard, one of the high priest's servant girls approached him. ⁶⁷When she saw Peter warming himself, she stared at him and said, "You also were with Jesus the Nazarene."

⁶⁸But he denied it saying, "I don't know or understand what you are talking about." Then he went outside into the front courtyard; and a rooster crowed.

⁶⁹When the servant girl saw him, she again began to tell those standing around, "This man is with them." ⁷⁰But he denied it again.

After a little while, those standing around said to Peter, "Surely you must be with them, for you are a Galilean. Even your speech makes it evident."

⁷¹Then he bound himself under a curse and swore, "I do not know this man you are talking about."

⁷²Immediately a rooster crowed for the second time. Peter remembered the words Jesus had spoken to him, "Before the rooster crows twice, you will deny knowing me three times." When he remembered, he was overwhelmed by weeping.

---

[i] Blasphemy is about speaking profanely of sacred things, to slander God, or to speak against him.

Mark 15:1

Jesus Handed over to Pilate

Chapter Fifteen

¹Shortly after that, in the early morning, the chief priests, with the elders, scribal scholars, and the whole Sanhedrin, took counsel together. They bound Jesus, led him away, and handed him over to Pilate.

²Pilate questioned him, "Are you the King of the Jews?" In response, Jesus said to him, "You yourself are saying it."

³The chief priests were bringing many accusations against him. ⁴But Pilate again questioned him asking, "Won't you respond to anything? Pay attention to the many charges they are bringing against you."

⁵But Jesus no longer responded to anything. This bewildered Pilate.

The Religious Leaders Persuade the Crowd

⁶Now during the feast, Pilate customarily released to them one prisoner whom they requested. ⁷There was one man named Barabbas in prison with the rebels; he had committed murder in the rebellion. ⁸The crowd shouted and began to ask that he do what he normally did for them during the feast.[i]

⁹So Pilate responded to them asking, "Do you want me to release the King of the Jews?" ¹⁰For he knew that the chief priests had handed him over because they were jealous. ¹¹But the chief priests stirred up the crowd that he might instead release Barabbas to them.

¹²Pilate again responded to them asking, "What do you wish that I do with the one you call King of the Jews?"

¹³In response, they again shouted, "Crucify him!"

¹⁴But Pilate asked them, "For what? What evil has he done?" But they shouted all the more, "Crucify him!"

---

[i] Since Jesus was arrested overnight in secret, the only bystanders present would have been those interested in clemency for Barabbas, not Jesus.

¹⁵Because Pilate wished to pacify the crowd, he released Barabbas to them, and after he whipped Jesus severely, he handed him over to be crucified.

The Soldiers Add to Jesus' Suffering

¹⁶The soldiers led him away into their courtyard, that is the Praetorium,[ii] and they called together the entire Roman cohort. ¹⁷They dressed him in a purple *cape*, and wove a crown made of thorny branches, and put it on him. ¹⁸They began to salute him, "Hail, King of the Jews." ¹⁹They repeatedly struck his head with a reed staff and kept spitting on him. They also knelt before him and bowed to him. ²⁰When they had finished mocking him, they took the purple cape off of him, and put his own clothing back on him. Then they led him out to crucify him.

Jesus is Crucified

²¹They pressed a man who had come from the countryside into their service to carry Jesus' cross. He had come from the countryside and was passing by—Simon of Cyrene, the father of Alexander and Rufus. ²²They brought him to the place called Golgotha, which means, "Place of the skull." ²³They gave him wine mixed with myrrh, but he did not take it. ²⁴They crucified him, and distributed his garments, throwing dice to decide what each soldier would get.

²⁵It was the third hour[iii] when they crucified him. ²⁶There was a notice of the accusation against him. It was inscribed, "King of the Jews."

²⁷Two rebels were crucified with him, one on his right and one on his left. ²⁸The Scripture was fulfilled that said,

"He was counted with the lawbreakers."[iv]

[ii] The Praetorium was the palace of the Roman governor.
[iii] About 9:00 AM.
[iv] Isaiah 53:12

²⁹Those who walked by ridiculed[i] him shaking their heads and saying, "Aha! This is the one who can destroy the temple and rebuild it in three days. ³⁰Come down from the cross and save yourself."

³¹Likewise, the chief priests and the scribal scholars were also mocking him among themselves saying, "He saved others. He does not have the power to save himself. ³²The Messiah! The King of Israel! Let him come down now from the cross so that we might see and believe." Even those who were crucified with him heaped scorn on him.

³³At the sixth hour, darkness fell across the whole land until the ninth hour.[ii] ³⁴At the ninth hour, Jesus cried out with a thundering voice, "Eloi, Eloi! Lama sabachthani?" When it is translated, it means,

> "My God, my God! Why have you abandoned me?"[iii]

³⁵Some who were standing nearby said, "Look, he is calling Elijah."

³⁶Then someone ran and filled a sponge with cheap wine. He put it on a reed stick and gave him a drink saying, "Allow me to do this![iv] Let us see if Elijah comes to take him down."

³⁷After Jesus released a piercing cry, he breathed out his last breath.

³⁸Then the curtain of the temple was split into two from top to bottom.

³⁹When the centurion who was standing facing Jesus, saw the way that he had breathed his last breath, he said, "Truly this man was the Son of God."

---

[i] Or, "blasphemed."

[ii] The sixth hour is noon. The ninth hour is 3:00 PM.

[iii] Psalm 22:1

[iv] In Matthew, the other soldiers also seek permission from the centurion, since the centurion had to give permission for it to happen.

Mark 16:3

The Faithful Few Continue to Watch and Serve

⁴⁰There were also women who were observing events from a distance. The group included Mary Magdalene; Mary the mother of Joseph and the less prominent James; and Salome. ⁴¹When Jesus was in Galilee, they followed him and served him. There were also many other women who traveled with him to Jerusalem.

⁴²Since evening was already upon them and it was the Day of Preparation[v]—the day before the Sabbath—⁴³Joseph from Aramathea, a prominent member of the Sanhedrin who was also waiting for the Kingdom of God, acted with courage; he approached Pilate to ask for the body of Jesus.

⁴⁴But Pilate was shocked that he had already died. He summoned the centurion and asked him if Jesus had already died. ⁴⁵When he learned the details from the centurion, he gave the body to Joseph.

⁴⁶Joseph bought a linen cloth, took Jesus down, wrapped him in the linen, and placed him in a tomb that had been chiseled out of rock. He also rolled a stone against the door of the tomb. ⁴⁷Mary Magdalene and Mary the mother of Joseph were watching where they laid him.

The Women Hear the Good News of Resurrection

Chapter Sixteen

¹After the Sabbath was over, Mary Magdalene, Mary the mother of James, and Salome brought spices that they might anoint Jesus' body. ²They came to the tomb very early on the first day of the week, as the sun began to rise. ³They were discussing among themselves, "Who will roll away the stone from the door of the tomb for us?"

---

[v] The day of Preparation (Friday) was the day one prepared for the Sabbath (Saturday)

⁴When they looked up, because the stone was very large, they saw that it had been rolled away. ⁵When they came to the tomb, they saw a young man sitting on the right side; he was wearing a white robe. The women were surprised.

⁶But the man said to them, "Do not be startled. You are seeking Jesus the Nazarene who was crucified. He has been raised to life; he is not here. Look at the place where they placed him. ⁷But go tell his disciples and Peter, 'He is going ahead of you into Galilee. You will see him there. It is just as he told you.'"

⁸They went out from the tomb and ran away, for trembling and spiritual ecstasy[i] had overwhelmed them. They said nothing to anyone because they were filled with awe.[ii]

Jesus Appears to Mary Magdalene

⁹When Jesus had arisen early on the first day of the week, he appeared first to Mary Magdalene, from whom he had cast out seven demons. ¹⁰She went and reported to those who had been with him. They were mourning and weeping. ¹¹But when they heard that he was alive and had been seen by her, they did not believe it.

Jesus Appears on the Road to Emmaus

¹²After these things, he appeared in a different guise to two of them while they were walking on their way to the country.[iii] ¹³They also went and reported to the others, but they did not believe them either.

Jesus Commissions His People

¹⁴Later, he appeared to the eleven while they were eating and rebuked their unbelief and hardness of heart, because they did not believe the ones who had seen him after he had risen.

---

[i] "Spiritual ecstasy" translates a Greek noun used when referring to spiritual ecstatic phenomena in ancient times.

[ii] Or, "reverence."

[iii] See Luke 24:13.

¹⁵He said to them, "When you go into all the world, preach the good news to all the creation. ¹⁶The one who has believed and has been baptized will be saved, but the one who has refused to believe will be condemned.

¹⁷"These confirmations will accompany those who have believed: In my name they will expel demons; they will speak with new languages; ¹⁸they will take up snakes with their hands; and should they drink any deadly thing, it will certainly not harm them;[iv] they will put their hands upon the sick, and they will be healthy."

¹⁹When the Lord Jesus had spoken with them, he was taken up into heaven and sat on the right hand of God.

²⁰Then they went out and preached everywhere. The Lord kept working with them and confirming the word through the signs that attended them.

[iv] Note in the first half of verse 18 that the issue is deadly poison, whether injected or ingested. Jesus is teaching that God's people can expect supernatural protection when these types of accidents occur.

LUKE

Luke Explains His Purpose in Writing

Chapter One

¹Since many have attempted to compile a record of the events that happened in our midst, ²as it was committed to us by those who from the beginning were eyewitnesses and servants of the word, ³it seemed appropriate that I write an orderly account to you, most excellent Theophilus. For I have investigated it all carefully for a long time, ⁴so that you may know how reliable the words are that you have been taught.

Gabriel Foretells the Birth of the Forerunner of Christ

⁵In the days that Herod was King of Judea, there was a certain priest by the name of Zechariah, from the division of priests known as Abijah. His wife came from the daughters of Aaron, and her name was Elizabeth. ⁶They were both righteous before God, walking faultlessly in all the commands and requirements of the Lord. ⁷But they did not have a child, because Elizabeth was barren *and unable to have children*, and they were both quite advanced in age.

⁸Then, as it happened, while his division of priests was on duty, and he was serving as priest before God, ⁹according to the tradition of the priesthood, he was chosen by lot to go in and burn incense in the temple of the Lord. ¹⁰All the multitude of the people were praying outside at the time that the incense was burned.

¹¹Then an angel of the Lord appeared to him, standing at the right of the altar of incense. ¹²When he saw it, Zechariah was shaken, and fear assailed him. ¹³Then the angel said to him, "Stop being afraid, Zechariah, for your request has been heard. Your wife, Elizabeth, will bear a son to you, and you will call his name John. ¹⁴He will be a joy and a cause of celebration for you, and many will rejoice at his birth, ¹⁵for he will be great in the sight of the Lord. He must not drink wine or beer, since he will be filled with the Holy Spirit while yet in his mother's womb. ¹⁶He will return many of the sons of Israel to the Lord their God. ¹⁷He is the one who will go before the Lord in the spirit and power of Elijah, to turn the hearts of the fathers to the children,[i] and the disobedient to the way that the righteous think. He will prepare a people who are being developed for the Lord."[ii]

¹⁸But Zechariah said to the angel, "What is the sign that this will happen for us? For I am an elderly man and my wife is advanced in age."

¹⁹The angel responded and said to him, "I am Gabriel, the one who stands before God. I was sent to speak with you and tell you this good news. ²⁰Now pay attention! You will lose the ability to speak, and you will not be able to speak again until these things happen, because you did not believe my words, which will be fulfilled at their appropriate time."

²¹By this time, the crowd was waiting for Zechariah, and they were wondering why he spent such a long time in the temple.

---

[i] See Malachi 4:5-6.

[ii] See Isaiah 40:3-5.

22But when he came out, he was unable to speak to them, and they recognized that he had experienced a visitation in the temple. He could only signal to them because he was deaf and mute.

23When the days of his service were fulfilled, he left for his home. 24Then, after these events, Elizabeth, his wife, conceived, and she hid herself for five months, saying, 25"The Lord has done this for me. At the time he took notice of me, he removed my disgrace among men."

Gabriel Foretells the Birth of the Christ

26Then, in the sixth month, the angel Gabriel was sent by God to a city in Galilee named Nazareth, 27to a virgin contracted for marriage to a man by the name of Joseph, who was from the house of David. The virgin's name was Mary. 28When he arrived, he said to her, "Rejoice, you who have received a gracious gift, the Lord is with you."

29But she was confused by his speech, and considered carefully what sort of greeting it could be. 30Then the angel said to her, "Stop being afraid, Mary, for you have found favor with God. 31Listen closely, you will conceive in your womb, and give birth to a son, and you will give him the name Jesus. 32He will be great, and will be called the son of the Most High; and the Lord God will give the throne of his father David to him. 33He will reign over the house of Jacob forever, and his kingdom will not end."

34Then Mary said to the angel, "How will this happen, since I am not having intimate relations with a husband?"

35The angel responded to her and said, "The Holy Spirit will come upon you, and the power of the Most High will overshadow you; as a result, the holy one who is born to you will be called the Son of God. 36Also, take note of your relative Elizabeth. She has conceived a son in her old age. This is the sixth month for her who was called barren. ³⁷For nothing God says is impossible."ⁱ

³⁸Then Mary said, "Look, I am the servant of the Lord. May it happen to me as you have promised." Then the angel left her.

Elizabeth Confirms the Angel's Promise

³⁹After these things, Mary left and eagerly went to a town of Judah in the hill country. ⁴⁰She entered the house of Zechariah, and greeted Elizabeth. ⁴¹As soon as Elizabeth heard Mary's greeting, the baby leaped in her womb, and Elizabeth was filled with the Holy Spirit. ⁴²She cried out with a loud shout, and said, "You are honored among women, and the child in your womb is also honored. ⁴³Now how has this happened to me, that the mother of my Lord would come to me? ⁴⁴Listen, when the sound of your greeting reached my ears, the baby in my womb leaped in joy. ⁴⁵Blessed is she who has believed that what was spoken to her by the Lord will be fulfilled."

Mary's Praise to the Lord

⁴⁶And Mary said,

> "My soul greatly honors the Lord, ⁴⁷and my spirit rejoices in God my Savior.
>
> ⁴⁸"For he has taken special notice of the humble position of his servant.
>
> "For certainly, from now on every generation will regard me as blessed.
>
> ⁴⁹"For the Able Oneⁱⁱ has done great things for me. Holy is his name.
>
> ⁵⁰"His mercy extends from generation to generation for those who fear him.
>
> ⁵¹"By his arm, he has done a mighty thing.

ⁱ More literally, "For every word from God is not impossible."
ⁱⁱ Or, "The Powerful One."

> "He scatters those who are arrogant in the thoughts of their heart.
>
> ⁵²"He has deposed rulers from their thrones, and exalted those who are humble.
>
> ⁵³"He has satisfied those who are hungry with good things, and sent those who are rich away empty-handed.
>
> ⁵⁴"He has taken up the cause of his servant Israel, remembering mercy, ⁵⁵just as he spoke to our fathers, to Abraham and his offspring, through the years."

⁵⁶Mary remained with Elizabeth about three months. Then she returned to her home.

Gabriel's Promise Fulfilled: The Birth of John

⁵⁷Now the time for Elizabeth to give birth arrived, and she bore a son. ⁵⁸Her neighbors and relatives heard that the Lord had multiplied his mercy to her, and they rejoiced with her.

⁵⁹As was usual, on the eighth day they came to circumcise the child, and they named him after his father, Zechariah. ⁶⁰But his mother responded and said, "Absolutely not! Instead, he will be called John."

⁶¹But they said to her, "No one from your family has that name."

⁶²So they gestured to his father about what he wanted to name him. ⁶³He asked for a small writing tablet[i] and wrote, "John is his name." And they were all surprised.

⁶⁴Then immediately his mouth was opened and his tongue freed, and he spoke praising God. ⁶⁵As a result, fear fell upon everyone living around them, and they were discussing all these supernatural things throughout the hill country of Judea.

---

[i] The pinakidion was a small writing tablet normally made of wood with a prepared wax surface.

⁶⁶Everyone who heard about it, treasured it in their heart asking, "What will this child become?" They asked this because the hand of the Lord was with him.

Zechariah's Prophecy

⁶⁷Then his father, Zechariah, was filled with the Holy Spirit and prophesied saying,

> ⁶⁸"Praise the Lord God of Israel, for he has visited us, and begun the redemption of his people.[ii]
>
> ⁶⁹"He has raised up a horn of salvation for us in the house of his child, David,[iii] ⁷⁰just as he spoke through the mouth of his holy prophets over the ages.
>
> ⁷¹"*He promised* deliverance from our enemies, and from the hand of all who hate us.
>
> ⁷²"*He promised* to show mercy to our fathers, and to remember his holy covenant.
>
> ⁷³"*He promised* to fulfill the oath which he swore to Abraham, our father, to give us ⁷⁴deliverance from the hand of our enemies, so we can serve him without fear ⁷⁵in holiness and righteousness before him all the days of our lives.
>
> ⁷⁶"Even you, my child, will be called a prophet of the Most High, for you will go in advance of the Lord to prepare his ways.[iv]
>
> ⁷⁷"You will give the knowledge of deliverance to his people in the forgiveness of their sins, ⁷⁸because of the compassionate mercy of our God. It is

---

[ii] Zechariah knows of impending birth of the Messiah, and how John and he will be linked.

[iii] See 2 Samuel 22:3 and Psalm 18:2.

[iv] See Isaiah 40:3.

the compassionate mercy of God by which the Dawn from on high will visit us, ⁷⁹and will shine light on those who are sitting in darkness and the shadow of death, and guide our feet in the way of peace."

⁸⁰The child grew and became strong in spirit. He lived in the wilderness until the day of his appearance to Israel.

Gabriel's Promise Fulfilled: The Birth of Jesus

Chapter Two

¹In those days an edict went out from Caesar Augustus that all the Roman world[i] be registered. ²This registration happened before Quirinius was governor of Syria.[ii] ³Everyone went to be registered, each to his own city.

⁴Joseph also went up from Galilee, from the city of Nazareth to Judea, to the city of David which is called Bethlehem, because he was from the house and family line of David. ⁵He went to register with Mary, who was formally engaged to marry him, and she was pregnant.[iii] ⁶While they were there, the days were completed for her to give birth. ⁷So, she gave birth to her firstborn son, and wrapped him in long strips of cloth and laid

---

[i] Or, "inhabited world," usually referring to the Roman world in the gospels and Acts.

[ii] Quirinius was governor in 6 A.D., many years after Jesus was born. Quirinius did order a much-hated registration, but Luke is pointing out that this was not the one that Quirinius did.

[iii] More than likely they traveled before Mary's pregnancy made it too dangerous to take on such a venture. They could have been in Bethlehem for quite some time before the birth of Jesus.

him in a feeding trough, because there was no place for mother and child[iv] in the guest room.[v]

The Angels Announce the Birth of the Messiah to Shepherds

[8]There were shepherds in the same area staying outside during the night, keeping watch over their flocks. [9]Without warning, an angel of the Lord stood by them, the glory of the Lord shone around them, and they were very afraid.

[10]The angel said to them, "Stop being afraid! Listen carefully, for I am bringing good news to you about a great joy that will be for all people. [11]For today, a Savior has been born for you in the city of David. He is Christ and Lord. [12]This is a sign for you. You will find an infant wrapped in long strips of cloth and lying in a feeding trough."

[13]Suddenly there were with the angel a large heavenly army praising God and saying,

> [14]"Glory to God in the highest heavens, and
> peace on earth among men who are
> recipients of his good pleasure."[vi]

[15]When the angels had gone away from them into heaven, the shepherds said to each other, "Let us now go over to Bethlehem and see this prophecy that has been fulfilled, which the Lord has made known to us."

[16]So they hurried along and searched until they found Mary, Joseph, and the infant lying in the feeding trough. [17]Then after visiting, they made known the promise which was spoken to

---

[iv] Or, "them."

[v] Though this word is often translated, "inn," it is not the normal Greek word for inn. If the couple was staying in a crowded guest room with relatives, Mary and Joseph would have been required to move so that the other guests would not become ceremonially unclean from the birth.

[vi] The Qumran discoveries have given insight on the meaning of "recipients of his good pleasure." Several Qumran Hymns read, "the sons of his [God's] good pleasure," and "the elect of his [God's] good pleasure." This was a well-known expression that referred to God's chosen.

them about this child. ¹⁸Everyone who heard was filled with wonder over what the shepherds had told them. ¹⁹But Mary kept all these things in mind and thought deeply about them in her heart. ²⁰Then the shepherds returned glorifying and praising God for all that they had heard and seen, just as it was told to them.

The Circumcision and Naming of Jesus

²¹When the eight days were fulfilled for his circumcision, he was named Jesus, the name he was called by the angel before he was conceived in Mary's womb.

The Sacrificial Redemption of Jesus as Firstborn Son

²²When the days of their purification were completed according to the law of Moses, they brought him to Jerusalem to place him at the disposal of the Lord. ²³This agrees with what is written in the Law of the Lord,

> "Every male who is first from the womb will be called holy to the Lord."[i]

²⁴They also came to offer the sacrifice as it is spelled out in the Law of the Lord, "A pair of doves or two young pigeons."[ii]

The Holy Spirit Provides Witnesses

²⁵Notably, there was a man in Jerusalem by the name of Simeon. He was righteous and devout, waiting for the Encouragement of Israel, and the Holy Spirit was upon him. ²⁶It had been revealed to him by the Spirit of God that he would not see death until he would see the Lord's Christ. ²⁷He came to the temple by the Spirit when the parents brought the child Jesus, that they might carry out the traditions of the Law for him. ²⁸He took the child into his arms, praised God, and said,

> ²⁹"Now Master let your servant depart in peace, according to your promise.

---

[i] Exodus 13:2, 12.

[ii] Leviticus 12:8

30"For my eyes have seen your salvation, 31the salvation you have prepared in front *of the eyes* of all peoples, 32a light of revelation for the nations, and glory for your people, Israel."

33Both his father and mother were surprised at what was spoken about him.

34Then Simeon blessed them and said to Mary his mother, "Listen closely, this child has been placed here for the downfall and elevation of many in Israel, and for a sign to be spoken against, 35that the thoughts from the hearts of many will be revealed; a sword will even pierce your very own soul."

36There was also a prophetess, Anna the daughter of Phanuel, from the tribe of Asher. She was quite advanced in age, having lived with her husband seven years after ending her virginity. 37She had been a widow for eighty-four years, never leaving the temple, but serving night and day with prayers and times of fasting.[iii] 38At that very hour, she came upon them and gave thanks to God. She spoke about the child to everyone who was waiting for the deliverance of Jerusalem.

The Family Returns to Nazareth

39When they had finished all the things detailed by the Law of the Lord, they returned to Galilee to their own city of Nazareth. 40Then the child grew, became strong, and was filled with wisdom. The grace of God was upon him.

Jesus Steps into the Affairs of His Father

41His parents used to go to Jerusalem each year for the Feast of Passover. 42When he turned twelve years old, they followed their normal practice and went up to the festival. 43After finishing their time at the festival, they left for home. However, the child Jesus stayed behind in Jerusalem, but they did not know it. 44They thought that he was with the rest of the

---

[iii] Or, "fastings and prayers."

returning pilgrims, so they went a day's journey before they began to look for him among their relatives and friends. ⁴⁵When they did not find him, they returned to Jerusalem to search for him. ⁴⁶After three days they found him in the temple. He was sitting in the company of the teachers listening to them and asking them questions. ⁴⁷Everyone who heard him was beside themselves with amazement at his understanding and responses.

⁴⁸When they saw him, they were overwhelmed with wonder, and his mother said to him, "My child, why have you behaved this way toward us? Your father and I were terribly worried and were searching for you."

⁴⁹But he said to them, "Why were you searching for me? Didn't you know that I needed to be about the affairs of my Father?"[i] ⁵⁰However, they did not understand the significance of what he was saying to them.

⁵¹Then he left with them and returned to Nazareth. He also willingly submitted to them; and his mother stored all these things in her heart. ⁵²Then Jesus continued to grow in wisdom and maturity, and in favor with God and men.

The Baptizer Steps into His Call and Purpose

Chapter Three

¹In the fifteenth year of the reign of Tiberius Caesar, when Pontius Pilate was governing Judea, Herod was governing as tetrarch of Galilee, Philip his brother was governing as tetrarch of the district of Ituria and Trachonitis, and Lysanias was governing as tetrarch of Abilene, ²at the time of the high priesthood of Annas and Caiaphas, the word of God came to John, son of Zechariah, in the desert. ³He went into all the region of the Jordan proclaiming a baptism of repentance for the forgiveness of sins. ⁴As it is written in the book of Isaiah the prophet,

---

[i] Or possibly, "in the house of my Father."

"A voice calling in the desert, 'Prepare the way of the Lord, make his paths straight, ⁵every valley will be filled in and every mountain and hill leveled, and the crooked places will become straight, and the uneven places a smooth road. And all flesh will see the salvation of God.'"[ii]

⁷Therefore, John often told the crowds that were coming out to be baptized by him, "You offspring of poisonous snakes, who told you to flee from the punishment[iii] to come? ⁸Now then, produce fruits worthy of repentance, and do not begin to say among yourselves, 'We have father Abraham.' For I am telling you that God is able to raise up children for Abraham from these stones. ⁹For already the ax is positioned at the root of the trees. Every tree that does not produce good fruit will be cut down and thrown into the fire."

¹⁰The crowds questioned him saying, "So what should we do?"

¹¹Then he responded and told them, "Let the one who has two tunics share with the one who does not have one, and let the one who has food do likewise."

¹²Then tax collectors came to be baptized, and they asked him, "Teacher, what should we do?"

¹³He said to them, "Do not collect more than what has been assigned to you."

¹⁴Then soldiers questioned him asking, "What can those like us do?"

He said to them, "Don't oppress others, do not bring a false charge against anyone, and be content with your wages."

¹⁵Now the people were waiting with anticipation and considering carefully in their hearts about whether John might be the Christ. ¹⁶John responded to them all and said, "I am the

---

[ii] Isaiah 40:3-5

[iii] Or, traditionally, "wrath."

one who baptizes you with water, but one who is greater than I am is coming. I am not worthy to loosen a strap of his sandals. He is the one who will baptize you with the Holy Spirit and fire. ¹⁷His winnowing fork is in his hand to thoroughly clean his threshing floor, and to gather the grain into his storehouse, but the chaff he will burn with unquenchable fire." ¹⁸So John exhorted the people with many other teachings, and preached the good news.

¹⁹But when Herod the tetrarch was rebuked by John about his brother Philip's wife, Herodias, and about all of the evil Herod was doing, ²⁰he also added this evil to them all: he confined John in prison.

The Spirit of God Empowers Jesus at His Baptism

²¹At that time, all the people were being baptized, Jesus also was baptized. While he was praying, the heaven opened, ²²and the Holy Spirit descended upon him in the physical form of a dove, and a voice came from heaven, "You are my cherished Son, in you I am well pleased."

Jesus, a Son of Adam

²³Jesus himself was about thirty years of age.

He was the son, as it was thought, of Joseph, the son of Eli,
²⁴the son of Matthat, the son of Levi, the son of Melchi, the son of Jannai, the son of Joseph,
²⁵the son of Mattathias, the son of Amos, the son of Nahum, the son of Hesli, the son of Naggai,
²⁶the son of Maath, the son of Matthias, the son of Semein, the son of Josech, the son of Joda,
²⁷the son of Joanan, the son of Rhesa, the son of Zerubbabel, the son of Shealtiel, the son of Neri,
²⁸the son of Melchi, the son of Addi, the son of Cosam, the son of Elmadam, the son of Er,

²⁹the son of Jesus,ⁱ the son of Eliezer, the son of Jorim, the son of Matthat, the son of Levi,
³⁰the son of Simeon, the son of Judah, the son of Joseph, the son of Jonam, the son of Eliakim,
³¹the son of Melea, the son of Menna, the son of Mattatha, the son of Nathan, the son of David,
³²the son of Jesse, the son of Obed, the son of Boaz, the son of Salmon, the son of Nahshon,
³³the son of Amminadab, the son of Admin, the son of Arni,ⁱⁱ the son of Hezron, the son of Perez, the son of Judah,
³⁴the son of Jacob, the son of Isaac, the son of Abraham, the son of Tera, the son of Nahor,
³⁵the son of Serug, the son of Reu, the son of Peleg, the son of Eber, the son of Shelah,
³⁶the son of Cainan, the son of Arphaxad, the son of Shem, the son of Noah, the son of Lamech,
³⁷the son of Methuselah, the son of Enoch, the son of Jared, the son of Mahalalel, the son of Cainan,
³⁸the son of Enosh, the son of Seth, the son of Adam, the son of God.

The Testing of Jesus

Chapter Four

¹Then Jesus, full of the Holy Spirit, returned from the Jordan and was guided by the Holy Spirit into the desert ²for forty days, all the while being tempted by the Accuser.ⁱⁱⁱ He did not eat for those days, and after they were over, he was hungry.

ⁱ The Hebrew name "Joshua" came into the Greek as "Jesus."

ⁱⁱ Or, "Ram."

ⁱⁱⁱ Traditionally, "devil." The name means to slander or accuse. For this reason, this word is most often translated "Accuser" in this Bible version.

³Then the Accuser said to him, "Since[i] you are the Son of God, speak to this stone so that it becomes bread."

⁴But Jesus responded to him, "It is written, 'Man will not live on bread alone, but on every word of God.'[ii]"

⁵After he led Jesus up to a higher point, he showed him all the kingdoms of the inhabited world[iii] in a moment of time. ⁶Then the Accuser said to him, "I will give you all this authority and all their glory, because it has been handed over to me, and I can give it to whomever I wish. ⁷Therefore, if you bow before me to honor me, it will all be yours."

⁸But Jesus responded and said to him, "It is written, 'Worship the Lord your God, and venerate him alone.'[iv]"

⁹Then he led him to Jerusalem, and Jesus stood upon the highest point of the temple. The Accuser said to him, "Since you are the Son of God, throw yourself down from here. ¹⁰For it is written,

> " 'He will command his angels concerning you to keep you safe,' ¹¹and 'they will lift you up in their hands, so that you do not strike your foot against a stone.'[v] "

¹²But Jesus responded and said to him, "It is said, 'You will not test the Lord your God.'[vi]"

¹³After he completed all the testing, the Accuser withdrew from him, awaiting a more critical time.

---

[i] Or, traditionally, "if," though the Accuser does not seem to be questioning who Jesus is, but attempting to get him to abandon the Father's path.

[ii] See Deuteronomy 8:3. The Greek word used here often refers to God's supernatural provision, as the Hebrew does in the Deuteronomy passage.

[iii] Or, "the Roman world."

[iv] Deuteronomy 6:13

[v] Psalm 91:11-12

[vi] Deuteronomy 6:16

Jesus Rejected in His Hometown

¹⁴Jesus returned to Galilee in the power of the Spirit. The report about him went out throughout the entire region. ¹⁵He was teaching in their synagogues and was praised by everyone. ¹⁶Then he went to Nazareth, where he had been raised. On the Sabbath, as he was accustomed, he went to the synagogue, and stood up to read. ¹⁷The scroll of the Prophet Isaiah was given to him. He unrolled the scroll and found the place where it was written,

> ¹⁸"The Spirit of the Lord is upon me, for he has anointed me to preach the good news to the poor, he has sent me to heal those with broken hearts,[vii] to proclaim freedom for the captives, and the restoration of sight to the blind, to send out in freedom those who are crushed by oppression, and ¹⁹to proclaim a year of the Lord's favor."[viii]

²⁰After he rolled up the scroll, he gave it back to the synagogue official and sat down. The eyes of everyone in the synagogue were fixed on him. ²¹Then he began to say to them, "Today, this Scripture stands fulfilled in your hearing."

²²At that, everyone began to talk about him; they were bewildered at the message about favor[ix] that came from his mouth; and many were beginning to ask, "This is the son of Joseph, isn't it?"

[vii] Some manuscripts drop, "to heal broken hearts." However, Jesus was reading from Isaiah 61:1, which most certainly includes this phrase.

[viii] Isaiah 61:1-2a

[ix] Traditionally, "they were astonished by his gracious words." But see Acts 14:3 and 20:32 where this exact expression is translated, "the message about grace" or "the message about favor."

²³So he said to them, "Doubtless you will tell me this proverb, 'Physician, heal yourself,' and 'Do also here in your hometown everything that we have heard you did in Capernaum.'"

²⁴Then he said, "I tell you the truth, no prophet is accepted in his hometown. ²⁵I am speaking only truth to you. There were many widows in Israel in the days of Elijah, when the sky was locked shut for three years and six months as an intense famine came upon the land, ²⁶but Elijah was sent to none of them. He was sent only to Zarephath in Sidon, to a woman who was a widow. ²⁷There were also many lepers in Israel at the time of Elisha the prophet, but none of them were cleansed except Naaman the Syrian."

²⁸Everyone in the synagogue who heard these things was consumed with a violent rage, ²⁹so that they rose up and drove him out of the city. They dragged him to a cliff on the hill on which their city was built in order to throw him off of it, ³⁰but Jesus passed through the middle of them and continued his journey.

Jesus Demonstrates the Kingdom: Authority over a Demon

³¹He went down to Capernaum, a city in Galilee, and continued to teach the people on the Sabbaths. ³²They were almost overwhelmed by his teaching, because his words had authority.

³³There was a man in the synagogue who had a spirit of an unclean demon, and he cried out with a loud voice, ³⁴"Stop! Why are you bothering me, Jesus of Nazareth? Have you come to destroy us? I know who you are—the Holy One of God."

³⁵But Jesus rebuked him saying, "Be silent and come out of him." The demon forced him to the ground in the middle of the congregation, but it came out of him without injuring him.

³⁶Everyone was filled with wonder, and they were discussing it with each other asking, "What is this message? For he commands the unclean spirits with authority and power, and

they come out." ³⁷As a result, the report about him spread into all the surrounding region.

Jesus Demonstrates the Kingdom: Healing the Sick and Demonized

³⁸Then Jesus left the synagogue and went into the house of Simon. But Simon's mother-in-law was afflicted with a high fever, and they approached him on her behalf. ³⁹He stood above her and rebuked the fever, and it left her. She got up immediately and began to serve them.

⁴⁰When *that Sabbath* ended at sundown, all those who had anyone who was sick with various illnesses brought them to Jesus. He laid his hands upon each one of them and healed them.

⁴¹Demons were also coming out from many people. They were shouting and saying, "You are the Son of God." But he rebuked them and would not allow them to speak, because they knew that he was the Christ.

Jesus' Defines His Purpose to His Followers

⁴²When daylight came, Jesus went out and journeyed to an uninhabited place, but the crowds were looking for him. They found him and tried to stop him from journeying away from them. ⁴³But he said to them, "It is imperative that I preach the good news[i] about the Kingdom of God to other cities. I was sent for this reason." ⁴⁴So, he continued preaching in the synagogues of the Jewish people.

---

[i] The Greek word can be translated "Gospel" or "Good News." The word gospel means good news. It is translated both ways in this Bible version.

Jesus Issues a Miraculous Call to His Disciples[i]

Chapter Five

¹Once when a crowd was pushing against him to hear the word of God, he was standing beside the Lake of Gennesaret. ²He spotted two boats moored beside the lake. The fishermen had left the boats and were washing their nets. ³He stepped into one of the boats, the one that belonged to Simon, and asked him to push off a little from the shore. Then he sat and taught the crowds from the boat.

⁴After he finished speaking, he said to Simon, "Put out into the deep water and let down your nets for a catch."

⁵But Simon responded, "Master, we have worked hard through the night and caught nothing. But at your word, I will let down the nets."

⁶When they did this, they caught a great multitude of fish, and their nets began to tear. ⁷They signaled their partners in the other boat to come and help them. When they came, they filled both boats so that they began to sink.

⁸When Simon Peter saw this, he fell down at Jesus' knees saying, "Depart from me, Lord, for I am a sinful man." ⁹For great fear had seized him and all those with him, because of the catch of fish that they had gathered. ¹⁰This included James[ii] and John, the sons of Zebedee, who were partners of Simon.

Jesus said to Simon, "Do not be afraid; from now on you will be catching people."

¹¹When they brought their boats to the shore, they left everything and followed him.

---

[i] The other gospels make it clear that Jesus had already called the disciples to be a part of his team. This was a far more official call that declared their future, and Jesus used the miraculous catch to emphasize its importance.

[ii] Greek text, "Jacob." James is the Anglicized form of Jacob used since the first English translations. Unless it refers to the patriarch Jacob, it will be translated as James in this New Testament.

Luke 5:21

Jesus Touches a Leper and Heals Him

12Then, while he was in one of the cities, surprisingly, there was a man full of leprosy. When he saw Jesus, he fell down on his face and begged him saying, "Lord, if you are willing, you are able to cleanse me."

13Jesus extended his hand and touched him, saying, "I am willing. Be cleansed." Immediately the leprosy left him.

14Then he instructed him not to tell anyone, "But go and show yourself to the priest, and present an offering for your cleansing, just as Moses commanded, as a testimony to them."

15But the report about him went out even more, and many crowds came together to hear him and to be healed of their sicknesses. 16Even then, he would withdraw into the uninhabited regions and pray.

Jesus Demonstrates the Power from God to Heal and Forgive

17On one of the days Jesus was teaching, there were Pharisees and teachers of the law evaluating him, who had come from all the villages of Galilee, and Judea and Jerusalem; and power from the Lord was there so that he could heal. 18At that point, some men who were carrying a paralyzed man on a stretcher tried to carry him inside to place him in front of Jesus. 19When they could not find any way that they might bring him in because of the crowd, they went up to the roof. They let him down with his stretcher, through the tiles, into the middle of the room in front of Jesus.

20Seeing their faith, he said, "Man, your sins are forgiven you."

21But the scribal scholars and the Pharisees began to discuss this saying, "Who is this man? He is speaking blasphemy[iii]. Who is able to forgive sins except God alone?"

[iii] Blasphemy is about speaking profanely of sacred things, to slander God, or to speak against him.

²²But Jesus knew of their discussions, and responded to them, "Why are you debating in your hearts? ²³What is easier, to say, 'Your sins are forgiven you,' or to say, 'Get up and walk'? ²⁴But so that you may know that the Son of Man has authority upon the earth to forgive sins," he said to the paralyzed man, "I say to you, get up, take your stretcher and go to your home." ²⁵He immediately rose up in front of them, took what he had been lying on, and went to his own home praising God.

²⁶Then everyone was overwhelmed by ecstatic joy[i], and they began glorifying God. They were filled with reverence and said, "We have seen incredible things today."

Jesus Demonstrates His Love for Outcasts

²⁷After these things, he went out and saw a tax collector by the name of Levi, sitting at the tax collection station. Jesus said to him, "Follow me." ²⁸Then he abandoned his position there, left the tax booth, and followed him.

²⁹At that time, Levi held a great banquet for Jesus in his house. There was a large crowd of tax collectors and others who were dining with them. ³⁰But the Pharisees and their scribal scholars were complaining to his disciples and said, "For what possible reason are you eating and drinking with tax collectors and sinners?"

³¹Jesus responded and said to them, "Those who are healthy do not have need of a physician, only those who have an illness. ³²I have not come to call the righteous, but sinners to repentance."

Preserving the Old and the New Spiritual Forms

³³Then they said to him, "John's disciples frequently fast when they participate in prayers; likewise, those who are Pharisees also *fast*. But your disciples eat and drink when they pray."

---

[i] "Ecstatic joy" translates a Greek noun used when referring to spiritual ecstatic phenomena in ancient times.

³⁴Then Jesus said to them, "You cannot make the guests[ii] at a wedding fast while the bridegroom is with them, can you? ³⁵But the days will come when the bridegroom is led away from them, they will fast at that time."

³⁶Then he told a parable to them, "No one tears a piece of cloth from a new garment and puts it on an old garment. If a person does so, the new piece of cloth will also tear, and the patch from the new cloth will not match the old garment. ³⁷And no one puts new wine into old inflexible wineskins. If a person does so, the fermenting wine will burst the wineskin; the wine will be lost, and the wineskin will also be ruined. ³⁸But new wine must be put into new flexible wineskins, and both are protected. ³⁹Again, no one who drinks old wine immediately wants new wine. For the old wine is very agreeable."

God's Desire for Mercy from His People

Chapter Six

¹On one Sabbath, when he was crossing through fields of grain, his disciples were picking the grains of wheat, vigorously rubbing them in their hands, and eating them. ²Then some of the Pharisees said, "Why are you doing things that are not lawful on Sabbath days?"

³Jesus responded to them by saying, "Haven't you read the things that David did when he and those with him were hungry, ⁴how he came into the house of God and took the bread of the presence, ate it, and gave it to those who were with him? This bread is not lawful for anyone to eat except the priests alone." ⁵Then he began to explain to them, "The Son of Man is Lord of the Sabbath."

[ii] Literally, "sons of the wedding hall."

Setting a Trap for Jesus

⁶On another Sabbath, he came into the synagogue and was teaching; and there was a man there whose right hand was withered and paralyzed. ⁷But the scribal scholars and the Pharisees were watching him closely to see if he would heal on the Sabbath, in order that they might find a reason to accuse him. ⁸But he knew their thoughts, so he said to the man who had the withering paralysis in his hand, "Get up and stand in the middle *of the congregation*." He arose and stood in their midst.

⁹Then Jesus asked them, "I ask you if it is lawful on the Sabbath to do good or to do evil, to save a life or destroy it?"

¹⁰After he looked around at all of them, he said to the man, "Extend your hand." The man did, and his hand was restored to health just like the other.

¹¹But the Pharisees and scribal scholars were themselves filled with unreasoning fury and discussed among themselves what they might do with Jesus.

Jesus Appoints Twelve Apostles

¹²About that time, he went out to a mountain to pray, and he spent the night in prayer to God. ¹³When daylight came, he called his disciples, and selected twelve of them, whom also he named apostles: ¹⁴Simon, whom he also named Peter, and Andrew his brother, James and John, Philip, Bartholomew, ¹⁵Matthew, Thomas, James son of Alphaeus, Simon who was called the Zealot, ¹⁶Judas son of James, and Judas Iscariot, who became a traitor.

Multitudes Come to Jesus and the Power of God Heals Them

¹⁷He went down with them and stood on a level area. There was a large crowd of his disciples, and a great multitude of people from all of Judea, Jerusalem, and the coastal region of Tyre and Sidon. ¹⁸They came to hear him, and to be healed of their sicknesses. Those who suffered from unclean spirits were

being made well. ¹⁹The whole crowd was trying to touch him, because power was going out from him and healing everyone.

The Sermon on the Plain and the Beatitudes

²⁰Then he directed his eyes toward his disciples and said,

"Blessed are the poor,
  for yours is the Kingdom of God.
²¹"Blessed are those who are hungry now,
  for you will be fed until you have as much as you want.
"Blessed are you who are weeping now,
  for you will laugh.
²²"Blessed are you when men hate you, when they exclude you, when they insult you and disparage your reputation as evil because of the Son of Man; ²³rejoice in that day and dance for joy, for take note of this, your reward in heaven is great. For their fathers used to treat the prophets in the same way.

²⁴"On the other hand,

"Woe to you who are wealthy,
  for you are receiving your encouragement now.
²⁵"Woe to you who are filled up with food now,
  for you will be hungry.
"Woe to those who are laughing now,
  for they will grieve and weep.
²⁶"Woe to you when all men speak well of you,
  for their fathers used to treat the false prophets in the same way.

Living as Kingdom People

²⁷"But I say to you who are listening, love your enemies, do good to those who hate you, ²⁸speak well of those who curse you, pray for those who mistreat you. ²⁹When someone strikes you upon one cheek, present the other cheek to him also; and when someone takes your outer garment, do not stop him from taking your shirt. ³⁰Give to everyone who asks you, and when someone

takes your things, do not demand them back. ³¹Treat men the same way that you want them to treat you.

³²"If you love those who love you, what grace does that provide you? For even sinners love those who love them. ³³For if you do good to those who do good to you, what grace does that provide you? Even sinners do the same. ³⁴If you lend money to those from whom you hope to receive benefit, what grace does that provide you? Even sinners lend money to other sinners so that they might receive future benefit. ³⁵But love your enemies, do good, and lend without expecting future benefit. Then your reward will be great, and you will be sons of the Most High; for he himself is good to ungrateful and evil people.

³⁶"Be merciful just as your Father is merciful.

Refuse to Criticize Others

³⁷"Do not judge, and you will never be judged. Do not condemn and you will never be condemned. Forgive, and you will be forgiven. ³⁸Give, and it will be given to you. They will pour a good measure, pressed down, shaken together, and overflowing into your carry pouch. For with the measure you measure things, it will be measured back to you."

Seek Teachers who Can See

³⁹Then he also spoke this parable to them, "A blind man is not able to guide a blind man, is he? They will both fall into a ditch, won't they?

⁴⁰"A disciple is not above his teacher; but everyone who is fully trained will be like his teacher."

Correct Yourself Before You Correct Others

⁴¹"So why do you see the small chip of wood in your brother's eye, but do not notice the beam of wood in your own eye? ⁴²How are you able to say to your brother, 'Brother, allow me to remove the small chip of wood in your eye,' when you yourself do not see the beam of wood in your own eye? Hypocrite, first remove the beam of wood from your eye, and then because you

are seeing clearly, you can remove the small chip of wood in your brother's eye.

Recognizing God's Servants by Their Fruit

⁴³"For a good tree does not produce worthless fruit, and likewise, a worthless tree does not produce good-looking fruit. ⁴⁴Each tree is known by its fruit. People do not gather figs from thorn bushes, nor do they pick grapes from brambles.

⁴⁵"The good man produces good from the good treasured in his heart; but an evil man produces evil from the evil treasured in his heart. For from that which is abundant in his heart, his mouth speaks.

Building a Life that Withstands Trials

⁴⁶"But why do you call me, 'Lord, Lord,' and do not do the things I am saying? ⁴⁷Everyone who comes to me, and after hearing my words also makes a habit of them, I will show you what he is like. ⁴⁸He is like a man building a house who dug down deep into the ground and laid the foundation on the rock. Then, when the river overflowed, and the rushing water slammed into that house, the water was not strong enough to shake it, because it was established upon the rock. ⁴⁹But the one who hears my words and does not make a habit of them is like a man building a house on the ground without a foundation; when the rushing water slammed into it, it immediately collapsed, and the house suffered catastrophic damage."

A Demonstration of Great Faith: The Centurion

Chapter Seven

¹When he had finished all his teaching in front of the people, he went to Capernaum. ²There a certain centurion had a servant who was ill and was about to die. The servant was dear to him. ³When he heard about Jesus, he sent Jewish elders to Jesus asking that he might come and heal his servant. ⁴When the elders arrived by Jesus, they earnestly appealed to him saying,

"He is worthy that you grant him this, ⁵for he loves our people, and he is the one who built the synagogue for us."

⁶Then Jesus started on his way with them. When he was not far from the house, the centurion sent friends who said to him, "Lord, do not trouble yourself, for I am not worthy that you come under my roof. ⁷For this very reason I did not consider myself worthy to come to you. But say the word, and my servant will be healed. ⁸For I also am a man deployed under authority, having soldiers under me. I say to this one, 'Go!' and he goes, to another, 'Come!' and he comes, to my servant, 'Do this!' and he does it."

⁹When Jesus heard these things, he was astonished by the centurion. He turned to the crowd that was following him and said, "I tell you; I have not found in all Israel a faith so great as this."

¹⁰When those who were sent returned to the house, they found the servant restored to health.

Raising the Dead to Life

¹¹After this, Jesus went to a city called Nain, and his disciples and a large crowd were traveling with him. ¹²As they drew near the city gate, at just that moment, a man who had died was carried out. He was the only son of his mother, and she was a widow. A notable crowd from the city was with her.

¹³When the Lord saw her, he was moved by compassion for her, and he said to her, "Stop weeping."

¹⁴He came up and touched the bier, and the ones who were carrying it stood still. Jesus said, "Young man, I say to you, wake up." ¹⁵The dead man sat up and began to speak, and Jesus returned him to his mother.

¹⁶Then everyone was filled with awe and glorified God saying, "A great prophet has arisen among us," and "God has visited his people." ¹⁷This report about him went out through all of Judea and the surrounding region.

John's Question About the Christ

¹⁸When John's disciples reported all of these things to him, he called for two of his disciples ¹⁹and sent them to Jesus asking, "Are you the One Coming, or should we wait for another?"

²⁰When they came to Jesus, the men said, "John the Baptizerⁱ sent us to ask you, 'Are you the One Coming, or should we wait for another?'"

²¹At that moment he was healing many people from sicknesses, diseases, and evil spirits, and was freely giving sight to many blind people. ²²So, he responded and said to them, "When you go, report to John what you see and hear. The blind see again, the crippled are walking, lepers are being cleansed and the deaf are able to hear, the dead are raised, and the poor hear the good news preached. ²³Blessed is the one who doesn't stumble over me."

Jesus Defends John

²⁴When John's messengers had gone, Jesus began to ask the crowds about John. "What did you come out into the desert to see? A stalk of grass blown by the wind? ²⁵But what did you come out to see, a man dressed in luxurious clothing? Listen, those in opulent clothing and living in luxury reside in royal mansions. ²⁶But what did you truly come out to see? A prophet? Yes, I tell you, much more than a prophet. ²⁷This is the one about whom it is written,

" 'Look, I am sending my messenger ahead of you. He will prepare your way before you.'ⁱⁱ

²⁸"I assure you, among those born of woman, there is no one greater than John. But the least important person in the Kingdom of God is greater than John.

²⁹"When all the people and tax collectors heard John, they agreed with the justice of God and were baptized with his

---

ⁱ Traditionally, "Baptist," The word describes action; so "Baptizer" here.
ⁱⁱ Malachi 3:1

baptism. ³⁰But the Pharisees and the legal experts rejected the purpose of God for themselves and were not baptized by John.

³¹"Therefore, what shall I compare to the men of this generation? What are they like? ³²They are like children sitting in the marketplace calling loudly to each other and say,

> " 'We played a flute for you, but you did not dance. We wailed in mourning, but you did not cry.'

³³"For John the Baptizer came, and he doesn't eat normal food or drink wine, and you say, 'He has a demon.' ³⁴But the Son of Man came, and he does eat *normally* and drink wine, and you say, 'Take note of this, a man who eats too much, and is a heavy drinker, a friend of tax collectors and sinners.' ³⁵Wisdom is proven by all of her children."

Responding to God's Love

³⁶Then a certain Pharisee kept asking Jesus to eat with him, so Jesus went to the house of the Pharisee and reclined at the table with him to dine. ³⁷At that time, a woman brought an alabaster jar of aromatic oil to the house. She was a sinner in that city, and had learned that Jesus was dining at the house of the Pharisee. ³⁸She stood behind Jesus, weeping by his feet. She began to wet his feet with her tears and was drying his feet with the hair on her head, kissing his feet, and anointing them with the aromatic oil.

³⁹When the Pharisee who had invited Jesus saw this, he said to himself, "If this man were a prophet, he would know who she is, what kind of woman is touching him, and that she is a sinner."

⁴⁰Jesus responded and said to him, "Simon, I have something to tell you." He replied, "Tell me, teacher."

⁴¹"Two people were in debt to a particular money lender. One owed five hundred denarii,[i] and the other owed fifty. ⁴²When they were not able to repay the money, he graciously forgave them both. Based on this fact, which of them will love him more?"

⁴³Simon responded and said to him, "I imagine the one to whom he forgave more." Jesus said to him, "You have judged correctly."

⁴⁴He turned to the woman and said to Simon, "Do you see this woman? I came into your house; you did not give me water for my feet. She has wet my feet with her tears and dried them with her hair. ⁴⁵You did not give me a kiss in greeting, but since I arrived, this woman has not stopped kissing my feet with heartfelt devotion. ⁴⁶You did not anoint my head with oil, but this woman has anointed my feet with aromatic oil. ⁴⁷Based on these things I tell you that her sins, many as they are, have been forgiven, as is evident from the great love she has shown. But when someone is forgiven a small amount, he loves a small amount."

⁴⁸Then he said to the woman, "Your sins have been forgiven."

⁴⁹Those reclining at the table with him began to say among themselves, "Who is this man who even forgives sins?"

⁵⁰But he said to the woman, "Your faith has rescued you. Go in peace."

The Women on Jesus' Team

Chapter Eight

¹After this, Jesus began to travel from one city or village to another. He was preaching and proclaiming the good news of the Kingdom of God. The twelve were with him. ²There were

---

[i] A denarius is a day's wage for a soldier or a day laborer. Five hundred denarii would be over eighteen month's wages. Fifty denarii would be about two month's wages.

also some women who had been delivered from evil spirits and illnesses. Mary, who was called Magdalene, from whom seven demons had come out, ³Joanna wife of Chuza, the steward of Herod's property, Susanna, and many others who were taking care of his needs using their own resources.

The Parable of the Planter and the Soils

⁴When a large crowd came together, and many were coming to him from the cities, he spoke through parables, ⁵"A planter went out to plant his seed. While he was broadcasting the seed, some fell beside the road and was trampled, and the birds of the air ate it all up. ⁶Other seed fell upon a layer of rock. When it grew, it withered because it did not have enough water. ⁷Some seed fell among the thorn plants. The thorns grew with the seed and crowded it out. ⁸Still other seed fell on good ground, and when it grew it produced a hundred times as much grain as was sown." While he was saying these things he called out, "The one who has ears to hear, let him understand."

⁹Later his disciples asked him what this parable meant. ¹⁰He explained, "You have been allowed to know the mysteries of the Kingdom of God, but to the rest it is revealed in parables, that

> " 'While seeing they might not see, and while
> hearing they might not understand.'ⁱ

The Parable of the Planter and the Soils Explained

¹¹"This is the meaning of the parable: the seed is the word of God. ¹²The seeds beside the road are the people who have heard, but then the Accuser comes and takes the word from their hearts, so that they may not believe and be rescued from harm. ¹³The seeds above the layer of rock are the people who, when they hear, receive the word with joy, but they have no root. They believe for a season, but in a season of testing, they stop believing. ¹⁴The seed that fell among the thorns are those who have heard, but as they live their lives, they are choked by worries, wealth, and the pleasures of this life, and do not bear

---

ⁱ Isaiah 6:9

mature fruit. 15But the seed in the rich soil are those who have sincere and good hearts; when they hear the word, they hold tightly to it, and by perseverance produce fruit.

The Kingdom Revealed

16"No one who lights a lamp covers it with a clay pot, or places it under a dining couch. Instead, they place it on a lampstand so that those who go inside might see the light. 17For there is nothing that is secret that will not become evident; there is nothing hidden that will not be made known and become clear.

The One Who Seeks Knowledge and Lives it, Will Get more

18"Therefore, pay attention to how you listen. For whoever has *understanding*, even more will be given; but whoever does not have it, even what he thinks he has will be taken away from him."

Jesus Redefines His Family

19Then his mother and brothers came to him, but they were not able to approach him because of the crowd. 20Then someone reported to him, "Your mother and your brothers are standing outside and wish to see you."

21But he responded to them, "These are my mother and my brothers, those who hear the word of God and do it."

Jesus Demonstrates Authority over Weather Patterns

22Jesus and his disciples embarked in a boat on one of those days, and he said to them, "Let us go over to the other side of the lake." So, they put out to sea. 23While they sailed, Jesus fell asleep, and a windstorm descended onto the lake. They began to founder and were in great danger.

24The disciples came to Jesus and woke him crying, "Master, Master, we are about to die." When he woke up, he rebuked the wind and the surging water, and they stopped, and it became calm. 25Then he said to them, "Where is your faith?"

They were terrified at first; and then they were shocked and said to each other, "Who then is this, that he even commands the winds and the water, and they obey him?"

Jesus Demonstrates Authority over the Demonic Realm

²⁶Then they sailed toward the country of the Gerasenes[i], which is opposite Galilee. ²⁷When he came to the shore, he met a man from the city who had demons. He had not worn a garment for a long time, and did not live in a house, but in the tombs. ²⁸When he saw Jesus, he shouted and fell down before him. He cried out with a loud voice, "Why are you harassing me, Jesus, Son of the Most High God? I am begging you, do not torment me." ²⁹He said this because Jesus had commanded the unclean spirit to come out from the man. It had seized him many times. He had been repeatedly bound with chains and shackles and kept under guard; yet he would break the bonds and be driven into the desolate areas by the demon.

³⁰Jesus asked him, "What is your name?"

Because many demons had entered into him, he responded, "Legion."[ii] ³¹The demons kept begging him not to command them to depart into the abyss.

³²A large herd of pigs was grazing there on the mountain. They begged him to allow them to go into them, and he allowed it. ³³The demons came out of the man and went into the pigs. Then the herd bolted down the side of the hill into the lake and drowned.

³⁴When those caring for the pigs saw what had happened, they ran away and reported the news in the city and throughout the countryside. ³⁵Then *those who had been told* came out to see what had happened; they approached Jesus and found the man from whom the demons had come out sitting at Jesus feet, clothed and sound of mind. It terrified them. ³⁶The ones who had seen how the demonized man was delivered, explained it to

---

[i] Or, "Gadarenes." Also in verse 37.

[ii] A Roman legion, though it varied in size, averaged about 5,000 men.

them. ³⁷All the crowd from the country of the Gerasenes asked him to depart from them, because they were overcome with a great fear. He boarded the boat and returned across the lake.

³⁸But the man from whom the demons had come out, kept asking to go with him; but Jesus sent him away, telling him, ³⁹"Return to your home and explain everything that God has done for you." He left and proclaimed everything Jesus had done for him throughout the entire city.

Jesus Demonstrates Authority over Sickness and Death

⁴⁰When Jesus returned, the crowd welcomed him, for they were all waiting for him. ⁴¹Notably, a man by the name of Jairus, who was a leader in the synagogue, came and fell down at his feet. He begged Jesus to come to his house ⁴²because his only daughter, who was about twelve years old, was dying.

While Jesus was going with him, the crowd pressed so hard against him he could hardly breathe. ⁴³There was a woman in the crowd who had a flow of blood for twelve years. She had spent all her financial resources on physicians but was not healed by any of them. ⁴⁴She came up from behind and touched the tassles on his garment, and her flow of blood stopped immediately.

⁴⁵Then Jesus said, "Who touched me?" When everyone denied it, Peter, and those with him, said, "Master, the crowds are pressing in and crowding up against you, and you ask, 'Who touched me?'"

⁴⁶But Jesus said, "Someone touched me. I know that power has gone out from me."

⁴⁷When the woman saw that she could not escape notice, she came trembling and fell down before him. In front of the entire crowd, she explained the reason she touched him, and that she was healed immediately. ⁴⁸Then Jesus said to her, "Daughter, your faith has rescued you. Go in peace."

⁴⁹While he was yet speaking, someone came from the household of the ruler of the synagogue and said, "Your daughter has died. Do not trouble the teacher any longer." ⁵⁰But when Jesus heard, he responded to him, "Do not give in to fear. Just believe and she will be saved."

⁵¹When they came to the house, he did not permit anyone to enter with him except Peter, John, James, and the young girl's father and mother.

⁵²Everyone was weeping and mourning for her. But he said, "Do not weep. For she has not died, but is sleeping." ⁵³But they laughed him to scorn, knowing that she had died.

⁵⁴Then, when he had sent them all outside, he seized her hand and spoke loudly, "Child, wake up!" ⁵⁵Her spirit[i] returned, and she immediately woke up. So, Jesus directed them to give her something to eat.

⁵⁶Her parents were overwhelmed with ecstatic joy,[ii] but Jesus commanded them to tell no one what had happened.

The Disciples Sent to Preach and Demonstrate the Kingdom

Chapter Nine

¹Jesus called the twelve together, and gave them power and authority over all demons, and to heal diseases. ²Then he sent them to preach the Kingdom of God and to heal the sick. ³He said to them, "Take nothing on the journey, neither cudgel,[iii] provision bag, bread, silver, nor even two shirts apiece. ⁴Remain

---

[i] Or, "breath."

[ii] "Overwhelmed with ecstatic joy" translates a Greek verb used when referring to spiritual ecstatic phenomena in ancient times.

[iii] This word (rhabdos) can mean a variety of things, including a walking staff or a cudgel. Matthew and Luke both forbid the rhabdos (staff or cudgel), though Matthew's wording makes it sound like the reference is to an extra walking staff. Luke, from a more Gentile understanding, is probably referring to a weapon (cudgel).

in whatever house you might enter until you leave that area. ⁵Whenever people do not accept you, shake the dust from your feet as you are leaving that city, as a witness against them."

Herod Responds to the Flurry of Kingdom Activity

⁶Then they went out and began to go from village to village preaching the good news and healing wherever they went. ⁷Herod the tetrarch heard everything that was happening, and was very confused, because some were reporting that John had been raised from the dead, ⁸others were reporting that Elijah had appeared, and still others that one of the ancient prophets had awakened.

⁹Then Herod said, "I beheaded John myself; but who is this man about whom I am hearing all these things?" So, he began trying to see Jesus.

Jesus Multiplies Loaves of Bread and Fish for Five Thousand

¹⁰When the apostles returned, they explained everything they had done in detail to him. He then took them aside and privately withdrew to a city called Bethsaida. ¹¹But when the crowds learned about it, they followed him. Jesus welcomed them and spoke to them about the Kingdom of God. He also was healing those who had need of healing.

¹²When the day began to draw to a close, the twelve came to him and said, "Send the crowd away so that they can go to the surrounding villages and countryside and might find lodging and something to eat. For we are in a desolate place."

¹³But he said to them, "You give them something to eat."

But they said, "We do not have anything more than five loves and two fish, unless we go and buy food for all these people." ¹⁴For there were about five thousand men.

But he said to his disciples, "Have everyone gather in groups of about fifty in order to eat."

¹⁵They did as he said, and everyone settled down to eat. ¹⁶Then he took the five loaves and the two fish, and looking up to heaven, he blessed them and broke all the loaves, and distributed them to his disciples to set before the crowd. ¹⁷Everyone ate and had as much as they wanted; and they picked up twelve baskets of leftover pieces of bread.

The Christ, the Son of the Living God

¹⁸Once while he was praying alone, his disciples met him, and he questioned them asking, "Who do the crowds say that I am?"

¹⁹They answered his question and said, "Some say John the Baptizer, but others Elijah, still others say that one of the ancient prophets has risen."

²⁰Then he asked them, "But who do you say that I am?"

Then Peter responded to his question and said, "The Christ of God."

Jesus Shares a Sacrificial View of the Future with His Disciples

²¹Jesus strongly warned them commanding that they not tell this to anyone. ²²He explained that it was necessary for the Son of Man to suffer many things, and to be rejected by the elders, chief priests, and the scribal scholars, to be killed, and to rise again on the third day.

²³He began to explain to all of them, "If anyone desires to follow after me, let him deny himself, take up his cross every day, and be my disciple. ²⁴For whoever wants to protect his soul,[i] will suffer loss to his soul; but whoever suffers loss to his soul for my sake, will save his soul. ²⁵For what does it benefit a man to gain the whole world, but lose or suffer loss to himself? ²⁶For whoever is ashamed of me and my words, the Son of Man will be ashamed of him when he comes in his glory, the glory of the Father and of the holy angels. ²⁷Now I tell you the truth, there

---

[i] The soul is the seat of the mind, emotions, and will.

are some standing here who will not taste death until they see the Kingdom of God."

Jesus' Transfiguration

²⁸About eight days after these teachings, Jesus took Peter, John, and James up on to a mountain to pray. ²⁹While he was praying, the appearance of his face changed, and his clothing was flashing white like lightning. ³⁰Suddenly, two men, Moses and Elijah, appeared in glory and were speaking with him. ³¹They were discussing his journey, which he was about to bring to completion in Jerusalem. ³²Peter and those with him had fallen asleep, but they jolted awake and saw his glory, and the two men standing with him. ³³As Moses and Elijah were leaving them, Peter, who did not know what he was saying, said to Jesus, "Master, it is good for us to be here. Let us make three tents, one for you, one for Moses, and one for Elijah."

³⁴While he was saying this, a cloud appeared and overshadowed them. The disciples were frightened as they entered into the cloud. ³⁵A voice came from the cloud and said, "This is my cherished Son[ii], my chosen one. Listen to him." ³⁶When the voice had finished, they found that Jesus was alone. The disciples kept quiet and did not tell anyone at that time what they had experienced.

A Demonstration of Little Faith: The Demonized Boy

³⁷On the next day, when they came down from the mountain, a large crowd met him. ³⁸At that time, a man from the crowd called out and said, "Teacher, I beg you to give attention to my son, for he is my only son. ³⁹Look, a spirit takes hold of him, and he suddenly screams. It also gives him convulsions and causes him to foam at the mouth. It hardly ever leaves him and is traumatizing him. ⁴⁰I begged your disciples to cast it out, but they were not able."

[ii] Some Greek manuscripts, "My Son." However, both Matthew and Mark have "cherished."

⁴¹Then Jesus responded and said, "Oh unbelieving and confused generation, how long will I be with you; how long must I put up with you? Bring your son here."

⁴²While the boy was still approaching, the demon threw him down in a convulsion, and shook him violently. Jesus rebuked the unclean spirit, healed the boy, and gave him to his father. ⁴³Everyone was overwhelmed with astonishment at the greatness of God.

More Revelation on Jesus' Mission and Future

But while they were wondering at all that he was doing, he said to his disciples, ⁴⁴"Let these words ring in your ears: the Son of Man is about to be delivered into the hands of men."

⁴⁵But they did not understand this statement. It was hidden from them so that they could not understand it, and they were afraid to ask him about it.

True Greatness in the Kingdom

⁴⁶Then a discussion began among them about who might be greater than the rest of them. ⁴⁷But Jesus, because he knew the thoughts of their heart, took a small child and placed this little one at his side. ⁴⁸He said to them, "Whoever welcomes this child in my name welcomes me; and whoever welcomes me welcomes him who sent me. For the one among all of you who is least important, this is the one who is great."

Discerning Allies in the Kingdom

⁴⁹John responded to this and said, "Master, we saw someone expelling demons in your name, and we tried to stop him, because he was not following along with us as a disciple."

⁵⁰But Jesus said to him, "Do not stop him. For the one who is not against you, is for you."

James and John Demonstrate the Wrong Spirit

⁵¹Then, when the days were drawing near for him to be taken up, he resolutely turned his face toward Jerusalem. ⁵²He sent

messengers before him. They went ahead and entered a Samaritan village to prepare for him. ⁵³But they did not welcome him, because he was headed to Jerusalem. ⁵⁴When the disciples James and John noted this, they asked, "Lord, do you want us to call for fire to come down from the sky and devour them as Elijah also did?" ⁵⁵But he turned, rebuked them, and said, "You do not know what kind of spirit you are. ⁵⁶For the Son of Man has not come to destroy men's souls, but to restore them to health." Then they went to another village.

The Difficulty of Journeying with Jesus

⁵⁷While they were traveling along the road, a man said to him, "I will follow you wherever you go."

⁵⁸Jesus said to him, "Foxes have dens, and birds of the sky have nests, but the Son of Man does not have anywhere that he might lay his head."

⁵⁹He said to another, "Follow me."

But he said, "Lord, permit me first to go bury my father."

⁶⁰But Jesus said to him, "Let those who are dead bury their own dead. But you come and proclaim the Kingdom of God."

⁶¹Another said, "I will accompany you, Lord, but first permit me to take leave of those in my house."

⁶²But Jesus said to him, "No one who has put his hand to the plow, and looks back, is fit for the Kingdom of God."

The Seventy Sent to Preach and Demonstrate the Kingdom

Chapter Ten

¹After these things, the Lord commissioned seventy others, and sent them two by two ahead of him into every city and place where he was about to go. ²He said to them, "The fact is that the harvest is large, but there are only few workers. Therefore, ask the Lord of the harvest to send out workers into his harvest.

³"Go! Pay close attention, I am sending you as lambs in the midst of wolves. ⁴Do not carry a wallet, a bag for provisions, or sandals, and do not greet anyone along the road.

⁵"Whenever you come into a house, first say, 'Peace to this house.' ⁶If there is a son of peace there, your peace will rest upon him; but if there is not one there, your peace will return to you. ⁷Remain in that house eating and drinking what they provide. For the workman is worthy of his pay. Do not move from house to house.

⁸"When you come into a city and they welcome you, eat what they set before you. ⁹Heal the sick in the city, and say to them, 'The Kingdom of God has drawn near you.' ¹⁰When you come into a city and they do not welcome you, go out into its streets and say, ¹¹'Even the dust that clings to our feet from your city, we wipe off as a sign against you; but know this, the Kingdom of God has drawn near.' ¹²I tell you, it will be more bearable for Sodom on that Day, than for that city.

¹³"Woe to you, Chorazin! Woe to you Bethsaida! If the miracles which were done in you had been done in Tyre and Sidon, they would have repented long ago, sitting in sackcloth and ashes. ¹⁴But it will be more bearable for Tyre and Sidon in the judgment than for you. ¹⁵You also, Capernaum, you will not be exalted to heaven, will you? You will descend as low as Hades.

¹⁶"The one who hears you hears me, and the one who rejects you rejects me; but the one who rejects me rejects the one who sent me."

The Report of the Seventy

¹⁷The seventy returned with joy and reported, "Lord, even the demons submitted to us in your name."

¹⁸Then he said to them, "I was watching Satan when he fell from the sky like lightning. ¹⁹Take note, I have given you authority to trample on snakes, scorpions, and upon all the power of the enemy; and by no means will anything harm you. ²⁰Nevertheless, do not rejoice in the fact that spirits submit to

you, rather rejoice that your names have been written in the heavens."

Jesus Celebrates Those who Receive Him

21At that time, Jesus overflowed with joy in the Holy Spirit and said, "I praise you Father, Lord of heaven and earth, because you have hidden these things from the wise and intelligent, and have revealed them to these little ones. Yes, Father, for this was pleasing before you. 22All things have been delivered over to me by my Father, and no one knows who the Son is except the Father, and who the Father is except the Son and those to whom the Son wishes to reveal him."

23He turned toward his disciples and said privately, "Blessed are your eyes, because they see what you see. 24For I tell you that many prophets and kings desired to see what you see, but they did not see it; and to hear what you hear, but they did not hear it."

How to Recognize Your Neighbor: The Good Samaritan

25In an unusual turn of events, a certain legal expert stood up to test him, asking, "Teacher, what must I do to inherit eternal life?"

26Jesus asked him, "What is written in the law? How do you read it?"

27He responded and said, "Love the Lord your God with all your heart, with all your soul, with all your strength, and with all your mind; and your neighbor as yourself."

28Jesus said to him, "You have answered correctly. Do this and you will live."

29Because he wished to justify himself, he asked Jesus, "But who is my neighbor?"

30Jesus took up the discussion and said, "A man went down from Jerusalem to Jericho and stumbled upon bandits. They stripped him and rained blows upon him. They went on their way leaving him nearly dead. 31By chance a priest was going down that road, but when he saw him, he passed by on the opposite side from him. ³²In the same way, when a Levite came to that place and saw, he also passed by on the other side. ³³Then a Samaritan, who was on a journey, came across the man. When he saw him, he was moved by compassion. ³⁴When he came to him, he poured oil and wine on his wounds and bandaged them. Then he put him upon his own riding animal[i] and brought him to a lodging place and took care of him. ³⁵On the next day, he paid the manager two denarii[ii] and said, 'Take care of him, and whatever you spend in addition to this, I will pay you when I return.'

³⁶"Which one of these three do you consider a neighbor to the man who encountered the bandits?"

³⁷He said, "The one who had mercy on him."

Jesus said to him, "Go. You do the same thing."

Choosing the Better Portion: Mary and Martha

³⁸While they were going along, Jesus came to a particular village where a woman by the name of Martha welcomed him as a guest. ³⁹She had a sister named Mary. She was seated near the Lord's feet and was listening to his message. ⁴⁰But Martha was occupied by all the preparations for the meal. She drew near and said, "Lord, aren't you concerned that my sister has left me without help to serve the tables? So then, speak to her so that she assists me."

⁴¹The Lord responded to her and said, "Martha, Martha, you are anxious and distressed about many things. ⁴²But one thing is necessary. Mary has chosen the better portion, and it will not be taken from her."

---

[i] This may have been a donkey or a horse.
[ii] A denarius was a day's wage for a soldier or a day laborer.

The Disciples Learn About Prayer

Chapter Eleven

¹Jesus was at a certain place praying. When he had finished praying, one of his disciples asked him, "Lord, teach us to pray, just as John taught his disciples."

The Prayer Pattern of the Kingdom

²So, he said to them, "When you are praying say,

" 'Father, let your name be honored as holy.
" 'Let your Kingdom come.
" 'Let your will manifest on earth as it is manifest in heaven.
³" 'Keep granting us each day our supply of bread for the dawning day.
⁴" 'Forgive to us our sins,
   for we ourselves also forgive everyone who has offended us.
" 'Do not bring us into testing,
   but deliver us from the evil one.'"

Jesus Encourages Persistence

⁵Then he said to them, "If any among you has a friend, and goes to him at midnight and says, 'Friend, give me three loaves of bread, ⁶because my friend has come to me from a journey, and I do not have anything to set before him.' ⁷When he responds from the inside he will say, 'Do not trouble me. The door is already closed, and my children and I are in bed. I cannot get up to give you bread.'

⁸"I tell you, even if he will not get up and give him bread because he is his friend, he will get up and give him as much as he needs in order to protect him from shame."[iii]

[iii] More literally, "On account of his shamelessness." Jesus' words could be taken to mean that the friend will get up in order to avoid the shame of refusing the request, or that he will get up to protect his friend from the shame of having no bread for a traveler.

⁹"I tell you, keep on asking, and it will be given to you; keep on seeking, and you will find; keep on knocking and it will be opened to you. ¹⁰For everyone who asks, receives; and the one seeking will find; and the door will be opened for everyone who knocks.

The Father Gives the Holy Spirit to Those who Ask

¹¹"But which of you fathers, if his son asks for a fish, would give him a snake instead of a fish? ¹²Or if he asks for a chicken egg, will give him a scorpion? ¹³Therefore, if you who are defective[i] know to give good gifts to your children, how much more will your Father give from heaven the Holy Spirit to those who ask him."

The Foolishness of Ascribing Kingdom Power to Satan

¹⁴Then Jesus began to drive out a demon that had caused a man to be mute. When the demon had gone, the mute person spoke, and the crowds were astonished. ¹⁵But some of them said, "He expels demons by Beelzebul,[ii] the prince of demons." ¹⁶Others, trying to test him, were seeking a sign in the sky from him.

¹⁷Then Jesus knew their thoughts and said to them, "Every kingdom divided against itself is lost, and every house divided against itself falls. ¹⁸You are saying that I expel demons by Beelzebul, but if Satan is divided against himself, how will his kingdom stand? ¹⁹Also, if I expel demons by Beelzebul, by whom do your sons expel them? So, they will be your judges. ²⁰However, if I expel demons by the finger of God, then the Kingdom of God has arrived among you.

²¹"When a strong man who is fully armed guards his walled estate, the things that he owns are not in danger. ²²But when a stronger man arrives and defeats him, the stronger one takes away the armor in which he trusted and distributes his possessions as plunder.

---

[i] Or, "evil."

[ii] Another name for Satan. Also in verses 18 and 19.

²³"The one who is not with me is against me, and the one not gathering people together with me is scattering them.

Jesus Warns Those Who Reject Him About Their Danger

²⁴"When an unclean spirit goes out from a man, it goes through dry places seeking rest but does not find it. Then it says, 'I will return to my house from which I came.' ²⁵When it comes, it finds it swept and put in order. ²⁶Then it sends for seven other spirits more evil than itself, brings them along, enters him, and lives there. The final state of that man is worse than the beginning."

Blessed are Those who Hear and Obey

²⁷While Jesus was saying these things, one of the women in the crowd lifted her voice and said to him, "Blessed is the womb that bore you, and the breasts from which you nursed."

²⁸But he said, "Yes, but blessed also are those who hear the word of God and obey it."

The Stubborn Request for more Signs

²⁹When the crowd had gotten larger, he began to speak, "This current generation is a stingy and envious generation. It is seeking a sign, but a sign will not be given it, except the sign of Jonah the prophet. ³⁰For just as Jonah became a sign to the Ninevites, so also will the Son of Man be a sign to this generation.

³¹"The queen of the south will rise up at the judgment with this generation and condemn them, because she came from the ends of the earth to hear the wisdom of Solomon; and consider this, a greater than Solomon is here.

³²"The men of Nineveh will rise up with this generation at the judgment and condemn it, for they repented at the preaching of Jonah; and be aware, a greater than Jonah is here.

Luke 11:33

Letting the Light Shine in You

³³"No one lights a lamp and puts it into hiding or under a basket, but they place it on a lampstand in order that those who come in might see the light.

³⁴"The lamp of the body is your eye. When your eye is generous, then your whole body is full of light. But when it is stingy and envious, your body is also full of darkness. ³⁵For this reason, check carefully that the light in you isn't darkness. ³⁶Therefore, if your whole body is full of light, not having any dark part, it will be completely full of light, as when a lamp shines its light upon you."

Jesus Condemns the Hypocrisy of the Pharisees

³⁷After he had spoken, a Pharisee asked him to have a meal with him. When they arrived at the house, he reclined at the table. ³⁸But when the Pharisee saw this, he was shocked that Jesus did not first baptize[i] his hands before the meal.

³⁹But the Lord said to him, "At present, you Pharisees clean the outside of the cup and the plate, but your insides are full of violent greed and habitual wickedness. ⁴⁰Foolish people, did not the one who made the outside also make the inside? ⁴¹However, give the things on the inside as generous gifts of righteousness, and know this, all things will be clean for you.

⁴²"Woe to you Pharisees, because you give a tenth of your mint, rue, and every garden herb, but you disregard justice and the love of God. It was necessary that you do the latter things, and not overlook doing the former things.

⁴³"Woe to you Pharisees, because you love the best seat in the synagogue, and greetings in the markets.

⁴⁴"Woe to you, because you are like unmarked tombs that men walk over and do not know it."

---

[i] He did not follow their ritual to ceremonial clean his hands.

Jesus Condemns the Hypocrisy of the Spiritual Legal Scholars

⁴⁵One of the legal experts responded and said to him, "Teacher, when you say these things, you also insult us."

⁴⁶Then Jesus said, "And woe to you legal experts, for you load men with heavy burdens that are difficult to carry; and you yourselves will not use even one of your fingers to lighten the load. ⁴⁷Woe to you, because you build the tombs of the prophets, but your fathers killed them. ⁴⁸Therefore, you are witnesses that you agree with the works of your fathers, for they killed them, but you build their tombs. ⁴⁹For this reason, the Wisdom of God also said, 'I will send to them prophets and apostles. Some of them they will kill, and some they will persecute' ⁵⁰This is so that the blood of all the prophets which has been poured out since the founding of the world may be required from this current generation, ⁵¹from the blood of Abel to the blood of Zechariah, who was killed between the altar and the house of God. Yes, I say to you, it will be required from this current generation.

⁵²"Woe to you legal experts, for you have taken the key of knowledge away. You yourselves have not entered, and you have hindered those who are entering."

⁵³When he left that place, the scribal scholars and the Pharisees began to hold a bitter grudge, and to ask hostile questions about many things ⁵⁴trying to trap him in something he might say.

The Leaven of Hypocrisy

Chapter Twelve

¹At that time, when countless thousands of people had gathered, so many that they were trampling on each other, Jesus began to speak primarily to his disciples.

"Protect yourselves from the leaven of the Pharisees, which is hypocrisy. ²There is nothing concealed that will not be revealed, nor is there anything secret that will not be known. ³So then, that which you have spoken in the dark will be heard in the light, and that which you have whispered in someone's ear in an interior room will be proclaimed from the rooftops.

Do Not Give into Pressure and Compromise on God's Things

⁴"I say to you, my friends, do not fear those that can kill the body, but after that have nothing more they can do. ⁵But I will show you whom you should fear. You should fear the one that after he has ended your life, has the authority to throw you into Gehenna.[i] Yes, I tell you, fear him.

⁶"Are not five sparrows sold for an assarion?[ii] Yet not one of them is forgotten before God. ⁷But even the hairs of your head are all numbered—do not be afraid—you have more value than many sparrows.

⁸"So I say to you, whoever confesses me before men, the Son of Man will also confess before the angels of God. ⁹But the one who denies me before men will be denied before the angels of God. ¹⁰Everyone who speaks a word against the Son of Man will be forgiven. But the one who speaks against[iii] the Holy Spirit will not be forgiven.

¹¹"When they bring you before synagogues, the rulers, or the authorities, do not worry how or what you will say in your defense, or what you will say in general; ¹²for the Holy Spirit will teach you in that hour what you must say."

A Warning Against Greed

¹³Then a person in the crowd called out to him, "Teacher, tell my brother to give part of the inheritance to me."

---

[i] A valley known as "the valley of the sons of Hinnom." It was the place of child sacrifice and gross impurity, and came to symbolize the place of eternal punishment.

[ii] An assarion was about a tenth of a denarius. A denarius was a day's wage for a soldier or day laborer.

[iii] Or, "blasphemes." To blaspheme is about speaking profanely of sacred things, to slander God, or to speak against him.

¹⁴But Jesus said to him, "Sir, who appointed me as judge or estate manager for you?" ¹⁵But to his disciples he said, "Take care and guard yourself against all types of greed, for even when a person has an overabundance, life is not about what you own."

¹⁶Then he shared a parable with them saying, "The land of a particular rich man produced an abundant harvest. ¹⁷So, he pondered within himself thinking, 'What shall I do? For I do not have a place that I can gather my harvest?'

¹⁸"Then he said, 'This is what I will do. I will tear down my barns and build larger ones, and I will gather all my grain and my goods there. ¹⁹Then I will say to my soul, "Soul,ⁱᵛ you have many goods stored up for many years. Relax! Eat, drink, and enjoy yourself."'

²⁰"But God said to him, 'Foolish man! Your soul will be demanded back from you this very night. Then who will get what you have prepared?'

²¹"This same thing happens to anyone who stores up treasure for himself but is not financially generous toward God."

The Foolishness of Worry About Possessions

²²Then he said to his disciples, "For this reason, I am telling you not to worry about your soul, what you will eat, or your body, what you will wear, ²³for your soul is much more than food, and your body is much more than your clothing. ²⁴Think about the ravens. They do not plant crops, and they do not harvest; they do not have a storeroom or a barn, yet God still feeds them. How much more valuable are you rather than birds?

²⁵"Who from among you, through worrying, is able to add a cubitᵛ to his stature? ²⁶Therefore, if you are not able to do this small thing, why worry about the rest?

ⁱᵛ The souls is the seat of the mind, emotions, and will.

ᵛ About eighteen inches.

27"Think about how the wildflowers grow. They do not labor, and they do not spin wool into yarn; but I say to you that not even Solomon in all his glory, clothed himself like one of these. 28So, if this is how God arrays the grass that is in the field today, but tomorrow is thrown into the oven, how much more valuable are you, you of little faith.

29"As for you, stop seeking what you will eat or what you will drink, and do not place so much importance on it that you are unsettled in your mind about it. 30For all the nations of the world pursue these things, but your Father knows that you need them. 31But seek his Kingdom, and these things will be added to you.

32"Stop being afraid, little flock, for your Father has willingly chosen to give you the Kingdom. 33Sell the things that belong to you and give charitable gifts to those in need. Make wallets for yourselves that do not wear out, an inexhaustible treasure in the heavens, where no thief comes near, and no moth destroys. 34For where your treasure is, there your heart will be also.

Always Be Prepared to Meet the Lord

35"Be properly dressed and ready and have your lamps burning. 36Be like men who are waiting for their master to return from a wedding celebration; when he comes and knocks, they are prepared to open the door to him immediately. 37Blessed are those servants whom their master finds watching when he comes. I tell you the truth, he will change his clothing and have them recline at the table, and he will come and serve them. 38If he finds them ready, even if he comes in the second or third watch, they will be blessed. 39But know this, if the owner of the house had known what hour the thief was coming, he would not have allowed his house to be forcibly entered. 40You also be prepared; the Son of Man will come at an hour you do not expect."

What the Lord Expects of His Disciples

⁴¹Then Peter asked him, "Lord, are you telling this parable to us, or to everyone?"

⁴²The Lord said, "Who then is the faithful and wise manager, whom his master puts in charge over his household, so that he gives everyone their provisions at the proper time? ⁴³Blessed is that servant whom, when his master comes, he finds doing this. ⁴⁴I tell you the truth, he will put him in charge over all his possessions.

⁴⁵"But if that servant says in his heart, 'My master's return is delayed,' and he begins to harm the male and female servants, and to eat and drink, and get drunk, ⁴⁶the master of that servant will come on a day when he does not expect, and at an hour that he does not know, and he will punish him severely, even assigning him the fate of an unbeliever.

⁴⁷"The servant who knew his master's will, but did not prepare or act in accord with it, will be punished severely; ⁴⁸the one who did not know his master's will, and does things worthy of punishment, will be punished less. To everyone to whom much is freely given, much will be sought from him; and to whom much is entrusted as an investment, they will require even more from him.

The Message of the Kingdom will Be Opposed

⁴⁹"I have come to set fire on the earth, and how I wish it was already ignited. ⁵⁰The fact is, I have to face a baptism, and how preoccupied I am until it is completed.

⁵¹"Do you think that I came to grant peace on the earth? Not peace, I tell you, but rather division. ⁵²For from now on, there will be five in one house who are divided, three against two, and two against three. ⁵³Father will be divided against his son and son against father, mother against daughter and daughter against mother, mother-in-law against her daughter-in-law and daughter-in-law against mother-in-law."

Luke 12:54

Knowing and Responding to the Signs of the Times

⁵⁴Then he began to tell the crowds, "When you see a cloud rising up in the west, you immediately say, 'A thunderstorm is coming,' and it happens just as you have said. ⁵⁵And when the south wind is blowing, you say, 'It will be a hot one today,' and it happens. ⁵⁶Hypocrites! You know how to interpret the appearance of the earth and the sky, but you do not know how to interpret this season of time?

⁵⁷"Why don't you judge what is right among yourselves? ⁵⁸For as you are going with your legal opponent to the magistrate, do your best to disengage from him, lest he drag you before the judge, and the judge hand you over to the court official, and the court official throw you into prison. ⁵⁹I tell you; you will not get out of prison until you have paid back the very last penny."[i]

Recognizing the Need for God's Protection at All Times

Chapter Thirteen

¹At that same time, there were some who had come who brought news to Jesus about the Galileans whose blood Pilate had mingled with their sacrifices. ²Jesus responded to them and said, "Do you think that these Galileans were more sinful than all other Galileans, because they suffered these things? ³No, I tell you, but if you do not repent, you will all die in a similar fashion. ⁴Or those eighteen who were killed when the tower of Siloam fell upon them, do you think that they owed a greater debt *to God* than all the men who live in Jerusalem? ⁵No, I tell you, but if you do not repent, you will all die in like manner."

Take Advantage of the Season for Repentance While it is There

⁶Then he told them this parable, "A certain man had a fig tree planted in his vineyard, and he came to it seeking fruit, but did not find any. ⁷Then he said to the horticulturist, 'See here, I have

---

[i] Or, "until you have paid the last lepton." A lepton is a coin of little value.

come seeking fruit from this fig tree for three years and have not found any. Cut it down. Why should it make this ground useless?' ⁸But horticulturist responded and said to him, 'Sir, let it remain for this year also, until I dig around it and add manure. ⁹If it produces fruit next season, good; but if not, then cut it down.'"

Jesus Heals a Woman on the Sabbath

¹⁰Later, Jesus was teaching in one of the synagogues on the Sabbath. ¹¹Notably, there was a woman who, for eighteen years, had a spirit that caused physical impairment. In her case, she was bent over and was not able to straighten up completely. ¹²But when Jesus saw her, he called out to her and said, "Woman, you are released from your physical impairment." ¹³He also placed his hands on her, and she immediately stood up straight and glorified God.

¹⁴But the synagogue officer was indignant that Jesus had healed on the Sabbath and said to the crowd, "There are six days that it is appropriate to work. So, come and be healed on those days, and not on the Sabbath day."

¹⁵But the Lord responded to him and said, "Hypocrite! Each of you unties his ox or donkey from its stall and leads it to get a drink on the Sabbath, don't you? ¹⁶But this woman is a daughter of Abraham; Satan has bound her, pay attention, for eighteen years! It is vital that she be freed from this bondage on the Sabbath day, isn't it?"

¹⁷When he said these things, all those who opposed him were filled with shame, but all the crowd was rejoicing over all the wonderful things he was doing.

A Parable of the Kingdom's Growth: The Mustard Seed

¹⁸Then he began speaking, "What is the Kingdom of God like, and to what shall I compare it? ¹⁹It is like a mustard seed which a man took and sowed in his own garden. It grew and transformed into a tree; and the birds of the air nested in its branches."

Luke 13:20

A Parable of Growing Kingdom Influence: The Yeast

²⁰Again, he said, "To what shall I compare the Kingdom of God? ²¹It is like yeast that a woman took and mixed into three large measures of flour until all of it has risen."

Enter Through the Narrow Door

²²Jesus began journeying through cities and villages teaching as he continued his journey to Jerusalem. ²³Someone asked him, "Lord, are there only a few who are being saved?"

Then he said to them, ²⁴"Work hard to enter in through the narrow door; for many, I tell you, will seek to come in and will not be able. ²⁵When the owner of the house gets up and closes the door, you will stand outside and knock on the door saying, 'Lord, open up for us.' He will respond and tell you, 'I do not know you or from where you have come.'

²⁶"Then you will explain, 'We ate and drank in your presence, and you taught in our streets.'

²⁷"But he will tell you, 'I do not know you, or from where you have come. Stay away from me, all you who work unrighteousness.'

²⁸"There will be weeping and gnashing of teeth when you see Abraham, Isaac, Jacob, and all the prophets in the Kingdom of God, but you yourselves being sent away. ²⁹They will come from the east, the west, the north, and the south to be seated at the table in the Kingdom of God. ³⁰Listen closely, those who are last will be first, and those who are first will be last."

Herod's Threat's Do not Change Jesus' Destination

³¹At this same time, some Pharisees came to Jesus and said, "Go away from here and leave the area, for Herod wants to kill you."

³²But he said to them, "When you have left here, tell that fox, 'Look, I am driving out demons and healing people today and tomorrow, and on the third day I will complete my work. ³³However, it is important that I travel today, tomorrow, and the

next day, for it is unthinkable for a prophet to die outside of Jerusalem.

³⁴"Jerusalem, Jerusalem, the one who kills the prophets and stones those sent to her; how often I wanted to gather your children like a hen gathers her chicks under her wings, but you did not allow it. ³⁵Be aware, your house is left to you abandoned. But I tell you, you will most certainly not see me until that time when you say, 'Blessed is the one coming in the name of the Lord.'"

It is Proper to Heal on the Sabbath

Chapter Fourteen

¹Once, when Jesus went into the house of one of the leaders of the Pharisees on the Sabbath to eat bread, they were observing him closely. ²Just at that time, a man was in front of him who was suffering from edema.ⁱ ³So, Jesus responded *to* this, and spoke to the legal experts and Pharisees asking, "Is it proper to heal on the Sabbath or not?" ⁴But they remained silent; so Jesus held the man firmly, healed him, and released him.

⁵He said to them, "Who among you, if your son or ox falls into a pit on a Sabbath day, will not immediately pull him out?" ⁶They were not able to reply to these things.

Demonstrating Humility

⁷Then he began to tell a parable to those who had been invited *to a dinner*, when he noticed how they chose the best seats. He said to them, ⁸"When you are invited by someone to a wedding celebration, do not take your place at the best seat, in case the host invited someone who is more distinguished than you. ⁹The one who invited both of you will come and say to you, 'Give this man your place.' Then you will be disgraced and have to take your place at the seat of least honor.

ⁱ Traditionally, "dropsy." More commonly known today as edema in the United States. Dropsy is the accumulation of large amounts of excess fluid below the surface of the skin or in some cavity of the body.

¹⁰"On the contrary, when you are invited, take the seat of least honor, so that when the one who invited you comes, he will say to you, 'Friend, come up to a better seat.' Then you will have honor in front of all those at the table with you. ¹¹For everyone who exalts himself will be humbled, and the one who humbles himself will be exalted."

Inviting the Disadvantaged

¹²Then he said to the one who had invited him, "When you host a lunch or dinner, do not invite your friends, your brothers, relatives, or wealthy neighbors, lest they also invite you back and that will be your repayment. ¹³But when you host a gathering, invite the poor, the crippled, those who cannot walk, and the blind, ¹⁴then you will be blessed, because they do not have the ability to repay you; for you will be repaid at the resurrection of the righteous."

Filling the Kingdom Banquet Hall

¹⁵When one of those who were dining with him heard these things, he said, "Blessed is anyone who will eat bread in the Kingdom of God."

¹⁶But Jesus said to him, "A certain man was making a great feast, and invited many people. ¹⁷He sent out his servants at the time of the feast to tell those who were invited, 'Come, for the feast is already prepared.'

¹⁸"But they all began, as one, to excuse themselves. The first said to him, 'I have bought some farmland, and I am obliged to go out and see it. I ask that you consider me excused.' ¹⁹Yet another said, 'I have bought five pairs of oxen, and I am going to check them. I ask that you consider me excused.' ²⁰And yet another said, 'I have married a woman, and for this reason I am not able to attend.'

²¹"The servant went to his master and reported these things. Then the master of the house became angry and said to his servant, 'Go out quickly to the streets and lanes of the city and

bring the poor, the crippled, those who cannot walk, and the blind here.'

²²"The servant said, 'Sir, what you ordered has been done, and yet there is still space.'

²³"The master said to his servant, 'Go out into the roads and country lanes and compel them to come in, that my house might be full. ²⁴For I tell you that not one of those men whom I invited will taste my feast.'"

Calculating the Cost of Following Jesus

²⁵At that time, large crowds were traveling with him. Jesus turned and said to them, ²⁶"If anyone comes to me and does not disregard the desires[i] of his own father, mother, wife, children, brothers, and sisters, even the desires of his own soul,[ii] he is not able to be my disciple. ²⁷Whoever does not carry his own cross and come after me, is not able to be my disciple.

²⁸"For who from among you, wanting to build a watchtower, doesn't first sit down and calculate what it will cost, to see if he has enough to finish it? ²⁹He does this so that he does not lay the foundation only to find he does not have the ability to complete it. When everyone sees it, they will begin to mock him ³⁰and say, 'This man began to build, but did not have the ability to complete it.'

³¹"Or what king going to meet another king in battle does not first sit down and take counsel about if he can, with ten thousand men, engage in hostilities against the one coming against him with twenty thousand men? ³²If not, while he is still far away, he sends a delegation and asks for terms of peace. ³³In just this way, any of you who does not leave all you have that is your own, is not able to be my disciple.

³⁴"Therefore, salt is good; but if even the salt has lost its flavor, with what will you season things? ³⁵It cannot be used for

---

[i] Or, "hate his own father … "

[ii] The soul is the seat of the mind, emotions, and will.

the soil or the manure pile, so they will throw it out. The one who has ears to hear, let him understand."

Recovering the Lost Ones

Chapter Fifteen

¹Now all the tax collectors and sinners were gathering around him to listen to him. ²In response, both the Pharisees and the scribal scholars began to grumble and were complaining, "This man welcomes sinners as guests and eats with them."

³But Jesus told this parable to them explaining, ⁴"What man from among you, if you have a hundred sheep, and lose one of them, will not leave behind the ninety-nine in the pasture and pursue the lost one until he finds it? ⁵Then, when he finds it, he places it upon his shoulders, celebrating. ⁶When he gets to his home, he calls together his friends and neighbors and says to them, 'Celebrate with me! For I have found my sheep that was lost.' ⁷I tell you that in this same way there will be celebration in heaven over one sinner who repents than over the ninety-nine righteous who did not need to repent.

⁸"Or what woman who has ten drachmas,[i] if she loses one drachma, will not light a lamp, sweep the house, and search diligently until she finds it? ⁹When she finds it, she calls together her friends and neighbors and says, 'Celebrate with me! For I found the drachma that I lost.' ¹⁰In this same way, I tell you, there is celebration in the presence of the angels of God over one sinner who repents."

Recovering the Rebellious Ones: The Lost Sons

¹¹Then he said, "A certain man had two sons. ¹²The younger of them said to his father, 'Give me the part of the property that falls to me.' So, he distributed his livelihood to them.

---

[i] A drachma is the equivalent of one denarius, which is a day's wage for a soldier or a day laborer. Also in verse 9.

¹³"It wasn't that many days later that the younger son gathered all his things and journeyed away to a far country. While he was there, he wasted his property by living a depraved lifestyle. ¹⁴Now when he had spent everything, a severe famine spread across that country, and he began to do without. ¹⁵So, he went and joined one of the citizens of that country, but *that man* sent him into the fields to feed the pigs; ¹⁶and he yearned to satisfy his hunger with the carob pods that the pigs were eating, because no one gave anything to him.

¹⁷"But when he came to himself, he said, 'How many of my father's hired laborers have an abundance of loaves of bread? But I am being destroyed by the famine in this place. ¹⁸I will get up and go to my father, and I will say to him: "Father, I have sinned against heaven and against you; ¹⁹I am no longer worthy to be called your son. Make me like one of your hired laborers."'

²⁰"So, he got up and went to his own father. But while he was still a long way away, his father saw him, and was filled with compassion. He ran, threw his arms around him,ⁱⁱ and kissed him.

²¹"Then his son said to him, 'Father, I have sinned against heaven and against you. I am no longer worthy to be called your son.'

²²"But his father said to his servants, 'Quickly, bring out the best robe and put it on him. Get a ring for his hand and sandals for his feet. ²³Bring the fattened calf, slaughter it, and let us eat and be glad; ²⁴for this son of mine was dead, but now he is alive, he had disappeared, but now he is found.'

"So, they began to celebrate, ²⁵but his older son was in the field, and as he was coming near the house, he heard music and a dancing chorus. ²⁶He called one of the childrenⁱⁱⁱ and questioned him about what was happening. ²⁷Then he told him, 'Your

---

ⁱⁱ Literally, "fell upon his neck," an idiom meaning to embrace or hug.

ⁱⁱⁱ This word literally means "children," but may also refer to servants.

brother has come, and your father slaughtered the fattened calf, because he has received him back unharmed.'

28"But he became angry and did not wish to go in. So, his father came out and began to encourage him. 29But he responded and said to his father, 'As you know, for many years I have served you and I have never ignored your commands, but you have never given me a young goat that I might celebrate with my friends. 30But when this son of yours has come, who has devoured your livelihood with prostitutes, you slaughter the fattened calf for him.'

31"Then the father said to him, 'My child, you are always with me, and everything I possess is yours. 32But we had to celebrate and rejoice, for this brother of yours was dead, and is alive; he had disappeared, but now he is found.'"

Using Worldly Possession Wisely in this Life

Chapter Sixteen

1Then he began to tell his disciples, "There was a certain wealthy man who had a household manager, and this manager was accused before his master with wasting his possessions. 2So, he called him in and said to him, 'What is this I hear about you? Give an account of your management, for you cannot be household manager any longer.'

3"The manager said to himself, 'What shall I do now that my master is removing me from my position? I am not strong enough to dig, and I am ashamed to beg. 4I know what I will do so that when I am removed from the management position, people will welcome me into their homes.'

5"He called each one of those who were in debt to his master, and said to the first, 'How much do you owe my master?'

⁶"Then the man said, 'One hundred baths[i] of olive oil.' Then he said to him, 'Take your bill, sit down quickly and write fifty.'

⁷"Then he said to another, 'And how much do you owe?' The man said to him, 'A hundred cors[ii] of wheat.' He said to him, 'Take your bill and write eighty.'

⁸"Then his master commended the unrighteous household manager because he acted insightfully. For the sons of this age are more clever in dealing with their own compatriots than the sons of the light.

⁹"But I tell you, use the illusory wealth of this world to make friends for yourself, in order that when it comes to an end, people will welcome you into eternal dwellings.

¹⁰"The one who is faithful with the smallest things is also faithful with much, and the one who is unrighteous in the smallest things is also unrighteous with much. ¹¹Therefore, if you have not been faithful with illusory wealth, who will trust you with things that have true value? ¹²And if you have not been faithful with the possessions of another person, who will give you your own?

¹³"No servant is able to serve two masters; for he will either hate the one and love the other, or he will be loyal to one, and treat the other indifferently. You are not able to serve God and wealth."

Pressing Forward into the Kingdom

¹⁴The Pharisees were listening to all these things, and because they loved wealth, they began to ridicule him.

¹⁵So, he said to them, "You are the ones who justify yourselves before men, but God knows your hearts; for the things that are exalted among men are repugnant to God. ¹⁶The law and the prophets were in effect until John; since then, the good news of the Kingdom of God has been proclaimed, and

---

[i] A bath was a jar capable of holding up to nine gallons of liquid.

[ii] A cor was about fifteen bushels.

everyone is pressing forward into it. ¹⁷But it is easier for heaven and earth to pass away than for the smallest part of one letter of the Law to fall from it.

¹⁸"Anyone who divorces his wife and marries another woman commits adultery; and anyone who marries this woman who is divorced from her husband commits adultery.[i]

The Importance of Paying Attention to the Word

¹⁹"There was a certain wealthy man who habitually dressed himself in purple cloth and fine linen and made himself happy each day living luxuriously. ²⁰But there was a very poor man named Lazarus who was laid at his gate who was covered in sores. ²¹He longed to fill his stomach from the scraps that would fall from the wealthy man's table; instead the dogs came and fed on the festering sores.

²²"But when the very poor man died, and he was carried by the angels to Abraham's side, the wealthy man also died and was buried. ²³While he was being tormented in Hades, he looked up, and saw Abraham from a distance, and Lazarus at his side. ²⁴So, he cried out and said, 'Father Abraham, have mercy on me and send Lazarus to dip the tip of his finger in water and cool my tongue, for I am in agony in this flaming fire.'

²⁵"But Abraham said, 'Child, remember that you received your good things in your life, and likewise, Lazarus received evil things, but now he is being consoled while you are in agony. ²⁶On top of everything else, a great chasm stands between us and you, so that those who wish to go over from here to you are not able to do so, nor can anyone cross over from there to us.'

²⁷"He responded, 'Then I ask you, father, that you send him to my father's house. ²⁸For I have five brothers that he can warn so that they do not also come to this place of torment.'

---

[i] The Pharisees had very lax divorce practices. This teaching is an example of how they allow for more than the letter of the law to disappear.

²⁹"But Abraham said, 'They have Moses and the Prophets. Let them pay attention to them.'

³⁰"But he responded, 'No, Father Abraham, but if someone from the dead goes to them, they will repent.'

³¹"Then Abraham said to him, 'If they will not pay attention to Moses and the Prophets, they will not be persuaded, even if someone rose from the dead.'"

Faith and Helping Those who Stumble

Chapter Seventeen

¹Then he said to his disciples, "It is not possible to avoid the things that cause people to stumble into sin; but woe to him through whom it comes. ²It would be better for him if a millstone were placed around his neck and he were thrown into the sea, rather than causing one of these little ones to stumble into sin.

³"Be concerned about yourself; if your brother sins rebuke him, and if he repents, forgive him. ⁴If he sins against you seven times in a day, and returns seven times saying, 'I repent,' you must forgive him."

⁵Then the apostles said to the Lord, "Increase our faith."

⁶But the Lord said, "If you have faith like a mustard seed, you can say to this mulberry tree, 'Be uprooted and be planted in the sea,' and it will obey you.

The Obligation to Serve

⁷"Who from among you, if you have a servant plowing or tending the sheep, when he has come in from the field, says to him, 'Sit down immediately and eat your meal'? ⁸Wouldn't you instead say to him, 'Prepare something so that I can eat my meal, then change your clothing and serve me while I am eating and drinking; when I am done, you may eat and drink'? ⁹He does not

show special favor to his servant because he does the things assigned to him, does he? I do not think so. ¹⁰It is the same with you; when you have done all the things assigned to you, say, 'We are undeserving servants. We have only done what we are under obligation to do.'"

Give Thanks, Even While Fulfilling the Obligation to Obey

¹¹While he was going to Jerusalem, he was passing through the area between Samaria and Galilee. ¹²While he was going into a certain village, ten men with leprosy drew near to him. They stood at a distance ¹³and together raised their voices calling, "Jesus, Master, have mercy on us."

¹⁴When he noticed them, he said to them, "Go present yourselves to the priests for examination." But while they were going, they were all cleansed.

¹⁵Then one of them, when he saw that he was healed, returned to Jesus, glorifying God with a loud voice. ¹⁶He fell down on his face at his feet, thanking Jesus, yet he was a Samaritan.

¹⁷Then Jesus responded to this and said, "Were there not ten cleansed? So where are the other nine? ¹⁸Were none found who returned to give thanks to God except this foreigner?" ¹⁹At that point he said to him, "Arise and go; your faith has rescued you."

The Kingdom of God Starts Without Obvious Exterior Signs

²⁰Now when he was asked by the Pharisees when the Kingdom of God was coming, he responded to them and said, "The Kingdom of God is not coming with careful observation. ²¹Nor will you say, 'See! It is here,' or, 'It is over there.' For listen closely, the Kingdom of God is within your reach."

²²Then he said to his disciples, "The time will come when you will very much desire to see one of the days of the Son of Man, but you will not see it. ²³They will say to you, 'See! It is there,' or, 'Listen! It is over here.' Do not follow, and do not pursue. ²⁴For it will be like lightning when it flashes; it lights up one end of

the sky to the other end of the sky. The Son of Man will do the same thing in his day. ²⁵But first, it is necessary that he suffer many things, and be rejected by this generation.

When the Son of Man is Revealed

²⁶"Then, just as it was in the days of Noah, it will also be in the days of the Son of Man. ²⁷They were eating, they were drinking, they were marrying, and being given in marriage, until the day Noah entered into the ark; and the cataclysm came and destroyed all of them.

²⁸"In the same way, it will be just like it was in the days of Lot; they were eating, they were drinking, they were buying, they were selling, they were planting, and they were building. ²⁹But on the day Lot went out from Sodom, fire and sulfur rained from the sky and destroyed all of them.

³⁰"It will be exactly the same on the day the Son of Man is revealed. ³¹On that day, one will be on the roof and his possession will be in the house. He must not go down to get them. Likewise, the one in the field must not go back. ³²Remember Lot's wife! ³³Whoever seeks to make his life[i] secure will suffer loss, but whoever suffers loss will make his life secure. ³⁴I tell you, on that night there will be two in one bed, one will be taken, and the other will be left. ³⁵Two women will be grinding on the same millstone, one will be taken, but the other will be left. ³⁶Two men will be in the field, one will be taken, and the other will be left."

³⁷"They responded to him and asked, "Where Lord?"

But he said to them, "Where there is a body, there also the eagles will be gathered."

---

[i] Or, "soul." The soul is the seat of the mind, emotions, and will.

Luke 18:1

God Answers Persistent Prayer: The Parable of the Tenacious Widow

Chapter Eighteen

¹Then he began to tell them a parable about the fact that that they must always pray, and never get discouraged. ²He said, "There was a judge in a certain town who did not fear God and had no regard for man. ³There was a widow in that town, and she kept coming to him petitioning, 'Grant me justice against my adversary.'

⁴"He refused for a time. But later he said to himself, 'Even though I do not fear God nor regard man, ⁵because this widow will continue to trouble me, I will grant her justice so that, in the end, she doesn't give me a black eye[i] by continuing to come to me.'"

⁶Then the Lord said, "Listen to what the unjust judge is saying. ⁷*Unlike the judge,* God will most certainly execute judgment for his elect[ii] who cry out to him day and night, won't he? Will he continue to endure their cries? ⁸I tell you that he will execute judgment for them quickly. Nevertheless, when the Son of Man comes, will he find faith upon the earth at that time?"

Trusting in Self Rather than God: The Parable of Proud Pharisee

⁹Then he also told this parable to some who trusted in themselves, believing they were righteous, and they had a low opinion of everyone else. ¹⁰"Two men went up to the temple to pray, one a Pharisee and the other a tax collector. ¹¹When the Pharisee stood up, he began to pray these things to himself: 'God, I thank you that I am not like the rest of men, vicious robbers, unrighteous, adulterers, or even like this tax collector. ¹²I

---

[i] This picturesque expression is most likely a metaphor for the fact that her repeated plea would cause him to lose honor before the people.

[ii] The term translated "elect" is used over twenty times in the New Testament and most often is a reference to those who are called by God to true faith that perseveres.

fast twice a week. I give a tenth of all my income, as much as I get.'

¹³"But the tax collector stood at a distance. He was unwilling even to lift his eyes toward heaven, but struck his chest and said, 'God, have mercy on me, a sinner.'

¹⁴"I tell you, this man went down to his house acquitted of his sin, rather than the other one. For the one who exalts himself will be humbled, and the one who humbles himself will be exalted."

The Priority of Little Ones

¹⁵At that time, they began to bring infants to him, so that he might hold them; but the disciples began scolding them. ¹⁶Then Jesus called them over saying, "Allow the children to come to me, and do not stop them; for the Kingdom of God is made up of those who are like these children. ¹⁷I tell you the truth, whoever does not receive the Kingdom of God like a child will most certainly never enter into it."

Wealth as a Potential Impediment to the Kingdom

¹⁸A certain ruler questioned him asking, "Good teacher, what shall I do to inherit eternal life?"

¹⁹But Jesus said to him, "Why do you call me good? No one is good except the one God. ²⁰You know the commandments: do not commit adultery, do not murder, do not steal, do not testify falsely, honor your father and your mother."

²¹But he responded, "I have kept all of these commandments from my youth."

²²When Jesus had heard, he said to him, "One thing is still deficient in your life. Sell everything, all that you have, and distribute it among the poor, and you will have treasure in the heavens; then come, follow me."

²³But when he heard these things, he was filled with sorrow, for he was extremely wealthy. ²⁴When Jesus saw him filled with

sadness, he said, "How difficult it is for those who have wealth[i] to enter into the Kingdom of God. ²⁵For it is easier for a camel to go through the eye of a needle than for a rich person to enter into the Kingdom of God."

²⁶Then those who were listening said, "But who is able to be saved?"

²⁷He said, "The things that are impossible for men are possible for God."

Giving Up All for the Kingdom: A Promise

²⁸Peter said, "See, we have left our possessions to follow you."

²⁹Then he said to them, "I tell you the truth, there is no one who has left home, wife, siblings, parents, or children on account of the Kingdom of God, ³⁰who will not receive many times more at this time; and in the age to come, eternal life."

Jesus Points to His Death and Resurrection

³¹After he took the twelve aside, Jesus explained to them, "Pay close attention. We are going up to Jerusalem, and all the things written through the prophets about the Son of Man will be fulfilled. ³²For he will be handed over to the Gentiles, and he will be mocked, abused, spit upon, ³³and when they have whipped him, they will kill him; but on the third day he will come back to life."

³⁴But they did not understand any of these things. The meaning of his message was hidden from them, and they did not comprehend what he was speaking about.

Jesus Responds to Persistent Faith: Opening Blind Eyes

³⁵Now when Jesus was in the vicinity of Jericho, a certain blind man was sitting beside the road begging.[ii] ³⁶When he

---

[i] Or, "possessions." Also in verse 24.

[ii] Matthew references two blind men. Luke only focuses on Bartimaeus, probably because he was known to the Church when Luke wrote this gospel.

heard the crowd passing through, he asked what was happening. ³⁷They told him that Jesus of Nazareth was passing by.

³⁸Then he shouted crying, "Jesus, Son of David, have mercy on me."

³⁹Those who were going ahead of Jesus rebuked him so that he would be quiet. But he shouted all the more, "Son of David, have mercy on me."

⁴⁰Then, when Jesus stopped, he ordered that the blind man be brought to him. When he came near, Jesus questioned him, ⁴¹"What do you want me to do for you?"

He said, "Lord, I want to see again."

⁴²Jesus said to him, "See again! Your faith has rescued you."

⁴³Immediately, he was able to see, and began to follow him, glorifying God; and all the people who saw it, gave praise to God.

Jesus Seeks Out the Ostracized: Zacchaeus

Chapter Nineteen

¹After Jesus entered Jericho, he began to walk around the city. ²At the same time, there was a man there by the name of Zacchaeus. He was an important tax collector and was wealthy. ³He was attempting to see who Jesus was, but he was not able to see because of the crowd, and because he was a man of small stature. ⁴So, he ran ahead of the crowd and climbed a sycamore fig tree so that he might see him, because he was about to pass through that way.

⁵When Jesus came to the place, he looked up and said to him, "Zacchaeus, come down here quickly, for today I must stay at your house."

⁶He quickly came down and welcomed him joyfully. ⁷When everyone saw it, they began to grumble, saying, "He has gone in to be the guest of a sinful man."

⁸But Zacchaeus stopped and said to the Lord, "Be aware, Lord, I usually give[i] half of all my possessions to the very poor; and if I have profited from anyone falsely, I always pay back four times what I took."

⁹Then Jesus said to him, "Today salvation has come to this household, since this man is also a Son of Abraham. ¹⁰For the Son of Man has come to search for those who are lost and rescue them."

The Importance of Being Engaged: Using Opportunities

¹¹While they were listening to these things, Jesus proceeded to tell them a parable because he was near Jerusalem, and they believed that the Kingdom of God was going to appear almost immediately. ¹²Therefore, he said, "A certain high-ranking man went to a far country to receive a kingdom for himself, and then return to it. ¹³He called ten of his servants and gave them ten minas[ii] and said to them, 'Tend to my business until I come back.'

¹⁴"But his citizens hated him and sent representatives behind him to state, 'We do not want this man to be king over us.'

¹⁵"When he received his kingdom, he returned and commanded that the servants to whom he had given the silver should be called before him, so that he might know what profit they had made.

¹⁶"The first one came and said, 'Lord, your mina has made ten more minas.'

¹⁷"Then the ruler said to him, 'Well done my good servant! Because you have been faithful in the smallest of things, you shall have authority over ten cities.'

---

[i] The Greek verbs are in the present tense. Not "I will give," but "I am (already) giving," "I am (always) paying back" (The normal or customary use of the present tense).

[ii] One mina was equivalent to about a hundred denarii, or about three and a half month's wages for a soldier or day laborer.

¹⁸"The second came and said, 'Your mina, my Lord, has made five minas.'

¹⁹"Again, the ruler said also to him, 'You are to have authority over five cities.'

²⁰"Then another came and said, 'My Lord, see, here is your mina which I stored away in a cloth napkin. ²¹For I was afraid of you, for you are a harsh man who takes what you did not give, and harvests where you did not plant.'

²²"The ruler said to him, 'I will judge you by what has come from your own mouth, you worthless servant. You knew that I am a harsh man, taking what I did not give, and harvesting where I did not plant? ²³Then why didn't you give my silver to the money changers? Then, when I came, I could have collected it with interest.'

²⁴"He said to those who were standing near him, 'Take the mina from him, and give it to the one who has the ten minas.'

²⁵"They said to him, 'Lord, he already has ten minas.'

²⁶'I tell you that to anyone who has, more will be given, but from the one who does not have, even what he has will be taken away from him. ²⁷But these enemies of mine who did not want me to reign over them, bring them here, and slaughter them in front of me.'"

The King Arrives in Jerusalem

²⁸After he said these things, he went on ahead going up to Jerusalem. ²⁹As he drew near to Bethphage and Bethany, near the mount that is called Olives, he sent two of his disciples ³⁰instructing them, "Go to the village we are approaching. While you are going into it, you will find a colt tied up, one on which no one has ever sat. Untie it and lead it here. ³¹But if someone questions you asking, 'Why are you untying it?' answer this way, 'The Lord has need of it.'"

³²So, those who had been sent went ahead and found it just as he had told them. ³³While they were untying the colt, its owners asked them, "Why are you untying the colt?"

³⁴They responded, "The Lord has need of it."

³⁵They led it to Jesus, threw their outer garments upon the colt, and put Jesus on it. ³⁶As they went along, they continued to spread their outer garments on the road. ³⁷When he was already drawing near the path down to the Mount of Olives, all the multitude of his disciples began to praise God with loud shouts because of all the miracles they had seen.

³⁸They were shouting,

> "Blessed is the King who is coming in the name of the Lord. Peace in heaven and glory in the highest."[i]

³⁹But some of the Pharisees from the crowd said to him, "Teacher, rebuke your disciples."

⁴⁰He answered them, "I tell you, if these disciples were silent, the stones would cry out."

⁴¹As he drew near Jerusalem, he saw the city and wept over it ⁴²saying, "If you had only known on this day the things that would bring you peace, but now it has been hidden from your eyes. ⁴³For the time will come upon you when your enemies will put up siege works around you, surround you, and lay siege against you on every side. ⁴⁴Then they will raze you to the ground, and your children within you. They will not leave one stone upon another in you because you did not know the time of your visitation."

Jesus Exercises His Authority at the Temple

⁴⁵When he entered the temple and began to drive out those who were buying and selling *in the temple*. ⁴⁶He told them, "It is written,

---

[i] Psalm 118:25-26

> " 'My house will be a house of prayer,'[ii], but you have made it a bandit's lair.'[iii] "

⁴⁷He began teaching each day in the temple. The chief priests, the scribal scholars, and the prominent leaders of the people were seeking a way to ruin him, ⁴⁸but they could not find anything that they could do, for the all the people were holding fast to his teaching as they listened to him.

Jesus' Authority Challenged

Chapter Twenty

¹On one of the days, he was teaching the people in the temple and preaching the good news, the chief priests and the scribal scholars, along with the elders, approached him. ²They said to him, "Explain to us, by what authority are you doing these things? Who is it who gave you this authority?"

³But he responded to them and said, "I will also ask you something, and you explain it to me. ⁴Was the baptism of John from Heaven or from men?"

⁵They discussed this with each other and concluded, "If we say, 'From Heaven,' he will ask, 'Why didn't you believe him?' ⁶But if we say, 'From men,' all the people will stone us because they are convinced that John was a prophet."

⁷So, they responded, "We do not know where it was from."

⁸Jesus said to them, "Neither will I tell you by what authority I am doing these things."

The Parable of the Tenant Farmers

⁹Then he began to tell the people this parable, "A certain man planted a vineyard, leased it out to tenant farmers, and left on a journey for a long time. ¹⁰At the appropriate time, he sent a

---

[ii] Isaiah 56:7

[iii] See Jeremiah 7:11.

servant to the farmers in order that they might pay him with some of the fruit from the vineyard. But they beat him and sent him away without anything. ¹¹The owner proceeded to send another servant, but they beat that one also, treated him dishonorably, and sent him away without anything. ¹²He also sent a third, but they wounded him and threw him out of the vineyard.

¹³"Then the vineyard's owner said, 'What shall I do? I will send my cherished son; they will most certainly show respect to him.'

¹⁴"But when the tenant farmers saw him, they discussed it among themselves and said, 'This is the heir. Let's kill him so that the inheritance might be ours.' ¹⁵So, they cast him out of the vineyard and killed him.

"Therefore, what will the vineyard's owner do to them? ¹⁶He will come and destroy these tenant farmers and will give the vineyard to others."

When they heard it, they said, "May that never be!"

¹⁷But Jesus looked at them and said, "What, therefore, is this that was written,

> " 'The stone which the builders rejected, this one
> has become the most essential cornerstone.'[i]

¹⁸"Everyone who falls upon that stone will be shattered, but if it falls on someone, it will grind him to powder."

¹⁹The scribal scholars and the chief priests sought to lay hands on him that very hour, for they knew that he told this parable about them, but they feared the people. ²⁰They kept a close watch on him and sent agents who pretended to be sincere. They wanted to catch him saying something wrong in order to hand him over to the authority and jurisdiction of the governor.

---

[i] Psalm 118:22

The Leaders Test Jesus: Paying the Poll Tax

²¹They questioned him asking, "Teacher, we know that you speak and teach correctly, and are not partial to anyone, but you teach the way of God in truth. ²²Is it right that we pay tribute to Caesar or not?"

²³But because he perceived their treachery clearly, he said to them, "Why are you testing me? ²⁴Show me a denarius.ⁱⁱ Whose image and inscription are on it?"

They said, "Caesar's."

²⁵So, he said to them, "Then give back the things of Caesar to Caesar, and the things of God to God."

²⁶They were not able to catch him in his words in front of the people. They were stunned by his answer and said nothing more.

The Sadducees Test Jesus: The Marriage Conundrum

²⁷Now some Sadducees, who oppose the idea of the resurrection and say there is no resurrection, came to him and questioned him. ²⁸They asked, "Teacher, Moses wrote to us, 'If someone's brother dies and leaves a widow, and she does not have children, that the brother should take her as his wife and raise up offspring for his brother.'ⁱⁱⁱ ²⁹Now there were seven brothers. The first took a wife but died childless. ³⁰The same thing happened to the second, ³¹and the third married her, but in just the same manner also the seven died and did not leave children. ³²Later, the woman also died.

³³"Therefore, at the resurrection whose wife will she be? For the seven had married her."

³⁴Jesus said to them, "The sons of this age marry and are given in marriage, ³⁵but those who are considered worthy to attain that age and the resurrection from the dead neither marry nor are given in marriage. ³⁶For they are no longer able to die,

---

ⁱⁱ A Roman coin worth a day's wage for a soldier or day laborer.

ⁱⁱⁱ See Deuteronomy 25:5.

because they are like the angels, and they are sons of God because they are sons of the resurrection. ³⁷But that the dead are raised, even Moses revealed it at the bush when he said that the Lord is the God of Abraham, the God of Isaac, and the God of Jacob. ³⁸For he is not the God of the dead, but of the living; for everyone is alive to him."

³⁹Then some of the scribal scholars responded and said, "Teacher, you have spoken well," ⁴⁰but they no longer dared to ask him anything.

A Test for the Leaders: Whose Son is Christ

⁴¹Then he said to them, "How come they say that the Christ is David's son? ⁴²For David said in the book of Psalms,

> " 'The Lord said to my Lord, "Sit at my right hand, ⁴³until I make your enemies a footstool for your feet." ' [i]

⁴⁴"Since David calls him Lord, how also is he his son?"

Jesus Condemns the Religious Leaders of Israel

⁴⁵While all the people were listening, he said to his disciples, ⁴⁶"Be on your guard against the scribal scholars. They like to walk around in special robes, and love greetings at the market, the seat of honor in the synagogues, and the place of honor at banquets. ⁴⁷They devour the houses of widows, and to make themselves look good, offer up long prayers. They will receive greater judgment."

The Greatest Offering

Chapter Twenty-One

¹When he looked up, he saw the wealthy putting their gifts into the temple offering box. ²He also saw a certain poor widow put

---

[i] Psalm 110:1

two lepta[ii] into the offering box. ³So, he said, "I tell you that this poor widow gave more than anyone. ⁴For everyone else gave gifts from their abundance, but she gave from her lack of resources, all that she has to live on."

Looking Ahead to the Destruction of Jerusalem and Beyond

⁵While some of them were speaking about the temple, that it was adorned with beautiful stones and gifts devoted to God, he said, ⁶"The days will come when these things which you now see will not be left stone upon stone. They will be cast down."

⁷They questioned him asking, "Teacher, so when will these things happen, and what will be the sign that these things are about to happen?"

Jesus Answers Their Question

⁸He told them, "See to it that you are not deceived; for many will come in opposition to my name saying, 'I am *the Christ*,' and, 'The time is near.' Do not follow after them. ⁹But when you hear of wars and disturbances, do not be terrified. For these things must happen first, but the end will not come immediately."

¹⁰Then he said to them, "People group will rise up against people group,[iii] and kingdom against kingdom. ¹¹There will be great earthquakes, and famines and plagues in various places. There will be terrifying things happening, and great signs from heaven.

¹²"But before all these things, they will arrest you and persecute you, handing you over to synagogues and prisons, taking you before kings and governors on account of my name. ¹³It will give you opportunity to witness for me. ¹⁴Therefore, fix in your hearts that you will not think ahead to how you will

---

[ii] A lepton was about one percent of a denarius, which was a day's wage for a soldier or day laborer.

[iii] Or, traditionally, "nation will rise against nation," though his next words about kingdom against kingdom would appear to address the nations.

defend yourselves. ¹⁵For I will give you what to say, and wisdom that none of those who oppose you will be able to resist or speak against. ¹⁶Even your parents, brothers, relatives, and friends will hand you over to those who oppose you, and they will kill some of you. ¹⁷You will be despised by everyone on account of my name, ¹⁸but not a hair from your head will ever be lost. ¹⁹You must gain your lives by your endurance.

²⁰"When you see Jerusalem encompassed by armed camps, then know that its desolation is near. ²¹Then those who are in Judea must flee to the mountains, and those who are inside of the city must leave it, and those in the country must not go back to the city. ²²They must do this because these are the days of punishment where all the things that have been written will be fulfilled. ²³Woe to those who are pregnant or nursing a child in those days; for there will be great distress upon our land, and punishment[i] for this people. ²⁴They will fall to the hunger of the sword and will be led as captives to all the nations. Jerusalem will be trampled underfoot by the Gentiles until the times of the Gentiles are fulfilled.

²⁵"There will be signs in the sun, moon, and stars—and upon the earth anxious perplexity among the nations at the roaring and shaking of the sea; ²⁶men will faint from fear and expectation of what is coming upon the inhabited world,[ii] for the powers of the heavens will be shaken. ²⁷Then they will see the Son of Man coming in the clouds with power and great glory. ²⁸When these things begin to happen, stand up straight and lift your heads, for your redemption is drawing near."

²⁹Then he told them this parable, "Observe the fig tree and all the trees. ³⁰As soon as they bring forth leaves, you see it and know by yourselves that summer is already near. ³¹So also, you, when you see these things happening, know that the Kingdom of God is near at hand.

---

[i] Or, traditionally, "wrath."

[ii] Or, "Roman world."

³²"I tell you the truth, this current generation will by no means pass away before all these things have happened. ³³Heaven and earth will pass away, but my words will never pass away.

³⁴"Watch carefully over yourselves so that your hearts are not weighed down with drunkenness, drunken behavior, and the worries of this life, so that day does not fall upon you unexpectedly ³⁵as a trap. For it will come upon everyone living in the land. ³⁶Keep watch at all times, praying that you have the strength to flee from these things that are about to happen, and to stand in the presence of the Son of Man."

³⁷During the day, Jesus taught in the temple, but at night he went out and spent the night at the mountain known as Olives. ³⁸All the people would get up early in the morning and go to him in the temple to hear him.

Passover Draws Near: Jesus' Enemies Plot His Death

Chapter Twenty-Two

¹Now the festival of unleavened bread, called the Passover, was drawing near. ²The chief priests and scribal scholars were seeking how they might legally do away with him, for they were afraid of the people.

Satan Incites Judas to Betray Jesus

³Then Satan entered Judas, who was also called Iscariot. He was numbered among the twelve. ⁴He went and spoke with the chief priests and military officers about how he might hand him over to them.[iii] ⁵They were filled with joy and agreed together to pay him in silver. ⁶So, he accepted their terms, and began to seek the right moment to hand him over to them when the crowds were not around them.

---

iii According to John 12:4-6, Judas had been the one who led the attack over when Mary anointed Jesus, because he was greedy for the money.

Luke 22:7

Jesus Blocks Judas' Ability to Disrupt the Last Supper

⁷Then the day of Unleavened Bread arrived. This was the day it was necessary to sacrifice the Passover lamb. ⁸Jesus sent Peter and John instructing them, "Go and prepare the Passover for us so that we may eat it."

⁹They asked him, "Where do you want us to prepare it?"

¹⁰He told them, "Listen closely. When you have gone into the city, a man will meet you who is carrying a jar of water. Follow him to the house that he enters. ¹¹Then you will tell the owner of the house, 'The teacher asks you, "Where is the guest room where I will eat the Passover with my disciples?" ' ¹²That man will show you a large furnished upstairs room. Prepare the Passover there."

¹³They went and found everything just as he said to them. So, they prepared the Passover.

Jesus Gives New Meaning to the Passover Meal

¹⁴When the hour had come, Jesus reclined ready for the meal, and the twelve apostles with him. ¹⁵Then he said to them, "I have had an intense desire to eat this Passover with you before I suffer. ¹⁶For I tell you that I will most certainly not eat it after this until it has been fulfilled in the Kingdom of God."

¹⁷After receiving the cup, he gave thanks and said, "Take this and divide it among yourselves. ¹⁸For I tell you, I will most certainly not drink from the fruit of the vine from now until the time that the Kingdom of God has come."

¹⁹After he took the bread and gave thanks, he broke it and gave it to them saying, "This is my body given on your behalf. Do this to remember me."

²⁰In just the same way, after they had eaten, he took the cup and said, "This cup is the new covenant in my blood, which is poured out on your behalf.

²¹"However, know this: the hand of the one who is giving me up *to my enemies* is with me on the table. ²²For, on the one hand, the

Son of Man is going on the path that has been appointed, however, woe to that man by whom he is delivered over *to that path*."

23Then they began to discuss among themselves who from among them might be the one who was going to do this. 24In addition, a dispute arose among them about who among them was considered the most important.

25But Jesus said to them, "The kings of nations act as masters over them, and those who have authority have themselves called benefactors. 26But you are not to act like them; on the contrary, let the one who is most important among you be like the least important, and the one who leads like one who serves. 27For who is more important, the one reclining at the table, or the one who is serving? Isn't it the one who is reclining? But I am among you as one who serves. 28Yet you are the ones who have remained with me through my trials. 29Just as my Father has entrusted a kingdom to me, I also entrust one to you, 30so that you may eat and drink at my table in my Kingdom and sit on thrones judging the twelve tribes of Israel."

Jesus Predicts the Failure of Peter and the Other Disciples

31Then the Lord said, "Simon, Simon, pay close attention: Satan's request to sift all of you like wheat has been granted. 32But I have prayed for you so that your faith does not falter; and when you have repented, strengthen your brothers."

33Then Peter said to him, "Lord, I am prepared to go with you to prison and to death."

34But Jesus said, "I tell you, Peter, the rooster will not crow today before you have denied that you know me three times."

35He said to them, "When I sent you without a wallet, bag for provisions, or sandals, you did not lack anything, did you?"

They responded, "Nothing."

36Then he added, "But now, let anyone who has a wallet or a bag for provisions bring it along. Let anyone who does not have a sword, sell his cloak and buy one. 37For I tell you I must fulfill this thing that is written, 'He was counted with the rebels,'[i] for the things written about me are being fulfilled."

[38]They said, "Lord, see, here are two swords."

Then he said to them, "That is sufficient."

Jesus' Struggle in Gethsemane

[39]He went out and traveled, as was his custom, to the Mount of Olives. His disciples also followed him. [40]When he reached the place, he said to them, "Pray that you do not fall into temptation."

[41]He withdrew from them about a stone's throw, knelt down, and began to pray saying, [42]"Father, if you are willing, remove this cup from me; only do not let my will, but yours be done." [43]Then an angel from heaven appeared to him and was strengthening him. [44]Because he was in a violent struggle for victory, he prayed with even more resolve, so that his sweat was like drops of blood falling on the ground.

[45]When he got up from praying and approached his disciples, he found them sleeping because of their grief. [46]He said to them, "Why are you sleeping? Wake up and pray so that you do not fall into temptation."

Jesus Betrayed and Arrested

[47]While he was still speaking, a crowd suddenly appeared. The one called Judas, one of the twelve, was showing them the way. He approached Jesus to kiss him. [48]Jesus said to him, "Judas, is it with a kiss that you hand over the Son of Man to his enemies?"

[49]When those who were around him saw the situation, they asked, "Lord, shall we attack them with our swords?" [50]Then one from among them struck the servant of the high priest and sliced off his right ear.

---

[i] Isaiah 53:12

⁵¹But Jesus responded to it and said, "Let this happen!" Then he touched the man's ear and healed him.

⁵²Jesus said to the chief priests, the temple's military officers, and the elders who had come for him, "Why have you come out with swords and clubs as you would for a rebel? ⁵³You did not lay your hands on me each day while I was with you in the temple. But this is your hour, and the hour of the ruler of the darkness."

Peter's Failure

⁵⁴After they arrested him, they left the garden and went into the house of the chief priest; but Peter followed at a distance. ⁵⁵When they had started a fire in the middle of the courtyard and sat down together, Peter settled among them. ⁵⁶Because of this, one of the female servants saw him sitting there near the light. She watched him closely and said, "This man was also with him."

⁵⁷But he denied it saying, "I do not know him, woman."

⁵⁸After a short time, another saw him and said, "You are also one of them."

But Peter said, "Man, I am not."

⁵⁹After about an hour, another man began to insist strongly saying, "Without a doubt, this man was also with him, for he is a Galilean."

⁶⁰But Peter said, "Man, I do not know what you are talking about." Immediately, while he was yet speaking, a rooster crowed. ⁶¹Then the Lord turned and looked at Peter. Peter remembered the Lord's warning to him when he said, "Before the rooster crows today, you will deny me three times." ⁶²When he had gone outside, he wept in bitter agony.

Jesus Tried and Condemned

⁶³Then the men who surrounded Jesus began to mock him and beat him. ⁶⁴They blindfolded him and quizzed him asking,

"Prophesy! Which one of us struck you?" ⁶⁵They also were saying many other things against him, disparaging him.

⁶⁶At daylight, they assembled the elders of the people, both the chief priests and the scribal scholars, and they led him to the Sanhedrin. ⁶⁷They questioned him, "If you are the Christ, tell us."

But he said to them, "If I tell you, you will certainly not believe it; ⁶⁸if I ask a question, you will most certainly not answer me or release me. ⁶⁹But from now on, the Son of Man will be seated at the right hand of God's power."

⁷⁰They asked, "So, are you the Son of God?"

Then he said to them, "You yourselves are declaring that I am."

⁷¹They said, "What additional testimony do we need? For we have heard it from his own mouth ourselves."

Jesus Handed over to Pilate

Chapter Twenty-Three

¹The whole assembly recessed their meeting and brought him to Pilate. ²Then they began to accuse him and say, "We found this man deceiving our nation and forbidding the people to pay taxes to Caesar. He also claimed that he himself is Messiah, a king."

³So, Pilate questioned him and asked, "Are you the king of the Jews?"

Jesus responded to him and said, "You yourself are saying it."

⁴Pilate said to the chief priests and the assembly, "I find no guilt in this man."

⁵But they were insistent, saying, "He began stirring up the people in Galilee, and has come here teaching everywhere in Judea."

⁶But when Pilate heard about Galilee, he asked if the man was a Galilean. ⁷When he found out that he was under the authority of Herod, he sent him to Herod, who was also in Jerusalem at that time.

⁸When Herod saw Jesus, he was very happy, for he had heard about him and wanted to see him for a long time. He was hoping to see him do some miracles. ⁹He peppered Jesus with many questions, but Jesus did not answer him. ¹⁰However, the chief priests and scribal scholars were fervently accusing him. ¹¹Then Herod and his soldiers treated him with contempt, mocked him, put bright clothing on him, and sent him to Pilate. ¹²Herod and Pilate became friends with each other on that very day; they had hated each other before this.

¹³Pilate called together the chief priests, the rulers, and the people ¹⁴and said to them, "You brought this man to me saying he stirred up the people, but see, I have examined him in front of you, and have not found him guilty of any of the charges you brought against him. ¹⁵In addition, neither has Herod, for he sent him back to us. Look, he has done nothing worthy of death. ¹⁶I will punish him and then release him," ¹⁷for he was obligated to release one prisoner to them during the Passover festival.

¹⁸But they shouted together, "Take this man away; release Barabbas to us." ¹⁹Barabbas was a man who had been thrown into prison for a riot in the city and for murder.

²⁰So, because Pilate wanted to release Jesus, he addressed them again. ²¹They cried out shouting, "Crucify, crucify him!"

²²He spoke to them a third time, "For what reason? What wrong has this man done? I have not found him guilty of anything that deserves death. So, I will punish him and then release him."

²³But they persisted and with loud voices they demanded that he be crucified. Their voices and those of the chief priests prevailed ²⁴and Pilate decided to grant their request. ²⁵He

released the one they were asking for, who had been thrown into prison for a riot and murder; but he delivered Jesus to their will.

Jesus is Crucified

²⁶As they led him away, they stopped Simon of Cyrene, who had come into Jerusalem from the country. They put the cross on him, and he carried it behind Jesus. ²⁷A great number of the people followed him, and the women were mourning and wailing for him.

²⁸Jesus turned to them and said, "Daughters of Jerusalem, stop weeping for me. Instead, weep for yourselves and for your children. ²⁹For, listen, the days are coming when you will say, 'Blessed are the childless women, the wombs that have not given birth, and the breasts that never nursed.' ³⁰Then they will cry out to the mountains, 'Cover us,' and to the hills, 'Hide us.' ³¹For if they do these things while the tree is green, what will happen when it is dry?"

³²They also brought two other criminals with him to be executed. ³³When they came to the place known as the Skull, they crucified him and the criminals, one on his right, and the other on his left.

³⁴Then Jesus said, "Father, forgive them, for they do not know what they are doing."

They cast lots for his clothing after they had divided them up. ³⁵The people stood near watching while the rulers scoffed at him and said, "He saved others, let him save himself if he is the Chosen One,[i] God's Messiah."

³⁶The soldiers also came up to him and mocked him. They brought him sour wine ³⁷and said, "If you are the King of the Jews, save yourself."

³⁸There was also a written notice above him in Greek, Latin, and Hebrew, "This man is the King of the Jews."

---

[i] Or, "Elect One."

³⁹One of the criminals hanging there spoke abusively to him, "You are the Christ, aren't you? Save yourself and us."

⁴⁰But the other criminal responded to him and rebuked him saying, "Don't you fear God, since you are under the same judgment? ⁴¹We are getting justice, for we are receiving the payment we deserve, but this man has done nothing wrong."

⁴²Then he said, "Jesus, remember me when you have entered into your Kingdom."

⁴³Jesus responded to him, "I tell you the truth, today you will be with me in paradise."

Signs and Portents Around Jesus' Suffering and Death

⁴⁴It was already about the sixth hour,[ii] and darkness fell upon the whole land until the ninth hour, ⁴⁵because the sun failed. Then the temple curtain was torn down the middle.

⁴⁶After Jesus called out with a loud cry, he said, "Father, into your hands I entrust my spirit." When he said this, he released his spirit.

⁴⁷When the centurion saw what had happened, he praised God and said, "Certainly this man was righteous."

⁴⁸All the crowds who had come together to witness this event, when they saw what happened, began beating their breasts and began to leave.

The Faithful Few Continue to Watch and Serve

⁴⁹All those who knew him stood at a distance. The women who had followed him from Galilee were also watching these things.

⁵⁰At about that time, there was a man by the name of Joseph, who was a member of the Sanhedrin and a good and righteous man. ⁵¹He was from Arimathea, a Jewish city, and was waiting for the Kingdom of God. He had not agreed with the council's plan or deeds.

[ii] The sixth hour is noon. The ninth hour is 3:00 PM.

⁵²He went to Pilate and requested the body of Jesus. ⁵³He took down Jesus' body and wrapped it in good quality linen cloth; he placed it in a tomb that had been chiseled in the rock, where no one was yet interred. ⁵⁴It was the Day of Preparation,ⁱ and the Sabbath was upon them.

⁵⁵The women, the ones who had come together with him from Galilee, followed Joseph. They saw the tomb and how his body was placed. ⁵⁶Then they returned and prepared spices and aromatic oils, but they rested on the Sabbath in accord with the commandment.

Jesus Rises from the Dead

Chapter Twenty-Four

¹On the first day of the week early in the morning, the women came to the tomb bringing the spices they had prepared. ²But they found the stone had been rolled away from the tomb. ³When they went in, they did not find the body of the Lord Jesus. ⁴While they stood there at a loss about this, at that moment, two men suddenly stood near them. They were dressed in dazzling white clothing. ⁵The women were afraid and bowed down prostrate on the ground, and the men said to them, "Why are you seeking the living one among the dead? ⁶He is not here but has been raised from the dead. Remember how he told you while you were still in Galilee? ⁷He explained *to you* that the Son of Man must be delivered into the hands of sinful men, be crucified, and rise again on the third day."

⁸Then they remembered his words. ⁹When they returned from the tomb, they reported all these things to the eleven and to everyone else. ¹⁰Those reporting these things to the apostles were Mary Magdalene, Johanna, Mary the mother of James, and the rest who were with them. ¹¹But these words appeared to be utter nonsense to them, and they did not believe them.

ⁱ The day of Preparation (Friday) was the day one prepared for the Sabbath (Saturday)

¹²However, Peter got up and ran to the tomb and when he stooped down, he saw only the linen cloths. He went away wondering to himself what had happened.

Jesus Reveals Himself on the Road to Emmaus

¹³Even more notable, on that same day, two of his followers were going to a village by the name of Emmaus, which was about sixty stadia[ii] from Jerusalem. ¹⁴They were speaking with each other about all these things that had happened. ¹⁵While they were conversing and debating them, Jesus himself drew near and began to travel with them; ¹⁶but their eyes were prevented from recognizing him.

¹⁷He asked them, "What are these things that you are discussing with each other while you are walking?"

Then they stopped and looked distressed. ¹⁸One, by the name of Cleopas, responded and said to him, "Are you only visiting Jerusalem and do not know the things that have happened in it these past days?"

¹⁹He said to them, "What things?"

They said to him, "The things concerning Jesus of Nazareth, who was a prophet, a man powerful in his actions and words before God and all the people, ²⁰and how our chief priests and rulers handed him over *to Pilate* for a verdict of death, and how they crucified him. ²¹We were hoping that he was the one who was going to redeem Israel. But in addition to all these things, it is the third day from when these things happened, ²²Even more, some women from among us also overwhelmed us when they went to the tomb early this morning ²³and did not find his body. They came saying that they had seen a vision of angels who said he is alive. ²⁴Some who were with us went to the tomb and found it just as the women had said, but they did not see him."

²⁵Then he said to them, "Oh foolish ones! You have hearts that are reluctant to believe all the prophets have spoken.

[ii] About 7 miles. A stadion was about 600 feet.

26Wasn't it necessary that the Christ suffer these things and enter into his glory?"

27Then beginning with Moses and all the prophets, he clearly explained to them the things concerning himself in all the Scriptures. 28When they drew near the village where they were going, he gave the impression that he was going further. 29But they appealed to him saying, "Remain with us, for the evening is approaching, and the day is already ending." So, he went in to stay with them.

30While he was eating with them, he took the bread, blessed it, broke it, and began to give it to them. 31Then their eyes were opened, and they knew him, but he vanished from their presence. 32They said to each other, "Were not our hearts burning in us as he spoke to us on the road, and he opened the Scriptures to us?"

Jesus Reveals Himself to His Disciples

33They got up that same hour and returned to Jerusalem. They found the eleven gathered together, and those with them. 34They said *to the two*, "The Lord has truly been raised, and he has appeared to Simon."

35Then they also began to share what had happened on the road, and how they recognized him by the breaking of bread. 36While they were sharing these things, Jesus himself stood in their midst and said to them, "Peace to you."

37But they were alarmed and very frightened; they thought they were seeing a spirit. 38He said to them, "Why are you distressed, and why do questions spring up in your heart? 39Look at my hands and my feet, for I myself am here. Touch me and see, for a spirit does not have flesh and bones as you see that I have."

40When he said this, he showed them his hands and his feet. 41Because they were so filled with joy and astonishment that they had difficulty believing, he said to them, "Do you have any food here?" ⁴²They gave him a piece of roasted fish. ⁴³He took it and ate it in front of them.

⁴⁴Then he said to them, "This was my message that I told you while I was yet with you; that it was necessary that everything written in the Law of Moses, the Prophets, and the Psalms concerning me be fulfilled."

⁴⁵Then he opened their minds to understand the Scriptures. ⁴⁶He said to them, "It is written in just this way, that the Christ would suffer and rise from the dead on the third day, ⁴⁷and that repentance for forgiveness of sins would be proclaimed in his name to all nations, beginning in Jerusalem. ⁴⁸You are witnesses of these things. ⁴⁹Also, be aware: I am sending the promise of my Father to you, so you must stay in the city until you are clothed with power from on high."

Jesus Ascends to the Father

⁵⁰Later, he led them out to the area around Bethany; there he raised his hands and blessed them. ⁵¹While he was blessing them, he moved away from them and was taken up into heaven.

⁵²When they had worshiped him, they returned to Jerusalem with great joy, ⁵³and they were in the temple all the time praising God.

TRANSLATOR'S PREFACE TO THE BOOK OF JOHN

The book of John provides a basic challenge to those who wish to translate its pages accurately. How does one understand John's repeated reference to the Jews? It is clear throughout the book that when John writes of the Jews, he is often referring to the Jewish religious leaders, not the Jewish people themselves. Two passages help demonstrate this fact:

> Nevertheless, no one spoke freely about him on account of their fear of the Jewish leaders. (John 7:13).

The crowd that is in focus consists of the Jewish pilgrims who had come to the Feast of Tabernacles. John says of them, "no one spoke freely" because of their fear of the Jews. It is clear that they were not afraid of their fellow pilgrims, but of their religious leaders.

Another passage that clearly demonstrates this is found in chapter 9:

> His parents said these things because they were afraid of the Jewish leaders; for the Jewish leaders had already decided that anyone who acknowledged Jesus as the Christ would be banished from the synagogue. (John 9:22)

The parents of the man born blind had this same fear. They did not speak openly because they were afraid of the Jews, again a clear reference to the Jewish religious leaders who would put anyone who supported Jesus out of the synagogue.

While there are other references that could be presented, these two passage clearly demonstrate the point.

For this reason, for contextual accuracy and absolute clarity, this translation most often translates "Jews" as "Jewish leaders" in the book of John, and in some other books of the New Testament.

This is especially important for religious leaders today. It is important that today's religious leaders in Christianity note how the religious leaders of Israel, the priests, the scribal scholars, and the Pharisees, moved from being the guardians of orthodoxy to resisting the Holy Spirit, and finally opposing him and the purposes of God. In the same way today, Christian religious leaders of every generation will be confronted with the "new" things that God is doing. As guardians of truth, they must examine all things and compare them to biblical teaching. The Book of John is a warning to those religious leaders that honest examination can easily move into stubborn refusal to believe. It is easier than we know to step from the role of defender of the truth into the role of an enemy of what God is doing today. The Book of John stands as a warning for every generation of God's people, and it is vital we understand it correctly so that we avoid this great error.

JOHN

All Things Came into Existence through Jesus

Chapter One

¹The Word was there at the beginning, and the Word was with God, and the Word was God. ²This man was with God at the beginning. ³All things came into existence through him, and apart from him not one thing came into existence. What came into existence ⁴through him was life,[i] and this life was the light of men. ⁵The Light is shining in the darkness—and the darkness has not overpowered it.

The Forerunner and the Christ

⁶There was a man who was sent from God; his name was John. ⁷This man came as a witness to give his testimony about the light, in order that everyone might believe through him. ⁸That man was not the light, but one who would give his testimony about the light.

⁹The true light that shines on every person was coming into the world. ¹⁰He was in the world, and the world came into existence through him, but the world did not recognize him.

---

[i] Light and Life are important themes of this book, as they are in Genesis 1.

¹¹He came to his own, but his own did not welcome him. ¹²But as many as received him, who believed in his name, he gave them power to become children of God; ¹³they were born not from blood, nor from the desire of the flesh, nor from the will of a husband, but from God.

¹⁴The Word became flesh and pitched his tent among us. We have seen his glory, his glory as the unique and only Son of the Father, full of grace and truth.

¹⁵John testified about him and called out saying, "This man was the one of whom I said, 'The one who is coming after me existed before me, for he is greater than me.'"

¹⁶For out of his fullness, we have all also received ever-increasing grace; ¹⁷for the Law was given through Moses, grace and truth came into existence through Jesus Christ. ¹⁸No one has ever seen God; God the unique and only Son, who is at the Father's side, has revealed him.

The Jewish Leaders Question John

¹⁹This is the testimony of John when the Jewish leaders from Jerusalem sent priests and Levites so that they might ask him, "Who are you?"

²⁰He acknowledged and did not deny it, but confessed, "I am not the Christ."

²¹They questioned him, "Then what? Are you Elijah?"

He responded, "I am not."

"Are you the prophet?"

He answered, "No."

²²Therefore, they said to him, "Who are you, so that we might give an answer to those who sent us? What do you say about yourself?"

²³He said,

" 'I am a voice crying in the wilderness, make the way of the Lord straight,'[i] just as Isaiah the prophet said."

²⁴Now they had been sent by the Pharisees. ²⁵They questioned him and asked, "Then why do you baptize if you are not the Christ, Elijah, or the prophet?"

²⁶John responded to them and said, "I am baptizing in water. There is one who stands in your midst whom you do not know. ²⁷He is the one who is coming after me. I am not worthy to untie the straps of his sandals."

²⁸These things happened in Bethany across the Jordan, where John was baptizing.

John Points to the Lamb of God

²⁹On the next day, John saw Jesus coming toward him and said, "Look, the Lamb of God, the one who takes away the sin of the world. ³⁰This man is the one I mentioned when I said, 'A man is coming after me who existed before me, for he is greater than me.' ³¹Even I did not recognize him, but for this reason I came baptizing in water so that he might be revealed to Israel."

³²John told what he had witnessed saying, "I saw the Spirit descending from heaven in the form of a dove and remain on him. ³³I did not know it was him, but the one who sent me to baptize in water said to me, 'The one upon whom you see the Spirit descend and remain, he is the one who baptizes in the Holy Spirit.' ³⁴I have seen this, and I testify that this man is the Son of God."

John Sends Disciples to Jesus

³⁵On the next day John was again standing with two of his disciples. ³⁶When he looked at Jesus while he was walking by, he said, "Look, the Lamb of God!"

---

[i] Isaiah 40:3

⁳⁷The two disciples heard John while he was speaking, and they followed Jesus. ³⁸When Jesus turned and saw them following, he said to them, "What are you trying to find?"

Then they said to him, "Rabbi," (which means Teacher when translated), "where are you staying?"

³⁹He said to them, "Come and see." So, they went and saw where he was staying, and they stayed with him that day. It was about the tenth hour.[i]

⁴⁰Andrew, the brother of Simon Peter, was one of the two who heard from John and followed Jesus. ⁴¹First, he found his own brother, Simon, and said to him, "We have found the Messiah" (which means Christ when translated). ⁴²He brought Peter to Jesus. When Jesus saw him, he said, "You are Simon, the son of Jonah; you will be called Cephas" (which is Peter[ii] when translated).

Jesus Adds Philip and Nathaniel

⁴³On the next day, Jesus wanted to leave for Galilee. He found Philip and said to him, "Follow me."

⁴⁴Now Philip was from Bethsaida, the same city as Andrew and Peter. ⁴⁵Philip found Nathaniel and said to him, "We have found the one Moses wrote about in the Law, and the prophets predicted; Jesus the son of Joseph—from Nazareth."

⁴⁶Nathaniel said to him, "Is any good able to come from Nazareth?"

Philip responded to him, "Come and see."

⁴⁷Jesus saw Nathaniel coming to him and said about him, "Look, here is truly an Israelite in whom there is no deceit."

⁴⁸Nathaniel asked him, "How do you know me?"

---

[i] About 4:00 PM.
[ii] Both Cephas and Peter mean "Rock."

Jesus responded and said to him, "Before Philip shouted to you while you were under the fig tree, I saw you."

⁴⁹Nathaniel answered him, "Rabbi, you are the Son of God. You are the King of Israel."

⁵⁰Jesus responded and said to him, "Because I told you what I saw when you were under the fig tree, you believe? You will see greater than these things." ⁵¹He said to him, "I am telling you the very truth, you will see heaven standing open and the messengers of God ascending and descending on the Son of Man."

Jesus Reveals His Glory to His Disciples: Changing Water into Wine

Chapter Two

¹On the third day, there was a marriage in Cana of Galilee, and Jesus' mother was there. ²Jesus and his disciples were also invited to the wedding feast. ³When the wine ran short, Jesus' mother said to him, "They have no wine."

⁴Jesus said to her, "Mother,[iii] what is that to us? My hour has not yet come."

⁵His mother said to the servants, "Whatever he may tell you, do it."

⁶There were six stone water jugs for the Jewish rites of cleansing, holding two or three measures.[iv] ⁷Jesus said to the servants, "Fill the water jugs with water," and they filled them to the top.

⁸He said to them, "Now draw some out and take it to the manager of the banquet."

[iii] Traditionally translated, "Woman." But, the word was a polite form of address to a woman in that culture, but not as much in modern culture. In current culture, the correct way to politely address one's mother is, "Mother."

[iv] A measure was about nine gallons. Each jug held eighteen to twenty-seven gallons.

Then they took it. ⁹When the manager of the banquet tasted the water that had changed to wine, he did not know where it was from—but the servants who had drawn the water knew—the manager of the banquet called out to the bridegroom ¹⁰and said to him, "Everyone serves the good wine first, and when they have drunk too much, they serve the lesser quality wine. But you have saved the good wine until now."

¹¹Jesus did this first of his miraculous signs in Cana of Galilee, and made his glory known; and his disciples believed in him.[i]

¹²After this, he went down to Capernaum, Jesus and his mother, his brothers, and his disciples, and he stayed there for a few days.

Jesus Exercises His Authority at the Temple

¹³The Passover of the Jews was near at hand, and Jesus went up to Jerusalem. ¹⁴In the temple, he found those selling oxen, sheep, and doves; and moneychangers were seated there. ¹⁵Jesus made a whip from cords and drove both the sheep and the oxen from the temple, and he poured out the coins of the moneychangers and overturned their tables. ¹⁶He said to those who were selling doves, "Take these things from here. Stop making my Father's house into a house of commerce."

¹⁷His disciples remembered that it was written,

"Zeal for your house will consume me."[ii]

¹⁸Therefore, the Jewish leaders responded and questioned him, "What miraculous sign will you show to us since you are doing these things?"

---

[i] Throughout the book of John, to believe "in" Jesus (using the preposition) means to have saving faith in him. To "believe Jesus" (using the dative case) means to intellectually acknowledge that what he is saying is true. That may include saving faith, but the context will tell.

[ii] Psalm 69:9

¹⁹Jesus responded and said to them, "Destroy this temple and in three days I will raise it."

²⁰So, the Jewish leaders said, "It has taken forty-six years to build this temple; and you will raise it in three days?"

²¹But he was speaking about the temple of his body. ²²Therefore, when he was raised from the dead, his disciples remembered that he had said this, and they believed the Scripture and the word which Jesus had spoken.

²³But while he was in Jerusalem at the Passover, at the Feast, many believed in his name because they saw his miraculous signs that he kept doing. ²⁴But Jesus himself would not entrust himself to them because he knew all men, ²⁵and because he had no need that anyone testify concerning man, for he himself knew what was in man.

Nicodemus Comes at Night

Chapter Three

¹There was a man from the Pharisees, Nicodemus was his name, who was a ruler of the Jewish leaders. ²This man came to Jesus at night and said to him, "Rabbi, we know that you have come from God as a teacher; for no one is able to do these miraculous signs which you are doing if God is not with him."

³Jesus responded and said to him, "I am telling you the very truth, unless one is born again,[iii] he is not able to see the Kingdom of God."

⁴Nicodemus asked him, "How is a man able to be born when he is old? He can't enter his mother's womb a second time to be born, can he?"

⁵Jesus answered, "I am telling you the very truth, unless someone is born from water and Spirit, he is not able to enter

---

[iii] Or, "born from above." The Greek word can mean either thing. In verse 31 it is clear that it should be translated "from above" in that verse.

into the Kingdom of God. ⁶The one who has been born from flesh is flesh, and the one who has been born from the Spirit is spirit. ⁷Do not wonder that I said to you that it is necessary that you *all*[i] be born again. ⁸The wind blows where it wants. You hear its sound, but you do not know from where it has come or where it is going. So also, is everyone who is born from the Spirit."

⁹Nicodemus responded and said to him, "How then can these things be?"

¹⁰Jesus answered and said to him, "You are the teacher of Israel and you do not know these things?" ¹¹I am telling you the very truth, we speak of what we know, and we testify to what we have seen, but you do not receive our testimony. ¹²If I have spoken to you of earthly things and you do not believe, how will you believe if I speak to you of heavenly things? ¹³Indeed, no one has gone up into heaven except the one who has come down from heaven, the Son of Man who is in heaven. ¹⁴Just as Moses lifted up the snake in the desert, so also it is necessary for the Son of Man to be lifted up ¹⁵in order that everyone who believes might in him possess eternal life."

¹⁶"For God loved the world so much that he gave his unique and only[ii] Son, so that everyone who believes in him might not be lost but possess eternal life. ¹⁷For God has not sent the Son into the world so that he might condemn the world, but so that the world might be saved through him. ¹⁸The one who believes in him is not judged; but the one who does not believe in him has been judged already, because he has not believed in the name of God's unique and only Son. ¹⁹This is the judgment, that the Light has come into the world, but men loved the darkness rather than the Light, for their actions were evil. ²⁰For everyone who works at evil hates the Light and does not come to the Light, so that his actions might not be exposed. ²¹But the one who makes a habit of the truth does come to the Light, in order

---

[i] Jesus uses the plural pronoun here.

[ii] Traditionally, "only begotten." The Greek word emphasizes the fact that this is the unique and only offspring.

that it might be evident that his works are being accomplished by God."

²²After these things, Jesus and his disciples arrived in the region of Judea where he stayed with them and was baptizing. ²³John was also baptizing in Aenon near Salim, because there were many waters there; people were coming and were being baptized ²⁴(for John had not yet been put into prison).

John Testifies on Behalf of Jesus

²⁵As a result, a debate arose between the disciples of John and a Jewish religious leader concerning ritual purification. ²⁶So, they came to John and said to him, "Rabbi, the man about whom you testified and who was with you across the Jordan, look, this man is baptizing, and everyone is going to him."

²⁷John responded and said, "A man isn't able to receive anything if it hasn't been given to him from heaven. ²⁸You yourselves can testify that I said, 'I am not the Christ,' but, 'I have been sent ahead of him.' ²⁹The man who has the bride is the bridegroom. But the friend of the bridegroom, who takes his stand and listens for him, joyfully rejoices at the bridegroom's voice. Therefore, my joy has been made complete. ³⁰He must grow *in influence*, but I must diminish."

³¹"The one who has come from above is above everything. The one who is from the earth is from the earth and speaks from the earth. The one who has come from heaven is above everything. ³²What he has seen and heard, he testifies about this, but no one receives his testimony. ³³The one who has received his testimony confirms that God is true. ³⁴For the one God sent speaks the words of God, for God did not limit him, *as if using* a measuring device, when he gave the Spirit to him. ³⁵The Father loves the Son and has given all things into his hand. ³⁶The one who believes in the Son possesses life eternal, but the one who refuses to believe the Son will not see life. On the contrary, the anger of God remains upon him."

Jesus Reveals Himself as Messiah to a Samaritan Woman

Chapter Four

¹Therefore, when Jesus learned that the Pharisees had heard that he was recruiting and baptizing more disciples than John— ²although Jesus himself wasn't baptizing, but his disciples—³he left Judea and withdrew again to Galilee.

⁴Now this required that he pass through Samaria. ⁵So, he came to a city in Samaria called Sychar, near the field Jacob gave to his son Joseph. ⁶Jacob's well was located there. So, because Jesus was tired from the journey, he was sitting just as he was at the well. It was about the sixth hour.ⁱ

⁷A Samaritan woman came to draw water. Jesus spoke to her, "Give me a drink, please."ⁱⁱ—⁸For his disciples had gone into the city in order to purchase food.

⁹So the Samaritan woman said to him, "How can you, a Jewish man, ask me, a Samaritan woman for a drink?"—For Jewish men do not deal with Samaritans.

¹⁰Jesus responded and said to her, "If you knew the gift of God and who it is who asked, 'Give me a drink, please,' you would ask him, and he would give you living water."

¹¹The woman said to him, "Sir, you do not have a bucket, and the well is deep. So, where do you get living water? ¹²You are not greater than our father, Jacob, are you? He gave this well to us, and he himself, his sons, and his animals drank from it."

¹³Jesus responded and said to her, "Everyone who drinks from this water will be thirsty again. ¹⁴But whoever drinks from the water which I will give to him will by no means ever be thirsty

---

ⁱ About noon.

ⁱⁱ The Greek is literally a command, "Give me a drink." However, in verse 9 the woman clearly states that Jesus had asked for a drink, not commanded her to give one. His tone of voice may have made the command into a polite question.

to the end of this age. Rather, the water which I will give him will be in him a well of water bubbling up for life eternal."

15The woman said to him, "Sir, please give me this water that I will not be thirsty, and so that I no longer have to come here to draw water."

16He said to her, "Go call your husband and come back here."

17She responded and said to him, "I do not have a husband."

Jesus said to her, "You have answered correctly, 'I do not have a husband.' 18For you have had five husbands, and the man you have now is not your husband. This you have answered correctly."

19The woman said to him, "Sir, I see that you are a prophet. 20Our fathers worshiped on this mountain, but you say that the place where we must worship is in Jerusalem."

21Jesus said to her, "Believe me, woman, a time is coming when neither on this mountain nor in Jerusalem will you worship the Father. 22You worship what you do not know. We worship what we do know, for salvation is from the Jewish people. 23But a time is coming, and now is here, when true worshipers will worship the Father in spirit and truth. For the Father is seeking those who worship him in this way. 24God is spirit and those who worship him must worship him in spirit and truth."

25The woman said to him, "I know that Messiah is coming, the one who is called Christ. When that one comes, he will tell us all things."

26Jesus said to her, "I, the one who is speaking to you, am he."

Jesus Teaches the Disciples About the Harvest

27At that point his disciples arrived. They were shocked that he was speaking with a woman; yet no one said, "What are you seeking," or "Why are you speaking to her?"

28So, the woman left her water jar and went to the city and said to the men, 29"Come see a man who told me everything, as much as I have done. This is not the Christ, is it?" ³⁰They went out of the city and began coming toward him.

³¹Meanwhile his disciples were encouraging him, "Rabbi, eat."

³²But he responded to them, "I have food to eat that you do not comprehend."

³³So, his disciples began to ask each other, "No one has brought him something to eat, have they?"

³⁴Jesus said to them, "My food is that I do the will of the one who sent me, and that I complete his work. ³⁵You yourselves say, 'There are still four months and then the harvest will come,' don't you? Listen, I say to you, lift up your eyes and observe the fields. They are white for harvest. ³⁶The one who reaps is already receiving his wages, and he is gathering fruit for life eternal, so that the one who sows and the one who reaps might rejoice together. ³⁷For in this way the saying is true, 'One sows and another reaps.' ³⁸I sent you to reap what you yourselves have not toiled over. Others have toiled and you have entered into their labor."

Many Samaritans Believe in Jesus as Messiah

³⁹Many of the Samaritans from that city believed in him because of the report of the woman who testified, "He told me everything that I have done." ⁴⁰So, when the Samaritans came to him, they repeatedly asked him to stay with them; he remained there two days. ⁴¹Then many more believed on account of his message.

⁴²They were telling the woman, "We no longer believe because of your words, for we ourselves have heard, and we now know that this is truly the Savior of the world, the Christ."

Jesus Demonstrates Authority over Sickness: The Official's Son

⁴³Then, after two days, he departed from there for Galilee. ⁴⁴For Jesus himself had testified that a prophet does not have honor in his own hometown. ⁴⁵When he arrived in Galilee, the

Galileans welcomed him, because they had seen all the things he had done in Jerusalem at the feast—for they themselves had also gone to the feast.

⁴⁶So, he went again to Cana of Galilee, where he had made water into wine. There was a certain royal officer whose son was sick in Capernaum. ⁴⁷When he heard that Jesus had come from Judea to Galilee, he went to him and was asking that he might come down and heal his son, for he was about to die.

⁴⁸For this reason, Jesus said to him, "Unless you see signs and wonders, you will not believe."

⁴⁹The royal officer said to him, "Lord, come down before my child dies."

⁵⁰Jesus said to him, "Go, your son lives."

The man believed the message that Jesus spoke to him, and he started on his way. ⁵¹Then, while he was already on his way, his servants met him and told him that his child was living. ⁵²So, he asked them the hour when he had recovered. They said to him, "Yesterday at the seventh hour the fever left him."

⁵³The father knew that it was the same hour when Jesus said to him, "Your son lives." Then he himself believed, and his whole house.

⁵⁴This again was the second miraculous sign Jesus had done when he came from Judea to Galilee.

The Healing at Bethesda: Confronting the Human Heart

Chapter Five

¹After these things there was a feast of the Jewish people, and Jesus went up to Jerusalem. ²There is in Jerusalem, at the Sheep Gate, a pool called Bethesda in the Hebrew dialect.[i] It had five colonnades. ³A great number of those who were ill, blind, lame,

---

[i] That is, Aramaic.

and paralyzed used to lie in these colonnades waiting for the movement of the water. ⁴For at certain times, an angel went down into the pool and troubled the water. Then the first person who entered the pool after the water was stirred became healthy, free from whatever sickness which was limiting him.

⁵There was a certain man there who was sick for thirty-eight years. ⁶When Jesus saw this man lying down, and knew that he had already been lying there for a long time, he said to him, "Do you want to be healthy?"

⁷The one who was sick responded, "Lord, I do not have a man to place me in the pool when the water is troubled. So, while I am on the way by myself, another goes in before me."

⁸Jesus said to him, "Arise, pick up your mat, and walk around."

⁹Immediately, the man was restored to health. He took up his mat and walked around, but that day was a Sabbath day. ¹⁰So, the Jewish religious leaders said to the man who was healed, "It is the Sabbath, and it is not lawful for you to carry your mat."

¹¹But he responded to them, "The one who made me healthy, that man said to me, 'Take up your mat and walk around.'"

¹²They questioned him, "Who is the man who said to you, 'Take your mat and walk?'"

¹³The one who was healed did not know who it was, for Jesus had left without being seen while there was a crowd there. ¹⁴Jesus found him in the temple after these things, and said to him, "Look, you are healthy. Do not sin any longer so that nothing worse happens."

Jesus Does What the Father is Doing

¹⁵The man went out and reported to the Jewish religious leaders that Jesus was the one who had made him healthy. ¹⁶Because of this, the Jewish leaders began to persecute Jesus because he was doing these things on the Sabbath. ¹⁷But Jesus

responded to them, "My Father is working even now, and I also am working."

¹⁸For this reason, the Jewish leaders were seeking even more diligently to kill him. Because, not only was he violating the Sabbath, but he was also calling God his own Father, making himself equal to God.

¹⁹So, Jesus responded to them and said, "I am telling you the very truth, the Son is not able to do anything by himself, only what he sees the Father doing; for whatever the Father does, these things the Son also does. ²⁰For the Father loves the Son, and he shows him all the things that he himself is doing. He will show him even greater works than these, so that you might be astounded. ²¹Just as the Father raises the dead and gives life, so also the Son gives life to those he desires. ²²For the Father judges no one, but has given all judgment to the Son, ²³in order that everyone will honor the Son just as they honor the Father. The one who does not honor the Son, does not honor the Father who sent him.

Possessing Eternal Life

²⁴"I am telling you the very truth, the one who hears my word, and believes the one who sent me, possesses eternal life and will not come into judgment. On the contrary, he has crossed over from death to life. ²⁵I am telling you the very truth, an hour is coming and is here, when those who are dead will hear the voice of the Son of God, and those who hear will come to life. ²⁶For just as the Father has life in himself, in the same way he has given life to the Son to have in himself. ²⁷He has given authority to him to execute judgment, because he is the Son of Man.

²⁸"Do not be astonished by this, for an hour is coming when all those in their graves will hear his voice ²⁹and will come out; those who have done good to the resurrection of life, and those who have practiced evil, to the resurrection of judgment.

30"I am not able to do anything on my own. I judge just as I hear, and my judgment is fair; for I do not seek my will, but the will of the one who sent me. 31If I testify about myself, my testimony is not trustworthy,[i] 32but there is one who testifies about me, and I know that the testimony which he gives about me is trustworthy.

John and the Father Testify on Jesus' Behalf

33"You sent an inquiry to John, and he testified to the truth. 34I do not accept testimony from man, but I say these things so that you might be saved. 35John was a lamp that was burning and providing light, and you were willing to delight in his light for a short time.

36"But I have an even greater testimony than John, for the works which the Father has given me to complete—the very same works that I am doing—they testify about me that the Father has sent me. 37The Father who sent me, he has testified about me. You have never heard his voice, nor have you seen his appearance. 38You do not have his word residing in you, for you do not believe the one whom he has sent. 39You carefully investigate the Scriptures, for you suppose you possess eternal life in them, but those Scriptures are the ones that testify about me—40and you are not willing to come to me so that you might possess life.

The Religious Leaders Reject Messiah and Moses

41"I do not accept approval from men, 42quite the opposite, I have come to find out about you, because you do not possess the love of God within you. 43I have come in my Father's name, and you do not accept me. If another one comes in his own name, you will accept him. 44How can you believe when you receive approval from one another, but you do not seek the approval that is from the only God?

---

[i] The Law of Moses required at least two witnesses in order for testimony to be considered trustworthy. But see John 8:14 for the intrinsic value of Jesus' testimony.

⁴⁵"Do not suppose that I will accuse you before the Father. The one who accuses you is Moses, the one in whom you have hoped. ⁴⁶For if you believed Moses, you would believe me, for he wrote about me. ⁴⁷But if you do not believe his Scriptures, how will you believe my words?"

Jesus Multiplies Loaves of Bread and Fish for Five Thousand

Chapter Six

¹After these things, Jesus went across the Sea of Galilee, *also known as* the Sea of Tiberias. ²A great crowd followed him, because they saw the miraculous signs which he was doing for those who were sick. ³Then Jesus went up a mountain and sat down there with his disciples.

⁴Now, the Passover, the feast of the Jewish people, was near at hand. ⁵So, when Jesus lifted up his eyes and observed that a great crowd had come to him, he said to Philip, "Where can we purchase loaves of bread so that these people may eat?" ⁶But he asked this to test him. For he already knew what he was about to do.

⁷Philip responded to him, "Two hundred denarii[ii] worth of bread loaves would not be enough so that each one might receive a little."

⁸One of his disciples, Andrew the brother of Simon Peter, added, ⁹"There is a youngster here who has five barley loaves and two fish, but what are these for so many?"

[ii] A denarius is a day's wage for a soldier or a day laborer. Two hundred denarii would be about eight month's wages.

¹⁰Jesus said, "Make the men settle down[i] on the ground." Now there was a great deal of grass in that place. So, the men settled down. They numbered around five thousand.[ii]

¹¹So, Jesus took the loaves, and when he had given thanks, he divided it to those who had settled down on the ground. In the same way, he distributed the fish, as much as they wanted.

¹²But when they were full, he said to his disciples, "Gather the leftover pieces, so that nothing is lost." ¹³So, they gathered them and filled twelve large baskets of the pieces from the five barley loaves that were left over by those who had eaten.

Jesus Walks Out to His Disciples on the Sea

¹⁴When the men saw the miraculous sign he had done, they were commenting, "This is truly the prophet, the one who is coming into the world." ¹⁵Then, when Jesus recognized that they were about to come and take him by force so that they might make him king, he withdrew again to the mountain alone by himself.

¹⁶But when evening had come, his disciples had gone down to the sea. ¹⁷They had embarked in a boat and begun to go across the sea to Capernaum. It had already grown dark, and Jesus had not yet gone out to them. ¹⁸The sea began to awaken because a strong wind was blowing. ¹⁹Then, when they had rowed twenty-five or thirty stadia,[iii] and when they noticed Jesus walking upon the sea coming near the boat, they were frightened. ²⁰But he called to them, "It is I; do not be afraid." ²¹So, they were willing to take him into the boat, and the boat immediately arrived at the shore where they had intended to go.

---

[i] More literally, "Make the men recline." Jewish custom was to recline on one elbow to eat meals (Also in verse eleven).

[ii] Estimates are that between fifteen and twenty thousand people were present.

[iii] That is, about three or four miles.

John 6:34

Jesus Reveals That He is the Bread of Life

22On the next day, the crowd that had stayed across the sea recognized that there had been no other boat there except the one, and that Jesus had not gone with his disciples into the boat. The disciples had departed alone. 23Other small boats came from Tiberias, which was near the place where they had eaten the bread after the Lord had given thanks. 24So, when the crowds recognized that neither Jesus nor his disciples were there, they embarked in the small boats and came to Capernaum seeking Jesus.

25When they found him across the sea, they asked him, "Rabbi, when did you get here?"

26Jesus answered and said, "I am telling you the very truth, you are seeking me, not because you saw miraculous signs, but because you ate the loaves of bread and your stomachs were filled. 27Don't work for food that does not last, but for the food which remains to life eternal, which the Son of Man will give to you, for God the Father has set his seal upon him."

28Then they asked him, "What should we do so that we might carry out the works of God?"

29Jesus answered and said to them, "This is the work of God, that you believe in that one whom he has sent."

30So, they asked him, "Then what miraculous sign will you do, that we might see and believe you? What work will you do? 31Our fathers ate manna in the wilderness, just as it is written, 'He gave them bread from heaven to eat.'[iv] "

32"Then Jesus said to them, "I am telling you the very truth, Moses did not give the bread from heaven to you, but my Father is giving you the true bread from heaven. 33For the bread of God is the one who comes down from heaven and gives life to the world."

34So, they said to him, "Lord, always give us this bread."

[iv] See Nehemiah 9:15.

John 6:35

35Jesus said to them, "I am the bread of life; the one who comes to me will most certainly never hunger, and the one believing in me will most certainly never thirst at any time. 36But I have said to you, 'You have seen me but do not believe.' 37Everything[i] the Father gives to me will come to me, and I will most certainly never send him away who comes to me. 38For I have come down from heaven, not that I do my own will, but the will of the one who sent me. 39This is the will of the one who sent me, that I do not lose anything that he has given to me; instead, I will raise it up on the last day. 40For this is the will of my Father, that everyone who recognizes the Son and believes in him might have life eternal, and I myself will raise him on the last day."

Jesus is the True Manna from Heaven

41Then the Jewish leaders began to grumble about him, because he said, "I am the bread that came down from heaven." 42They were saying, "This is Jesus the son of Joseph, isn't it? We know his father and mother. How can he now say that he has come down from heaven?"

43Jesus responded and said to them, "Stop complaining to each other. 44No one is able to come to me if the Father who sent me does not compel him. Then I will raise him on the last day. 45It is written in the prophets,

> " 'And everyone will be instructed by God.'[ii]

"Everyone who has heard and learned from the Father, comes to me. 46Not that anyone has seen the Father except the one who is from God; this one has seen the Father. 47I am telling you the very truth, the one who believes possesses eternal life.

48"I am the bread of life. 49Your fathers ate the manna in the wilderness; even so they died. 50This is the bread that is coming down from heaven, so that one can eat of it and not die. 51I am

---

[i] "Everything" is a neuter adjective, so Jesus is intentionally not saying, "Everyone" in this verse. He uses "Everyone" in verse 40.

[ii] See Isaiah 54:13.

the living bread that has come down from heaven. If someone eats from this bread, he will live to the coming age. The bread that I will give for the life of this world is my flesh."

⁵²Then the Jewish leaders began to quarrel with one another asking, "How is this man able to give us his flesh to eat?"

⁵³So, Jesus said to them, "I am telling you the very truth, if you do not eat the flesh of the Son of Man, and drink his blood, you do not have life within you. ⁵⁴The one who consumes my flesh and drinks my blood possesses eternal life, and I will raise him on the last day. ⁵⁵For my flesh is genuine food, and my blood is genuine drink. ⁵⁶The one who consumes my flesh and drinks my blood lives in me and I in him. ⁵⁷Just as the living Father has sent me, and I am living because of the Father, the one who consumes me will live because of me. ⁵⁸This is the bread which has come down from heaven, it is not like *the bread* the fathers ate and died; the one who consumes this bread will live to the coming age." ⁵⁹He said these things while teaching in a synagogue in Capernaum.

Even Though Many Desert, Peter and the Disciples Hold Fast

⁶⁰Then many from among his disciples who had heard said, "This is a challenging teaching. Can anyone understand it?"

⁶¹But Jesus knew within himself that his disciples were complaining about this and questioned them, "Does this make you stumble? ⁶²Therefore, what if you see the Son of Man going up to where he was at first? ⁶³The Spirit is the one who gives life, the flesh contributes nothing. The words which I have spoken to you are spirit and life. ⁶⁴But there are some from among you who do not believe."

For from the beginning, Jesus knew the ones who did not believe, and the one who would hand him over to his enemies. ⁶⁵He also added, "This is why I mentioned to you that no one is able to come to me if it is not granted to him by the Father."

John 6:66

⁶⁶From this point, many from among his disciples turned back and no longer walked with him. ⁶⁷So, Jesus asked the twelve, "You do not also want to go away, do you?"

⁶⁸Simon Peter answered him, "Lord, to whom would we go? You have the words of life eternal, ⁶⁹and we have believed, and understand, that you are the Holy One of God."

⁷⁰Jesus responded to them, "I myself have chosen you, the twelve, haven't I? And even one from among you is a devil." ⁷¹But Jesus was speaking about Judas, the son of Simon Iscariot. For this man, one of the twelve, was soon to hand him over to his enemies.

Jesus Brothers' Do Not Accept Jesus' Divine Mission

Chapter Seven

¹After these things, Jesus was walking about in Galilee, for he did not want to travel about in Judea because the Jewish leaders were looking for a way to kill him. ²Now the Jewish Feast of Tabernacles was near at hand. ³So, his brothers said to him, "Move on from here and go into Judea, so that your disciples can see the works that you do. ⁴No one does anything in secret when he is seeking to be well known. If you are doing these things, reveal yourself to the world." ⁵For his brothers did not believe in him.

⁶So, Jesus said to them, "My opportune time has not yet come, but your time is always at hand. ⁷The world is not able to hate you, but it hates me because I testify about it that its actions are evil. ⁸You go up to the feast. I am not yet going up to this feast because my time still has not fully arrived."

⁹Then, when he had shared these things, he remained in Galilee.¹⁰But his brothers went up to the feast. Then Jesus himself went up, not openly but in secret. ¹¹So, the Jewish leaders were seeking him at the feast and asking, "Where is that man?"

¹²There was much controversy about him in the crowds. On the one hand, they were saying, "He is a good man."

But others were also saying, "No! Instead, he is deceiving the public." ¹³Nevertheless, no one spoke freely about him on account of their fear of the Jewish leaders.

Jesus Confronts the Lawbreakers

¹⁴But when the feast was half over, Jesus went up to the temple and began to teach. ¹⁵Then the Jewish leaders were startled, and said, "How has this man acquired an education, since he has not had formal training?"

¹⁶So, Jesus responded to them and explained, "My teaching is not mine, but *it is from* the one who sent me. ¹⁷If anyone wants to do his will, he will know about my teaching, whether I am speaking from God or I am speaking on my own. ¹⁸The one who speaks from himself is seeking his own glory, but the one seeking the glory of the one who sent him, this one is honest, and there is no unrighteousness in him. ¹⁹Moses gave you the Law, didn't he? But no one carries out the Law. Why are you seeking to kill me?"

²⁰The crowd responded, "You have a demon! Who is seeking to kill you?"

²¹Jesus responded to them and said, "I have done one healing,[i] and you are all filled with wonder. ²²Moses gave you circumcision —not that it came from Moses, but from the fathers—and for this reason you circumcise a man on the Sabbath. ²³If a man can receive circumcision on the Sabbath and the Law of Moses is not compromised, why are you angry with me because I made a whole man healthy on the Sabbath? ²⁴Do not judge by external appearance, but judge with righteous judgment."

Dissension About Jesus

²⁵Then some of the people from Jerusalem were asking, "This is the one they are seeking to kill, isn't it? ²⁶Now look, he is

---

[i] More literally, "I have done one work," referring to healing at Bethesda.

speaking freely and they are not saying anything to him. The rulers haven't actually recognized that he is the Christ, have they? ²⁷But we already know where this man is from; but when the Christ comes, no one will know where he is from."

²⁸So, Jesus cried out while he was still teaching in the temple, and said, "You know me and you know where I am from. I have not come on my own, but the one who has sent me is true. You yourselves do not know him. ²⁹I myself know him, because I am from him, and he sent me."

³⁰Therefore, they were seeking to arrest him, but no one laid a hand on him, because his hour had not yet come. ³¹But many from the crowd believed in him and repeatedly asked, "When the Christ comes, will he do more miraculous signs than what this man has done?"

³²The Pharisees heard the crowd creating controversy over these things, and the chief priests and Pharisees sent officers to arrest him.

³³Then Jesus said, "I am with you for a little time yet, then I am going to the one who sent me. ³⁴You will seek me, but you will not find me, and where I am, you will not be able to come."

³⁵Then the Jewish leaders asked one another, "Where is this man about to go that we will not find him? He isn't about to go to the Diaspora[i] among the Greeks in order to teach the Greeks, is he? ³⁶What is this statement that he made, 'You will seek me, but you will not find me,' and 'Where I am, you will not be able to come'?"

³⁷Now on the last great day of the feast, when Jesus took a stand, he cried out and said, "If anyone has a thirst, let him come to me and drink. ³⁸The one who believes in me, just as the Scripture states, rivers of living water will flow from his

---

[i] The Diaspora refers to the dispersion of the Jewish people among the Gentiles throughout the Mediterranean world.

midsection.ⁱⁱ" ³⁹But he said this in reference to the Spirit, whom those who believed in Jesus were about to receive; for the Spirit was not yet *given*, because Jesus was not yet glorified.

⁴⁰Then, when *some* from the crowd heard these words, they began to say, "This is truly the Prophet.ⁱⁱⁱ"

⁴¹Others began to say, "This is the Christ."

But others were asking, "No. The Christ will not come from Galilee, will he? ⁴²The Scripture says that the Christ comes from the seed of David, and from Bethlehem, the village where David was *born*, doesn't it?"

⁴³Therefore, there was dissension in the crowd because of him. ⁴⁴In fact, some from among them wanted to arrest him, but no one laid their hands on him. ⁴⁵Then the officers came to the chief priests and Pharisees, and these *leaders* said to them,

"Why haven't you brought him?"

⁴⁶The officers answered, "No man has ever spoken in this way."

⁴⁷Then the Pharisees responded to them, "You aren't also deceived, are you? ⁴⁸No one has believed in him from among the rulers or from among the Pharisees, have they? ⁴⁹But this crowd which does not know the Law, they are under a curse."

⁵⁰Nicodemus, the one who came to him earlier, and was one of them, asked them, ⁵¹"Our Law does not condemn a man unless first it hears from him and investigates what he is doing, does it?"

⁵²They responded and said to him, "You aren't also from Galilee, are you? Search it out and see that a prophet does not arise from Galilee."

ⁱⁱ Midsection is a translation of a word that generally means belly, or inner parts of the torso.

ⁱⁱⁱ See Deuteronomy 18:15. The Prophet like Moses.

⁵³Then, each of them went to his *own* home, ⁸:¹but Jesus went out to the Mount of Olives.

The Pharisees Test Jesus: The Woman Caught in Adultery

Chapter Eight

²At daybreak, he again arrived at the temple, and all the people came to him. When he sat down, he began to teach them. ³The scribal scholars and Pharisees led in a woman who had been arrested while committing adultery, and when they placed her in the middle *of the people*, ⁴they questioned him, "Teacher, this woman was arrested while in the act of committing adultery. ⁵Now, Moses commanded in the Law to stone such a woman as this; therefore, what do you say?"

⁶But they were asking this to test him, so that they might bring charges against him. Then Jesus bent forward to the ground and began to write on it with his finger. ⁷So, when they continued to question him, he looked up and said, "Let the one who is without fault throw the first stone at her." ⁸Then again, he bent forward and wrote on the ground.

⁹But when her accusers heard, and because they were convicted by their conscience, they began to leave one by one, beginning with the elders, until he was left alone; and the woman was still in the middle of the people. ¹⁰Then, Jesus looked up and asked her, "Woman, where are they, those who spoke against you? No one has condemned you, have they?"

¹¹So, she said, "No one, Lord."

Then Jesus said to her, "Neither do I condemn you. Go, and from this time forward, stop committing *this* sin."

The Light of the World

¹²Then again, Jesus spoke to them and said, "I am the light of the world. The one who follows me will most certainly never walk about in darkness; instead he will have the light of life."

¹³Therefore, the Pharisees said to him, "You yourself give testimony about yourself. Your testimony is not trustworthy."

¹⁴Jesus responded and said, "Even if I am giving testimony about myself, my testimony is trustworthy, for I know where I have come from, and where I am going. But you do not know where I have come from or where I am going. ¹⁵You judge according to the flesh; I am not judging anyone. ¹⁶Even if I should pass judgment, my judgment is true, for I am not alone; on the contrary, I and the Father who sent me *would be the ones passing judgment.* ¹⁷In your own Law it is written that the testimony of two men is trustworthy. ¹⁸I am the one giving testimony about myself, and the Father who sent me also bears testimony about me."

¹⁹So, they began asking him, "Where is your father?"

Jesus answered, "You do not know me nor my Father. If you knew me, you would also know my Father." ²⁰He spoke these words while teaching by the offering boxes in the temple, yet no one arrested him, because his hour had not yet come.

²¹Then again, he said to them, "I myself am going away, and you will seek me, but you will die in your sins. Where I am going you are not able to come."

²²So, the Jewish leaders began to ask, "He will not kill himself, will he? For he has said, 'Where I myself am going, you are not able to come.'"

²³He was also telling them, "You are from that which is below, I am from that which is above; you are from this world, I am not from this world. ²⁴For this reason, I told you that you will die in your sins, for if you do not believe that I am he, you will die in your sins."

²⁵So, they were asking him, "Who are you?"

Jesus replied to them, "What I was telling you from the beginning. ²⁶I have much to say about you, and to judge, but the one who sent me is truthful, and what I have heard from him, these things I am telling the world."

²⁷They did not understand that he was speaking of the Father to them. ²⁸So, Jesus said to them, "When you lift up the Son of Man on high, then you will know that I am he, and I am doing nothing by myself; but I am sharing these things in the same way as the Father has taught me. ²⁹The one who sent me is also with me, he has not left me alone; for I always do the things that are pleasing to him."

Some Believe in Jesus, Some Believe About Jesus

³⁰While he was saying these things, many believed in him. ³¹Therefore, Jesus said to the Jewish leaders who had believed about him,ⁱ "If you remain in my word, you are truly my disciples, ³²and you will know the truth, and the truth will give you freedom."

³³They responded to him, "We are Abraham's offspring, and have never been enslaved by anyone. How can you say, 'You will become free,'?"

³⁴Jesus answered them, "I am telling you the very truth, everyone who makes a habit of sin is a slave of sin, ³⁵but the slave does not remain in the house forever. The Son does remain forever. ³⁶So, if the Son gives you freedom, you are really free. ³⁷I know that you are Abraham's offspring; but you are seeking to kill me, because my word is not getting through to you. ³⁸I am speaking the things which I have seen at the side of my Father; therefore, you also do the things which you have heard at the side of your father."

Jesus Identifies the True Father of These Religious Leaders

³⁹They responded and said to him, "Our father is Abraham."

ⁱ Throughout the book of John, to believe "in" Jesus (using the preposition) means to have saving faith in him. To "believe Jesus" (using the dative case) means to intellectually acknowledge that what he is saying is true. That may include saving faith, but the context will tell.

Jesus said to them, "If you are children of Abraham, you are obligated to do the works of Abraham. ⁴⁰But right now, you are seeking to kill me, a man who has spoken the truth to you, truth which I heard at the side of God. Abraham did not do this. ⁴¹You are doing the works of your father."

Then they said to him, "We were not born as the result of an illicit sexual relationship; we have one Father, God."

⁴²Jesus said to them, "If God were your Father, you would love me, for I have come from God and am now present here. I have not come on my own, but he sent me. ⁴³Why don't you understand my speech? It is because you are not able to understand my Word. ⁴⁴You are from your father, the Accuser,ⁱⁱ and you want to do the will of your father. He was a murderer from the beginning, and he does not stand in the truth, because there is no truth in him. When he speaks the lie, he is speaking from what is his own, because he is a liar and the father of the lie. ⁴⁵But because I am telling the truth, you do not believe me."

⁴⁶"Who from among you can bring proof that I have sinned? If I am speaking truth, why don't you yourselves believe me? ⁴⁷The one who is from God hears the words of God; for this reason, you do not hear, because you are not from God."

⁴⁸The Jewish leaders responded and said to him, "We are right when we say that you are a Samaritan and have a demon, aren't we?"

Jesus Promises That Those who Believe will not See Death

⁴⁹"Jesus answered, "I do not have a demon, but I honor my Father, and you dishonor me. ⁵⁰But I am not seeking my glory; there is one who is seeking *it*, and he is the one who judges. ⁵¹I am telling you the very truth, if anyone keeps my Word, he will most certainly never see death."

ⁱⁱ Traditionally, "devil." The name means to slander or accuse. For this reason, this word is most often translated "Accuser" in this Bible version.

⁵²Then the Jewish leaders said to him, "Now we know that you have a demon. Abraham died, and the prophets; yet you say, 'If anyone keeps my Word, he will most certainly never taste death.' ⁵³You are not greater than our father Abraham who died, are you? The prophets also died. What are you making yourself?"

⁵⁴Jesus answered, "If I give glory to myself, my glory is nothing; my Father is the one who gives me glory. He is the one that you say is your God, ⁵⁵even though you do not know him. But I know him, and if I say that I do not know him, I will be a liar like you. However, I do know him, and I keep his word. ⁵⁶Your father Abraham rejoiced that he might see my day. He saw it and was glad."

⁵⁷Then the Jewish leaders said to him, "You have not yet lived fifty years, and you have seen Abraham?"

⁵⁸Jesus said to them, "I am telling you the very truth, before Abraham existed, I AM."[i]

⁵⁹Then they gathered stones so that they might throw them at him, but Jesus hid himself and left the temple.

Jesus Heals a Man on the Sabbath who was Blind from Birth

Chapter Nine

¹While Jesus was leaving *the temple*, he saw a man who was blind from birth. ²His disciples questioned him asking, "Rabbi, who sinned, this man or his parents, that he was born blind?"

³Jesus answered, "Neither this man nor his parents *sinned*, but it is so that the works of God might be revealed in him. ⁴We must do the works of the one who sent me while the day lasts; night is coming when no one is able to work. ⁵When I am in the world, I am the light of the world."

⁶After he said these things, he spat on the ground and made mud from the saliva, and he anointed the man's eyes with the

---

[i] Compare Exodus 3:14. This was a clear statement of deity.

mud. ⁷Then he said to him, "Go wash in the pool of Siloam" (which is translated "Sent"). So, he went away and washed *in the pool*, and came away seeing.

⁸Therefore, his neighbors and those who had seen him previously, because he was a beggar, were asking, "This is the man who was sitting and begging, isn't it?"

⁹Some were saying, "This is *the man*."

Still others said, "No, but it is someone like him."

That man kept saying, "I am that man."

¹⁰So, they continued to ask him, "Then how were your eyes opened?"

¹¹That man answered, "The man named Jesus made mud, anointed my eyes with it, and said to me, 'Go and wash in Siloam.' So, I went away and when I washed, I was able to see."

¹²They also asked him, "Where is that man?" He said, "I do not know."

The Trial of the Man Born Blind

¹³They brought the man who was once blind to the Pharisees, ¹⁴for the day on which Jesus made mud and opened his eyes was a Sabbath. ¹⁵So, the Pharisees questioned him once more about how he could see. Then he said to them, "He put mud on my eyes; I washed and I can see."

¹⁶Therefore, some from among the Pharisees were saying, "This man is not from God, for he does not keep the Sabbath."

But others asked, "How is a sinful man able to do miraculous signs such as these?" And there was dissension among them.

¹⁷So, they asked the blind man again, "What do you say about him, for he opened your eyes?"

Then he said, "He is a prophet."

¹⁸Because the Jewish leaders did not believe *the report* about him, that he had been blind and received his sight, they called

John 9:19

the parents of the man who had received his sight. [19]They questioned them asking, "Is this man your son, who you say was born blind? Then how can he see now?"

[20]Then his parent answered and said, "We know that this man is our son, and that he was born blind, [21]but how he is able to see now, we do not know; or who opened his eyes, we ourselves do not know. Ask him. He has standing."

[22]His parents said these things because they were afraid of the Jewish leaders; for the Jewish leaders had already decided that anyone who acknowledged Jesus as the Christ would be banished from the synagogue. [23]For this reason, his parents said, "He has standing, ask him."

[24]Then they questioned the man who was blind a second time, and said to him, "Give glory to God. We know that this man is a sinner."

[25]Therefore, that man said, "If he is a sinner, I do not know. I do know one thing, that I was blind but now I see."

[26]Then they asked him, "What did he do to you? How did he open your eyes?"

[27]He responded to them, "I told you already, and you did not listen. Why do you want to hear again? You don't want to become his disciples also, do you?"

[28]Then they raged against him and said, "You are a disciple of that man, but we are disciples of Moses. [29]We ourselves know that God spoke to Moses, but we do not know where this man is from."

[30]The man responded and said to them, "Truly this is shocking; you do not know where he is from, yet he opened my eyes. [31]We know that God doesn't listen to sinners, but if anyone is a sincere worshiper of God and does his will, God hears him. [32]Never, from time eternal, has anyone heard that someone opened the eyes of a man who was born blind. [33]If this man was not from God, he would not be able to do anything."

³⁴They responded and said to him, "You were born in sins, your entire being, and you are teaching us?" Then they banished him *from the synagogue.*

³⁵Jesus heard that they had banished him, and when he found him, he asked, "Do you believe in the Son of Man?"

³⁶That man responded and said, "Who is he, sir, that I might believe in him?"

³⁷Jesus said to him, "You have seen him, and the one speaking with you is that one."

³⁸Then he said, "I believe, Lord;" and he worshiped him.

³⁹Jesus also said, "I have come into this world for judgment, in order that those who do not see might see, and those who see might become blind."

⁴⁰Those who were with him from among the Pharisees heard these things and asked, "We are not blind also, are we?"

⁴¹Jesus said to them, "If you were blind, you would not have sin; but now you say, 'We see,' your sin remains.

The Pharisees did not Recognize the Good Shepherd

Chapter Ten

¹"I am telling you the very truth, the one who does not come into the sheep pen through the gate, but goes in some other way, that man is a thief and a robber. ²The man who comes in through the gate is the shepherd of the sheep. ³The gatekeeper opens the gate for this man, and the sheep hear his voice. He calls his own sheep by name, and he leads them out. ⁴When he leads all of his own *sheep* out, he goes in front of them and the sheep follow after him, because they know his voice. ⁵But they will never follow a stranger; instead, they will flee from him, because they do not know the stranger's voice."

⁶Jesus shared this proverb with them, but they did not understand what it was that he was telling them. ⁷So, Jesus said

again, "I am telling you the very truth, I am the gate for the sheep. ⁸All, the many that came before me, were thieves and robbers, but the sheep did not listen to them. ⁹I am the gate. If anyone enters through me, he will be saved. He will go in and he will go out and find pasture. ¹⁰The thief only comes that he might steal, slaughter, and destroy. I have come that they might have life, and that they might have it in overflowing abundance."

¹¹"I am the good shepherd; the good shepherd dedicates his life on behalf of the sheep. ¹²When one who is hired, who is not the shepherd and does not own the sheep, sees a wolf coming, he abandons the sheep and flees. Then the wolf plunders them and scatters them. ¹³He abandons them because he is a hired hand, and he is not concerned about the sheep."

¹⁴"I am the good shepherd. I know my own, and those who are mine know me; ¹⁵just as the Father knows me and I know the Father, and I dedicate my life on behalf of the sheep. ¹⁶I also have other sheep that are not from this sheep pen. I must also bring them, and those sheep will hear my voice; there will be one flock, and one shepherd. ¹⁷For this reason, my Father loves me, because I dedicate my life so that I might receive it back again. ¹⁸No one takes it from me, but I dedicate it on my own. I have authority to dedicate it, and I have authority to take it again. I received this command from my Father."

¹⁹Dissension arose again among the Jewish leaders because of these words. ²⁰Many from among them said, "He has a demon and is experiencing demonic rapture.ⁱ Why are you listening to him?"

²¹Others were saying, "These words are not from a man who is demon possessed. A demon is not able to open the eyes of the blind, is it?"

ⁱ This Greek word was often used to describe spiritual ecstatic phenomena, in this context, they refer to an experience caused by demons, not God.

Jesus and the Father are One

²²At the time that the festival of Hanukkah[ii] took place in Jerusalem. It was winter. ²³Then Jesus was walking about in Solomon's Colonnade at the temple. ²⁴So the Jewish leaders surrounded him and kept questioning him, "When will you lift the suspense? If you are the Christ, tell us candidly."

²⁵Jesus responded to them, "I told you, but you did not believe. The works that I am doing in the name of my Father, these things testify about me; ²⁶but you do not believe, because you are not from among my sheep. ²⁷My sheep have come to know my voice, I know them, and they follow me. ²⁸I give life eternal to them, and they will certainly never stray *from me* in this age; and no one is able to steal them from my hand. ²⁹My Father, the one who gave them to me, is greater than all, and no one is able to steal them from the hand of the Father. ³⁰I and the Father, we are one."

The Blind Leaders Attempt to Stone the Good Shepherd

³¹Again, the Jewish leaders collected stones so that they might stone him. ³²Jesus responded to them, "I showed you many praiseworthy works from the Father; for which of them are you planning to stone me?"

³³The Jewish leaders responded to him, "We are not stoning you for your morally excellent work, but for blasphemy, and that you, being a man, make yourself a god."

³⁴Jesus responded to them, "It is written in your law, 'I have said you are gods,'[iii] isn't it? ³⁵If he called them gods, to whom the word of God came—and the Scripture cannot be proven false—³⁶what about the one whom the Father dedicated and sent into the world? Why do you say, 'You are blaspheming,'[iv]

[ii] Or, "the Festival of Dedication," that is, Hanukkah.

[iii] Psalm 82:6

[iv] Blasphemy is about speaking profanely of sacred things, to slander God, or to speak against him.

because I said, 'I am the Son of God'? ³⁷If I am not doing the works of my Father, do not believe me. ³⁸But if I am doing them, even though you do not believe me, believe the works, that you might come to know and understand that the Father is in me, and I am in the Father."

³⁹Therefore, they began to seek a way to restrain him by force, but he escaped from their hands.

Many Put Their Faith in Jesus

⁴⁰Then he went again across the Jordan to the place where John was baptizing at the beginning; and he remained there. ⁴¹Many people came to him, and they were saying, "John did not do any miraculous signs, but everything John said about this man was true;" ⁴²and many believed in him there.

Lazarus Dies

Chapter Eleven

¹There was a certain man, named Lazarus, who was sick. He was from Bethany, the village of Mary and her sister, Martha. ²It was Mary's brother, Lazarus, who was sick. She was the one who anointed the Lord with aromatic oil and wiped his feet with her hair. ³Because he was sick, the sisters sent a message to Jesus that said, "Lord, look, the one whom you love is sick."

⁴When Jesus heard the message, he sent a reply,ⁱ "This sickness isn't so that Lazarus dies, but for the glory of God, so that the Son of God might be glorified through it."

⁵Jesus loved Martha, her sister, and Lazarus. ⁶Therefore, when he heard that Lazarus was sick, he then stayed in the place where he was two days. ⁷After this, he said to his disciples, "Let us go to Judea again."

ⁱ Verse 40 demonstrates that he sent this reply to the sisters.

John 11:22

⁸The disciples said to him, "Rabbi, the Jewish religious leaders are now watching for you to stone you, and you are going there again?"

⁹Jesus responded, "There are twelve hours in a day, aren't there? If a man walks during the day, he will not stumble, because he sees *by* the light of this world. ¹⁰But if a man walks during the night, he will stumble because the light is not available to him."

¹¹After Jesus said these things, he said to them, "Our friend Lazarus has fallen asleep, but I am going in order that I might wake him."

¹²Then his disciples responded to him, "Lord, if he has fallen asleep, he will get well again." ¹³Jesus had been speaking about his death, but they thought that that he was speaking about normal sleep.

¹⁴Then Jesus spoke to them clearly, "Lazarus has died, ¹⁵and for your sakes, I am glad that I was not there, so that you might believe. Now let us go to him."

¹⁶Then Thomas, who was called Twin,ⁱⁱ said to his fellow disciples, "Let us also go, that we might die with him."

Jesus is the Resurrection and the Life

¹⁷When Jesus came, he found that Lazarus had already been in the grave four days. ¹⁸Bethany was near Jerusalem, about fifteen stadia,ⁱⁱⁱ ¹⁹so, many of the religious leaders had come to Martha and Mary in order that they might comfort them about their brother. ²⁰Because of this, when Martha heard that Jesus was coming, she went out to meet him; but Mary remained seated at the house.

²¹Then Martha said to Jesus, "Lord, if you had been here, my brother would not have died, ²²but even now, I know that anything you ask God, God will give to you."

ⁱⁱ The Greek word for "Twin" is "Didymus."

ⁱⁱⁱ This is less than two miles.

²³Jesus said to her, "Your brother will rise again."

²⁴Martha said to him, "I know that he will rise in the resurrection at the last day."

²⁵Jesus said to her, "I am the resurrection and the life. Anyone who believes in me will live, even though he has died; ²⁶and everyone who is living and believes in me will never ever die. Do you believe this?"

²⁷She said to him, "Yes, Lord, I believe that you are the Christ, the Son of God, the one coming into the world."

²⁸After she said this, she went and called her sister Mary secretly and said, "The teacher is here and is asking for you." ²⁹When she heard it, she quickly got up and went to meet him. ³⁰Jesus had not yet come into the village but was still in the place where Martha had met him.

³¹So, when the Jewish leaders, who were with her in the house comforting her, saw Mary get up quickly and leave, they followed her, believing that she was going to the tomb so she could weep there.

³²When Mary arrived where he was and saw him, she fell at his feet and said to him, "Lord, if you had been here, my brother would not have died."

³³When Jesus saw her weeping, and the Jewish leaders who had come with her weeping, he became angry in his spirit and shook himself. ³⁴He asked, "Where have you buried him?"

They said to him, "Lord, come and see."

³⁵Jesus broke into tears.

³⁶So, the Jewish religious leaders began to say, "Look how he loved him."

³⁷But some from among them responded, "Could not this man, who opened the eyes of the blind man, have also done something so that this man would not have died?"

Jesus Demonstrates His Authority over Death: Raising Lazarus

38So, Jesus was again angry within himself as he arrived at the tomb. It was a cave, and a stone was covering the entrance. 39Jesus said, "Take away the stone."

Martha, the sister of the one who had died, said to him, "Lord, there is already a bad smell, for it has been four days."

40But Jesus said to her, "Did I not tell you that if you believed you will see the glory of God?"

41So, they took away the stone. Then Jesus raised his eyes upward and said, "Father, I give thanks to you that you have heard me. 42I know that you always hear me, but on account of the crowd standing around, I am saying this, in order that they might believe that you sent me."

43After he said these things, he called out with a loud voice, "Lazarus, come out!"

44The one who had died came out, with his feet and hands still bound with strips of cloth, and his face still wrapped with a burial cloth.

Jesus said to them, "Untie him and let him go."

Caiaphas Prophesies the Reason for Jesus' Death

45Then, many of the Jewish leaders who had come to Mary, and saw what he had done, believed in him; 46but some from among them went to the Pharisees and told them what Jesus had done. 47So, the chief priests and the Pharisees called together the Sanhedrin.

They said, "How are we to act since this man is doing many miraculous signs? 48If we permit him *to go on* like this, everyone will believe in him, and the Romans will come and take away our place and our nation."

49Then one who was from among them, Caiaphas, who was the high priest that year, said to them, "You do not know anything! 50Nor do you consider that it is better for you that one man die on behalf of the people so that the whole nation doesn't perish."

⁵¹But he did not speak this by himself, rather, because he was high priest that year, he prophesied that Jesus was about to die on behalf of the nation; ⁵²and not on behalf of the nation alone, but so that he might also gather the children of God, who had been scattered abroad, into one *family*.

The Religious Leaders Plan to Kill Jesus

⁵³So, from that day, they made plans so that they might kill him. ⁵⁴Therefore, Jesus no longer walked freely among the Jewish leaders, but left there for the region close to the wilderness, to a city named Ephraim; and he remained there with his disciples.

⁵⁵Now the Jewish Passover was close, and many were going up to Jerusalem from the country for the Passover, in order that they might purify themselves. ⁵⁶They were looking for Jesus, and as they stood in the temple, they kept asking one another, "What do you think? He has certainly come to the feast, hasn't he?" ⁵⁷But the chief priests and the Pharisees had given orders that if anyone found out where he was, he was to reveal it so that they might arrest him.

Jesus Prepared for His Burial

Chapter Twelve

¹Then Jesus came to Bethany six days before the Passover. This was where Lazarus lived, the one who had died, whom Jesus raised from among the dead. ²So, they made a dinner for him there, and Martha was serving, but Lazarus was one of those who was reclining *at the table* with him. ³Then Mary took a Roman pound[i] of very valuable genuine aromatic oil of nard,

---

[i] An ancient Roman pound, which was about 12 ounces or a bit less than half a liter by volume.

anointed Jesus' feet, and wiped his feet with her hair. The house was filled with the aroma of the perfumed oil.

⁴But Judas, son of Simon Iscariot, one of his disciples, who was about to hand him over to his enemies asked, ⁵"Why wasn't this aromatic oil sold for three hundred denarii[ii] and *the money given to the poor?* ⁶Now he said this, not because the poor concerned him, but because he was a thief; and since he kept their wallet, he often stole the money that was put into it.

⁷Therefore, Jesus said, "Leave her alone. She has saved it for this day of my burial preparation. ⁸For you will always have the poor people with you, but you will not always have me."

Jesus and Lazarus Draw a Crowd

⁹Then a large crowd from among the Jewish people recognized that he was there, and came, not only on account of Jesus, but also in order that they might see Lazarus whom he raised from among the dead. ¹⁰Then, the chief priests took counsel that they might also kill Lazarus, ¹¹because on account of him many from among the Jewish people were beginning to leave *them* and believe in Jesus.

The King Arrives at Jerusalem

¹²The next day, when the large crowd that had come to the festival heard that Jesus was coming into Jerusalem, ¹³they took the branches of palm trees and went out to meet him. They were shouting,

> "Hosanna! Blessed is the one coming in the name of the Lord. He is the King of Israel."[iii]

¹⁴When Jesus found a young donkey, he sat upon it, just as it is written,

---

[ii] A denarius is a day's wage for a soldier or a day laborer. Three hundred denarii would be about a year's wages.

[iii] Psalm 118:25-26

¹⁵"Stop being afraid, Daughter of Zion; Look, your king is coming sitting on the colt of a donkey."ⁱ

¹⁶His disciples did not recognize these things at first, but when Jesus was glorified, then they remembered that these things were written about him, and they had done these things to him.

¹⁷The crowd that was with him when he called Lazarus out of the tomb and raised him from among the dead, began to share their testimony *about* it. ¹⁸So, the crowds met him, for they had heard that he had done this miraculous sign. ¹⁹Then, the Pharisees said among themselves, "You all see that you are not helping at all. Look, the world has gone after him."

The Greeks are a Sign of Jesus' Impending Death

²⁰Now there were some Greeks from among those who had gone up that they might worship at the festival. ²¹Then they came to Philip, who was from Bethsaida in Galilee, and they made a request of him asking, "Sir, we want to see Jesus." ²²Philip came and spoke to Andrew; Andrew and Philip came and spoke to Jesus.

²³Then Jesus responded to them saying, "The hour has arrived that the Son of Man might be glorified. ²⁴I am telling you the very truth, if a grain of wheat does not fall into the ground and die, it will remain alone. But if it dies, it will bear much fruit. ²⁵The one who loves his life will lose it, and the one disregarding his life in this world will preserve it for life eternal. ²⁶If anyone serves me, he must follow me, and where I am, my servant will also be there. If anyone serves me, the Father will honor him.

²⁷"At present, my soul is troubled. So, what shall I say? 'Father, rescue me from this hour?' On the contrary, for this reason I have come to this hour. ²⁸Father, glorify your name."

Then a voice came from heaven, "I have glorified it and I will glorify it again." ²⁹Then the crowd that was standing there and

---

ⁱ See Zechariah 9:9.

heard it kept saying it had thundered; others were saying, "An angel has spoken to him."

30Jesus responded and said, "This voice did not happen for me, but for you. 31Now the judgment of this world has come. Now the ruler of this world will be cast out. 32And I, if I am lifted up on high from the earth, I will attract all men to myself." 33But he was saying this indicating what kind of death he was about to experience.

34Then the crowd responded to him, "We have heard from the Law that the Christ will remain to the coming age, so how can you say that it is necessary that the Son of Man be lifted up on high? Who is this Son of Man?"

35So, Jesus said to them, "For a little while the light will remain among you. Keep walking while you have the light, so that darkness will not overtake you. The one who is walking in darkness does not know where he is going. 36While you have the light, believe in the light in order that you might be sons of the light." Jesus spoke these things, then he went away and hid himself from them.

The Majority Reject Jesus, but Some Believe

37Even with as many miraculous signs as he had done in front of them, they would not believe in him, 38so that the word of Isaiah the prophet was fulfilled which said,

> "Lord who has believed our report? And to whom has the Arm of the Lord been disclosed?"[ii]

39For this reason, they were not able to believe, because again Isaiah said,

> 40"He has blinded their eyes and made their heart stubborn, so that they might not see with their eyes, understand with their heart, and turn around so I might heal them."[iii]

[ii] Isaiah 53:1

[iii] Isaiah 6:10

⁴¹Isaiah said these things because he saw Jesus' glory and spoke concerning him.

⁴²Nevertheless, many from among the rulers also believed in him, but they did not publicly acknowledge him on account of the Pharisees, in order that they not be banished from the synagogue; ⁴³for they preferred the approval of men more than the approval of God.

⁴⁴Then Jesus shouted out and said, "The one who believes in me does not believe in me, but in the one who sent me. ⁴⁵The one who sees me sees the one who sent me. ⁴⁶I myself have come as a light into the world, so that everyone who believes in me will not remain in darkness. ⁴⁷If someone hears my words and does not keep them, I myself do not judge him. For I have not come that I might judge the world, but so that I might rescue the world. ⁴⁸The one who rejects me as false, and does not receive my words, does have one judging him; the word which I have spoken, it will judge him on the last day. ⁴⁹For I have not spoken from myself, but from the Father who sent me. He has given a command to me about what I say and what I speak. ⁵⁰I also know that his command is life eternal. Therefore, what I am speaking, I speak in the very same way as the Father spoke to me."

Jesus Teaches His Disciples to Serve Each Other

Chapter Thirteen

¹Then, before the festival of Passover, because Jesus knew that the hour had come that he would cross over from this world to the Father, and because he loved his own who were in the world, he demonstrated his love for them to the end.

²While supper was being served and the Accuser had already put into the heart of Judas, the son of Simon Iscariot to hand him over to his enemies, ³and because Jesus knew that the Father had given all things into his hands, and that he had come from God and was going to God, ⁴he arose from the supper, set

aside his garments and took a towel and wrapped it around himself. ⁵Then he put water into the washbasin and began to wash the feet of the disciples and dry them with the towel which was wrapped around him.

⁶Then he came to Simon Peter. Simon said to him, "Lord, are you going to wash my feet?"

⁷Jesus responded and said to him, "What I am doing, you will not understand right now, but you will understand it after these things."

⁸Peter said to him, "You will never wash my feet, ever!"

Jesus answered him, "If I do not wash you, you have no fellowship with me."

⁹Simon Peter said to him, "Lord, not my feet alone, but also my hands and head."

¹⁰Jesus said to him, "The one who has been bathed does not have need to wash except for his feet, in fact he is entirely clean. You also are clean, but not every one." ¹¹For he knew the one who was handing him over to his enemies. For this reason, he said, "Not all of you are clean."

¹²So, after he washed their feet and had taken his garments, he reclined at the table again. He asked them, "Do you know what I have done to you? ¹³You call me, 'Teacher' and 'Lord,' and you are correct, for I am. ¹⁴If then, I, your Lord and Teacher, have washed your feet, then you also ought to wash one another's feet. ¹⁵For I have given an example to you so that you also do just as I have done to you. ¹⁶I am telling you the very truth, a servant is not greater than his Lord, nor is an apostle greater than the one who sent him. ¹⁷Since you know these things, you are blessed if you do them.

Jesus Predicts His Betrayal

¹⁸"I am not speaking about all of you. I know whom I have chosen, but *this is* in order that the Scripture may be fulfilled,

" 'The one consuming my bread has lifted up his heel against me.'[i]

[19]"But now I am telling you before it happens, so that you may believe that I AM[ii] when it happens. [20]I am telling you the very truth, the one who receives anyone I send, receives me. The one who receives me, receives the one who sent me."

[21]After he said these things, Jesus was unsettled in his spirit and bore witness *to it*. He said, "I am telling you the very truth, that one from among you will hand me over *to my enemies.*"

[22]The disciples began staring at one another because they were perplexed about whom he was speaking. [23]One from among his disciples, the one whom Jesus loved, was reclining at the table next to Jesus' chest. [24]So, Simon Peter nodded his head at this disciple to ask, "Who is the one about whom he is speaking?"

[25]Then that one leaned back upon Jesus' chest and asked him, "Lord, who is it?"

[26]Jesus answered, "He is the one for whom I will dip this piece of bread, then I will give it to him." So, when he dipped the piece of bread, he took it and gave it to Judas, son of Simon Iscariot. [27]Then, after he took the piece of bread, Satan entered into him.

So, Jesus said to him, "What you are doing, do as soon as possible." [28]But none of those reclining at the table knew why he said this to him; [29]for some assumed, since Judas kept the wallet, that Jesus was saying to him, "Buy what we need for the feast," or that he should give something to the poor people. [30]Then, after he received the piece of bread, he immediately left; and night had come.

The New Command to Love One Another

[31]So, when he went out, Jesus said, "Now the Son of Man is glorified and God is glorified in him. [32]If God is glorified in

---

[i] Psalm 41:9

[ii] Compare Exodus 3:14. This was a clear statement of deity.

him, God will also glorify him in himself; and he will glorify him immediately.

³³"Children, I am with you for a little while yet. You will seek me, and just as I told the Jewish leaders, I am now telling you also. 'Where I am going you are not able to come.'

³⁴"I am giving a new command to you, that you love one another; just as I have loved you so that you also love one another. ³⁵Everyone will know by this that you are my disciples, if you have love for one another."

³⁶Simon Peter asked him, "Lord where are you going?"

Jesus answered him, "Where I am going you are not able to follow me now, but you will follow me later."

³⁷Peter asked him, "Lord, why am I not able to follow you now? I will give[iii] my life for you."

³⁸Jesus responded, "Will you give your life for me? I am telling you the very truth; a rooster will most certainly not crow until you deny that you know me three times."

Preparing a Place for His Disciples

Chapter Fourteen

¹"Do not allow your[iv] heart to remain unsettled. Have faith in God, also have faith in me. ²There are many places to stay in my Father's house. If this were not true, would I have told you that I am going to prepare a place for you? ³If I go and prepare a place for you, I am coming again and I will take you for myself, in order that where I am, you also may be. ⁴You also know the way I am going."

[iii] Or, "dedicate." Also in verse 38.

[iv] This pronoun is plural.

The Way, the Truth, and the Life

⁵Thomas asked him, "Lord, we do not know where you are going, how can we know the way?"

⁶Jesus said to him, "I am the way, the truth, and the life. No one comes to the Father except through me. ⁷If you have known me, you will also know my Father, and from this time forward, you do know him and you have seen him."

⁸Philip said to him, "Lord, show the Father to us, and it is enough for us."

⁹Jesus asked him, "Haven't you come to know me, Philip, even after I have been with you for such a long time? The one who has seen me has seen the Father. How can you say, 'Show us the Father'? ¹⁰Do you not believe that I am in the Father and the Father is in me? The words which I am speaking to you I am not speaking on my own; but the Father abiding in me is doing his work. ¹¹Believe me, that I am in the Father, and the Father is in me; but if not that, believe because of the works themselves.

Jesus' Disciples Will Do Greater Works

¹²"I am telling you the very truth, the one who believes in me will also do the works I am doing; he will do even greater *works* than these, because I am going to the Father. ¹³Then, whatever you ask in my name, this I will do, in order that the Father might be glorified in the Son. ¹⁴If you ask me anything in my name, I will do it."

Jesus Promises the Paraclete

¹⁵"If you love me, you will keep my commands. ¹⁶I will ask the Father, and he will give another Paraclete,[i] in order that he will be with you throughout this age. ¹⁷*He is* the Spirit of Truth, whom the world is not able to receive, because it does not see

---

[i] Paraclete is a title for the Holy Spirit. In 1 John 2:1 John writes that Jesus is also a paraclete on our behalf. It could be translated, Helper, Counselor, or Advocate. The word encompasses aspects of all three of these titles, as well as that of comforter or encourager. Also verse 25.

him or know him. You know him, for he lives with you and will be in you.

The Disciples Will See Jesus after His Death

[18] "I will not leave you orphans; I am coming to you. [19] In a little while, the world will no longer see me, but you will see me; because I am living, you also will live. [20] In that day, you yourselves will know that I am in my Father, and you are in me, and I am in you. [21] The one who has my commands and keeps them, that is the one who loves me; and the one who loves me will be loved by my Father, and I will love him and reveal myself to him."

[22] Judas—not Iscariot—asked him, "Lord, what has happened that you are about to reveal yourself to us, but not to the world?"

[23] Jesus answered and said to him, "If anyone loves me he will keep my word, and my Father will love him and come to him, and we will make a dwelling place with him. [24] The one who does not love me does not keep my words, and the word which you are hearing is not mine, but the Father's who sent me.

[25] "I have spoken these things to you while I remain with you. [26] But the Paraclete, the Holy Spirit, whom the Father will send in my name, that one will teach you all things, and will remind you of all the things which I have spoken to you. [27] I am leaving peace with you, my peace I am giving to you. I am not giving to you as the world gives. Let not your hearts be unsettled or dismayed.

[28] "You have heard that I said to you, 'I am going away, but I will come to you.' If you have loved me, you would be filled with joy that I am going to the Father, because the Father is greater than I. [29] Even now I have spoken to you before it happens, that when it happens you believe. [30] I will no longer speak extensively with you, for the ruler of the world is coming; but he has nothing in me. [31] But I carry out exactly what the Father

commands me in order that the world might know that I love the Father.

"Stand up; let us go from here.

Staying Connected to Jesus: The Vine and Branches

Chapter Fifteen

¹"I am the authentic vine, and my Father is the farmer. ²Every branch in me that does not bear fruit, he takes it away; and every one that bears fruit, he prunes it so that it might bear more fruit. ³You are already pruned because of the word which I have spoken to you. ⁴Remain in me, and I *will be* in you. Just as the branch is not able to bear fruit by itself, unless it remains in the vine, in the same way you cannot *bear fruit* unless you remain in me.

⁵"I am the vine, you are the branches. The one who remains in me, and I in him, this is the one who bears much fruit; for apart from me, you can do nothing. ⁶If anyone does not remain in me, like the branch he is tossed outside and he dries out. Then they gather the dry branches and throw them into the fire, and they are burned. ⁷If you remain in me, and my words remain in you, ask whatever you wish, and for you, it will happen. ⁸My Father is glorified by this, and the result is that you bear much fruit and become my disciples.

⁹"Just as the Father has loved me, I also love you. Remain in my love. ¹⁰If you keep my commands, you will remain in my love, just as I have kept my Father's commands and remain in his love. ¹¹I have spoken these things to you so that my joy may be in you, and your joy might be filled to the full. ¹²This is my command, that you love one another just as I have loved you.

No Longer Servants, But Friends

¹³"No one has greater love than this, that he dedicates his life for his friends. ¹⁴You are my friends if you do what I command you. ¹⁵I no longer refer to you as servants, for the servant does not know what his master is doing. But I have referred to you as

friends, because everything I have heard from the Father I have made known to you. ¹⁶You did not choose me, but I chose you and commissioned you that you go and bear fruit, and that your fruit remain, so that whatever you ask the Father in my name, he will give to you. ¹⁷These things I am commanding you so that you might love one another.

But Not Friends with the World

¹⁸"If the world hates you, know that it hated me before you. ¹⁹If you were from the world, the world would befriend its own; but because you are not from the world, even more, because I have chosen you out of the world, the world hates you. ²⁰Remember the word I have spoken to you. A servant is not greater than his master. If they persecute me, they will also persecute you. If they have kept my word, they will also keep yours. ²¹But all these things they will do to you on account of my name, because they do not know the one who sent me. ²²If I had not come and spoken to them, they would not have sin; but now they do not have a valid excuse for their sin. ²³The one who hates me also hates my Father. ²⁴If I had not done the works among them that no other has done, they would not have sin. But now they have both seen and hated both me and my Father. ²⁵In fact, *this has happened* in order that the word which was written in their Law might be fulfilled, 'They hated me for no reason.'[i]

²⁶"When the Paraclete[ii] comes, who I will send to you from the Father, the Spirit of truth who goes out from the Father, he will testify about me. ²⁷You also are testifying, because you have been with me from the beginning.

Chapter Sixteen

¹"I have spoken these things to you so that you might not stumble. ²They will expel you from the synagogues, even worse,

---

[i] See Psalm 35:19 and 69:4.

[ii] This title of the Holy Spirit could be translated, "Helper," "Advocate," or "Counselor." See footnote for John 15:15. Also in 16:7.

an hour is coming when everyone who kills you will think that he is offering worship to God. ³They will do these things because they have not known the Father or me. ⁴However, I have spoken these things to you so that when their hour comes, you might remember that I spoke to you about them. I did not tell you these things at the beginning, because I was with you.

The Role of the Paraclete

⁵"But I am now going to the one who sent me, and none of you is asking me, 'Where are you going?' ⁶In fact, because I have spoken these things to you, grief has filled your heart. ⁷But I am telling you the truth, it is better for you that I go away. For if I do not go away, the Paraclete will not come to you. But if I go, I will send him to you. ⁸When that one comes, he will convict the world about sin, about righteousness, and about judgment: ⁹about sin, because they did not believe in me; ¹⁰about righteousness, because I am going away to the Father and you will no longer see me; ¹¹about judgment, because the ruler of this world has been judged.

¹²"I still have many things to say to you, but you are not able to bear it now. ¹³But when that one, the Spirit of truth, comes, he will instruct you in all truth. For he will not speak by himself, but as much as he hears, he will speak and he will report to you the things that are coming. ¹⁴He will glorify me, because he will receive from me and report it to you. ¹⁵All things, as much as the Father has, are mine. For this reason I said that he will receive from me and will report to you.

¹⁶"Just a little longer, and you will no longer see me; and again a little while, and you will see me."

Grief Turned to Joy

¹⁷Then some from among his disciples asked each other, "What is this that he is saying to us, 'A little while and you will not see me, and again a little while and you will see me'? And, 'I am going to the Father'?" ¹⁸So, they were discussing, "What is

John 16:30

this that he is saying, 'a little while'? We do not know what he is speaking about."

[19]Jesus knew that they wanted to question him, and he said to them, "Are you discussing this with one another because I said, 'A little while and you will not see me, and again a little while and you will see me'? [20]I am telling you the very truth, that you will weep and mourn, but the world will rejoice. You will grieve, but your grief will be transformed to joy. [21]When a woman is bearing a child, she has grief, because her hour has come. But when she bears a child, she no longer remembers the hardship because of her joy that a *new* person[i] has been born into the world. [22]So, also you have grief now, but I will see you again, and your heart will rejoice, and no one will take your joy from you.

Answered Prayer from the Father in Jesus' Name

[23]"In that day you will not ask me anything. I am telling you the very truth, whatever you request of the Father in my name, he will give to you. [24]Until the present time, you have requested nothing in my name; ask and you will receive, so that your joy will be complete.

[25]"I have spoken these things to you using obscure speech. An hour is coming when I will no longer speak to you with obscure speech, but I will tell you openly about the Father. [26]In that day, you will ask in my name, and I am not saying that I will ask the Father for you; [27]for the Father himself loves you, because you have loved me and believed that I have come from God. [28]I have come from the Father and come into the world; again, I am leaving the world and going to the Father."

The Disciples Believe

[29]His disciples said to him, "Look, now you are speaking openly and you are saying nothing with obscure speech. [30]Now we know that you know all things and you have no need for

---

[i] Or, "a human being."

anyone to question you. By this we believe that you have come from God."

³¹Jesus responded to them, "Do you believe now? ³²Listen, an hour is coming and has come, when you will be scattered, each to his own home, and you will leave me alone. But I am not alone because the Father is with me. ³³I have spoken these things to you in order that you might have peace in me. In the world you will have tribulation, but be courageous, I have overcome the world."

Jesus Prays: To Be Glorified in order to Glorify the Father

Chapter Seventeen

¹Jesus spoke these things, and then lifted up his eyes to heaven and said, "Father, the hour has come. Glorify your Son that the Son might glorify you; ²for you have given him authority over all flesh, so that all whom you have given to him, to them he may give life eternal. ³Now this is eternal life, that they may know you, the only true God, and Jesus Christ, whom you have sent. ⁴I have glorified you on the earth by finishing the work you gave me to do. ⁵Now also glorify me, Father, at your side with the glory that I had with you before the world came into being.

Jesus Prays: For His Disciples

⁶"I have made your name known to the men whom you have given me out of the world. They were yours, you gave them to me, and they have kept your word. ⁷Now they have recognized that all things, as much as you have given to me, are from you, ⁸for I have given the words to them that you gave to me, and they have received them. They also genuinely understood that I have come from you, and they believe that you are the one who sent me. ⁹I am praying for them. I am not praying for the world, but for those whom you have given to me, for they are yours. ¹⁰Everything that is mine is yours, and everything that is yours is mine, and I have been honored by them. ¹¹I am no longer in the world; they are in the world and I am coming to you.

"Holy Father, protect them by your name which you gave to me, so that they might be one just as we are one. ¹²While I was with them, I was protecting them by your name which you gave to me, and I guarded them and not one from among them was destroyed except the son of destruction, that the Scripture might be fulfilled. ¹³But now I am coming to you, and I am speaking these things in this world so that they might have my joy filling them completely. ¹⁴I have given them your word, and the world has hated them because they are not from the world, just as I am not from the world. ¹⁵I am not asking that you take them from the world, but that you protect them from the evil one. ¹⁶They are not from the world just as I am not from the world. ¹⁷Set them apart[i] by the truth; your word is truth. ¹⁸Just as you sent me into the world, I am also sending them into the world. ¹⁹I am also setting myself apart for their sake, that they might also themselves be set apart by truth.

Jesus Prays: For Future Believers

²⁰"I am not asking for these alone, but also for those who will believe in me through their report, ²¹that they all might be one, just as you, Father, are in me and I am in you; that they themselves might be one in us, so that the world might believe that you have sent me. ²²I also have given them the glory that you have given to me, that they might be one just as we are one; ²³I in them and you in me, that they might achieve perfect unity, in order that the world might know that you sent me and have loved them just as you loved me.

²⁴"Father, I desire that those whom you have given me might be where I am, in order that they might see my glory which you have given to me, because you loved me before the founding of the world.

²⁵"Righteous Father, the world does not know you, but I know you, and these men know that you sent me. ²⁶I have made your name known to them, and I will make it known, so that the

---

[i] Traditionally, "Sanctify" which means "Set apart." Also in verse 19.

love with which you have loved me might be in them, and I in them."

Jesus Betrayed and Arrested

Chapter Eighteen

¹When Jesus had spoken these things, he went out with his disciples across the Wadi Kidron[i] where there was a garden. He and his disciples went into it. ²But Judas, the one who was handing him over to his enemies, also knew the place, for Jesus often met with his disciples there. ³So, Judas, when he had received a troop of Roman soldiers and officers from the chief priests and from the Pharisees, came there with torches, lamps, and weapons.

⁴Then, because Jesus knew all the things coming upon him, he went out and asked them, "Whom do you seek?"

⁵They answered him, "Jesus the Nazarene."

He said to them, "I AM"[ii]

Judas, the one who was handing him over, took his stand with them. ⁶When Jesus said to them, "I AM," they staggered back and fell to the ground.

⁷Therefore, he asked them again, "Whom do you seek?"

Then they said, "Jesus the Nazarene."

⁸Jesus answered, "I told you that I AM. So, if you are seeking me, allow these men to go."

⁹This was to fulfill the word which he spoke,

---

[i] The Wadi Kidron is a valley that runs from Jerusalem to the Dead Sea. A seasonal stream flows through it.

[ii] This also could be translated, "I am he," or "It is I." But it is clear from the reaction to Jesus' statement that he was revealing the power of "I AM" as he spoke. See Exodus 3:14 and John 8:58. Also in verses 6 and 8.

"*Those* whom you have given to me, I have not lost any from among them."iii

¹⁰So, Simon Peter, since he had a sword, drew it and struck the servant of the high priest, and sliced off his right ear. The name of the servant was Malchus. ¹¹Then Jesus said to Peter, "Put your sword into its sheath. I need to drink the cup which the Father has given me, don't I?" ¹²So, the troop of Roman soldiers, the tribune, and the Jewish officers arrested Jesus, bound him, ¹³and led him to Annas first, for he was the father-in-law of Caiaphas who was high priest that year. ¹⁴It was Caiaphas who had counseled the Jewish leaders that it was better that one man die for the people.

Peter's First Denial

¹⁵Simon Peter was following Jesus, along with another disciple. That disciple was well known to the high priest and went with Jesus into the courtyard of the high priest. ¹⁶But Peter stood near the door outside. So, the other disciple who was well known to the high priest, went out and spoke to the gatekeeper, and brought Peter in.

¹⁷Then the servant girl who was the gatekeeper asked Peter, "You aren't also among the disciples of this man, are you?" He said, "I am not."

¹⁸Because it was cold, the servants and officers were standing around a charcoal fire they had made, warming themselves. Peter was standing with them warming himself.

Jesus Questioned by Annas

¹⁹So, the *former* high priest questioned Jesus concerning his disciples and concerning his teaching.

²⁰Jesus responded to him, "I have spoken openly to the world. I have always taught in synagogues and in the temple where all the Jewish leaders gather together. I spoke nothing in secret.

---

iii John 6:39

²¹Why are you questioning me? Ask those who heard what I have spoken to them. Look, these men know what I spoke."

²²Because he said these things, one of the officers standing near him struck him with his open hand and said, "Is this how you respond to the high priest?"

²³Jesus said to him, "If I have spoken wickedly, testify concerning that wickedness; but if I spoke rightly, why did you hit me?"

²⁴So, Annas sent him bound to Caiaphas the high priest.

Peter's Second and Third Denials

²⁵Now Simon Peter was standing and warming himself. Then they said to him, "You aren't also from among his disciples, are you?"

Peter denied it and said, "I am not."

²⁶One from among the servants of the high priest, a relative of the one whose ear Peter had cut off, asked, "I saw you in the garden with him, didn't I? ²⁷So, Peter again denied it, and immediately the rooster crowed.

Jesus' Trial Before Pilate

²⁸Then they led Jesus from the house of Caiaphas to the Praetorium.ⁱ But it was early, and they did not go into the Praetorium so that they might not be defiled, but eat the Passover.

²⁹Therefore, Pilate went out to them and asked, "What charge are you bringing against this man?"

³⁰They responded and said to him, "If this man was not doing evil, we would not have handed him over to you."

³¹Then Pilate said to them, "Take him yourselves and judge him according to your laws."

ⁱ The Praetorium was the palace of the Roman governor. Also verse 33 and 19:9.

The Jewish leaders said to him, "It is not lawful for us to condemn anyone to death." ³²This was to fulfill the word of Jesus which he spoke making known what kind of death he was about to die.

³³So, Pilate went into the Praetorium again, and addressed Jesus and asked him, "Are you the King of the Jews?"

³⁴Jesus responded, "Are you saying this by yourself, or did others speak to you about me?"

³⁵Pilate answered, "I am not a Jewish leader, am I? Your own nation and the chief priests handed you over to me. What have you done?"

³⁶Jesus answered, "My kingdom is not from this world. If my kingdom were from this world, my attendants would have fought so that I was not handed over to the Jewish leaders. But at this time my Kingdom is not from this place."

³⁷Then Pilate asked him, "So you are a king then?"

Jesus answered, "You yourself are saying that I am king. For this reason I was born, and for this I have come into the world, that I might testify to the truth. All who are of the truth hear my voice."

³⁸Pilate asked him, "What is truth?"

After he said this, he again went out to the Jewish leaders and said, "I find no grounds for an accusation against him. ³⁹But you have a custom that I release one person to you during the Passover. So, do you desire that I release to you the King of the Jews?"

⁴⁰Then they cried out again saying, "Not this man but Barabbas." Now Barabbas was a rebel.

John 19:1

Jesus Mocked and Condemned

Chapter Nineteen

¹Then Pilate took Jesus and scourged him. ²The soldiers wove a crown from thorny weeds and placed it on his head. They put a purple *military* cloak around him ³and began to call to him, "Greetings, King of the Jews!" They also gave him open-handed blows to his face.

⁴Pilate again came out and said to them, "Look, I am bringing him out to you so that you might know that I find no grounds for the charge against him."

⁵Then Jesus came outside, wearing the crown made of thorns and the purple cloak. Pilate said to them, "Look at the man."

⁶Then, when the chief priests and officers saw him, they shouted out saying, "Crucify! Crucify!"

Pilate said to them, "You take him yourselves and crucify him, for I find no grounds for the charge against him."

⁷The Jewish leaders answered him, "We have our own law, and according to the Law he deserves to die for he made himself the Son of God."

⁸When Pilate heard this report, he was even more afraid, ⁹and he went into the Praetorium again and said to Jesus, "Where are you from?" But Jesus did not give an answer to him. ¹⁰So, Pilate said to him, "Why aren't you speaking to me? Don't you know that I have authority to free you or to crucify you?"

¹¹Jesus responded to him, "You would not have any authority over me except it was given to you from above. For this reason, the one who handed me over to you has committed a greater sin."

¹²From that moment, Pilate sought to free him, but the Jewish leaders shouted out saying, "If you free this man, you are not a friend of Caesar. Anyone who makes themselves a king is speaking against Caesar."

John 19:23

¹³Therefore, when Pilate heard this statement, he brought Jesus out and sat down on the judgment seat at a place called the Stone Pavement—which in the Hebrew dialect[i] is Gabbatha.

¹⁴It was about the sixth hour[ii] of the Day of Preparation[iii] *during* the Passover celebration. Pilate said to the Jewish leaders, "Behold your king!"

¹⁵Then, they cried out, "Do away with him! Do away with him! Crucify him!"

Pilate responded to them, "I should crucify your king?"

The chief priests countered, "We have no king except Caesar."

Jesus is Crucified

¹⁶Then he handed Jesus over to them in order that he might be crucified. The soldiers took Jesus under their authority. ¹⁷He carried his own crossbeam and went out to the *crucifixion site* called "Place of the Skull," which is called "Golgotha" in the Hebrew dialect. ¹⁸ This was where they crucified him, and two others with him, one on each side with Jesus in the middle.

¹⁹Pilate also wrote a notice and placed it on the cross, "Jesus the Nazarene, King of the Jews."

²⁰Many of the Jewish people read this notice, for the place where Jesus was crucified was near the city, and it was written in the Hebrew, Roman, and Greek languages. ²¹Therefore, the Jewish chief priests complained to Pilate, "Do not write, "King of the Jews," but rather that he said, "I am king of the Jews.""

²²Pilate answered, "What I have written, I have written."

²³Then, when the soldiers crucified Jesus, they divided his clothing into four portions, a portion for each soldier, and the

---

[i] Aramaic (also in verses 17 and 20).

[ii] By Roman reckoning, about 6:00 AM.

[iii] The day of Preparation (Friday) was the day one prepared for the Sabbath (Saturday).

inner garment. But the inner garment was seamless, woven from the top down. ²⁴So, they said to one another, "Let us not tear it, but cast lots for it to determine who will get it."

This happened so that the Scripture would be fulfilled that says,

> "They divided my clothing among themselves,
> and cast lots for my garment."[i]

Therefore, the soldiers did these things.

²⁵The mother of Jesus was standing by his cross, along with his mother's sister, Mary the wife of Clopas, and Mary Magdalene. ²⁶So, when Jesus saw his mother and the disciple whom he loved standing near, he said to his mother, "Mother,[ii] look to your son." ²⁷Then he said to the disciple, "Look to your mother." From that hour, the disciple took her into his own home.

The Lamb of God Lays Down His Life

²⁸After this, when Jesus recognized that all things had already been completed, in order that the Scripture might be fulfilled, said, "I am thirsty." ²⁹A container full of sour wine was lying there. So, they attached a sponge full of sour wine to a hyssop branch and brought it to his mouth.

³⁰Then, when Jesus received the sour wine he said, "It is completed." After he bowed his head, he gave up his spirit.

³¹Then the Jewish leaders, because it was the Day of Preparation, in order that their bodies would not remain on the cross during the Sabbath—for that Sabbath day was a high sabbath[iii]—asked Pilate that their legs might be broken and taken away. ³²So, the soldiers came and broke the legs of the first

---

[i] Psalm 22:18

[ii] Traditionally translated, "Woman." But, the word was a polite form of address to a woman in that culture, but not as much in modern culture. In current culture, the correct way to politely address one's mother is, "Mother."

[iii] When a festival fell on a Sabbath, it was a "High Sabbath."

man and the legs of the other man crucified with him. ³³But after they came to Jesus, when they saw he had already died, they did not break his legs, ³⁴instead one of the soldiers jabbed his spear into his side, and immediately blood and water flowed out.

³⁵The one who saw this has testified, and his testimony is trustworthy; and he knows that he is speaking the truth so that you also might believe. ³⁶For these things happened so that the Scripture might be fulfilled,

> "Not a bone of his will be broken."[iv]

³⁷Again, another Scripture also says,

> "They will look at the one whom they have pierced."[v]

Jesus is Buried

³⁸Then, after these things, Joseph of Arimathea, who was a disciple of Jesus, but secretly for fear of the Jewish leaders, asked that he might take away the body of Jesus; and Pilate allowed it. So, he came and took away his body. ³⁹Nicodemus also came, the man who had first come to him at night. He was carrying a mixture of myrrh and aloes, about a hundred *Roman* pounds.[vi] ⁴⁰So, they took the body of Jesus and bound it up in linen cloth with the spices, as is the custom among the Jewish people to prepare for burial.

⁴¹Now there was a garden in the place where he was crucified, and in the garden there was a new tomb in which no one had ever been placed. ⁴²Therefore, because it was the Day of Preparation for the Jewish people, and the tomb was near, they placed Jesus there.

[iv] Exodus 12:46; Numbers 9:12

[v] Zechariah 12:10

[vi] Since an ancient Roman pound was about 12 ounces, this is about 75 pounds of spices.

Jesus Rises from the Dead

Chapter Twenty

¹On the first day of the week, early in the morning while it was still dark, Mary Magdalene came to the tomb. She noticed that the stone had been moved away from the tomb. ²So, she ran and went to Simon Peter and the other disciple whom Jesus loved. She said to them, "They have removed the Lord from the tomb, and we do not know where they have put him."

³Then Peter and the other disciple went out and headed to the tomb. ⁴The two were running together, but the other disciple ran ahead faster than Peter, and came to the tomb first. ⁵He bent down and saw the linen cloths lying there, but did not go in. ⁶Then Simon Peter, who was following behind him, arrived and went into the tomb, and also saw the linen cloths lying there, ⁷as well as the smaller cloth that had covered Jesus' head. It was not near the linen cloths but was rolled up by itself in a separate place. ⁸So, then the other disciple who had arrived first, also entered the tomb. He saw, and he believed[i] ⁹(they did not yet understand the Scripture, that it was necessary that Jesus rise from the dead).

Jesus Reveals Himself to Mary Magdalene

¹⁰The disciples went back again to the others, ¹¹but Mary stood outside near the tomb weeping. While she was still crying, she bent down to look into the tomb, ¹²and she saw two angels in white sitting, one near the head, and the other near the feet, where the body of Jesus had been lying.

¹³They asked her, "Woman, why are you crying?"

She said to them, "They have carried my Lord away, and I do not know where they have put him." ¹⁴After she said this, she turned around and saw Jesus standing there, but she did not know that it was Jesus.

---

[i] In this context, "he believed Mary's report." John explicitly states that they did not understand about the resurrection at this time.

¹⁵Jesus said to her, "Woman, why are you weeping? Whom are you seeking?"

She thought that he was the gardener, and said to him, "Sir, if you have carried him away, tell me where you have put him, and I will go get him."

¹⁶Jesus said to her, "Mary."

Mary turned and said to him in the Hebrew dialect,[ii] "Rabboni!"[iii]—which means "Teacher."

¹⁷Jesus said to her, "Stop holding on to me,[iv] for I have not yet ascended to my Father. But go to my brothers and tell them, 'I am ascending to my Father and your Father, to my God and your God.'"

¹⁸Mary Magdalene came and announced to the disciples, "I have seen the Lord." She also reported the things he had said to her.

Jesus Reveals Himself to His Disciples

¹⁹Then, when it was evening on that day, the first day of the week, and the doors were closed where the disciples were for fear of the Jewish leaders, Jesus came and stood among them and said to them, "Peace be with you." ²⁰When he said this, he showed his hands and his side to them. When they saw the Lord, the disciples rejoiced. ²¹Then, Jesus said to them again, "Peace be to you. Just as the Father sent me, I also am sending you."

[ii] Aramaic

[iii] The word used is "Rabboni," a form of the word "Rabbi," which means "Teacher." However, Rabboni itself is more personal. It means "My Rabbi," (My Teacher).

[iv] Or, "Stop clinging to me." Like the women in Matthew who saw Jesus after his resurrection (see Matthew 28:9), Mary had naturally begun to cling to Jesus.

John 20:22

The Church is Born: The Disciples Receive the Holy Spirit

²²After he said this, he breathed on them and said, "Receive the Holy Spirit. ²³If you forgive anyone their sins, they have been forgiven them, if you hold anyone's *sin against them*, they have been held."

²⁴But Thomas, one from among the twelve, who was called Twin,[i] was not with them when Jesus came. ²⁵So, the other disciples kept telling him, "We have seen the Lord."

But he said to them, "Unless I see in his hands the nail wounds, and put my finger in the nail wounds, and put my hand into his side, I will never believe."

Jesus Reveals Himself to Thomas

²⁶Then after eight days, his disciples were again inside, and Thomas was with them. Even though the doors were shut, Jesus came and stood among them and said, "Peace be with you." ²⁷Then he said to Thomas, "Put your finger here and see my hands, and take your hand and place it in my side. Stop being faithless, but believe."

²⁸Thomas answered and said, "My Lord and my God."

²⁹Jesus said to him, "Is it only because you have seen me that you believe? Blessed are those who have not seen but have believed."

The Purpose of the Miracles Recorded in the Book of John

³⁰Now Jesus did many other miraculous signs in the presence of his disciples, which are not written in this book. ³¹But these have been written so that you might believe that Jesus is the Christ, the Son of God, and so that by believing you may possess life in his name.

---

[i] The Greek word for "Twin" is "Didymus." Also in 21:2.

Jesus Reveals Himself to His Disciples in Galilee

Chapter Twenty-One

¹After these things, Jesus revealed himself to the disciples again at the Sea of Tiberias. He revealed himself in this way. ²Simon Peter, Thomas, who was called Twin, Nathaniel, who was from Cana in Galilee, the sons of Zebedee and two others from among his disciples were together. ³Simon Peter said to them, "I am going fishing."

They responded to him, "We are also coming with you." They went outside and embarked in his boat, but they caught nothing that night.

⁴But when daylight was already breaking, Jesus stood on the shore; however, the disciples did not know that it was Jesus. ⁵Then Jesus said to them, "Children, you don't have any fish[ii] to eat, do you?"

They responded to him, "No."

⁶Then he said to them, "Cast your net on the right side of the boat and you will catch some." So they cast the net, but they did not have the strength to haul it in because of the great amount of fish.

⁷Because of this, that disciple whom Jesus loved said to Peter, "It is the Lord." When Simon Peter heard that it was the Lord, he tied his outer garment around himself, for he wasn't wearing any clothing, and he threw himself into the sea. ⁸But the other disciples came with the boat, for they were not far from the land, only about two hundred cubits,[iii] and they were dragging the net with the fish. ⁹When they stepped out onto land, they saw a charcoal fire[iv] prepared, and fish and bread cooking on it.

[ii] The word Jesus uses could be used of any food eaten with bread, but in this context, the focus is fish.

[iii] A cubit was about eighteen inches in length; so, about 300 feet.

[iv] The only other time a charcoal fire is specifically mentioned by John was in 18:18, when Peter was warming himself at the time he denied Jesus.

¹⁰Jesus said to them, "Bring some of the fish which you have just caught."

¹¹Then Simon Peter got up and dragged the net ashore. It was full of large fish, one hundred and fifty-three. Even with so many in it, the net did not tear.

¹²Jesus said to them, "Come and have breakfast." None of his disciples dared to ask him, "Who are you?" because they knew it was the Lord.

¹³Jesus came, took the bread and gave it to them, and in the same way he gave them the fish. ¹⁴This was already the third time that Jesus was revealed to his disciples after he was raised from the dead.

Peter Publicly Reinstated by Jesus

¹⁵When they had eaten breakfast, Jesus said to Simon Peter, "Simon, son of John, do you love me more than these others?"

He responded, "Yes Lord, you already know that I have deep affection for you."[i]

He said to him, "Tend to my lambs."

¹⁶Jesus questioned him again a second time, "Simon, son of John, do you love me?"

Peter answered him, "Yes Lord, you already know that I have deep affection for you."

Jesus said to him, "Guide my sheep."

¹⁷Jesus spoke to him a third time, "Simon, son of John, do you have deep affection for me?"

Peter was grieved that he asked him the third time, "Do you have deep affection for me?" so he said to him, "Lord, you

---

[i] The Greek verbs agapeo (ἀγαπάω) and phileo (φιλέω), both which can be translated "love," are used by Jesus and Peter in this section. However phileo can simply be a reference to deep affection, and is translated that way here to show the interplay between Jesus and Peter.

already know all things. You know that I have deep affection for you."

Jesus said to him, "Tend to my sheep."

¹⁸"I am telling you the very truth, when you were younger you fastened a belt on yourself and walked where you desired. But when you grow old, you will stretch out your hands, and another will fasten a belt on you and bring you where you do not desire." ¹⁹Now Jesus said this to make known by what kind of death Peter would glorify God. After he had said this, he said to him, "Follow me."

²⁰When Peter turned, he saw the disciple whom Jesus loved following them. He was also the one who leaned back on Jesus' chest at the supper and asked, "Lord, who is the one handing you over to your enemies?" ²¹So, when Peter saw him, he asked Jesus, "Lord, what about this man?"

²²Jesus said to him, "If I want him to remain until I am come, what is that to you? You follow me."

²³Then this report went out to the brothers, that this disciple would not die. But Jesus did not say that he would not die, but "If I want him to remain until I am come, what is that to you?"

²⁴This is the disciple who testifies concerning these things, and has written these things, and we know[ii] that his testimony is trustworthy.

²⁵But there are also many other things that Jesus did, which if they were written point by point, I suppose that the world itself could not contain the books that would be written.

[ii] Or, "I certainly know that his testimony is trustworthy."

ACTS

Luke Continues His Report

Chapter One

¹I wrote the first report, O Theophilus, about all the things that Jesus began to do and to teach, ²until the day he was taken up to heaven, after he gave instructions through the Holy Spirit to the apostles whom he had chosen. ³After his suffering, he revealed to them that he was alive with many sure proofs. He appeared to them over a period of forty days, telling them things that concerned the Kingdom of God. ⁴While he was eating together with them, he commanded them, "Do not leave Jerusalem, but wait for the promise of the Father which you have heard about from me. ⁵For John baptized with water, but you will be baptized in the Holy Spirit before too many days have passed."

Jesus Ascends to Heaven

⁶Therefore, when they had gathered around him, they were questioning him, asking, "Lord, are you going to restore the kingdom of Israel at this time?"

⁷But he said to them, "It isn't yours to know the times or the strategic opportunities that the Father has established by his

own authority. ⁸But you will receive power when the Holy Spirit has come upon you, and you will be my witnesses in Jerusalem, in all of Judea and Samaria, and unto the most distant parts of the earth."

⁹When he had said these things, and while they were watching, he was lifted up and a cloud took him up away from their sight.

¹⁰They were staring intently into the sky as he was going, when suddenly two men stood by them in white clothing. ¹¹They said, "Men of Galilee, why are you standing and looking into the sky? This Jesus who has been taken up from you into heaven, will come in the same way you watched him go into heaven."

Gathered with One Passion

¹²Then they returned to Jerusalem from the mountain known as Olives, which is near Jerusalem, a Sabbath's walk from it. ¹³When they arrived in the city, they went up to the second-story room where they were staying. Peter, John, James,ⁱ Andrew, Phillip, Thomas, Bartholomew, Matthew, James son of Alphaeus, Simon the Zealot, and Judas the son of James were there. ¹⁴They were all, with one passion, continually joining together in prayer, along with the women, Mary the mother of Jesus, and his brothers.

Replacing the Betrayer

¹⁵During this time, Peter arose in the midst of the brothers— a group of about 120 people—and said, ¹⁶"Men, brothers, the Scriptures must be fulfilled which the Holy Spirit foretold through the mouth of David, concerning Judas who served as guide to those who arrested Jesus. ¹⁷Because he was counted as one of us, he received his share in this ministry." ¹⁸(Now this man had purchased a field with the reward for his unrighteous

---

ⁱ Greek text, "Jacob." James is the Anglicized form of Jacob used since the first English translations. Unless it refers to the patriarch Jacob, it is translated as James in this New Testament.

actions. When he fell headfirst, his midsection burst open and all his internal organs spilled out. ¹⁹This became known to everyone living in Jerusalem, so that field came to be known, in their own language as Akeldama, that is, Field of Blood.) ²⁰"For it is written in the book of Psalms:

> " 'Let his house be a desert,
>   and let no one live in it.'[i]

"And

> 'Let another take his office of leadership.'[ii]

²¹"Therefore, it is necessary that one from the men who traveled with us during all the time the Lord Jesus went in and out among us, ²²beginning from the baptism of John until the day he was taken up from us, one of them must become a witness with us of his resurrection."

²³They selected two, Joseph who was called Barsabbas—also called Justus—and Matthias. ²⁴As they prayed, they said, "You, Lord, know everyone's heart. Show which one of these two you have chosen ²⁵to receive this place of service and the office of apostle that Judas gave up to go to his own place."

²⁶So, they threw lots for them, and the lot fell to Matthias, and he was counted with the eleven apostles.

Jesus Pours Out His Spirit: Pentecost

Chapter Two

¹When the day of Pentecost was being observed, they were all together in the same place. ²Suddenly, a sound came from heaven like a gusting, mighty wind, and it filled the whole house where they were sitting. ³Something like tongues of fire—tongues that divided themselves—appeared to them. It settled upon each one of them. ⁴They were all filled with the Holy

---

[i] Psalm 69:25

[ii] Psalm 109:8

Spirit and began to speak in foreign languages[iii] as the Holy Spirit was giving them things to declare.

⁵There were Jews residing in Jerusalem, devout men from every nation under the heavens. ⁶When this sound came from heaven, a great number of people gathered, and they were confused because each one heard them speaking in their own language. ⁷They were swept up in ecstatic amazement[iv] and astonished. They said, "Listen! Are not all of those who are speaking Galileans? ⁸How are we hearing them each in our own language to which we were born? ⁹Partheans, Medes, and Elamites; those living in Mesopotamia, Judea, Cappadocia, Pontus, and Asia, ¹⁰Phrygia, Pamphylia, Egypt, and the districts of Libya near Cyrene, as well as the Romans who are visiting, ¹¹both Jews and proselytes, Cretans and Arabs—we hear them sharing the mighty things of God in our own languages."

¹²Then everyone was overwhelmed with wonder, and they were perplexed. They were asking each other, "What does this mean?"

¹³But others joked about them saying, "They have indulged in too much sweet wine."

Peter Confronts the Crowds

¹⁴But when Peter stood with the eleven, he raised his voice and spoke out loudly and clearly to them, "Men of Judea and everyone who lives in Jerusalem, let this be known to you, and listen carefully to my words. ¹⁵For these men are not drunk as you suppose, it is only the third[v] hour of the day. ¹⁶This is what God spoke through the prophet Joel,

---

[iii] Traditionally: "Tongues." When referring to the physical organ, this word means tongue (compare verses 3 and 26). When referring to what is spoken, it means languages, as the context demonstrates here.

[iv] Swept up in ecstatic amazement" translates a Greek verb used when referring to spiritual ecstatic phenomena in ancient times. Also verse 12.

[v] 9:00 AM

17" 'This will happen in the last days, I will pour from my Spirit upon all flesh, and your sons and your daughters will prophesy, your young men will see visions, and your elders will dream dreams.

18" 'And surely I will pour out from my Spirit on my male servants and on my female servants in those days, I will pour out from my Spirit —and they will prophesy.

19" 'I will display wonders in the skies above, and signs upon the earth below, blood, fire, and hazy smoke.

20" 'The sun will be turned to darkness and the moon into blood before the great and magnificent day of the Lord comes.

21" 'And this will happen; all who call on the name of the Lord will be saved.'[i]

22"Men of Israel, listen to these words: Jesus of Nazareth, a man for whom God demonstrated his approval to you with miracles, wonders, and signs—God did these things through him in your midst, just as you yourselves know—23this man, who was delivered up by God's settled plan and foreknowledge, you killed by crucifying him at the hands of lawless men. 24But God raised him up again, having unchained him from the birth pains of death, because it was impossible for him to be held by death. 25For David said of him,

" 'I was looking ahead, and I saw the Lord with me through everything. He is at my right hand so that I will not be shaken.

26" 'Because of this, my heart is glad, and my tongue rejoices, and even more, my body will live in hope,

---

[i] Joel 2:28-32

27" 'For you will not forsake my soul to Hades,
nor allow your Holy One to see decay.

28" 'You have made known to me the ways of life;
you will fill my joy completely with your
presence.'ⁱⁱ

²⁹"Men, brothers, I can say to you with confidence about the Patriarch David, that he died and was buried, and his tomb is with us even today. ³⁰Surely he was a prophet, and knew that God had sworn an oath to him to seat one who came from his loins upon his throne;ⁱⁱⁱ ³¹he looked ahead and spoke concerning the resurrection of the Christ, that His soul was not forsaken to Hades, nor did his flesh see decay. ³²God restored this Jesus to life, and we are all witnesses of this.

³³"Therefore, having been exalted to the right hand of God, and having received the promise of the Holy Spirit from the Father, he has poured out this that you see and hear. ³⁴For David did not ascend into the heavens, but he said,

" 'The Lord said to my Lord, "Sit at my right
hand, ³⁵until I place your enemies under your
feet."'

³⁶"Therefore, let all the house of Israel know with absolute certainty that God has made him Lord and Christ—this Jesus whom you crucified."

³⁷When they heard, they were pierced through to the heart, and said to Peter and the rest of the apostles, "Men, brothers, what shall we do?"

³⁸Then Peter said to them, "Repent, and let each of you be baptized in the name of Jesus Christ for the forgiveness of your sins, and you will receive the gift of the Holy Spirit. ³⁹For the

---

ⁱⁱ Psalm 16:8-11

ⁱⁱⁱMany manuscripts, "Surely he was a prophet, and knew that God had sworn an oath to him that he would raise up one from his loins (with respect to the flesh), the Christ, and seat him upon his throne." It should be noted that Luke may have added this himself in later copies of Acts.

promise is for you and your children, and all those who are far away, as many as the Lord our God will call."

⁴⁰With many other words he continued to earnestly testify to them and encourage them saying, "Let yourself be delivered from this crooked generation!"

Three Thousand Souls Added to the Christian Fellowship

⁴¹Then those who received his message were baptized, and over three thousand souls were added that day. ⁴²They continued to hold fast to the apostles' teaching and the fellowship, to the breaking of bread and the prayers. ⁴³A sense of awe was overwhelming everyone, and many wonders and signs were done through the apostles.

⁴⁴At that time, everyone who believed began to gather together in one place, and they considered all their belongings of little value—⁴⁵they used to sell their property and possessions and share them with everyone as anyone had need.

⁴⁶Each day, they joined together with one passion in the temple,[i] breaking bread from house to house, taking part in meals with joy and simplicity of heart. ⁴⁷They were praising God and had favor with all the people. The Lord added to those being saved each day at that same place.

A Demonstration of Kingdom Authority: Healing a Crippled Man

Chapter Three

¹At another time, Peter and John were going up to the temple at the ninth hour, the hour of prayer. ²At that same time, a man who had been unable to walk from the time he was born was also being transported to the temple. They placed him at the gate that was called Beautiful each day, so that he might ask for charitable gifts from those who were going into the temple.

---

[i] This was a Jewish congregation that saw Jesus as the expected Messiah, but still practiced Judaism. They were originally seen as a sect within Judaism. The Gentile mission had not started.

³When he saw Peter and John about to enter the temple, he began to ask for contributions. ⁴Then Peter fixed his eyes upon him, and together with John said, "Look at us!"

⁵Then the man turned his attention to them expecting to receive a contribution from them. ⁶Peter said, "I do not have any silver or gold with me, but what I have I will give to you. In the name of Jesus Christ of Nazareth, get up and walk!"

⁷Then he firmly grasped his right hand and lifted him up. At that moment his feet and ankles became strong. ⁸The man vaulted up, stood on his feet, and walked about. Then he went with them into the temple walking, jumping, and praising God. ⁹All the people saw him walking and praising God. ¹⁰When they began to realize that he was the one who sat by the Beautiful Gate at the temple seeking charitable gifts, they were filled with amazement and ecstatic joy,[ii] because of what had happened to him.

Peter Points to the Times of Restoration of All Things

¹¹Then, while he was holding tightly to Peter and John, all the people were filled with awe and rushed together toward them at the covered walkway called Solomon's Colonnade. ¹²But when Peter saw this, he began to respond to the crowd, "Men, Israelites, why are you astonished at this healing, and why are you looking at us as if by our own power or godliness we have made him walk? ¹³The God of Abraham, Isaac, and Jacob, the God of our fathers, has glorified his Servant,[iii] Jesus, whom you handed over and denied in the presence of Pilate, even though he had decided to free Jesus. ¹⁴You denied the Holy and Righteous One and asked that a man who was a murderer be given to you! ¹⁵You killed the founder of life, the one whom God raised from the dead. We are witnesses of his resurrection.

[ii] Ecstatic joy" translates a Greek noun used when referring to spiritual ecstatic phenomena in ancient times.

[iii] Or, "Son." Peter is using a word which can mean "servant" or "son." Also in verse 26.

¹⁶"Now these things have been done by faith in the name of Jesus. The name of Jesus has strengthened this man whom you see and know. That faith, which is through Jesus, has given him this complete healing in front of all of you."

¹⁷"But now, brothers, I know that you acted in ignorance, just as your leaders also did. ¹⁸But God announced beforehand, through the mouth of all the prophets, the things his Christ would suffer. He has fulfilled those prophecies in this way. ¹⁹Therefore, repent and turn back to God so that your sins might be wiped away, ²⁰so that times of refreshing might come from the presence of the Lord, and so that he might send the one he chose for you, Jesus, the Christ. ²¹Heaven will honor him as its guest until the times of the restoration of everything that God spoke through the mouth of his holy prophets long ago. ²²Moses said,

> " 'The Lord your God will raise up for you a prophet like me from among your brothers. You must listen to him, to everything he speaks to you.
>
> ²³" 'But it will come about that every soul who does not listen to that prophet will be rooted out from among the people.'[i]

²⁴"In addition, all the prophets starting with Samuel and continuing on—all who spoke—foretold these days. ²⁵You are the sons of the prophets, and of the covenant which God gave to your fathers, saying to Abraham,

> " 'And in your seed all the families of the earth will be blessed.'[ii]

²⁶"God raised up his Servant first for you, and sent him to bless you by turning each of you from your evil ways."

---

[i] See Deuteronomy 15:18-19.
[ii] Genesis 22:18

The Religious Leaders Warn Peter and John

Chapter Four

¹But while they were speaking to the people, the priests, the commander of the temple guard, and the Sadducees violently restrained them. ²They were very angry because Peter and John were teaching the people and proclaiming in Jesus the resurrection from the dead. ³They arrested them and put them in jail until the next day, for it was already evening. ⁴Then, many of those who had heard the message believed it, and the number of men grew to about five thousand.

⁵On the next day, the rulers, the elders, and the scribal scholars were gathered in Jerusalem; ⁶the high priest, Annas, was there, as well as Caiaphas, John, Alexander, and all the family members of the high priest. ⁷They placed Peter and John in the middle and began to question them, "By what power, or by what name have you done this?"

⁸Then Peter was filled with the Holy Spirit and said to them, "Rulers and elders of the people, ⁹if we are undergoing a judicial inquiry today because of a good deed done for a sick man, because you want to know how he has been healed, ¹⁰let it be known to all of you and to all the people of Israel that it is by the name of the Nazarene, Jesus Christ, whom you crucified, whom God raised from the dead, by his name this man stands in front of you whole. ¹¹He is the stone, the one rejected by you, the builders, the one which has become the chief cornerstone.[iii] ¹²There is no salvation in anyone else; for there is no other name under heaven given to men by which we can be saved."

¹³When they saw the bold clarity of Peter and John, and understood that they were uneducated and did not have religious training, they were astonished, and they began to realize that they had been with Jesus. ¹⁴However, since they saw the man who had been healed standing with them, they did not have anything to say in response. ¹⁵After they commanded them

---

[iii] See Psalm 118:22.

to step outside of the Sanhedrin, they conferred with each other. ¹⁶They asked, "What shall we do with these men? For it is obvious to everyone living in Jerusalem that a remarkable miracle has been done through them, and we cannot deny it. ¹⁷But in order that it is not spread further among the people, we will forbid them, under threat of punishment, to speak any longer to anyone in this name."

¹⁸When they had summoned them, they commanded them not to speak or teach at all in the name of Jesus. ¹⁹But Peter and John responded and said to them, "Whether it is right in God's sight to obey you rather than God, you must judge. ²⁰For we are not able to stop speaking about what we have seen and heard."

²¹When they had threatened them even more, they released them. They could not discover a way to punish them, because all the people were glorifying God for what had happened; ²²for the man who received this miracle of healing was over forty years old.

The Believers Pray for Boldness and Miracles

²³After they were released, they went to their fellow believers and reported everything the chief priests and the elders had said to them. ²⁴When they heard it, they raised their voices to God with one passion and said, "Oh Absolute Ruler, you who have made the heaven and the earth, the sea and all the things in them. ²⁵You spoke by the Holy Spirit through the mouth of our father, your servant David,

> " 'Why are the nations in such tumult, and why do the people dwell on foolishness?
>
> ²⁶" 'The kings of the earth make themselves ready, and the rulers were brought together at the same location against the Lord and against his Christ.'[i]

²⁷For most assuredly, both Herod and Pontius Pilate—along with the Gentiles and the people of Israel—were brought

---

[i] Psalm 2:1-2

together in this city against your holy servant Jesus, whom you anointed. ²⁸They were brought together to do everything your hand and your counsel had decided in advance would be done. ²⁹And now, Lord, pay attention to their threats, and give your servants the ability to speak your word with all boldness, ³⁰while you stretch forth your hand for healing, signs, and wonders to be done through the name of your holy servant Jesus."

³¹When they had prayed, the place they were gathered was shaken, and they were all filled with the Holy Spirit and continued speaking the word of God with boldness.

The Believers Value Each Other more Than Possessions

³²The multitude of those who believed were of one heart and soul. None of them said that his possessions were his own, but everything was of little value to them. ³³The apostles continued to testify about the resurrection of the Lord Jesus with great power, and great grace continued upon all of them. ³⁴For there were none among them who were needy; those who owned fields or houses regularly sold them, and brought the proceeds of the sales ³⁵and placed it beside the feet of the apostles. They distributed to each person according to what they needed.

³⁶Then Joseph, who was called Barnabas by the apostles—which is translated Son of Encouragement—a Levite raised in Cyprus, ³⁷*also* sold a field that he owned and brought the money and placed it at the feet of the apostles.

The Danger of Lying to the Holy Spirit: Ananias and Sapphira

Chapter Five

¹But another man by the name of Ananias, along with his wife Sapphira, sold a property ²and embezzled[ii] from the proceeds. His wife also was aware of it. Ananias brought a portion of the proceeds and placed it at the feet of the apostles.

---

ii Ananias had committed the full proceeds of the sale to the believers, but then secretly withheld (embezzled) some of the proceeds.

³Peter said, "Ananias, how has Satan filled your heart to the point you lied to the Holy Spirit, and embezzled from the proceeds of the field? ⁴While it remained unsold was it not your possession? When it was sold, wasn't the money yours to control? Why did you plan this deed in your heart? You did not lie to men but to God."

⁵When Ananias heard these words, he fell down and expired.[i] At that, great fear came upon all who heard of it. ⁶Then the young men got up, wrapped his clothing around him, and carried him out to bury him.

⁷After a span of about three hours, his wife came in. She did not know what had happened. ⁸Then Peter asked her, "Tell me, was this what you received for the field?"

She responded, "Yes, that is how much we received."

⁹Peter said to her, "How could you agree to test the Spirit of the Lord? Look, the feet of the men who buried your husband are at the door, and they will carry you out also."

¹⁰She immediately fell at his feet and expired. The young men came in and found her dead, and they carried her out and buried her with her husband. ¹¹Then great fear came upon the whole church and upon everyone who heard about these things.

Jesus Stretches Out His Hand with Healings, Signs and Wonders

¹²Many signs and wonders were done among the people through the hands of the apostles. They kept on meeting with one passion in Solomon's Colonnade; ¹³none of the rest of those there dared to join them, but the people held them in honor. ¹⁴Even more, multitudes of those who came to faith, both men and women, were being added to the Lord, ¹⁵with the result that they carried the sick into the wider streets and place them upon stretchers and mats so that when Peter came by his shadow might overshadow some of them. ¹⁶Multitudes of those around the city of Jerusalem also came to the city bringing those who

---

[i] Or, "breathed out his last breath." Also in verse 10.

were sick and oppressed by unclean spirits, and all of them were being healed.

The Religious Leaders Punish the Apostles

17But the High Priest and all those with him, those who were from the sect of the Sadducees, made their move, because they were filled with concern. 18As a result, they laid their hands on the apostles and threw them into the city jail. 19But an angel of the Lord opened the doors of the prison during the night, brought them out and said, 20"Go, take your stand, and speak the whole message about this life to the people in the temple!"

21When they heard this, they went into the temple at dawn and began to teach.

After the High Priest and those with him arrived, they called the Sanhedrin—the whole council of elders of the sons of Israel—and sent a message to the jail that the apostles be brought to them. 22But when their assistants arrived, they did not find them in the prison. They returned and reported this. 23They said, "We found the prison closed with full security, and the guards stationed at the door. But when we opened it, we did not find anyone inside."

24As the commander of the temple guard and the chief priests were listening to these words, they were extremely perplexed about them, and wondered what this might mean. 25At that time, someone came and reported to them, "Listen, the men whom you put in the prison have taken a position in the temple and are teaching the people."

26Then the commander came with his officers and led them away, but not with force, because they were afraid the people might stone them. 27When they had brought them, they stationed them in the Sanhedrin, and the High Priest questioned them 28asking, "Didn't we command you not to teach in this name? Now look, you have filled Jerusalem with your teaching. You want to bring the blood of this man on us."

²⁹Peter and the apostles responded and said, "We are required to obey God rather than men. ³⁰The God of our fathers raised Jesus, whom you killed by hanging him on a tree. ³¹God exalted him to his right hand as Leader and Savior to grant repentance and the forgiveness of sins to Israel. ³²We are witnesses to these things, as is the Holy Spirit whom God gave to those who obey him."

³³When they had listened, they were furious, and they wanted to kill them. ³⁴But a certain Pharisee by the name of Gamaliel stood up in the Sanhedrin. He was honored as a teacher of the law by all the people. He ordered that the men be put outside for a little while. ³⁵He said to them, "Men, Israelites, take stock of your actions against these men and what you are about to do. ³⁶For in the past, Theudas rose up claiming to be someone himself. About four hundred men joined him. He was killed and everyone who had believed him were scattered and came to nothing. ³⁷After this, Judas the Galilean arose in the days of the census and led people after him in revolt. He also was killed, and all those who had believed him were scattered. ³⁸Now I speak to you about the present situation. Free these men and stay away from them. For if this counsel or activity is from men it will come to an end. ³⁹But if it is from God, you cannot destroy them, lest you also find yourselves fighting against God."

They were persuaded by him. ⁴⁰When they summoned the apostles, they beat them and commanded them not to speak in the name of Jesus. Then they released them.

⁴¹The apostles were rejoicing as they departed from the Sanhedrin, because they had been considered worthy to suffer dishonor for the sake of the Name. ⁴²Every day in the temple and from house to house they did not stop teaching and proclaiming the good news about Jesus the Messiah.[i]

---

[i] Or, "Christ."

The Apostles Build Their Ministry Team to Handle the Growth
Chapter Six

¹In those days, when the numbers of the disciples were multiplying, the Hellenistic Jews[ii] grumbled against the Hebrew Jews because their widows were being overlooked in the daily food service. ²Then the twelve called the multitude of the disciples and said, "It is not proper for us to forsake the word of God to serve meals. ³So, brothers, carefully select seven men from among you who are of good reputation, who are full of the Spirit and wisdom. We will appoint them to this need. ⁴Then we will focus on prayer and preparing the food of the word."

⁵The plan pleased all of the multitude of believers, and they chose Stephen, a man full of faith and the Holy Spirit, Philip, Prochorus, Nicanor, Timon, Parmenas, and Nicolas, a proselyte from Antioch. ⁶They had them stand in front of the apostles, and after they prayed, they laid hands on them.

⁷The word of God was spreading, and the number of disciples in Jerusalem was greatly increasing; and a great number of priests were becoming obedient to the faith.

Signs and Wonders Move Beyond the Apostles: Stephen

⁸Then Stephen, full of grace and power, was performing signs and great miracles among the people. ⁹But some rose up from the synagogue called Libertinus,[iii] both Cyrenians and Alexandrians, as well as others from Cilicia and Asia. They were arguing with Steven, ¹⁰but they were not strong enough to resist the wisdom and the Spirit by which he spoke.

¹¹Then they bribed men who said, "We have heard him speaking blasphemous words against Moses and against God."

[ii] Greek speaking Jews from other parts of the Roman world who had returned to Jerusalem.

[iii] "Libertinus" is a Latin word which means freed man. It refers to someone freed from slavery, perhaps because the synagogue was founded by freed slaves.

¹²They stirred up the people, the elders, and the scribal scholars. They attacked him, seized him, and brought him to the Sanhedrin. ¹³Then they presented false witnesses who said, "This man has not stopped speaking declarations against this holy place and the law. ¹⁴For we have heard him say that this Jesus of Nazareth will destroy this place and change the customs that Moses has handed down to us."

¹⁵When they looked at him, everyone sitting in the Sanhedrin saw his face look like the face of an angel.

Stephen Testifies to the Sanhedrin

Chapter Seven

¹Then the High Priest said, "Are these things true?"

²Then Stephen responded, "Men, brothers and fathers, listen carefully! The God of glory appeared to our father Abraham while he was still in Mesopotamia, before he lived in Haran. ³He said to him, 'Go out from your land and from your relatives and move to the land that I will show to you.'

⁴"Then he moved from the land of the Chaldeans and lived in Haran. From there, after his father died, God resettled him in this land where we now live. ⁵But he did not give him an inheritance in it, not even a square foot. Yet, while he did not have a child, God promised to give it as a possession to him and to his descendants after him. ⁶God explained it this way, that his descendants would be resident aliens in a foreign land, and they would be enslaved and treated badly for four hundred years. ⁷But the nation which they will serve, 'I will judge,' God said, 'and after these things I will bring them out and they will worship me in this place.' ⁸He then gave them the covenant of circumcision; and in this way Abraham became the father of Isaac and circumcised him on the eighth day. Isaac became the father of Jacob, and Jacob became the father of the twelve patriarchs.

⁹"The patriarchs were jealous of Joseph and sold him into Egypt; but God was with him. ¹⁰He delivered him from all his difficulties, and gave him grace and wisdom before Pharaoh, king of Egypt. Pharaoh made him ruler over Egypt, and over his whole household.

¹¹"Then a famine came upon the whole land of Egypt and Canaan, along with great difficulty. Our fathers could not find food. ¹²When Jacob heard that there was grain in Egypt, he sent our fathers there the first time. ¹³On the second trip, Joseph made himself known to his brothers, and Joseph's lineage was made known to Pharaoh. ¹⁴Then Joseph sent a message and summoned his father Jacob, and all his relatives, seventy-five souls in all. ¹⁵Jacob came down to Egypt, and he and all our fathers died. ¹⁶They brought them from there to Shechem, and buried them in the tomb that Abraham had paid the asking price in silver to the sons of Hamor in Shechem.

¹⁷"When the time of the promise God had given Abraham drew near, the people grew and multiplied in Egypt, ¹⁸until the time that another king arose in Egypt who did not know Joseph. ¹⁹This king took advantage of our people and mistreated our fathers forcing them to expose their infants so that they would not survive.

²⁰"Moses was born at a strategic time, and he was beautiful to God; he was raised for three months in his father's home. ²¹Then, when he was exposed, the daughter of Pharaoh took him and raised him as her own son. ²²Moses was instructed in all the wisdom of Egypt; he was powerful in his words and achievements.

²³"When he was forty years old, a desire rose in his heart to visit his brothers, the sons of Israel. ²⁴When he saw one of them being harmed, he defended him and took vengeance on the one mistreating him, striking the Egyptian down. ²⁵Moses thought his brothers would understand that God was giving them deliverance through his hand; but they did not understand. ²⁶On the next day, he presented himself to them while some

were fighting among themselves. He tried to reconcile them in peace saying, 'Men, you are brothers; why are you harming each other?' ²⁷But the one who was hurting his neighbor pushed Moses forcefully away asking, 'Who made you a ruler and judge over us? ²⁸You don't want to kill me in the same way you killed the Egyptian yesterday, do you?' ²⁹Then, at this question, Moses fled and became an exile in the land of Midian—where he had two sons.

³⁰"After forty years had passed, an angel appeared to him in the desert of Mount Sinai in the flame of a burning bush. ³¹Moses saw it and wondered at the sight. When he drew near to investigate it, the Lord's voice came to him, ³²'I am the God of your fathers, the God of Abraham, Isaac, and Jacob.' Moses shook with fear and did not dare to investigate it.

³³"The Lord said to him, 'Remove the sandals from your feet, for the place where you are standing is holy land. ³⁴I have surely seen the suffering of my people who are in Egypt, and I have heard their groans. I have come to rescue them. Now come, I am sending you to Egypt.'

³⁵"This is the Moses, whom they rejected saying, 'Who appointed you ruler and judge?' God sent him ruler and liberator by the hand of the angel who appeared to him in the thorn bush. ³⁶This man led them out by doing wonders and signs in land of Egypt, in the Red Sea, and in the desert for forty years.

³⁷"This is the Moses who said to the Sons of Israel, 'God will raise up a prophet like me from your brothers.' ³⁸This is the one who was with the congregation[i] and our fathers in the wilderness, and with the angel who spoke to him on Mount Sinai. He received living revelation to give to us. ³⁹Our fathers did not want to be obedient to him. They refused to listen and turned to Egypt in their hearts. ⁴⁰They said to Aaron, 'Make gods for us who will go before us. For this Moses, who led us

---

[i] The Greek word is ekklesia, (ἐκκλησία) which is most often translated "church" in other contexts.

out of Egypt, we do not know what has happened to him.' ⁴¹They made an idol in the form of a calf in those days, and they brought a sacrifice to the idol. They rejoiced in the works of their hands. ⁴²But God turned away and handed them over to worship the host of the heavens, just as it is written in the book of the prophets:

> " 'You did not offer sacrificial animals and offerings to me for forty years in the desert, did you, O house of Israel? ⁴³You took up the tent of Moloch, and the star of your god, Rephan,[ii] the images which you made to worship them, so I will resettle you beyond Babylon.'[iii]

⁴⁴"The tabernacle of the testimony was with our fathers in the desert. The one who spoke to Moses commanded him to make it according to the pattern which he saw. ⁴⁵When they received possession of it, our fathers brought it with Joshua when they took possession of the nations, whom God drove out from before our fathers until the time of David. ⁴⁶He found favor before God, and asked to secure a temple for the house of Jacob, ⁴⁷but Solomon built the house for him.

⁴⁸"But the Most High does not live in things made with human hands, just as the prophet said,

> ⁴⁹" ' "Heaven is my throne, and the earth is a footstool for my feet. What kind of house will you build for me," asks the Lord, "or what place for my rest? ⁵⁰Has not my hand made all these things?" '[iv]

⁵¹"You are just like your fathers, stiff-necked and uncircumcised in heart and ears; you are always resisting the Holy Spirit. ⁵²Were there any of the prophets your fathers did

---

[ii] Rephan or Remphan, generally thought to refer to worship involving the planet Saturn.

[iii] See Amos 5:25-27. Septuagint (Greek translation of the Hebrew Bible).

[iv] Isaiah 66:1-2

not persecute? They killed those who foretold the coming of the Righteous One. Now you have become his betrayers and murderers, ⁵³you who received the law by the decrees of angels, but did not obey it."

The Religious Mob Stones Stephen

⁵⁴When they heard these things, their hearts were enraged, and they gnashed their teeth at him. ⁵⁵But Stephen was filled with the Holy Spirit. He fixed his eyes on heaven and saw the glory of God, and Jesus standing at the right hand of God. ⁵⁶He said, "Listen closely, I see the heavens opening and the Son of Man standing at the right hand of God."

⁵⁷They shouted with a great cry, covered their ears, and they rushed at him with one intent. ⁵⁸They expelled him from the city and began to stone him. The witnesses put their garments at the feet of a young man named Saul.

⁵⁹They were stoning Stephen while he was calling out saying, "Lord Jesus, receive my spirit." ⁶⁰Then, when he fell to his knees, he cried out with a loud voice, "Lord, do not hold this sin against them." When he said this, he fell asleep.

Chapter Eight

¹Saul was pleased at his execution.

On that day, a great persecution broke out against the church in Jerusalem. Everyone was scattered across the regions of Judea and Samaria except the apostles. ²Devout men made arrangements for Stephen's burial, and they mourned deeply over him. ³But Saul began to destroy the church. He was searching from house to house, and dragged both men and women away and put them in prison.

Signs and Wonders Multiply in the Church

⁴Then those who had been scattered traveled about proclaiming the good news of the word. ⁵Philip went down to the city of Samaria and preached Christ to them. ⁶With one

focus, the crowds were paying attention to what Philip was saying while they heard and saw the miracles he was doing. [7]For many of those who had unclean spirits were cleansed, and the demons came out with loud shouting; many who were paralyzed and those who were unable to walk also were being healed. [8]As a result, there was much joy in that city.

Simon the Sorcerer Experiences the Kingdom

[9]There was a certain man whose name was Simon who previously had practiced sorcery in the city. He had overwhelmed the people of Samaria with wonder, claiming to be someone great. [10]Everyone from the least to the greatest had paid attention to him saying, "This man is the Power of God, which is called Great." [11]They had paid attention to him because he had overwhelmed their senses with his sorcery for a long time. [12]When they believed the good news that Philip was proclaiming about the Kingdom of God and the name of Jesus Christ, men and women were both being baptized. [13]Simon himself also believed and was baptized and served Philip personally. He was beside himself with joy when he saw the signs and the great miracles that were happening.

[14]When the apostles in Jerusalem heard that the Samaritans had received the word of God, they sent Peter and John to them. [15]They came down and prayed for them that they might receive the Holy Spirit, [16]for He had not yet fallen upon any of them. They had only been baptized in the name of the Lord Jesus. [17]Then they laid their hands on them, and they received the Holy Spirit.

[18]When Simon saw that the Holy Spirit was given through the laying on of the hands of the apostles, he offered money to them. [19]He said, "Give this authority to me also, so that when I lay hands on someone, they may receive the Holy Spirit."

[20]But Peter said to him, "May your silver go with you to ruin, for you thought to obtain the gift of God through money. [21]There is no part or share for you in this message, because your heart is not right before God. [22]Therefore, repent from this evil

of yours, and ask the Lord if perhaps this ambition of your heart might be forgiven, ²³for I see that you are filled with bitter envy and shackled to unrighteousness."

²⁴Then Simon responded and said, "You yourselves pray to the Lord for me so that nothing that you have said comes upon me."

²⁵After they warned them and spoke the word of the Lord, they began their journey back to Jerusalem, but proclaimed the good news in many villages of the Samaritans.

The Ethiopian Eunuch is Saved and Baptized

²⁶Then an angel of the Lord spoke to Philip and told him, "Arise and go south on the road that goes down from Jerusalem to Gaza—this is the desert road." ²⁷Philip arose and went. Unexpectedly, he encountered a man, an Ethiopian Eunuch, a court official of Candace, queen of Ethiopia. He was over all her treasury, and he had come to worship in Jerusalem. ²⁸He was on his way home and was sitting on his traveling-chariot[i] reading the prophet Isaiah. ²⁹The Spirit said to Philip, "Go and follow this chariot closely."

³⁰When Philip had run up to the chariot, he heard him reading the prophet Isaiah and asked, "Do you understand what you are reading?"

³¹But the official said, "Truly, how can I, if someone does not instruct me?" Then he invited Philip to come up and sit with him.

³²The passage of Scripture he was reading was this:

> "He was led as a sheep to slaughter, and as a lamb before those shearing him is silent, so he did not open his mouth. ³³Because of his low status, he was denied justice; who can

---

[i] As opposed to a war chariot.

speak of his descendants? For his life was taken from the earth."[ii]

³⁴The official responded to Philip and said, "I ask you, about whom was the prophet saying this? About himself or someone else?" ³⁵Then Philip opened his mouth and, beginning from this Scripture, he proclaimed the good news about Jesus to him.

³⁶As they were traveling down the road, they came upon some water. The official asked, "See, there is water. What would stop me from being baptized?" ³⁷Philip said, "If you believe with all your heart, it is permitted." He responded and said, "I believe that Jesus Christ is the Son of God."

³⁸He gave the command to stop the chariot, and both the official and Philip went down into the water, and Philip baptized him. ³⁹When they came up from the water, the Spirit of the Lord caught Philip away, and the official did not see him any longer. Then he went on his way rejoicing. ⁴⁰But Philip found himself in Azotus. As he passed through, he proclaimed the good news to all the cities until he came to Caesarea.

Jesus Calls Saul into the Kingdom of God

Chapter Nine

¹While this was happening, Saul was still breathing out threats and murder against the disciples of the Lord. He went to the high priest ²and asked for letters from him to the synagogues in Damascus, that if he found any who belonged to the Way, whether men or women, he might arrest them and bring them to Jerusalem. ³While he was going, as he drew near to Damascus, a light from heaven suddenly flashed around him. ⁴He fell to the ground and heard a voice speaking to him, "Saul, Saul, why are you persecuting me?"

[ii] Isaiah 53:7-8

⁵He responded, "Who are you, Lord?"

"I am Jesus who you are persecuting. ⁶Now get up, go into the city, and you will be told what you must do."

⁷The men who were traveling with him stood speechless. They heard the voice but did not see anyone. ⁸Then Saul got up from the ground. When he opened his eyes he could see nothing. They brought him into Damascus leading him by the hand. ⁹He was there for three days. He was unable to see, and did not eat or drink.

¹⁰In Damascus, there was a certain disciple named Ananias. The Lord spoke to him in a vision, "Ananias!" He responded, "Here I am, Lord."

¹¹Then the Lord said to him, "Get up and go to the street called Straight Street and ask at Judas' house for a man from Tarsus named Saul. For—and take note of this—he is praying ¹²and he saw a man in a vision by the name of Ananias come in and lay hands on him so that he might see again."

¹³Ananias responded, "Lord, I have heard from many people about this man and how much harm he has done to your saints in Jerusalem; ¹⁴and he has authority here from the chief priests to arrest everyone who calls upon your name."

¹⁵But the Lord said to him, "Go. This man is my select vessel to carry my name before nations, kings, and the sons of Israel. ¹⁶For I myself will show him how much he is required to suffer for my name."

¹⁷Then Ananias went and entered the house, placed his hands upon him and said, "Brother Saul, the Lord Jesus, who appeared to you on the road by which you came, has sent me so that you might get your sight back and be filled with the Holy Spirit." ¹⁸Immediately, something like flakes of skin fell from Saul's eyes and he regained his sight. Then he arose and was baptized.

¹⁹When he had taken some food, he regained his strength. He remained with the Damascus disciples for a number of days,

²⁰and immediately began to proclaim Jesus in the synagogues, that he is the Son of God. ²¹Everyone who heard him was overwhelmed with shock, and repeatedly asked, "Isn't this the man who destroyed those who were calling upon this name in Jerusalem? And didn't he come here for the very purpose of arresting them and taking them back to the High Priest?" ²²Saul kept growing stronger and confounding the Jews who lived in Damascus, proving that Jesus is the Christ.

Saul Escapes Damascus and Returns to Jerusalem

²³After much time had gone by, the Jewish leaders began to make plans to charge him with a capital offense, ²⁴but their plan was revealed to Saul. Then they began to watch the gates closely every day and every night, so that they might execute him. ²⁵But his disciples took him by night and lowered him in a basket through an opening in the wall.

²⁶When he came to Jerusalem, he attempted to join the disciples, but everyone was afraid of him, and did not believe he was a disciple. ²⁷Then Barnabas took firm hold of Saul and led him to the apostles. He explained in detail to them how he saw the Lord on the road, and that the Lord spoke to him; and how Saul spoke openly in the name of Jesus in Damascus.

²⁸Then Paul stayed with them, going in and out of Jerusalem speaking openly in the name of the Lord. ²⁹He also was speaking and debating with the Greek speaking Jews, but they were planning to execute him. ³⁰When the brothers found out, they brought him down to Caesarea and sent him away to Tarsus.

The Lord Grants Peace to the Church

³¹As a result, the church throughout all of Judea, Galilee, and Samaria had peace. The church multiplied because it built on, and moved forward in, the fear of the Lord and the encouragement of the Holy Spirit.

Peter Demonstrates the Kingdom with Power

³²While Peter was traveling throughout the countryside, he also went down to visit the saints who lived in Lydda. ³³He found a certain man by the name of Aeneas who had been confined to his bed for eight years because he was paralyzed. ³⁴Peter said to him, "Aeneas, Jesus Christ is healing you. Get up and make your own bed." He immediately got up. ³⁵Everyone who lived in Lydda and Sharon saw him and turned to the Lord.

³⁶In Joppa, there was a certain female disciple by the name of Tabitha (that is Dorcas when translated into Greek). She was full of good works and acts of charity; and was continually involved in doing them. ³⁷During that time, she got sick and died. After they washed her, they placed her in an upstairs room. ³⁸When the disciples heard that Peter was in Lydda, and since Lydda is near Joppa, they sent two men to him pleading, "Do not delay in coming to us."

³⁹Then Peter got up and went with them. When he arrived, they brought him into the upper room. All the widows stood with him crying and showing him the inner and outer garments that Dorcas made when she was with them.

⁴⁰After Peter sent them all out, he got on his knees and prayed. He turned to the body and said, "Tabitha, get up." She opened her eyes, and when she saw Peter, she sat up. ⁴¹He gave her his hand and helped her up. When he had called the saints and the widows, he presented her to them alive. ⁴²This became known all-around Joppa, and many believed in the Lord. ⁴³Peter stayed many days in Joppa with a tanner named Simon.

The Kingdom Mission Expands to the Gentiles

Chapter Ten

¹There was a certain man in Caesarea by the name of Cornelius, a centurion from a *Roman* military unit called the Italian

Cohort.[i] ²He was pious, and he and his entire household feared God.[ii] He made many charitable contributions to the people and prayed to God about everything. ³About the ninth hour[iii] of the day, he clearly saw an angel of God come to him in a vision. The angel called, "Cornelius!"

⁴He stared at the angel and was filled with fear. He asked, "What is it, Lord?"

Then the angel said to him, "Your prayers and your charitable contributions have ascended to heaven as a memorial before God. ⁵Now send men to Joppa and summon Simon, who is also called Peter. ⁶This man is the guest of a certain Simon the tanner, who has a house beside the sea.

⁷As soon as the angel who was speaking to him left, he called two of his personal servants and a pious soldier who was loyal to him. ⁸When he had explained everything to them, he sent them to Joppa.

Peter's Ecstatic Vision Prepares Him to Go to Gentiles

⁹On the next day at about the sixth hour,[iv] while they were journeying and drawing near the city, Peter went up to the roof to pray. ¹⁰But he became hungry and wanted to eat. While they were preparing the food, he experienced an ecstatic vision.[v] ¹¹He saw heaven opening and a vessel like a great sail being let down by its four corners to the earth. ¹²It contained all the quadrupeds

---

[i] A Roman military cohort was about 600 soldiers.

[ii] This description indicates that Cornelius was a believer in the true God, but did not know about Jesus.

[iii] 3:00 PM

[iv] Noon

[v] An ecstatic vision" translates a Greek noun used when referring to spiritual ecstatic phenomena in ancient times.

and creeping things of the earth, as well as birds of the air. ¹³A voice came to him, "Get up, Peter. Slaughter them and eat."

¹⁴But Peter said, "Most certainly not, Lord. I have never eaten anything that was not kosher[i] or that was unclean."

¹⁵Again, the voice came to him a second time, "You must not make what God has cleansed into something that isn't kosher." ¹⁶This happened three times and the vessel was immediately taken up into heaven.

¹⁷Peter was at a loss as he struggled with what the vision which he had seen might mean. At just that moment, the men sent by Cornelius had learned where Simon's house was, and they were now standing at the entrance. ¹⁸They called out and asked if a Simon who was called Peter was a guest there.

¹⁹While Peter was still thinking seriously about the vision, the Spirit said to him, "Listen, three men are asking for you. ²⁰But get up, go down to them, and go with them. Do not doubt that I have sent them myself."

²¹Then Peter went down to the men and said, "Look here, I am the one you are seeking. What is the reason you have come?"

²²They said, "The centurion Cornelius, a righteous and God-fearing man, who is spoken well of by the entire nation of the Jews, was directed by a holy angel to summon you to his house, and to hear a message from you." ²³As a result, he invited them in and gave them lodging.

On the next day, he got up and went with them; and some of the brothers from Joppa accompanied him. ²⁴The day after that, he arrived in Caesarea. Cornelius was expecting them and called together his relatives and close friends. ²⁵When Peter entered the house, Cornelius met him, fell at his feet, and paid homage to him.

---

[i] More literally, "Common," as in common for all people, but not for Israel. Also in verse 15 and 11:9.

²⁶But Peter raised him to his feet saying, "Stand up. I am also a man myself." ²⁷After he conversed with him, he went in and found many people gathered together.

²⁸He told them, "You understand that it is unlawful for a Jewish man to closely associate with a foreigner or to become a close friend with them. But God has shown me not to call any man common or unclean. ²⁹For this reason, I also came without any objection when I was summoned. Therefore, may I ask for what reason you have sent for me?"

³⁰Then Cornelius explained, "Four days ago at this very hour, I was praying during the ninth hour[ii] at my house, when, suddenly, a man stood in front of me in bright clothing. ³¹He said, 'Cornelius, your prayer has been heard, and your charitable contributions have been remembered before God. ³²Therefore, send to Joppa and summon Simon, who is called Peter. He is staying in a house by the sea as a guest of Simon the tanner.'

³³"So I immediately sent for you, and you have graciously responded and have come. Now we have all come before God to listen to everything that the Lord has commanded you to share."

The Holy Spirit Pours Out on the Gentiles

³⁴Then Peter began to speak and said, "Beyond all doubt, I understand that God does not discriminate between people. ³⁵He accepts those from every nation who fear him and work at doing what is right. ³⁶He sent this message to the people of Israel. He proclaimed the good news of peace through Jesus Christ. Jesus is Lord of everyone. ³⁷You yourselves know the things that happened through all of Judea, beginning from Galilee after the baptism which John preached; ³⁸how God anointed Jesus of Nazareth with the Holy Spirit and power, and how he went everywhere doing good and healing everyone who

---

[ii] Starting at 3:00 PM.

was oppressed by the accuser,[i] because God was with him. ³⁹We are witnesses of everything that he did in the land of the Jewish people and also in Jerusalem. Then they executed him by hanging him on a tree. ⁴⁰God raised this man up on the third day, and allowed him to be seen, ⁴¹not by all the people, but by witnesses chosen by God beforehand. He was seen by us who ate and drank with him after his resurrection from the dead. ⁴²He commanded us to preach to the people and to testify that this man is the one who is appointed by God as judge of the living and the dead. ⁴³All the prophets testify about him, that everyone who believes in him receives the forgiveness of sins through his name."

⁴⁴While Peter was speaking these words, the Holy Spirit fell upon everyone who had heard the message. ⁴⁵The believers who were circumcised, who had come with Peter, were overwhelmed with joy[ii] that the gift of the Holy Spirit was poured out also upon the Gentiles. ⁴⁶They heard them speaking with language gifts[iii] and praising God.

Then Peter interjected, ⁴⁷"Certainly no one is able to object to these people being baptized with water; they have received the Holy Spirit just as we have." ⁴⁸So, he ordered them to be baptized in the name of Jesus Christ. Then they asked him to remain with them for a number of days.

Peter Explains the Gentile Mission in Jerusalem

Chapter Eleven

¹Then the apostles and brother who lived throughout Judea heard that the Gentiles also had received the word of God. ²When Peter went up to Jerusalem, those who were circumcised

---

[i] Traditionally, "devil." The name means to slander or accuse. For this reason, this word is most often translated "Accuser" in this Bible version.

[ii] "Overwhelmed with joy" translates a Greek verb used when referring to spiritual ecstatic phenomena in ancient times.

[iii] See Acts 2:3.

began to argue with him ³asserting, "You entered a house with uncircumcised men and ate with them."

⁴Peter began to make things clear to them in a logical fashion, ⁵"I was in the city of Joppa praying, and I had an ecstatic vision. I saw a vessel like a great sail being let down by its four corners from heaven, and it came right up to me. ⁶When I focused on it, I began to study it and saw the quadrupeds of the earth, as well as the wild animals, the creeping things, and the birds of the air. ⁷Then I heard a voice speaking to me, 'Peter, slaughter them and eat.'

⁸"But I said, 'Most certainly not, Lord; for nothing that is not kosher or that is unclean has ever entered my mouth.'

⁹"Then the voice from heaven responded a second time, 'You must not make what God has cleansed into something that isn't kosher.'

¹⁰"This happened three times before everything was drawn back up into heaven. ¹¹Significantly, at just that moment, three men stopped at the house where I was. They had been sent from Caesarea for me. ¹²The Spirit told me to go with them and not to doubt them. These six brothers came with me and we went into the man's house. ¹³He told me how he saw an angel standing in his house telling him, 'Send to Joppa and summon Simon who is called Peter. ¹⁴He will share a message with you by which you will be saved, you and your house.'

¹⁵"But when I had begun to speak, the Holy Spirit fell upon them just as he also first fell upon us. ¹⁶Then I remembered the words of the Lord when he said, 'John baptized with water, but you will be baptized in the Holy Spirit.' ¹⁷Therefore, if God gave the same gift to them that he gave to us who had believed in the Lord Jesus Christ, how could I get in God's way?"

¹⁸When they heard these things, they stopped questioning him and praised God saying, "So then, God has also given Gentiles repentance into life."

The Church in Antioch is Established

¹⁹The Jews who had been scattered by the persecution that had happened at the time of Stephen had traveled up to Phoenicia, Cyprus, and Antioch. They shared the word only with the Jewish people. ²⁰However, there were some from among them, men of Cyprus and Cyrene, who came to Antioch and spoke also to the Hellenistic Jews[i] preaching the good news about the Lord Jesus. ²¹The hand of the Lord was with them, and a large number believed and turned to the Lord.

²²The report about them got the attention of the church in Jerusalem, and they sent Barnabas to Antioch. ²³When he arrived and saw the grace of God, he rejoiced and encouraged everyone to stay connected to the Lord with focused hearts, ²⁴for Barnabas was a good man, full of the Holy Spirit and faith. A good number of people were also added to the Lord.

²⁵Then he went to Tarsus to look for Saul. ²⁶When he found him, he brought him to Antioch. As it happened, they met with the church for a full year and taught a good number of people. The disciples were first called Christians in Antioch.

A Prophetic Prediction from Agabus About Famine

²⁷During that time prophets from Jerusalem came down to Antioch. ²⁸One of them, by the name of Agabus, arose and through the Spirit predicted a severe famine that was about to come upon the whole Roman world.[ii] This happened during Claudius' reign.

²⁹Then the disciples, any who were well off, each determined to send assistance to the brothers who were living in Judea. ³⁰They carried this out and sent it to the elders by the hand of Barnabas and Saul.

---

[i] Greek speaking Jews from other parts of the Roman world outside of Judea and Jerusalem.

[ii] Or "inhabited world," usually referring to the Roman world in the gospels and Acts.

Herod Begins to Kill the Apostles

Chapter Twelve

¹At that time, King Herod laid hands on certain individuals from the church in order to persecute them. ²He had James the brother of John executed with a sword. ³When he saw that it pleased the Jewish leaders, he also proceeded to arrest Peter. This was during the days of Unleavened Bread.ⁱⁱⁱ ⁴After he had arrested him, he put him in prison with four squads of four soldiers to guard him. He planned to bring him out to the people after the Passover.

⁵Therefore, because Peter was being kept in the prison, the church was praying earnestly to God on his behalf.

An Angel Rescues Peter

⁶On the night before Herod was going to bring him before the people, Peter was sleeping between two soldiers where he was bound with two chains, and guards were at the door watching over the prison. ⁷Suddenly, an angel of the Lord drew near, and a light shone in the room. He struck Peter's side, woke him, and said, "Get up quickly!" Then the chains fell off his hands.

⁸The angel said to him, "Arrange your clothing and put on your sandals." Peter did just this. The angel said to him, "Wrap your outer garment around you and follow me."

⁹He followed him out of the cell, but he did not know if what the angel was doing was truly happening. He thought he was seeing a vision. ¹⁰They went past the first guard, and the second, and came to the iron gate that would bring them into the city. It opened automatically for them, and they came out and went down one street. Suddenly, the angel left him.

ⁱⁱⁱ The Feast of Unleavened Bread, a seven-day festival observing the Israelites departure from Egypt, begins the day after the Passover celebration.

¹¹Then Peter came to himself and said, "Now I know for certain that the Lord sent his angel and rescued me from the hand of Herod, and from all the Jewish people were expecting."

¹²When he recognized this, he went to the house of Mary, the mother of John, who was also called Mark. Many people had gathered and were praying there. ¹³When he knocked on the door of the gate, a servant girl named Rhoda came in response. ¹⁴She recognized Peter's voice and was so joyful that she did not open the door but ran to report that Peter was standing at the gate.

¹⁵They said to her, "You are experiencing spiritual rapture."[i] However, she kept on insisting that it was true. They responded, "It's his angel."

¹⁶Meanwhile, Peter kept knocking. When they opened the door, they saw him and were overwhelmed with ecstatic joy.[ii]

¹⁷He motioned with his hand for them to be silent and explained to them how the Lord brought him out from the prison. He told them, "Tell James and the brothers these things." Then he left them and went to another place.

¹⁸When the light of day came, there was no minor disturbance among the soldiers about what had happened to Peter. ¹⁹Then Herod searched for Peter but did not find him. He interrogated the guards and ordered that they be executed.

Herod went down to Caesarea and stayed there. ²⁰He was involved in an angry quarrel with the leaders of Tyre and Sidon. With one intent they came to him. They had convinced Blastus, the king's palace chamberlain, to support them. They were seeking peace because they received their food from the king's territory.

---

[i] The Greek word was often used to describe spiritual rapture. Because it was often associated with pagan activity, it was not the normal word used for spiritual rapture in the New Testament.

[ii] This Greek verb is the normal verb used when referring to a spiritual ecstatic phenomenon experienced in the early church.

²¹On the appointed day, Herod put on his royal robes, and when he had taken his place upon his judgment seat, he began to deliver a public speech to them. ²²Then the people began to cry out, "This is the voice of a god, and not a man."

²³Immediately, an angel of the Lord struck him severely because he did not give the glory to God. He was eaten by worms, and he expired.[iii]

²⁴However, the word of God kept on growing and multiplying.

²⁵Then Barnabas and Saul returned after fulfilling their ministry in Jerusalem. They brought John, who was called Mark, back with them.

Saul and Barnabas Commissioned and Sent Out

Chapter Thirteen

¹There were in Antioch, in the church there, prophets, Barnabas, Simeon, who was called Niger, and Lucius from Cyrene; and teachers, Manaen, who was brought up with Herod the Tetrarch, and Saul. ²While they were ministering to the Lord and fasting, the Holy Spirit said, "Set apart Barnabas and Saul for me at this time, to the work to which I have called them."

³Then, when they had fasted and prayed, they laid hands on them and released them from their ministry. ⁴Since they had been sent out by the Holy Spirit, they went down to Seleucia; and from there they sailed to Cyprus.

⁵When they arrived in Salamis, they began to proclaim the word of God in the Jewish synagogues, and they had John as their assistant.

[iii] Or, "breathed his last breath."

Acts 13:6

Paul Confronts a False Prophet

⁶When they had passed through the whole island and arrived in Paphos, they found a certain man who was a magus,ⁱ a Jewish false prophet by the name of Bar-Jesus. ⁷He was with the proconsul, Sergius Paul, who was an intelligent man. The proconsul summoned Barnabas and Saul intending to hear the word of God. ⁸But Elymas the magus, for this was how his name was interpreted, resisted them and attempted to turn the proconsul away from the faith. ⁹But Saul, who was also called Paul, was filled with the Holy Spirit and looked steadily at him. ¹⁰He said, "You who are full of every deceit and wrongdoing, son of the Accuser and enemy of all righteousness. Will you never stop making the straight path of the Lord crooked? ¹¹Now look, the hand of the Lord is against you, and you will be blind, unable to see the sun for a season."

Immediately mist and darkness fell on him, and he began looking for someone to lead him around by the hand. ¹²When the proconsul saw what happened, he believed and was astonished at the teaching of the Lord.

Paul and Barnabas in Pisidian Antioch

¹³When Paul and those with him had set sail from Paphos, they arrived in Perga in Pamphylia. There John deserted them and returned to Jerusalem. ¹⁴But Paul and Barnabas traveled from Perga and arrived in Pisidian Antioch. They went into the synagogue on the Sabbath day and sat down. ¹⁵After the reading of the Law and the Prophets, the synagogue officers sent a message to them that said, "Men, brothers, if you have any word of encouragement for the people, share it."

¹⁶Paul stood up and motioned with his hands for everyone to be quiet. Then he said, "Men, Israelites and you who are God

---

ⁱ Magus is the singular of magi. While the magi were associated with a religious caste in Parthia, in popular language those who practiced magic arts were also called magi. See Matthew 2 for the role the Parthian magi played at the birth of Jesus.

fearing, listen to me. ¹⁷The God of this people, Israel, chose our fathers and exalted them during their sojourn in the land of Egypt, and led them out of it with his uplifted arm. ¹⁸For about a forty-year period of time, he put up with them in the desert. ¹⁹He overthrew seven nations in Canaan and gave them the land as their inheritance.

²⁰"After these things, for about four hundred and fifty years, he gave them judges until *the time of* Samuel the prophet. ²¹At that time, they asked for a king, and God gave them Saul, Son of Kish, a man from the tribe of Benjamin who reigned for forty years. ²²After he removed Saul, he raised up David as a king for them, about whom he testified and said, 'I have found David the son of Jesse a man in accord with my heart. He will do all that I desire.'

²³"From the seed of this man, according to his promise, God raised up for Israel a Savior, Jesus. ²⁴Before he appeared, John had proclaimed a baptism of repentance for all the people of Israel. ²⁵As John was ending his race, he began to say, 'Who do you think that I am? I am not the Messiah.[ii] But listen, one is coming after me. I am not worthy to untie the sandals on his feet.'

²⁶"Men, brothers, sons of Abraham's family, and those among you who fear God; the message of this salvation has been sent to us. ²⁷For, those living in Jerusalem and their rulers were ignorant of this. They fulfilled the words of the prophets that are read every Sabbath by condemning him. ²⁸They found no basis for a death sentence, yet they asked Pilate to execute him. ²⁹When they had carried out all the things that were written about him, they took him off the tree and put him in a tomb. ³⁰Then God raised him from among the dead. ³¹He appeared over many days to those who traveled with him from Galilee to Jerusalem. They now are his witnesses to the people.

---

ii John 1:20

³²"We proclaim the good news to you about the promise that was given to the fathers. ³³God has fulfilled this promise to us their children by raising Jesus up. As it is written in the second Psalm,

> " 'You are my Son. Today I have become your Father.'[i]

³⁴"But that he raised him from among the dead, no longer subject to decay, he has said,

> " 'I will give you the holy and sure blessings of David.'[ii]

³⁵"Therefore, he also says in another Psalm,

> " 'You will not let your Holy One see decay.'[iii]

³⁶"For when David served the will of God in his own generation, he fell asleep and was buried with his fathers and saw decay. ³⁷But the one God raised, he did not see decay.

³⁸"Therefore, let it be known to you, men and brothers, that through this man the forgiveness of sins is proclaimed to you, forgiveness from all the things that you were not able to be justified by the Law of Moses; ³⁹in him, everyone who believes is justified. ⁴⁰Therefore, watch that what the prophets spoke does not happen to you,

> ⁴¹" 'Pay attention, you who look down on everything, be amazed and fade from sight, for I am working a thing in your days, a work that no one will believe if someone tells it to you.'[iv]"

⁴²When they were leaving, the leaders urged them to speak these words to them on the next Sabbath. ⁴³When the synagogue service ended, many of the Jews and the devout

---

[i] Psalm 2:7

[ii] Isaiah 55:3

[iii] Psalm 16:10

[iv] Habakkuk 1:5

proselytes followed Paul and Barnabas. They continued to speak to them and were persuading them to remain in the grace of God.

⁴⁴On the following Sabbath, almost all the city came together to hear the word of God. ⁴⁵When the Jewish leaders saw the crowds, they were filled with deep concern for their ways. They argued against and slandered the things being spoken by Paul.

⁴⁶Then Paul and Barnabas spoke fearlessly, "It was necessary to speak the word of God to you first. Since you have refused it, and do not judge yourselves worthy of eternal life, look, we are turning to the Gentiles. ⁴⁷For this is how the Lord has commissioned us,

> " 'I have made you a light to the Gentiles, so that
> you might be for salvation to the ends of the earth.'ᵛ"

⁴⁸When the Gentiles had heard this, they rejoiced and glorified the word of the Lord; and as many as had been appointed to eternal life believed.

⁴⁹The word of the Lord was spreading throughout the whole region. ⁵⁰Then the Jewish leaders incited the devout women who were prominent, and the foremost men of the city. They stirred up a persecution against Paul and Barnabas and expelled them from their region. ⁵¹But after they shook the dust from their feet against them, they went to Iconium. ⁵²The disciples were filled with joy and the Holy Spirit.

Paul and Barnabas in Iconium

Chapter Fourteen

¹In Iconium, they went into the Jewish synagogue together and spoke in such a way that a great number of both Jews and Greeks believed. ²But the Jews who refused to believe stirred up

---

ᵛ Isaiah 49:6

the souls[i] of the Gentiles and turned them against the brothers. ³Then they remained for a long time sharing openly about the Lord. He continued to bear witness to his word of grace by giving signs and wonders that were done through their hands. ⁴The assembly in the city was divided; some of its members were with the Jews, and some were with the apostles. ⁵But when the Gentiles and Jews, along with their leaders, made up their minds to treat them with contempt and stone them, ⁶they found out about it and fled to the region of Lycaonia around the cities of Lystra and Derbe. ⁷They also preached the good news there.

Paul and Barnabas in Lystra: Healing the Lame Man

⁸A certain man was sitting in Lystra, he had no strength in his feet. He was lame from his mother's womb and had never walked. ⁹This man heard Paul speaking. Paul looked intently at him and saw that he had faith to be healed.[ii] ¹⁰In a loud voice he said, "Get up and stand straight upon on your feet!" Then he jumped up and walked around.

¹¹When the crowds saw what Paul had done, they raised their voices and in the Lycaonian language said, "The gods have come down to us in the likeness of men." ¹²They called Barnabas, Zeus, and they called Paul, Hermes, because he was the one who led in the word. ¹³The priests of Zeus had a temple in front of the city. They brought bulls and garlands to the city gates planning to hold a sacrifice with the crowds.

¹⁴When the apostles Barnabas and Paul heard *this*, they tore their garments and rushed out into the crowd shouting ¹⁵and saying, "Men, why are you doing these things? We are men who feel the same things you feel and are proclaiming the good news to you about turning from these pointless things to the living God, who made heaven, earth, the sea, and everything in them. ¹⁶In past generations, he allowed all the nations to go their own way. ¹⁷Yet by doing good, he did not leave himself without a

---

[i] The soul is the seat of our mind, emotions, and will.

[ii] Or, "saved."

witness, giving rains and fruitful seasons to you, filling you with food and gladness of heart." ¹⁸By saying these things, they, with difficulty, stopped the crowds from sacrificing to them.

¹⁹Then the Jews came from Antioch and Iconium. After persuading the crowds, they stoned Paul and dragged him outside the city thinking that he was dead. ²⁰When the disciples surrounded him, he arose and went into the city. The next day he left with Barnabas for Derbe.

Paul and Barnabas Strengthen the New Believers

²¹They proclaimed the good news in that city, and a considerable number of people became disciples. They returned to Lystra, Iconium, and Antioch ²²strengthening the souls of the disciples, encouraging them to continue in the faith, and telling them, "Through much tribulation we must enter into the Kingdom of God."

²³They appointed elders for them in each church, and after they prayed with fasting, they presented them to the Lord in whom they had believed.

²⁴When they had passed through Psidia, they came to Pamphylia. ²⁵When they had spoken the word in Perga, they went down to Attalia. ²⁶From there they sailed to Antioch, where they had been delivered over to the grace of God for the work they had completed. ²⁷When they had arrived and gathered the church, they reported everything that God had done through them, and that he had opened the door of faith to the Gentiles. ²⁸They remained with the disciples for quite some time.

The Council About the Gentiles in Jerusalem

Chapter Fifteen

¹Certain men came down from Judea and were teaching the brothers, "Unless you are circumcised according to the custom of Moses, you cannot be saved." ²This caused no little amount of

argument and debate between them and Paul and Barnabas. The church appointed Paul and Barnabas and some others from among them to go up to the apostles and elders in Jerusalem about this dispute. ³So, they were sent on their way by the church and passed through Phoenicia and Samaria telling of the conversion of the Gentiles. They brought great joy to all the brothers. ⁴When they had come to Jerusalem, they were received by the church, the apostles, and the elders; and they reported all that God had done with them.

⁵Then some of those who had believed from the party of the Pharisees stood up and said, "We must require that the Gentiles be circumcised and keep the Law of Moses."

⁶The apostles and the elders gathered together to look into this matter. ⁷After a great deal of debate had occurred, Peter arose and said to them, "Men, brothers, you know that already from ancient times God made a choice among us that the Gentiles would hear the message of the gospel[i] from my mouth and believe. ⁸The God who knows hearts also gave testimony on their behalf by giving the Holy Spirit to them just as he also gave the Spirit to us. ⁹He did not distinguish between us and them, having cleansed their hearts by faith.

¹⁰"Therefore, why are you now testing God by placing this yoke upon the necks of the disciples, a yoke which neither we nor our forefathers were able to bear? ¹¹On the contrary, we believe that it is through the grace of our Lord Jesus we are saved, just like they are."

¹²Then all the many who were gathered fell silent, listening to Barnabas and Paul recounting all the miracles and wonders God did through them among the Gentiles.

¹³After they had stopped speaking, James responded and said, "Men, brothers, listen to me. ¹⁴Simon has recounted how at first

---

[i] The Greek word can be translated "Gospel" or "Good News." The word gospel means good news. It is translated both ways in this Bible version.

God chose to take a people for his name from the Gentiles. ¹⁵The words of the prophets agree, just as it is written,

> ¹⁶" ' "After these things I will return and rebuild the tent of David that has fallen. I will rebuild that which was torn down.
>
> " ' "I will build it up again ¹⁷in order that the remnant of men might seek the Lord—all the Gentiles who have been called by my name," says the Lord who does these things, ¹⁸things that are known from eternity.' ⁱⁱ

¹⁹"Therefore, I judge that we should not cause extra difficulty for those from among the Gentiles who are turning to God, ²⁰but that we write them to keep away from food defiled by idols, from illicit sexual relationships, from things that are strangled, and from blood. ²¹For Moses has been preached in every city from past generations and has been read in the synagogues each Sabbath."

²²Then it seemed good to the apostles and elders with the whole church, to send men chosen from among them to Antioch with Paul and Barnabas. They chose Judas who is called Barsabbas, and Silas, leading men among the brothers. ²³They wrote by their own hand,

> "The apostles and elders, your brothers, to the brothers who are among the Gentiles in Antioch, Syria, and Cilicia. Greetings.

²⁴"Since we have heard that some have gone out from us who troubled you with words that distressed your souls, to whom we did not give instructions, ²⁵it seemed good to us, who have come together with one intent, to send to you men we have chosen, along with our cherished Paul and Barnabas, ²⁶men who have been willing give up their lives for the name of our Lord Jesus Christ. ²⁷Therefore, we sent Judas and Silas so they might bring the same news

---

ⁱⁱ Amos 9:11-12

through their report. ²⁸For it seemed good to the Holy Spirit and to us not to place any more burden on you except these necessary things: ²⁹Keep away from food defiled by idols, from blood, from things that are strangled, and from illicit sexual relationships. If you keep yourselves from these things, you will be acting properly.

"Be well."

³⁰So, they were sent off and went down to Antioch. They gathered the assembly and presented the letter. ³¹When they had read it, they rejoiced at the encouragement. ³²Both Judas and Silas were themselves prophets, and they encouraged and strengthened the brothers through much discussion. ³³After they had stayed for a time, the brothers released them with peace to go back to those who had sent them. ³⁴However, it seemed good to Silas that he remain there.

³⁵Paul and Barnabas also stayed in Antioch teaching and proclaiming the good news about the word of the Lord along with many others.

Paul and Barnabas Go in Different Directions

³⁶After some time, Paul said to Barnabas, "Let's return and visit the brothers in every city where we proclaimed the word of the Lord to see how they are doing."

³⁷Barnabas also wanted to take along John, called Mark. ³⁸But Paul preferred that they not take the one who had forsaken them in Pamphylia, and had not participated in the work with them. ³⁹They had such a sharp difference of opinion that they separated from each other. Barnabas took Mark and sailed to Cyprus. ⁴⁰Paul chose Silas and departed, having been committed to the grace of the Lord by the brothers. ⁴¹He passed through Syria and Cilicia strengthening the churches.

Paul, Silas, and Timothy Strengthen the Churches

Chapter Sixteen

¹They came to Derbe and to Lystra. On an important note, there was a certain disciple by the name of Timothy who was there. His mother was a Jewish woman who believed, but his father was Greek. ²The brothers of Lystra and Iconium spoke well of him. ³Paul wanted to have him come with him. He took him and circumcised him because of the Jews who lived in that area; for they all knew that his father was a Greek.

⁴Then, as they passed through the cities, they delivered the decrees that had been decided by the apostles and elders in Jerusalem for them to keep. ⁵So the churches were strengthened in the faith, and they increased in number each day.

The Macedonian Call

⁶They passed through the region of Phrygia and Galatia, but the Holy Spirit prevented them from speaking the word in Asia. ⁷When they came to Mysia, they attempted to go into Bithynia, but the Spirit of Jesus did not permit them. ⁸When they passed by Mysia, they came down to Troas. ⁹A vision appeared to Paul in the night, a certain man of Macedonia was standing and exhorting him saying, "Cross over to Macedonia and help us." ¹⁰When he saw the vision, he immediately endeavored to go over to Macedonia because he concluded that God had called us to preach the good news to them.

¹¹We sailed from Troas straight to Samothrace, and the next day arrived in Neapolis. ¹²From there we went to Philippi, which is a prominent city in that district of Macedonia and a Roman colony. We remained in that city for some days.

Lydia and Her Family are Saved

¹³On the Sabbath day we went outside of the gates of the city, near the river where we assumed prayers would be offered. We sat down and spoke to the women who had gathered together there. ¹⁴A certain woman by the name of Lydia was

listening. She was a seller of purple from Thyatira who worshiped God. The Lord opened her heart to pay attention to the things that Paul was speaking. ¹⁵When she and her household were baptized, she invited them saying, "If you consider me to be faithful to the Lord, come to my house and stay." So, she convinced us.

Paul Expels a Spirit of Divination

¹⁶At one time, while we were going to the prayer meeting, a certain slave girl who had a spirit of python[i] met us. She provided her masters much income by telling fortunes. ¹⁷She was following behind Paul and us, and kept shouting, "These men are servants of God Most High. They are proclaiming the way of salvation to you."

¹⁸She kept doing this for many days. Paul grew very angry, and turned to the spirit and said, "I command you, in the name of Jesus Christ to come out from her." The spirit went out from her at that moment.

Paul and Silas Beaten and Imprisoned

¹⁹When her masters saw that their hope of making money was gone, they seized Paul and Silas and dragged them to the rulers in the marketplace. ²⁰They brought them to the chief magistrates and said, "These men, who are Jews, are stirring up our city. ²¹They are teaching customs that are not lawful for us to believe or to do, since we are Romans."

²²When the crowd joined in the attack against them, the chief magistrates stripped off their clothing and ordered that they be beaten with rods. ²³After they had inflicted many blows on them, they threw them into prison and commanded the jailer to guard them closely. ²⁴Because he had received such a

---

[i] According to Greek legend, Python was the name of the dragon that Apollo killed at Delphi so that it became a place of divination (The Oracle at Delphi). As a result, Python became synonymous with a demon of divination.

command, he put them in the inner prison and fastened their feet in the stocks.

The Jailer at Philippi and His Family are Saved

25 At around midnight, while Paul and Silas were praying, they were singing hymns to God, and the other prisoners were listening to them. 26 Suddenly a great earthquake occurred. It was so large that the foundations of the prison were shaken. Immediately, all the doors and all the shackles were opened. 27 When the jailer awoke and saw that the doors of the prison were open, he drew his sword and was about to kill himself, believing that the prisoners had escaped. 28 But with a loud voice Paul called out shouting, "Do not harm yourself. For we are all here."

29 The jailer called desperately for lights and rushed into the prison. He shook with fear and fell down in front of Paul and Silas. 30 When he brought them outside, he said, "Lords,[ii] what must I do so that I am saved?"

31 They said, "Believe on the Lord Jesus, and you will be saved, you and your family." 32 Then they shared the word of the Lord with him and with all those in his household. 33 He took them and washed their wounds at that hour of the night, and immediately he and all those who were a part of his household were baptized. 34 He brought them into his house and set a meal before them. He was extremely joyful because he and his whole family believed in God.

Paul the Roman Citizen

35 When it was daylight, the magistrates sent the lictors[iii] to say, "Release those men." 36 The jailer reported these instructions to Paul because the magistrates had sent this word that they might go, "Now then, when you leave, go in peace."

[ii] Used as a title of respect. In the next verse they direct him to the "Lord" who can save.

[iii] A lictor is an officer of the magistrates.

37But Paul said to them, "They beat us openly without a proper trial even though we are Roman citizens, and they threw us into prison—and now they wish to send us away in secret? Certainly not! Let them come and usher us out."

38The lictors reported these statements to the magistrates. When the magistrates heard that they were Roman citizens, they were afraid. 39The magistrates came to the prison and apologized. When they ushered them out of the prison, they asked that they leave the city. 40When they left the prison, they went to the house of Lydia. When they had seen the brothers, they encouraged them and left.

Paul and Silas in Thessalonica

Chapter Seventeen

1After they had traveled around Amphipolis and Apollonia, they came to Thessalonica, where there was a synagogue for the Jewish people. 2As was Paul's custom, he went to the Jewish people, and for three sabbaths he debated with them from the Scriptures 3and explained and proved that the Christ had to suffer and rise from the dead. He said, "This Jesus whom I am declaring to you is the Christ." 4Some of them were persuaded and a great multitude of pious Greeks joined Paul and Silas, and not a few of the leading women.

5But the Jews were envious and recruited some of the worthless men from the marketplace. They gathered a crowd and caused an uproar in the city. They attacked the house of Jason, hoping to bring Paul and Silas out to the people. 6When they did not find them, they dragged Jason and some of the brothers to the politarchs[i] crying out, "The ones who have incited trouble around the Roman world[ii] have also come here. 7Jason has welcomed them as his guests, but these men are all acting

---

[i] Politarchs were the chief officers of the city.

[ii] Or "inhabited world," usually referring to the Roman world in the gospels and Acts.

contrary to the decrees of Caesar, saying there is another king named Jesus."

⁸When they heard these things, the politarchs and the crowd were troubled. ⁹They released Jason and the rest after he had posted a bond.

Paul and Silas in Berea

¹⁰Immediately the brothers sent Paul and Silas to Berea during the night. When they arrived, they went to the Jewish synagogue. ¹¹The Bereans were more fair-minded than the people in Thessalonica, and they listened to the word eagerly. They investigated the Scriptures each day to determine if these things were true. ¹²Therefore, many of them believed, along with not a few of the prominent Greek men and women.

¹³But when the Jews from Thessalonica found out that the word of God was being preached by Paul in Berea, they also came there and incited and agitated the crowds. ¹⁴Then the brothers immediately sent Paul away to the sea, but Silas and Timothy remained there.

Paul in Athens

¹⁵Those who escorted Paul brought him as far as Athens. They left when they received directions *from Paul* that Silas and Timothy should come to him as quickly as possible. ¹⁶While Paul was waiting for them in Athens, he was stirred to anger in his spirit when he saw the city was full of idols. ¹⁷Therefore, he spoke in the synagogue with the Jews and the God-fearing Greeks, but in the marketplace each day with those who chanced to be there. ¹⁸Then some of the Epicurean and Stoic philosophers began debating him. Some were saying, "What is this pseudo-intellectual chatterbox trying to say?" Others said, "He seems to be heralding gods that foreigners worship." They said this because Paul was proclaiming the good news about Jesus and the resurrection. ¹⁹They took hold of him and led him to the Areopagus saying, "Are we permitted to know what this new teaching is that you are proclaiming? ²⁰For you are bringing

some things that sound strange to our ears. We want to know what these things mean?" ²¹All the Athenians and the foreigners who lived there enjoyed spending time in nothing other than sharing or listening to new ideas.

²²So Paul took a stand in the middle of the Areopagus and said, "Men, Athenians, I see that in all things you are very religious. ²³For while I was visiting your city and observed your objects of worship and was giving thought to them, I also found an altar with this inscription, 'To An Unknown God.' So you worship what you do not know. This is what I am proclaiming to you. ²⁴The God who made the world and all the things in it, he is the Lord of heaven and earth. He does not dwell in temples made with human hands. ²⁵He also is not served by human hands, as if needing something. He gives life and breath and all things to everyone. ²⁶He made from one man all the peoples of mankind to dwell upon all the face of the earth, having determined their appointed times and the boundaries that they should occupy. ²⁷He did this so they would seek God, and perhaps feel him and discover him; and yet he is not far from each of us. ²⁸For in him we live, move, and exist. As also some of your own poets have said, 'For we are his offspring.'

²⁹"Therefore, since we are the offspring of God, we should not think that the divine nature is like gold, silver, or stone, a sculpture made by the craftsmanship and thought of man. ³⁰In the past he overlooked times of ignorance, now God is directing all men everywhere to repent, ³¹because he has set a day in which he will judge the inhabited world in righteousness, by a man he has appointed, having provided proof to everyone by raising him from the dead."

³²When they heard of the resurrection from the dead, some began to make fun of him, but others said, "We will hear you again concerning this." ³³In this way Paul went out from among them. ³⁴But some men joined him and believed. Among them were Dionysius, who was a member of the Areopagus, a woman by the name of Damaris, and others with them.

Paul Joins with Aquila and Priscilla in Corinth

Chapter Eighteen

¹After these things, he left Athens for Corinth. ²He found a certain Jew by the name of Aquila, a native of Pontus, and his wife, Priscilla. They had recently come from Italy because Claudius had ordered all the Jews to leave Rome. Paul came to them ³and, because they had the same trade, he stayed with them and began working with them; for they were tentmakers by trade. ⁴His custom was to speak in the synagogue each Sabbath persuading both Jews and Greeks, ⁵but when Silas and Timothy came down from Macedonia, Paul began to focus on the word, earnestly testifying to the Jews that Jesus was the Christ.

⁶But when they resisted, and began to verbally abuse him, he shook out his garment and said to them, "Your blood is on your own head. I am clean. From now on I will go to the Gentiles."

⁷When he left there, he went into the house of a God-fearing man by the name of Titius Justus, whose house was next door to the synagogue. ⁸Crispus, the synagogue officer, believed in the Lord, along with his whole house. Many other Corinthians heard, believed, and were being baptized.

⁹The Lord spoke to Paul in a vision during the night, "Do not be afraid, but speak and do not be silent, ¹⁰For I am with you, and no one will attack you and harm you, for many people belong to me in this city." ¹¹So, he settled there for a year and six months, teaching the word of God among them.

Gallio Gives Christians Room to Operate Under Roman Law

¹²While Gallio was proconsul of Achaia, the Jewish people rose up against Paul with one intent, and they brought him before the judgment seat, ¹³and said, "This man is persuading men to worship God against the Law."

¹⁴But when Paul was about to open his mouth, Gallio said to the Jews, "If this were about a breach of *Roman* law, or *other*

malicious crime, oh Jewish men, there would be a reason to put up with you—¹⁵but if it is about differences of opinions about a message, names, and your own law, you take responsibility for it. I am not willing to be the judge of these things."

¹⁶After that, he drove them away from the judgment seat. ¹⁷Then the people seized Sosthenes, the synagogue officer, and beat him in front of the judgment seat, but Gallio was concerned about none of these things.

Paul, Aquila, and Priscilla in Ephesus

¹⁸When Paul had remained for some time with the brothers, he left and set sail for Syria, along with Priscilla and Aquila. He cut his hair in Cenchrea, for he was keeping a vow. ¹⁹They arrived at Ephesus, and he left Priscilla and Aquila there. He himself went into the synagogue speaking with the Jews. ²⁰When they asked him to stay a longer time, he did not agree. ²¹But as he departed, he said, "I will come back to you again if God is willing," and he sailed from Ephesus. ²²He went down to Caesarea, went up to greet the church, and went down to Antioch.

²³After he spent some time there, he went out and passed through the regions of Galatia and Phrygia—in that order—strengthening all the disciples.

²⁴A certain Jew by the name of Apollos, an Alexandrian by birth and a learned man, arrived in Ephesus. He was particularly capable in the Scriptures. ²⁵This man was thoroughly instructed in the way of the Lord, and he spoke and taught accurately about the things concerning Jesus because he was overflowing in the Spirit, but he was only acquainted with the baptism of John. ²⁶He began to speak confidently in the synagogue, but when Priscilla and Aquila heard him, they took him aside and explained the way of God more fully to him.

²⁷When he wished to go to Achaia, the brothers wrote to the disciples urging them to welcome him. When he arrived, he was a great help to those who had believed through grace; ²⁸for he

vigorously refuted the Jews in public, demonstrating from the Scriptures that Jesus is the Christ.

Paul Returns to Ephesus

Chapter Nineteen

¹While Apollos was in Corinth, Paul passed through the interior highlands and arrived in Ephesus. He found some disciples there ²and asked them, "Did you receive the Holy Spirit when you believed?" They responded to him, "Not at all, we have not heard that there is a Holy Spirit."

³Paul asked, "So, into what were you baptized?"

They said, "Into the baptism of John."

⁴Paul said, "John baptized with the baptism of repentance, telling people that they should believe in the one coming after him. That is, in Jesus."

⁵When they heard this, they were baptized into the name of the Lord Jesus. ⁶After Paul laid his hands on them, the Holy Spirit came upon them; they began to speak with language gifts,[i] and to prophesy. ⁷There were about twelve men in all.

⁸Then Paul entered the synagogue and spoke boldly for about three months. He dialogued with them and worked to persuade them about the Kingdom of God. ⁹But when some of them began to harden themselves and refused to believe, slandering the Way in front of the congregation, Paul withdrew from them and took his disciples away. He began speaking each day in the School of Tyrannus. ¹⁰This continued for two years, with the result that all of those who lived in Asia heard the word of the Lord, both Jews and Greeks.

¹¹God was performing miracles through the hands of Paul— of a type not normally experienced. ¹²Towels and aprons that had touched his skin were even carried away and placed upon

---

[i] See Acts 2:3.

the sick, and they were freed from their diseases, and the evil spirits left them.

¹³Some among the Jewish exorcists who traveled about from place to place, attempted to call out the name of the Lord Jesus over those who suffered from evil spirits. They would say, "I invoke Jesus against you, whom Paul proclaims." ¹⁴Now seven sons of a certain Sceva, a Jewish chief priest, were doing this same thing. ¹⁵The evil spirit answered and said to them, "I know Jesus, and I know about Paul, but who are you?" ¹⁶Then the man in whom the evil spirit dwelled jumped on and overpowered the two[i] that were there, and overcame each of them so that they fled from that house naked and bleeding. ¹⁷This became known to everyone who lived in Ephesus, both Jews and Greeks, and fear fell upon them all, and they held the name of Jesus in high honor.

¹⁸Many of those who had believed came to confess and admit their deeds. ¹⁹A large number of those who had practiced magic brought their scrolls and burned them in front of everyone. They added up the value of the scrolls and found that it was fifty thousand pieces of silver. ²⁰Thus, the word of the Lord increased and strengthened in power.

²¹After these things happened, Paul purposed in his spirit to pass through Macedonia and Achaia and go to Jerusalem. He said, "After I have been there, I must go to see Rome." ²²But after he sent Timothy and Erastus, two of those who were ministering with him, to Macedonia, he focused for a time on Asia.

The Silversmiths' Disturbance

²³At that time a significant disturbance about the Way developed. ²⁴There was a man by the name of Demetrius, a silversmith who made silver shrines for Artemis[ii] that brought

---

[i] More literally, "the both of them." The Greek is clear that only two of the seven were present at the time.

[ii] Known in Latin as Diana.

the craftsmen more than a little profit. ²⁵He gathered those who did similar work together and said, "Men, you understand that our prosperity comes from this business. ²⁶You have seen and heard that this Paul has persuaded a considerable number of people, not only in Ephesus, but throughout almost all of Asia, and turned them away saying that gods made by hand are not gods. ²⁷This not only puts our trade at risk of coming under serious criticism, but also that the temple of the great goddess Artemis be regarded as nothing, and that the majesty of the one whom the whole of Asia and the inhabited world worships, will be overthrown."

²⁸When they had heard this, they were filled with rage and began to cry out, "Great is Artemis of the Ephesians." ²⁹The city was filled with an uproar. They seized Aristarchus and Gaius, Paul's traveling companions from Macedonia, and rushed with one intent to the theater. ³⁰Paul desired to go into the assembly, but the disciples would not let him. ³¹Some of the high-ranking provincial officials who were friends of Paul, sent messages to him urging him not to sacrifice himself in the theater.

³²So, some were shouting one thing, and some another, for the assembly was confused and most did not know why they had come together. ³³Some from the crowd explained *what was happening* to Alexander because the Jews pushed him forward. Alexander wanted to make a defense to the assembly, so he motioned for attention with his hand. ³⁴But when they recognized that he was Jewish, they all cried with one voice for over two hours shouting, "Great is Artemis of the Ephesians."

³⁵Then the town secretary quieted the crowd and said, "Men, Ephesians, who among you does not know that the city of Ephesus is the keeper of the temple of the great Artemis and the stone that fell from heaven? ³⁶Therefore, since these are indisputable facts, you ought to restore order and not do anything rash. ³⁷For you have brought these men here though they have not robbed our temple nor spoken against our goddess. ³⁸Therefore, if Demetrius and the craftsmen who are with him have an issue with anyone, the market courts are open,

and the proconsuls are there. Let them bring charges against each other there. ³⁹If you seek anything more, it will be resolved in a lawful assembly. ⁴⁰For we are in danger of being accused of rioting concerning what has happened today. We would not be able to give an explanation of this disorderly mob since there is no reason for it." ⁴¹After he said these things, he dismissed the assembly.

Paul Visits Macedonia and Greece

Chapter Twenty

¹After the riot had come to an end, Paul sent for the disciples and encouraged them. He bid them farewell and left to go to Macedonia. ²He traveled through that region and encouraged them through much discussion. Then he came to Greece. ³He stayed there three months. When a plot was conceived against him by the Jews just as he was about to sail to Syria, he decided to return through Macedonia. ⁴He was accompanied by Sopater son of Pyrrhus of Berea, the Thessalonians Aristarchus and Secundus, Gaius of Derbe, and Timothy, Tychicus and Trophimus of Asia. ⁵These men had gone ahead of us and stayed in Troas. ⁶After the days of Unleavened Bread,[i] we sailed from Philippi and came to them in Troas in five days. We stayed there with them seven days.

Paul Raises Eutychus from the Dead

⁷On the first day of the week while we were gathered to break bread, Paul began speaking to them because he was about to leave the next day. He extended his speech until midnight, ⁸but there were a number of torches in the upstairs room where they were meeting. ⁹There was a certain young man by the name of Eutychus sitting in the window. He was falling into a deep sleep while Paul spoke at length. When he was overcome by sleep, he fell from the third story to the ground. He was picked up dead. ¹⁰But Paul went down and fell upon him, embraced

---

[i] See Acts 12:3 for the Feast of Unleavened Bread. It began after Passover.

him and said, "Stop being afraid, for his soul is in him." ¹¹After he went back upstairs, he broke bread, and ate a bit of food. Then he conversed with them until daybreak and left. ¹²They took the boy away alive, and they were very much comforted.

Paul Greets the Elders of Ephesus

¹³But we went ahead to the ship and set sail to Assos, planning to pick Paul up there; for he had arranged this, planning that he would go by land. ¹⁴When he met us in Assos, we took him aboard and sailed to Mitylene. ¹⁵We set sail from there, and arrived the next day opposite Chios, and the next day we sailed to Samos. The day after, we arrived in Miletus, ¹⁶for Paul had made the decision to sail by Ephesus, so that he might not have to spend time in Asia. *He did this*, because he was eager, if possible, to be in Jerusalem by the day of Pentecost. ¹⁷From Miletus Paul sent a message to Ephesus that they bring the elders of the church.

¹⁸When they came to him, he told them, "You are familiar with how I lived among you from the first day that I arrived in Asia, and for the entire time. ¹⁹I served the Lord with all humility and many tears through the trials that came upon me because of the plots of the Jews *who opposed me*, ²⁰but I did not draw back from proclaiming the things that were beneficial to you, and taught you in public and in one house after another. ²¹I solemnly testified to Jews and Greeks about repentance toward God and faith in our Lord Jesus.

²²"Now pay close attention, I am bound by the Spirit to go to Jerusalem, not knowing the things that will come upon me there, ²³except that the Holy Spirit testifies to me in every city saying that prison and tribulation await me. ²⁴But this message does not change my behavior, and I do not consider my life precious to me as I finish my race and the ministry that I received from the Lord Jesus, to testify to the good news of the grace of God.

²⁵"Now be aware of this, I know that all of you among whom I have traveled about preaching the Kingdom will never again

see my face. ²⁶Therefore, I am testifying to you today that I am unstained by the blood of any one. ²⁷For I most certainly have not been reticent about proclaiming the whole counsel of God to you. ²⁸Give careful attention to yourselves and to all the flock among which the Holy Spirit has placed you as those who give oversight.ⁱ Do this so that you might shepherd the church of God, which he won with his own blood. ²⁹I know that after I leave, vicious wolves will come in among you, and they will not spare the flock. ³⁰Even from among you who are gathered here, men will rise up twisting the truth in order to lead disciples away to follow after them. ³¹Therefore, stay alert, remembering that night and day for three years I did not stop admonishing each one of you with tears.

³²"And now I commend you to God and the word of His grace, which is able to build you up and give you an inheritance among all those who have been sanctified. ³³I have not longed for anyone's gold, silver, or clothing. ³⁴You yourselves know that these hands have supported me and those who were with me. ³⁵By working in this manner, I have shown you that in everything we must be concerned about the weak, remembering the words the Lord Jesus himself spoke, 'It is more blessed to give than to receive.'"

³⁶After he said these things, he got down on his knees and prayed with all of them. ³⁷They shed many tears and fell upon Paul's neck, kissing him. ³⁸What especially caused them pain were the words he had spoken that they would never see his face again. Then they escorted him to his ship.

Paul Travels to Jerusalem

Chapter Twenty-One

¹When we had torn ourselves away from them, we set sail. We sailed straight to Kos, the next day to Rhodes, and from there to

---

ⁱ Or, "overseers." This term refers to those who watch over God's flock.

Patara. ²When we found a ship sailing over to Phoenicia, we boarded and set sail. ³When Cyprus came into view, we ignored it and sailed to its southern side to Syria and came down to Tyre; for the ship was going to unload its cargo there. ⁴After we sought out the disciples, we stayed there seven days. Through the Spirit, they repeatedly told Paul not to go to Jerusalem. ⁵But when the seven days had passed, we went out of the city and were leaving. They all accompanied us, along with their wives and children. Then we knelt upon the beach and prayed. ⁶We said farewell to each other, and we embarked in the ship while they returned to their homes.

⁷But we continued the voyage from Tyre and arrived at Ptolemais. We greeted the brothers and remained with them one day. ⁸On the next day, we departed and arrived at Caesarea. We entered into the house of Philip the evangelist, one of the seven, and stayed with him. ⁹He had four virgin daughters who prophesied.

¹⁰After we stayed a good number of days, a prophet arrived from Judea by the name of Agabus. ¹¹He came over to us, took Paul's belt, and bound his own feet and hands and said, "The Holy Spirit says this, 'The Jews in Jerusalem will bind the man who owns this belt in this same way, and they will deliver him into the hands of the Gentiles.'"

¹²As soon as we heard these things, we and the people there began to beg him not to go up to Jerusalem. ¹³But Paul responded, "Why are you weeping and breaking my heart? For I am ready, not only to be bound, but also to die in Jerusalem for the name of the Lord Jesus." ¹⁴Since we could not persuade him, we stopped trying and said, "Let the will of the Lord be done."

¹⁵After this time, we got ready and went up to Jerusalem. ¹⁶Some of the disciples from Caesarea also came with us. They were bringing us to Mnason the Cypriot, a disciple from the beginning. We were staying with him.

Acts 21:17

The Brothers in Jerusalem Welcome Paul and His Companions

17After we arrived in Jerusalem, the brothers welcomed us gladly. 18On the next day Paul went in with us to James. All of the elders were present. 19After he greeted them, he began to explain carefully, each in its turn, what God had done among the Gentiles through his ministry.

20When they had heard, they began to glorify God. Then they said to him, "You see, brother, how there are many thousands among the Jews who have believed, and they are all zealots for the Law. 21They have been taught that you are teaching rebellion against Moses to all the Jews who live among the Gentiles, by teaching them not to circumcise their children or live according to the customs. 22What, therefore, is to be done? A multitude *of them* will certainly assemble, for they will hear that you have come. 23So, do these things that we tell you to do. There are four men with us who have taken a vow. 24Take these men, and you perform the purification rites with them and pay their expenses so that they might shave their heads. Then everyone will know that what they have been taught about you is not correct, but that you live in conformity to our standards, and that you yourself keep the Law.

25"But about those who have believed among the Gentiles; after we made a decision, we wrote them that they should avoid that which is offered to idols, blood, the meat of strangled animals, and sexual misconduct."

26On the next day, Paul took the men, and when he had been purified with them, went into the temple. He gave notice when the days of purification would be completed, and the sacrifice would be presented for each one of them. 27But when the seven days were almost over, the Jews from Asia noticed him in the temple and began to stir up all the people so that they seized Paul. 28They shouted, "Men, Israelites, help! This is the man who is teaching everyone everywhere against our people, our Law, and this place. Even more, he has brought Greeks into the temple and has defiled this holy place." 29For they had previously seen Trophimus the Ephesian in the city with him, and they thought that Paul had brought him into the temple.

30The entire city was set in motion, and the people assembled quickly. They took Paul and dragged him outside of the temple; and immediately the doors were shut.

Paul Rescued by the Romans

31While they were attempting to kill him, a report that the whole of Jerusalem was stirred up came to the tribune of the Roman cohort. 32He immediately took soldiers and centurions and ran down among them. When the crowd saw the tribune and the soldiers, they stopped beating Paul.

33When he drew near, the tribune seized Paul and ordered that he be bound with two chains. Then he began asking who he was and what he had done. 34But some from the crowd were answering one thing and some another thing. When he was not able to determine something definite because of the noise, he ordered that he be brought into the fortress. 35When Paul arrived at the stairs, he was carried by the soldiers because of the violence of the crowd, 36for the majority of the people were following shouting, "Away with him!"

37When he was about to be brought into the fortress, Paul asked the tribune, "Am I permitted to say something to you?" He responded, "Do you know Greek? 38Then you are not the Egyptian who incited a rebellion and led four thousand terrorists into the desert not long ago?"

39Paul said, "I am a Jewish man, from Tarsus in Cilicia, a citizen of no insignificant city. I beg you, permit me to speak to the people."

40When he gave him permission, Paul stood up on the stairs and signaled with his hand to the crowd. When there was a complete silence, Paul began to address them in the Hebrew dialect.[i] He said,

---

[i] Aramaic. Also in 22:2.

Chapter Twenty-Two

¹"Men, brothers and fathers, listen now to my defense before you." ²When they heard that he spoke to them in the Hebrew dialect, they became even more calm.

Paul said, ³"I am a Jewish man, born in Tarsus of Cilicia, but educated in this city at the feet of Gamaliel strictly according to the law of our fathers, zealous for God just as all of you are today. ⁴I persecuted *those who believed in* this Way to the death, arresting and putting in prison both men and women, ⁵as also the high priest and all the Council of elders can testify on my behalf. I also received letters to the brothers and began to journey to Damascus to bring those who were there as prisoners to Jerusalem in order that they might be punished.

⁶"But while I was traveling to Damascus and approaching it about noon, a bright light from the sky suddenly flashed around me. ⁷I fell to the ground and heard a voice saying to me, 'Saul, Saul, why are you persecuting me?'

⁸"I responded, 'Who are you, Lord?'

"He said to me, 'I am Jesus of Nazareth, whom you are persecuting.' ⁹Those who were with me saw the light and were afraid, but they did not understand the voice of the one speaking to me.

¹⁰"Then I said, 'What should I do, Lord?'

"The Lord answered me, 'Get up and go into Damascus, and there you will be told about all the things that have been ordained for you to do.'

¹¹"But since I was not able to see because of the glory of that light, I was led by the hand into Damascus by those who were with me. ¹²A certain Ananias, a devout man with respect to the Law, who was spoken well of by all the Jews who were living there, ¹³came to me, stood above me, and said, 'Brother Saul, see again!' At that moment, I *was able to* look up at him.

¹⁴"Ananias continued, 'The God of our fathers has chosen you to know his will, and to see the Righteous One, and to hear his voice from his mouth; ¹⁵for you will be a witness to all men of what you have seen and heard. ¹⁶Now what are you waiting for? Get up, baptize yourself, and wash your sins away calling on his name.'

¹⁷"Then, when I returned to Jerusalem and I was praying in the temple, I fell into an ecstatic vision[i] ¹⁸and saw Jesus saying to me, 'Hurry! Leave Jerusalem quickly; for they will not receive your testimony about me.'

¹⁹"I said, 'Lord, they know that I used to go from synagogue to synagogue to imprison and beat those who believed in you; ²⁰and when the blood of your witness Stephen was being poured out, I also consented, standing and guarding the cloaks of those who were killing him.'

²¹"But he said to me, 'Go, for I am sending you far away to the Gentiles.'"

²²They listened to him until this point, then they lifted their voices and said, "Purge the earth of such a man! For it isn't right to let him live." ²³They were shouting, waving their cloaks, and throwing dust into the air.

The Tribune Realizes Paul is a Roman Citizen

²⁴The tribune ordered that he be brought into the fortress, saying that he would be interrogated with flogging in order that he might know why they were shouting at him in this way.[ii] ²⁵But when they had stretched him out for the flogging, Paul asked the centurion who was standing there, "Is it lawful for you to flog a Roman citizen who has not been found guilty?"

---

[i] An ecstatic vision translates a Greek noun used when referring to spiritual ecstatic phenomena in ancient times.

[ii] The tribune did not understand because Paul spoke in Aramaic.

²⁶When the centurion heard this, he went to the tribune and brought the news asking, "What are you about to do? For this man is a Roman citizen."

²⁷The tribune came and said to him, "Are you a Roman citizen?"

He answered, "Yes."

²⁸The tribune responded, "I bought this citizenship with a large amount of capital."

But Paul said, "I myself was born a citizen."

²⁹Those who were about to interrogate him immediately stepped away from him, and the tribune was afraid when he learned that Paul was a Roman citizen, and that he had bound him with chains.

Paul Appears Before the Sanhedrin

³⁰On the next day, because he wanted to know without any doubt why Paul was being accused by the Jews, he released him and ordered the chief priests and all the Sanhedrin to come together. Then he brought Paul and stood him in front of them.

Chapter Twenty-Three

¹When Paul had looked directly at the Sanhedrin, he said, "Men, brothers, I have lived as a citizen with a totally clear conscience before God to this very day." ²But the high priest, Ananias, ordered those standing near him to strike him on the mouth.

³Then Paul called to him, "God is about to strike you, you whitewashed wall. How can you yourself sit judging me according to the Law, and then command that I be struck in violation of the Law?"

⁴Those standing beside him said, "Are you reproaching God's high priest?"

⁵Paul said, "I did not know, brothers, that he is the high priest; for it is written, 'Do not speak negatively about a ruler of the people.'"

⁶Then Paul, because he knew that one part of the assembly was Sadducees, and the other was Pharisees, shouted in the Sanhedrin, "Men, brothers, I am a Pharisee, the son of a Pharisee. I am being accused because of my hope, the resurrection of the dead."

⁷When he said this, a disturbance broke out between the Pharisees and the Sadducees, and the gathering was divided. ⁸For the Sadducees say there is no resurrection, and neither angel nor spirit; but the Pharisees profess them both. ⁹When a great outcry began, some of the scribal scholars who were from the party of the Pharisees stood up and protested strongly saying, "We find nothing wrong with this man. What if a spirit or angel has spoken to him?"

¹⁰When a great quarrel broke out, the tribune feared that Paul would be torn to pieces by them. He ordered his squad to go down and seize him from their midst and take him to the fortress.

¹¹On the following night, the Lord stood near him and said, "Take courage! For as you have testified to these things about me in Jerusalem, it is necessary that in the same way you testify in Rome."

The Plan to Kill Paul Prevented

¹²When the next day dawned, certain Jews formulated a secret plan and placed themselves under a curse saying that they would not eat or drink until they had killed Paul. ¹³There were more than forty men who joined this conspiracy. ¹⁴When they came to the chief priests and the elders they said, "We have placed ourselves under an oath that we will not eat until we have killed Paul. ¹⁵So, you and the Sanhedrin bring formal charges to the tribune—as if you were about to investigate more precisely the

things concerning him—so that he will bring him to you; but before he gets close, we are prepared to kill him."

¹⁶However, when the son of Paul's sister heard about the plot, he came to the fortress and went in to tell Paul. ¹⁷Paul summoned one of the centurions and said, "Bring this young man to the tribune. He has something to report to him."

¹⁸The centurion took him and brought him to the tribune and said, "The prisoner, Paul, called me over and asked me to bring this young man to you because he has something to tell you."

¹⁹The tribune took him by the hand and led him aside to question him privately, "What is it that you have to report to me?"

²⁰He said, "The Jews agreed to petition you so that you might bring Paul down to the Sanhedrin tomorrow, as if they were going to investigate his case more precisely. ²¹But you should not be persuaded by them, for more than forty men from among them are lying in wait for him. They have put themselves under an oath not to eat or drink until they have killed him. They are now prepared and are awaiting your consent."

²²Then the tribune dismissed the young man, ordering him, "Tell no one that you have informed me of these things."

²³He called two of the centurions and said, "Prepare two hundred soldiers so that they might go to Caesarea with seventy cavalrymen and two hundred light infantry by the third hour of the night. ²⁴Also provide mounts to put Paul on so that he might be taken safely to Felix the governor."

²⁵He wrote a letter which had this message:

²⁶"Claudius Lysias to his excellency governor Felix.

"Greetings.

²⁷"When this man was seized by the Jews, and he was about to be killed by them, I came with the troops and rescued him when I learned that he was

a Roman. ²⁸Because I wanted to know the legal basis for the accusations against him, I brought him down to their Sanhedrin, ²⁹where I found he was being accused about questions of their law, but not any accusations that are worthy of death or imprisonment.

³⁰"When I received confidential information that there was a plot against this man, I sent him to you immediately, and ordered his accusers to present what they had against him to you.

"May you be well."

³¹Then the soldiers, following their orders, took Paul and brought him through the night to Antipatris. ³²But on the following day, they allowed the cavalry to leave with Paul, and returned to the fortress. ³³When they arrived in Caesarea and delivered the letter to the governor, they also presented Paul to him.

³⁴When he had read it and asked from what province Paul hailed, he learned that he was from Cilicia. ³⁵He commanded that Paul be kept in Herod's Praetorium.ⁱ "I will hear your case," he said, "when your accusers also arrive."

Paul Tried by Governor Felix

Chapter Twenty-Four

¹After five days, the high priest Ananias came down with some of the elders and an attorney named Tertullus. They presented the things they had against Paul to the governor. ²After Paul was summoned, Tertullus began to accuse him stating, "We have experienced much peace through you and through the reforms being carried out in this nation through your oversight. ³We welcome this on every side and in every place, most excellent Felix, with all thankfulness.

ⁱ The Praetorium was the palace of the Roman governor.

⁴"But in order that I not weary you further, I request that, with your forbearance, that you hear us briefly. ⁵For we have found this man to be a plague, and one who stirs up strife among all the Jews throughout the Roman world.ⁱ He is also a leader of the Nazarene sect. ⁶He even tried to desecrate the temple, which is when we seized him, and wanted to judge him by our Law, ⁷but Lysias the tribune, using a great deal of force, came and took him out of our hands. ⁸He commanded Paul's accusers to come before you. When you question Lysias yourself concerning all of these things, you will discover the truth of the things of which we are accusing him."

⁹The Jewish leaders also joined in the attack, declaring that these things were true.

¹⁰When the governor motioned to Paul to speak, he responded, "I cheerfully present my defense, because I know that for many years you have been a judge in this nation. ¹¹You will be able to find out that not more than twelve days ago, I went up to Jerusalem to worship. ¹²They did not find me having arguments with anyone in the temple, nor stirring up riots in the crowd, the synagogues, or anywhere in the city. ¹³They are not able to prove to you the things of which they are now accusing me. ¹⁴But I do confess this to you, that according to the Way, which they call a sect, I serve the God of our fathers, and believe all that is in accord with the Law and written in the Prophets. ¹⁵I have hope in God, which these men also accept, that there will be resurrection of the righteous and the unrighteous. ¹⁶Because of this, I do my best always to keep a blameless conscience before God and before men.

¹⁷"After some years, I came to bring charitable gifts to my nation and to make offerings. ¹⁸They found me doing this in the temple after I was purified. I was not with a crowd, and there was no riot. ¹⁹But there are some from among the Asian Jews who ought to be here bringing charges before you, if they have

---

ⁱ Or "inhabited world," usually referring to the Roman world in the gospels and Acts.

anything against me. ²⁰Or let these men themselves declare what wrongdoing they found when I stood before the Sanhedrin, ²¹unless concerning this one statement which I shouted while I stood among them, 'I am being accused before you today because of the resurrection from the dead.'"

²²Then Felix adjourned them because he had an accurate understanding of the Way. He said, "When the tribune Lysias arrives, I will examine your case more thoroughly."

²³He commanded the centurion to continue to hold him in custody, but to give him some liberty, and not to hinder his associates from supplying his needs.

²⁴After some days, Felix came with Drusilla, his wife who was Jewish. He sent for Paul and listened to him speak about faith in Christ Jesus. ²⁵But while he explained about righteousness, self-control, and the coming judgment, Felix was frightened and said, "Go away for now. When I have the opportunity, I will summon you." ²⁶At the same time, he was hoping that Paul would give him money, so he sent for him frequently to converse with him.

²⁷After two years had gone by, Felix was succeeded by Porcius Festus. Because Felix desired to do a favor for the Jews, he left Paul in confinement.

Paul Tried by Governor Festus

Chapter Twenty-Five

¹Then Festus arrived in the province. Three days later, he went up to Jerusalem from Caesarea. ²The chief priests and prominent men among the Jews brought charges to Festus against Paul and began pressuring him. ³They kept asking a favor at Paul's expense, that he might be summoned and brought to Jerusalem. At the same time, they were planning an ambush to kill him along the way. ⁴Festus responded that Paul was being kept in Caesarea, but that he himself was about to go there in short

order. ⁵"Therefore, let competent men from among you go with me," he said, "and if there is any wrong in this man, let them bring charges against him."

⁶After remaining with them for no more than eight or ten days, he left for Caesarea. On the next day he sat upon the judge's seat and ordered that Paul be brought. ⁷When Paul arrived, the Jewish leaders who had come down from Jerusalem stood around him bringing many serious accusations, ones they could not prove.

⁸Paul defended himself, "I have not committed any sin against the Law of the Jews, the temple, or against Caesar."

⁹Then Festus, wishing to grant a favor to the Jewish leaders, replied to Paul and asked, "Are you willing to go up to Jerusalem to be tried before me on these charges?"

¹⁰But Paul said, "I am standing before the judgment seat of Caesar, where it is appropriate that I be judged. I have done no harm to the Jews, as you quite well know. ¹¹If I am wrong and have done something that deserves death, I am not refusing to die; but if there is nothing to what these men are accusing me, no one is able to hand me over to them. I appeal to Caesar."

¹²Then, after Festus had conferred with his council, he replied, "You have appealed to Caesar, to Caesar you will go."

Festus Seeks Advice from King Agrippa

¹³After several days had gone by, King Agrippa and Bernice arrived in Caesarea to give Festus their greetings. ¹⁴While they were staying there a number of days, Festus explained to the king the case against Paul saying, "There is a certain man who was left a prisoner by Felix. ¹⁵When I went to Jerusalem, the chief priests and the elders of the Jews brought charges and requested that I condemn him. ¹⁶I let them know that it is not Roman custom to hand over any man until the one who is being accused meets his accusers face to face and receives an opportunity to defend himself against the charges.

¹⁷"So, when they had come together here, I did not wait, but took my place on the judgment seat the next day and ordered the man be brought. ¹⁸When his accusers stood up, they did not bring accusations against him of the type of crimes I suspected, ¹⁹but only some differences of opinion they had with him about their own religion, and about a certain Jesus, who had died, but that Paul claims is alive. ²⁰Since I was at a loss at how to investigate these things, I checked to see if he might want to go to Jerusalem to be tried there on these matters. ²¹But when Paul appealed to be held for the decision of the Emperor, I ordered him to be held until I send him to Caesar."

²²Then Agrippa said to Festus, "I also wish to hear this man for myself."

"Tomorrow," he replied, "you shall hear him."

Paul's Defense Before King Agrippa

²³Therefore, on the next day, Agrippa and Bernice came with great pomp and ceremony, and entered the audience hall with the tribunes and important men of the city. When Festus issued the command, Paul was brought in. ²⁴Festus explained, "King Agrippa and all the men who are with us, you see this man about whom the whole multitude of the Jews have petitioned me, both in Jerusalem and here, shouting out that he no longer deserved to live. ²⁵But I discovered that he had done nothing that deserved death. When he appealed to the Emperor,[i] I decided to send him. ²⁶But I do not have anything to write about him to our lord with certainty, therefore I have brought him before all of you, and especially you, King Agrippa, so that after the examination has taken place, I might have something to write. ²⁷For it seems irrational to me to send a prisoner, and not also indicate the charges against him."

---

[i] Or, "Augustus." This title was conferred on the emperors in 27 B.C.

Chapter Twenty-Six

¹At that point, Agrippa said to Paul, "You have permission to speak for yourself." Then Paul extended his hand and began to make his defense.

²"I consider myself blessed, King Agrippa, that I am about to make my defense before you today concerning all of the things of which I am accused by the Jews—³especially since you are knowledgeable about all the Jewish customs and disputes. Therefore, I beg that you listen to me patiently.

⁴"All the Jews know of my way of life from my youth, where from the beginning I was with them in my nation and in Jerusalem. ⁵Since they have known me from the first, if they are willing, they can testify that I lived according to the strictest sect of our beliefs as a Pharisee. ⁶Now I am standing trial because of the hope of the promise given by God to our fathers, ⁷to which our twelve tribes hope to attain by earnestly serving night and day. It is for this hope, King Agrippa, that I am being accused by the Jews—⁸why do any of you think it is unbelievable that God raises the dead?

⁹"I myself, therefore, thought that it was necessary to act with great hostility against the name of Jesus of Nazareth, ¹⁰which is also what I did in Jerusalem. I myself was instrumental in getting many of the saints locked up in prison after I received authority from the chief priests. I even cast my vote against them when they were being executed. ¹¹I went often to all the synagogues punishing them; I was trying to get them to blaspheme.ⁱ I was overwhelmed with insane rage against them so that I also pursued them to foreign cities.

¹²"I was doing just this, going to Damascus with the authority and complete power from the chief priests, ¹³when in the middle of the day while on the road, O King, I saw a light from heaven brighter than the sun shining around me and those

---

ⁱ Blasphemy is about speaking profanely of sacred things, to slander God, or to speak against him.

who were traveling with me. ¹⁴When we had all fallen to the ground, I heard a voice speaking to me in the Hebrew dialect,[ii] 'Saul, Saul, why are you persecuting me? It hurts you when you kick against the goads.' ¹⁵Then I said, 'Who are you, Lord?' The Lord said, 'I am Jesus whom you are persecuting. ¹⁶But stand up and get on your feet. I have appeared to you for this reason, to appoint you as a servant and a witness, both of what you have seen of me, and what I will show you. ¹⁷I will rescue you from your people and the Gentiles to whom I am sending you. ¹⁸I will open their eyes to turn them from darkness to light, and from the authority of Satan to God, so that they might receive forgiveness of sins and an inheritance among those sanctified by faith in me.'

¹⁹"From that point, O King Agrippa, I was not disobedient to the vision from heaven, ²⁰but I have constantly proclaimed, first in Damascus, then in Jerusalem, all of the region of Judea, and to the Gentiles, that they are to repent and turn to God, producing deeds worthy of repentance. ²¹For these reasons, the Jews seized me while I was in the temple and tried to kill me. ²²So, because I obtained help from God, I stand to this day testifying to both the common man and the elite, saying nothing beyond what the Prophets and Moses said was going to happen: ²³that the Christ would have to suffer, that he would be first of among those who would rise from the dead, and that he must proclaim light to this people and to the Gentiles."

²⁴While Paul was presenting these things in his defense, Festus shouted out with a loud voice, "Paul, you are out of your mind with religious rapture! Your great learning is leading you toward a break with reality.[iii]"

²⁵But Paul said, "I am not experiencing religious rapture, most excellent Festus, but I am speaking out clearly with true and reasonable words. ²⁶For the king knows about these things. I

[ii] Aramaic

[iii] The two related Greek words that Festus uses (one noun and one verb) were often used to describe spiritual ecstatic phenomena.

am speaking with boldness because I am convinced that none of these things has escaped his notice; for this has not been done in a corner. ²⁷King Agrippa, do you believe the prophets? I know that you believe."

²⁸But Agrippa responded to Paul, "You are attempting to convince me to become a Christian with so few words?"

²⁹Paul said, "I pray to God that whether with few words or many, that not only you, but everyone who is listening to me today would become just what I am, except without these chains."

³⁰Then the king stood up, along with the governor and Bernice and all those with them. ³¹When they had departed, they began talking to one another and said, "This man is doing nothing that is worthy of death or imprisonment."

³²Agrippa said to Festus, "This man could have been set free if he had not appealed to Caesar."

Paul is Sent to Rome

Chapter Twenty-Seven

¹After it was determined that we would sail to Italy, they turned Paul and some other prisoners over to a centurion of the Imperial[i] Cohort by the name of Julius. ²When we had boarded a ship from Adramyttium that was about to sail along the ports on the coast of Asia, we put out to sea. Aristarchus, a Macedonian from Thessalonica, was also with us. ³On the next day, we put in at Sidon. Julius treated Paul kindly and allowed him to go to his friends and obtain what he needed. ⁴From there we put out to sea and sailed in the shelter of Cypress because the winds were against us. ⁵After we sailed across the open sea along Cilicia and Pamphylia, we arrived at Myra in Lycia. ⁶There the centurion found an Alexandrian ship sailing for Italy, so he put us aboard it. ⁷We sailed slowly for a number of days and arrived,

---

[i] Or, "the Augustinian Cohort."

with difficulty, at Cnidus. Since the wind did not allow anything else, we sailed under the shelter of Crete and Salmone. ⁸We sailed along it with difficulty, and came to a place called Fair Havens, which was near the city of Lasea.

⁹Since much time had been lost, and the voyage was now dangerous—it was already past the Day of Atonement[ii]—Paul began to give them advice, ¹⁰telling them, "Men, I see that the coming voyage will be filled with disaster and much loss, not only to the cargo and ship, but also to our souls." ¹¹But the centurion was more persuaded by the captain and the ship owner than by what Paul was saying. ¹²Since the harbor was not suitable for spending the winter, the majority decided to put out to sea from there, hoping that they might somehow reach Phoenix, a harbor of Crete with entrances to the southwest and northwest. They planned to spend the winter there.

Caught in a Violent Storm

¹³When a south wind began to blow gently, they thought it was just what they needed to get to Phoenix, so they weighed anchor and sailed along Crete. ¹⁴It didn't take long for a violent wind, called the Northeaster,[iii] to rush down from the island ¹⁵and catch the ship. Since we were not able to head into the wind, we yielded to the wind and were driven along by it. ¹⁶When we were running along under the shelter of a small island called Cauda, we were able, with great difficulty, to get the skiff under control. ¹⁷After they had hoisted it on board, they began fastening rope supports under the ship to brace it; and because they were afraid that they might run aground near Syrtis, they lowered the anchors[iv] and were driven along. ¹⁸When we were still being violently tossed by the storm on the next day, they began to throw things overboard; ¹⁹and on the third day, they threw the ship's equipment overboard with their own hands. ²⁰When neither the sun nor the stars appeared over the course

---

[ii] Or, "the Fast," which referred to the Day of Atonement in Autumn.

[iii] A storm from the northeast that would push the ship west.

[iv] This phrase could also refer to lowering the sails.

of many days, and it was apparent that it was not a small storm that was battering us, all hope that we would be saved was lost.

²¹Because many of the passengers had lost their desire for food, Paul stood in their midst and spoke, "Men, you would have spared yourself this disaster and loss if you had listened to me when I said we should not have sailed from Crete. ²²Now I urge you to cheer up. For there will be no loss of life among you, but only the ship will be lost. ²³For this night, an angel of the God to whom I belong and whom I serve stood by me ²⁴and said, 'Do not be afraid, Paul, it is necessary that you stand before Caesar; and listen, God has graciously given you the lives of everyone sailing with you.' ²⁵Therefore, cheer up, men, for I believe God. It will happen in just the way it has been explained to me. ²⁶But we will run aground on some island."

Making it Safely to Shore

²⁷When the fourteenth night arrived, we were being driven along in the Sea of Adria. In the middle of the night, the sailors suspected that they were drawing close to some dry land. ²⁸When they took a sounding of the water, they found it was twenty fathoms[i] deep. When they had gone a little farther, they again took a sounding of the water, and found it was fifteen fathoms deep. ²⁹Because they were afraid that we might run aground on some rocky place, they dropped four anchors from the stern praying that daylight would come. ³⁰The sailors began looking for a way to flee from the ship, and lowered the skiff into the sea, pretending that they were about to affix anchors from the bow. ³¹Paul said to the centurions and the soldiers, "If these men do not remain on the ship, you cannot be saved." ³²Then the soldiers cut the ropes from the skiff and let it fall away.

³³From then until daylight, Paul kept encouraging everyone to eat some food, saying, "Today is the fourteenth day of constant apprehension and no food; you have eaten nothing.

---

[i] A fathom is 6 feet; the first reading was 120 feet deep, then 90 feet.

³⁴For this reason, I urge you to take some food so that you survive, for not a hair from your head will be lost." ³⁵When he had said these things, he took bread and gave thanks to God in front of everyone. Then he broke it and began to eat. ³⁶They were all encouraged, and they took some food themselves. ³⁷We were, in all, 276 souls on the ship. ³⁸When they had eaten their fill, they began to lighten the ship by throwing the grain into the sea.

³⁹When daylight came, they did not recognize the land; but they did notice a bay that had a beach. They were planning to drive the ship into it if they could. ⁴⁰They cut away the anchors and left them in the sea. At the same time they released the ropes on the rudders and hoisted the mainsail into the wind and headed for the shore. ⁴¹But they unexpectedly ran the ship aground at a place where two currents met. The bow stuck fast and remained immovable, and the stern began to break apart under the force of the waves.

⁴²The soldiers planned to kill the prisoners so that none of them could swim away and escape, ⁴³but because the centurion wished to rescue Paul, he prevented them from carrying out their plan. He commanded that those who were able to swim should jump overboard first and get to land, and ⁴⁴the rest were to go on planks or other items from the ship. In this fashion everyone arrived safely on the land.

Marooned on Malta

Chapter Twenty-Eight

¹After we were safe, we discovered that the island was called Malta. ²The indigenous people demonstrated unusual hospitality to us, welcoming us all as guests, and kindling a fire because it was rainy and cold. ³After Paul had gathered a number of sticks and was placing them on the fire, a viper was driven out by the heat and fastened onto his hand. ⁴When the people of the island saw the creature hanging from his hand, they said to each other,

"Certainly this man is a murderer. He escaped from the sea, but justice has not allowed him to live." ⁵Then Paul shook the creature off into the fire and suffered no negative effects. ⁶They were expecting him to fall sick with a fever or suddenly fall down dead. But after they waited for a long time and did not see anything unusual happen to him, they changed their minds and began to say that he was a god.

⁷In the region around that place, the lands were owned by the first man[i] of the island. His name was Publius. He welcomed us in a friendly manner and entertained us as guests for three days. ⁸The father of Publius was confined to bed, sick with fevers and dysentery. Paul went to visit him. He prayed, placed his hands on him, and healed him. ⁹After this had happened, the rest of those on the island who had sicknesses came and were healed. ¹⁰They honored us with many gifts, and when it was time to set sail, they provided the things that we needed.

Resuming the Trip to Rome

¹¹After three months on the island, we set sail in a ship that had spent the winter there. It was an Alexandrian ship with the Twins, Castor and Pollux, as the figurehead. ¹²After we put in at Syracuse, we stayed there three days. ¹³From there we weighed anchor and arrived in Rhegium. After a day, a south wind came up, and on the second day we came to Puteoli. ¹⁴We found some brothers there and were invited to stay with them for seven days; and this is the way we came to Rome. ¹⁵When the brothers there heard the reports about us, they came as far as the Forum of Appius and the Three Taverns to meet us. When Paul saw them, he gave thanks to God and took courage.

Paul Arrives in Rome

¹⁶When we arrived in Rome, Paul was permitted to stay by himself with the solder who was guarding him. ¹⁷After three days, he called together those who were leading men among the Jews. When they had come together, he began explaining to

---

[i] A recognized leader on the island, either an official or leading citizen.

them, "Men, brothers, even though I have done nothing against our people or the traditions of our fathers, I was handed over into the custody of the Romans as a prisoner from Jerusalem. ¹⁸When the Romans had examined me, they were willing to release me because there were no grounds for the death penalty in my case. ¹⁹But when the Jews opposed this, I was forced to appeal to Caesar—not as if I had charges to bring against my people. ²⁰Therefore, because of this accusation, I called you together to see you and to speak to you. For it is because of the hope of Israel that I am wearing these chains."

²¹But they said to him, "We have not received letters about you from Judea, nor has anyone who has come reported about you or spoken anything bad about you. ²²But we value the opportunity to hear from you about your views, because we know that this sect is spoken against everywhere."

Paul Presents His Defense Before the Jewish Leaders in Rome

²³When they had set a time with him, many came to him at the place he was staying. He began to explain and testify to them about the Kingdom of God, and from morning until evening he tried to convince them from the Law of Moses and the prophets about Jesus. ²⁴Some were convinced by what he was saying, but others did not believe. ²⁵When they were unable to agree with each other, they began to leave after one statement Paul had made, "The Holy Spirit correctly spoke through Isaiah the prophet to our fathers ²⁶when he said,

> " 'Go to this people and say, "You will listen carefully, but not understand; you will watch closely, but you will not see." ²⁷For the heart of this people has become hard. They listen with impervious ears and have closed their eyes, lest they see with their eyes, and hear with their ears, and understand with their heart, and return, and I will heal them.'[ii]

[ii] Isaiah 6:9-10

28"Therefore, let it be known to you that this deliverance from God has been sent to the Gentiles, and they will listen."

29When he had spoken these things, the Jews left, but continued to have a major argument among themselves.

30However, Paul remained two full years in his own rented home. He welcomed everyone who visited him. 31He preached the Kingdom of God and taught the things that concerned the Lord Jesus Christ with all openness and without hindrance.

ROMANS

Chapter One

¹Paul, a servant of Christ Jesus, a called apostle separated for the good news[i] of God, ²which He promised long ago through his prophets in the Holy Scriptures; ³the good news concerns his Son, who came from the seed of David (with respect to the flesh), ⁴and who, according to the Spirit of Holiness, was revealed in power to be the Son of God through his resurrection from the dead, Jesus Christ our Lord. ⁵It is through Jesus that we have received grace and the apostolic authority among all the Gentiles to call them to the obedience of faith for his name. ⁶You also are among those called by Jesus Christ—

⁷To all those who are cherished by God in Rome, chosen saints:

Grace to you and peace from God our Father and the Lord Jesus Christ.

---

[i] Note: The Greek word can be translated "Gospel" or "Good News." Gospel means good news. It is translated both ways in this version.

Paul's Desire to Visit the Roman Christians

⁸First, I give thanks to my God through Jesus Christ for all of you because your faith is being reported throughout the whole world. ⁹For God, whom I serve with my spirit through the good news of his Son, is my witness as I remember and make mention of you without ceasing, ¹⁰always asking at my prayer times if I might somehow now at last, by the will of God, succeed in coming to you.

¹¹For I eagerly desire to see you, that I might share some spiritual grace gift with you for your strengthening, ¹²that is, to be encouraged together with you on account of each other's faith, both yours and mine. ¹³I do not want you to be uninformed, brothers, that I have often intended to come to you so that I might have some fruit among you, just as I also have among the rest of the Gentiles; but I have been forbidden to do so until now.

¹⁴I am obligated to both Greeks and barbarians, both to the wise and to the foolish. ¹⁵So, in line with my *purpose*, I am eager also to proclaim the good news to you in Rome. ¹⁶For I am not ashamed of the gospel, because it is the power of God for salvation to everyone who believes, both for the Jew first, then also the Greek. ¹⁷For the righteousness of God is revealed from faith to faith in the gospel. Just as it is written,

> "The righteous will live from faith."[i]

How God's Anger is Revealed on the Earth

¹⁸For the anger of God is being revealed from heaven upon all ungodly activity and lawlessness of men who hold back the truth by their lawlessness. ¹⁹Because what may be known about God is easily known by them; for God made it plainly known to them. ²⁰For from the creation of the world, his invisible qualities, his eternal power and divine nature, have been clearly seen,

---

[i] Habakkuk 2:2

being understood by what was created, so that they have nothing to present in their defense.

21Therefore, although they recognized God, they did not honor him as God or give him thanks, but they have been given over to nonsense in their discussions, and their half-witted hearts have been darkened. 22Confidently claiming that they are wise, they have demonstrated that they are fools. 23They substituted images in the likeness of corruptible man, birds, animals, and reptiles, for the glory of the incorruptible God.

24Therefore, God handed them over to moral impurity in accord with the sexual lusts of their hearts, so that they treated their bodies shamefully with one another. 25They exchanged the truth of God for the lie, and worshiped and served the creation instead of the one who created, who is praised forever. Amen.

26Because of this, God handed them over to dishonorable passions, for their females exchanged their natural sexual function for that which is contrary to nature, 27and likewise, also their males left their natural sexual function with females and were consumed with their passion for each other; males with males doing what is shameful and receiving in themselves the preordained payment for their error.

28Since they did not think it was worthwhile to acknowledge God, God handed them over to a worthless mind, to do things that are not proper. 29They are filled with all unrighteousness, evil, sexual greed, and wickedness. They are full of envy, murder, strife, and deceit. They are mean-spirited, gossips, 30slanderers, and hate God. They are insolent, arrogant, boastful people who invent ways to do evil. They are disobedient to their parents 31and are without understanding. They break their promises, lack normal human affection, and are without mercy. 32They are people who, although they know God's righteous requirement that those who practice such things are worthy of death, not only do these same things, but are pleased with those who indulge in them.

Paul Confronts Human Hypocrisy

Chapter Two

¹Therefore, you have no excuse, O Man, all of you who condemn others, because at the place you condemn others, you are condemning yourself—for you do the very things that you condemn! ²We know that the judgment of God, in accord with truth, is upon those who practice such things as these. ³Do you think this, O Man, you who condemn those who practice such things but do the same thing? Do you think that you will escape the judgment of God? ⁴Or do you feel contempt for the riches of his kindness, patience, and forbearance, not knowing that the kindness of God leads you to repentance?

⁵But owing to your stubbornness and your unrepentant heart, you are storing up punishment[i] for the day of punishment, when the righteous judgment of God is made fully known. ⁶God will repay to each one according to his actions.[ii] ⁷To those who, by perseverance in good works are seeking glory, honor, and an undying nature, he will give life eternal; ⁸but to those who out of selfishness refuse to believe the truth and pursue unrighteousness, he will give wrath and fierce anger. ⁹There will be tribulation and difficult circumstances for every human soul who does evil, both for the Jew first, then also the Greek; ¹⁰but glory, honor, and peace for everyone who works at doing good, both for the Jew first, then also the Greek—¹¹for God does not have biased judgment.

¹²Those who sin without the Law will also die without the Law, and those who sin with the Law, will be judged by the Law; ¹³for those who hear the Law are not righteous before God, but those who do the Law will be justified. ¹⁴For when Gentiles who do not have the Law, naturally do the things the Law requires, these people who do not have the Law are law for themselves. ¹⁵They demonstrate the obligations of the Law are

---

[i] Traditionally, "Storing up wrath for the day of wrath."
[ii] Psalm 62:12, Proverbs 24:12.

written in their hearts, their conscience will bear testimony about each of their thoughts, accusing or defending them—all of this ¹⁶on the day when God judges the secrets of men through Christ Jesus, as my gospel proclaims.

¹⁷But if you regard yourself a Jew, depend on the Law, and glory in God, ¹⁸if you know his will, and approve of the things that really matter because you have learned them from the Law, ¹⁹if you yourself are confident that you are a leader of the blind, a light for those in darkness, ²⁰an instructor of the foolish, a teacher of infants, because you have the system of knowledge and truth in the Law; ²¹therefore, you who teach others, do you teach yourself? You who preach not to steal, do you steal? ²²You who say, "Do not commit adultery," do you commit adultery? You who detest idols, do you profit from pagan temples? ²³You who glory in the Law, do you dishonor God by your violation of the Law? ²⁴"For the Law of God is spoken against[iii] among the Gentiles because of you,"[iv] just as it is written.

True Circumcision

²⁵For circumcision is beneficial if you practice the Law, but if you violate the Law, your circumcision becomes uncircumcision. ²⁶Therefore, if an uncircumcised man keeps the requirements of the Law, his uncircumcision will be counted for circumcision, will it not? ²⁷The physically uncircumcised man who keeps the Law will judge you who violate the Law, especially because you have the letter of the Law and circumcision.

²⁸For someone is not a Jew on the outside, nor is circumcision on the outside in flesh. ²⁹But someone is a Jew on the inside, and circumcision is of the heart—not by the letter but by the Spirit. Such a man does not receive praise from men, but from God.

[iii] Or, blasphemed. To blaspheme is about speaking profanely of sacred things, to slander God, or to speak against him.

[iv] Isaiah 52:5, Ezekiel 36:20-22.

The Benefit of Being Jewish

Chapter Three

¹So, what is special about being Jewish? Or what benefit is there for the circumcised? ²There is much benefit in every respect. For first, they were trusted with the revelation of God. ³To what end? If some were not faithful, their unfaithfulness will not cancel God's faithfulness, will it? ⁴May that never be! Let God be true, and every man a liar,[i] as it is written:

> "So that you might be justified in your words, and
> gain victory when you yourself are judged."[ii]

⁵But if our unrighteousness puts God's righteousness on display, what shall we say? That God is unrighteous for imposing his punishment? I am speaking as a man thinks. ⁶May that never be! Otherwise, how will God judge the world?

⁷But if, because of my lie, the truthfulness of God overflows to his glory, why am I yet judged as a sinner? ⁸Also why not say, "Let us do evil that good might come"? This is what some people have said that we say as they slander us. Their condemnation is appropriate.

There is No Spiritual Advantage of Being Jewish

⁹What then? Do we have an advantage? Not at all. For we have charged previously that all people, both Jews and Greeks, are all under sin. ¹⁰Just as it is written,

> "There is no one righteous, not one."[iii]
> ¹¹"There is no one who understands, there is no one
> who is seeking God. ¹²All have turned away, they
> have together become worthless; there is no one
> who is acting with virtue, not even one."[iv]

---

[i] Psalm 116:11

[ii] Psalm 51:4

[iii] Ecclesiastes 7:20

[iv] Psalm 14:2-3

> [13]"Their throats are like an opened grave; they keep deceiving with their tongues."[v]
> "The poison of asps is under their lips."[vi]
> [14]"Their mouths are full of cursing and bitterness."[vii]
> [15]"Their feet are quick to shed blood. [16]Destruction and misery are on their roads, [17]they have not known the way of peace."[viii]
> [18]"There is no fear of God before their eyes."[ix]

[19]Now we know that as much as the Law says, it says to those under the Law in order that every mouth might be silenced, and all the world be accountable to God. [20]Therefore, no flesh will be justified by the works of law before him; for the knowledge of sin comes through law.

The Righteousness of God Revealed for Jews and Gentiles

[21]But now a righteousness from God that is separate from law has been revealed. The Law and the Prophets are witnesses of it; [22]and the righteousness from God is through faith in Jesus Christ for all those who believe. There is no distinction between them, [23]for all have sinned and lack God's approval,[x] [24]and are justified freely by his grace through the redemption that is in Christ Jesus. [25]God offered him as the means by which sins are forgiven,[xi] through faith in his blood. He did this to demonstrate his righteousness, because in his forbearance, he had let the sins which had been committed prior to Christ[xii] go unpunished. [26]So, God offered him as a demonstration of his righteousness

---

[v] Psalm 5:9

[vi] Psalm 140:3

[vii] Psalm 10:7

[viii] Isaiah 59:7-8

[ix] Psalm 36:1

[x] Or, "fall short of God's glory." The word can mean "glory" or "approval."

[xi] Or, "as a propitiation."

[xii] "Prior to Christ" is more literally, "before hand" or "previously," indicating sins committed before the cross.

at the present time. He is just, and the one who justifies anyone who has faith in Jesus. ²⁷Therefore, where is boasting? It is excluded. On account of what kind of law? Of works? No, but on account of a law of faith. ²⁸For we believe that a man justified by faith apart from works of law. ²⁹Or is God the God of Jews alone? And not also the God of Gentiles? Yes, he is also the God of the Gentiles. ³⁰Since God is one, he will justify the circumcised by faith and the uncircumcised through faith. ³¹So, do we cancel the law through faith? May that never be! Instead, we validate the law.

Abraham as the Example of Faith

Chapter Four

¹What shall we say that Abraham, our forefather (with respect to the flesh) found out? ²For if Abraham was justified by works, he had a reason for pride, but not before God. ³For what does the Scripture say? "Abraham believed God, and it was credited to him for righteousness."[i]

⁴Now wages are not credited as a gift to him who works, but as a debt. ⁵But to the one who does not work, but believes in the one who justifies the ungodly, his faith is credited for righteousness. ⁶It is just how David describes the blessing of the man to whom God credits righteousness apart from works:

> ⁷"Blessed are those whose lawlessness is forgiven, and whose sins are covered. ⁸Blessed is the man whose sin the Lord does not record."[ii]

⁹Therefore, is this blessing on the circumcised or on the uncircumcised? For we say, "His faith was credited to Abraham for righteousness."

---

[i] Genesis 15:6. Also verse 9.

[ii] Psalm 32:1-2

¹⁰Then, how was it credited? Was it while he was uncircumcised or while he was circumcised? It was not while he was circumcised, but while he was uncircumcised. ¹¹He received the sign of circumcision *as* a seal of the righteousness of the faith which he had while uncircumcised. This was so that he might be the father of all who believe though they are uncircumcised, that righteousness could be credited to them. ¹²He is also father of the circumcised, of those who are not only circumcised but also walk in the footsteps of the faith of our father Abraham when he was uncircumcised.

¹³For it is not through law that the promise came to Abraham or his offspring that he would inherit the world, but through the righteousness that is by faith. ¹⁴For if those who follow the Law are heirs, faith is made powerless, and the promise is invalidated. ¹⁵For the law results in punishment, but where there is no law, there is no violation of the law.

¹⁶For this reason, it is by faith, in order that it might be in agreement with grace; this is so that the promise might be valid for all his offspring, not just to those who are of the Law, but also to those who are of the faith of Abraham, who is the father of us all. ¹⁷Just as it is written,

"I have made you a father of many nations."[iii]

This was in the presence of the one whom he believed, of God who makes the dead alive and calls forth the things that do not exist so that they come into existence.

¹⁸Beyond hope, but in the power of hope, he believed that he would become a father of many nations according to what had been told him, "So shall your offspring be."[iv] ¹⁹He did not have weakness in faith even when he observed that his own body was already impotent—since he was about a hundred years old—and that Sarah's womb was barren. ²⁰He did not talk himself out of the promise of God in unbelief, but he was empowered by faith

---

[iii] Genesis 17:5

[iv] Genesis 15:5-6. Also verse 22.

and gave glory to God; ²¹he was absolutely certain that what God had promised, he was also able to do. ²²Therefore, "it was credited to him for righteousness." ²³Now it was not written on account of him alone that "it was credited to him," ²⁴but also for us, to whom it would be credited, to those who believe in the one who raised Jesus our Lord from the dead. ²⁵He was delivered over because of our offenses, and he was raised for our justification.

Standing in Grace, Rescued by His Blood

Chapter Five

¹Therefore, because we have been justified by faith, we have peace with God through our Lord Jesus Christ, ²through whom also we have continuing admission, by faith, into this grace in which we stand; and let us boast in the hope of the glory of God.

³Not only this, but let us also boast in our tribulations, knowing that tribulation produces endurance, ⁴endurance produces tested character, and tested character produces hope; ⁵and hope does not cause us embarrassment, for the love of God is poured out in our hearts through the Holy Spirit who was given to us.

⁶For while we were still helpless, yet at the right time, Christ died for the ungodly. ⁷Someone, with difficulty, might die for a righteous person, and for a good person someone might possibly have the courage to die; ⁸but God has made his own love known to us by his actions, for while we were still sinners Christ died for us.

⁹How much more, since we have been justified by his blood, will we be rescued through him from punishment. ¹⁰For if while we were enemies, we were reconciled to God through the death of his Son, how much more will we, since we are reconciled, be rescued by his life. ¹¹Not only this, but we also boast in God

through our Lord Jesus Christ, through whom we now have received his reconciliation.

Death Entered the World Through Adam, Life Through Jesus Christ

¹²Therefore, just as through one man sin entered into the world, and death entered through his sin, and in this way, death has passed through all mankind, upon all who have sinned—

¹³For before law, sin was in the world, but sin is not charged against anyone while there is no law. ¹⁴But death reigned from Adam until Moses, even over those who did not sin in the same manner that Adam had violated the law. He is a type of the one who was to come. ¹⁵But the gift of grace is also not like the offense; for if by the offense of the one the many died, how much more has the grace of God overflowed to the many, along with the gift by the grace of the one man, Jesus Christ. ¹⁶The gift is not like what happened when the one man sinned. For the judgment came after one offense and brought punishment, but the gift of grace came after many offenses and brought justification. ¹⁷For if by the offense of the one man, death reigned through the one man, how much more will those who receive the abundance of grace and the gift of righteousness reign in life through the one man, Jesus Christ.

¹⁸—So then, just as through the one offense punishment came upon all men, so also through the one act of righteousness the justification that brings life came to all men. ¹⁹For just as through the disobedience of the one man the many were made sinners, in this same way, through the obedience of the one man, the many will be made righteous.

²⁰So, law slipped in to increase the offense; but where sin increased, grace overflowed even more, ²¹so that just as sin reigned in death, in just this way grace might reign through righteousness that results in eternal life, through Jesus Christ our Lord.

United with Christ Jesus in His Death and Resurrection

Chapter Six

¹Therefore, what shall we say? Shall we continue to sin so that grace might multiply? ²May that never be! We are those who have died to sin, how can we still live in it? ³Or do you not know that all of us who have been baptized into Christ Jesus have been baptized into his death? ⁴Therefore, we have been buried with him through baptism into his death, in order that, just as Christ was raised from the dead through the glory of the Father, in the same way we also might walk in a brand new life.

⁵For if we have been united with him in the likeness of his death, how much more will we also be united with him in the likeness of his resurrection. ⁶For we know this, that our old man was crucified with him, in order that our sinful body might be rendered inoperative, and that we might no longer be slaves to sin—⁷for anyone who has died is acquitted of sin.

⁸But if we have died with Christ, we believe that we will also live with him. ⁹We know that since Christ was raised from among the dead, he can no longer die; death no longer rules over him. ¹⁰For the death he died, he died to sin once for all; but the life he is living, he is living to God.

No Longer Letting Sin Reign in our Bodies

¹¹In this way you also must regard yourselves as those who are dead to sin but living for God in Christ Jesus. ¹²Therefore, do not let sin reign in your physical body so that you obey its desires; ¹³and do not continue to present the parts of your body to sin as tools of unrighteousness. Instead, present yourselves to God as those who were among the dead and are now living; and present the parts of your body to God as tools of righteousness. ¹⁴For sin will not rule over you, for you are not under law, but under grace.

¹⁵Therefore, what shall we do? Should we sin because we are not under law, but under grace? May that never be! ¹⁶Don't you know that when you present yourselves as a slave to someone so that you obey them, you become slaves to the one you obey? This is true

whether you become slaves to sin that results in death, or slaves to obedience that results in righteousness. [17]But thanks be to God that although you were slaves of sin, you have now obeyed from the heart the pattern of teaching which has been given to you.

The Path to Life or the Path to Death

[18]Now, since you have been set free from sin, you have been made slaves to righteousness. [19]I am speaking in a human way on account of the weakness of your flesh; for just as you presented the parts of your body as slaves to moral impurity and lawlessness that leads to even more lawlessness, so now present the parts of your body as slaves to righteousness that leads to holiness.

[20]For when you were slaves of sin, you were free men with respect to righteousness; [21]so, what results did you have then from the things for which you are now ashamed? For the end result of those things is death. [22]But now, since you have been freed from sin and become slaves to God, you are producing your fruit, which leads to holiness; and the end result is life eternal. [23]For the reimbursement for sin is death, but the gift of God's grace is life eternal in Christ Jesus our Lord.

Paul Illustrates the Christian's Separation from Law

Chapter Seven

[1]Or do you not know, brothers (since I am speaking to those who know the Law), that the Law rules over a man only for the time he lives? [2]For the married woman is bound by law to her husband while he is living, but if her husband dies, she is free from the regulation concerning her husband. [3]So then, while her husband is living, she will be called an adulteress if she lives with another man. But if her husband dies, she is free from the regulation and is not an adulteress if she marries another man.

[4]In this way, my brothers, you were also put to death to the Law through the body of Christ so that you might live for another; for him who was raised from the dead. This has

happened so that you might bear fruit for God. ⁵For when we were living in the flesh, the sinful passions which were stirred through the Law were working in the parts of our body to produce fruit that results in death. ⁶But now we are free from the Law, since we have died to that which restrained us, so that we serve in the fresh way of the Spirit, and not the stale way of the letter.

The Law Reveals Sin and Sin Takes Advantage of Law

⁷Therefore, what shall we say? Is the Law sin? May that never be! On the contrary, I would not have recognized sin except through the Law. For I would not have recognized lust if the Law had not said, "Do not lust!"ⁱ ⁸Then, through the commandment, sin took the opportunity and created every lust in me. For apart from law, sin is dead. ⁹Once I was living apart from law, but when the commandment came, sin came back to life and I died; ¹⁰and I found that the commandment which was intended for life resulted in death. ¹¹For sin took the opportunity given through the commandment and deceived me, and through it, killed me. ¹²So, the Law is holy, and the commandment is holy and righteous and good.

¹³So, did this good thing become lethal to me? May that never be! But sin, in order that it might be revealed as sin, was working death in me through what is good. This was so that sin might become extremely sinful through the commandment.

Our Flesh Reveals the Absolute Need to be Empowered by Christ

¹⁴We certainly know that the Law is spiritual, but I am made of flesh and sold into slavery to sin. ¹⁵I do not realize what I am doing, for I do not behave in the way I want; what I hate, I end up doing. ¹⁶But if I end up doing what I do not want to do, I agree with the Law, that it is good. ¹⁷But now I am no longer doing it, but the sin living in me. ¹⁸For I know that good does not live in me, that is, in my flesh. For the desire to do good is present in me, but the ability to do the good is not. ¹⁹For it isn't the good that I

ⁱ Exodus 20:17; Deuteronomy 5:21

want that I am doing, but rather the evil that I do not want, this I end up acting out. ²⁰But if I am doing what I do not want to do, I am no longer the one bringing it about, but the sin living in me.

²¹I am discovering then, this principle: evil is present in me even though I want to do good. ²²For I joyfully agree with the law of God with my inner man, ²³but I see another law in the parts of my body. It is waging war against the law in my mind and taking me captive because of the law of sin which is in the parts of my body. ²⁴I am a miserable man! Who will deliver me from this body owned by death? ²⁵But thanks be to God, who has delivered me through Jesus Christ our Lord. So, then I myself with my mind serve the law of God, but on the other hand, I serve the law of sin in my flesh.

Freedom from Punishment in Christ Jesus

Chapter Eight

¹Now then, there is no punishment for anyone who is in Christ Jesus. They do not walk according to the flesh, but according to spirit.ⁱⁱ ²For the law of the spirit of life in Christ Jesus sets you free from the law of sin and death. ³For what the law was unable to do, in that it was weak on account of the flesh, God did by sending his own Son in the likeness of sinful flesh, and he punished sin in the flesh *of his Son* because of our sin.

⁴*He did this* in order that the legal requirement of the law might be fulfilled in us who are not walking according to flesh, but according to spirit. ⁵For those who live only in flesh think of fleshly things, but those who live according to spirit think of spiritual things. ⁶For the thoughts of the flesh release death, but the thoughts of the spirit release life and peace. ⁷So, the thoughts of the flesh are hostile to God because the flesh is not

---

ⁱⁱ Some Manuscripts (and most modern translations) omit: "They do not walk according to the flesh, but according to the spirit." Since this sentence appears in verse 4 as a clause, it is clearly in the apostle's mind as he writes, and thus, this translation retains it in verse 1.

submitted to the law of God; for it is unable to do so. ⁸And those who are living according to their flesh are not able to please God.

The Spirit's Activity Among His People

⁹However, you *Romans*[i] are not living according to flesh, on the contrary, you are living according to spirit, since the Spirit of God dwells in your midst. If anyone does not have the Spirit of Christ, he does not belong to Christ. ¹⁰If Christ is in your midst, the body has death *working in it* on account of sin, but the spirit has life *working in it* on account of righteousness. ¹¹In fact, if the Spirit of the one who raised Jesus from the dead lives in your midst, the one who raised Christ from the dead will also release life to your perishable bodies through his Spirit dwelling in your midst.

Divine Adoption in the Spirit

¹²Now then, brothers, we are in debt, not to the flesh to live according to fleshly principles, ¹³for if you live according to fleshly principles, you will certainly die. But if instead you put to death the fleshly deeds of the body with the Spirit, you will live, ¹⁴since as many as are led by the Spirit of God are sons of God. ¹⁵For you did not receive a spirit that is in bondage to the fear of death, but you received a spirit of divine adoption by which we cry, "Abba Father!"

¹⁶The Spirit himself bears witness with our spirit that we are children of God. ¹⁷Now if we are children *of God*, then we are also heirs; heirs of God and joint heirs with Christ, if indeed we suffer together *with him* in order that also we might share in glory *together with him*.

Creation Awaits the Revelation of the Sons of God

¹⁸I consider that the sufferings of this present time are not worth comparing to the glory that will be revealed in us. ¹⁹For the creation is filled with confident expectation as it eagerly awaits the revealing of the sons of God. ²⁰The creation has been

---

[i] Or, "But you all." Paul is referring to the Roman congregation.

subjected to hopeless futility, not willingly, but because the one who subjected it to this futility *did so* in expectation ²¹that the creation itself will be released from slavery to decay, and will be brought into the freedom and the splendor of the children of God.

²²We know that the whole creation together groans and suffers even until the present time. ²³But creation isn't the only one, we who have the firstfruits of the Spirit, we also groan in ourselves awaiting adoption as sons, the freeing of our body.[ii] ²⁴For this hope we have been rescued, but it is no longer hope when you can see it. Who hopes for what he sees? ²⁵But if we hope for what we do not see, we are patiently waiting.

The Holy Spirit Makes Appeals on our Behalf

²⁶Likewise, the Spirit also helps with our weakness. For we do not understand the things it is absolutely necessary that we pray, but the Spirit himself appeals on our behalf with inexpressible groans. ²⁷The one who examines hearts knows what the thoughts of the Spirit mean, because it is by the will of God that the Spirit makes his appeals on behalf of the saints.

God is Working for the Good

²⁸Now we know that all things work together for good for those who love God, for those who are the called according to his purpose.[iii] ²⁹Because those he foreknew, he also predestined to conform to the image of his Son, so that he would be the firstborn among many brothers; ³⁰and those he predestined, he also called; and those he called, he also pronounced righteous; and those he pronounced righteous,[iv] he has also given honor.

[ii] Since "Body" in singular, and the possessive pronoun (our) is plural, this may be a reference to the Body of Christ.

[iii] Also possible, "Now we know that God works with those who love him so that all things result in good; he works with those who are called according to his purpose."

[iv] Or "Justified."

Romans 8:31

It is Impossible to Sever God's People from the Love of God

³¹Therefore, what shall we say to these things? If God is for us, who can oppose us? ³²Indeed, he did not spare his own Son, but delivered him up on behalf of us all; how will he not also, working with his Son, freely give all things to us?

³³Who would dare bring an accusation against God's elect?[i] God is the one who has declared them righteous! ³⁴Who would dare bring a guilty verdict? Christ Jesus, the one who died, and more than that, was raised to life, he is also on the right hand of God and he is always pleading *before the throne* on our behalf.

³⁵Who can divorce us from the love of Christ? Will tribulation, difficult circumstances, harassment, famine, nakedness, peril or threat of sword be able to do it? ³⁶Just as it is written:

> "For your sake we are put to death the entire day; we are counted as sheep for slaughter."[ii]

³⁷But in all these things we are completely and overwhelmingly victorious through the one who loved us. ³⁸For I am fully persuaded that neither death nor life, neither angels nor principalities, neither current events nor future events, neither earthly powers, ³⁹nor powers in the heavens above or in the depths below, and nothing else in all of creation is able to divorce us from the love of God which is in Christ Jesus our Lord.

---

[i] The term translated "elect" is used over twenty times in the New Testament and is a reference to those who are called by God to true faith that perseveres.

[ii] Psalm 44:22

Paul's Desire for the Salvation of the Israelites

Chapter Nine

¹I am speaking truth in Christ, I am not lying, my conscience verifies it for me in the Holy Spirit, ²that I have great sadness and constant sorrow in my heart. ³For I almost wished that I myself might be cut off from the Messiah[iii] for the sake of my brothers, my relatives (with respect to the flesh), ⁴those who are Israelites. They have the adoption of sons, the glory, the covenants, the giving of the Law, the worship, and the promises. ⁵They have the fathers; and with respect to the flesh, from them comes the Christ, who is God over all things, blessed forever. Amen.

Discerning the Children of Promise

⁶But it isn't as if the Word of God has failed. For not all those who have descended from Israel are Israel, ⁷nor because they are Abraham's offspring are they all his children, but "Through Isaac your offspring will be named."[iv] ⁸That is, it is not the children of the flesh who are these children of God, but it is the children of the promise who are counted for offspring. ⁹For this was the word of promise, "I will come at this time, and Sarah will have a son."[v]

¹⁰Not only this, but Rebecca also, from one sexual encounter with our father Isaac *conceived two boys*, ¹¹then before *the twins* were born, before they did anything good or bad—in order that the purpose of God with respect to election might endure, ¹²not through works, but through him who calls—she was told, "The older will serve the younger."[vi] ¹³Just as it is written, "I have loved Jacob, but I have despised Esau."[vii]

[iii] Or, "the Christ."
[iv] Genesis 21:12
[v] Genesis 18:10
[vi] Genesis 25:23
[vii] Malachi 1:2-3

The God who Makes His Choice

¹⁴Then what shall we say? There is no unrighteousness in God, is there? May that never be! ¹⁵For he said to Moses,

> "I will have mercy on whom I have mercy, and I will have compassion on whom I have compassion."[i]

¹⁶So then, it isn't about the one who wants it, nor the one who is striving for it, but it is about the God who has mercy. ¹⁷For the Scripture says to Pharaoh,

> "For this very reason, I have given you a place in history, so that I might put my power on display through you, and that my name might be proclaimed in all the earth."[ii]

¹⁸So then, he has mercy on those whom he wishes, and he hardens those whom he wishes.

¹⁹Therefore, will you say to me, "Why then, does he still blame anyone? For who opposes his will?" ²⁰On the contrary, oh man, who are you to criticize God in response? Does what is created say to its creator, "Why have you made me like this?" ²¹Or doesn't the potter have the authority over his clay to make from the same lump one vessel of high value, and another with little value?

²²But what if God, because he wanted to put his wrath on display and make his power known, endured with much patience vessels of wrath who have prepared themselves[iii] for destruction? ²³What if he did this to make the riches of his glory known to the vessels of mercy, which he prepared ahead of time for glory, ²⁴even to us whom he has called, not only from among the Jews, but also from the Gentiles? ²⁵As also he said in Hosea,

---

[i] Exodus 33:19

[ii] Exodus 9:16

[iii] Or "who are prepared for destruction?"

"I will call those who aren't my people, 'My people,' and those not loved, 'Loved;'[iv] ²⁶and it will come to pass in the place where it was said to them, 'You are not my people,' there they will be called, 'sons of the Living God.'"[v]

²⁷Isaiah cried out concerning Israel,

"Even if the number of the sons of Israel be as the sand of the sea, the remnant are the ones who will be saved; ²⁸for the Lord will fulfill his word on the earth completely and without hesitation."[vi]

²⁹As Isaiah foretold,

"If the Lord who leads armies had not left us offspring, we would have become like Sodom, and been compared to Gomorrah."[vii]

³⁰So then, what shall we say? That Gentiles who have not pursued righteousness have discovered righteousness, but a righteousness which is from faith; ³¹but Israel, who has been pursuing law to achieve righteousness, has not reached that law. ³²Why? Because they did not pursue it from faith, but as if it were by works; they took offense over the stumbling stone. ³³Just as it is written,

"Look, I will place a stone of stumbling in Zion and a rock of offense, and anyone who believes him will never be ashamed."[viii]

[iv] Hosea 2:23

[v] Hosea 1:10

[vi] Isaiah 10:22-23

[vii] Isaiah 1:9

[viii] Isaiah 8:14; 28:16

Paul's Prayer for Israel's Salvation

Chapter Ten

¹Brothers, certainly the delight of my heart, and my prayer to God for them is salvation. ²For I testify about them that they have zeal for God, but it is not in agreement with knowledge. ³Because they are ignorant of the righteousness of God, and because they seek to establish their own righteousness, they did not submit themselves to the righteousness of God. ⁴For Christ was the purpose of the Law, resulting in righteousness for everyone who believes.

⁵Moses wrote about the righteousness which is from the Law,

"The man who does them will live by them."[i]

⁶But the righteousness from faith says it in this way: "Do not say in your heart, 'Who will go up to heaven?' That is, to lead Christ down. ⁷Or, 'Who will go down to the abyss?' That is, to lead Christ up from the dead. ⁸But what does it say? 'The word is near you, in your mouth and in your heart.'"[ii] This is the word of faith that we are proclaiming—⁹that if you acknowledge with your mouth that Jesus is Lord, and believe in your heart that God raised him from the dead, you will be saved, ¹⁰For a person believes with the heart, resulting in righteousness, and acknowledges with the mouth, resulting in deliverance.

¹¹The Scripture says,

"Everyone who believes on him will never be ashamed."[iii]

¹²There is no distinction between Jew and Greek, for the same Lord is over all people. He is rich toward all those who call on him. ¹³For everyone who calls on the name of the Lord will be saved!

---

[i] Leviticus 18:5

[ii] Verses 6-8 are based on Deuteronomy 30:12-14.

[iii] Isaiah 28:16

The Need to Proclaim the Gospel of Christ

¹⁴So, how will they call on him in whom they have not believed? And how will they believe in him about whom they have not heard? And how will they hear apart from someone proclaiming the message? ¹⁵And how will they proclaim the message unless they are sent? Just as it is written,

> "How beautiful are the feet of those proclaiming the good news!"[iv]

¹⁶But not everyone has been obedient to the good news. For Isaiah says,

> "Lord, who has believed our report?"[v]

¹⁷Therefore, faith comes from what is heard, but what is heard comes through the word of Christ. ¹⁸But I ask, they have heard, haven't they? Of course!

> "Their voice has gone out into all the earth, and their words to the ends of the world."[vi]

¹⁹But I ask, Israel did not know, did they? First Moses says,

> "I will make you jealous over what is not a nation, I will make you angry over a nation without understanding."[vii]

²⁰Isaiah is so bold as to say,

> "I was found by those who were not seeking me, I became visible to those who were not inquiring about me."[viii]

[iv] Isaiah 52:7

[v] Isaiah 53:1

[vi] Psalm 19:4

[vii] Deuteronomy 32:21

[viii] Isaiah 65:1

²¹But concerning Israel he says,

> "All the day long, I have extended my hands to a people who disobey me and speak against me."[i]

God's Promises for Israel Stand

Chapter Eleven

¹I ask then, God did not push his people aside, did he? May that never be! For I also am an Israelite, from the seed of Abraham, of the tribe of Benjamin. ²God did not reject his people, whom he foreknew. Or do you not know what the Scripture about Elijah states how he interceded with God against Israel?

> ³"Lord, they have killed your prophets, they have razed your altars, and I alone am left, and they are seeking my life."[ii]

⁴But how does God respond to him?

> "I have left for myself seven thousand men who have not bent the knee to Baal."[iii]

⁵In this way, then, at this time, there is also left a remnant according to the election of grace. ⁶But if it is by grace, it is no longer gained by works, otherwise grace is no longer grace.

⁷What then? What Israel was seeking, Israel did not attain; but the elect[iv] have attained it, and the rest were hardened. ⁸Just as it is written,

> "God gave them a spirit of bewilderment, eyes not able to see, and ears not able to hear, to this very day."[v]

---

[i] Isaiah 65:2

[ii] I Kings 19:10, 14

[iii] 1 Kings 19:18

[iv] On the term "elect" see Romans 8:33 footnote.

[v] Deuteronomy 29:4; Isaiah 29:10

⁹David says,

"Let their table be a snare and net, even a stumbling block and repayment to them. ¹⁰Let their eyes be darkened, not able to see, and bend their back through it all."[vi]

¹¹I say then, they did not make this blunder so that they might fall beyond recovery, did they? May that never be! But by their trespass, salvation has come to the Gentiles in order to make them jealous. ¹²But if their trespass brings riches for the world, and their failure brings riches for the Gentiles, how much more will their full measure bring!

¹³Now I am speaking to you Gentiles, inasmuch as I myself am an apostle to the Gentiles. I emphasize my ministry ¹⁴that in some way I might make my people jealous and save some from among them. ¹⁵For if their loss means reconciliation for the world, what will their addition be if not life from among the dead? ¹⁶Now if the firstfruits is holy, so is the whole lump of dough. If the root is holy, so are the branches.

Gentiles are Grafted on to the Promises

¹⁷But if some of the branches have been broken off, and you who are a wild olive tree have been grafted in among them and have become partners in the rich overflow of the root of the olive tree, ¹⁸do not look down on the branches; but if you do look down on them, give thought to the fact that you do not sustain the root, but the root sustains you. ¹⁹So you will say, "Branches were broken off that I might be grafted on." ²⁰Very well, they were broken off by unbelief, but you stay in place by faith; do not be haughty, but rather have profound reverence; ²¹for if God did not spare the natural branches, neither will he spare you.

²²Therefore, note the kindness and severity of God; on the one hand, to those who fell, severity, but on the other hand, to you, the kindness of God—if you remain in his kindness, since

---

[vi] Psalm 69:22-23

you also can be cut off. ²³As for them, if they do not remain in unbelief, they will be grafted on, since God is able to graft them on again. ²⁴For if you were cut out of what is by nature a wild olive tree, and contrary to nature were grafted on to a cultivated olive tree, how much more will they be grafted on to what is by nature their own olive tree.

Understanding the Future of Israel

²⁵For I do not want you to be ignorant, brothers, about this mystery, so that you might not be wise in your own view. The mystery is that a partial hardening has come upon Israel until the time that the full measure of Gentiles has come in. ²⁶Even in this way, all Israel will be rescued, just as it is written,

> "The one who rescues will come out of Zion, he
> will turn ungodliness away from Jacob. ²⁷This
> is my covenant with them,[i] when I take away
> their sins."[ii]

²⁸On the one hand, and in agreement with the gospel, they are enemies because of you, but on the other hand, and in agreement with election, they are cherished because of the fathers; ²⁹for the grace gifts and the call of God are permanent. ³⁰For just as you formerly refused to believe God, but now you have received mercy through their disobedience, ³¹in this same way, they also now have refused to believe that they might now be shown mercy through the mercy given to you. ³²For God has caught everyone in the net of disobedience, in order that he might show mercy to everyone.

³³Oh, the depth of the riches, wisdom, and knowledge of God; how far beyond our understanding are his judgments, and untraceable are his paths! ³⁴For who has known the mind of the Lord? Or who has become his counselor?[iii] ³⁵Or who has given

---

[i] Isaiah 59:20-21

[ii] Isaiah 27:9

[iii] Isaiah 14:13-14

first to him, so that it might be paid back to him?[iv] 36Since from him and through him and to him are all things; to him be glory unto the ages. Amen.

Be Transformed as Living Sacrifices
Chapter Twelve

1Therefore, I encourage you, brothers, through the mercies of God, to present your bodies as a holy living sacrifice that is pleasing to God; that is your spiritual sacrifice. 2Stop contorting yourself to fit the pattern of this age; instead, be transformed[v] by the renewing of your minds so that you can test what is the will of God, which is good, pleasing to him, and perfect.

3For through the grace given to me, I say to everyone who is living among you, do not think more highly of yourself than what it is necessary, rather think of yourself sensibly, in accord with the measure of faith which God has apportioned to each person. 4For just as we have many body parts in one body, and all the parts do not have the same task, 5in the same way, we are many in one body, in Christ, and each one of us are members of each other.

Use the Spiritual Gifts God has Given

6But we have different grace gifts according to the grace given to us. If it is prophecy, use it in agreement with the faith; 7if it is service, use it in serving; if you are one who teaches, use it in teaching; 8if you are one who encourages, use it in encouragement; if you are one who gives, use it with generosity; if you are one who leads, use it with eager readiness; if you are one who shows mercy, use it with cheerfulness.

[iv] See Job 35:7; 411

[v] This word could also be translated, "transfigured," as it is in the accounts of Jesus' transfiguration (see Matthew 17:2 and Mark 9:2). It refers to an obvious change, a metamorphosis.

Romans 12:9

How to Live as a Spiritual Sacrifice

⁹Love is without hypocrisy, abhors evil, and clings to the good. ¹⁰Be affectionate to each other with brotherly affection; excel above one another in showing honor. ¹¹Do not shrink away from eager devotion, but overflow in the Spirit while serving the Lord. ¹²Rejoice in hope. Endure through tribulation. Persevere in prayer. ¹³Share in the needs of the saints. Press forward with hospitality.

¹⁴Speak well of those who persecute you, speak well of and do not curse. ¹⁵Rejoice with those who rejoice; weep with those who weep. ¹⁶Have the same view of one another, not a haughty view, but be willing to fellowship with those of low position. Do not be wise in your own opinion.

¹⁷Do not pay back evil for evil to anyone; give thought to what is good in the judgment of all men. ¹⁸If you are able, as far as it depends on you, live in peace with all men. ¹⁹Do not avenge yourselves, cherished friends, but leave a place for the vengeance of God. For it is written,

> " 'Vengeance belongs to me, I will pay back,' says the Lord."[i]

²⁰Rather,

> "If your enemy is hungry, feed him. If he is thirsty, give him a drink; for while you are doing this, you are heaping up fiery coals upon his head."[ii]

²¹Do not be conquered by evil, rather conquer the evil with the good.

---

[i] Deuteronomy 32:35
[ii] Proverbs 25:21-22

A Christians Relationship to Authority

Chapter Thirteen

¹Every soul must submit himself willingly to those who have authority over them, for there is no authority except from God, and the ones that exist are appointed by God. ²So, the one who resists authority takes a stand against the command of God. Those who have taken such a stance will be subject to legal action.

³The rulers, then, are not a concern for good activity, but for evil activity. If you do not want to be afraid of the authority, do good, and you will receive appreciation from them. ⁴For the ruler is a servant of God for you for your good. But if you practice evil, be afraid. For he does not carry a sword in vain; he is an avenging servant of God to visit punishment[iii] on those who practice evil. ⁵Therefore, it is absolutely necessary *that we* submit, not just because of the punishment, but also because of conscience.

⁶For this reason, you also pay taxes, for rulers are public servants who devote themselves to this service. ⁷Pay back your debts to everyone; tax to whom tax is owed, tribute to whom tribute is owed, respect to whom respect is owed, and honor to whom honor is owed.

Loving Your Neighbor

⁸Owe nothing to anyone, except *the debt* to love one another; for the one who loves another has fulfilled the law. ⁹For these things, "Do not commit adultery, do not murder, do not steal, do not covet,"[iv] and if there is any other command, it is summed up by this, "Love your neighbor as yourself."[v] ¹⁰Love does no harm to a neighbor; therefore, love is a fulfillment of the law.

[iii] Traditionally, "wrath." Also in verse 5.

[iv] Exodus 20:13-17; Deuteronomy 5:17-21

[v] Leviticus 19:18

¹¹Do this, understanding the time, for it is already the hour for you to wake up from your slumber; for deliverance is nearer to us now than when we came to faith. ¹²The night is drawing to a close, and the day has drawn near. So, let us put away the works of darkness and put on the armor of light. ¹³Let us conduct ourselves with propriety, not with orgies and drunkenness, not with sexual encounters and unrestrained sensuality, not with strife and envy, ¹⁴but put on the Lord Jesus Christ, and do not make any provision for the flesh and its lusts.

Christian Freedom

Chapter Fourteen

¹Welcome the one whose faith is weak into your fellowship, *but* not so that you can argue about *their* doubts. ²On the one hand, one person has faith to eat everything, but another who is weak eats only food from the garden. ³The one who eats *everything* should not look down on the one who does not eat *everything*, and the one who does not eat everything should not judge the one who eats *everything*; for God has welcomed him into fellowship. ⁴Who are you to judge another person's household servant? To his own master he stands or falls; but the Lord is able to make him stand.

⁵Yes, there are some who regard one day as more important than another day, but there are others who regard every day *the same*. Let each person be convinced in his own mind. ⁶The one who regards the day *as important*, does so for the Lord. The one who eats *everything*, does so for the Lord, for he gives thanks to God; and the one who does not eat everything does so for the Lord, and gives thanks to God. ⁷For none of us lives for himself, and no one dies for himself. ⁸For if we should live, we are living for the Lord, and if we should die, we are dying for the Lord. Therefore, if we should live or die, we are the Lord's.

Do Not Judge Each Other

⁹For this purpose, Christ died and now lives, that he might be Lord of those who are dead and those who are living. ¹⁰But you, why do you judge your brother? Or you, why do you look down on your brother? For we will all stand before the judgment seat of God. ¹¹For it is written,

> " 'I myself am living,' says the Lord, 'Every knee will bend, and every tongue will offer praise to God.' "[i]

¹²So then, each one of us will give an account about himself to God.

¹³Therefore, we must no longer judge each other, but rather you must resolve to do this: Do not place a stumbling stone or impediment in front of your brother. ¹⁴I understand and I am convinced in the Lord Jesus that nothing is impure by itself; but for the one who considers it to be impure, it is impure for him. ¹⁵For if your brother feels grief on account of food, you are no longer walking in accord with love. Do not cause harm over your food *choices* for the one for whom Christ died.

¹⁶Therefore, do not let your good thing be slandered as bad; ¹⁷for the Kingdom of God does not consist in food or drink, but it does consist of righteousness, peace, and joy in the Holy Spirit. ¹⁸The one who serves Christ in this way is pleasing to God and is considered worthy by men.

¹⁹So then, let us pursue the things that concern peace and that build one another up. ²⁰Do not destroy the work of God because of food. All things are certainly clean, but they are harmful for the man who eats while causing offense. ²¹It is good not to eat meat, drink wine, or do whatever your brother stumbles over, takes offense at, or has doubts[ii] about.

---

[i] Isaiah 45:23

[ii] Or, "is weakened by."

²²You yourself have a belief about this; keep it between yourself and God. Blessed is the one who does not condemn himself by what he approves. ²³But the one who doubts is condemned if he eats, because he is not eating from faith; and everything that is not from faith is sin.

Glorify God with One Passion

Chapter Fifteen

¹But we who are strong must bear with the doubts[i] of those who are not strong, and not desire to please ourselves. ²Each of us must please his neighbor for his good to build him up. ³For even Christ did not please himself, but just as it is written,

> "The reproach of those who insulted you fell on me."[ii]

⁴For everything written in the past was written for our education, in order that through endurance and the encouragement of the Scriptures, we might have hope.

⁵Now may the God of endurance and encouragement give you the same view of one another in accord with Jesus Christ, ⁶so that with one passion and one voice you may glorify the God and Father of our Lord Jesus Christ.

⁷Therefore, welcome one another into fellowship, just as Christ also welcomed you into fellowship for the glory of God. ⁸For I tell you that Christ has become a servant to the circumcised in defense of God's truthfulness, to prove that that the promises to the fathers were reliable, ⁹and to prove that the Gentiles would glorify God for his mercy. Just as it is written,

---

[i] Or, "weaknesses."

[ii] Psalm 69:9

"For this reason I will acknowledge you among the Gentiles, and I will sing a song of praise to your name."[iii]

¹⁰Again it says,

"Rejoice, you Gentiles, with his people."[iv]

¹¹And again,

"Praise the Lord, all you Gentiles, and let all the peoples praise him."[v]

¹²And again, Isaiah says,

"The root of Jesse will appear, even the one who rises up to rule the Gentiles; Gentiles will hope in him."[vi]

¹³Now may the God of hope fill you with all joy and peace in the one you believe, so that you overflow with hope by the power of the Holy Spirit.

Paul's Confidence in the Roman Christians

¹⁴But I myself am also convinced about you, my brothers, that you yourselves are filled with goodness, since you have been filled with all knowledge and are able to impart understanding to one another. ¹⁵Indeed, I have written to you with great daring on some points, as I remind you again of those things, through the grace that was given me by God ¹⁶to be a minister of Christ Jesus to the Gentiles. I am acting as a priest for the gospel of God, so that my sacrificial offering of the Gentiles might be acceptable, since it has been sanctified by the Holy Spirit.

¹⁷Therefore, I take pride in Christ Jesus about my work for God. ¹⁸For I will not dare to speak anything that Christ has not

---

[iii] 2 Samuel 22:50; Psalm 18:49

[iv] Deuteronomy 32:43

[v] Psalm 117:1

[vi] Isaiah 11:10

accomplished through me, by my word and work, resulting in the obedience of the Gentiles. ¹⁹He has done this through the power of signs and wonders, *and* through the power of the Spirit of God; so that from Jerusalem and around to Illyricum I have completely proclaimed the gospel of Christ.

Paul Hopes to Come to Rome

²⁰In this way, also, I have made it my ambition to preach the good news *in places* where Christ was not already named, so that I would not build upon a foundation that belonged to someone else. ²¹But just as it is written,

> "To those who did not have a report of him, they will see; and the ones who did not hear, they shall understand."[i]

²²Therefore, I have been hindered many times from coming to you. ²³But now, since I no longer have an opportunity in these regions, and I have had a desire to come to you for many years. ²⁴I intend to come to you as I journey to Spain. For I hope that while I am passing through that I will see you and be helped on my way there, after I first have enjoyed your company for a while.

²⁵At this time, I am journeying to Jerusalem to serve the saints. ²⁶For Macedonia and Achaia were very pleased to make a fellowship offering to the poor among the saints in Jerusalem. ²⁷Indeed, they were very pleased to *give*, and they are under obligation to them; for if the Gentiles have shared in their spiritual things, they are also under obligation to minister to them with physical things.

²⁸Then, after I have completed this, and delivered this fruit safely to them, I will leave for Spain by way of you. ²⁹I know that when I come to you, I will come with the full measure of the blessing of Christ.

³⁰But I urge you, brothers, through our Lord Jesus Christ and through the love of the Spirit, to fight together with me by your

---

[i] Isaiah 52:15

prayers to God on my behalf, ³¹that I be delivered from those who are disobedient in Judea, and that my service in Jerusalem might be acceptable to the saints; ³²so that, after I have come to you in joy through the will of God, I might be refreshed with you. ³³Now, the God of peace be with all of you. Amen.

Greetings from the Brothers and Sisters with Paul

Chapter Sixteen

¹I recommend to you our sister, Phoebe, a deaconess of the church in Cenchrea, ²so that you welcome her in the Lord in a manner worthy of the saints, and so that you supply her in whatever way she may have need from you. For she has been patroness to many, and to me also.

³Greet Priscilla and Aquila, my fellow workers in Christ Jesus, ⁴who risked their own necks for my life. I do not thank them alone, but also all the churches of the Gentiles *join with me*; ⁵also greet the church that is in their house.

Greet Epaenetus, my cherished friend, who is the firstfruits for Christ in Asia.

⁶Greet Mary, who has labored much for you.

⁷Greet Andronicus and Junias, my relatives and my fellow prisoners, who are eminent among the apostles, and also were in Christ before me.

⁸Greet Ampliatus, my cherished friend in the Lord.

⁹Greet Urbanus, our fellow worker in Christ, and Stachys my cherished friend.

¹⁰Greet Apelles, the one who stood the test in Christ. Greet those from the household of Aristobulus. ¹¹Greet Herodian, my relative.

Greet those from the household of Narcissus who are in the Lord.

¹²Greet Tryphena and Tryphosa, who labored much in the Lord.

Greet Persis, my cherished friend who worked hard in the Lord.

¹³Greet Rufus, the elect[i] one in the Lord, and his mother and mine.

¹⁴Greet Asyncritus, Phlegon, Hermes, Patrobas, Hermas, and the brothers with them.

¹⁵Greet Philologus and Julia, Nereus and his sister, and Olympas and all the saints with them.

¹⁶Greet one another with a holy kiss. All the churches of Christ greet you.

Watch for Those who Cause Divisions and Create Obstacles to Faith

¹⁷I encourage you, brothers, to take special notice of those who cause divisions and create stumbling blocks over the teaching you have learned. Turn away from them. ¹⁸For such men as these are not serving our Lord Christ, but their own bellies. They deceive the naïve through their fine words and flattering speech.

¹⁹*News of* your obedience has become known to everyone, so I am rejoicing over you; but I desire that you be wise in what is good, and uncontaminated by what is evil. ²⁰Then the God of peace will quickly crush Satan under your feet. The grace of our Lord Jesus be with you.

²¹Timothy, my fellow worker greets you, as well as Lucius, Jason, and Sosipater, my relatives.

²²I, Tertius, the one writing this letter, greet you in the Lord.

²³Gaius, who has acted as host to me and the whole church, greets you.

---

[i] On the term "elect" see Romans 8:33 footnote.

Erastus, the city manager, and Quartus greet you.

24The grace of our Lord Jesus Christ be with you all. Amen.

25Now to him who is able to make you strong through my gospel and the preaching of Jesus Christ, according to the revelation of the mystery which was kept secret in ages past, 26but now has been revealed and made known to all nations through the prophetic Scriptures—by the command of the eternal God—resulting in the obedience that stems from faith; 27to the only wise God, through Jesus Christ, be the glory for all ages. Amen.

1 CORINTHIANS

Chapter One

¹Paul, a called apostle of Christ Jesus by the will of God, and Sosthenes your brother:

²To the church of God which is in Corinth, to those who have been made holy in Christ Jesus, to the called saints, along with all those who call on the name of our Lord Jesus Christ in every place, their *Lord* and ours.[i]

³Grace to you and peace from God our Father and our Lord Jesus Christ.

Paul Gives Thanks for the Corinthian Christians

⁴I am always giving thanks to my God about you, over the grace of God that was given to you in Christ Jesus, ⁵because in everything you were made wealthy in him, in all your reasoning and in all your knowledge. ⁶In the same way, the testimony of Christ was validated among you ⁷in that you did not lack any grace gift while you eagerly await the revelation of our Lord Jesus Christ. ⁸He will also validate you as blameless to the very

---

[i] Grammatically, "theirs and ours" could also be translated, "their place and ours."

end on the day of our Lord Jesus Christ. ⁹God is trustworthy, through whom you were called into fellowship with his Son, Jesus Christ our Lord.

Paul's Warning Against Divisions in the Church

¹⁰Now I encourage you, brothers, through the name of our Lord Jesus Christ, that you all may speak in agreement, and that there be no divisions among you, but that you may be restored to the same mind and to the same intent. ¹¹For those *who came* from Chloe have told me about you, my brothers, that there are quarrels among you. ¹²I am speaking about this: Each of you says, "I am with Paul," or, "I am with Apollos," or, "I am with Cephas," or, "I am with Christ." ¹³Has Christ been divided? Paul wasn't crucified for you, was he? Or were you baptized into the name of Paul?

¹⁴I give thanks to God that I did not baptize any of you except Crispus and Gaius, ¹⁵so that no one may say that they were baptized into my name. ¹⁶Of course, I also baptized the household of Stephanas. I do not know if I baptized anyone else in addition *to them*. ¹⁷For Christ did not send me to baptize, but to proclaim the good news, not with skillful speech, so that the cross of Christ might not be emptied of power.

The Cross is the Power of God

¹⁸For this talk of the cross is nonsense to those who are lost, but it is the power of God for those of us who are being saved. ¹⁹For it is written,

> "I will destroy the wisdom of the wise, and I will set aside the understanding of the insightful."[ii]

²⁰Where is the wise man? Where is the man of letters? Where is the man who uses words to debate in this age? God has made the wisdom of this world into nonsense, hasn't he? ²¹For since, in the wisdom of God, the world did not know God through its wisdom, God was pleased through the "nonsense" of our

---

[ii] Isaiah 29:14

preaching to save those who believe. ²²For Jews ask for a sign, and Greeks seek wisdom, ²³but we preach Christ crucified, offensive to the Jews and nonsense to the Gentiles, ²⁴but to the called, both Jews and Greeks, Christ the power of God and the wisdom of God. ²⁵Because the nonsense of God is wiser than men, and the weakness of God is stronger than men.

²⁶Indeed, take note of your calling, brothers. Not many were wise according to the flesh, not many were powerful, not many were of high rank. ²⁷But God chose the foolish things of the world to shame the wise. God chose the weak things of this world to shame the powerful. ²⁸God chose the insignificant things of this world, and the disregarded things, the things that are unimportant, so that he may render powerless the things that are important, ²⁹so no one[i] may boast in the presence of God. ³⁰But you are in Christ Jesus because of him. He was born to us as wisdom from God, our righteousness, holiness, and redemption; ³¹so that, just as it is written, "Let the one who boasts, boast in the Lord."

Proof of the Holy Spirit's Power

Chapter Two

¹When I came to you, brothers, I did not come with outstanding speech or wisdom while I was preaching the mystery of God to you. ²For I made up my mind not to know anything except Jesus Christ and him crucified. ³I approached you with weakness, fear, and much trembling, ⁴and my speech and my preaching were not filled with convincing words of wisdom, but with proof of the Holy Spirit and power, ⁵so that your faith might not be in the wisdom of men, but in the power of God.

⁶However, we are speaking wisdom among those who are adults. It is not a wisdom of this age, nor of the rulers of this age, who are being rendered powerless, ⁷but we are speaking God's

---

[i] Or, more literally, "no flesh may boast."

wisdom, which was hidden in mystery; and which God predestined for our glory before the ages. ⁸None of the rulers of this age recognized this wisdom, for if they had recognized it, they would not have crucified the Lord of glory. ⁹But as it is written,

> "What eye has not seen, and ear has not heard,
> what has not arisen in the heart of man, God
> has prepared for those who love him."ⁱⁱ

¹⁰God has revealed to us through his Spirit.

Speaking Things Taught by the Holy Spirit

For the Spirit investigates everything, even the depths of God. ¹¹For who among men knows the things of a man except the man's spirit that is in him? In this same way, no one knows the things of God except the Spirit of God. ¹²But we have not received the spirit of the world, but the Spirit who is from God, so that we may know the things that have been graciously given to us by God. ¹³We are also speaking of these things, not with words taught by human wisdom, but with those taught by the Spirit, matching spiritual *truths* to spiritual words. ¹⁴But the soulish manⁱⁱⁱ does not accept the things of the Spirit of God, for they are nonsense to him, and he cannot understand because they are spiritually evaluated. ¹⁵The spiritual manⁱᵛ evaluates all things, but he himself is not evaluated by anyone. ¹⁶For

> "Who has known the mind of the Lord, who
> will instruct him?"ᵛ

But we have the mind of Christ.

ⁱⁱ Isaiah 64:4

ⁱⁱⁱ One who is led by his soul (his own mind, emotion, or will) rather than his spirit (See Romans 8:14; Galatians 5:18).

ⁱᵛ One who is led by the Spirit of God in his spirit.

ᵛ Isaiah 40:13

Divisions Corrupt God's Temple

Chapter Three

¹I could not speak to you, brothers as spiritual, but as fleshly,[i] like infants in Christ. ²I gave you milk, not *adult* food, for you were not yet able *to digest it*; but even now you are not yet able, ³for you are still fleshly. For are you not fleshly, and do you not walk in the manner of men since there is jealousy and strife among you? ⁴For when someone says, "I am with Paul," and another, "I am with Apollos," are you not fleshly?

⁵Therefore, who is Apollos? Who is Paul? We are servants through whom you believed, and each as the Lord has granted the opportunity. ⁶I planted, Apollos watered, but God causes the growth. ⁷So, it is not the one who plants or the one who waters who is anything, but God who is causing the growth. ⁸The one planting and the one watering are one, but each one will receive their own reward corresponding to his own labor. ⁹For we are God's fellow workers, you are God's field, God's building.

¹⁰According to the grace of God which was given to me, I laid a foundation as a skilled master builder, but another is building *on it*. But each one must take note of how he is building. ¹¹For no one can lay another foundation beside the one that is laid, which is Jesus Christ. ¹²But if anyone is building on the foundation using gold, silver, valuable gems, wood, grass, or straw, ¹³each one's workmanship will become visible, for the Day will make it known, because it will be revealed by fire. Then the fire itself will assess each man's workmanship. ¹⁴If anyone's work which he has built lasts, he will receive his reward. ¹⁵If anyone's work is burned down, he will forfeit *his reward*. He himself will be saved, but only as *having passed* through fire.

---

[i] Those who are led by the desires of their flesh rather than the Spirit of God. Also verses 3 and 4.

¹⁶Do you not know that you *together*[ii] are the temple of God, and that the Spirit of God dwells in you? ¹⁷If anyone corrupts the temple of God, God will corrupt him. For the temple of God is holy. You yourselves are that temple.

¹⁸Let no one deceive himself. If anyone among you presumes to be wise in this age, he must become foolish so that he might become wise. ¹⁹For the wisdom of this world is nonsense in the sight of God. For it is written,

> "He is the one who catches the wise in their cleverness."[iii]

²⁰And again,

> "The Lord knows the discussions of the wise, for they are worthless."[iv]

²¹For this reason, let no one boast in men, for all things are yours, ²²whether Paul, or Apollos, or Cephas, or the world, or life, or death, or what is present, or what is future. All things are yours, ²³and you are Christ's, and Christ is God's.

Paul as an Apostle of Christ

Chapter Four

¹A man should regard us as officers of Christ and administrators of the mysteries of God. ²In this connection, among administrators, it is required that each of them be found faithful. ³But for me, it is insignificant that I might be examined by you or at any human day of reckoning; in point of fact, I do not even examine myself. ⁴For I know of nothing that is against me, but I am not justified by this; the Lord is the one who examines me. ⁵So, do not judge anything before the proper time, prior to the

---

[ii] You" is plural in this verse. Paul is referring to believers together as God's temple. Also in verse 17.

[iii] Job 5:13

[iv] Psalm 94:11

time when the Lord comes. He will bring to light the hidden things of darkness, and will reveal the intentions of hearts. Then each man's praise from God will be evident.

⁶But these things, brothers, I have applied rather freely to myself and Apollos on your behalf, so that in us you might learn not to go beyond what is written, and so that none of you become puffed up as you prefer one of us against the other. ⁷For who prefers you? What do you have that you did not receive? If you also received it, why are you boasting like you did not receive it?

⁸Are you already satisfied? Are you already wealthy? Are you reigning as kings without us? If only you were truly reigning, that we also might reign with you. ⁹For I think God has appointed those of us who are apostles last, as those who are under sentence of death, for we have become players on a stage for the world, for angels, and for men. ¹⁰We are fools for the sake of Christ, but you are wise in Christ. We are weak, but you are strong. You are famous, but we are unknown. ¹¹Until this exact hour, we are hungry, we are thirsty, we are wearing ragged clothing, we endure beatings, and have no home. ¹²We are growing tired working with our own hands. When we are abused, we bless; when we are persecuted, we endure; ¹³when we are slandered, we encourage. We are like the world's scape goats, bearing the filth of all men, even to this present time.

¹⁴I am not writing these things to make you ashamed, but to instruct you as cherished children. ¹⁵For if you have a myriad of those who guide and lead you in Christ, you do not have many fathers; for in Christ Jesus I became your father through the gospel.ⁱ ¹⁶So, I encourage you, become imitators of me. ¹⁷For this reason, I have sent Timothy to you, who is my cherished child, and trustworthy in the Lord. He will remind you of my ways of life which are in Christ Jesus, as I teach everywhere in every church.

ⁱThe Greek word can be translated "Gospel" or "Good News." The word gospel means good news. It is translated both ways in this Bible version.

The Kingdom is About Power

¹⁸Some are becoming arrogant, as though I were not coming to you. ¹⁹But I will come to you soon, if the Lord desires, and I will gain an understanding, not of the speech of those who are arrogant, but of their power. ²⁰For the Kingdom of God is not about speech, but about power. ²¹What do you want? Should I come against you with a rod, or with love and a spirit of gentleness?

Protecting the Congregation from an Immoral Brother

Chapter Five

¹One actually hears that there is an illicit sexual relationship among you, and it is sexual misconduct of such a kind that it is not common even among the Gentiles; for some man has his father's wife. ²And you are puffed up with pride! Shouldn't you have grieved instead, so that the one who has done this thing might be removed from your midst?

³For I, though I am absent in the body but present in the spirit, I have already passed judgment on the one who has acted in this way, just as if I were present. ⁴In the name of our Lord Jesus Christ, when you have gathered together and my spirit is there with the power of our Lord Jesus, ⁵hand such a man as this over to Satan for the destruction of his flesh, so that his spirit might be saved on the day of the Lord Jesus.

⁶Your boasting is not good. Don't you know that a small amount of yeast permeates the whole batch of dough? ⁷Clean out the old yeast, so that you may be a new batch of dough, without yeast, just as you are. For Christ, our Passover lamb, has also been offered as a sacrifice. ⁸For this reason, let us celebrate the Festival *of Passover*,[ii] not with old yeast, nor with the yeast of wickedness and evil, but with the unleavened bread of purity and truth.

[ii] More literally, "let us celebrate the festival." However, Passover is in view.

⁹I have written to you in my letter not to associate with sexually immoral people, ¹⁰not completely *avoiding* those who are sexually immoral in this world, or greedy people, or those who extort money, or idolaters, since you would then need to escape from the world. ¹¹But right now I am writing to you not to associate with anyone who is called a brother, but is sexually immoral, an idolater, one who insults others, one who gets drunk, or one who extorts money; with such a one as this do not even eat. ¹²For why should I judge those on the outside? You judge those on the inside, don't you? ¹³But God judges those who are outside. Remove the evil man from among you!

Taking Fellow Believer to Court

Chapter Six

¹Do any of you, when you have something of significance against another, presume to litigate it before the unrighteous and not before the saints? ²Or do you not know that the saints will judge the world? If the world will be judged by you, are you not worthy to judge the insignificant cases? ³Do you not know that we will judge angels, not to mention the matters of everyday life? ⁴Therefore, if you have a legal case about business matters, do you appoint those men who are rejected by the church to judge? ⁵I am speaking to your shame. So, is there not even one wise man among you who is able to decide between each brother? ⁶Instead, brother goes to court against brother, and this happens in front of those who do not believe.

⁷So, actually, it is already a failure for you, because you have legal actions against each other. Why not rather suffer injustice? Why not rather be swindled? ⁸But you yourselves commit injustice and swindle *others*, and this even with brothers!

Those who are Outside the Kingdom

⁹Or do you not know that the unrighteous will not inherit the Kingdom of God? Do not be mislead, neither the sexually immoral, nor idolaters, nor adulterers, nor passive homosexuals,

nor dominant homosexuals, ¹⁰nor thieves, nor the greedy, nor habitual drunkards, nor slanderers, nor robbers will inherit the Kingdom of God. ¹¹Even some of you used to do these things, but you were washed, but you were sanctified, but you were justified in the name of the Lord Jesus Christ and by the Spirit of our God.

The Disastrous Implications of Sexual Immorality

¹²All things are lawful for me, but not all things are in my best interest; all things are lawful for me, but I will not be overpowered by anything. ¹³Food for the stomach, and the stomach for food, but God will free us from the stomach and food. The body is not for illicit sexual entanglement, but for the Lord, and the Lord for the body.

¹⁴Now God has also raised the Lord, and he will raise us up through his power. ¹⁵Do you not know that your bodies are parts of Christ? So, shall I take the parts of Christ and make them parts of a prostitute? May that never be! ¹⁶Or do you not know that the one who joins himself together with a prostitute becomes one body *with her*? For it says, "The two will be one flesh."[i] ¹⁷But the one who joins himself to the Lord is one spirit *with him*.

¹⁸Steer clear of illicit sexual entanglement. Every sin a man does is outside of the body, but the one who indulges in *such* sexual misconduct is committing sin in his own body. ¹⁹Or do you not know that your body is a temple of the Holy Spirit who is among you, whom you have from God, and none of you belong to yourselves? ²⁰For you have been redeemed at a price, therefore glorify God in your body.

---

[i] Genesis 2:24

1 Corinthians 7:1

Paul Begins to Answer Their Questions: A Question on Marriage

Chapter Seven

¹Now concerning the questions about which you wrote, it is morally acceptable for a man not to have sexual intimacy with a woman, ²but because of *the temptation toward* illicit sexual entanglement, each man should have his own wife, and each woman should have her own husband. ³The husband must perform his *sexual* obligation to his wife, and likewise, the wife to her husband. ⁴The wife does not have authority over her own body, but the husband has that authority. Likewise, the husband does not have authority over his own body, but the wife has that authority. ⁵Stop stealing from one another, except by agreement for a time, so that you might have time for prayer; but join together again in sexual fulfillment, so that Satan does not tempt you because of your lack of inner strength.

⁶Now, I am giving this answer as an accommodation, not as a command. ⁷For I wish all men were also as I myself am. But each man has his own gift of grace from God, one in this way, another in another way.

Paul's Instruction to the Once Married and Currently Married

⁸But I say to the formerly married,[i] and to the widows, it is morally acceptable for them that they remain as I am;[ii] ⁹yet, if they cannot live a life of sexual abstinence, let them marry. For it is better to marry than to burn with passion.

¹⁰To those who are married[iii] I give this instruction, not just I, but the Lord *also said this*, a wife must not divorce her husband, ¹¹but if she does divorce, let her remain formerly married, or let

---

[i] The Greek word speaks of those who have already been married (not just those who are unmarried). Compare verse 34 where a virgin does not belong to this category of formerly married people, or verse 11 where a divorced person is considered formerly married.

[ii] That is, single. Paul had never been married. For this reason, he does not use the term "formerly married" of himself.

[iii] Paul is addressing Christians who are currently married to each other.

her be reconciled to her husband. A husband also must not divorce his wife.

Paul's Instruction to Those with Mixed Faith Marriage

¹²To the rest[iv] I say this myself, the Lord did not *make mention of this*,[v] if any brother has an unbelieving wife, and she is willing to live with him, he must not divorce her. ¹³If a wife has an unbelieving husband, and this man is willing to live with her, she must not divorce her husband. ¹⁴For the unbelieving husband is purified by his wife,[vi] and the unbelieving wife is purified by the *believing* brother, since otherwise your children would be impure; but now they are holy.

¹⁵But if the unbelieving spouse divorces, let that one divorce. The brother or sister is not obligated by such behavior, for God has called you to peace—¹⁶for how do you know, wife, that you will save your husband? Or how do you know, husband, that you will save your wife?

¹⁷Only let each one walk in the way that the Lord has assigned, as God has called each person. I give this instruction in this way to all the congregations. ¹⁸Was anyone called who was circumcised? He should not conceal it. Was anyone called while he was uncircumcised? Let him not be circumcised. ¹⁹Circumcision is nothing, and uncircumcision is nothing; what is important is keeping the commands of God. ²⁰Let each man remain in the calling he had when he was called. ²¹If you were a slave when you were called, do not let it concern you. But if you can become free, do that instead. ²²For the one who was called

---

[iv] Paul is speaking to the rest, that is, those who have become believers, but their spouses did not.

[v] When Jesus discussed marriage, it was always in the context of two people under the covenant of Moses. Mixed marriages were not something he addressed.

[vi] Paul has previously said that joining the parts of Christ to a prostitute was unthinkable (6:15). He is helping believing spouses understand that this is not a problem while married to an unbelieving spouse.

by the Lord as a slave is the Lord's freedman. Likewise, the one who was called while free is Christ's slave. ²³You have been redeemed at a price, therefore do not become slaves of men. ²⁴Brothers, let each one remain with God in the calling he had when he was called.

Answering a Question About Engagements

²⁵Now concerning your question about virgins, I have no command from the Lord, but I am giving my opinion as one who was shown mercy by the Lord in order to be trustworthy. ²⁶So, I believe this is an acceptable view because of the present distress: It is good for a man to remain as he is. ²⁷If you are engaged to a woman, do not seek to be break the engagement. If you have been divorced from a woman, stop seeking a wife. ²⁸But even if you have married, you have not sinned, and if a virgin has married, she has not sinned. But those who do get married will have hardship in their marriage,[i] and I am trying to spare you.

²⁹But this I say, brothers, the time is running out. So those who have wives should live like those who do not have wives for the remaining time. ³⁰Those who are grieving should live like those who are not grieving, those who are celebrating should live like those who are not celebrating, those who are buying should live like those who do not have possessions, ³¹and those who make use of the world should live like those who have no use for it. For the pattern of life in this world is passing away.

³²Yet I want you to be free from care. One who is not married is concerned for the things of the Lord, how he can please the Lord. ³³But the one who has married is concerned about the things of the world, how he can please his wife, ³⁴and his focus is divided. The formerly married woman and the virgin are concerned about the things of the Lord, that she might be holy also in body and spirit, but the woman who has married is concerned about the things of this world, how she can please her

---

[i] More literally, "in their flesh." Marriage is the "one flesh" relationship.

husband. ³⁵I am saying this for your own benefit, not that I place restrictions on you, but so that you are honorable, and devoted to the Lord without being distracted.

³⁶But if anyone believes that he is acting improperly toward his fiancée,[ii] if he has strong passions, and thus he believes it is necessary, let him do what he wants. He is not sinning. Let him marry. ³⁷But he who has taken a firm stand in his heart, and has no compulsion, but has authority over his own desire, and has decided this in his own heart, to keep her a virgin, he does what is morally acceptable. ³⁸So, the one who marries his fiancée does well, and the one who does not allow the marriage does better.

³⁹A wife is bound in marriage for as long a time as her husband is living. But if her husband falls asleep *in death*, she is free to be married to whomever she wishes, only in the Lord. ⁴⁰But, in my opinion, she is happier if she does not get married, and I think that I also have the Spirit of God.

Answering a Question About Food Sacrificed to Idols

Chapter Eight

¹Now concerning your question about food that has been sacrificed to idols. We know that we all have knowledge. Knowledge makes a person arrogant, but love builds people. ²If anyone believes he knows something, he does not yet know what he must know. ³But if anyone loves God, this one is known by God.

⁴So, to your question about food that has been sacrificed to idols, we know that an idol has nothing to do with world order, and there is no God but one. ⁵For since there are those that are called gods, whether in heaven or on the earth (as there are many gods and many lords), ⁶but to us, there is one God, the Father. All things are from him, and we are in him. There is also

---

[ii] More literally, "his virgin." Also in verse 38.

one Lord Jesus Christ, all things exist through him, and we exist through him.

⁷But all men do not have this understanding. Some, because it was once their custom *to sacrifice* to an idol, even now when they eat food that has been sacrificed to an idol, their conscience is violated because it is weak. ⁸But food does not consecrate us before God. We do not fall short if we do not eat, nor do we advance if we do eat.

⁹Only watch that this authority of yours does not in some way become a stumbling stone to the weak. ¹⁰For if someone sees you who have understanding, sitting at a table in an idol's temple, won't his conscience be hardened to eat food that has been sacrificed to idols even though he believes it is wrong?ⁱ ¹¹Then the one who is weak, this brother for whom Christ died, is lost by your knowledge. ¹²In this way, by sinning against the brothers and harming their weak conscience, you are sinning against Christ. ¹³Therefore, if food causes my brother to stumble into sin, I will never eat meat in this age, so that I do not cause my brother to stumble.

Be Willing to Give Up Rights for the Gospel

Chapter Nine

¹I am free, aren't I? I am an apostle, aren't I? I have seen Jesus, haven't I? You are my work in the Lord, aren't you? ²If I am not an apostle to others, at least I am to you. For you are my seal of apostleship in the Lord.

³My defense to those who question me is this: ⁴We have the freedom to eat and drink, don't we? ⁵We have the freedom to travel with a *believing* sister as a wife, like the rest of the apostles, the brothers of the Lord, and Cephas, don't we? ⁶Or is it only Barnabas and I who do not have the freedom to forgo working at a trade? ⁷Who has ever served as a soldier providing his own

---

ⁱ "He believes it is wrong" is more literally "He has a weak conscience."

salary? Who plants a vineyard and does not eat its fruit? Or who shepherds a flock and does not partake of the milk of the flock?

The Financial Rights of Those Who Minister with the Gospel

⁸I am not speaking these things on the basis of human *understanding*, doesn't the law also say these things? ⁹For in the Law of Moses it is written,

> "Do not muzzle an ox while it is threshing grain."ⁱⁱ

It isn't about oxen that God is concerned, is it? ¹⁰Or is he speaking especially on our account? He is speaking on our account, for it is written, "The plowman ought to plow in hope, and the thresher thresh in hope of a share *of the harvest*."ⁱⁱⁱ ¹¹If we planted spiritual things among you, is it surprising that we ourselves reap material things from you? ¹²If others enjoy this freedom from you, we deserve it more, don't we? But we did not make use of this freedom, rather we endured all things so that we might not erect any obstacle to the gospel of Christ. ¹³You know, don't you, that those who work at the temple eat the food from the temple, and those who perform their duties at the altar share in what is offered at the altar? ¹⁴In the same way, the Lord also has commanded those who preach the gospel to make their living from the gospel.

¹⁵But I have not made use of any of these things, and I have not written these things so that it will happen this way for me. For it would be better for me to die rather than have anyone empty my boast of power. ¹⁶For when I am proclaiming the good news, there I have no boast, since *the Lord* has placed an obligation upon me. Woe to me if I do not proclaim the good news! ¹⁷For if I do this willingly, I have a reward. But if I am unwilling, I have still been given the responsibility to manage it. ¹⁸So, what is my reward *when I do it willingly*? It is that while I am proclaiming the good news, I can offer the gospel free of

---

ⁱⁱ Deuteronomy 25:4

ⁱⁱⁱ Paul quotes from an unknown source from his era.

charge! The result is that I have not used my freedom in the gospel for myself.

¹⁹For although I am a free man[i] among all men, I make myself a slave to all men, in order that I might win more of them. ²⁰I became like a Jew to the Jews, in order that I might win Jews. To those who are under the Law, I became like one under the Law (though I myself am not bound by the Law), so that I might gain those under the Law. ²¹To those who are without the Law, I became like one who does not have the Law (though I am not without the law of God, but I am obedient to the law of Christ), in order that I win those who are without the Law. ²²I have become weak to those with a weak conscience, in order that I might win those with a weak conscience. I have become all things to all men, in order that I might most certainly save some of them. ²³I am doing all things for the sake of the gospel, so that I might be a partner in the gospel.

Focused on the Prize

²⁴Do you not know that all those who are running in the arena run, but one receives the prize? Run in a way that you may obtain the prize. ²⁵Everyone who contends for the prize exercises self-control in all things. So those who compete do it that they might receive a victor's wreath that will wilt, but we receive one that will never wilt. ²⁶Therefore, I am so running in this way, like a runner focused on the goal; in the same way, I am boxing like a boxer who doesn't throw wild punches into the air. ²⁷On the contrary, I give my body a black eye and bring it under my control so that after I have preached to others, I myself do not lose the race.

---

[i] A free Roman citizen with all rights and privileges.

Warnings Against Misusing Christian Freedoms

Chapter Ten

¹For I do not want you to be uninformed, brothers, that all our fathers were under the cloud and all of them passed through the sea. ²All of them were baptized into Moses in the cloud and in the sea, ³and all of them ate the same spiritual food, ⁴and all of them drank the same spiritual drink. For they were drinking from the spiritual rock following them, and the rock was Christ. ⁵However, God was not pleased with the majority of them, for they were cut down in the wilderness.

⁶Now these things happened as a moral example for us, so that we would not be those who long for evil things, as they longed for them. ⁷Do not be idolaters, as some of them were; as it is written,

> "The people sat to eat and drink, and arose to indulge in sensual dancing."[ii]

⁸We must not indulge in illicit sexual relationships, as some of them practiced such relationships, and twenty-three thousand fell in one day. ⁹We must not test the Christ, as some of them tried him and were destroyed by serpents. ¹⁰You must not grumble, as some of them grumbled and were put to death by the angel of destruction. ¹¹Now these things happened to them as typical examples, and they are written to admonish us, to whom the purposes of the ages have fallen. ¹²Therefore, he who believes he is standing secure must watch carefully that he does not fall. ¹³No temptation has taken hold of you that is not normal for human beings; but God is trustworthy, he will not permit you to be tempted beyond what you can handle, but with the temptation he will also provide an escape route so that you are able to cope with it.

¹⁴Therefore, my cherished friends, flee from idolatry. ¹⁵I am speaking as to wise men. You yourselves must judge what I am saying. ¹⁶The cup of blessing which we bless, it is fellowship[iii] in the blood of Christ, isn't it? The bread which we break, it is

---

[ii] Exodus 32:6

[iii] Or, "koinonia." Used twice in this verse.

fellowship in the body of Christ, isn't it? ¹⁷Since there is one loaf of bread, we, the many, are all one body, for we all share together from the one loaf of bread.

Do Not Share Fellowship with Demons

¹⁸Look at physical Israel, those who eat the sacrifices are partners[i] at the altar, aren't they? ¹⁹So, what am I saying? That food sacrificed to idols is anything, or that an idol is anything? ²⁰On the contrary, *I am saying* that what they sacrifice, they sacrifice to demons and not to God, and I do not want you to be partners with demons. ²¹You cannot drink the cup of the Lord and the cup of demons, you cannot share in the table of the Lord and the table of demons. ²²Or, do we want to make the Lord jealous? We are not stronger than him, are we?

Evaluating the Use of Christian Freedom

²³All things are lawful, but not all things are in my best interest; all things are lawful, but not all things are constructive. ²⁴Let no one pursue his own interests, but rather the interests of the other person. ²⁵Eat anything for sale in the meat market, while not inquiring about matters of conscience, ²⁶for

> "The earth belongs to the Lord, and all that is in it."[ii]

²⁷If any of the unbelievers invites you, and you are willing to go, eat everything presented to you without inquiring about matters of conscience. ²⁸But if any *of them* say to you, "This is meat offered in sacrifice," do not eat it, on account of that one who revealed it, and on account of conscience. ²⁹I am not speaking of your own conscience, but the other person's conscience. For what reason is my freedom judged by the conscience of another? ³⁰If I partake with thankfulness, why am I slandered about that for which I give thanks?

---

[i] Or, "in fellowship" at the altar. Also verse 20, "in fellowship" with demons.

[ii] Psalm 24:1

Doing Everything for God's Glory

³¹Therefore, whether you eat or drink, or whatever you do, do all things for the glory of God. ³²Be blameless to Jews, Greeks, and the church of God, ³³as I also please all men in all things, not pursuing my own benefit, but the benefit of the many, in order that they might be saved. ¹¹:¹Be imitators of me, just as I also imitate Christ.

Chapter Eleven[iii]

Avoiding Offense When Possible

²Now I applaud you, because you have remembered me in all things, and hold firmly to the traditional teachings, just as I gave them to you. ³But I want you to recognize that Christ is the head of every man, and the head of a woman is her husband,[iv] but God is the head of Christ.

⁴Every man who prays or prophesies while wearing a head covering, puts his head to shame. ⁵But every woman who prays or prophesies with her head unveiled,[v] puts her head to shame—for she is one and the same as a woman with a shaved head. ⁶In fact, if a woman does not wear a veil, she should cut her hair; but if it is unattractive for a woman to cut or shave her hair, she should veil herself. ⁷For a man should not wear a veil on his head, since he possesses the image and glory of God; but the woman is the glory of her husband. ⁸For man was not *taken* from woman but woman was *taken* from man. ⁹In fact, man was not created on account of the woman, but woman was created on

---

[iii] See previous paragraph for verse 1 of this chapter.

[iv] "Husband" could also be "male." The context determines whether the word means male or husband. Also in verses 7 and 11.

[v] Jewish custom—the traditional regulation—was that women wore veils. The Greeks did not have this custom, which is why there was contention in Greek Corinth.

account of man. ¹⁰For this reason—because of the angels—the woman should have freedom of choice[i] over her *own* head. ¹¹Nevertheless, a man is not distinct from his wife, nor is a woman distinct from her husband in the Lord. ¹²for just as the woman was created from man, and just as man is born from woman, all things are from God.

¹³Determine for yourselves, is it fitting that an unveiled woman pray to God? ¹⁴Our outward appearance itself teaches us that when a man wears long hair, it is demeaning, doesn't it? ¹⁵But *it also teaches that* when a woman wears long hair, it is for her glory, doesn't it? For her hair has been given to her for clothing. ¹⁶But if someone is determined to disagree, we have no custom such as this, nor do the congregations of God.[ii]

Abuses of the Fellowship Meal with the Lord's Supper

¹⁷As I give this next instruction, I do not applaud you, because you are not gathering together for the better, but for the worse. ¹⁸For first, when you gather together as a church, I hear that there are divisions that exist among you; and to some degree, I believe it. ¹⁹For it is essential that factions exist among you, in order that those who are genuine might become obvious to you. ²⁰Therefore, when you gather together at the same place, it is not to eat the Lord's Supper, ²¹for when you eat, each person takes their own supper before everyone else, and some go hungry while some drink to intoxication.

²²Come now, don't you have homes to eat and drink in? Or do you show contempt for the congregation of God, and embarrass those who have nothing? What can I say to you? Shall I applaud you? I cannot applaud you about this.

---

[i] Or, "authority over her own head." Many translations add the word "symbol" to this verse, changing the meaning of the verse. The word "symbol" is not found in the verse.

[ii] By appealing to custom, Paul helps us understand that the issue is to prevent offense in a cultural context.

23For I received from the Lord what I handed on to you. On the night on which he was betrayed, the Lord Jesus took bread, 24and when he had given thanks, he broke it and said, "This is my body, which is broken for you; do this to remember me." 25In the same way *he* also *took* the cup after they ate saying, "This cup is the new covenant in my blood; do this as often as you drink it, to remember me." 26For as often as you eat this bread and drink the cup, you declare the Lord's death until he comes.

The Danger of Dividing the Body over the Lord's Supper

27So, the result is that whoever eats the bread or drinks the cup of the Lord unworthily, will be guilty *of an offense* against the body and blood of the Lord. 28But let a man examine himself, and in this way let him eat from the bread and drink from the cup. 29For whoever eats and drinks without discerning the body, eats and drinks judgment on himself. 30For this reason, many among you are weak and sick, and a considerable number have fallen asleep. 31Now if we evaluated ourselves, we would not be judged. 32But when we are judged by the Lord, we are being disciplined so that we are not condemned with the world.

33So, my brothers, when you gather together to eat, wait for each other. 34If anyone is hungry, let him eat at home, in order that your meetings do not result in judgment. But I will address the rest of these issues when I come.

Answering a Question About Spiritual Gifts

Chapter Twelve

1Now about your question about spiritual gifts, brothers, I do not want you to be uninformed, 2since you know how, when you were pagans, you were carried away and would be led to speechless idols. 3Therefore, I am letting you know that no one speaking by the Spirit of God says, "Jesus is cursed," and no one is able to say, "Jesus is Lord," except by the Holy Spirit.

The Roles of the Father, Son, and Holy Spirit in the Gifts

⁴Now there are a variety of grace gifts, but the same Spirit. ⁵There are a variety of ministry tasks, but the same Lord. ⁶There are a variety of supernatural effects, but the same God works all of them in everyone.

Gifts Given for the Common Good

⁷But to each one the manifestation of the Spirit is given for the most benefit. ⁸For to one a word of wisdom is given through the Spirit, but to another a word of knowledge by that same Spirit, ⁹to another faith by the same Spirit, and to another grace gifts of healings by the one Spirit, ¹⁰to another supernatural works of power, to another prophecy, to another *gifts of distinguishing of spirits*, to another families of languages,ⁱ and to another the interpretation of languages. ¹¹The one and same Spirit energizes all these things, distributing them to each person individually just as he desires.

¹²For just as the body is a single unit, and it has many parts, but all the parts of the body, although they are many are one body, so also is Christ. ¹³For we all were also baptized by one Spirit into one body, whether Jews or Greeks, slaves or free men, and we were all given one Spirit to drink. ¹⁴For the body is not one part, but many. ¹⁵If the foot should say, "Because I am not a hand, I am connected to the body," it is not, because of this, not connected to the body. ¹⁶If the ear should say, "Because I am not an eye, I am not connected to the body," it is not, because of this, not connected to the body. ¹⁷If the whole body were an eye, where would the hearing be? If the whole body were for hearing, where would the sense of smell be? ¹⁸But now God has placed the parts, each one of them, in the body just as he desired. ¹⁹If they all were the same part, where would the body be? ²⁰Now there are many parts, but one body.

ⁱ Traditionally, "Tongue." When referring to the physical, this word means the physical organ. When referring to what is spoken, it means languages.

²¹The eye cannot say to the hand, "I have no need of you," or again, the head cannot say to the foot, "I have no need of you." ²²On the contrary, to a much greater degree, the parts of the body thought to be easily damaged are essential. ²³The parts we think are less honorable, we show these parts more honor, and our unattractive parts are made even more attractive. ²⁴But the parts of the body that are already attractive have no need of this. For God has arranged the body giving more abundant honor to the parts that lacked it, ²⁵in order that there might be no division in the body, but that the parts of the body might have the same concern for one another. ²⁶Then, if one part suffers, all the parts suffer with it; if one part is honored, all the parts are honored with it. ²⁷Now, you are the body of Christ, and a part of the whole *body*.

The Order of Offices and Gifts in the Church

²⁸In the Church, God has first appointed those who are apostles, second prophets, and third teachers;ⁱⁱ then power gifts, grace gifts of healing, helps, government gifts, and families of languages. ²⁹All are not apostles, are they? All are not prophets, are they? All are not teachers, are they? All are not workers of power, are they? ³⁰All do not have grace gifts of healing, do they? All do not speak with language gifts, do they? All do not interpret, do they?

The Excellent Way of Using Spiritual Gifts in Love

³¹But you are yearning for the greater grace gifts, and yet, let me show you a way that is more excellent.

Chapter Thirteen

¹If I speak with the languages of men and angels, but have not love, I have become an echoing brass gong or a resonating cymbal. ²If I have prophecy and I know all the mysteries and all

---

ⁱⁱ Since "teachers" can include Pastors who teach congregations, as well as Evangelists who teach unbelievers, this list agrees with Ephesians 4:11.

knowledge, and if I have all the faith necessary to transplant mountains, but I do not have love, I am nothing. ³If I distribute all my possessions, and I hand over my body that I might be burned, but I do not have love, I have no benefit.

The Actions of Love

⁴Love demonstrates patience. Love shows kindness. It doesn't envy. Love doesn't boast. It is not puffed up with pride. ⁵Love doesn't behave improperly. It does not seek its own things. It is not carried away by anger. It does not focus on the harm done. ⁶It does not rejoice over unrighteousness, but rejoices with the truth. ⁷It endures all things quietly. It believes all things, hopes all things, perseveres in all things.

The Greatness of Love

⁸Love never falls short. But if there are prophecies, they will be rendered of no effect; if there are languages, they will stop; if there is knowledge, it will be rendered of no effect. ⁹For we know a part, and we prophesy from that part, ¹⁰but when the complete thing comes, the things known from the part will lose their importance. ¹¹When I was a child, I spoke like a child, I thought like a child, and I reasoned like a child; when I became a man, I put an end to these things from my childhood. ¹²For at this time, we see by means of a mirror in riddles, but then face to face.ⁱ Now I know just a portion, but then I will know just as I am known.

¹³But now these three things remain: faith, hope, and love; but love is the greatest of these.

Comparing Prophecy and Language Gifts

Chapter Fourteen

¹Pursue love, and yearn for spiritual gifts—now more than ever, so that you might prophesy. ²For the one speaking with a

---

ⁱ See Numbers 12:8.

language gift does not speak to men, but to God;[ii] for no one understands. He speaks mysteries with his spirit. ³But the one who prophesies speaks to men to build up, to encourage, or to comfort. ⁴The one speaking with a language gift builds up himself, but the one prophesying builds up the Church. ⁵I want you all to speak with language gifts, but even more that you may prophesy; for the one who prophesies is greater than the one speaking with language gifts, unless he interprets so that the Church may be built up.

⁶But now, brothers, if I come to you speaking with a language gift, what help am I to you unless I speak either with a revelation, a word *of knowledge*, a prophecy, or a teaching? ⁷In the same way, even things that are not alive, whether a flute or harp, while making a sound, if they do not make a distinction in their tones, how will what is played on the flute or the harp be understood? ⁸For if the trumpet also makes an unrecognizable sound, who will prepare himself for war? ⁹It works this way with you also, unless you make a recognizable statement through your language gift, how will what you have spoken be understood? For you will be speaking into the air. ¹⁰It is possible that there are, perhaps, a great many families of spoken languages in the world, and none that do not communicate. ¹¹So, if I do not understand the function[iii] of the sound, I will be a barbarian to the one speaking, and the one speaking will be a barbarian to me. ¹²It is the same way with you, since you are zealots for things of the Spirit, keep seeking that you might overflow *in gifts* that build up the church.

Pray to Interpret Language Gifts

¹³Therefore, the one speaking with a language gift should pray that he may interpret it. ¹⁴For if I should pray with a

---

[ii] When the language gift is used without interpretation, God is the only audience. See also 14:28.

[iii] Or, "understand the power." This Greek word is also translated "power." A spoken word has no power if it is not understood.

language gift, my spirit is praying, but my mind is not being effective. ¹⁵So what is happening? I will pray with my spirit, but I will also pray with my mind. I will sing with my spirit, but I will also sing with my mind. ¹⁶So, if you give thanks with your spirit, how can the one in the position of a spiritual novice[i] say, "Amen," over your prayer of thanksgiving? *He cannot* because he does not know what you are saying. ¹⁷For, on the one hand, you are giving thanks suitably, but the other person is not being built up.

¹⁸I thank God I speak with language gifts more than all of you. ¹⁹But in the church, so that I may teach others, I want to speak five words with my mind rather than ten thousand words with a language gift.

²⁰Brothers, do not be children in your understandings. Be infants with respect to evil, but mature in your understandings. ²¹In the Law it is written,

> " 'I will speak to this people through those who speak strange languages, and through the lips of foreigners, but not even then will they listen to me?' says the Lord."[ii]

²²So, the language gifts are an authenticating sign, not for those who believe, but for the unbelieving. Prophecy is not for the unbelieving, but for those who believe.

²³So, if the whole church gathers together at the same place, and everyone speaks with a language gift, and if the spiritual novice and unbeliever come in, they will say that you are out of your minds with religious rapture,[iii] won't they? ²⁴But if everyone prophesies, and the unbeliever or the spiritual novice come in, they will be convicted by everyone, he will be examined by

---

[i] Paul is referring to a person who is untrained or new to the things of the Spirit. Also in verses 23 and 24.

[ii] Isaiah 28:11-12

[iii] The Greek word was often used to describe religious ecstatic phenomena or spiritual rapture.

everyone, ²⁵and the hidden things of his heart will be revealed. In this way, he will fall on his face and worship God, declaring that God is truly among you.

Orderly Use of Gifts in the Church

²⁶What, then, is happening, brothers? Whenever you gather together, each one has a psalm. Each one has a teaching. Each one has a revelation. Each one has a language gift. Each one has an interpretation. Let all these things happen for building up. ²⁷If anyone speaks with a language gift, *it should be done* by two or three at the most. But *they must do it* in turn, and let one interpret. ²⁸But if there is no interpreter, let him stop speaking to the church, and let him continue to speak to himself and to God.ⁱᵛ

²⁹But let two or three prophets speak, and let the others interpretᵛ it. ³⁰But if the interpretation is revealed to another who is seated, let the first man stop speaking. ³¹For you can all prophesy, each one in turn, so that everyone may learn, and everyone may be encouraged. ³²The spirits of prophets are to submit themselves willingly to prophets, ³³for he is not the God of confusion, but of peace.

As in all the congregations of the saints, ³⁴the wivesᵛⁱ are to be quiet in the congregations. For speaking was not entrusted to them. Rather, they are to submit themselves willingly, just as the Law says.ᵛⁱⁱ ³⁵But if they wish to find something out, let them

---

ⁱᵛ This is a clear instruction that the one using the language gift should continue to use it even when it is not interpreted, but to change its focus (and volume) in such a way so that God is the primary audience. See also 14:2.

ᵛ Or, "judge." However this word means "to interpret" when it refers to revelation of any sort.

ᵛⁱ "Wives" could also be "women." The context determines whether the word means woman or wife. The context of verses 34-35 helps us understand that wives are in focus, not women in general. Also, in verse 35.

ᵛⁱⁱ Christians are not under the Law, but Paul's concern is for the synagogues which still observed the Law of Moses. He did not want Christians to needlessly offend them by their practice. See also verse 36.

ask their own husbands[i] at home. For it is embarrassing for a wife to speak in the congregation.

[36]Did the word of God arise among you? Or has it come only to you?[ii] [37]If anyone thinks he is a prophet or a spiritual man, let him observe that the things I am writing to you are the commandment of the Lord. [38]But if anyone does not pay attention *to this*, pay no attention to him.

[39]So, my brothers, eagerly desire to prophesy, and do not forbid speaking with language gifts, [40]but let it all be done properly and by taking turns.

The Resurrection of Christ is the Most Important Thing

Chapter Fifteen

[1]Now I want you to understand, brothers, the gospel which I preached as good news to you, which you also received, on which you have taken a stand. [2]Through this gospel you are also saved, if you hold firmly to the good news, the message I proclaimed to you—unless you have believed to no purpose.

[3]For, as the most important thing, I handed over to you what also I received, that Christ died for our sins according to the Scriptures, [4]and that he was buried, and that he was raised to life on the third day, according to the Scriptures. [5]That he also appeared to Cephas, then to the Twelve, [6]then he appeared to over five hundred of the brothers at one time, of whom the majority remain alive even now, but some have fallen asleep. [7]After that, he appeared to James,[iii] then to all the apostles, [8]and

---

[i] "Husbands" could also be "males." The context determines whether the word means male or husband. In this instance, the context demands "husband," also helping us understand that verse 34 is about wives.

[ii] Another reference which shows that Paul is concerned about the ones with whom the word did arise, the Jewish people.

[iii] Greek text, "Jacob." James is the Anglicized form of Jacob used since the first English translations.

last of all he appeared also to me, as though to one born in an abnormal way.

⁹For I am the least of the apostles. I am not worthy to be called an apostle, because I persecuted the church of God. ¹⁰But by the grace of God I am what I am, and his grace toward me was not without purpose. On the contrary, I worked much harder than all of them, but not I, rather it was the grace of God that was with me. ¹¹Then whether it was I or they, we preach in this way, and in this way you believed.

¹²But if it is preached that Christ has been raised to life from the dead, how are some among you saying that there is no resurrection from the dead? ¹³If there is no resurrection to life from the dead, then Christ has not been raised. ¹⁴But if Christ has not been raised to life, then our preaching has no purpose, and your faith also has no purpose, ¹⁵and we are exposed as false witnesses about God, because we testified about God that he raised the Christ, which he did not if the dead are not raised. ¹⁶For if the dead are not raised, then Christ was not raised to life, ¹⁷and if Christ has not been raised to life, your faith is pointless; you are still in your sins, ¹⁸and then those who have fallen asleep in Christ are lost. ¹⁹If we have hope in Christ only in this life, we are more pitiful than all other men.

²⁰But now Christ has been raised to life from the dead, a firstfruits of those who are still asleep. ²¹For since death came through a man, the resurrection of the dead comes through a man. ²²For just as in Adam everyone died, so also in Christ everyone will be made alive. ²³But each one in his own rank, Christ the firstfruits, after that those who belong to Christ at his visitation.[iv] ²⁴Then the goal *will be achieved*, when he delivers over the Kingdom to our God and Father, at that time when he has put an end to all dominion, all authority, and power.

[iv] Or, "parousia." Parousia is a technical term that can mean coming, presence, or visitation.

²⁵For he must reign until the Father has placed all his enemies under his feet.ⁱ ²⁶Death, a last enemy, is *already* being rendered inoperative. ²⁷For

> "He has placed all things in submission under
> his feet;"ⁱⁱ

but when he says, "All things were placed in submission," it is obvious that the one who placed all things under him is excluded. ²⁸But when all things have been placed in submission to him, then the Son himself will be in submission to the one who placed all things in submission to him, so that God may be all things in all respects.

²⁹But if the dead are not actually raised, why are people also baptized on their behalf? Then what will those who are baptized on behalf of the dead do? ³⁰Why are we also exposing ourselves to danger every hour? ³¹I swear by my rightful pride for you, which I have in Christ Jesus our Lord, that I face death each day. ³²If I fought wild beasts in Ephesus for human reasons, what benefit do I have? If the dead are not raised,

> "Let us eat and drink, for tomorrow we die."ⁱⁱⁱ

³³Do not be deceived: Evil companions spoil good habits. ³⁴Shake off your mental confusion and stop sinning, for some have no understanding about God. I am speaking to your shame.

Anticipating a Changed Body

³⁵But someone will ask, "How are the dead raised?" And with what kind of body are they coming?" ³⁶You foolish man! What you plant does not spring to life unless it dies; ³⁷and what are you planting? You are not planting the grown plant that will be sprouting, but the bare kernel, possibly of grain or some other seed. ³⁸But God, as he wishes, will give it a form; and *he will give* each of the seeds a form of their own. ³⁹All bodies are not the

---

ⁱ See Psalm 110:1.

ⁱⁱ Psalm 8:6.

ⁱⁱⁱ See Isaiah 22:13.

same form. There is one type of body for men, another body for animals, another for birds, and another for fish.

⁴⁰There are also celestial bodies and terrestrial bodies, but the glory of the celestial bodies is different than that of the terrestrial bodies. ⁴¹There is one glory for the sun, another glory for the moon, and another glory for the stars; for star differs from star in glory.

⁴²This is the way the resurrection from the dead is also. The physical body is planted in decay, it is raised never to decay; ⁴³it is planted without dignity, it is raised in glory; it is planted in weakness, it is raised in power; ⁴⁴it is planted a physical body,ⁱᵛ it is raised a spiritual body. If there is a physical body, there is also a spiritual one. ⁴⁵So it is also written,

> "The first man, Adam, became a living soul,"ᵛ

the last Adam became a life-giving spirit. ⁴⁶But the spiritual body is not first, but first the natural,ᵛⁱ then the spiritual. ⁴⁷The first man was from the dust of the earth, the second man is from heaven. ⁴⁸As the one from the dust, so also are those who are of the dust; and as the heavenly one, so also are those who are of heaven. ⁴⁹Just as we have worn the image of the one from the dust, we shall also wear the image of the heavenly.

The Transformation of the Body

⁵⁰But I say this, brothers, that flesh and blood are not able to inherit the Kingdom of God, nor is the body that decays able to inherit the body that does not decay. ⁵¹Pay close attention, I am telling you a mystery. We will not all sleep, but we will all be transformed, ⁵²in an instant, in the blink of an eye, at the final trumpet; for he will sound the trumpet and the dead will be raised immortal, and we will be transformed. ⁵³For this body that decays must put on one that does not, and this mortal body

---

ⁱᵛ Or, "a soulish body."

ᵛ Genesis 2:7

ᵛⁱ Or, "the soulish."

must put on immorality. ⁵⁴But when this body that decays puts on the one that does not, and this mortal body puts on immortality, then the word that is written will be fulfilled,

> "Death is swallowed up in victory."[i]
> ⁵⁵"Where, O death is your victory?
> Where, O death, is your sting?"[ii]

⁵⁶For sin is the sting of death, and the authority of sin is the Law. ⁵⁷But thanks be to God, because he is giving us the victory through our Lord Jesus Christ.

⁵⁸So, my cherished brothers, be firm, immovable, and always overflowing in the work of the Lord, because you know that your labor in the Lord is not foolish.

Answering a Question About the Special Offering

Chapter Sixteen

¹Now about your question regarding the collection for the saints, as I instructed the churches in Galatia, so also you should do. ²On the first day of every week, each of you on his own, as he has financial success, should make a deposit and store it away, so that when I come no collections need to be made. ³Then, when I arrive, whomever you may approve, I will send with letters *of introduction* to take your gift to Jerusalem. ⁴If it is appropriate that I should also go, they will journey with me.

Travel Plans

⁵But I will come to you when I have traveled through Macedonia, for I am going through Macedonia, ⁶It is also possible that I will remain with you, or even spend the winter, so you may send me on my way wherever I might go. ⁷For I do not wish to see you now in passing, for I hope to remain with you for some time if the Lord permits. ⁸But I will remain in Ephesus

---

[i] Compare Isaiah 25:8

[ii] Compare Hosea 13:14.

until Pentecost, ⁹for a significant and effective door has opened to me, but many are hostile.

¹⁰If Timothy should come, see that he can be with you without concern, for he is doing the work of the Lord just as I am. ¹¹Therefore, let no one look down on him. But send him on his way in peace, that he may come to me, for I am expecting him with the brothers.

Answering a Question About Apollos

¹²Now about your question concerning our brother Apollos: I encouraged him strongly that he should go to you with the brothers. It was definitely not his will to come at this time, but he will come when he has the time.

¹³Stay alert! Stand firm in the faith. Behave yourselves like men. Be strong. ¹⁴Let all your *activities* be done in love.

¹⁵You know the household of Stephanas, that it was the firstfruits of *those who believe in* Achaia, and they have devoted themselves for ministry to the saints. Now, I encourage you, brothers, ¹⁶that you also willingly submit to men such as these, and to everyone who is assisting in the work and laboring diligently. ¹⁷I was glad at the coming of Stephanas, Forunatus, and Achaicus, because these men supplied what was missing from you. ¹⁸For they have refreshed my spirit as well as yours. Therefore, recognize such men as these.

Greetings from the Brothers and Sisters with Paul

¹⁹The churches of Asia greet you, Aquila and Priscilla greet you enthusiastically in the Lord, along with the church at their house. ²⁰All the brothers greet you. Greet each other with a holy kiss. ²¹This greeting is in my, Paul's, hand.

²²If anyone does not love the Lord, let him be under a curse. O Lord, come!

²³The grace of the Lord Jesus be with you.

²⁴My love is with all of you in Christ Jesus. Amen.

2 CORINTHIANS

Chapter One

¹Paul, an apostle of Christ Jesus by the will of God, and Timothy our brother:

To the church of God which is in Corinth, with all the saints who are in all of Achaia.

²Grace to you, and peace from God our Father and the Lord Jesus Christ.

The God who Encourages

³Blessed is the God and Father of our Lord Jesus Christ, the Father of mercies, and the God of all encouragement.[i] ⁴He is the one who encourages us in all our trials so that we are able to encourage those in every trial with the encouragement which we ourselves were given by God. ⁵For just as the sufferings of Christ overflow in us, so also our encouragement also overflows through Christ. ⁶But if we suffer hardship, it is for your encouragement and deliverance; if we are encouraged, it is for your encouragement, which is activated when you endure the

---

[i] Or, traditionally, "comfort." This word can be translated either way. Also in verse 4-7.

same suffering which we also are experiencing. ⁷Our hope for you is certain, because we know that just as you are partners in our sufferings, in the same way *you are* also *partners* with our encouragement.

⁸For we do not want you to be uninformed, brothers, about the trial that we experienced in the province of Asia, for we were exceptionally burdened, even beyond our capability, so that we gave up hope of even living. ⁹We ourselves carried the sentence of death within us, so that we had no trust in ourselves, but in the God who raises the dead. ¹⁰He rescued us from such overpowering death, and will rescue us. He is the one on whom we have placed our hope that he will always rescue us. ¹¹You also join in helping us when you pray for us, so that the gift of grace in us is received with thanksgiving by many people—through the prayers of many on our behalf.

Paul's Planned Visit to Corinth

¹²For this is our boast, the testimony of our conscience: it is that we conducted ourselves in this world—and even more toward you—with sincerity and godly purity, not by fleshly wisdom, but by the grace of God. ¹³For we write nothing other than what you can read or understand. But I hope that you will understand completely, ¹⁴even as you understand us to some degree *now*, that on the day of the Lord Jesus we will be your boast as you also will be ours.

¹⁵In this confidence, I wanted to come to you first in order that you might have a second *visit of* grace. ¹⁶I wanted to pass through Corinth[ii] on into Macedonia, and again to return to you from Macedonia, and to be helped on my way to Judea by you.

¹⁷So, when I wanted this, I wasn't acting capriciously, was I? Or what I plan, do I plan in the flesh so that with me it is both yes, yes, and no, no? ¹⁸But God is faithful, because our word to you is not yes and no; ¹⁹for the Son of God, Jesus Christ, who

---

[ii] Paul uses the pronoun "you" instead of the city name.

was preached among you by us—by me, Silas, and Timothy—was not yes and no, but is yes in him. ²⁰For as many promises as God has given, in Jesus they are all yes. Therefore, also through him, there is an "Amen" to God's glory through us. ²¹God is the one who establishes us with you in Christ, and has anointed us. ²²He also sealed us and gave us the down payment of the Holy Spirit in our hearts.

Paul's Desire to Avoid Confrontation

²³But I call on God, the witness over my soul, that it was because I wanted to spare you that I did not come to Corinth. ²⁴Not that we rule over your faith, but we are fellow workers for your joy, for by faith you have taken your stand.

Chapter Two

¹In fact, I decided this for myself; I would not come again in sorrow to you. ²For if I grieve you, then who is there to cheer me, except the one who was grieved by me? ³I have written this same thing, that when I came, I might not experience grief from those who should give me joy. I had confidence in all of you, that my joy is also your joy. ⁴For from much trouble and distress of heart, I have written to you with many tears, not in order to give you grief, but that you may know the overflowing love that I have for you.

Restoring the Repentant Brother

⁵But if someone has caused grief, he has not caused grief to me, but to all of you to some degree—not that I want to burden him *further*. ⁶This punishment by the majority *of you* is sufficient for such a case as this, ⁷so that now you should rather forgive and encourage *him*, so that someone like this is not overwhelmed by excessive grief. ⁸So, I encourage you to confirm your love for him. ⁹For I have also written for this reason, that I might come to know your character, whether you are obedient in all things. ¹⁰But if you forgive anyone of anything, I also *forgive*, and what I have forgiven—if I needed to forgive anything—I

have forgiven in the presence of Christ for your sake, ¹¹so that we would not be outmaneuvered by Satan, for we are not uninformed of his intentions.

Releasing an Aroma of Life or an Aroma of Death

¹²Now when I went to Troas for the gospel of Christ, and when a door was open for me by the Lord, ¹³I had no rest for my spirit when I did not find my brother Titus. Instead, after I took my leave of them, I left for Macedonia.

¹⁴But thanks be to God, who always reveals who we are in Christ, and makes the fragrance of the knowledge of Christ known through us in every place. ¹⁵For we are the fragrance of Christ to God among those who are being saved, and among those who are perishing; ¹⁶to the one, we are a smell of death for death, to the other we are an aroma of life for life. Who is adequate for these things? ¹⁷For we are not like the many who traffic in the word of God for profit, but we speak *the word* in Christ. *We speak* in the presence of God like those who have purity; like those who are from God.

Servants of the New Covenant

Chapter Three

¹Are we beginning to put ourselves on display again? Or do we require a letter of introduction to you or from you, as some do? ²You are our letter, inscribed in our hearts, known and read by all men. ³It has become known that you are a letter of Christ because you have received ministry from us. This letter is not written with ink, but with the Spirit of the Living God, not on tablets of stone, but on tablets of human hearts.

⁴But we have such confidence as this through Christ in accord with God. ⁵Not that we are adequate in ourselves to presume that anything originates in us, but our adequacy is from God. ⁶He also made us adequate as servants of the new

covenant, not of the letter but of the Spirit; for the letter kills, but the Spirit makes alive.

The Glorious New Covenant

⁷Now if the ministry of death, engraved on stones with letters, came into existence with glory, so that the sons of Israel were not able to fix their eyes on Moses' face because of the glory of it, a glory which was losing its power, ⁸how can the ministry of the Spirit not exist in more glory? ⁹For if there is glory in the ministry of condemnation, then the ministry of righteousness will overflow with much more glory. ¹⁰For in this respect, the thing that had glory has no glory because of this surpassing glory. ¹¹For if the one that loses power came with glory, how much more *does* the one that remains in glory.

¹²So, since we have such a hope as this, we act with great confidence, ¹³and we are not like Moses, who put a veil over his face so that the sons of Israel could not look closely at the final state of what was losing power.

¹⁴But their minds were hardened. For to this day, the same veil remains when the old covenant is read. It is not removed because it is only ended in Christ. ¹⁵Instead, to this day when Moses is read, a veil is resting on their heart, ¹⁶but when someone turns to the Lord, the veil is taken away. ¹⁷Now the Lord is the Spirit, and where the Spirit of the Lord is, there is freedom. ¹⁸We all, with unveiled faces, are seeing a reflection of the glory of the Lord, and are being transformed into the same image from glory to glory. This also is from the Spirit of the Lord.

The Hidden Nature of New Covenant Glory

Chapter Four

¹For this reason, since we have this ministry because we have received mercy, we do not become discouraged, ²and we have rejected dishonorable hidden methods *of ministry*. We do not

use devious techniques that taint the word of God. On the contrary, we recommend ourselves to every man's conscience in the presence of God with the open proclamation of the truth. ³If our gospel is hidden, it is hidden to those who are being lost. ⁴The god of this age has blinded the thoughts of the unbelieving so that the light of the gospel, the glory of Christ, who is the image of God does not shine in them. ⁵For we do not preach ourselves, but Jesus Christ as Lord, and ourselves as your servants because of Jesus. ⁶For the God who said, "Light will shine out of darkness,"[i] is the one who let the light of the knowledge of the glory of God in the face of Jesus Christ shine in our hearts.

⁷But we have this treasure in clay containers, so that the extraordinary amount of power might be from God, and not from us. ⁸We suffer hardship in every way, but are not constrained by them. We are at a loss about what to do, but do not give up hope. ⁹We suffer persecution, but are not abandoned. We are injured, but we are not destroyed. ¹⁰We always carry the death of Jesus around in this body, in order that the life of Jesus might become visible in our body. ¹¹For we who are living are always being handed over to death on account of Jesus, so that the life of Jesus might become visible in our perishable flesh. ¹²So, death is working in us, but life is working in you.

¹³We have the same spirit of faith *that is described in* what has been written, "I have believed, therefore I have spoken." We believe, and therefore we are also speaking, ¹⁴and we understand that the one who raised the Lord Jesus will also raise us with Jesus, and will commend us with you. ¹⁵For all these things are on your account, so that the grace which is multiplying through many people may cause thanksgiving to overflow to the glory of God.

¹⁶Therefore, we do not become discouraged, but even if our exterior man is losing the battle to death, yet our interior man is being renewed day after day. ¹⁷Our current limited trouble is producing for us an eternal weight of abundant and

---

[i] Compare Genesis 1:3.

immeasurable glory. ¹⁸So, we do not focus on the things which are seen, but the things that are not seen. For the things that are seen are momentary, but the things that are not seen are eternal.

The Reality of our Heavenly Bodies

Chapter Five

¹For we know that if our temporary earthly house is dismantled, we have a substantial structure from God, a house in the heavens that human hands did not make. ²For in this place we sigh with longing, yearning to be clothed with our heavenly dwelling,[i] ³because we know that if we are clothed with our heavenly dwelling, we will never be embarrassed by a lack of clothing. ⁴For while we are in this temporary dwelling, we sigh because we are burdened by it. We do not want to have our clothing removed, but we wish to have even more clothing, so that the perishable is swallowed by life. ⁵The one who has made us for this very purpose is God, who gave us his Spirit as a down payment *on our new dwelling.*

⁶So we are always confident and know that while we are at home in this body, we are sojourning away from the Lord; ⁷for we walk by faith and not by external appearances, ⁸and are so confident that we prefer instead to be sojourning away from the body and at home with the Lord. ⁹Therefore, we aspire to be pleasing to him whether we are home or away, ¹⁰for we are all destined to appear before the judgment seat of Christ, so that everyone will bring the things that they have done in the body before him, whether good or bad.

The Message of Reconciliation

¹¹Therefore, because we know the fear of the Lord, we persuade men and are known to God. Now I hope also that we

---

[i] The Greek word translated "dwelling" (oiketerion) is only used here in the New Testament, and in Jude 6. It is more than ironic that the fallen angels in Jude 6 abandoned the very thing Paul longs for.

are also known in your consciences. ¹²We are not putting ourselves on display to you again, but are giving you an opportunity to boast about us, so that you have a response to those who boast about surface things, but not about the inner things of the heart. ¹³For if we are experiencing religious ecstasy,[ii] it is for God; if we are demonstrating self-control, it is for you. ¹⁴For the love of Christ constrains us, because we have concluded this, that one man died for all and so all died. ¹⁵He died on everyone's behalf, so that those who live no longer live for themselves, but on behalf of the one who died for them and was raised up.

¹⁶For this reason, from this point on, we for our part do not know anyone by their flesh, since *in the past* we have known Christ by his flesh, but now we no longer know him in this way —¹⁷and so we know that if someone is in Christ, he is a new creation; the old things have passed away; look, the new things have materialized. ¹⁸Now this is all from God, who reconciled us to himself through Christ Jesus, and gave us the ministry of reconciliation, ¹⁹because God was in Christ reconciling the world to himself, not adding their offenses to their account, and he has entrusted to us the message of reconciliation. ²⁰Therefore, we serve as official ambassadors on Christ's behalf, as if God were appealing to you through us. We beg you on Christ's behalf, be reconciled to God. ²¹God made *him* sin on our behalf, the one who did not know sin, so that we might become the righteousness of God in him.

Chapter Six

¹We are working together with him, and encouraging you not to receive God's grace to no purpose. ²For he says,

> "I answered you at an acceptable time, and I
> helped you in the day of deliverance. Look,

[ii] "Experiencing religious ecstasy" translates a word that was often used to describe ecstatic religious experiences in the bible and in ancient times.

now is the opportune time to be accepted; see, now is the day of deliverance."[i]

Demonstrating what it Means to be Servants of Christ

³We give no grounds for offense to anyone in any way, so that our ministry would provide no grounds for criticism. ⁴But we put ourselves on display as servants of God in all things. We did this in much endurance, in tribulations, in troubles, in difficult circumstances, ⁵in beatings, in imprisonments, in mob violence, in tiresome labors, in nights without sleep, and in times of fasting. ⁶*We did this* in purity, in knowledge, in patience, in kindness, in the Holy Spirit, in genuine love, ⁷in a truthful message, and in the power of God. *We did this* through the weapons of righteousness on the right and on the left, ⁸through glory and dishonor, and through defamation and honor. We are like those who deceive, but are true, ⁹like those who are ignored, but are known, like those who are dying, but unexpectedly, we live. We are like those who are disciplined, but not put to death, ¹⁰like those who are grieving, but who always rejoice, like those who are poor, but make many people rich, and like those who have nothing, but possess everything.

¹¹We speak plainly to you,[ii] O Corinthians, our heart is opened wide. ¹²You are not pressured by us, but you are pressured by your own feelings. ¹³Now as equivalent repayment, I am speaking as if you are children, you also open your hearts wide to us.

Getting Rid of Everything that Defiles the Temple of God

¹⁴Do not be yoked together with unbelievers, for what fellowship do righteousness and lawlessness share? Or what fellowship does light have with darkness? ¹⁵What agreement is there between Christ and Belial?[iii] Or what do a believer and an unbeliever share in common? ¹⁶What agreement does God's

---

[i] Isaiah 49:8

[ii] More literally, "Our mouth is open to you."

[iii] A Jewish name for the Accuser.

temple have with idols? For you are the temple of the living God, as God said,

> "I will live and walk among them, and I will be their God, and they themselves with be my people."[iv]

¹⁷Therefore,

> " 'Come out from among them and be separated,' says the Lord, 'and stop touching what is unclean, and I will accept you;' "[v]
>
> ¹⁸" 'I will be a Father to you, you yourselves will be my sons and daughter,' says the Lord, the Ruler of all things."[vi]

Chapter Seven

¹Therefore, since we have these promises, cherished friends, we should clean ourselves from everything that defiles flesh and spirit, aiming at holiness in the fear of God.

The Corinthians Fill Up Paul's Joy

²Put up with us; we harmed no one, we did not corrupt anyone, we did not take greedy advantage of anyone. ³I am not speaking to censure you, for I mentioned earlier that you are in our hearts so that we would die with you or live with you. ⁴I have great confidence concerning you. I have great pride concerning you. I have been filled with encouragement. I am overflowing with joy through all our troubles.

⁵For when we arrived in Macedonia, our flesh had no relief, but we were being troubled by everything. We experienced controversy on the outside, and fear on the inside. ⁶But the God who encourages those who are despondent, encouraged us by the arrival of Titus. ⁷It wasn't only by his presence with us, but

---

[iv] Leviticus 26:12

[v] Isaiah 52:11

[vi] Compare 2 Samuel 7:14 and 1 Chronicles 17:13.

also by the encouragement he received because of you. He recounted for us your longing, your mourning, and your ardent affection for me, so that I rejoiced all the more. ⁸For if I grieved you by my letter, I am not sorry, though I was beginning to regret it. For I became aware that the letter did grieve you, but only for a short time. ⁹Now I am glad, not because you were grieved, but because you were grieved to the point of repentance. For you were grieved by God's will, that you might not suffer loss in any way from us.

¹⁰For sorrow that is by the will of God works repentance that results in salvation without need of regret, but the sorrow of the world brings about death. ¹¹For look at how much eagerness this very thing—this sorrow by the will of God—has accomplished in you; how eager you are to defend yourselves, how indignant, how anxious, what longing and ardent zeal *you feel*, and how eager you are to clear *yourselves*. In everything you have shown yourselves to be innocent in this matter. ¹²So, even if I wrote to you, it was not because of the one who did wrong, nor was it because of the one who was harmed, but it was so that your eagerness on our behalf might be made known to you in the sight of God. ¹³For this reason, we have been encouraged.

But in addition to our encouragement, we rejoiced even more over the joy of Titus, because his spirit was refreshed by all of you. ¹⁴If I boasted to him of anything about you, I was not embarrassed. On the contrary, just as we spoke all things to you truthfully, so our boasting in the presence of Titus was also truthful. ¹⁵His affections are focused on you to a greater measure as he remembers how all of you obeyed, and how you welcomed him with respect approaching fear.ⁱ ¹⁶I am rejoicing because I have confidence in you in every way.

ⁱ More literally, "with fear and trembling," an idiom which can be translated as above.

The Special Offering for the Jerusalem Saints

Chapter Eight

[1] Now, I will tell you, brothers, about the grace of God that was given to the churches in Macedonia, [2] because in a difficult trial involving distressing circumstances, the overflowing abundance of their joy, even with their profound poverty, overflowed into the riches of their generous response. [3] For I can attest that they gave voluntarily according to their capability, and even beyond their capability. [4] They begged us and repeatedly pleaded for the joy of partnership in this service to the saints. [5] They not only did it in the way we had hoped, but first gave themselves to the Lord, then to us by the will of God. [6] For this reason, we urged that Timothy, since he had begun this gracious giving activity among you, might also carry it to its conclusion. [7] But just as you overflow in everything, in faith, in doctrine, in knowledge, in all eagerness, as well as the love that flowed from us to you, be diligent that you also overflow in this gracious giving activity.

Complete the Offering with Generosity

[8] I am not giving a command, but I am testing the genuineness of your love through the eagerness that others *demonstrate*. [9] For you know the grace of our Lord Jesus Christ, that although he was rich, for your sake he became poor, so that you, by that poverty, might become rich. [10] I am also giving my understanding on this topic, for this is in your best interest. You not only began to do this last year, but you also were glad to do it.

[11] Now then, carry out to its conclusion what you started. Just as you were eager and willing *at the beginning*, also carry it to its completion using *the resources* that you have. [12] For if the willingness is itself present, the offering is acceptable according to *the resources that* you have, not according to what you do not have. [13] For our goal is not that others rest while you suffer hardship, but so that everything is fair. [14] At the present time, your abundance is to provide their need, so that their abundance

might provide for your need, so that everything can be fair. ¹⁵As it is written,

> "He who gathered much did not have more than he needed, and he who gathered little, did not have less than they needed."[i]

Titus Sent to Carefully Administer the Offering

¹⁶But thanks be to God, who placed the same eagerness *that I have* on your behalf within the heart of Titus. ¹⁷For he received my request, and he was even more eager *than I hoped*, and traveled to you by his own choice. ¹⁸We also sent a brother with him whose *work* in the gospel is recognized through all the churches. ¹⁹This wasn't the only reason we sent him, but he also was chosen by the churches as our traveling partner while we care for this gracious gift. *We are motivated* by our desire to help and to give glory to the Lord, ²⁰so we avoid the possibility that anyone could find fault in how we care for this generous gift. ²¹For we take care to do what is good, not only in the sight of the Lord, but also in the sight of men.

²²We also have sent with them our brother whom we have often tested. He has proven eager to help in all matters, and now he is even more eager to help because of his great confidence in you. ²³If anyone asks about Titus, he is my partner and a fellow worker for you. If anyone asks about our brothers, they are apostles of the churches, and a credit to Christ. ²⁴Therefore, show them the proof of your love, and the reason for our personal boasts about you to the churches.

Chapter Nine

¹For it isn't necessary that I write to you about this service to the saints, ²since I know how eager you are. I boast about you to the Macedonians, *sharing with them* that Achaia has been ready since last year, and your commitment has spurred on most of

---

[i] Exodus 16:18

them. ³But I have sent the brothers so that our boasting about you in this respect might not prove empty, and that you may be prepared just as I was telling them. ⁴For it may happen that some Macedonians come with me and find you unprepared, then we on our part—not to mention you—would be embarrassed by this confidence. ⁵So, I considered it necessary to encourage the brothers, that they might go to you and prepare this blessing you had promised earlier, in order that this gift would be ready as a blessing, and not as one that is limited by greed.

Sowing Enough Seed for a Lavish Harvest

⁶But know this, he who sows seed in a stingy manner will also reap a stingy harvest, and he who sows seed in a lavish manner will also reap a lavish harvest. ⁷Each one, *should do* as he has decided ahead of time in his heart, not with a heavy heart or feeling pressure, for God loves a cheerful giver. ⁸Now God is able to make every grace overflow on you, so that in all things you always have all the things that you need, and that you might overflow in every good work. ⁹Just as it is written,

"He has scattered, he has given to the poor;
His righteousness endures forever."[ii]

¹⁰The one who provides seed for sowing and bread for food will supply and multiply your seed and increase the harvest of your righteousness. ¹¹You are being made rich in everything, so that you can be generous at all times. Your generosity will produce thanksgiving to God through us. ¹²For this charitable service is not only supplying what is lacking for the saints, but it is also overflowing with many thanksgivings to God. ¹³Because of the evidence offered by this charitable giving, they will glorify God over your obedience to your vow, and over the good news of Christ and the generosity of your fellowship with them and everyone else. ¹⁴They also have great affection for you in their

---

[ii] Psalm 112:9

prayers on your behalf, because of the surpassing grace of God that is upon you. ¹⁵Thanks be to God for his indescribable gift!

Paul's Power on Display When Needed

Chapter Ten

¹I, Paul, I myself encourage you with the gentleness and patient self-control of Christ. I do not flaunt my power when I am face to face with you, but when I am absent, I confidently demonstrate my power *as I write* to you. ²Now I am asking that when I come, I do not have to demonstrate my power with the confidence that I consider necessary against some who think that we walk according to the flesh. ³For though we walk in flesh, we do not wage war according to our flesh. ⁴For the weapons of our warfare are not physical, but are God's powerful weapons for the destruction of fortified places. ⁵We are destroying lines of reasoning and every high tower that has raised itself up against the knowledge of God, and we are taking every thought captive to the obedience of Christ—⁶and we are prepared to punish every disobedience once your obedience is completed.

⁷You are looking only at the appearance of things. If anyone is convinced in himself that he belongs to Christ, let him think this through for himself again, because just as he belongs to Christ, so also do we. ⁸For even if I am boasting a bit more about our authority, which the Lord gave for building you up and not for tearing you down, I will not be embarrassed. ⁹I do not want it to appear like I wanted to intimidate you by my letters, ¹⁰for "His letters," they say, "are fierce and powerful, but his physical presence has no power, and his speech is of little value." ¹¹Let such a person consider this, that the same way we are in our discourse through our letters while we are absent, we will also be in our action when we are present.

¹²For we do not dare to class ourselves in the same category as, or compare ourselves with, some who recommend themselves. When they measure themselves by themselves, and compare themselves with themselves, they have no self-awareness.

¹³But we will not boast about things without a measure *for reference*, but we will use the measure of the territory which God has assigned to us, a measure that reached even to you. ¹⁴For we are not pushing beyond our measure, as though we did not reach you. We were the first to reach as far as you with the gospel of Christ. ¹⁵We are not boasting about things without a measure— *as if* boasting in the work of others—but we have hope that as your faith is growing, our territory among you might be greatly increased, ¹⁶so that we might preach the good news in the territories beyond you. For we do not boast about the territory of other men, over the things they have done. ¹⁷But let the one who boasts, boast in the Lord. ¹⁸For it is not that one who recommends himself who is authentic, but the one whom the Lord recommends.

Paul's Concern for the Corinthians

Chapter Eleven

¹If only you would go along with me in a bit of foolishness, and yet you must go along with me. ²For I am jealous for you with a godly jealousy, for I promised you in marriage to one husband, to present you as a pure virgin to Christ. ³But I am afraid, lest, as the serpent led Eve astray by his craftiness, your minds might be enticed away from the simplicity and purity of this engagement to Christ. ⁴For if someone comes and preaches another Jesus whom we did not preach, or you welcome another spirit which you have not received, or another gospel which you did not believe, you go along with that happily.

Paul's Response to the Imitation Apostles

⁵Now I do not consider myself inferior to these wonderful apostles. ⁶But even if I am untrained in my speech, I am certainly not untrained in my knowledge; unquestionably, we have made this known to you in every way and in all things.

⁷Did I sin when I humbled myself so that you might be exalted, because I proclaimed the good news of the gospel of God to you as a gift? ⁸Did I rob other churches by taking wages *from them* to provide ministry to you? ⁹When I was with you, and I was in need, I did not burden anyone, for when the brothers arrived from Macedonia, they supplied what I needed. So, I kept myself from being a burden to you in anything, and I will keep doing so. ¹⁰The truth of Christ is in me. This boasting on my own behalf will not be silenced in the regions of Achaia. ¹¹Why? Is it because I do not love you? God knows *the answer*.

¹²But what I am doing, I will also continue to do, in order that I might remove any opportunity of those who desire an opening to boast. They want to boast so that through it they come across as just like us. ¹³For such men as these are false apostles and malicious workers who transformed themselves into apostles of Christ. ¹⁴There is no need to wonder at this, for Satan himself transforms himself into an angel of light. ¹⁵So, it is not surprising that his servants transform themselves to look like servants of righteousness. The outcome of their lives will match their actions.

Paul Dares to Boast in His Suffering

¹⁶Again I say, let no one think that I am foolish; but if you do, welcome me as foolish, so that I also may boast a bit. ¹⁷What I am saying I am not saying for the Lord, but in foolishness by this trust in my boasting. ¹⁸Since many people boast in agreement with their flesh, I also will boast. ¹⁹For you gladly go along with the foolish because you are so insightful. ²⁰In fact, you go along with it if someone makes you into slaves, if someone devours you, if someone takes you as a trophy, if someone exalts himself, or if someone hits you in the face. ²¹I

say, to my shame, that in comparison to them, we ourselves have been weak. However, in other areas where some may dare to go, I am speaking in foolishness, I also will dare to go.

²²Are they Hebrews? I am also. Are they Israelites? I am also. Are they seed of Abraham? I am also. ²³Are they servants of Christ? I am even more (I am speaking as one who is foolish). I have been in more troubles, in more prisons, in more severe beatings, and often faced death. ²⁴Five times I received from the Jews forty lashes minus one. ²⁵I was beaten with rods three times, and I was stoned once. I have been shipwrecked three times, and I have been adrift a night and day in the open sea. ²⁶I have often been on journeys, facing danger from rivers, facing dangers from bandits, facing dangers from my own people, facing danger from the Gentiles, facing dangers in the city, facing dangers in the wilderness, facing dangers in the sea, and facing dangers among false brothers. ²⁷I have experienced wearisome labor and toil, many sleepless nights, and hunger and thirst—often without any food. I have been cold and naked. ²⁸Quite apart from other matters, there is the pressure that rests on me each day, namely my concerned thoughts for all the churches. ²⁹Who is weak and I am not weak? Who stumbles into sin, and I am not burning with concern?

³⁰If it is necessary that I boast, I will boast about the things that display my weakness. ³¹The God and Father of our Lord Jesus Christ knows, the one who is blessed forever, he knows that I am not lying. ³²When I was in Damascus, the governor[i] appointed by King Aretas was keeping the city of the Damascenes under watch in order to arrest me. ³³Then I was lowered in a braided rope basket through a window in the wall, and escaped his hands.

---

[i] More literally, "the ethnarch."

Caught Up to the Third Heaven

Chapter Twelve

¹It is necessary that I keep boasting, though it is not helpful. But I will go on to visions and revelations from the Lord. ²I am aware of a man in Christ, who fourteen years ago was caught away—I am not aware if he was in the body, nor am I aware if he was out of the body, God knows—this man was caught away to the third heaven. ³I am aware that this man was caught away—I am not aware of whether he was in the body or apart from the body, God knows—⁴I am aware that he was caught away to Paradise and heard things that cannot be spoken, things that a man is not permitted to speak. ⁵On behalf of such a man as this I will boast, but I will not boast on my own behalf, except in my weaknesses. ⁶For if I wanted to boast, I would not be foolish, for I would be speaking the truth. But I avoid it so that no one will think that I am more than they see in me or hear from me; ⁷and *so that they do not think this* because of the extraordinary nature of these revelations.

Because of their extraordinary nature, in order that I might not become arrogant, a thorn in the flesh was given to me, an angel[i] of Satan, that he might batter me; *this is* so that I might not become arrogant. ⁸I called out to the Lord three times about this so that he might depart from me. ⁹But he said to me, "My grace is enough for you. For my power comes to maturity in weakness." Therefore, I will boast even more gladly about my weaknesses so that Christ's power takes up residence in me. ¹⁰Therefore, because of Christ, I am pleased by weakness, by insults, by troubled times, by persecutions, and by difficult circumstances; for whenever I am weak, then I am powerful.

---

[i] Traditionally, "Messenger." The Greek word is the normal word for angel, but can also refer to a human messenger. The word is used over 170 times in the New Testament, and never refers to anything other than a human messenger or supernatural angel (good or evil). For this reason, it is very probable that Paul's thorn was an agent sent from the enemy, not a sickness, disease, or impediment.

The Corinthians Witnessed Authenticating Miracles by Paul

11 I have become foolish. You forced me yourselves. For I deserve to be recommended by you, since I am not less than these wonderful apostles, even if I am nothing. 12 The authenticating signs of an apostle were thoroughly demonstrated among you in all perseverance by signs, by wonders, and by miracles. 13 For in what way were you treated worse than the rest of the churches, except that I myself did not become a burden to you? Forgive me this injustice.

Paul Took No Advantage of the Corinthians

14 Look, I am ready to come to you for this third time, and I will not be a burden to you. For I do not seek your things, but you. Since the children are not obligated to store up for their parents, but the parents for the children, 15 I will most gladly spend and be completely spent on behalf of your souls. If I love you more, am I myself loved less? 16 Then let it be so, but I did not burden you. And yet, since I am a crafty man, did I take hold of you by deceit? 17 I did not take advantage of you through any of those men I sent to you, did I? 18 I encouraged Titus to go, and I sent the brother with him. Titus did not take advantage of you, did he? We walked in the same spirit, didn't we? We followed the same steps, didn't we?

19 Have you been thinking all this time that we are defending ourselves to you? We are speaking by Christ in the presence of God, and all these things, my cherished ones, are on your behalf to build you up. 20 For I am afraid that when I come I will not find you as I wish, and that you might find that I am not as you wish. I am afraid that there will be strife, envy, anger, selfishness, evil speech, gossip, arrogance, and confusion. 21 I am afraid that when I come again, my God may humble me before you, and I will be sad about the many who previously sinned but did not repent of the moral impurity, illicit sexual relationships, and the unrestrained sensuality in which they have indulged.

Two or Three Witnesses

Chapter Thirteen

¹This is the third time I will be coming to you. Every matter must be verified by the testimony of two witnesses or three. ²I have said this before, when I was present with you during my second visit, and I say it now in advance while I am absent, that should I come again, I will not spare those who have sinned previously, nor any of the rest, ³since you are seeking proof that Christ is speaking in me. He is not weak toward you, but powerful among you. ⁴For he was crucified because of weakness, but he lives because of the power of God. We also are weak in him, but we will live with him because of the power of God *we will demonstrate* among you.

Testing to See if You are in the Faith

⁵Test yourself to check whether you are in the faith, prove yourselves! Or do you not know this about yourselves, that Jesus Christ is in you? Unless you fail the test. ⁶But I hope that you will find out that we ourselves have not failed the test. ⁷Now we pray to God that you do not do anything harmful, not that we may look like we passed the test, but that you may do what is good, even if it looks like we have not passed the test.

⁸For we cannot do anything against the truth, but only for the sake of the truth. ⁹For we rejoice when we are weak ourselves, but you are powerful. We pray also for this, your full equipping. ¹⁰For this reason, I am writing these things while I am absent, so that when I am present with you, I will not need to be severe when I use the authority that the Lord gave to me for building up, and not for tearing down.

Greetings from Those with Paul

¹¹Finally, brothers, be glad. Be fully equipped. Be encouraged. Be of like mind. Be in peace, and the God of love and peace will be with you.

¹²Greet each other with a holy kiss.

¹³All the saints greet you.

¹⁴The grace of our Lord Jesus Christ, the love of God, and the fellowship of the Holy Spirit be with all of you. Amen.[i]

---

[i] Addended at the end of many manuscripts: "The second letter to the Corinthians was written from Philippi in Macedonia through the hands of Titus and Lucas."

GALATIANS

Chapter One

¹Paul, an apostle—sent not by men or through men, but through the Lord Jesus Christ and God the Father, who raised him from among the dead—²and all the brothers with me.

To the congregations in Galatia:

³Grace to you and peace from God our Father and the Lord Jesus Christ. ⁴He gave himself for our sins in order that he might rescue us from the present evil age according to the will of God our Father, ⁵to whom be glory forever and ever. Amen.

Turning to a Counterfeit Gospel

⁶I am surprised that you are so quickly turning away in this way from the one who called you by the grace of Christ, to another gospel[i]—⁷which is not another gospel—except that there are some who are confusing you, and who want to turn the gospel of Christ into something else. ⁸But even if we or an angel from heaven proclaims a gospel to you different from the gospel we proclaimed to you, let him be under a curse. ⁹As I have just

---

[i] The Greek word can be translated "Gospel" or "Good News." The word gospel means good news. It is translated both ways in this Bible version.

stated, and now say again, if anyone is proclaiming a gospel to you unlike what you received, let him be under a curse.

¹⁰For am I now trying to convince men or God? Or am I seeking to please men? If I was still in the habit of pleasing men, I could not be a servant of Christ.

The Source of Paul's Gospel: Revelation from Christ

¹¹For I am letting you know, brothers, the gospel that I preached is not from man. ¹²For I did not receive it from man, nor was I taught it, but I received it through a revelation of Jesus Christ. ¹³For you heard of my way of life when I was in Judaism, that I persecuted the church of God to an extreme degree, and tried to destroy it. ¹⁴I also continually made progress in Judaism beyond many of my people who were my age, and was more zealous for the traditions of my fathers. ¹⁵But when God, who separated me from my mother's womb for his service, and called me by his grace, was pleased ¹⁶to reveal his Son in me, so that I might preach the good news about him among the Gentiles, I did not immediately take counsel with flesh and blood, ¹⁷nor did I go up to Jerusalem to those who were apostles before me, but I went away to Arabia and then returned again to Damascus.

¹⁸Then after three years I went up to Jerusalem to get to know Cephas,[ii] and I stayed with him fifteen days, ¹⁹but I did not see the other apostles except for James[iii] the brother of the Lord. ²⁰Take note! I assure you before God that I am not lying about what I am writing. ²¹Then I went to the regions of Syria and Cilicia, ²²but I was not known in person to the congregations in Judea which were in Christ; ²³they only kept hearing, "The one who formerly persecuted us is now proclaiming the good news of the faith which he once tried to destroy." ²⁴So, they praised God for me.

[ii] Peter

[iii] Greek text, "Jacob." James is the Anglicized form of Jacob used since the first English translations. Unless it refers to the patriarch Jacob, it is translated as James in this New Testament.

The Apostles Accept Paul and His Mission

Chapter Two

¹Then, after fourteen years, I went up again to Jerusalem with Barnabas. We also took Titus along with us. ²But I went up because of a revelation; and I explained to them the gospel that I preached among the Gentiles, but privately to those who were considered prominent, concerned that I was running, or had run the race in vain. ³But even Titus, who was with me and is a Greek, wasn't compelled to be circumcised. ⁴This happened on account of those who pretended to be brothers. They secretly joined us to spy on the freedom that we have in Christ Jesus so that they might enslave us. ⁵We did not yield in submission to them for even a moment, so that the truth of the gospel might be preserved for you.

⁶But from those who were considered prominent—what they once were made no difference to me, for God does not treat one person better than another—but those who were considered prominent did not impart anything to me. ⁷On the contrary, when they saw that I had been entrusted with the gospel for the uncircumcised just as Peter had been entrusted with the gospel for the circumcised—⁸for the one who had worked in Peter in his apostolic office also worked in me for the Gentiles, ⁹and because they recognized the grace that was given to me, James, Cephas, and John, those who were considered prominent pillars gave the right hand of fellowship to me and Barnabas, so that we might go to the Gentiles, and they to the circumcised. ¹⁰They only asked that we might remember the poor and respond appropriately, the very thing I have always been eager to do.

Paul Confronts Peter with the Gospel

¹¹But when Cephas came to Antioch, I opposed him to his face because he stood exposed as wrong. ¹²For before some men came from James, he was accustomed to eating with the Gentiles; but when they came, he began to draw back and separate himself because he was afraid of those from the circumcision group. ¹³The rest of the Jews also joined him and

acted like hypocrites, so that even Barnabas was led astray in their hypocrisy. ¹⁴But when I saw that they were not walking in line with the truth of the gospel, I spoke openly to Cephas in front of everyone, "If you, a Jew, live like a Gentile and not according to Jewish custom, how can you expect the Gentiles to live like Jews? ¹⁵For we ourselves are Jews by birth—not sinners from among the Gentiles—¹⁶but because we know that a man is not justified by the works of law, but only through faith in Jesus Christ, we also believe in Christ Jesus. We do this in order that we might be justified by faith in Christ and not by the works of law, because no one will be justified by works of law."

¹⁷But if, while we are seeking to be justified in Christ, we ourselves are also found to be sinners, then is Christ a servant of sin? May that never be! ¹⁸For if the things I once did away with I again am building, I alone prove to be a lawbreaker. ¹⁹For through law I myself died to the law, in order that I might live for God. ²⁰I have been crucified with Christ, and I myself am no longer living, but Christ is living in me. What I now am living in this flesh, I am living by faith in the Son of God, who loved me and delivered himself over on my behalf. ²¹I will not reject the grace of God. For if righteousness came through obeying law, then Christ died for no reason.

The Spirit and His Miracles Come through Faith not Law

Chapter Three

¹You foolish Galatians, who has put you under their spell? To whom, in front of your eyes, Jesus Christ was vividly portrayed as crucified? ²This alone I wish to learn from you: Did you receive the Spirit from obeying a principle of law or from responding[i] with faith? ³Are you this foolish? You began by the Spirit and now you finish in the flesh? ⁴Did you experience so much in vain? If, indeed, it was in vain. ⁵So, does the one who

---

[i] Or, "hearing," but the word refers to hearing and obeying.

supplies the Spirit to you and works miracles among you do it through obedience to a principle of law or through responding with faith? ⁶In just the same way,

> "Abraham believed God, and it was counted to him as righteousness."[i]

⁷Know this, then, that those who live by faith are themselves the sons of Abraham. ⁸The Scripture, foreseeing that God would justify the Gentiles by faith, proclaimed the gospel in advance to Abraham,

> "All the nations will be blessed in you."[ii]

⁹So that those who live by faith are blessed with the believer, Abraham.

¹⁰For all who depend on the works of law live under a curse; for it is written,

> "Cursed is everyone who does not abide by everything written in the book of the Law, and do them."[iii]

¹¹It is obvious that no one is justified by the Law before God, because

> "The righteous will live by faith."[iv]

¹²But the Law is not by faith, but

> "The one who does them will live by them."[v]

¹³Christ redeemed us from the curse of the Law by becoming a curse on our behalf; for it is written,

> "Cursed is everyone who is hung on a tree."[vi]

---

[i] Genesis 15:6

[ii] Genesis 12:3

[iii] Deuteronomy 27:26

[iv] Habakkuk 2:4

[v] Leviticus 18:5

[vi] Deuteronomy 21:23

¹⁴He did this in order that the blessing of Abraham might come to the Gentiles through Christ Jesus, so that we might receive the promise of the Spirit through faith.

The Law Does Not Nullify the Promise

¹⁵Brothers, I am speaking of human things: after all, no one nullifies a human contract that has already been signed, or adds further stipulations to it. ¹⁶But in this case, the promises were spoken to Abraham and his seed. He does not say, "And to seeds," as to many, but to one, "And to your seed,"[vii] who is Christ. ¹⁷I am saying this: the Law that came into existence four hundred and thirty years after the covenant validated by God, does not invalidate the covenant or render the promise ineffective. ¹⁸For if the inheritance was by means of law, it is no longer by means of promise; but God gave it to Abraham through a promise.

¹⁹So, why is there Law? It was added on account of violations of law. It was ordained through angels by the hand of a mediator until the Seed would come to whom it was promised. ²⁰But a mediator is not needed for a one-party contract, and God is one.

²¹So, is the Law against the promises of God? May that never be! For, if a law had been given that was able to give life, then righteousness would be by law. ²²But the Scripture has bound everyone up in the net of sin, in order that the promise which is by faith in Jesus Christ might be given to those who believe.

²³Before the faith came, we were kept guarded by law, being bound in the net until the coming faith was revealed, ²⁴so that the Law had become our nanny until Christ, in order that we might be justified through faith. ²⁵But since faith has come, we are no longer under a nanny.

Sons of God and Clothed with Christ

²⁶For in Christ Jesus, you are all sons of God through faith; ²⁷since all of you who were baptized into Christ are wearing

---

[vii] See Genesis 17:19

Christ in the same manner as clothing. ²⁸There is no longer Jew or Greek, slave or free, male or female; for all of you are one in Christ Jesus. ²⁹If you belong to Christ, then you are the seed of Abraham, heirs according to promise.

Sons and Heirs

Chapter Four

¹Now, I say, as long as the heir is a child, he is no different than a slave though he is master of everything; ²but he is under guardians and household managers until the time set by his father. ³This is just like us. When we were children, we were enslaved by the rudimentary principles of the world; ⁴but when the fullness of time arrived, God sent forth his Son, born of woman, born under law, ⁵in order that he might redeem those under law so that we might be adopted as sons. ⁶Because we are sons, God sent out the Spirit of his Son into our hearts calling, "Abba, Father!" ⁷For this reason, you are no longer a slave, but a son; and since you are a son, through God's initiative, you are also an heir.

Becoming Enslaved to the Law

⁸But at the time when you did not know God, you were enslaved to those things that are in essence not gods. ⁹Now that you know God, or rather, that you are known by God, how are you turning back again to the weak and poverty-inducing rudimentary principles to which you want to be enslaved all over again? ¹⁰You are keeping days, months, seasons, and years—¹¹I fear for you, lest somehow I have wearied myself over you in vain.

¹²I beg you, become as I am, brothers, for I also became like you. You did not mistreat me, ¹³rather, you know that it was because of a physical weakness that I proclaimed the good news to you the first time. ¹⁴You did not despise or reject the trial my body brought upon you, but you received me as an angel of God —as Christ Jesus! ¹⁵That being so, where did all your happiness

go? For I can testify to you that if it were possible, you would have torn out your eyes and given them to me. ¹⁶So, have I become your enemy by telling you the truth? ¹⁷They are not devoted to you for the right reasons; but they want to separate you from me so that you are devoted to them. ¹⁸It is always good to be devoted to me for the right reasons, but not only when I am present with you. ¹⁹My children, with whom I am again suffering birth pains until Christ is formed in you, ²⁰I want to be present with you now and change my tone, for I am at a loss about how to help you.

Slavery versus Freedom: Hagar and Sarah

²¹Tell me, those of you who desire to be under law, don't you understand the law? ²²For it is written that Abraham had two sons, one from the slave girl and one from the free woman. ²³But the one from the slave girl was born by human design,ⁱ and the one from the free woman was born through promise. ²⁴This has been taken as an allegory, for these women are two covenants. One is from Mount Sinai and bears children who will be slaves. That is Hagar, ²⁵for Hagar is Mount Sinai in Arabia. She corresponds to Jerusalem now, for she is serving as a slave with her children. ²⁶But the Jerusalem above is free; she is our mother. ²⁷For it is written:

> "Rejoice, you sterile woman who has not borne children. You who have not experienced birth pains break forth and shout, for the children of the desolate woman are more than the one who has a husband."ⁱⁱ

²⁸But we, brothers, like Isaac, are children of promise; ²⁹and just like it was then, the one born according to human design persecuted the one born according to the Spirit. So it is now. ³⁰But what does the Scripture say?

ⁱ Or, "according to the flesh." Also in verse 29.

ⁱⁱ Isaiah 54:1

> "Cast out the slave girl and her son; for the son of the slave girl will not receive an inheritance with the son of the free woman."[i]

³¹For this very reason, brothers, we are not children of the slave girl but of the free woman.

Falling from the Grace Principle

Chapter Five

¹For freedom Christ has set us free. Therefore, take your stand and do not again become entangled with the yoke of slavery.

²Look, I, Paul, tell you that if you are circumcised because of the Law, Christ will not benefit you. ³I again testify to every man who is circumcised because of the Law, that he is under obligation to keep the whole Law. ⁴Whoever is justified by law no longer operates connected to Christ. You have fallen from grace. ⁵For we ourselves are waiting for the hope of righteousness by the Spirit through faith. ⁶For in Christ Jesus neither circumcision nor uncircumcision have any power, only faith exerting itself through love.

⁷You were running well; who prevented you from believing the truth? ⁸That persuasion does not come from the one who called you. ⁹A little leaven leavens the whole lump of dough. ¹⁰I am confident in the Lord about you, that you will have no other opinion. But the one who is confusing you will bear the judgment, whoever he might be. ¹¹But I, brothers, if I still preach circumcision, why am I still being persecuted? Then the scandal of the cross is ended. ¹²If only the ones who are misleading you would also castrate themselves.

¹³For you were called to freedom, brothers, only do not use your freedom as an opportunity for your flesh, but serve each other through love. ¹⁴For all law is fulfilled by one sentence, by this:

---

[i] See Genesis 21:10.

"Love your neighbor as yourself."[ii]

¹⁵However, if you are biting and tearing each other to pieces, watch that you are not destroyed by each other.

Avoiding the Desires of the Flesh

¹⁶But I say, walk by the Spirit and you will certainly not carry out desires of flesh, ¹⁷for the flesh desires what is against the Spirit, and the Spirit desires what is against the flesh, for these two are at odds with each other, so that you should not do the things you might desire. ¹⁸But if you are led by the Spirit, you are not under law. ¹⁹However, the activities of the flesh are obvious. They include illicit sexual relationships, impure activities, unrestrained sexual excess, ²⁰idolatry, drug-fueled witchcraft,[iii] hatred, strife, jealousy, anger, seeking only what is best for oneself, divisions, factions, ²¹envy, drunkenness, orgies, and things like these. I am warning you about these things, just as I told you before, that those who practice such things cannot inherit the Kingdom of God.

Embracing the Fruit of the Spirit

²²But the fruit of the Spirit is love, joy, peace, patience, kindness, goodness, faithfulness, ²³gentleness, and self-control; there is no law against such things as these. ²⁴Those who belong to Christ Jesus have crucified the flesh with its passions and desires. ²⁵If we are living by the Spirit, let us also agree with the Spirit. ²⁶Let us not become a person with empty opinions, provoking each other and refusing to give in to each other.

[ii] Leviticus 19:18

[iii] Attempting to access the spiritual realm or achieve spiritual insight using drugs or potions.

Restoring Those who have Stumbled

Chapter Six

¹Brothers, if anyone is taken by surprise in any fault, let those of you who are spiritual[i] restore such a person to repentance with a gentle spirit, taking care that you also are not tempted. ²Carry each other's burdens and, by this, fulfill Christ's law. ³For if anyone believes that he is someone when he is nothing, he has deceived himself. ⁴Let each one test his own work for authenticity, and then he can boast to himself alone, but not to anyone else, ⁵for each person will carry his own weight.

Sharing All Good Things with Instructors in the Word

⁶The one who is instructed in the word should share all good things with the one doing the instructing. ⁷Do not be deceived, God cannot be disrespected, for what a man sows, this he also reaps; ⁸for the one sowing on behalf of his own flesh, from that flesh will reap deterioration. The one sowing on behalf of the Spirit, will from the Spirit reap life eternal. ⁹Do not become tired of doing good, for at exactly the right time for each person, we will reap a harvest if we do not grow discouraged and give up. ¹⁰Therefore, as we have the strategic opportunity, let us carry out what is good for everyone, and especially the household of faith.

The Thing that Really Matters: A New Creation

¹¹Look at the large characters of the alphabet I am writing with my own hand. ¹²In just the same way, some wish to make a good impression with physical things. They force you to be circumcised for one reason, so that they will not be persecuted for the cross of Christ. ¹³Those who are circumcised do not even keep the Law themselves, but they want you to be circumcised so that they may boast in your flesh. ¹⁴But may I never boast except in the cross of our Lord Jesus Christ, through whom the world has been crucified to me, and I to the world. ¹⁵For

---

[i] Or, "led by the Spirit."

circumcision isn't anything, nor is uncircumcision, but a new creation is what matters.

¹⁶Peace and mercy upon everyone who agrees with this standard of truth, even upon the Israel of God.

¹⁷Finally, let no one cause trouble for me, for I bear the marks of Jesus on my body.[ii]

¹⁸The grace of our Lord Jesus Christ be with your spirit, brothers. Amen.

[ii] While Paul may be referring to other marks, it is also apparent that being stoned and beaten with rods (2 Corinthians 11:25) would have left obvious marks.

EPHESIANS

Chapter One

¹Paul, an apostle of Christ Jesus through the will of God,

To the saints who live in Ephesus and are faithful in Christ Jesus.

²Grace to you, and peace from God our Father, and the Lord Jesus Christ.

The Father is Worthy of Praise because He Has Blessed Us

³The God and Father of our Lord Jesus Christ is worthy of praise. He has blessed us with every spiritual blessing in the heavenly realms in Christ Jesus, ⁴since, in love, he chose us in him before the founding of the world to be holy and without blemish in his sight. ⁵Through Jesus Christ, he has predestined us to be adopted as his sons; this was his delight and his desire, ⁶for the praise of his wondrous grace, which he graciously gifted to us in the one he loved. ⁷In him we have been redeemed; we have been forgiven of our misdeeds through his blood, in harmony with the richness of his grace, ⁸which he lavishly provided for us with all wisdom and understanding. ⁹He made known to us the mystery of his will, in accord with his good

pleasure displayed in Christ, ¹⁰for managing the ending of the ages and bringing all things together in Christ, things in the heavens, and things on the earth.

¹¹In Christ, we were also appointed as his inheritance, having been predestined according to the purpose of the one working all things according to the focus of his will, ¹²so that we, who were first to hope in Christ, might be the praise of his glory. ¹³When you heard the word of truth, the good news[i] of your rescue, and believed, you were also marked by him with a seal, the down payment of the Holy Spirit. ¹⁴He is a deposit guaranteeing our inheritance until the full redemption of the people God has acquired, to the praise of his glory.

His Divine Energy Working in His People

¹⁵On account of this, and because I heard about your faith in the Lord Jesus and your love for all the saints, ¹⁶I have not stopped giving thanks for you, making mention of you at my prayer times. ¹⁷I pray that the God of our Lord Jesus Christ, the Father of Glory, might give you a spirit of wisdom and revelation in your knowledge of him. ¹⁸I pray that he might give light to the eyes of your heart so that you know what is the hope of his calling, what are the riches of the glory of his inheritance in the saints, ¹⁹and what is his exceedingly great power in us who have believed. That power is in accord with the divine energy[ii] of his mighty strength ²⁰which he worked in Christ when he raised him from the dead and seated him on his right hand in the heavenly realms, ²¹far above all, rule, authority, power, dominion, and every rank that can be named; not only in this age, but also in the age to come. ²²He also placed all things under his feet, and appointed him head over all things for the Church, ²³which is his body, the fullness of the one who fills all things in every respect.

---

[i] The Greek word can be translated "Gospel" or "Good News." The word gospel means good news. It is translated both ways in this Bible version.

[ii] The Greek word "energeia" refers to supernatural energy. It refers to God's energy at work in us, or Satan's energy at work in the world.

Saved by Grace through Faith

Chapter Two

¹Your history is that you also were dead in your offenses and your sins, ²by which you once walked in agreement with the supernatural forces of this world, in step with the ruler of the spiritual authorities in the second heaven,ⁱ the spiritual being who is now working in those distinguished by stubborn disobedience. ³We all also once walked with them, subject to the desires of our flesh, following its will and impulses. Like everyone else we were, by nature, angry people.

⁴But God, because he is rich in mercy, and because of his great love with which he loved us, ⁵and even though we were dead in our offenses, made us alive together with Christ—by grace you have been saved—⁶he also raised us with him and seated us in the heavenly realms with him in Christ Jesus. ⁷He did this, so that in the ages to come, he might show the extraordinary wealth of his grace revealed in his kindness toward us in Christ Jesus. ⁸For by grace you have been saved, through faith; and you are not the source of this salvation, it is a gift of God. ⁹It is not derived from human effort so that no one can boast. ¹⁰For we are his creative work, crafted in Christ Jesus with a view to the good works that God prepared in advance so that we might walk in them.

One New Man in Christ

¹¹Therefore, remember that you who are Gentiles physically, called "uncircumcised" by those who are called "circumcised" (a procedure in the flesh by the human hand), ¹²remember that once you were separate from Christ, cut off from citizenship in Israel, and strangers to the covenants of promise. You did not have hope, and you had no understanding of God in this world. ¹³But now in Christ Jesus, you who were once far away are now near through the blood of Christ.

ⁱ Or, "the air." The ancients believed the air (the second heaven) was the abode of demons.

14For he himself is our peace, the one who made the two one, and destroyed in his flesh the barrier, the separating wall of human hostility. 15He canceled the Law of the commandments and regulations, in order that he, in himself, might make the two into one new man, and establish peace; 16and that he might reconcile them both to God in one body through the cross, having put the hostility to death by it. 17When he came, he proclaimed the good news of peace to you who were far, and peace to those who were near; 18for through him we both have admission to the presence of the Father by one Spirit.

19So then, you are no longer foreigners or resident aliens. Rather, you are fellow citizens with the saints and belong to God's household, 20having been built upon the foundation of the apostles and prophets, with Christ Jesus being its most essential cornerstone. 21In him the whole building is being fitted securely together and is growing into a holy temple in the Lord. 22In him you also are being built together into a dwelling place of God in spirit.

Paul as a Steward of the Mystery of the One New Man

Chapter Three

1For this reason, I Paul, the prisoner of Christ Jesus on behalf of the Gentiles—2for surely you have heard of the provision of God's grace that was given to me for you, 3that according to revelation, the mystery was made known to me just as I have written about previously in a brief fashion. 4By reading about this, you can understand my knowledge of the mystery of Christ, 5which was not made known in other generations to the sons of men as it has now been revealed by the Spirit to his holy apostles and prophets. 6That mystery is that through the good news the Gentiles are joint heirs, fellow members of one body, and share in the promises in Christ Jesus.

7I became a servant of this good news through the gift of the grace of God which was given to me in accord with the working of his supernatural power. 8This grace was given to me, the least of all the saints, to proclaim the good news of the incomprehensible riches of Christ to the Gentiles; ⁹and to bring to light for everyone the details of this mystery which was hidden for ages in the God who created all things. ¹⁰He did this in order that the multifaceted wisdom of God might be made known now to the rulers and the authorities in the heavenly places through the church, ¹¹in accord with the eternal purpose which he performed in Christ Jesus our Lord. ¹²In him we have boldness and confident admission to his presence through faith in Christ Jesus. ¹³On account of this, I ask you not to be discouraged over my tribulations on your behalf, which are your glory.

Paul's Prayer that Ephesians Comprehend God's Love

¹⁴For this reason, I bend my knees to the Father, ¹⁵for whom every family in heaven and on earth is named. ¹⁶I ask, in accord with the riches of his glory, that he might grant that you be strengthened with power through his Spirit in your inner man, ¹⁷so that Christ dwell in your hearts through faith. I also pray that having been rooted and established in love, ¹⁸that you might be able to fully comprehend, along with all the saints, what is the breadth, length, height, and depth of it, ¹⁹and that you know the love of Christ that transcends our knowledge. I also pray that you might be filled with all the fullness of God.

²⁰Now to the one who is able to do all things beyond our ability to measure, beyond anything that we could ask or think, through his power at work in us, ²¹to him be the glory in the Church, and in Christ Jesus, unto all the generations, forever and ever. Amen.

Walking in a Manner Worthy of Our Calling

Chapter Four

¹Therefore, as a prisoner for the Lord, I encourage you to walk in a manner worthy of the calling to which you have been invited. ²Walk with all humility, gentleness, and patience, putting up

with each other in love; ³being diligent to keep the unity of the Spirit within the constraint of peace. ⁴There is one body and one Spirit, just as also you were called in one hope to your calling; ⁵one Lord, one faith, one baptism, ⁶one God and Father of all, who is over all, through all, and in all.

Equipping the Body of Christ

⁷Now to each one of us grace has been given corresponding to the measure of the gift of Christ. ⁸Therefore, it says,

"When he ascended to the heights, he took many captives with him, and gave gifts to men."ⁱ

⁹For what does, "He ascended" mean, if not that he also descended unto lowest parts of the earth? ¹⁰The one who himself descended is also the one who ascended far above all the heavens, in order that he might fill all things.

¹¹At that time, he himself gave some for apostles, others for prophets, evangelists, pastors, and teachers, ¹²to prepare the saints for the work of ministry so that the Body of Christ is built up. ¹³This will continue until we all achieve the unity of the faith and the knowledge of the Son of God, becoming a fully mature adult, attaining the measure of maturity that comes with the fullness of Christ.

¹⁴We must become fully mature adults so that we are no longer tossed back and forth in the waves like infants, carried about like babies by every wind of teaching that comes from the games of men, which they play with cunning and crafty deceptions. ¹⁵Then, proclaiming the truth in love, we will grow in all things into him who is our head, Christ. ¹⁶In him the entire body is fitted and joined together as each ligament provides support, and each part contributes to make the body grow according to its measure of divine energy,ⁱⁱ so that the body builds itself up in love.

ⁱ Psalm 68:18

ⁱⁱ See footnote at Ephesians 1:19.

Ephesians 4:17

Do Not Live Like the Pagans Live

17Therefore, I say—and I affirm this in the Lord—that you must no longer walk in the way that the Gentiles walk, in the futility of their thinking. 18They are darkened in their understanding, and excluded from the life of God, because of their inner ignorance caused by their hardness of heart. 19Because they have lost the ability to feel shame, they have given themselves over to sensual excess, to the practice of every sordid activity as they sexually exploit each other. 20But you did not become acquainted with the Christ in that way, 21for surely you have truly come to know him, and have been taught by him, because truth is in Jesus. 22You were taught, with respect to your former way of life, to put away the old man, which was being morally corrupted through enticing lusts, 23and to be renewed in your mind by the Spirit, 24and to put on the new man, created for God in righteousness and true holiness.

25Therefore, because you have put away the lying nature, each of you must speak truth to his neighbor, for we are members of each other. 26When you are angry, do not sin. Do not let the sun set while you are incensed; 27do not give the Accuser[i] space to operate. 28Anyone who is stealing, must steal no longer, rather he must work at doing good, toiling at a job with his hands, in order that he might share with those in need. 29Let no harmful speech come out of your mouth, but only what is good for building up according to the need at hand, in order that it might release grace to those who are listening. 30Also, do not grieve the Holy Spirit of God, by whom you were sealed for the day of redemption; 31let all bitterness, violent emotion, anger, uproar, and slander be taken from you, along with every hateful feeling. 32Instead, be kind and compassionate to each other, being gracious with each other, just as also God was gracious to you in Christ.

---

[i] Traditionally, "devil." The name means to slander or accuse. For this reason, this word is most often translated "Accuser" in this Bible version.

Be Imitators of God

Chapter Five

¹Therefore, be imitators of God as dearly loved children; ²and walk in love, just as also the Christ loved us and gave himself for us as an offering and a sacrifice, a sweet-smelling aroma to God.

³But let illicit sexual relationships, impurity of every kind, and sexual exploitation not be named among you, as is fitting for those who are holy. ⁴Instead of shameful talk, foolish words, and vulgar speech that is not becoming, practice giving thanks. ⁵For you can be certain of this, that no immoral, impure, or greedy person—especially since greed is a form of idolatry—you can be certain that those who practice these things do not have an inheritance in the Kingdom of the Christ and God. ⁶Let no one deceive you with empty words, for on account of these things the vengeance of God comes upon the sons of disobedience, ⁷therefore, do not be in league with them.

Walk as Children of Light

⁸For you were once darkness, but now you are light in the Lord. Walk as children of light—⁹for the fruit of the light is found in all goodness, righteousness, and truth—¹⁰learning what is pleasing to the Lord. ¹¹Do not have fellowship with the fruitless works of darkness, but rather bring them into the light. ¹²For it is embarrassing to mention the things done in secret by the children of darkness. ¹³But everything brought into the light will be made visible by the light, ¹⁴for anything that makes things visible is light. Therefore, it says,

> "Get up, you who are sleeping, and rise from the
> dead, and the Christ will shine on you."[ii]

¹⁵Therefore, watch carefully how you walk, not as fools, but as wise; ¹⁶redeeming every opportunity, since these are oppressive days. ¹⁷On account of this, do not be unwise, but understand what the

---

[ii] This may have been an early Christian baptismal hymn with roots in Isaiah. See Isaiah 9:2; 26:19; 51:17; 52:1; and Isaiah 60:1.

Lord's will is. ¹⁸Also, do not be intoxicated with wine, which destroys self-control; instead be filled with the Spirit. ¹⁹Speak to each other with psalms, songs of praise, and spiritual songs, singing and making music in your heart to the Lord. ²⁰Give thanks at all times to our God and Father for everything in the name of our Lord Jesus Christ.

Voluntary Submission in the Body of Christ: Husbands and Wives

²¹Submit willingly[i] to each other out of sincere respect for Christ. ²²Wives, *submit willingly*[ii] to your husbands as to the Lord, ²³because the husband is head of the wife as also the Christ is head of the church, he himself is Savior of *the people belonging to* his body. ²⁴As the Church willingly submits to Christ, so also wives should submit willingly to their husbands in everything.

²⁵Husbands, sacrificially love your wives, just as also Christ loved the church and gave himself on her behalf. ²⁶He did this in order that he might make her holy, having cleansed her with the washing of water by the word, ²⁷so that he might present her to himself a magnificent church, having no stain or wrinkle, or any other such thing, but that she be holy and blameless. ²⁸Thus, husbands also ought to sacrificially love their wives as their own bodies. The one loving his own wife loves himself. ²⁹For no one ever hates his own physical body, but feeds it and takes care of it, just as also Christ the Church, ³⁰because we are members of his Body.

> ³¹"For this reason, a man will leave his father and
> his mother and will be united to his wife,
> and the two will be one flesh."[iii]

---

[i] The verb translated "submit willingly" implies an orderly submission to each other which allows the Body of Christ to function. Submission is a volitional act.

[ii] The verb is not repeated in verse 22 because the two parts of the sentence are governed by the first verb, "submit willingly." It works better in English to add the verb again.

[iii] Genesis 2:24

³²This is a great mystery; but I am speaking to Christ and to the Church. ³³However, I am also speaking to you as individuals. Let each husband love his own wife, just as he loves himself, and his wife should respect her husband.

Voluntary Submission in the Body of Christ: Children and Parents

Chapter Six

¹Children, obey your parents in the Lord, for this is righteous.

²"Honor your father and mother,"[iv]

which is the first commandment given with a promise,

³"that it may be well with you, and you will live a long time on the earth."

⁴Fathers, do not make your children angry, but raise them with the training and understanding of the Lord.

Voluntary Submission in the Body of Christ: Slaves and Masters

⁵Slaves, obey your earthly masters with respect approaching fear,[v] with sincerity of your heart as to Christ. ⁶Don't just look the part, as those who try to gain favor with men, but as slaves of Christ doing the will of God from your soul. ⁷Serve with goodwill as serving the Lord and not men, ⁸knowing that whatever good anyone might do, he will receive this back from the Lord, whether he is slave or free.

⁹Masters, also do the same things with them, abandoning threats, knowing that your Master and theirs is in the heavens, and he does not show favoritism.

Be Empowered by the Lord

¹⁰Finally, be empowered by the Lord and by the might of his strength. ¹¹Put on the full armor of God, with which you are

---

[iv] Exodus 20:12; Deuteronomy 5:16. Also in 6:3.

[v] More literally, "with fear and trembling," which is an idiom which can be translated as above.

able to stand against the crafty scheming of the Accuser. ¹²For our fight is not against flesh and blood, but it is against the rulers, the authorities, the spiritual world rulers of this dark age, and against the evil spiritual beings in the heavenly realms. ¹³Therefore, take up the full armor of God, so that you are able to put up a fight on the day of trouble; and when you have done everything to thoroughly prepare yourself, make your stand.

Walking in the Armor of God

¹⁴Therefore, take your stand, having wrapped your sexual life[i] in truth, and having put on the body armor of righteousness. ¹⁵Fasten the readiness of the gospel of peace to your feet; ¹⁶and in addition to everything else, take up the shield of faith, with which you are able to quench all the flaming arrows of the evil one. ¹⁷Take also the helmet of salvation, and the sword of the Spirit, which is the word of God. ¹⁸Pray at all times in the Spirit with every type of prayer and petition. To this end, keep watch with all diligence, and pray on behalf of all the saints.

¹⁹Pray on my behalf that a message might be given to me when I open my mouth, to boldly make known the mystery of the gospel, ²⁰for which I am an ambassador in chains. Pray in order that I might speak clearly; that is essential when I speak.

Closing Greetings

²¹Now Tychicus will tell you everything, so that you might know how things are with me, and what I am doing. He is my cherished brother and faithful servant in the Lord. ²²I am sending him to you for this very reason, that you might know about us, and that he might encourage your hearts.

²³Peace to the brothers, and love with faith, from God our Father, and the Lord Jesus Christ.

²⁴Grace be with all those who love our Lord Jesus Christ with a love that will never perish. Amen.

---

[i] Or, "having wrapped your loins." The loins are the procreative region of the body.

PHILIPPIANS

Chapter One

¹Paul and Timothy, servants of Christ Jesus,

To all the saints in Christ Jesus who are in Philippi, along with those who give oversight[i] and the deacons.

²Grace to you and peace from God our Father and the Lord Jesus Christ.

Paul's Joy over the Believers in Philippi

³I am giving thanks to my God over every memory of you. ⁴I am always praying with joy in my every prayer for all of you, ⁵over your fellowship in the gospel[ii] from the first day until now. ⁶I am certain of this, that the one who began a good work in you will continue to do so until it is finished on the day of Christ Jesus.

⁷It is right for me to think this way regarding all of you, because I have you in my heart; you are all partners of grace with me, both in my imprisonment and in the defending and

---

[i] Or, "the overseers." This term refers to those who watch over God's flock.
[ii] The Greek word can be translated "Gospel" or "Good News." The word gospel means good news. It is translated both ways in this Bible version.

establishing of the gospel. ⁸For God is my witness of how I have great affection for all of you with the compassion of Christ Jesus. ⁹I am also praying this, that your love overflows yet more and more in knowledge and all discernment, ¹⁰so that you will be able to approve those things that are essential. I pray this in order that you might be sincere and blameless until the day of Christ Jesus, ¹¹filled with the fruit of righteousness that comes through Jesus Christ, for the glory and praise of God.

Paul's Circumstances Advance the Gospel

¹²I want you to know, brothers, that the things that have happened to me have advanced the gospel even more than before, ¹³so that my imprisonment for Christ has become evident among the whole palace guard and to all the rest of the people. ¹⁴In addition, most of the brothers in the Lord have gained confidence because of my imprisonment, and have resolved to speak the word even more fearlessly.

¹⁵To be sure, some are proclaiming Christ from jealousy and discord, but others also from good will. ¹⁶The latter do so out of love, knowing that I live for the defense of the gospel; ¹⁷the former proclaim Christ out of self-interest, not sincerely. They think that they can add to my trouble during my imprisonment.[i] ¹⁸For what reason? That doesn't matter. The only thing that does is that by every means, whether from pretense or from truth, Christ is proclaimed—in this I am rejoicing—most definitely, I will be glad.

Paul's Choice to Remain and Serve

¹⁹For I know that this will lead to my release, on account of your prayers and help from the Spirit of Jesus Christ. ²⁰This is in accord with my intense expectation and hope that I will not be brought to shame in any way. I have every confidence that, just as in the past, and now at this time, Christ will be exalted in my body, whether through my life or through my death. ²¹For to me,

---

[i] Verses 16 and 17 are in reverse order in many Greek manuscripts. The order here aligns with the traditional rendering.

to live is Christ, and to die is gain. ²²But if there is fruitful work for me by living in this body, I do not know what I will choose. ²³I am pulled in two directions. I have the desire to depart and be with Christ, for that is much more beneficial, ²⁴but it is necessary for your sake that I remain in the body. ²⁵Since I am convinced of this, I know that I will stay, and remain here with you all for your growth and joy in the faith, ²⁶so that your pride in me might overflow in Christ Jesus because I am coming to you again.

²⁷Only lead your lives worthy of the gospel of Christ. Do this so that whether I come and see you, or whether I am absent, I hear about you, that you stand firm in one spirit, with one soul[ii] fighting together for the faith of the gospel; ²⁸and so that you are not intimidated by anything done by those who oppose you. This is evidence to them of their ruin and your deliverance. This also is from God. ²⁹For it has been granted to you, on behalf of Christ, not only to believe in him, but also to suffer on his behalf. ³⁰You are experiencing the same struggle that you saw in me, and now have heard is still with me.

Demonstrating Humility in the Body of Christ

Chapter Two

¹Therefore, if there is any encouragement in Christ, if there is any comfort in his love, if there is any fellowship by his Spirit, if there is any tenderness and compassion, ²bring my joy to fullness by having the same thoughts, the same love, being united and having one understanding. ³Do nothing from selfishness or empty boasting, but with humility, regarding one another as more valuable than yourselves. ⁴Each one should not only watch over his own welfare, but also each other's welfare.

⁵Have this mindset among you, one which was also in Christ Jesus:

[ii] The concept of soul includes the mind, emotions, and will.

⁶Who, because he was the visual expression of God, did not consider it an illegal appropriation to be equal to God. ⁷But he emptied himself, and took the visual expression of a servant, and was made in the likeness of men.
Since he was found in his outward form as a man, ⁸he humbled himself and became obedient to the point of death, even death from a cross.
⁹Therefore, God highly exalted him, and freely gave him the name that is above all names, ¹⁰so that at the name of Jesus everyone in heaven, on earth, and under the earth will bend the knee, ¹¹and every tongue will confess that Jesus Christ is Lord, for the glory of God the Father.

Shining Radiantly in this Dark World

¹²So, my cherished friends, just as you have always obeyed, not just when I am with you, but now much more in my absence, continue working out your salvation with respect approaching fear;[i] ¹³for it is God who is working in you to desire and accomplish his good pleasure.

¹⁴Do everything without complaint or contention, ¹⁵so that you might be blameless and pure, children of God who are unblemished in the midst of a crooked and confused generation. You shine among them like radiant lights in the world ¹⁶as you hold to the word of life. For this will be my boast on the Day of Christ, that I did not run and weary myself for no purpose. ¹⁷On the contrary, if I also am being poured out as a drink offering upon the sacrifice and service of your faith, I am glad and rejoice with you all. ¹⁸You do the same and be glad and rejoice with me.

Paul's Fellow Workers on behalf of the Philippians

¹⁹I hope in the Lord Jesus to send Timothy to you soon, so that I might be encouraged by knowing what is happening among you. ²⁰For I have no one else of a like mind, who is genuinely concerned about what is happening among you.

---

[i] More literally, "with fear and trembling," an idiom which can be translated as above.

²¹Everyone is seeking their own welfare, and not the welfare of Jesus Christ. ²²For you know his proven character, that he served with me in the gospel like a child with his father. ²³Therefore, I hope to send him as soon as I find out what is ahead for me. ²⁴I am convinced in the Lord, that I myself will also be coming to you before long.

²⁵But I considered it necessary to send Epaphroditus to you. He is my brother, fellow worker, and fellow-soldier, and your apostle and minister to my need. ²⁶I considered it necessary because he was longing for you all, and troubled that you had heard he was sick. ²⁷For he was sick and came close to death, but God had mercy on him, and not only on him, but also on me, that I might not have grief upon grief. ²⁸So, I eagerly sent him so that when you see him again, you might rejoice, and I might have less concern. ²⁹Therefore, receive him in the Lord with all joy, and hold those who are like him in honor; ³⁰for he came close to death on account of the work of Christ. He risked his life so that he could supply the things that were lacking from you in your service to me.

Chapter Three

¹In addition, my brothers, rejoice in the Lord. To write the same things to you is not a bother to me, and a safe course for you.

Warnings About Those who Depend on the Flesh

²Be aware of the dogs, the evil workers, the ones who mutilate the flesh. ³For we are the circumcision, those who worship by the Spirit of God, who boast in Christ Jesus, and who are not confident in our flesh—⁴though I myself might have confidence in the flesh. If someone has confidence in the flesh, I have more reason for confidence: ⁵circumcised on the eighth day, from the family of Israel, of the tribe of Benjamin, a Hebrew of Hebrews, a Pharisee according to the Law, ⁶zealously persecuting the church, and blameless with regard to the righteousness that is in the Law.

⁷But whatever was to my gain, I regard these things as a dead loss for the sake of Christ. ⁸Even more so, I count all things to be a dead loss on account of the unsurpassable knowledge of Christ Jesus my Lord. I have suffered the loss of all things for him. I count them as dung that I might gain Christ ⁹and be found in him not having a righteousness of my own that is from law, but that which is through faith in Christ. This is the righteousness that comes from God by faith; ¹⁰I count it all loss so that I may know him and the power of his resurrection, as well as the fellowship with his sufferings, and that I might die in a manner similar to his death; ¹¹so that I might somehow attain to the resurrection, the one out from among the dead.[i]

Running to Go Higher in Christ

¹²Not that I have already received it, or that I have already become mature, but I run after it so that I might take possession of that for which Christ Jesus took possession of me. ¹³Brothers, I do not consider that I have overtaken it, but one thing I do: forgetting what is behind and stretching toward what is ahead, ¹⁴I run toward the goal for the prize of the invitation of God to come higher in Christ Jesus.

¹⁵Therefore, those of us as are mature should think in this way. If in anything you think in any other way, God will reveal this to you. ¹⁶Nevertheless, let us live in accordance with what we have attained.

¹⁷Brothers, join together and imitate me, and pay attention to those who are walking according to the pattern you have from us. ¹⁸For many, as I told you often, and now say while weeping, many are walking as enemies of the cross of Christ. ¹⁹The outcome of their lives will be destruction. Their god is their appetite, and they glory in disgraceful things because they focus their attention on earthly issues. ²⁰For our citizenship is in the heavens. We await a Savior from there, the Lord Jesus Christ, ²¹who will transform our lowly body to share like form with his

---

[i] The word here translated "resurrection" is only used here in the New Testament. It emphasizes the "out from among" the dead idea.

glorious body. He will do this by the divine energy[ii] by which he is able to make all things submit to him.

Chapter Four

¹Therefore, my cherished brothers whom I long to see, my joy and my crown, in this way stand firm in the Lord, my cherished ones.

Closing Instructions

²I urge Euodia and I urge Syntyche to think the same way in the Lord. ³Yes, I am asking you also, my tested fellow worker, join in helping them. They have toiled at my side for the gospel, along with Clement and the rest of my fellow workers, whose names are in the Book of Life.

⁴Rejoice in the Lord always. I say again, rejoice. ⁵Let your gracious forbearance be known to all men. The Lord is near. ⁶Do not worry about anything, but in everything, by prayer and by requests mixed with thanksgiving, let your desires be known to God. ⁷Then the peace of God, which is better than all understanding, will protect your hearts and your thoughts in Christ Jesus.

⁸In addition, brothers, whatever is true, whatever is worthy of respect, whatever is righteous, whatever is pure, whatever is pleasing, whatever is commendable, if anything is virtuous or worthy of praise, think deliberately about these things. ⁹What you have learned, accepted, heard, and seen in me, practice these things; and the God of peace will be with you.

Thanksgiving for the Philippian's Support

¹⁰I have rejoiced much in the Lord that you are now once again in position to take thought on my behalf. You were thinking of me, but you had no opportunity to do anything.

[ii] The Greek word "energeia" refers to supernatural energy. It refers to God's energy at work in us, or Satan's energy at work in the world.

¹¹Not that I am speaking out of need, for I have learned to be content in all situations. ¹²I know also how to live in humble circumstances, and I know how to live in abundance. I have learned the secret of living in every and all circumstances, being filled and being hungry, having abundance and experiencing scarcity. ¹³I am able to do all things in the one who strengthens me.

¹⁴Nevertheless, you have done well in partnering with me in my hardship. ¹⁵You Philippians know that at the very beginning when I shared the gospel with you, after I left Macedonia, no other church partnered with me by giving a gift or a payment into my account except you alone. ¹⁶Even in Thessalonica, you supplied for my needs once or twice. ¹⁷Not that I am seeking a gift, but I am seeking fruit that will multiply in your account. ¹⁸Now I have received everything, and I have more than enough. I have been provided for completely since I received from Epaphroditus the things you sent. They are a sweet-smelling aroma, an acceptable sacrifice, pleasing to God; ¹⁹and my God will fill every area you have need, according to his riches in glory in Christ Jesus. ²⁰To our God and Father be glory for all the ages. Amen.

Closing Greetings

²¹Greet every saint in Christ Jesus. The brothers who are with me send their greetings to you.

²²All the saints send their greetings to you, especially the ones from Caesar's household.

²³The grace of the Lord Jesus Christ be with your spirit. Amen.

COLOSSIANS

Chapter One

¹Paul, an apostle of Christ Jesus through the will of God, and our brother Timothy.

²To the holy and faithful brothers in Colosse:

Grace to you and peace from God our Father and the Lord Jesus Christ.

The Gospel Bearing Fruit Throughout the World

³We give thanks to the God and Father of our Lord Jesus Christ while we continually pray for you, ⁴because we heard of your faith in Christ Jesus, and the love which you have for all the saints, ⁵on account of the hope that is safely stored in the heavens. You heard of this beforehand in the word of truth, the gospel[i] ⁶that is present in you. It is also present in all the world bearing fruit and growing, as it has been in you from the day that you heard and actually recognized the grace of God. ⁷You learned it in this way from Epaphras, our cherished fellow

---

[i] The Greek word can be translated "Gospel" or "Good News." The word gospel means good news. It is translated both ways in this Bible version.

bondservant, who is a faithful servant of Christ on your behalf. ⁸He also told us about your love by the Spirit.

Paul's Continued Prayer for those in Colosse

⁹For this reason, from the day we heard this, we also have not stopped praying for you and asking that you might be filled with the knowledge of his will in all spiritual wisdom and understanding. ¹⁰We do this so that you walk worthy of the Lord and always please him by bearing fruit in every good work, growing in the knowledge of God, ¹¹and being strengthened with all power through his glorious might, which will result in all endurance and patience. ¹²All while you are giving thanks to the Father with joy because he has qualified you for a share of the ministry of the saints in the light. ¹³He has saved us from the ruler of the darkness, and transplanted us to the Kingdom of his cherished Son. ¹⁴In him we possess redemption, the forgiveness of our sins.

The Firstborn of All Creation

¹⁵He is the visible likeness of the invisible God, firstborn of all creation. ¹⁶For by him all things were created in the heavens and upon the earth, visible and invisible, whether thrones, lordships, rulers or authorities—all things were created through him and for him. ¹⁷He is before all things, and in him all things continue to exist. ¹⁸He alone is also head of the body, the Church. He is the starting point, firstborn from the dead, in order that he might take preeminence in everything. ¹⁹For God was pleased for all fullness to abide in him, ²⁰and through him to reconcile all things to himself, having made peace through the blood of his cross. Whether it is the things upon the earth or the things in the heavens, it is all through him.

²¹You once were estranged and hostile in your thoughts as demonstrated by your evil activities, ²²but now he has reconciled you in his physical body[i] through death to present you holy, without spot, and blameless before him—²³since indeed you

---

[i] More literally, "the body of his flesh."

remain established and firm in your faith and are not shifting away from the hope of the gospel about which you have heard. This gospel has been proclaimed in all creation that is under heaven, and of which I myself became a servant.

The Hope of Glory: Christ in Us

²⁴Now I rejoice in the afflictions I suffer on your behalf, and I complete in my flesh what is lacking in the sufferings of Christ for his body, which is the Church. ²⁵I myself was made a servant of the Church for you, according to the stewardship role that God gave to me: to completely reveal the Word of God, ²⁶namely, the mystery that was hidden from the ages and the generations, but now has been made known to his saints. ²⁷God desired to make known to them the riches of the glory of this mystery among the Gentiles, which is Christ in you, the hope of glory.

²⁸We also proclaim him, imparting understanding to every person, and teaching everyone with all wisdom, so that we might present everyone as an adult in Christ. ²⁹For this reason, I am working hard, fighting in accord with his energy,[ii] the energy that is working in me with power.

Paul's Great Fight for the Believers

Chapter Two

¹For I want you to know how great a fight I am having on your behalf, on behalf of those in Laodicea, and on behalf of all those who have not seen my face in person. ²I am working hard that their hearts might be encouraged, united in love, and growing into all the richness of complete understanding, and into all the knowledge of the mystery of God, that is, Christ. ³In him all the treasures of wisdom and knowledge are hidden.

[ii] The Greek word "energeia" refers to supernatural energy. It refers to God's energy at work in us, or Satan's energy at work in the world. Also in 2:12.

⁴I am saying this so that no one deceive you with enticing arguments. ⁵For since I am absent in person, but with you in spirit, I am rejoicing as I see your good order, and the firm nature of your faith in Christ.

⁶Therefore, in the same way that you have received Christ Jesus the Lord, continue walking in him, ⁷rooted and built up in him, and being confirmed in the faith, just as you were taught, while overflowing in thanksgiving.

Made Alive in Christ

⁸Watch that no one carry you away as their prize through philosophy and empty pleasures that are in line with human regulations and the rudimentary principles of the world, and not in line with Christ. ⁹For in him all the fullness of the deity inhabits a physical form, ¹⁰and you have been filled by him, who is the head over all rule and authority.

¹¹In him you were also circumcised with a circumcision done without hands, in the putting off the body of the flesh through the circumcision of Christ. ¹²You were buried with him in baptism, by which you were also raised with him through faith in the supernatural energy of God, who raised him from among the dead. ¹³While you were dead in the offenses and the uncircumcision of your flesh, he made you alive together with him, having forgiven us all our offenses. ¹⁴He blotted out the hand-written record of the debt which was against us. He has taken it from our midst, nailing it securely to the cross. ¹⁵When he disarmed the rulers and authorities, he openly put them to shame, since he had triumphed over them by the cross.

Do Not Let People Judge Your Freedom in Christ

¹⁶Therefore, let no one judge you about food or drink, nor regarding a religious holiday, the new moon, or your sabbaths. ¹⁷These are a shadow of things that were coming, but the person casting the shadow is the Christ. ¹⁸Do not let anyone deprive you of your victory by insisting on self-abasement, an obsession with angels, or what he has seen when he entered the heavenly

court.[i] He is puffed up for no reason by his carnal mind. [19]He is not holding fast to the head, from whom all the body is supplied and held together through the joints and ligaments and grows with the growth of God.

[20]Since you died with Christ to the rudimentary principles of this world, why are you affirming its rules as if you are living in the world? [21]"Do not have marital intimacy, do not taste, do not embrace!" [22]All of these things are the commandments and teachings of men and refer to things that are subject to moral corruption as they are used. [23]These restrictions have a reputation for wisdom in their self-imposed ideas of worship, their constant debasements, and their demanding treatment of the body, but they have no value in restraining the gratification of the flesh.

Pursue the Things Above

Chapter Three

[1]Therefore, since you have been raised together with Christ, pursue the things above, where the Christ is sitting at the right hand of God. [2]Give your mind to the things above, not earthly things. [3]For you have died and your life has been hidden with Christ in God. [4]When Christ our life appears, then you also will be displayed with him in glory.

[5]Therefore, put to death the parts of you that are on the earth, illicit sexual relationships, sexual impurity, licentious passion, lust-filled desires, and sexual greed, which is idolatry. [6]On account of these the vengeance of God is coming upon the sons of disobedience. [7]You also once walked in them when you were living immersed in these things. [8]But now also, put away all of them, anger, rage, morally defective behavior, slander, and shameful speech from your mouth. [9]Do not lie to each other,

---

[i] The Greek word, embateuo, refers to a visionary experience in which some among the Colossians experienced entrance into the heavenly sanctuary.

since you have taken off the old man with its activities, ¹⁰and you have put on the new man that is being renewed in knowledge according to the pattern of its Creator. ¹¹Because of this, there is no Greek or Jew, circumcised or uncircumcised, barbarian, Scythian, slave, or free, but Christ is everything and in everyone.

Living as One Body

¹²Therefore, as God's elect ones,[i] holy and cherished by him, put on heartfelt compassion, kindness, humility, gentleness, and patience. ¹³If anyone has a complaint against another, bear with one another and forgive each other. Just as also the Lord has forgiven you, so also you should forgive. ¹⁴Above all these things add love, which produces a mature bond. ¹⁵Let the peace of Christ rule in your hearts. You were called to this as one body; and be thankful. ¹⁶Let the word of Christ richly live among you while you are teaching and admonishing each other with all wisdom, singing psalms, hymns, and Spirit songs with thankfulness in your hearts toward God. ¹⁷In all that you do by word or action, do everything in the name of the Lord Jesus, giving thanks to God the Father through him.

Voluntary Submission in the Body of Christ

¹⁸Wives, submit willingly[ii] to your husbands as is proper in the Lord. ¹⁹Husbands, sacrificially love your wives and do not become bitter toward them.

²⁰Children, obey your parents in all things, for this is pleasing to the Lord. ²¹Fathers, do not irritate your children, so that they will not be discouraged.

---

[i] The term translated "elect" is used over twenty times in the New Testament and most often is a reference to those who are called by God to true faith that perseveres.

[ii] The verb translated "submit willingly" implies an orderly submission to each other which allows the Body of Christ to function. Submission is a volitional act.

²²Slaves, obey your earthly[iii] masters in all things, not just for appearances as someone who wants to please people, but with sincerity of heart out of reverent fear for the Lord. ²³Whatever you do, work from your soul as serving the Lord, and not men; ²⁴you know that you will receive the reward of your inheritance from the Lord. Continue serving our Lord Christ, ²⁵for the one who does wrong will receive back what he has done wrong, and the Lord Christ does not show favoritism.

Chapter Four

¹Masters, provide justice and equal treatment to your slaves, knowing that you also have a Master in heaven.

Strategic Opportunities and Prayer

²Persevere in prayer, being watchful as you pray with thanksgiving; ³praying also at the same time about us, that God might open a door to us for the word, so we can share the mystery of Christ. It is for this message that I am chained. ⁴Pray that I might explain it understandably, as I am required to speak.

⁵Walk in wisdom with those outside, redeeming every opportunity. ⁶Let your words always be filled with grace while being flavored with salt; knowing how we are required to respond to one another.

Tychicus and Onesimus will Give Further Insights

⁷Tychicus, our cherished brother, faithful servant, and fellow bondslave in the Lord will make known to you all the details concerning me. ⁸I have sent him to you for this reason, so that you might know the things about us, and so he might encourage your hearts. ⁹I have sent him with Onesimus, our faithful and cherished brother, who is one of you. They will let you know everything that is happening here.

[iii] Or, "obey your masters according to the flesh."

Colossians 4:10

Greetings from Those with Paul

¹⁰My fellow-prisoner, Aristarchus, sends his greeting to you, as does Mark, the cousin of Barnabas—you have received instructions concerning him: If he comes to you, receive him—¹¹and Jesus, who is called Justus sends his greeting. These are the only coworkers from the circumcision in the Kingdom of God. They have been a help to me.

¹²Epaphras, who is one of you and a servant of Christ Jesus, sends his greeting to you. He is always fighting for you in his prayers, that you be planted firmly in the will of God, mature and completely certain. ¹³For I bear witness for him that he has labored much for you and those in Laodicea and Hierapolis.

¹⁴Luke, my cherished physician, sends his greeting to you, and also Demas.

¹⁵Greet the brothers in Laodicea, and Nympha and the church that meets in her house.

¹⁶When this letter is read publicly to you, make arrangements that it also be read publicly among the church of the Laodiceans, and you also read the letter from Laodicea publicly.

¹⁷Tell Archippus, "See to the ministry that you have received in the Lord, that you fulfill it."

¹⁸This greeting is by my own hand—Paul. Remember my chains. Grace be with you.

1 THESSALONIANS

Chapter One

¹Paul, Silas, and Timothy,

To the church of the Thessalonians in God the Father and the Lord Jesus Christ.

Grace to you and peace.

Paul Gives Thanks for the Christians in Thessalonica

²We always give thanks to God concerning all of you, making mention of you at our prayer times, ³while remembering your work of faith, your taxing labor of love, and your hope-filled endurance before our God and Father, through your hope in our Lord Jesus Christ. ⁴We are aware, brothers loved by God, of your election, ⁵because our gospel did not come to you by word alone, but also with power. It came with the Holy Spirit, and with complete certainty, because you knew how we conducted ourselves among you for your sake.

⁶You also became imitators of us, and of the Lord, when you received the word with the joy of the Holy Spirit in the midst of much tribulation. ⁷Because of this, you became an example to all those who believe in Macedonia and Achaia. ⁸For the word of

the Lord rang out from you, not only in Macedonia and Achaia, but in every place the report of your faith toward God has gone out; so that we have no need to say anything about it. ⁹For they themselves share the report about us, about what kind of access we had with you, and how you turned to God from idols; how you serve the living and true God; ¹⁰and how you wait expectantly for his Son from the heavens, whom he raised from the dead, Jesus. He is the one who is saving you from the punishment to come.

Paul's Hard Work among the Thessalonians

Chapter Two

¹For you yourselves know, brothers, that our stay with you was not without impact, ²but after we suffered and were deprived of our rights in Philippi—as you know—with God's help we had the confidence to share the gospel of God with you in the face of strong opposition. ³For our message does not come from error, impurity, or deception, ⁴but we have been proven genuine by God and entrusted with the gospel. We speak, not in order to please men, but to please the God who tests our hearts. ⁵We did not come with a flattering message, as you know, nor as a pretense for greed. God is our witness. ⁶We also did not seek human approval, either from you or from others, ⁷though as apostles of Christ we have the right to be a burden, but instead we were innocent as children among you. Like a nursemaid caring for her children, ⁸we were fond of you, and we were delighted to share with you not only the gospel of God, but also our very lives, because you became our cherished friends.

⁹For you remember, brothers, our hard work and toil, working night and day so not to be a burden to any of you as we preached to you the gospel of God. ¹⁰You—and God—are our witnesses, as to how holy, righteous, and blameless we were to those who believed. ¹¹As you know, we encouraged, comforted, and testified to each one of you as a father to his children, ¹²so that you walk worthy of the God who is calling you into his kingdom and glory.

¹³We also continuously give thanks to God, because when you received the word of God that you heard from us, you accepted it not as the word of men, but—as it truly is—the word of God, which also is releasing its energy in you who believe. ¹⁴For you, brothers, became imitators of the churches of God in Judea that are in Christ Jesus, because you suffered in the same way from your own countrymen, just as they did from those in Judea ¹⁵who killed the Lord Jesus and the prophets, and persecuted us severely. They are not pleasing God, and are a hindrance to everyone ¹⁶when they prevent us from speaking to the Gentiles so that they might be saved. The result is that they heap up their sin each time they do this, and the end time punishment has already drawn near them.ⁱ

Paul's Desire to See the Thessalonians in Person

¹⁷But we, brothers, have felt orphaned by our separation from you for a short season of time, in person not in affection, but we eagerly desired to see you in person. ¹⁸We wanted to come to you—I, Paul, wanted to come several times—but Satan blocked us. ¹⁹For who will be our hope, our joy, or crown of triumph in the presence of the Lord Jesus at his coming, if it is not you? ²⁰You are our glory and our joy.

Timothy's Joyous Report

Chapter Three

¹Therefore, when we could no longer endure it, we were happy to be left in Athens alone. ²We sent Timothy, our brother and God's fellow worker in the gospel of Christ, to strengthen you and encourage you in your faith, ³so that no one would be deceived by these tribulations. For you yourselves know that we are appointed to this. ⁴Even when we were with you, we told you in advance that we were about to suffer persecution, just as it also happened, as you know. ⁵For this reason, when I could no

---

ⁱ From Paul's perspective, he was in the end times as the predicted destruction of Jerusalem drew near (see Matthew 24).

longer endure it, I sent to learn about your faith, concerned that the tempter had trapped you, and that our labor had been in vain.

⁶But now Timothy has come to us from you and brought the good news about your faith and love to us, telling us that you always have good memories of us, and that you desire to see us, just as we also desire to see you. ⁷Thanks to this, brothers, we found comfort in you through all our distress and affliction because of your faith. ⁸Now we live again, since you are standing firm in the Lord. ⁹How can we adequately thank God for you, and for all the joy that we have felt over you before our God? ¹⁰We have prayed night and day, more times than we can count, that we might see you in person and complete what is lacking in your faith.

¹¹Now may our God and Father himself, and our Lord Jesus, direct our path to you, ¹²may the Lord increase you and cause you to overflow with love for each other, and for everyone else, just as we also do for you, ¹³so that your hearts are strengthened, and you are blameless in holiness before our God and Father at the coming of our Lord Jesus with all his holy ones.

Walk in a Way that Pleases God

Chapter Four

¹Now in addition, brothers, we ask and encourage you in the Lord Jesus, that just as you learned from us how you can walk in the way that pleases God—just as you are doing. We ask and encourage you to increase even more in this. ²For you know what commands we gave to you through the Lord Jesus. ³It is God's will that you all grow in holiness, abstaining from illicit sexual relationships; ⁴that each one of you learn how to acquire a sexual partner in holiness and honor, ⁵not in sexual passion like the nations that do not know God; ⁶and that no one cross the line and take greedy advantage of his brother in this matter. For the Lord is the avenger in all such matters, just as we told you

before and warned you about. ⁷For God has not called us to impurity, but to holiness. ⁸Therefore, the one who sets this teaching aside does not set man aside, but the God who gives his Holy Spirit to you.

Excel in Brotherly Love

⁹Now about brotherly love, you have no need that anyone write to you. For you yourselves are taught by God to love one another. ¹⁰That is obvious because you demonstrate love to all the brothers in all of Macedonia. But we encourage you, brothers, to excel even more at this. ¹¹In addition, make it your goal to lead a quiet life, to pay attention to your own affairs, and to work with your hands, just as we commanded you. ¹²Do this in order that you walk in a way that is pleasing to those who are outside the church, and so that you do not have need of anything.

When the Lord Comes Again: Resurrection and Transformation

¹³Now, I do not want you to be ill-informed, brothers, about those who are sleeping, so that you do not grieve like the rest of men who do not have hope. ¹⁴For since we believe that Jesus died and rose again, in this same way, God through Jesus will also bring with him those who have fallen asleep. ¹⁵For we tell you this by the word of the Lord, that we who are living and still survive at the coming of the Lord, will certainly not precede those who sleep. ¹⁶For the Lord himself will descend from heaven with a cry of command, with the voice of the archangel and with the trumpet of God; and the dead in Christ will rise first. ¹⁷Then we who are living, who have survived, will be caught away with them in the clouds to meet the Lord in the air. For this reason, we will always be with the Lord. ¹⁸So then, encourage one another with these words.

The Day will Not Surprise Those Walking in the Light

Chapter Five

¹Now about the times and strategic seasons, brothers, you do not need me to write to you. ²For you yourselves know perfectly that the day of the Lord will come just like a thief in the night. ³When they are saying, "Peace and security," then ruin will come upon them suddenly like labor pains upon a woman who is pregnant, and they will surely not escape.

⁴But you, brothers, are not in the darkness, so that the day surprises you like a thief. ⁵For you all are sons of the light and sons of the day. We are not of the night, nor of the darkness. ⁶So therefore, let us not sleep as the rest do, but let us stay alert and clearheaded. ⁷For those who are sleeping, sleep at night; and those who get drunk, get drunk at night. ⁸But since we are of the day, let us be clearheaded, having put on a breastplate of faith and love, and a helmet, the hope of deliverance. ⁹For God has not assigned us to punishment, but to possess salvation through our Lord Jesus Christ, ¹⁰who died for us, in order that whether we are alert in life or asleep in death, we will live together with him. ¹¹Therefore, encourage each other and build one another up, just as you are doing.

Closing Instructions

¹²Now we ask you, brothers, to acknowledge those who labor among you, who preside over you in the Lord and admonish you. ¹³Esteem them highly in love on account of their work. Be at peace among yourselves.

¹⁴We encourage you, brothers, admonish those who avoid their responsibilities, console those who are discouraged, give attention to those who are weak, be patient with everyone. ¹⁵See that no one repay evil for evil, but always pursue the good for one another and everyone.

¹⁶Rejoice always; ¹⁷pray relentlessly; ¹⁸give thanks in all things; for this is the will of God in Christ Jesus for you.

Do Not Suppress the Spirit and His Gifts

[19] Do not suppress the Spirit, [20] do not treat prophecy as if it had no value, [21] but test all of them; hold fast to the good, [22] and keep away from every expression of evil.

[23] But may the God of peace himself sanctify you through and through, and may the complete you, spirit, soul, and body, be preserved blameless at the coming of our Lord Jesus Christ. [24] The one who called you is faithful, and he also will accomplish it.

Closing Greetings

[25] Brothers, pray also concerning us.

[26] Greet all the brothers with a holy kiss.

[27] I place you under obligation, before the Lord, that this letter be read to all the brothers.

[28] The grace of our Lord Jesus Christ be with you. Amen.

2 THESSALONIANS

Chapter One

¹Paul, Silas, and Timothy,

To the church of the Thessalonians which is in God our Father and the Lord Jesus Christ.

²Grace to you and peace from God our Father and the Lord Jesus Christ.

Paul's Thankfulness for the Thessalonians

³We ought to give thanks to God concerning you at all times, brothers, as is appropriate, because your faith is continuing to grow, and the love of each one of you for each other is growing. ⁴As a result, we ourselves boast about you in the congregations of God, telling about your patience and faith in all your persecutions, and the tribulations that you are enduring.

⁵This is proof of God's righteous judgment, that he considered you worthy of the Kingdom of God, for which you are also suffering. ⁶Since it is righteous for God to give back trouble to those who trouble you, ⁷and to give relief to you who are troubled along with us, he will do so when the Lord Jesus is revealed from heaven with his powerful angels ⁸in flames of fire.

He will punish those who were strangers to God, and those who did not obey the gospel of our Lord Jesus. ⁹They will pay the penalty, eternal death, separated from the Lord's presence and from the glory of his power. ¹⁰This will happen on that day when he comes to be glorified with his saints, and to be marveled at by all those who believed, including you, because our testimony among you was believed.

Paul's Prayer for the Thessalonians

¹¹For this reason, we always pray concerning you, that our God consider you worthy of the calling, and that he will, in power, bring your every good intent and every work of faith to completion. ¹²We pray this so that the name of our Lord Jesus might be glorified in you, and you in him, according to the grace of our God and the Lord Jesus Christ.

The Day of the Lord and the Man of Lawlessness

Chapter Two

¹We ask you, brothers, concerning the coming of our Lord Jesus Christ and our meeting with him, ²that you not be easily agitated so that you no longer think clearly, nor are disturbed on account of a spiritual gift, a message, or letter stating that we believe the Day of the Lord has already begun. ³Let no one deceive you in any way, for the apostasy[i] must come first, and the man of lawlessness must be revealed, the son of destruction. ⁴He is the one who opposes, and rises up in pride against, all that is called god or is an object of worship; therefore, he will sit in the house of God proclaiming that he is a god.

⁵Do you remember that I explained these things to you while I was with you? ⁶You also know what is now restraining him, so that he will be revealed in his time. ⁷For the mystery of lawlessness is already working, but only until the one now holding it back is taken away. ⁸Then the lawless one will be

---

[i] Or, "the falling away must come first."

revealed, whom the Lord Jesus will remove by the breath of his lips,[i] and render ineffective when he appears at his coming.[ii] ⁹The coming of the lawless one will be accompanied by the supernatural activity[iii] of Satan with all types of power, lying miracles, and wonders, ¹⁰and in every kind of unrighteousness that delights those who are lost. They are lost because they did not retain the love of the truth so that they might be saved. ¹¹For this reason, God sends a supernatural delusion to them so that they believe what is false, ¹²in order that everyone will be condemned who did not believe the truth, but were pleased by unrighteousness.

¹³But we ought always to thank God concerning you, brothers loved by the Lord, because God chose you from the beginning for salvation[iv] through the sanctifying efforts of the Spirit and trust in the truth. ¹⁴He also called you to this through our gospel so that you might obtain the approval of our Lord Jesus Christ. ¹⁵So then, brothers, keep standing, and continue to hold the traditions that you were taught, whether through our speech or by our letter.

¹⁶Now may our Lord Jesus Christ himself, and God our Father who has loved us, and by his grace has given eternal encouragement and good hope, ¹⁷encourage your hearts and strengthen you in good actions and beneficial speech.

---

[i] See Isaiah 11:4.

[ii] Or, "parousia." Parousia is a technical term that refers to Christ's return. It is also the word Paul uses in verse 9 to speak of Satan's counterfeit parousia, or coming.

[iii] The Greek word "energeia" refers to supernatural energy. It refers to God's energy at work in us, or Satan's energy at work in the world. Also in verse 11.

[iv] Or, "because God chose you as firstfruits of salvation."

Paul's Prayer Request

Chapter Three

¹In addition, brothers, pray for us, that the word of the Lord spread quickly, and is honored as it also was among you; ²and that we might be delivered from warped and evil men. For not everyone has faith. ³The Lord is faithful, he will strengthen you and keep you from the evil one. ⁴We have confidence in the Lord about you, that what we commanded, you are doing and will continue to do. ⁵Now may the Lord guide your hearts into the love of God and the endurance of Christ.

Paul's Example of Hard Work

⁶But we command you, brothers, in the name of our Lord Jesus Christ, to stay away from every brother who is living irresponsibly, and not according to the traditions which they received from us. ⁷For you yourselves know that it is vital to imitate us, since we did not live irresponsibly among you, ⁸nor did we eat bread from anyone without paying for it. We worked night and day in toil and labor so that we would not burden any of you. ⁹It isn't that we did not have the right to receive support, but we did this in order that we might give you an example so that you would imitate us.

Paul Warns Those who are not Willing to Work

¹⁰Even when we were with you, we repeatedly commanded you about this; if anyone is not willing to work, he should not eat, either. ¹¹Now we hear that some are living among you in disorder; they are not working but are meddling in other people's affairs. ¹²In the Lord Jesus Christ, we command and urge such people to live quietly, and work so that they can eat their own bread.

¹³But you, brothers, do not be discouraged in doing good things. ¹⁴However, if anyone will not listen to our message in this letter, pay special attention to that person, and do not associate with him in order that he might be ashamed. ¹⁵Do not regard him as an enemy but correct him as a brother.

Closing Greetings

[16] Now may the Lord of peace himself give you peace through all things in every way. The Lord be with all of you.

[17] This written greeting is by my—Paul's—hand. This is a distinctive sign in every letter. This is how I write.

[18] The grace of our Lord Jesus Christ be with all of you. Amen.

1 TIMOTHY

Chapter One

¹Paul, an apostle of Christ Jesus, in accord with the command of God our Savior, and of our hope, Christ Jesus.

²To Timothy, a true child in faith:

Grace, mercy, and peace from God our Father and Christ Jesus our Lord.

The Problem of False Teachers

³As I encouraged you while I was leaving for Macedonia, remain in Ephesus in order that you might command certain men not to teach inaccurate doctrines, ⁴nor to turn their attention to myths and unending genealogies, which produce endless questions, rather than the plan of God which is by faith. ⁵But the goal of this command is love from a clean heart, a good conscience, and a faith without hypocrisy. ⁶When certain men have abandoned these, they have turned aside to empty chatter. ⁷They want to be teachers of law while they understand neither what they are saying, nor the things about which they give such firm assurances.

⁸But we know that the Law[i] is good, if one uses it as it was meant to be used. ⁹We know this, that law does not exist for the righteous, but for those who ignore law and rebel against it, for the ungodly and sinners, for the unholy and impure, for those who kill their fathers or mothers, for murderers, ¹⁰for those who are sexually immoral, homosexuals, human traffickers, liars, perjurers, and whatever other thing is in conflict with accurate teaching ¹¹that is in accord with the gospel about the glory of blessed God, with which I have been entrusted.

God's Mercy for Paul

¹²I give thanks to Christ Jesus our Lord, who has strengthened me, because he regarded me as faithful and has appointed me to service, ¹³in spite of the fact that I was a slanderer, a persecutor and insolent. But I was shown mercy because I did not understand and acted in unbelief, ¹⁴and the grace of our Lord overflowed in abundance with the faith and love that are in Christ Jesus.

¹⁵This is a faithful message and worthy of full acceptance: that Christ Jesus came into the world to save sinners, among whom I am most prominent. ¹⁶But I was shown mercy on account of this, so that in me, the most prominent of sinners, Christ Jesus might prove his full patience as an example to those who will believe in him for life eternal. ¹⁷Now to the King of the ages, incorruptible, invisible, the only God, be honor and glory forever and ever. Amen.

Fighting the Good Fight

¹⁸I commit this command to you, Timothy my son, according to the prophecies previously given concerning you, in order that with them you might fight the good fight, ¹⁹while you hold to faith and a good conscience, which certain men have pushed away and have shipwrecked their faith. ²⁰Among whom are Hymenaeus and Alexander, whom I have handed over to Satan

---

[i] Or, "law."

so that they might be disciplined and not continue to slander[ii] us.

Instructions to Timothy About Prayer

Chapter Two

¹Therefore, I encourage you, as a first priority, to make requests, prayers, intercession and thanksgiving for all men, ²for kings and all those who are in authority, so that we may pursue a quiet and peaceful life with all godliness and proper behavior. ³This is good, and welcome in the sight of God our Savior, ⁴who wants all men to be saved and to come to an understanding of truth. ⁵For there is one God, also one mediator between God and men, Christ Jesus, a man ⁶who gave himself a ransom on behalf of many, the testimony at its critical time; ⁷for which I myself was appointed a herald and apostle. I speak the truth, I am not lying. I am a teacher of the Gentiles by faith and truth. ⁸So, I want men in every place to pray, while lifting up holy hands apart from anger or doubt.

Worship Propriety

⁹In the same way, I also want women[iii] to make themselves attractive with a respectable outward appearance, with modesty and sensible action; not with elaborate hair styles, gold, pearls, or expensive clothing, ¹⁰but through good works, which is fitting for women who profess reverence for God.

¹¹Let a wife learn in quietness with all deference, ¹²for I do not entrust teaching to a wife, nor should she dominate her husband, but rather she should live with a tranquil spirit. ¹³For Adam was formed first, and then Eve; ¹⁴and Adam was not

---

[ii] Or, "blaspheme."

[iii] Or, "wives." The Greek word can mean women in general, or wives. In this context where Paul has just spoken to men in general, "women" is the best translation. However, in verse 11, where Paul speaks of the woman's husband, "wife" is the best translation.

deceived, but when his wife was deceived, she became disobedient. ¹⁵But a wife will find prosperity in raising children, if the husband and wife[i] abide in faith, love and holiness mixed with sensible action.

Requirements for Church Leadership and Ministry

Chapter Three

¹This is a faithful saying: If anyone sets his sights on being a leader of God's people, he desires an honorable calling. ²Therefore, it is required that the one who gives oversight[ii] be above criticism, a husband to one wife, restrained in the use of wine, sensible, respectable, hospitable, qualified to teach, ³not one who abuses alcohol, not a violent person, but reasonable, not quarrelsome, and not one who loves money. ⁴He must manage his own house well and have obedient children who demonstrate proper behavior. ⁵If someone doesn't understand how to manage his own house, how can he have charge of the church of God? ⁶He must not be a new convert, so that he does not become so proud that he fall under the same judgment as the Accuser.[iii] ⁷He must also have a good name among those on the outside, so that he does not fall under reproach and into the Accuser's trap.

⁸Deacons, in the same way, must be respectable, not two-faced, not devoted to wine, not filled with undisguised greed, ⁹but must hold to the mysteries of the faith with a clean conscience. ¹⁰But these men must also be examined first, then let those who are blameless serve as deacons.

¹¹In the same way, the women who serve must be respectable, not those who engage in slander, restrained in their use of wine, and trustworthy in everything.

---

[i] Or, "they abide in faith, love and holiness . . ." The pronoun has no obvious antecedent.

[ii] Or, "the overseer." This term refers to those who watch over God's flock.

[iii] Traditionally, "devil." The name means to slander or accuse. For this reason, this word is most often translated "Accuser" in this Bible version.

¹²Deacons must be the husband of one wife, one who manages his children and his own household well. ¹³For those who serve well as deacons attain for themselves a good reputation and much boldness in the faith in Christ Jesus.

Teaching People How to Behave in the Church

¹⁴I am writing these things to you hoping to come to you quickly. ¹⁵But if I am delayed, I write so that you know how one must behave in the house of God, which is the church of the living God, the pillar and foundation of the truth.

¹⁶Without any doubt, the mystery of godliness is great:

> God was revealed in flesh;
> He was vindicated by the Spirit;
> He was seen by messengers;
> He was proclaimed in the nations;
> He was believed by the world;
> He was taken up in glory.

Warnings to Timothy About Teachings of Demons

Chapter Four

¹But the Spirit distinctly says that in latter times certain men will revolt against the faith, paying attention to deceiving spirits and teachings of demons. ²These teachings will come through the hypocrisy of liars, each of them whose conscience has been branded with a hot iron. ³They will prevent people from marrying. They will also tell people to stay away from foods which God created to be received with thanksgiving by those who believe and know the truth ⁴that all that God created is good, and that nothing is to be thrown away when it is received with thanksgiving; ⁵for it is consecrated through the word of God and prayer.

⁶By demonstrating these things to the brothers, you will be a good servant of Christ Jesus, being nourished by the words of faith and the good teaching which you have carefully

investigated. ⁷But avoid profane and foolish myths—the type that old women tell. Instead, discipline yourself for godliness; ⁸for physical training is beneficial to a small degree, but godliness is beneficial in all things, since it holds the promise of life now and in the future. ⁹This is a trustworthy report, and worthy of full approval. ¹⁰It is for this purpose that we labor and spare no effort, for we have confidence in the living God, who is a Savior for all men, especially for those who believe.

Personal Instruction to Timothy

¹¹Continue to give commands about these things and teach them. ¹²Let no one think less of you because of your youth, but be an example in word, lifestyle, love, faith, and purity to those who are faithful. ¹³Until I come, continue to give yourself to public reading of the Scripture, encouragement, and teaching. ¹⁴Do not neglect the grace gift in you, which was given to you through prophecy accompanied by the laying on of the hands of the elders.

¹⁵Practice these things, live in them so that your progress might be visible to everyone. ¹⁶Keep yourself and your teaching in check, and continue to do these things; for while doing this you will rescue yourself and those who listen to you.

Relating to Different Age Groups

Chapter Five

¹Do not reprimand an older man, but admonish him as a father. Admonish younger men as brothers, ²older women as mothers, and younger women as sisters, in all purity.

Giving Financial Support to Widows

³Give financial honor[i] to widows who are actually widows. ⁴But if any widow has children or grandchildren, they must first

---

[i] The word "honor" often contained the idea of financial support. In this context, and in verse 17, this is clearly the meaning.

learn to show loyalty to their own house and pay back a pension to compensate their parents. For this is good and welcome in the sight of God. ⁵But the widow who is an actual widow, and who has been left alone, puts her hope in God and perseveres night and day in requests and prayers. ⁶Nevertheless, the widow who lives in self-indulgent luxury has died already, even while she is alive. ⁷Continue to give commands about these things so that they might be above criticism. ⁸But if anyone does not take care of his own, especially those of his household, he has denied the faith and is worse than an unbeliever.

⁹Put a widow on the support list if she was born at least sixty years ago, was the wife of one husband, ¹⁰has a reputation attested by her good works, has brought up children, has shown hospitality to strangers, has washed the feet of the saints, has assisted those who are afflicted, and has pursued every good work.

¹¹But refuse to put a young widow on the support list. For when they are moved by sensual passions, they desire to marry despite their commitment to Christ, ¹²and they are condemned by others because they abandoned their former promise.[ii] ¹³At the same time, they learn also to be idle, going around from house to house; and not only idle, but also chatterboxes and meddlers, saying things that they should not be saying. ¹⁴For this reason, I want young widows to marry, to bear children, to manage a household, and to give the adversary no opportunity for abusive slander. ¹⁵For already some have turned aside after Satan. ¹⁶If any believing woman has widows in the family, she must help them so that the church is not burdened, so that it might help those who are actual widows.

[ii] Paul's advice in verse 14 is that young widows remarry instead of making the commitments necessary to being on the widows' list. He is concerned that most will back out of such a commitment.

1 Timothy 5:17

Financial Support of Elders who Manage

¹⁷The elders who manage well are worthy of double financial honor,[i] especially those who labor in word and teaching. ¹⁸For the Scripture says,

> "Do not muzzle the ox while he is threshing grain,"[ii]

and

> "The worker is worthy of his wage."[iii]

¹⁹Do not believe an accusation against an elder, except upon the testimony of two or three witnesses. ²⁰Rebuke those who are found to be sinning in front of everyone, so that the rest may have reverential fear.

Various Instructions to Timothy

²¹I declare before God, Christ Jesus, and the elect angels, that you should obey these things without jumping to conclusions, and without doing anything from favoritism.

²²Do not act too quickly to lay hands on anyone, and in this way share in the sins of others.[iv] Keep yourself pure.

²³From now on, do not drink water alone, but mix in a little wine on account of your stomach and your frequent sicknesses.

²⁴The sins of some men are plain to see, leading the way before them into judgment, but for other men, their sins pursue them into judgment. ²⁵In the same way, good works are plain to see; even those that are not plain to see cannot be hidden.

---

[i] See the footnote for verse 3.

[ii] Deuteronomy 25:4

[iii] Matthew 10:10

[iv] The second half of this verse is not a new thought. It explains the reason for the prohibition in the first part of the verse.

Advice for Masters and Slaves

Chapter Six

¹All who are under the yoke of compelled service[v] must regard their own masters as worthy of all honor, so that the name of God and our teaching are not slandered. ²Those who have believing masters must not think less of them because they are brothers, but must serve them more than ever, because those who receive the service are believers and cherished friends.

Keeping Free from Overfondness for Money

Teach these things and encourage with them. ³If anyone spreads a different teaching and does not assent to the trustworthy words of our Lord Jesus Christ and with teaching that agrees with godliness, ⁴he is proud and understands nothing, but has a sick desire for debates and arguments about words. Out of such things come jealousy, discord, slanders, evil assumptions, ⁵and the constant arguing of men whose minds do not function and who are robbed of the truth. They think that godliness is a means of earning a living.

⁶But when accompanied by contentment, godliness is a great means of earning a living. ⁷For we brought nothing into the world, and since we cannot carry anything out, ⁸if we have food and covering,[vi] we shall be satisfied with these. ⁹But those who desire to become rich fall into temptation and a trap, and into many foolish and harmful desires, which drown men in the depths of ruin and destruction. ¹⁰For an overfondness for money is a root of all the evils, which some by being devoted to it, have been led away from the faith and have pierced themselves with severe grief.

How Timothy Should Live

¹¹But you, O man of God, flee these things and pursue righteousness, godliness, faith, love, perseverance, and gentleness. ¹²Fight the good fight of faith. Take firm hold of the eternal life

---

[v] Or, "slavery."

[vi] The Greek word could refer to clothing or shelter.

to which you were called when you also made your good confession in front of many witnesses. ¹³I command you in the sight of God, who gives life to all things, and Christ Jesus, who gave testimony before Pontius Pilate—the good confession— ¹⁴that you keep the command without blemish and beyond criticism until our Lord Jesus Christ appears. ¹⁵He will put his appearance on display at his own strategic time, he who is the blessed and only Sovereign, the King of kings and Lord of lords, ¹⁶who alone possesses immortality, and is dwelling in unapproachable light, whom no man has seen nor is he able to see. To him be honor, and eternal authority. Amen.

Appropriate Use of Wealth

¹⁷Command those who are wealthy in this present age not be haughty, nor to place their hope in the uncertainty of wealth, but rather upon God who richly gives us all things to enjoy. ¹⁸Command them to do good, to be rich in good works, to be generous and prepared to share. ¹⁹By doing this, they will store up for themselves a good foundation for what is about to come, so that they might take hold of that which is genuinely life.

Closing Thoughts

²⁰O Timothy, guard the truth deposited in you by avoiding profane and foolish talk, and the opposing arguments of what is falsely called knowledge. ²¹Some, by professing this, have wandered from the faith. Grace be with you.

2 TIMOTHY

Chapter One

¹Paul, an apostle of Christ Jesus through the will of God, in agreement with the promise of life in Christ Jesus,

²To Timothy, my cherished child:

Grace, mercy, and peace from God our Father and Christ Jesus our Lord.

Timothy's Sincere Faith

³I am grateful to God, whom I worship with a clean conscience in the same way my ancestors did, as night and day I always make mention of you in my prayers. ⁴Because I have remembered your tears, I long to see you so that I might be filled with joy. ⁵I have remembered your sincere faith, which first lived in your grandmother Lois, and in your mother Eunice, and I am convinced that it is also in you.

⁶For this reason, I remind you to rekindle the flames of the gift of God's grace, which is in you because I laid my hands on you. ⁷God has not given you a spirit of cowardice, but a spirit of power, love, and good sense.

2 Timothy 1:8

Never Be Ashamed of the Ways of the Lord

⁸Therefore, do not be ashamed of the testimony of our Lord nor of me, his prisoner, but join in suffering for the gospel through the power of God. ⁹He has saved us and called us to a holy calling, not through our works, but through his own intention and grace, which was given to us in Christ Jesus before time began. ¹⁰But now it has been made known through the appearance of our Savior Christ Jesus, who rendered death ineffective and brought life and immortality to light through the gospel, ¹¹for which I was appointed a herald, apostle, and teacher. ¹²It is for this reason that I also suffer these things, but I am not ashamed; for I know him whom I have believed, and I am convinced that he is able to guard my life's deposit until that day.

¹³Hold on to the pattern of trustworthy words, which you have heard from me, in the faith and love that are in Christ Jesus. ¹⁴You must guard, through the Holy Spirit who is living in us, the good deposit entrusted to you.

¹⁵You know this, that everyone in Asia turned away from me, Phygelus and Hermogenes included. ¹⁶May the Lord grant mercy to the household of Onesiphorus, because he often refreshed me and was not ashamed of my chains, ¹⁷but when he came to Rome, he sought diligently for me and found me; ¹⁸and you know very well all the ways he served in Ephesus. May the Lord grant this to him, that he find mercy from the Lord on that day.

Be Strong in God's Grace

Chapter Two

¹You then, my child, be strong in the grace that is in Jesus Christ, ²and what you have heard from me among many witnesses, entrust these things to faithful men who will be qualified to teach others. ³Unite with me in suffering as a good soldier of Christ Jesus. ⁴No one who is serving as a soldier gets

involved in the normal pursuits of life, so that he can please the one who recruited him. ⁵In addition, if anyone competes in an athletic contest, he is not crowned the winner unless he competes according to the rules. ⁶The farmer who toils in the field must be the first to receive the fruit of that field. ⁷Understand what I am saying properly, for the Lord will give you such understanding in everything.

⁸Remember Jesus Christ, from the seed of David, and who was raised from the dead. This is according to my gospel ⁹for which I endure suffering even up to being imprisoned as a criminal, but the word of God is not bound. ¹⁰For this reason, I endure all things because of the elect,ⁱ so that they also might obtain the salvation that is in Christ Jesus along with eternal glory.

¹¹This is a reliable message, namely that:

> If we die with him, we will also live with him.
> ¹²If we endure, we will also reign with him.
> If we deny him, he will also deny us.
> ¹³If we are unfaithful, he remains faithful,
>   for he is not able to deny Himself.

¹⁴Make mention of these things while you are testifying in the sight of God, and do not argue about words, which is not useful, and in addition it ruins those who are listening. ¹⁵Make every effort to present yourself trustworthy to God, a worker who has no need to be ashamed, one who shares the word of truth without distortion. ¹⁶But avoid profane and foolish words, for they will greatly increase ungodliness, ¹⁷and their message will eat away like a cancer, as happened with Hymenaeus and Philetus, ¹⁸who have wandered away from the truth, saying that the resurrection has happened already, and they have overthrown the faith of some people. ¹⁹Nevertheless, the firm foundation of God stands, having this seal,

---

ⁱ The term translated "elect" is a reference to those who are called by God to true faith that perseveres.

"The Lord knows those who are his,"[i]

and

"Everyone who calls on the name of the Lord must separate from unrighteousness."[ii]

Keeping a High Value Spiritual House

²⁰Now in a large house, there are not only gold and silver vessels, but also wood and clay vessels. Some are of high value, and some have little value. ²¹So, if anyone has cleansed himself from these things of lesser value, he will be a valuable vessel, sanctified, useful to the Master, equipped for every good work.

²²Flee from the passionate desires of youth, and pursue righteousness, faith, love, and peace, along with all those who call upon the Lord from a clean heart. ²³Avoid foolish and ignorant debates because you know that they produce quarrels. ²⁴For the Lord's servant must not be quarrelsome, but he is to be gentle to everyone, qualified to teach, and patient in the face of evil. ²⁵He must humbly instruct those who oppose him so that God might grant them repentance unto the knowledge of truth, ²⁶and that they may regain their senses and be freed from the snare of the Accuser,[iii] since they were captured by him to do his will.

Those with an Appearance of Godliness but No Power

Chapter Three

¹But know this, that in the last days there will be dangerous times. ²For men will be self-centered, lovers of wealth, boastful, proud, slanderous, disobedient to parents, ungrateful, unholy, ³unloving, unwilling to reconcile with others, accusers, without

---

[i] Numbers 16:5 Septuagint (a Greek translation of the Hebrew Bible)

[ii] This quote may be from an early baptismal formula.

[iii] Traditionally, "devil." The name means to slander or accuse. For this reason, this word is most often translated "Accuser" in this Bible version.

self-control, untamed, haters of the good, ⁴betrayers, thoughtless, swollen with conceit, and lovers of pleasure rather than lovers of God. ⁵They will have an appearance of godliness, but they will deny its power. Keep away from these men.

⁶For among them are those who make their way into households and take foolish women captive, women who are given over to sins and are led by a variety of passions. ⁷These men are always learning and never able to come to the knowledge of truth. ⁸But in like manner Jannes and Jambres resisted Moses. In the same way also, these men oppose the truth. They are men whose minds are destroyed by perversity. They are useless to the faith. ⁹But they will not make much progress, for just as with those men, their folly will be evident to everyone.

Everyone who Desires to Live a Godly Life will Face Opposition

¹⁰Now you have followed my teaching, my manner of life, my purpose, my faith, my patience, my love, my endurance, ¹¹my persecutions, and my sufferings, such as the things that happened to me in Antioch, Iconium, and Lystra. You know what sort of persecutions I endured, and the Lord rescued me from them all. ¹²But all those who want to live a godly life in Christ Jesus will also be persecuted, ¹³and evil men and charlatans will become even worse, deceiving and being deceived. ¹⁴Now you must remain in those things you have learned and come to trust, knowing those from whom you have learned them, ¹⁵because you have known the holy Scriptures from childhood. These Scriptures are able to make you wise for salvation through faith that is in Jesus Christ.

All Scripture is Inspired by God

¹⁶All Scripture is inspired by God, and useful for teaching, for reproof, for correction, for training in righteousness, ¹⁷so that a man of God might be proficient, equipped for every good work.

Preach the Word

Chapter Four

¹I solemnly charge you before God and Christ Jesus, who is going to judge the living and the dead, and who will appear in his Kingdom—²you must preach the word. Press forward when it is convenient and when it is inconvenient, reprove, rebuke, and encourage with all patience and teaching. ³For there will be a time when people will not have patience for accurate teaching, but they will accumulate for themselves teachers who will tickle their ears according to their own passions. ⁴They will turn from listening to the truth and will go astray following myths. ⁵But you, stay clearheaded in all things; endure suffering, do the work of an evangelist, be intent on fulfilling your ministry.

⁶For I am already being poured out as a drink offering, and the time of my departure is at hand. ⁷I have fought the good fight, I have completed the race, I have kept watch over the faith. ⁸Still, there is a crown of righteousness reserved for me, which the Lord, the righteous judge will confer on me on that day, and not only me, but also all those who have loved *the fact* that he will appear.

Closing Instructions

⁹Make it your goal to come to me soon, ¹⁰for Demas, because he loved this present age, has deserted me and gone to Thessalonica. Crescens has gone to Galatia. Titus has gone to Dalmatia. ¹¹Luke is the only one with me. Take Mark along and bring him with you, for he is useful to me in ministry. ¹²I have also sent Tychicus to Ephesus. ¹³When you come, bring the cloak which I left in Troas with Carpus, and the scrolls, most of all the parchments.

¹⁴Alexander the coppersmith has caused much harm to me. The Lord will repay him according to his works. ¹⁵Look out for him yourself, for he strongly opposed our teachings.

¹⁶No one came to my assistance at my first defense, but everyone deserted me. May it not be counted against them.

¹⁷But the Lord was present with me and gave me strength, so that through me the proclamation of the gospel might be presented completely, and all the Gentiles might hear; and I was rescued from the lion's mouth. ¹⁸The Lord will rescue me from every evil work and will deliver me safely into his heavenly kingdom. To him be glory forever and ever. Amen.

Closing Greetings

¹⁹Greet Priscilla, Aquila, and the household of Onesiphorus.

²⁰Erastus remained in Corinth, and I left Trophimus behind in Miletus because he was sick.

²¹Make every effort to come before winter.

Eubulus greets you, also Pudens, Linus, Claudia, and all the brothers.

²²The Lord be with your spirit. Grace be with you.

TITUS

Chapter One

¹Paul, a servant of God, and an apostle of Jesus Christ, in agreement with the faith of God's elect,[i] and the understanding of truth that aligns with godliness ²and the hope of eternal life. God, who does not lie, promised this before time began, ³but he revealed his word at his own strategic time through preaching. I was entrusted with this preaching by the command of God our Savior.

⁴To Titus, a true child in the common faith.

Grace and peace from God our Father and Christ Jesus our Savior.

Requirements for Church Leadership and Ministry

⁵I left you in Crete for this purpose, so that you might put the items that were left to do in order and appoint elders in each city. As I instructed you, ⁶an elder must be blameless, a husband of one wife, with believing children who are not open to the charge of being uncontrolled or rebellious. ⁷For the one who

---

[i] The term translated "elect" is a reference to those who are called by God to true faith that perseveres.

gives oversight[ii] as God's manager, must be blameless, not brazen, not inclined to anger, not one who abuses alcohol, not a violent person, and not filled with undisguised greed. ⁸On the contrary, he must be hospitable, one who loves what is good, sensible, just, godly, one who has sexual self-control, ⁹and holds tightly to the faithful word that agrees with my teaching, so that he also has the ability to encourage with accurate teaching, and to rebuke those who speak against it.

¹⁰For there are many rebellious men, meaningless talkers and deceivers, especially those from the circumcised, ¹¹who must be silenced. They overthrow whole households by teaching what they should not for the sake of shameful gain. ¹²One from among them, a prophet of their own has said,

> "Cretans are always liars, evil untamed beasts, unproductive appetites."[iii]

¹³This testimony is true. For this reason, rebuke them harshly so that they may become sound in the faith, ¹⁴no longer paying attention to Jewish myths and commandments of men who are turning from the truth. ¹⁵All things are clean to the clean, but to the defiled nothing is clean. On the contrary, both their mind and their conscience are defiled. ¹⁶They confess that they know God, but they deny him with their actions. They are detestable and disruptive, and of no value for any good work.

Practical Advice for Various Groups in the Congregation

Chapter Two

¹But you, speak what is suitable for sound doctrine. ²Older men must be restrained in their use of wine, respectable, sensible, sound in faith, in love, and in patience.

[ii] Or, "the overseer." This term refers to those who watch over God's flock.

[iii] The phrase appears in a proverb that is attributed to the Cretan Epimenides in the 6th century B.C.

³Older women, in just the same way must have a reverent disposition, not given to slander, not in bondage to much wine, and teaching what is good, ⁴so that they may teach the young women to love their husbands, to love their children, ⁵and to be sensible, pure, and good homemakers who willingly submit to their own husbands so that the word of God might not be slandered.

⁶Likewise, encourage the young men to use good sense ⁷in all circumstances. Put yourself on display as a pattern of good deeds, by teaching that is solid, with proper behavior, ⁸and with sound speech that cannot be condemned, so that anyone who opposes you will be put to shame because they do not have anything bad to say about us.

⁹Encourage slaves to willingly submit to their own masters in everything, to be pleasant and not to argue with them. ¹⁰Encourage them not to embezzle, but to demonstrate all good faith, so that they will make the teaching of God our Savior attractive in all things.

¹¹For the grace of God has appeared, bringing deliverance to all men, ¹²training us so that we disregard ungodliness and worldly desires, and live sensibly, righteously, and in a godly manner in this current age, ¹³while we look to the blessed hope and the time when the glory of our great God and Savior, Jesus Christ, appears. ¹⁴He gave himself for us to redeem us from all lawlessness, and to purify for himself a people as a treasured possession who are zealous for good works.

¹⁵Speak these things, encouraging and rebuking with all authority. Let no one disregard you.

Chapter Three

¹Remind them to be willing to submit to rulers and authorities, to be obedient, to be prepared for every good work, ²to slander no one, not to be quarrelsome, to be kind, and to demonstrate every kindness to all men.

God's Kindness and Love Freed Us from Foolishness and Hatred

³For we too were once foolish ourselves, disobedient, being deceived and enslaved by various kinds of desires and pleasures, spending our lives in wickedness and jealousy, hated, and hating each other. ⁴But when the kindness and love for mankind of God our Savior appeared, ⁵he saved us, not by works of righteousness which we ourselves have done, but by his mercy. He saved us through the washing of rebirth, and renewal by the Holy Spirit, ⁶whom he richly poured out upon us through Jesus Christ our Savior, ⁷so that, being justified by the Savior's grace, we might become heirs of eternal life in accord with our hope. ⁸This is a trustworthy message, and I want you to speak with certainty about these things, so that those who have believed in God might give serious consideration to devoting themselves to good works. These things are good and profitable for men.

Closing Instructions and Greetings

⁹But avoid foolish debates, genealogies, arguments, and the quarrels of legal experts; for they offer no advantage and are worthless. ¹⁰Refuse to associate with such a divisive[i] man after a first and second warning, ¹¹knowing that such a person as this is perverted, committing sin, and stands self-condemned.

¹²When I send Artemas or Tychicus to you, make every effort to come to me in Nicopolis, for I have made up my mind to spend the winter there. ¹³Do your best to help Zenas, the legal expert, and Apollos on their way, so that they do not lack anything they need. ¹⁴Our people must also learn to devote themselves to good works in order to meet urgent needs, so that they are not unfruitful.

¹⁵Everyone who is with me sends their greetings. Greet those who love us in the faith.

Grace be with all of you.

---

[i] Or, "heretical."

PHILEMON

¹Paul, a prisoner of Christ Jesus, and Timothy our brother,

To Philemon, our cherished friend and fellow worker, ²and to Apphia, our sister, and Archippus, our fellow soldier, and the church that meets in their house.

³Grace to you and peace from God our Father and the Lord Jesus Christ.

Paul's Thanksgiving for Philemon

⁴I give thanks to my God, always making mention of you at my prayer times. ⁵I have heard of your love and your faith which you have for the Lord Jesus and for all the saints. ⁶I pray that the fellowship produced by your faith might be energized by the knowledge of every good thing which is in us for Christ; ⁷for I have much joy and encouragement because of your love, and because the hearts of the saints have been refreshed through you, brother.

Paul's Request for Onesimus

⁸Therefore, although I have much confidence in Christ to command you to do what is appropriate, ⁹because of love, I encourage you instead—since I am such a one as Paul, an old

man, and now also a prisoner of Christ Jesus—¹⁰I encourage you concerning my child, whom I have borne in my chains, Onesimus.ⁱ ¹¹He was once worthless to you, but now he is worthwhile to both you and me.

¹²I have sent him back again to you, the one who is my heart, ¹³whom I desired to withhold for myself, in order that he might serve me in my chains for the gospel on your behalf. ¹⁴But I did not desire to do anything apart from your input, so that your goodness might not result from compulsion, but from free will. ¹⁵For perhaps he was parted for a season for this reason, so that you might receive him back eternally, ¹⁶no longer as a slave, but more than a slave, a cherished brother, especially to me, but how much more to you, both in the flesh and in the Lord.

¹⁷Therefore, if you are a partner with me, receive him as you would me. ¹⁸But if he has harmed you in anything, or owes a debt, charge it to my account. ¹⁹I, Paul, have written this with my hand. I will compensate you for damages. I need not remind you that you also owe yourself to me in return. ²⁰Yes, brother, I would like to rejoiceⁱⁱ over you in the Lord; refresh my heart in Christ.

Closing Instructions and Greetings

²¹I have written to you convinced of your obedience, knowing that you will do even more than I have asked.

²²But in addition, prepare a guest room for me. For I hope that through your prayers I will be graciously given to you.

²³Epaphras, my fellow-prisoner in Christ Jesus, sends his greetings to you, ²⁴as well as my fellow workers, Mark, Aristarchus, Demas, and Luke.

²⁵The grace of our Lord Jesus Christ be with your spirit. Amen.

ⁱ The name "Onesimus" means "the useful one," or "the worthwhile one."

ⁱⁱ Paul is using a wordplay. The word he uses to speak of rejoicing is onimamai, which is the word that Onesimus' name is built upon.

HEBREWS

God Has Spoken through His Son

Chapter One

¹God spoke to our fathers long ago by the prophets at many times and in a variety of ways. ²In these last days he has spoken to us by his Son, whom he appointed as heir of all things—through whom also he made the ages. ³He is the reflection of God's glorious light, the express image of his invisible reality, who maintains all things by the word of his power. When he had made cleansing for sins available, he sat on the right hand of the Majesty on high. ⁴He became so much greater than the angels in the same way that he inherited a far more valuable name than theirs.

The Son is Far above the Angels

⁵For to whom among the angels has he said at any time,

"You are my Son. Today I have fathered you"?[i]

And again,

---

[i] Psalm 2:7

"I will be a Father to him, and he will be a Son to me"?[ii]

⁶Then, again when he brought the firstborn into the inhabited world, he said,

"And let all the angels of God show him reverence."[iii]

⁷He also said of the angels,

"He who makes his angels winds, and his ministers flames of fire."[iv]

⁸But about the Son,

"Your throne, O God, is forever and ever, and the righteous scepter is the scepter of your kingdom. ⁹You have loved righteousness and hated lawlessness. For this reason God, your God, has anointed you with the oil of gladness above your associates."[v]

¹⁰And,

"At the beginning you, O Lord, you established the earth, and the heavens are the work of your hands. ¹¹They will cease to exist, but you remain; and all things will become obsolete like a garment, ¹²and like a cloak you will roll them up, as a garment they will also be altered. But you are the same, and your years will never fail."[vi]

¹³But to whom among the angels has he said at any time,

[ii] 2 Samuel 7:14

[iii] See Psalm 97:7 and Deuteronomy 32:14 Septuagint (a Greek translation of the Hebrew Old Testament).

[iv] Psalm 104:4

[v] Psalm 45:6-7

[vi] Psalm 102:25-27

"Sit at my right hand until I appoint your enemies as a footstool for your feet."[i]

¹⁴Are not all of them serving spirits sent out for service on account of those who will inherit salvation?

God Testified to Salvation in Jesus

Chapter Two

¹For this reason, we must pay special attention to the things that we have heard, so that we do not slip away from the faith. ²For if the message that was spoken through angels was reliable, and every violation and disobedience received just payment, ³how will we escape punishment if we refuse to acknowledge so great a salvation? This salvation first began to be spoken through the Lord, and has been confirmed for us by those who heard it. ⁴God was also testifying to this salvation with signs, wonders, various miracles, and allotments of the Holy Spirit given according to his will.

Jesus Became Like His Brothers

⁵For he did not subject the world that was to exist to angels—the inhabited world about which we are speaking. ⁶But someone has testified somewhere saying,

"What is man that you remember him, or a son of man that you watch over him? ⁷You have made him a little less than angels, you have crowned him with glory and honor, and have appointed him over the works of your hands. ⁸You placed all things in subjection under his feet."[ii]

For when he made all things subject to him, he left nothing that wasn't subject to him. Now we do not yet see all things

---

[i] Psalm 110:1

[ii] Psalm 8:4-5

placed in subjection to him. ⁹But we do see Jesus, the one who was made a little less than the angels, having been crowned with glory and honor on account of his suffering and death, so that by the grace of God he might taste death in everyone's place.

¹⁰For it was proper for him, for whom and through whom all things exist, and who will bring many sons to glory, to bring the founder of their salvation to complete maturity through suffering. ¹¹For both the one who sanctifies and those who are sanctified are all from one *Father*. For this reason, he is not ashamed to call them brothers, ¹²and said,

> "I will report your name to my brothers, in the midst of the assembly I will praise you."[iii]

¹³And again,

> "I will put my trust in him;"[iv]

and again,

> "Look, I and the children that God has given to me."[v]

¹⁴Therefore, since the children share blood and flesh, he himself also shared them, in order that through death he might render the one who held power over death powerless; that is the Accuser,[vi] ¹⁵and might liberate them, namely, those who were subject to slavery all their lives through the fear of death. ¹⁶For surely he did not take on the nature of angels, but he took on the nature of Abraham's seed. ¹⁷Therefore, he was obligated to be like his brothers in every way, so that he might become a merciful and faithful high priest focused on the things of God, to make atonement for the sins of the people. ¹⁸Because of what he himself suffered when he was tempted, he is able to help those who are being tempted.

[iii] Psalm 22:22

[iv] Isaiah 8:17

[v] Isaiah 8:18

[vi] Traditionally, "devil." The name means to slander or accuse.

Jesus is Worthy of more Honor than Moses

Chapter Three

¹Therefore, holy brothers, you who participate in a heavenly calling, pay attention to Jesus, the apostle and high priest of our confession of faith. ²He was faithful to the one who commissioned him, as also Moses was in his entire house. ³For he was considered worthy of more honor than Moses, in just the same way as the builder of the house has more honor than the house. ⁴For every house is built by someone, but the builder of all things is God. ⁵Moses also was faithful in all his house as a servant, for a testimony of the things that would be spoken in the future, ⁶but Christ was faithful as a son over his house. We are his house, if we hold firmly to our confidence and our hope, which is our pride and joy.

The Consequence of Unbelief

⁷Therefore, just as the Holy Spirit says,

> "Today, if you hear his voice, ⁸do not harden your hearts, as in the rebellion, during the day of testing in the wilderness, ⁹where your fathers tried me by testing me, though they saw my works for ¹⁰forty years. Therefore, I was indignant with that generation and said, 'They are constantly mislead by their heart, and they did not understand my ways.' ¹¹As I swore in my anger, they will not enter into my rest."[i]

¹²Watch, my brothers, so that none of you have an evil and unbelieving heart that falls away from the living God. ¹³But encourage each other each day, as long as it is called "Today," so that none of you is hardened by sin's pleasures. ¹⁴For we have become partners of Christ, if we hold firmly to our initial confidence steadfast until the end—¹⁵as was stated,

---

[i] Psalm 95:7-11

"Today, if you hear his voice, do not harden your hearts, as in the rebellion."[ii]

[16]For who rebelled when they heard? Certainly, it was all those who came out of Egypt because of Moses, wasn't it? [17]With whom was he angry for forty years? It was those who sinned, whose corpses littered the desert, wasn't it? [18]And to whom did he swear that they could not enter into his rest, if not those who refused to believe? [19]Now we see that they were not able to enter because they refused to believe.

Stepping into Sabbath Rest

Chapter Four

[1]Therefore, while a promise remains to enter into his rest, be careful that none of you appear to have failed to attain it. [2]For we also have had the good news shared with us, just as they also did, but the message they heard did not benefit them, since it was not mingled with faith by those who heard. [3]For we who have believed enter that rest, just as he has said,

"As I swore in my anger, they will not enter into my rest,"[iii]

and yet his works have been established from the founding of the world. [4]For he has spoken somewhere about the seventh day in this way,

"And God rested on the seventh day from all of his works."[iv]

[5]And again in this Scripture,

"They will not enter into my rest."[v]

[ii] Psalm 95:7-8
[iii] Psalm 95:11
[iv] Genesis 2:2
[v] Psalm 95:11

⁶Therefore, since there is still an opening for some to enter it, and those who earlier had the good news shared with them did not enter into it because of stubborn disobedience, ⁷he again appoints a certain day, "Today," saying by David after so much time, just as it was said before,

> "Today, if you hear his voice, do not harden your hearts."[i]

⁸For if Joshua had brought them to a place of rest, he would not have spoken concerning another day after these things. ⁹So, a Sabbath rest is still available for the people of God. ¹⁰For the one who has entered into his rest, also himself rests from his works, just as God did from his own. ¹¹Therefore, let us do our best to enter into that rest, so that no one fall by following the same pattern of stubborn unbelief.

¹²For the Word of God is living and energized, sharper than every two-edged sword, penetrating so far as to divide the soul and spirit, both the joints and marrow, discerning the thoughts and intents of the heart; ¹³there is nothing in creation hidden from God's sight, for all things are naked and exposed to his eyes, the one to whom we give account.

Approaching the Throne of Grace with Boldness

¹⁴Therefore, since we have a great high priest who has passed through the heavens, Jesus the Son of God, let us hold on to our confession of faith. ¹⁵For we do not have a high priest who is not able to sympathize with our weaknesses, but one that was tempted in everything just like us, yet without sin. ¹⁶So, let us continue to come near to the throne of grace with boldness, so that we might receive mercy and find grace to help us at just the right time.

---

[i] Psalm 95:7-8

A High Priest who Understands Our Weaknesses

Chapter Five

¹For every high priest chosen from among men is appointed for men over the things that concern God, so he can offer gifts and sacrifices for sins. ²He is in a position to sympathize with the ignorant and deceived, since he himself is also prone to weakness. ³Because of this, he is obligated to offer sacrifices for sins, not only for the people, but for himself in just the same way. ⁴In addition, no one takes this honor for himself, but he is called by God, just as Aaron was.

⁵In this same way Christ also did not honor himself in order to become a high priest, but the one who spoke said to him,

"You are my Son. Today I have fathered you."[ii]

⁶As he also says in another Scripture,

"You are a priest forever according to the order of Melchizedek."[iii]

⁷In the days of his flesh, Jesus offered both prayers and requests, with an intense outcry and tears, to the one who was able to deliver him from death; and he was heard because of his reverential fear. ⁸Though he was a Son, he learned obedience from what he suffered. ⁹When he was made complete, he became the source of eternal salvation for all those who obey him. ¹⁰He is addressed by God as a priest according to the order of Melchizedek.

The Importance of Solid Food

¹¹We have much to share about this, but it is difficult to explain, since you have become careless in how you listen. ¹²For by this time, you should be teachers, instead, you again need someone to teach you the foundational principles of God's revelations; you need milk instead of solid food. ¹³For

---

[ii] Psalm 2:7

[iii] Psalm 110:4

anyone who partakes of milk remains inexperienced in the message of righteousness, for he is a child. ¹⁴But solid food is for adults, the ones who have, by their practice, trained their senses to distinguish both good and evil.

Growing Toward Maturity

Chapter Six

¹Therefore, after we have left the foundational teaching about Christ, let us continue to progress toward maturity, not building again the foundation of repentance from lifeless works, faith in God, ²teaching about baptisms, the laying on of hands, the resurrection from death, and eternal judgment. ³We will do this, if God permits.

The Danger of Falling Away

⁴For it is impossible for those who were once given light, who have tasted the heavenly gift, who have become partners of Holy Spirit, ⁵and who have tasted the delightfulness of the word of God and the powers of the age to come, ⁶when they fall away, to bring them back again to repentance. It is impossible because they are personally crucifying the Son of God and exposing him to scorn. ⁷For land that has drunk the rain that often falls upon it, and has born plants appropriate for those who cultivate it, receives the blessing of God; ⁸but land that brings forth thorns and thistles is useless and near to a curse. Its destiny is burning fire.

⁹But we are convinced of better things about you, cherished friends, things that result in salvation, although we are speaking in this way. ¹⁰For God is not unjust, and will not forget your work and the love you have shown for his name, since you have served his saints, and are still serving them. ¹¹But we desire that each of you show the same eagerness to have the full assurance of hope until the end, ¹²in order that you do not become careless, but imitators of those who inherit the promises through faith and patience.

Holding Firmly to the Promises of God

¹³For when God made a vow to Abraham, since he had no one greater by whom he could swear, he swore by himself ¹⁴saying,

> "I will surely bless you, and I will surely multiply you."ⁱ

¹⁵In this way, after Abraham had demonstrated patience, he attained the promise.

¹⁶For men swear by one who is greater than they are, and with them, the oath provides a confirmation to end every dispute. ¹⁷In the same way, because God wanted to show the heirs of his promise the unchangeable character of his purpose even more clearly, he guaranteed it with an oath. ¹⁸He did this so that through two unchangeable things, in which it is impossible for God to lie, we who have taken refuge in him have strong encouragement to hold firmly to the hope that is in view. ¹⁹We have this hope as an anchor for our souls, safe and certain, and which enters the Most Holy Place behind the veil, ²⁰where Jesus, who has gone before us as a forerunner, has entered on our behalf; since he has become a high priest forever according to the order of Melchizedek.

Melchizedek

Chapter Seven

¹For this Melchizedek, king of Salem, priest of the Most High God, met together with Abraham, who was returning from cutting the kings to pieces, and blessed him. ²Abraham shared a tenth of everything with him. His name first means "king of righteousness," and then king of Salem, which means "king of peace." ³Without father, without mother, without traceable lineage, having no beginning of his days nor end to his life, but similar to the Son of God, he remains a priest without ceasing.

ⁱ Genesis 22:17

⁴Now you see how great this man was, to whom the patriarch Abraham gave a tenth from the best of the plunder. ⁵On the one hand, the sons of Levi who receive the priestly office have a command in the Law to receive a tenth from the people, that is, from their brothers, even though they come from the loins of Abraham. ⁶But the one whose lineage is not traced from them received a tenth from Abraham, and blessed the one who had the promises. ⁷Now, without any argument, the lesser is blessed by the greater. ⁸In the case of the priests, men who face death receive the tenth, but in the case of Melchizedek, the tenth is received by the one who is certified as alive. ⁹And, so to speak, even Levi who receives the tenth, paid the tenth through Abraham, ¹⁰for he was still in the loins of his father when Melchizedek met together with him.

Jesus is a Priest Like Melchizedek

¹¹Therefore, if moral perfection came through the Levitical priesthood (for the people were given the Law at the time of the priesthood), what need was still there for another priest to arise according to the order of Melchizedek, and not one identified with the order of Aaron? ¹²Indeed, when the priesthood is changed, it must follow that there is also a change of law. ¹³For the one of whom these things are spoken was the member of another tribe, one from which no one had devoted himself to service at the altar. ¹⁴It is plain to see that our Lord originated from Judah, and with respect to that tribe, Moses said nothing about the priesthood. ¹⁵This is still more clear if another priest is raised up according to the likeness of Melchizedek, ¹⁶one who has not come to this priesthood through the law's requirement of physical descent, but through the power of an indestructible life. ¹⁷For it is said of him,

> "You are a priest forever, according to the order of Melchizedek."[i]

---

[i] Psalm 110:4

¹⁸For on the one hand, the command that came before was nullified because it is weak and useless ¹⁹(for the law did not perfect anyone), but it is also an introduction of a better hope through which we draw near to God.

²⁰And it certainly was not without an oath—for Levitical priests became priests apart from an oath—²¹but he became a priest with an oath through the one who said to him,

> "The Lord has sworn, and will not regret it, 'You are a priest forever.'"[ii]

²²Jesus has become the guarantor of a better covenant by this oath.

Jesus is a Permanent High Priest

²³There are many priests who have served, because they were restrained by death from continuing in office, ²⁴but because Jesus will remain forever, he holds his priesthood permanently. ²⁵Therefore, he is able to save altogether and forever those who draw near to God through him, since he always lives to intercede for them.

²⁶For it was fitting that we should have such a high priest as this, holy, free from evil, undefiled, separated from sinners, and exalted higher than the heavens; ²⁷he does not have a daily need, like those high priests, to offer sacrifices for his own sins first, then for the people, for he did this once for all when he offered up himself. ²⁸For the Law appoints men as high priests who have weakness, but the word of the oath, the one that came after the Law, appoints a Son who has been made perfect forever.

[ii] Psalm 110:4

High Priest of a New and Better Covenant

Chapter Eight

¹But the main point of what has been said is this, we have a high priest such as this, who sat down at the right hand of the throne of Majesty in the heavens, ²a minister of the sanctuaries and of the genuine tabernacle, the one the Lord founded, not man.

³For every high priest is appointed to offer gifts and sacrifices, so this high priest must also have something which he can offer. ⁴Therefore, if he were on earth, he would not even be a priest since they offer their gifts according to the Law. ⁵They serve a copy and shadow of the heavenly things, just as Moses, when he was about to set up the tabernacle, was warned, for God said,

> "See that you make everything according to the pattern which was shown you on the mountain."[i]

⁶But now he has attained a more distinguished ministry, in as much as also he is mediator of a better covenant, which was founded on better promises.

⁷For if that first covenant was without defect, there would have been no reason to look for a second, ⁸but God found fault with the people and said,

> " 'Listen, the days are coming,' says the Lord, 'when I will ratify a new covenant for the house of Israel and the house of Judah. ⁹It will not be like the covenant which I made with the fathers on the day when I took them by the hand and led them out of Egypt, for they did not remain under my covenant, and I paid no attention to them,' says the Lord.
>
> ¹⁰" 'For this is the covenant which I will make with the house of Israel after those days,' says the Lord. 'I will put my laws into their minds, and I will write them upon their hearts, and I will be

---

[i] Exodus 25:40

their God, and they will be my people. ¹¹And no man will teach his countryman, nor any man his brother saying, "Know the Lord," for everyone will know me, from the least to the greatest of them; ¹²for I will be merciful on their unrighteousness, and I will not remember their sins any longer.'"ⁱⁱ

¹³When he spoke of a new covenant, he declared the first obsolete. But what has become obsolete and weak with age is about to disappear.

Tabernacle Worship Could Not Cleanse the Conscience

Chapter Nine

¹Now even the first covenant had requirements for worship and the sanctuary on earth. ²For when a tabernacle was built, the first part contained the lampstand, the table, and the presentation of the loaves in it. This is called the Holy Place. ³Then, behind the second veil was a part of the tent called the Holy of Holies. ⁴It had a golden altar of incense and the ark of the covenant overlaid on all sides with gold; in it were a golden vessel containing manna, Aaron's staff which budded, and the tablets of the covenant. ⁵But the glorious cherubim were above it all, overshadowing the mercy seat. At the present, we cannot speak about each of these items.

⁶Then, when these things had been set up in this way, the priests continually entered the first part of the tabernacle completing their sacrificial duties, ⁷but the high priest alone enters the second part of the tabernacle once every year. He does not enter without blood, which he offers for himself, and for the unwitting faults of the people. ⁸By this, the Holy Spirit is making it clear that the way into the holy places had not yet been fully revealed since the first tabernacle still exists. ⁹This is a

---

ⁱⁱ Jeremiah 31:31-34

parable for the present time. Consequently, the gifts and sacrifices that are being offered are not able to make the conscience of the one who worships whole. ¹⁰These offerings consist only of food, drink, and different ceremonial washings,[i] regulations for our flesh imposed by the Law until the time of the true and proper order.

The Blood of Christ Cleanses the Conscience

¹¹But when Christ—the high priest of the good things that have come—came through the greater and more perfect tabernacle that was not made with human hands (that is, not of this creation), ¹²he did not enter through the blood of goats and calves, but through his own blood. He entered once for all into the holy places after gaining eternal redemption. ¹³For if the blood of goats and bulls, and ashes of a heifer that are sprinkled on those who are ritually unclean, purify them so that they are clean in their flesh, ¹⁴how much more will the blood of Christ, who through the eternal Spirit offered himself without blemish to God, cleanse our conscience from lifeless actions so that we might serve the living God?

¹⁵For this reason, since his death was to pay for the transgressions committed under the first covenant, he is also the mediator of a new covenant, so that those who have been called might receive the promised eternal inheritance.

¹⁶For where a last will and testament is in effect, it is necessary to provide evidence of the death of the one who made it. ¹⁷For a last will and testament is established at the death of those who made it, since it never has authority while the one who made it is living. ¹⁸For this reason, the first covenant was not inaugurated without blood. ¹⁹For after every command from the law had been spoken by Moses to all the people, he took the blood of calves and goats, with water, scarlet wool, and hyssop, and sprinkled the scroll itself, and all the people. ²⁰He said,

---

[i] Or, "different baptisms."

"This is the blood of the covenant which God commanded for your sake."[ii]

²¹Then, in the same way also, the tabernacle and all the vessels of the priestly ministry were sprinkled with blood. ²²According to the Law, almost everything is cleansed with blood, and apart from the shedding of blood there is no forgiveness.

Jesus Offered Once for All

²³Therefore, the copies of the things in the heavens needed to be cleansed with these sacrifices, but the heavenly things themselves with better sacrifices than these. ²⁴For Christ has not entered holy places made with human hands, copies of the genuine ones, but into heaven itself to appear at this time in the presence of God on our behalf. ²⁵He did not enter it to offer himself frequently, like the high priest enters into the holy places each year with blood that is not his own, ²⁶since it would have repeatedly been necessary for him to suffer from the founding of the world. But now he has appeared once and for all, at the completion of the ages, to abolish sins through the sacrifice of himself. ²⁷Just as it is appointed for men to die once, then after this there is judgment, ²⁸in the same way Christ has been offered once so that he might bear the sins of many, and he will appear a second time—separated from sin—to those who are waiting for him for salvation.

The Law was Only a Shadow

Chapter Ten

¹For since the Law projects a shadow of the good things that are coming, but it is not the image of the things itself, it can never bring those who come near to perfection through the same sacrifices which they offer year after year without ceasing. ²Otherwise, would they not have stopped bringing offerings,

---

[ii] Exodus 24:8

since the ones who worshiped, when they were cleansed once, would no longer have a conviction of sins? ³But by those sacrifices, there is a reminder of sins year after year, ⁴for it is impossible for the blood of bulls and goats to take away sins.

⁵Therefore, when he came into the world he said,

> "You did not desire sacrifice and offerings, but you have prepared a body for me. ⁶You have not enjoyed burnt offering and sin offerings.
>
> ⁷"Then I said, 'See, I have come. It is written about me in the Bible scroll. My desire is to do your will, O God.'"ⁱ

⁸After he said that, "Sacrifice, offerings, burnt offerings, and offerings for sin you did not desire, nor did you enjoy them," (those offered according to the Law), ⁹then he said, "See, I have come to do your will." He repeals the first in order that the second might stand. ¹⁰By that will, we are sanctified through the offering of the body of Jesus Christ once and for all.

Jesus was the Reality that Made Forgiveness Permanent

¹¹Every priest also stands ministering and repeatedly offering the same sacrifices day after day. These can never take away sins, ¹²but this man, having offered one sacrifice for sins permanently, sat at the right hand of God ¹³waiting from that time on until his enemies are appointed as a footstool for his feet. ¹⁴For by one offering he has permanently perfected those who are being sanctified.

¹⁵Now the Holy Spirit also testifies to us, for after he said,

> ¹⁶" 'This is the covenant that I will make with them after those days,' says the Lord. 'I will put my laws in their hearts, and I will write them on their minds.'"ⁱⁱ

ⁱ Psalm 40:6-8

ⁱⁱ Jeremiah 31:33

17He also said,

> "I will not remember their sins and their lawless actions any longer."iii

18Now where there is forgiveness of these things, there is no longer an offering for sin.

Confidence to Access the Holy Place

19Therefore, brothers, since we have confidence to access the holy places by the blood of Jesus, 20that new and living way he opened for us through the veil, that is, by his flesh, 21and since we have a great priest over the house of God, 22let us draw near with genuine hearts in absolute certainty of faith, and with our hearts sprinkled clean from a bad conscience, and our bodies washed with pure water. 23Let us hold tightly to the confession of our hope without bending; for the one who has promised is faithful.

Moving Closer Through Congregational Meetings

24Let us understand each other, so that we may motivate each other to show love and good deeds. 5We can accomplish this by not abandoning our congregational meetings, as is the habit with some of you. Instead, encourage each other—and you must do this even more as you see the Day drawing near.

26For if we deliberately continue sinning after we have received the knowledge of the truth, there is no longer a sacrifice left for sins, 27but a certain terrible expectation of judgment and fierce fire that will devour those who oppose him. 28Anyone who refused to recognize the validity of the Law of Moses was put to death without mercy on the testimony of two or three witnesses. 29How much more severe a punishment do you think such a one will deserve, since he has trampled the Son of God under foot, and has regarded the blood of the covenant by which he was sanctified as unclean, and has arrogantly insulted the Spirit of grace? 30For we know the one who said,

---

iii Jeremiah 31:34

"The right to avenge is mine, I will repay."[i]

And again,

"The Lord will judge his people."[ii]

³¹It is a terrible thing to fall into the hands of the living God.

³²But remember your earlier days when you were brought to the light. You endured a great contest with sufferings. ³³You did this, on the one hand, by being publicly shamed with insults and hardships, and at other times by becoming partners with those who were so abused. ³⁴For you shared the suffering of those in prison, and accepted the theft of your possessions with joy, since you know that you have a better property, one that endures.

³⁵Therefore, do not throw away your confidence, which has a great reward. ³⁶For you have need of endurance, so that when you have done the will of God you may obtain the promise, ³⁷since,

"In just a little while, the one who is coming will come, and he will not delay; ³⁸but my righteous one will live by faith, but if he draws back, my soul will not be pleased with him."[iii]

³⁹But we are not those who shrink back and are ruined, but we are those who have faith and whose souls are preserved.

How People of Faith Live

Chapter Eleven

¹Now faith is the reality of the things we hope for, it is the evidence of events not yet seen. ²For by this faith the men who lived in ancient times obtained a good testimony.

---

[i] Deuteronomy 32:35

[ii] Deuteronomy 32:36

[iii] Habakkuk 2:3-4

³By faith we understand that the ages were set in order by the spoken word of God, so that what is seen did not come from that which was visible.

⁴By faith Abel brought a better sacrifice to God than Cain. Through faith he obtained the testimony that he was righteous when God bore testimony about his gifts, and through faith he still speaks though he has died.

⁵By faith Enoch was transformed so that he did not see death, and he was not found because God transformed him. For before his transformation, he was attested as pleasing to God. ⁶But apart from faith, it is impossible to please him; for the one who comes to God must believe that he exists, and that he rewards those who fervently seek him.

⁷By faith Noah, when he was given a revelation about that which was not yet seen, reverently obeyed and built an ark for the salvation of his household. By doing this, he condemned the world, and he became an heir of the righteousness that is by faith.

⁸By faith Abraham, after he was called to go to a place he would receive for an inheritance, obeyed. He went out without knowing where he was going. ⁹By faith he lived as a resident alien in the land of promise, dwelling as a foreigner in tents along with Isaac and Jacob, who were fellow heirs of the same promise. ¹⁰For he was awaiting the city which has foundations whose craftsman and builder is God.

¹¹By faith—even though Sarah herself was barren—he received power to conceive even beyond the proper season of life, since he counted the one who had promised as faithful. ¹²Therefore, even after these reproductive things had died, of this one man was born descendants that numbered as many as the stars of heaven, and innumerable as the sand that is beside the shore of the sea.

¹³Every one of these people died in faith, not having received the promises, but having seen them from afar, and embracing

them also while testifying that they were foreigners and temporary residents on the earth. ¹⁴For those who say such things make it plain that they are seeking a homeland. ¹⁵But if they were remembering that country from which they came, they had opportunity to return. ¹⁶But instead, they were striving for a a better one, that is a heavenly one. Therefore, God is not ashamed to be called their God. For he prepared a city for them.

¹⁷By faith Abraham, when he was tested, offered Isaac. The one who had received the promises of many descendants, attempted to sacrifice his one and only son. ¹⁸Abraham had been told, "Your seed will be named through Isaac."ⁱ ¹⁹So, Abraham reasoned that God is able to raise people from the dead. As a parable, he had received Isaac back from death.

²⁰It was also by faith that Isaac blessed Jacob and Esau, revealing what was to come.

²¹By faith Jacob, while he was dying, blessed each of the sons of Joseph, and worshipped upon the top of his staff.

²²By faith Joseph, while approaching his death, reminded the sons of Israel about the exodus, and gave instructions about his bones.

²³By faith Moses, when he was born, was hidden by his parents for three months, because they saw the beauty of the child, and they did not fear the king's command.

²⁴By faith Moses, when he had become a man,ⁱⁱ refused to be called the son of Pharaoh's daughter, ²⁵choosing to suffer with the people of God rather than to enjoy the transitory pleasure of sin. ²⁶He considered disgrace for the Messiah greater than the treasures of Egypt; for he was looking toward his reward. ²⁷By faith he left Egypt behind, not fearing the anger of the king, for he endured because he saw what was not visible. ²⁸By faith he instituted the Passover along with the smearing of blood on the

---

ⁱ Genesis 21:12

ⁱⁱ More literally, "when he had become great." While this phrase most likely speaks of his maturity, it may also speak to his position.

doorposts, in order that the Destroyer might not touch their firstborn.

²⁹By faith the people crossed over the Red Sea, as if crossing over on dry land; but when the Egyptians attempted it, they were swallowed up.

³⁰By faith the walls of Jericho fell when they were circled for seven days.

³¹By faith the prostitute Rahab was not destroyed with those who refused to believe, because she welcomed the spies in peace.

³²And what more can I add? For time will run out if I tell about Gideon, Barak, Samson, Jephthah, as well as David, Samuel, and the prophets. ³³Through faith they overcame kingdoms, worked justice, obtained promises, shut the mouths of lions, ³⁴quenched the power of fire, escaped the cutting edge of the sword, were strengthened when they were weak, became powerful in war, and put foreign armies to flight. ³⁵Women received their dead when they arose; but others were tortured, not expecting deliverance, in order that they might experience a better resurrection. ³⁶Still others experienced the testing of mocking and whipping, and even chains and prison. ³⁷They were stoned to death. They were sawn in two. They were tempted, they were murdered, and died by the sword. They went about in sheepskins and goatskins, lacking provision, while being harassed and mistreated. ³⁸The world was not worthy of them. They wandered in desolate regions, mountains, caves, and underground chambers.

³⁹All of these, although they received a positive report on account of their faith, did not obtain the promise, ⁴⁰because God had planned in advance for an even better plan for us, in order that they would not reach their goal apart from us.

Hebrews 12:1

Remembering the Great Cloud of Faithful Witnesses

Chapter Twelve

¹Therefore, since we have so great a cloud of witnesses surrounding us, let us lay down every impediment and the sin that easily distracts us, and let us run the race that lies before us ²by focusing our eyes on Jesus, the one who founded and completed our faith. For the joy that was clearly visible to him, he endured the cross, showed disdain for its shame, and sat at the right hand of the throne of God.

³Think carefully about him who endured such defiance against him from sinners, so that you do not become exhausted, and your souls weary. ⁴In your struggle against sin, you have not yet stood in opposition against it to the point of bloodshed. ⁵You also have forgotten the encouragement that is spoken to you as sons,

> "My son, do not think lightly of the discipline of the Lord, nor grow weary when corrected by him; ⁶for those whom he loves, the Lord disciplines, and he applies corrective punishment to every son whom he welcomes."[i]

Enduring Discipline as a Son

⁷You are suffering patiently to achieve discipline. God is treating you as sons. For is there a son whom his father does not discipline? ⁸But if you have not been disciplined—and all people have been involved in discipline—but if not, then you are illegitimate children and not sons. ⁹Besides this, we have had imperfect fathers as instructors, and we respected them. How much more, then, shall we willingly submit to the Father of spirits and live? ¹⁰For they disciplined us for a few days as it seemed right to them, but he disciplines us for our benefit, so that we might share in his holiness. ¹¹Now, no discipline is

---

[i] Proverbs 3:11-12

enjoyable at the moment, but painful; and later it produces the peaceful fruit of righteousness in those who have been trained by it.

¹²Therefore, restore your disabled hands and frozen knees, ¹³and make straight paths for your feet, so that the lame do not go astray, but rather find healing.

Pursue Peace and Grow in Holiness

¹⁴Pursue peace with everyone, and growing holiness; without it no one will see the Lord. ¹⁵Take care that no one fall away from the grace of God, that no root of bitterness grows up to cause trouble (many are defiled through a root of bitterness), ¹⁶that no one is sexually immoral or profane like Esau, who sold his birthright for one meal. ¹⁷For you know that even afterwards when he wanted to inherit the blessing, he was rejected as unworthy, for he did not find any possibility for a change of mind, though he sought it earnestly with tears.

The Church of the Firstborn

¹⁸Therefore, you have not come to a mountain that may be touched, to burning fire, a thick cloud, darkness, and a whirlwind, ¹⁹to the sound of the trumpet, and to the sound of spoken words, which when they heard it, they begged that not another word be added. ²⁰For they could not accept the clear command, "If even an animal should touch the mountain, it must be stoned."[ii] ²¹What they saw was so terrible, Moses said, "I am terrified and trembling."[iii] ²²However, you have come to Mount Zion and the city of the living God, a heavenly Jerusalem and countless thousands of angels, to a joyful gathering, ²³to the church of the firstborn whose names are recorded in the heavens, to God the Judge of all, to the spirits of the righteous who have reached their goal, ²⁴to Jesus, the mediator of a new covenant, and to the sprinkled blood that is speaking more effectively than the blood of Abel.

[ii] See Exodus 19:12-13.

[iii] Deuteronomy 9:19

Hebrews 12:25

Do Not Disregard God's Invitation to the Unshakeable Kingdom

25 Watch that you do not disregard the one who is speaking, for if those at the mountain did not escape when they disregarded the one who warned them on the earth, how much more culpable are we when we turn away from the one who is speaking from the heavens. 26Then his voice shook the earth, but now he has promised saying,

> "Yet once and for all I will shake not only the earth, but also the heaven."[i]

27But the words, "yet once and for all," reveal the removal of the things that are shaking, that had been created, in order that the things that are not shaking might remain. 28Therefore, since we are inheriting an unshakeable kingdom, let us have gratitude. It is through gratitude that we may worship God acceptably with reverence and awe; 29for our God is a devouring fire.

Living as a Part of the Unshakeable Kingdom

Chapter Thirteen

1Let brotherly love endure. 2Do not neglect hospitality, for by doing this, some people have received angels as guests. 3Remember the prisoners as though you are imprisoned with them. Remember those who are being physically mistreated because you also live in a body that can suffer physical abuse.

4Marriage must be honored in every way, and the sexual relationship[ii] in marriage must be kept pure, for God will judge the sexually immoral and adulterers.

---

[i] Haggai 2:6

[ii] More literally, "the marriage bed," a euphemism for the sexual relationship.

⁵Your character must be free from the love of money, be content with your possessions. For God himself said, "I will never abandon you or forsake you."ⁱⁱⁱ ⁶So, we can boldly say,

> "The Lord is my helper, I will not be afraid, what will man do to me?"ⁱᵛ

⁷Remember those who are leading you, who spoke the word of God to you; observe the result of their way of life closely, and imitate their faith. ⁸Jesus Christ is the same yesterday, today and forever. ⁹Do not be led away by various strange teachings, for it is good for the heart to be strengthened by grace, not by *rules about* foods. Those who observe such things are not benefitted.

¹⁰We have an altar from which those who serve in the tabernacle have no authority to eat. ¹¹For the high priest offered the blood of animals for sin in the holy places, but their bodies were burned outside the camp. ¹²Therefore, Jesus also suffered outside of the gate, so that he might sanctify the people through his own blood. ¹³So, let us go to him outside the camp, bearing his disgrace. ¹⁴For here on earth, we do not have a city that continues, but we are seeking the city that will come. ¹⁵Through him, then, let us offer up a sacrifice of praise to God in every circumstance, this is the fruit of lips that confess his name. ¹⁶Do not neglect good works and charitable contributions, for with such sacrifices as this, God is pleased.

Trusting and Praying for those who Lead

¹⁷Trust the ones leading you, and submit to them. For they take care of your souls as those who will give an account. Let them do this with joy, and not with distress. For that would be unprofitable to you.

¹⁸Pray for us, for we are convinced that we have a good conscience, and want to behave well in all situations; ¹⁹but I encourage you to do this even more, so that I might be restored to you soon.

ⁱⁱⁱ Deuteronomy 31:6

ⁱᵛ See Psalm 118:6-7.

A Prayer for Equipping

20Now may the God of peace, who raised the great Shepherd of the Sheep from the dead through the blood of the eternal covenant, our Lord Jesus, 21may he equip you with every good thing so that you might do his will, which is at work in us in his sight through Jesus Christ, to him be glory forever and ever. Amen.

22I encourage you, brothers, accept this word of encouragement, for I have written briefly.

Closing Greetings

23You should know that our brother Timothy has been released. If I come to you soon, I will see you and him.

24Greet all your leaders and all the saints. Those from Italy greet you.

25Grace be with all of you.

JAMES

Chapter One

¹James,[i] a servant of God and the Lord Jesus Christ,

To the twelve tribes in the Diaspora:[ii]

Greetings.

The Value of Trials and Tests

²Regard it as the utmost joy, my brothers, when you encounter various kinds of tests, ³because you know that the authentication of your faith develops perseverance. ⁴Allow perseverance to complete its work, so that you might be mature, without defect, and lacking nothing. ⁵If any of you lacks wisdom, let him request it from the God who provides generously to everyone without complaining, and it will be given to him. ⁶But let him ask with faith, without talking himself out of it; for anyone who talks himself out of it is like a wave of the sea

---

[i] Greek text, "Jacob." James is the Anglicized form of Jacob used since the first English translations. Unless it refers to the patriarch Jacob, it is translated as James in this New Testament.

[ii] The Diaspora refers to the dispersion of the Jewish people among the Gentiles throughout the Mediterranean world.

driven and blown by the wind. ⁷That man should not assume that he will receive anything from the Lord, ⁸he is a man of two minds, undecided in all his ways.

⁹Let the brother who finds himself in a humble position glory in his exalted position. ¹⁰But let the wealthy man glory in his humble position, seeing that like the blossom of a plant, he will fade away. ¹¹For the sun rises with its summer heat and withers the plant. Its blossom falls off, and its beauty is ruined. This is just like the wealthy man who wastes his life on his business trips.

¹²Blessed is a man who perseveres through a test, for when he is authenticated, he will receive the crown of life that the Lord promised to those who love him. ¹³No one should say while being tested, "I am being tested by God!" For God is not experienced with evil, and he doesn't test anyone with evil. ¹⁴But each man is tested by his own desires, when he is lured and hooked by them. ¹⁵Then, after desire has conceived, it gives birth to sin, and sin, when it has grown up, produces death.

¹⁶Do not be deceived *about this*, my cherished friends, ¹⁷everything good that is given, and every perfect gift is from above, descending from the Father of lights. There is no change of intensity or eclipses in his orbit.[i] ¹⁸It was his considered desire to bring us forth by the Word of Truth, so that we might be a kind of firstfruits of his created beings.

The Word is Able to Cleanse the Soul if We Act on It

¹⁹You already know, my cherished friends, that everyone should be quick to hear, slow to speak, and slow to respond in anger. ²⁰For the angry responses of man do not produce the righteousness of God. ²¹Therefore, in humility, keep on fighting off all filthy thoughts and remnant evil. Receive the word that was implanted in you and is able to deliver your souls from these things.

---

[i] James uses the image of the monthly waxing and waning of the moon's light as a contrast to the non-changing light of the Father.

²²So, be one who does that word, and not only hearers who deceive themselves. ²³If anyone is a hearer of the word, and not one who does the word, he is like a man who observes his existing face in a mirror, ²⁴that is to say, he sees himself and turns away, immediately forgetting the type of person he is. ²⁵But the one who pays close attention to freedom's perfect law and perseveres in it, and does not become a hearer who forgets, and is one who does the work, this man will be blessed by what he does.

Our Speech Puts our Commitment on Display

²⁶If anyone thinks he committed to his religious faith, but does not bridle his tongue, he deceives his heart; his religious faith is useless. ²⁷This is pure and undefiled religious faith in the opinion of God our Father: to care for orphans and widows when they are in trouble, and to keep yourself unstained by this world.

Stop Showing Favoritism

Chapter Two

¹My brothers, stop mixing faith in our glorious Lord Jesus Christ with favoritism. ²For if a man with a gold ring and fine clothing comes into your synagogue,[ii] and a poor man in filthy clothing also comes in, ³and you are attentive to the man wearing the fine clothing, "You sit here in this nice spot," but you say to the poor man, "You stand there, or sit by my footstool," ⁴have you not made distinctions among yourselves and become judges who issue bad decisions?

⁵Listen, my cherished friends, has not God chosen those who appear poor to this world to be rich in faith and heirs of the Kingdom, which he has promised to those who love him? ⁶You have treated the poor person shamefully. The wealthy cause you

---

[ii] This is the normal word for synagogue used throughout the New Testament. James wrote to Jewish Christians in the Diaspora.

severe hardship and they also drag you into court, don't they? [7]They are slandering the good name by which you are known, aren't they?

[8]If you really fulfill the royal law recorded in the Scripture, "Love your neighbor as yourself," you do well. [9]But if you show favoritism, you are committing sin and are proved by that law to be lawbreakers. [10]For whoever fulfills the entire law but stumbles on one issue is subject to liability for all of it. [11]For the one who said, "Do not commit adultery," also said, "Do not commit murder." If you do not commit adultery, but do commit murder, you have become a lawbreaker.

[12]Speak and act like you are about to be judged by freedom's law, [13]for there will be strict and merciless judgment for those who do not demonstrate mercy. Mercy is much superior to judgment.

Faith and the Actions of Faith

[14]What is the profit, my brothers, if someone claims to have faith, but has no actions of faith? The belief is not able to help him, is it? [15]If a brother or sister happens to have no clothing and lacks daily food, [16]and one from among you says to them, "Go in peace, warm yourself and be fed well," but does not give them the necessities for their body, what profit is that? [17]In just the same way, belief that does not have actions, is by itself dead. [18]Indeed, someone will say, "You have belief, but I have actions." Show me your belief apart from actions, and I will show you my belief by my actions. [19]You believe that God is one. You do well. Even the demons believe that, and tremble."

[20]Do you want to know, you foolish man, why belief apart from actions doesn't work? [21]Wasn't Abraham our father vindicated by his actions when he offered up Isaac his son upon the altar? [22]You see that belief was working together with his actions, and his belief matured through his actions. [23]Then the Scripture was fulfilled that says, "Abraham believed God, and it

was reckoned to him as righteousness,"[i] and he was called a friend of God. ²⁴You can see that a man is vindicated by his actions, and not by belief without actions. ²⁵Likewise, wasn't Rahab the prostitute vindicated by her actions when she welcomed the messengers and sent them on another road? ²⁶For just like the body without breath[ii] is dead, so also, belief apart from actions is dead.

Teachers Must Watch Their Words

Chapter Three

¹Do not raise up many teachers, my brothers, because you know that we will receive greater accountability, ²and we all make many mistakes. If anyone does not make a mistake in his speech, he is a mature man, able to hold his whole body in check. ³Now if we put bits in the mouths of horses so that they obey us, we also turn their whole body. ⁴Look also at ships, although they are so great and are driven by strong winds, they are steered by a small rudder wherever the pilot prefers to direct it.

⁵So also, the tongue is a small part of the body, but it makes extraordinary boasts. See how a great forest is set ablaze by a little fire. ⁶The tongue is also a fire, a world of unrighteousness. The tongue is appointed over our members, the thing that corrupts the whole body and sets on fire the course of our existence; and it is set on fire by Gehenna.[iii]

⁷For every species of wild animal, bird, reptile, and sea creatures is tamed and has been tamed by the human race. ⁸But no man is able to tame the tongue. It is an unstable evil full of deadly poison; ⁹with it we bless our Lord and Father, and with it we curse the men who are born according to God's likeness.

---

[i] Genesis 15:6

[ii] Or, "spirit." The Greek word can mean "breath" or "spirit."

[iii] A valley known as "the valley of the sons of Hinnom." It was the place of child sacrifice and gross impurity, and came to symbolize the place of eternal punishment.

¹⁰Blessing and cursing come out of the same mouth. My brothers, these types of things should not coexist. ¹¹Does a spring pour out fresh and salt water from the same source? ¹²My brothers, a fig tree cannot bear olives or a grapevine figs, can they? Nor can a salt spring produce fresh water.

Godly Wisdom versus Soulish Wisdom

¹³Who is wise and well informed among you? Let him show it by his good conduct and by his actions done with the gentleness of wisdom. ¹⁴If you have bitter envy or selfishness in your heart, do not act superior to everyone else and depart from the truth. ¹⁵This "wisdom" does not come down from above, on the contrary it is earthly, soulish,ⁱ and how demons act. ¹⁶For where there is envy and selfishness, there is turmoil and every moral evil.

¹⁷But the wisdom from above is first pure, then peaceful, reasonable, willing to listen, full of mercy and good fruits, and free from prejudice and hypocrisy. ¹⁸This fruit of righteousness is sown in peace by those who make peace.

The Source of Fights and Quarrels

Chapter Four

¹What is the source of these quarrels and battles among you? Isn't it from your fleshly desires that wage war among your members? ²You long for something, but do not get it. You murder and covet, but you cannot have it. You fight and quarrel, but you do not have because you do not ask. ³You ask, but you do not receive because you ask incorrectly, so that you can spend it on your fleshly desires.

⁴You adulteresses! Don't you know that friendship with the world is hatred toward God? So, whoever wants to be a friend of the world makes himself an enemy of God. ⁵Or do you suppose

---

ⁱ The term "soulish," refers to someone who is led by their mind, emotions, or will, rather than the Spirit of God (see Romans 8:14; Galatians 5:18).

that the Scripture states to no purpose, "The Spirit who dwells in us is intensely jealous."[ii] ⁶But isn't he giving a greater grace? For this reason, it says,

> "God opposes the proud, but gives grace to the humble."[iii]

Draw Near to God and He will Draw Near You

⁷Therefore, submit willingly to God, but oppose the Accuser,[iv] and he will flee from you. ⁸Draw near to God and he will draw near to you. Cleanse your hands, you sinners, and purify your hearts, you people of two minds. ⁹Be sorrowful, grieve, and weep. Let your laughter be turned to mourning and your joy to sadness. ¹⁰Be humble before the Lord and he will exalt you.

Stop Judging Each Other

¹¹Brothers stop speaking evil of each other. The one speaking evil of his brother or judging his brother speaks evil of the law and judges the law. But if you judge the law, you are not keeping it, but judging it. ¹²There is one Lawgiver and Judge who is able to rescue and destroy. But you who judge your neighbor, who are you?

Demonstrate Dependence on the Lord

¹³Come now, those who say, "Today or tomorrow we will go to this or that city, stay there a year, do business, and make a profit." ¹⁴You do not know about tomorrow, what your life will be like. You are a mist that appears for a little while, and then disappears. ¹⁵Instead, you should say, "If the Lord is willing, we will live and do this or that."

¹⁶But as it stands, you boast in your pretentious pride. All such boasting is worthless. ¹⁷Indeed, the one who knows the good he should do, but doesn't do it, commits a sin.

[ii] See Exodus 20:5.

[iii] Proverbs 3:34

[iv] Traditionally, "devil." The name means to slander or accuse.

Hoarding Wealth in Times of Great Need

Chapter Five

¹Come now you wealthy people, weep and cry out loud over the hardship that is coming upon you. ²Your wealth is destroyed, and your garments have been ruined by moths. ³Your gold and silver are tarnished, and their tarnish will be a testimony against you and will consume your flesh like fire. You have treasured up wealth in the last days![i]

⁴Look, the wages of the workers who reaped your fields, whom you defrauded, cry out against you; and the cries of those who harvested have reached the ears of the Lord, the one who leads armies.[ii] ⁵You have lived a life of self-indulgence and luxury upon the earth, you have fed your heart's desires in the day of slaughter. ⁶You have condemned, you have put a righteous man to death; he was not opposing you.[iii]

Growing in Patience

⁷Therefore, be patient, brothers, until the visitation[iv] of the Lord. See, the farmer waits for the valuable fruit of the ground. He is patient about it until it receives the early and late rains. ⁸You also be patient, strengthen your hearts, for the visitation of the Lord is near. ⁹Do not moan and complain about each other, brothers, so that you are not judged. Be aware, the Judge has taken his place by the door.

¹⁰For an example of suffering and patience, take the prophets who spoke in the name of the Lord. ¹¹Look, we pronounce a blessing on those who have endured; you have heard about the

---

[i] One of the main themes of the book of Acts, and of Paul's letter, is providing for the needs of the saints in Jerusalem during the last days of Jerusalem. James may be confronting those who preferred to hoard rather than to help others.

[ii] Or, "the Lord Sabaoth," which refers to the Lord who leads armies.

[iii] James may be addressing a specific injustice of which he was aware.

[iv] Or, "parousia." Parousia is a technical term that can mean coming, presence, or visitation. Also verse 8.

patience of Job, and you have seen the purpose of the Lord, that the Lord is very compassionate and merciful.

Let Your Yes be Yes

12Above everything, my brothers, do not continue to swear, neither by heaven nor by earth, nor any other oath. Let your "yes" be yes, and your "no," no, in order that you do not fall under judgment.

Calling the Elders for Healing Prayer

13Is anyone among you suffering hardship? Let him pray. Is anyone encouraged? Let him sing songs of praise. 14Is anyone among you sick? Let him call the elders of the church, and let them pray over him and anoint him with oil in the name of the Lord.

The Power of the Prayer of Faith

15The prayer of faith will rescue the one who is sick, and the Lord will raise him up; and if he has committed sins beforehand, it will be forgiven him. 16Therefore, admit your sins to each other, and pray for each other so that you may be healed. The supernaturally empowered prayer of the righteous person prevails against much.

17Elijah was a man who felt the same things we feel. But he prayed with persistence that it would not rain, and it did not rain upon the land for three years and six months. 18Then again, he prayed, and the skies gave rain, and the land produced its fruit.

Rescue the Straying

19My brothers, if any among you is led away from the truth, and someone brings him back to it, 20let him know that the one who brings back a sinner from the error of his path rescues his soul from death and conceals a multitude of sins.

1 PETER

Chapter One

¹Peter, an apostle of Jesus Christ,

To the elect[i] who are resident aliens in the Diaspora[ii] throughout Pontus, Galatia, Cappadocia, Asia, and Bithynia, ²chosen by the foreknowledge of God the Father, through the sanctifying efforts of the Holy Spirit, to yield to the will of Jesus Christ and to be sprinkled with his blood;

May grace and peace be multiplied in you.

Born from Above into Living Hope

³Blessed be the God and Father of our Lord Jesus Christ, who, in agreement with his great mercy, has caused us to be born from above[iii] into a living hope through the resurrection of Jesus Christ from the dead, ⁴into an inheritance that cannot perish or fade. This inheritance is kept in the heavens for you ⁵who are

---

[i] The term translated "elect" is a reference to those who are called by God to true faith that perseveres.

[ii] The Diaspora refers to the dispersion of the Jewish people among the Gentiles throughout the Mediterranean world.

[iii] Or "to be born again." The word has both meanings. Also verse 23.

protected by the power of God through faith, until the revelation of the salvation prepared for the last time.

⁶In this you are overjoyed, even though now it may have been necessary to be grieved for a little while by a variety of trials. ⁷This has happened to demonstrate that your faith is genuine. Your faith is more valuable than perishable gold, and even it is tested by fire. When your faith is found to be genuine, it will result in praise, glory, and honor at the revelation of Jesus Christ. ⁸Though you have not seen him, you love him; and though you do not see him now, you believe in him, and rejoice with unspeakable and glorious joy ⁹as you obtain the goal of your faith, the deliverance of your souls.

¹⁰About this salvation, the prophets who prophesied concerning the grace which was coming to you, sought diligently and investigated carefully, ¹¹tracking down what person or what time the Spirit of Christ in them was indicating while he was predicting the sufferings of Christ, and the glories after these sufferings. ¹²It was revealed to them that they were not serving themselves, but you. These same things have now been announced to you by the Holy Spirit who was sent from heaven. He announced them through those who shared the good news with you. These are the things into which angels desire to look.

Think Clearly About Holiness

¹³Therefore, after you have secured the disordered parts of your mind, stay clearheaded, fully expecting the grace that will be brought to you at the revelation of Jesus Christ. ¹⁴As obedient children, stop contorting yourself to fit your former lusts that you pursued in ignorance, ¹⁵but in the same way that the one who called you is holy, you also be holy in all your ways of life, ¹⁶because it is written, "Be holy, for I am holy."[iv]

¹⁷Now, since you call on a Father who judges each person's work without showing favoritism, live your life with reverential fear during your time as a resident alien. ¹⁸For you know that

---

[iv] Leviticus 11:44-45; 19:2; 20:7

you were not redeemed with perishable things such as gold or silver from the futile way of life received from your fathers, [19]but with the costly blood of Christ, who was like a lamb without blemish or spot. [20]For he was chosen before the founding of the world, but has been made known in these last times for your sake. [21]Through him you are believers in God, who raised him from the dead and gave him glory, so that your faith and hope are in God.

[22]Since you have purified your souls by obedience to the truth, and have a sincere love for the brothers, love each other continuously from a pure heart. [23]For you have been born from above, not by perishable seed, but with imperishable through the living and prevailing word of God.

[24]For,

> "All flesh is like grass, and all its glory is like the flowers in the grass. The grass withers and the flowers fall, [25]but the word of the Lord endures forever."[i]

Now this is the word which was proclaimed as good news to you.

Desire the Genuine Spiritual Milk of the Word

Chapter Two

[1]Therefore, after you have removed all wickedness, deceit, hypocrisy, jealousy, and evil speech, [2]like newborn infants, thirst for genuine spiritual milk, so that by it you may grow in your salvation; [3]since you have tasted that the Lord is kind.

Jesus, the Living Stone

[4]Because you are coming to him who is a living stone, rejected by men but chosen and esteemed before God, [5]you also, as living stones, are being built into a spiritual house to be a holy

---

[i] Isaiah 40:6-8

priesthood, to offer up spiritual sacrifices that are welcome by God through Jesus Christ. ⁶For this is included in Scripture,

> "Look I have laid a stone in Zion, an essential cornerstone, chosen and esteemed, and the one who believes in him will never be ashamed."[ii]

⁷So, to you who believe, the stone is of value. But for those who do not believe, it is,

> "The stone which those who build rejected, this stone has been made into the most essential cornerstone."[iii]

⁸And

> "A stone of stumbling and a rock of offense."[iv]

They take offense because they refuse to believe the word; they were set in place for this purpose.

A People For God's Own Possession

⁹But you are an elect[v] race, a royal priesthood, a holy nation, a people for God's possession, so that you might make known the virtues of the one who called you out of darkness into his wonderful light. ¹⁰At one time you were not a people, but now you are people of God. At one time you did not receive mercy, but now you have received mercy.

¹¹Cherished friends, I encourage you as resident aliens and temporary residents to stay at a distance from the physical lusts[vi] which are engaged in personal combat against your soul. ¹²Maintain such a good way of life among the Gentiles, that

---

[ii] Isaiah 28:16

[iii] Psalm 118:22

[iv] Isaiah 8:14

[v] The term translated "elect" is a reference to those who are called by God to true faith that perseveres.

[vi] Or, "fleshly lusts."

when they speak evil of you as criminals, they might glorify God on the day of his visitation because they have seen your good works.

Living in Godly Submission

¹³Therefore submit willingly to every living person because of the Lord, whether kings as those who are preeminent, ¹⁴or governors, as those who were sent by the king to punish criminals and receive the appreciation of those who are upright. ¹⁵For this is the will of God, that by doing good you muzzle the ignorant talk of men who lack wisdom. ¹⁶Conduct yourself as free men, but do not hold on to your liberty as a pretext for evil, instead hold on to it as servants of God. ¹⁷Honor everyone. Love the brothers. Fear God. Honor the king.

¹⁸Household servants, submit willingly to your masters in all things with respect; not only to the good and kind ones, but also to the unprincipled ones. ¹⁹For when a person endures undeserved suffering on account of his sensitive conscience before God, this receives grace. ²⁰For what kind of honor do you receive if you endure a beating because you have sinned? But if you endure suffering when you have done what is good, this receives grace from God.

²¹For you have been called for this, since Christ also suffered for you, leaving behind an example for you, so that you can follow in his footprints. ²²He had committed no sin, nor was deceit found in his mouth;[i] ²³when they raged against him, he did not rage against them in return. While he was suffering, he did not threaten them, but kept committing himself to the one who judges justly. ²⁴He himself bore our sins in his body on the tree, so that after we died to sin, we might live for righteousness. You have been healed by the welts[ii] he received when he was

---

[i] See Isaiah 53:9.

[ii] The Greek word is a clear reference to the type of wounds a slave would receive if beaten.

beaten. ²⁵For you were, like sheep, wandering away, but now you have returned to the Shepherd and Guardian[iii] of your souls.

Chapter Three

¹In like manner, wives submit willingly[iv] to your own husbands, so that even if any refuse to believe the word, they may be won without words by the behavior of their wives, ²because they have watched how pure your behavior is, mixed with respect. ³The things which make you attractive must not *only* be on the outside —the styling of hair, wearing of gold jewelry or certain clothing— ⁴but it should be the hidden you that is in your heart, with a gentle and quiet spirit that will never pass away, which is of great value in God's sight. ⁵For in this way, the holy women of former times who hoped in God, also made themselves attractive, submitting willingly to their own husbands, ⁶as Sarah obeyed Abraham and called him lord. You have become her children if you do good and are not frightened or intimidated in any way.

⁷In a similar fashion, husbands live in marital intimacy[v] with your wives in the knowledge that as a woman, she is a physically weaker sexual partner. Show her honor as a joint heir of the grace of life, so that your prayers are not hindered.

Be Devoted to Doing Good

⁸In addition, everyone should be like-minded, sympathetic, one who loves the brothers, compassionate, and humble. ⁹Do not pay back evil with evil or insult with insult, but instead repay with blessing, because you were called to this, so that you might inherit a blessing. ¹⁰For

> "The one who desires life, to love and see good
> days, must stop his tongue from speaking evil,

[iii] Or, "Overseer." This term refers to those who watch over or guard.

[iv] The verb translated "submit willingly" implies an orderly submission to another. Submission is a volitional act.

[v] This Greek word strongly includes the idea of having marital relations.

and his lips from speaking deceitfully. ¹¹He must avoid evil and do good. He must seek peace and pursue it. ¹²For the eyes of the Lord are on upon the righteous, and his ears are listening to their prayers, but the face of the Lord is against those who do evil."[i]

¹³Who will harm you if all of you are devoted to what is good? ¹⁴But even if you should suffer for doing what is right, you are blessed. Do not be afraid of the things people fear, and do not be distressed,[ii] ¹⁵but dedicate yourselves to Christ as Lord in your hearts. Always be ready to offer an explanation to anyone who asks you about the reason you are filled with hope, doing so with kindness and respect. ¹⁶Hold on to a good conscience, so that when you are slandered, those who speak evil of your good behavior in Christ will be ashamed. ¹⁷For it is better, if it conforms to the will of God, to suffer for doing good than for doing evil.

¹⁸For Christ also suffered for sins once and for all, the righteous for the unrighteous, so that he might bring you to God. He was put to death in flesh, but made alive by the Spirit, ¹⁹by whom he also went and preached to the spirits in prison, ²⁰to those who refused to believe in the past when divine patience waited in the days of Noah while the ark was being constructed. In it, a few, that is eight souls, were saved through water. ²¹This water is a picture of the baptism that now saves you. It is not about the removal of dirt from the body, but it is about the promise of a good conscience before God through the resurrection of Jesus Christ, ²²who is at the right hand of God since he journeyed to heaven after angels, authorities, and powers were made subject to him.

---

[i] Psalm 34:12-16

[ii] See Isaiah 8:12.

Understanding the Intent of Suffering

Chapter Four

¹Therefore, since Christ suffered in his flesh, you also must arm yourselves with the same intent. The one who has suffered in his flesh has made an end of sin, ²so that during the rest of their time in the flesh, they no longer live by human desires, but by the will of God. ³For the time is long over when it was normal for you to do the will of the Gentiles and live in sensual excesses, lusts, parties with excessive wine, orgies, binge-drinking, and the disgusting worship of idols. ⁴Because of this, they are astonished by your strange behavior because you do not join with them in the same floods of decadence, so they slander you. ⁵They will give an account to the one who is ready to judge the living and the dead. ⁶For this reason, the good news has also been preached to the dead,[iii] so that, on the one hand, although they were condemned in their flesh by men, they may now live in spirit by God's will.

Use Your Spiritual Gifts for Each Other

⁷But the end[iv] of all things is near. Therefore, use good sense and be clearheaded so that you can pray. ⁸Above everything, have sincere love for each other, for "love conceals a great number of sins."[v] ⁹Be hospitable to one another without complaining. ¹⁰To the degree that each one of you has received a grace gift, serve one another with them as good managers of the various kinds of God's grace. ¹¹If someone speaks, let him speak as one speaking the revelations of God. If someone serves, let him do so as one serving by the strength that God supplies, in order that God may be glorified in all things through Jesus Christ, to whom is the glory and the power forever and ever. Amen.

[iii] This is a difficult verse, but appears that Peter is speaking of those who heard the gospel before they died.

[iv] Or, "goal of all things."

[v] See Proverbs 10:12.

Sharing in the Sufferings of Christ

¹²Cherished friends do not be puzzled at the fire that is kindled among you in order to test you. It is not as if some strange thing were happening to you. ¹³But to the degree that you share in the sufferings of Christ, rejoice, so that you also may be filled with joy and rejoice at the time his glory is revealed. ¹⁴Blessed are you when you are insulted in the name of Christ, for the glory and the Spirit of God rest on you. ¹⁵So then, let none of you suffer as a murderer, thief, criminal, or as one who meddles in the affairs of others; ¹⁶but if someone suffers as a Christian, he must not be ashamed, but glorify God in this name. ¹⁷For it is an opportune time for judgment to start with the household of God. If it starts first with us, what will be the result for those who refuse to believe the gospel of God? ¹⁸And

> "If the righteous are not easily delivered, what will happen to the ungodly man and the sinner?"[i]

¹⁹So also, those who are suffering according to the will of God must entrust their souls to their faithful creator by doing good.

Encouragement to Congregational Leaders

Chapter Five

¹Therefore, I encourage the elders among you, as a fellow elder and witness of the sufferings of Christ, and a partaker of the glory that is about to be revealed, ²shepherd the flock of God that is with you, exercising your position of oversight, not because you are compelled to do so, but willingly in agreement with God's plan; not motivated by greed, but eager to serve. ³Do not act as if you are exercising dominion over those who are your responsibility, but instead act as examples to the flock. ⁴Then,

---

[i] Proverbs 11:31

when the Chief Shepherd is revealed, you will receive the unfading crown of glory.

Be Humble Toward One Another

⁵In the same way, young men, submit willingly to the elders. Let everyone put on the clothing of humility toward one another, for

> "God opposes the proud, but gives grace to the humble."ⁱⁱ

⁶Therefore, be humble under the strong hand of God, in order that he may exalt you at an opportune time ⁷after you have put all your concerns on him, because he concerns himself with you. ⁸Be self-controlled and watchful. Your opponent, the Accuser,ⁱⁱⁱ is walking about like a roaring lion seeking people to devour. ⁹Oppose him, firm in your faith, knowing that the same type of suffering is being endured by your brothers everywhere in the world. ¹⁰But the God of all grace, the one who called you to his eternal glory in Christ Jesus, after a little suffering, will himself restore you, make you firm, strengthen you, and give you solid foundations. ¹¹The power is his forever and ever. Amen.

Closing Greetings

¹²I have written to you briefly through the pen of Silas our faithful brother—I think of him in this way—encouraging and testifying that this is the genuine grace of God, for which you must stand firm.

¹³She who is in Babylon, who is chosen also with you, sends greetings, as does Mark, my son.

¹⁴Greet each other with the kiss of love.

Peace to all who are in Christ.

ⁱⁱ Proverbs 3:34

ⁱⁱⁱ Traditionally, "devil." The name means to slander or accuse. For this reason, this word is most often translated "Accuser" in this Bible version.

2 PETER

Chapter One

¹Simon Peter, a servant and apostle of Jesus Christ,

To those who have received a faith with the same privileges as ours, by the righteousness of our God and Savior Jesus Christ;

²Grace and peace be multiplied to you by the knowledge of God and of Jesus our Lord.

Growing in Usefulness for Jesus Christ

³He has given all things to you through his divine power, things pertaining to life and godliness. He has done this through true knowledge of the one who called you by his own glory and moral excellence. ⁴Through these things he has given us precious and great promises, so that through them you may become participants in the divine nature, having escaped the destruction of this world caused by lust.

⁵For this very reason, working with all eagerness, supplement your faith with notable service, your notable service with knowledge, ⁶your knowledge with self-control, your self-control with patience, your patience with godliness, ⁷your godliness with brotherly love, and your brotherly love with sacrificial love. ⁸For

when you possess these things, and increase in them, they will keep you from being useless—producing no fruit—in the knowledge of our Lord Jesus Christ. ⁹For whoever does not have these things is nearsighted and blind and has forgotten that he has been cleansed of his former sins.

Confirm Your Calling and Election

¹⁰Therefore, even more brothers, do your best to confirm your calling and election for yourself; for while you are doing these things, you will never stumble. ¹¹For in this same way, you will be provided rich access into the eternal Kingdom of our Lord and Savior Jesus Christ.

A more Certain Prophetic Word

¹²Therefore, I will always remind you about these things, even though you know them and are firmly established in the truth that is available to you. ¹³As long as I am in this temporary dwelling, I consider it fair that I stir you to wakefulness through this reminder, ¹⁴because I know that I will soon lay aside my temporary dwelling, as our Lord Jesus Christ has made known to me. ¹⁵I will also do my best so that at any time after my departure, you may be able to remember these things.

¹⁶For we did not follow artfully designed myths as we made known to you the power and presence[i] of our Lord Jesus Christ, but we were eyewitnesses of his majesty. ¹⁷For when he received honor and glory from God the Father, this special message was spoken to him by the Majestic Glory: "This is my Son, the one I love, with whom I am well-pleased."[ii]

¹⁸We ourselves heard this voice that came from heaven while we were with him on the holy mountain, ¹⁹but we have the prophetic word that is more certain, to which you do well to devote yourselves, as to a lamp shining in a dark place, until the day dawns and the morning star might rise in your hearts. ²⁰Know this first, no prophecy of Scripture was created by the

---

[i] Or, "parousia." Parousia is a technical term that can mean coming, presence, or visitation.

[ii] Matthew 17:5

writer's private analysis; ²¹for prophecy was never brought into existence by the will of man, but holy men spoke from God while they were carried away by the Holy Spirit.

The Danger of False Teachers

Chapter Two

¹There were also false prophets among the people, just as there will also be false teachers among you. They will discreetly introduce destructive factions,ⁱ and so deny the Master who bought them. This will bring swift destruction upon themselves. ²Many will also follow their sensual excesses, and the way of truth will be slandered because of them. ³In their greed, they will cheat you with false teachings; their long-awaited judgment is not idle, and their destruction is not asleep.

The Judgment of False Teachers

⁴For if God did not spare angels when they sinned, but he delivered them to Tartarus,ⁱⁱ where they are kept chained in darkness for punishment; ⁵and if he did not spare the ancient world, but preserved Noah, a preacher of righteousness, along with seven others when he brought a cataclysm upon the world of the ungodly; ⁶and if he condemned the cities of Sodom and Gomorrah to destruction by turning them to ashes, making them an example to those who intend to live in an ungodly way; ⁷and if he rescued righteous Lot, who was oppressed by the unrestrained sexual conduct of lawless men ⁸(for this righteous man experienced torment in his righteous soul day after day by what he saw and what he heard while living among them because of their lawless activities), ⁹then the Lord knows how to rescue the godly from temptation, and how to guard unrighteous

---

ⁱ Or, "heresies."

ⁱⁱ Peter's reference is to the ancient Book of Enoch, where it is recorded that the angels who fell at Noah's time (recorded in Genesis 6), were judged and imprisoned in Tartarus, a place under the earth. Later Greek legends described it as a place the demigods were imprisoned.

men who are being punished until the day of judgement. ¹⁰This is even more true about those who pursue the flesh with its impure desire, and who show contempt for authority. Reckless and brazen, they do not tremble with fear when they speak against[iii] heavenly beings. ¹¹In contrast, angels who are greater in strength and power, do not bring a slanderous judgment against them before the Lord.

¹²But these men, like irrational animals, which are born as natural creatures to be captured and destroyed, speak against things they do not understand. They will also be destroyed by their depravity, ¹³and will be treated to harm as payment for doing harm. They consider it a delight to indulge themselves in the daytime. They are stains and blemishes reveling in their pleasures even while they feast with you. ¹⁴They have eyes full of adultery and they are always watching for opportunities to sin. They seduce unstable souls. They have a heart trained in sexual exploitation. They are children of the curse. ¹⁵After they left the straight way, they were deceived and have followed after the way of Balaam, the son of Beor, who loved unrighteous wages, ¹⁶but he received a rebuke for his own evil actions when a speechless donkey, speaking with the voice of a man, hindered the madness of the prophet.

¹⁷They are springs without water, and clouds being driven by a storm, for whom the gloom and darkness have been reserved. ¹⁸For while they are speaking arrogant and empty words, they seduce—by lusts of the flesh and unrestrained sensuality—those who are barely beginning to escape from those who live in error. ¹⁹They promise them freedom while they themselves are slaves of depravity, for the depravity that overcomes a person is the thing by which he is enslaved. ²⁰For if they escape the world's impurities by knowledge of our Lord and Savior, Jesus Christ, but again become entangled in these things and are overcome, they are in worse condition at the end than at the beginning.

[iii] Or, "blaspheme." To blaspheme is speaking profanely of sacred things, to slander, or to speak against another. Also in verse 12.

²¹For it would be better for them not to have known the way of righteousness, than after knowing it, to turn back from the holy commands that were taught to them. ²²What the true proverb says has happened to them, "A dog returns to its own vomit, and after a sow has washed, it returns to rolling in the sewage."

The Heavens and the Earth Scheduled for Judgment

Chapter Three

¹This, my cherished friends, is already the second letter I have written to you, by which, through this reminder, I am stirring your thinking toward purity.

²Remember the words spoken in advance by the holy prophets, and the commands of the Lord and Savior spoken by your apostles. ³Know this first, that in the last days mockers will come with their ridicule. They will live in agreement with their own lusts ⁴and say, "Where is the promise of his coming?[i] For from the time the fathers fell asleep, all things continue in the same way they always have from the beginning of creation." ⁵For they purposely do not notice this thing, that by the word of God the heavens have existed for a long time, and the earth was formed out of water and through water, ⁶through which the world at that time was destroyed when it was flooded with water. ⁷But at this time, the heavens and the earth are being stored away by that same word, being kept for fire on the day of judgment, as well as for the destruction of ungodly men.

The Lord's Patience Waiting on Repentance

⁸So you, my cherished friends, notice this one thing, that one day with the Lord is as a thousand years, and a thousand years is as one day. ⁹The Lord does not delay his promises, as some count delay, but he is patient with you, not wanting anyone to perish, but everyone to make a place for repentance. ¹⁰But the day of

---

[i] Or, "parousia." Parousia is a technical term that can mean coming, presence, or visitation.

the Lord will come like a thief, the heavens will pass away with a loud rushing noise, and the elements will be destroyed with fervent heat, and the earth and the deeds in it will be revealed.[ii]

Looking Forward to the Day of the Lord

[11]Since all these things will be destroyed in this way, what sort of people should you be while you are living a life of holiness and godliness? [12]You should look with hope toward it, and hasten the coming of the day of God. On that day, the heavens will be destroyed by burning, and the elements will melt in fervent heat. [13]But in agreement with his promise, we expect new heavens and a new earth, a place where righteousness is at home.

[14]Therefore, cherished friends, since we are looking for these things, do your best to be discovered spotless by him, unblemished, and in peace. [15]Regard the patience of our Lord as salvation, just as our cherished brother Paul wrote to you according to the wisdom given to him. [16]As in all his letters, he also speaks in them about these things. Some things that he says are difficult to understand, which the ignorant and unstable pervert, as they also do to the rest of Scriptures to their own ruin.

[17]Therefore, you my cherished friends, since you are aware of this in advance, be on guard so that you are not carried away by the deception of lawless men and fall from your fixed position. [18]Instead, grow in the grace and knowledge of our Lord and Savior Jesus Christ.

To him is the glory, now and to the eternal day. Amen.

[ii]The Greek word means that the things of the earth will be discovered or found out.

1 JOHN

The Word of Life Made Known

Chapter One

¹What was from the beginning, what we have heard, what we have seen with our eyes, what we have observed, and what our hands have felt, concerning the Word of Life: ²this life was made known, and we have seen, testify, and proclaim to you this Eternal Life. He was with the Father and made known to us. ³What we have seen and heard, we proclaim also to you that you also might have fellowship with us; and our fellowship is with the Father, and with his Son, Jesus Christ. ⁴We ourselves have written these things so that our joy might be complete.

Having Fellowship with the God who is Light

⁵This is the message which we have heard from him, and we proclaim to you, that God is light and not one bit of darkness is in him. ⁶If we say that we have fellowship with him, and keep walking in darkness, we are lying and do not put the truth into practice. ⁷But if we keep walking in the light as he himself is in the light, we have fellowship with each other, and the blood of his Son, Jesus, cleanses us from every sin.

⁸If we say that we do not have sin, we deceive ourselves and the truth is not in us. ⁹If we confess our sins, he is trustworthy and righteous so that he might forgive us our sins and cleanse us from all unrighteousness. ¹⁰If we say that we have not sinned, we make him a liar, and his word is not in us.

Jesus is Our Champion

Chapter Two

¹My children, I am writing these things to you so that you do not sin. But if someone does sin, we have a Champion[i] before the Father, Jesus Christ the righteous. ²He is also the sacrifice that atones[ii] for our sins, but not for our sins alone, but also for the whole world.

Walking in the Lord's Commands

³We also know that we have come to know him by this, that we continue to keep his commands. ⁴The one who says, "I have come to know him," but does not continue to keep his commands, is a liar and the truth is not in him. ⁵But whoever continues keeping his word, truly the love of God has reached its goal in him. We know that we are in him by this: ⁶the one who says that he abides in him ought himself to walk just as he walked.

⁷Cherished friends, I am not writing a new commandment to you, but an old commandment which you had from the beginning; the old commandment is the word which you have heard. ⁸Furthermore, I am writing a new commandment to you, which is true in him and in you, because the darkness is passing away and the authentic light is already shining.

---

[i] Or, more literally, "Paraclete." In the gospel of John this word refers to the Holy Spirit and his role (See John 14:16). However, here it refers to Jesus and his role as our champion.

[ii] Or, "He is also the propitiation for our sins."

⁹The one who claims to be in the light, but hates his brother is in darkness even now. ¹⁰The one who continues loving his brother lives in the light and there is no stumbling block in him. ¹¹But the one who continues hating his brother is in darkness and is walking in darkness; he does not know where he is going, because the darkness has blinded his eyes.

> ¹²I am writing to you, children, because your sins have been forgiven on account of his name.
>
> ¹³I am writing to you, fathers, because you have known the one who is from the beginning.
>
> I am writing to you, young men, because you have conquered the evil one.
>
> I am writing to you, children, because you have known the Father.
>
> ¹⁴I have written to you, fathers, because you have known the one who is from the beginning.
>
> I have written to you, young men, because you are strong, the word of God lives in you, and you have conquered the evil one.

Do Not Love the World

¹⁵Do not love the world, nor the things in the world. If anyone loves the world, the love of the Father is not in him, ¹⁶because everything in the world, the lust of the flesh, the lust of the eyes, and the pretentious pride over our material resources,[i] is not from the Father, but from the world. ¹⁷The world is passing away, along with its desire, but the one who makes a habit of the will of God remains to the coming age.

---

[i] Traditionally, "the pride of life." However, it is a word that speaks of our material resources for life. See 1 John 3:17 for the same word used for material possessions or worldly resources.

Identifying Antichrists and Liars

¹⁸Children, it is the last hour, and just as you have heard that antichrist is coming, also now many antichrists have come. Therefore, we know that it is the last hour. ¹⁹They went out from us but were not from us. For if they were from us, they would have remained with us; they went out from us to show that every one of them was not from us.

²⁰You have an anointing from the Holy One, and you all understand. ²¹I have not written to you because you do not know the truth, but because you know it, and because every lie does not come from the truth. ²²Who is the liar, if not the one who denies that Jesus is the Christ? This one is the antichrist, the one who denies the Father and the Son. ²³Everyone who denies the Son also does not have the Father. The one who acknowledges the Son also has the Father. ²⁴What you have heard from the beginning, let it remain in you. If what you have heard from the beginning remains in you, you also will remain in the Son and in the Father. ²⁵This is the promise which he himself promised us, eternal life.

²⁶I have written these things to you about those who are misleading you. ²⁷The anointing which you yourselves received from him lives in you, and you have no need that someone should teach you; but as his anointing teaches you about all things, and is true and not a lie, just as it also has taught you, remain in him.

²⁸Now also, children, remain in him, in order that when he appears we might have confidence and not be rejected by him in his presence.[ii] ²⁹If you know that he is righteous, you also know that everyone who makes a habit of righteousness is born of him.

[ii] Or, "parousia." Parousia is a technical term that can mean coming, presence, or visitation.

Living as Children of God

Chapter Three

¹Take note of the kind of love the Father has given to us, that we are called children of God; and we are! For this reason, the world does not recognize us, because it does not know him. ²Cherished friends, we are now children of God, but what we will be has not yet been revealed. We know that when he appears, we will be like him, because we will see him just as he is. ³Everyone who has this hope in him, cleanses himself, just as he is clean.

⁴Everyone who makes a habit of sin also makes a habit of lawlessness; sin is lawlessness. ⁵You also know that he appeared in order to take away our sins, and there is no sin in him. ⁶Everyone who lives in him does not make a habit of sin, but everyone who makes a habit of sin has not seen him, and neither have they known him.

⁷Children, let no one deceive you, the one who makes a habit of righteousness is righteous, just as he is righteous. ⁸The one who makes a habit of sin is from the Accuser,[i] for from the beginning the Accuser made a habit of sin. For this reason, the Son of God appeared, that he might destroy the activities of the Accuser. ⁹Everyone who has been born of God does not make a habit of sin, for God's seed lives in him, and he is not able to continue in sin because he has been born of God. ¹⁰By this the children of God and the children of the Accuser are revealed: Everyone who does not make a habit of righteousness is not from God, as well as the one who does not love his brother.

¹¹For this is the message which you have heard from the beginning, "Let us love one another." ¹²We are not like Cain, who was from the evil one and brutally murdered his brother. Why did he murder him? Because his activities were evil, and his brother's were righteous.

---

[i] Traditionally, "devil." The name means to slander or accuse. For this reason, this word is most often translated, "Accuser." Also in verse 10.

¹³Do not be shocked, brothers, if the world hates you. ¹⁴We ourselves know that we have permanently crossed over from death into life because we love the brothers. The one who does not love remains on the side of death. ¹⁵Everyone who hates his brother is a murderer, and you know that no murderer has eternal life living in him.

Living with Authentic Love

¹⁶By this we know love, that he dedicated his life on our behalf, and we ought to dedicate our lives on behalf of our brothers. ¹⁷For example, whoever has the material resources of this world and sees his brother in need, and locks his compassions away from him, how can the love of God live in him?

¹⁸My children, let us not love only with a word or a speech, but with action and truth. ¹⁹It is in this way, we know that we have come from the truth, and it is how we soothe our hearts in his presence ²⁰when our heart convicts us. For God is greater than our hearts and knows all things. ²¹Cherished friends, if our heart does not convict us, we have confidence before God ²²and whatever we may ask, we receive from him, for we keep his commands and do the things that are pleasing before him. ²³This is his command, that we believe in the name of his Son, Jesus Christ, and love one another, just as he commanded us.

²⁴The one who keeps his commands lives in him, and he lives in them. This is the way that we know he lives in us, from the Spirit he gave to us.

Examining the Spirit of a Prophet

Chapter Four

¹Cherished friends, do not believe every spirit, but examine whether the spirits are from God, because many false prophets have gone out into the world. ²By this you know the Spirit of

God: Every spirit who openly acknowledges that Jesus Christ has come in the flesh is from God. ³But every spirit who does not openly acknowledge Jesus is not from God. This is the spirit of antichrist, which you have heard is coming, and now is already in the world.

⁴You are from God, children, and you have overcome them, because greater is the one in you than the one in the world. ⁵They themselves are from the world. Because of this, they speak from the world and the world hears them. ⁶We ourselves are from God. The one who knows God hears us. Whoever is not from God does not hear us; by this we know the Spirit of truth and the spirit of deception.

Revealing God's Love in Us

⁷Cherished friends, let us love each other, for love is from God, and everyone who loves has been born from God and knows God. ⁸The one who does not love does not know God, for God is love. ⁹The love of God is revealed among us by this, that God sent his unique and only Son into the world in order that we might be saved through him. ¹⁰In this is love, not that we loved God, but that he himself loved us and sent his Son as a sacrifice that atones[i] for our sins. ¹¹Cherished friends, since God so loved us, we also ought to love each other. ¹²No one, to this point, has seen God; if we love each other, God lives in us and his love is fulfilled in us.

¹³In this way we know that we live in him and he in us, for he has given from his Spirit to us. ¹⁴We have seen and we testify that the Father has sent the Son as Savior of the world. ¹⁵If someone openly acknowledges that Jesus is the Son of God, God lives in him, and he in God. ¹⁶We have come to know, and have trusted the love which God has for us. God is love, and the one abiding in his love abides in God, and God abides in him. ¹⁷In this way the love of God is fulfilled with us, so that we may have confidence on the day of judgment; because just as that one

---

[i] Or, "sent his Son as a propitiation for our sins."

is, we also are in this world. ¹⁸There is no fear in love, but mature love casts out fear, for fear is connected to punishment. But the one who is afraid has not matured in love.

¹⁹We ourselves love because he first loved us. ²⁰If someone says, "I love God," but despises his brother, he is a liar. For the one who does not love his brother whom he sees, is not able to love God whom he does not see. ²¹This is the command we have from him, that the one who loves God must also love his brother.

Born of God

Chapter Five

¹Everyone who believes that Jesus is the Christ has been born of God; and everyone who loves the one who has borne us, also loves the one that is born of him. ²We know that we love the children of God when we love God and we make a habit of his commands. ³For this is the love of God, that we keep his commands, and his commands are not a burden, ⁴because whatever is born of God gains the victory over the world. This is the victory that has overcome the world, our faith. ⁵But who is the one who gains the victory over the world, if not the one who believes that Jesus is the Son of God?

The Testimony of the Spirit, the Water, and the Blood

⁶This is the one who has come through water and blood, Jesus the Christ. He did not come by water alone, but by water and blood. The Spirit is the one who testifies because the Spirit is the truth. ⁷For there are three who testify in heaven, the Father, the Word, and the Holy Spirit, and these three are one. ⁸There are also three who testify on the earth, the Spirit, the water, and the blood, and the three are one in testimony. ⁹If we receive the testimony of men, the testimony of God is greater because this is the testimony of God which he has testified about his Son. ¹⁰The one who believes in the Son of God has this testimony in himself. The one who does not believe God

has made him a liar, because he has not believed in the testimony which God has given about his Son. ¹¹This is the testimony, that God has given life eternal to us, and this life is in his Son. ¹²The one who has the Son has this life; the one who does not have the Son of God does not have this life.

Closing Instructions

¹³I have written these things to you who believe in the name of the Son of God, in order that you might know that you possess life eternal. ¹⁴This is the confidence which we have before him, that if we ask anything according to his will, he hears us. ¹⁵If we know that he hears us, whatever we ask, we know that we possess the requested things which we have asked from him.

¹⁶If anyone sees his brother committing a sin that doesn't end in death, he can ask and God will give life to him, to those who are committing a sin that does not end in death. There is sin that ends in death.ⁱ I am not saying that he should ask about that kind. ¹⁷All unrighteousness is sin, but there is sin that does not end in death.

¹⁸We know that everyone who has been born from God does not make a habit of sin, but the one who was born of God guards him, and the evil one is not able to touch him.

¹⁹For we know that we are from God, and the whole world exists under the influence of the evil one.

²⁰We know that the Son of God has come and has given understanding to us, in order that we know the True One; and we are in the True One, in his Son, Jesus Christ. This one is the true God and life eternal.

²¹Children, protect yourselves from idols.

ⁱ In 1 Corinthians 11:30 the apostle Paul teaches that dividing the people of God can result in death. This may be an example of the type of sin to which John refers.

2 JOHN

¹The Elder,

To the elect[i] lady and to her children, whom I love in truth. I'm not the only one who loves them, but everyone who knows the truth also does, ²because the truth lives in us and will be with us to the coming age.

³Grace, mercy, and peace will be with us from Father God and from Jesus Christ, the Son of the Father, in truth and love.

Walking According to His Commands

⁴I was overjoyed that I found those from among your children walking in truth, just as we have received direction from the Father. ⁵And now I am asking you, lady, not as writing a new command to you, but one which we have had from the beginning, "Let us love each other!" ⁶This is love, that we walk according to his commands. This is the command, just as you have heard from the beginning, that you might walk in it.

---

[i] The term translated "elect" is a reference to those who are called by God to true faith that perseveres. Also in verse 13.

2 John 7

Do Not Share in the Evil Activities of Deceivers

⁷Many who deceive have gone out into the world—those who do not openly acknowledge that Jesus Christ has come in the flesh. This type is the deceiver and the antichrist. ⁸Because of this, watch yourselves, that you do not lose what we have accomplished, but rather that you receive full payment.

⁹Everyone who goes ahead and does not remain in the teaching of Christ, does not have God. The one who remains in this teaching, this one has the Father and the Son. ¹⁰If someone comes to you and does not bring this teaching, do not receive him into your house or speak to him in greeting, ¹¹for the one who wishes him well shares in his evil activities.

¹²Although I have many things to write to you, I do not want to be limited to pen and ink, but I hope to come to you and speak face to face, so that our joy might be completed.

¹³The children of your elect sister greet you.

3 JOHN

¹The Elder,

To my cherished friend Gaius, whom I love in truth.

²Cherished friend, I am praying that you prosper and enjoy good health, just as your soul is prospering. ³For I was overjoyed at the coming of the brothers and their testimony to your faithfulness, because you are walking in truth. ⁴I do not have any greater joy than this, when I hear that my children are walking in the truth.

Recognizing Coworkers in Christ

⁵Cherished friend, you are acting faithfully in what you have done for the brothers, even as strangers. ⁶They have testified to your love in front of the church. You will do well whenever you send them on their way in a manner worthy of God. ⁷For they went out for the sake of the Name and did not receive anything from the Gentiles. ⁸Therefore, we ought to provide for such men as these, in order that we might be coworkers with truth.

An Example of a Divisive Spirit

⁹I have written something to the church, but Diotrephes, who is fond of being first, has not welcomed us. ¹⁰For this

reason, if I come, I will remind him of the things that he is doing: he is talking nonsense with bad reports about us, and isn't satisfied just with this, he also does not welcome the brothers, and hinders those who desire to welcome them. He even puts them out of the church.

[11]Cherished friends, do not imitate this evil, but rather what is good. The one who does good is from God; the one who does evil has not seen God. [12]Demetrius has been endorsed by everyone, and even by the truth itself. We also endorse him, and you know that our testimony is true.

[13]I have much to write to you, but I do not want to be limited to pen and ink as I communicate with you. [14]I am hoping to see you soon, then we can speak face to face.

Peace be with you. Your friends greet you. Greet our friends by name.

JUDE

¹Jude, a servant of Jesus Christ and brother of James;[i]

To those who are called, loved by God our Father, and watched over by Jesus Christ.

²May mercy, peace, and love increase among you.

Contending for the Faith Against Infiltrators

³Cherished friends, while I was making every effort to write to you about our common salvation, I was constrained instead to write to you and encourage you to contend for the faith that was once for all handed over to the saints. ⁴For certain men have infiltrated your ranks whose judgment was written about long ago. They are ungodly men who transform the grace of God into sensual license, and so deny our only Sovereign and Lord, Jesus Christ.

⁵I want to remind you, although you know all these things, that the Lord once delivered a people out of the land of Egypt, but afterward destroyed those who did not believe. ⁶He has also

---

[i] Greek text, "Jacob." James is the Anglicized form of Jacob used since the first English translations. Unless it refers to the patriarch Jacob, it is translated as James in this New Testament.

Jude 7

kept the angels who did not stay in their own realm, but deserted their own dwelling,[i] in eternal imprisonment covered by darkness for punishment on the Great Day. ⁷Sodom and Gomorrah and the cities around them, in similar manner as these angels, engaged in sexual immorality and pursued other flesh. They are now on display as an example of those who suffer the punishment of eternal fire.

⁸In like manner, because of dreams, these men defile their flesh and rebel against authority by speaking against heavenly beings. ⁹But Michael the archangel, when he was arguing with the Accuser[ii] and contending about the body of Moses, did not presume to impose any disparaging judgment, but said, "The Lord rebuke you." ¹⁰But these men disparage anything they do not understand, and just like unreasoning animals, they are destroyed by anything they do by nature understand. ¹¹Woe to them, for they have journeyed on the path of Cain, they have given themselves over to Balaam's error for illicit wages, and they perish in Korah's rebellion. ¹²These men are a hidden danger[iii] at your love feasts, eating together with you irreverently, feeding only themselves. They are clouds without water who are blown along by the wind, unfruitful autumn trees that have died twice and been uprooted. ¹³They are wild sea waves causing their shameless deeds to foam up. They are wondering stars for whom the gloom and darkness of hell has been reserved forever.

¹⁴Enoch, the seventh from Adam, prophesied about these men saying,

> "Look! The Lord comes with myriads of his holy ones ¹⁵to release judgment among all

---

[i] The Greek word translated "dwelling" (oiketerion) is only used here in the New Testament, and in 2 Corinthians 5:2. It is more than ironic that the fallen angels abandoned the very thing Paul longs to be clothed with in 2 Corinthians.

[ii] Traditionally, "devil." The name means to slander or accuse. For this reason, this word is most often translated "Accuser" in this Bible version.

[iii] The word translated "hidden danger" refers to hidden rocks that threaten a ship in the water, or to hidden blemishes that threaten the purity of a product.

people, and to convict every soul concerning all their ungodly works which they have done in their wicked ways, and concerning all the harsh things which ungodly sinners have spoken against him."[iv]

They are Grumblers who Find Fault with Everything

[16]These men are grumblers who find fault with everything and pursue their own ungodly desires. Their mouths speak pompously as they flatter people to gain an advantage.

[17]But you, cherished friends, remember the words spoken ahead of time by the apostles of our Lord Jesus Christ [18]when they said to you, "There will be mockers in the last age who pursue their own ungodly desires."[v] [19]These men cause divisions; they follow their soulish[vi] thoughts because they do not have the Spirit.

Build Up in the Faith

[20]But you, cherished friends, continue to build yourselves up in the holy faith and continue praying with the Holy Spirit. [21]Keep yourselves in the love of God while waiting for eternal life and the mercy of our Lord Jesus Christ.

[22]Show mercy to those who doubt [23]Deliver those you are snatching away from the flames. Show mercy with a blend of fear, despising even the shirt stained by their sinful flesh.

[24]Now to the one who is able to keep you free from stumbling, and to make you stand in the presence of his glory blameless and rejoicing, [25]to the only God our Savior through Jesus Christ our Lord, be glory, majesty, power, and authority before every age, even now, and through all the ages. Amen.

[iv] Quoted from the non-canonical Book of Enoch.

[v] See 2 Peter 3:3.

[vi] The term "soulish," refers to someone who is led by their mind, emotions, or will, rather than the Spirit of God (see Romans 8:14; Galatians 5:18).

REVELATION

Chapter One

¹A revelation of Jesus Christ, which God gave him to show his servants the things that must shortly take place. He made it known in advance by sending his angel to his servant John, ²who has borne witness to the Word of God and the testimony of Jesus Christ, to everything that he saw. ³Blessed is the one who reads, and those who hear, the words of this prophecy, and who watch for the things written in it; for the time is near.

Greetings

⁴John,

To the seven churches that are in Asia;

Grace to you and peace from the One who is, and who was, and who is coming, and from the Seven Spirits[i] who are before his throne, ⁵and from Jesus Christ, the faithful witness, the firstborn of the dead, and the ruler of the kings of the earth.

---

[i] A title of the Holy Spirit.

To him who loves us and set us free from our sins by his blood, ⁶and made us a kingdom, priests to his God and Father, to him be the glory and the power forever and ever. Amen.

⁷Look, he is coming with the clouds, and every eye will see him, even those who pierced him through, and all the tribes of the land will mourn over him. Yes! Amen!

⁸"I am the Alpha and the Omega, the beginning and end," says the Lord God, "the one who is, the one who was, and the one who is coming, the Ruler of all things."

John's Commission for this Book

⁹I, John, your brother and partner in the tribulation, the kingdom, and the patience that we have in Jesus, was on the island that is called Patmos, because of the Word of God and the testimony of Jesus. ¹⁰I was in spirit on the Lord's Day, and I heard a loud voice behind me. It was loud as a trumpet. ¹¹The voice said, "Write what you see in a book and send it to the seven churches in Ephesus, Smyrna, Pergamum, Thyatira, Sardis, Philadelphia, and Laodicea."

The Son of Man

¹²Then I turned to see the voice that was speaking to me, and when I turned, I saw seven golden lampstands, ¹³and in the middle of the lampstands was one like the Son of Man. He was clothed in a robe down to his feet, and a golden sash was tied around his chest. ¹⁴His head and his hair were white like white wool or snow, and his eyes were like a flame of fire. ¹⁵His feet were like fine bronze glowing in a smelting furnace. His voice was like the sound of many waters. ¹⁶In his right hand he held seven stars, a sharp two-edged sword extended from his mouth, and his face shone like the sun shining at full strength.

¹⁷When I saw him, I fell at his feet like a corpse. He placed his right hand upon me and said, "Stop being afraid! I am the First and the Last, ¹⁸the Living One. I was dead, but see, I am living forever and ever, and I have the keys of death and of Hades. ¹⁹Therefore, write what you have seen, what you are

seeing, and what is about to happen after these things. ²⁰This is the answer to the mystery of the seven stars which you saw in my right hand, and the seven golden lampstands: the seven stars are the seven angels of the seven churches, and the seven lampstands are the seven churches.

A Letter to the Church in Ephesus

Chapter Two

¹"To the angel[i] of the church[ii] in Ephesus write:

"He who holds the seven stars in his right hand, who is walking in the middle of the seven golden lampstands, says these things.

²"I know your activities, your trouble, and your patience, and that you are not able to tolerate wicked men. You test those who call themselves apostles even though they are not, and you have discovered that they are liars. ³You have patience and have endured for my name without growing tired.

⁴"But I have something against you, you have divorced[iii] your first love. ⁵Therefore, be aware of how you have fallen, repent, and return to your first activities. But if you do not, I am coming to you, and unless you repent, I will remove your lampstand from its place. ⁶Yet you do hold on to this, you hate the activities of the Nicolaitans, which I also hate.

⁷"He who has ears, let him understand what the Spirit is saying to the churches. To the one who overcomes, I will allow him to eat from the tree of life, which is in garden of God.

A Letter to the Church in Smyrna

⁸"Also write to the angel of the church in Smyrna:

---

[i] The Greek word can also be translated "messenger." For this reason, this may be referencing a heavenly being or a leader at the congregation.

[ii] The Greek word, ekklesia (ἐκκλησία), means "church" or "congregation."

[iii] The Greek word can mean to dismiss, forsake, or divorce.

"The First and the Last, who was dead and came to life, is saying these things.

⁹"I am aware of your hardship and your poverty, but you are rich! I know the slander of those who say they are Jews and are not, but are instead a synagogue of Satan. ¹⁰Do not be frightened by the things you are about to suffer. Be alert to this, the Accuser[iv] is about to throw some of you into prison so that you might be tested. You will have ten days of tribulation. Be faithful even unto death and I will give you the crown of life.

¹¹"He who has ears, let him understand what the Spirit is saying to the churches. He who overcomes will never be harmed by the second death.

A Letter to the Church in Pergamum

¹²"Also write to the angel of the church in Pergamum:

"He who has the sharp two-edged sword is saying these things.

¹³"I know where you are dwelling, where the throne of Satan is located. You have held tightly to my name, and you did not deny my faithfulness even in the days of Antipas, my witness, my faithful one, who was killed among you where Satan is dwelling.

¹⁴"But I have a few things against you, you have those there who adhere to the teaching of Balaam, who taught Balak to put a stumbling block in front of the sons of Israel, so that they ate food sacrificed to idols and indulged in illicit sexual relationships. ¹⁵In this same way, you also have those who adhere to the teaching of the Nicolaitans. ¹⁶Therefore, repent. But if you will not, I am coming to you soon, and I will wage war against them with the sword of my mouth.

¹⁷"He who has ears, let him understand what the Spirit is saying to the churches. I will give him who overcomes the hidden

---

[iv] Traditionally, "devil." The name means to slander or accuse. For this reason, this word is most often translated "Accuser" in this Bible version.

manna, and I will give him a white stone, and a new name will be written on it that no one knows but the one who receives it.

A Letter to the Church in Thyatira

18"Also write to the angel of the church in Thyatira:

"The Son of God, the one who has eyes like a flame of fire, and his feet are like fine bronze, is saying these things.

19"I know your works, your love, faithfulness, service, and endurance, and that your most recent works are greater than your first works.

20"But I have something against you, you pardon the woman Jezebel, who calls herself a prophetess. She teaches and deceives my servants so that they indulge in illicit sexual relationships and eat things sacrificed to idols. 21I have given her time so that she might repent, but she is not willing to repent of her illicit sexual behavior. 22Be aware, I will confine her to her bed, and those who commit adultery with her will fall into great tribulation unless they repent for her actions. 23I will also kill her children with plague, and all the churches will know that I am the one who examines minds and hearts, and I will give to each of you in accord with your actions.

24"But I tell the rest of you in Thyatira, all of you who do not hold this teaching, who have not come to know the deep things of Satan, as they refer to them, I am putting no other burden on you, 25except that you hold fast to what you have until I come.

26"He who overcomes and keeps my works until the end, I will give him authority over the nations, 27and he will shepherd them 'with a rod of iron, as clay vessels are shattered,'[i] just as I also have received authority from my Father. 28I will also give him the morning star.

29"He who has ears, let him understand what the Spirit is saying to the churches."

---

[i] See Psalm 2:9

A Letter to the Church in Sardis

Chapter Three

¹"Also write to the angel of the church in Sardis:

"The one who has the Seven Spirits of God and the seven stars is saying these things.

"I am aware of your works. You have a reputation that you are alive, but you are dead. ²Be alert and strengthen the things that remain that are about to die, for I have not found that your works are satisfactory in the sight of my God. ³Therefore, remember how much you have received and heard; pay attention to it, and repent. If then you are not alert, I will come like a thief, and you will not know at what hour I will come to you.

⁴"But you have a few reputable people[ii] in Sardis who have not stained their garments. They will walk with me in white because they are worthy. ⁵He who overcomes will, in this same way, be clothed in white garments, and I will never strike his name from the scroll of life, and I will confess his name before my Father and his angels.

⁶"He who has ears, let him understand what the Spirit is saying to the churches.

A Letter to the Church in Philadelphia

⁷"Also write to the angel of the church in Philadelphia:

"The True One, the Holy One, the one who has the key of David, who opens doors that no one can shut, and he shuts doors that no one can open, is saying these things.

⁸"I know your activities. Listen, I have given you a door that is open, and no one can shut it. You have a little power, but you have paid attention to my word, and you have not denied my name. ⁹Pay close attention, I am making those from the synagogue of Satan, those who say they are Jews and are not, but are lying—see I will make them come and bow down at your

---

[ii] Or, "a few names." In Greek culture, "name" often referred to "reputation."

feet, and they will recognize that I have loved you. ¹⁰Because you have paid attention to my message of endurance, I also will keep you from the hour of testing that is about to come on the entire inhabited world[i] to test those who are dwelling in the land.

¹¹"I am coming soon. Hold tightly to what you have, so that no one may take your crown. ¹²He who overcomes, I will make him a pillar in the temple of my God, and he will never depart from it ever; and I will write upon him the name of my God, and the name of the city of my God, the new Jerusalem that is coming down from heaven from my God. I will also write my new name upon him.

¹³"He who has ears, let him understand what the Spirit is saying to the churches.

A Letter to the Church in Laodicea

¹⁴"Also write to the angel of the church in Laodicea:

"The faithful and true witness, the ruler of God's creation is saying these things.

¹⁵"I know your activities, that you are neither cold nor hot; if only you were cold or hot! ¹⁶So, because you are lukewarm and neither hot nor cold, I am about to vomit you out of my mouth. ¹⁷Because you say, 'I am rich,' and, 'I have become rich and I have nothing that I need,' but you do not know that you are pathetic, in need of pity, poor, blind, and naked. ¹⁸I advise you to buy from me gold refined by fire so that you might be rich; and white garments, that you might put on clothing so the shame of your nakedness might not be open to view; and eye salve to anoint your eyes so that you might see.

¹⁹"As many as I love, I correct and discipline; so, be eager and repent. ²⁰Look, I have taken a stand at the door, and I am knocking. If anyone hears my voice and opens the door, I will come into him and I will dine with him, and he with me.

---

[i] "Inhabited world," usually referring to the Roman world.

²¹"He who overcomes, I will give him the right to sit with me on my throne, as I also overcame and sat with my Father on his throne.

²²"He who has ears, let him understand what the Spirit is saying to the churches."

A Door Standing Open to Heaven

Chapter Four

¹After these things, suddenly, I saw a door that stood open in heaven, and the first voice that I heard—as loud as a trumpet—was speaking with me saying, "Come up here, and I will show you what must happen after these things."

The Throne Room in Heaven

²Immediately, I was in spirit, and notably, there was a throne positioned in heaven, and someone was sitting on it. ³He who was seated was like a jasper or carnelian stone in appearance, and a rainbow was all around the throne. The rainbow was like an emerald in appearance. ⁴Around the throne were twenty-four thrones, and twenty-four elders were seated upon the thrones clothed in white garments, with golden crowns on their heads. ⁵Flashes of lightning, voices, and crashes of thunder emanated from the throne, and seven flaming torches were burning before the throne, which are the Seven Spirits of God. ⁶There was something like a sea of glass in front of the throne, similar to crystal.

In the middle of the throne and around the throne were four living beings full of eyes in front and in back. ⁷The first living being was like a lion, the second living being was like an ox, the third living being had a face like a man, and the fourth living being was like an eagle that was flying. ⁸The four living beings, each one of them, had six wings full of eyes all around and within; and day and night they never stop saying,

> "Holy, holy, holy is the Lord God, the Ruler of all things, who was, who is, and who is coming."

⁹Whenever the living beings give glory, honor, and thanks to him who sits on the throne, to him who lives forever and ever, ¹⁰the twenty-four elders fall down before him who sits on the throne, and worship him who lives forever and ever; and they throw their crowns before the throne saying,

> ¹¹"You are worthy, our Lord and God, to receive glory, honor, and power, for you created all things, and by your will they exist and were created."

The Scroll in Heaven

Chapter Five

¹Then I saw, in the right hand of him who sits on the throne, a scroll inscribed on the front and back; it was sealed with seven seals. ²I also saw a powerful angel proclaiming with a loud voice, "Who is worthy to open the scroll and to break its seals?" ³But no one in heaven, upon the earth, or under the earth was able to open the scroll or to examine it, ⁴and I began to wail loudly, because no worthy person was found to open the scroll or examine it.

The Lamb is Worthy

⁵One from among the elders said to me, "Stop wailing, for look, the Lion who is from the tribe of Judah, the Root of David, has overcome so that he can open the scroll and its seven seals."

⁶Then I saw a Lamb who appeared to have been slaughtered as a sacrifice. He had taken a stand between the throne and the four living beings and the elders. He had seven horns and seven eyes, which are the Seven Spirits of God who are sent out into all the earth. ⁷Then he came and took the scroll from the right hand of him who sits on the throne, ⁸and when he had taken the scroll, the four living beings and the twenty-four elders fell

down in front of the Lamb. Each of them was holding a harp and golden bowls filled with incense, which are the prayers of the saints.

⁹Then they sang a new song calling,

"Worthy are you to take the scroll and to open its seals,
for you were slaughtered as a sacrifice, and with your blood you purchased people for God from every tribe, language, people, and nation. ¹⁰And you have made them a kingdom and priests for our God, and they will reign upon the earth."

¹¹Then I looked, and I heard the sound of many angels around the throne, and of the living beings and the elders, and the number of them was ten thousands of ten thousands,ⁱ and thousands of thousands. ¹²They were speaking very loudly,

"Worthy is the Lamb who was slaughtered as a sacrifice,
to receive power, wealth, wisdom, strength, honor, glory, and blessing."

¹³Then I heard every creature that is in heaven, on the earth, under the earth, and upon the sea, and all the things in them saying,

"To him who sits on the throne and to the Lamb, let there
be blessing, honor, glory and power forever and ever."

¹⁴The four living beings kept saying, "Amen;" and the elders fell down and worshiped.

Opening the Seals on the Scroll

Chapter Six

¹Then, when the Lamb opened the first of the seven seals, I saw and heard one of the four living beings speak. It was like a sound of thunder, "Set out!" ²I also looked, and immediately a white horse

---

ⁱ Or, "myriads of myriads."

appeared; and the one sitting on it held a bow, and a crown was given to him. He went out conquering, and so that he might conquer.

³When he opened the second seal, I heard the second living being speak, "Set out!" ⁴Then another horse, a flaming red one, went out; and an assignment was given to the one who was sitting upon it to take the peace from the earth so that men would slaughter each other; and a large sword was given to him.

⁵When he opened the third seal, I heard the third living being speak, "Set out!" I looked, and immediately a black horse appeared; the one sitting on it held a pair of scales in his hand; ⁶and I heard something like a voice in the middle of the four living beings speaking, "A ration[i] of wheat for a denarius, and three rations of barley for a denarius, but do not damage the olive oil and the wine."

⁷When he opened the fourth seal, I heard the voice of the fourth living creature speaking, "Set out!" ⁸I looked, and immediately a pale gray horse appeared; and the name of the one sitting on it was Death; and Hades followed after him. Authority was given to him over the fourth part of the earth to kill by sword, by famine, by plague, and by the animals of the earth.

⁹When he opened the fifth seal, I saw under the altar the souls of those who had been put to death because of the word of God and the testimony which they held tightly. ¹⁰They cried out with a loud voice saying, "How long will it be, holy and true Sovereign, until you judge those who dwell on the earth and avenge our blood?" ¹¹Then a white robe was given to each of them. They were also told that they should rest a little while yet, until those who were about to be killed as they had been, both from their fellow servants and their brothers, was completed.

---

[i] A ration (choinix) is considered a proper provision for one man. A denarius was a day's wage for a working man. These prices indicate rising prices for basic commodities.

¹²I looked when he opened the sixth seal, and there was a great earthquake, and the sun was black like sackcloth made of hair, and the whole moon was like blood. ¹³The stars of heaven also fell to the earth, in the same way that late season figs fall from a fig tree when it is shaken by a strong wind. ¹⁴The sky split open like a scroll being rolled up, and every mountain and island was moved from its place.

¹⁵Then the kings of the earth, the nobility, the high ranking military officers, the wealthy, the powerful, and every slave and free man, hid themselves in the caves and among the rocks of the mountains. ¹⁶They said to the mountains and to the rocks, "Collapse on us," and "Hide us from the sight of him who sits on the throne, and from the vengeance of the Lamb; ¹⁷for the great day of their vengeance has come, and who is able to stand?"

Sealing the One Hundred Forty-Four Thousand

Chapter Seven

¹After this I saw four angels taking a stand at the four corners of the earth. They were holding the four winds of the earth so that the wind would not blow on the earth, the sea, or any tree. ²Then I saw another angel coming up from the sunrise. He held a seal of the living God, and he called out with a loud voice to the four angels who were given authority to harm the earth and the sea. ³He said, "Do not harm the earth, the sea, or the trees until we seal the servants of our God on their foreheads.

⁴I also heard the number of those who were sealed, one hundred forty-four thousand. They were sealed from every tribe of the sons of Israel.

⁵Twelve thousand were sealed from the tribe of Judah,
twelve thousand from the tribe of Reuben,
twelve thousand from the tribe of Gad,
⁶twelve thousand from the tribe of Asher,
twelve thousand from the tribe of Naphtali,
twelve thousand from the tribe of Manasseh,

⁷twelve thousand from the tribe of Simeon,
twelve thousand from the tribe of Levi,
twelve thousand from the tribe of Issachar,
⁸twelve thousand from the tribe of Zebulun,
twelve thousand from the tribe of Joseph, and
twelve thousand from the tribe of Benjamin were sealed.

Those Clothed in White from the Great Tribulation

⁹After these things I looked, and at that moment there was a large crowd that no one was able to count, from every nation, tribe, people, and language. They had taken a stand before the throne and before the Lamb. They were clothed in white robes and had palm branches in their hands. ¹⁰They cried out with a loud voice and said,

> "Salvation is in our God who sits on the throne,
> and in the Lamb!"

¹¹All the angels also took their stand around the throne, the elders, and the four living beings, and they fell on their faces before the throne and worshiped God ¹²and said,

> "Amen. Blessing, glory, wisdom, thanksgiving,
> honor, power, and strength be to our God
> forever and ever. Amen."

¹³Then one from among the elders responded and said to me, "These clothed in white robes, who are they and from where have they come?"

¹⁴I said to him, "My lord, you know."

He said to me, "These are those who are coming from the great tribulation. They have washed their robes and made them white in the blood of the Lamb. ¹⁵For this reason, they are before the throne of God, and they serve him day and night in his temple; and he who sits on the throne will build his tabernacle over them. ¹⁶They will never hunger or thirst again, nor will the sun shine down upon them with any oppressive heat; ¹⁷for the Lamb in the middle of the throne will shepherd them and guide them to springs of living water. God will wipe away every tear from their eyes."

Opening the Seventh Seal
Chapter Eight

¹Then, when he opened the seventh seal, there was a silence in heaven for a half an hour or so. ²I saw the seven angels, the ones who have taken a stand before God, and seven trumpets were given to them.

³Another angel came and was stationed at the altar holding a golden censer, and much incense was given to him so that he would offer it with the prayers of all the saints on the golden altar before the throne. ⁴Then the smoke of the incense from the right hand of the angel arose with the prayers of the saints before God. ⁵The angel took the censer, filled it from the fire of the altar, threw it to the earth, and there were crashes of thunder, voices, flashes of lightning, and an earthquake.

Sounding the Seven Trumpets

⁶The seven angels who held the seven trumpets prepared themselves so that they might sound them. ⁷Then the first angel sounded his trumpet, and there was hail and fire mixed with blood, and it was thrown to the earth, and a third of the earth burned, a third of the trees burned, and all the green grass burned.

⁸Then the second angel sounded his trumpet, so that a great mountain burning with fire was also thrown into the sea, and a third of the sea became blood. ⁹A third of the things created in the sea, those things that had life, died; and a third of the ships were completely destroyed.

¹⁰Then the third angel sounded his trumpet, and a great star burning like a torch fell from the sky. It fell upon a third of the rivers and on the springs of water. ¹¹The name of the star is

called Wormwood,[i] and a third of the waters became bitter, and many men died from the waters because they were made bitter.

¹²Then the fourth angel sounded his trumpet, and a third of the sun, a third of the moon, and a third of the stars were struck down so that a third of them were dark, and the light of the day did not shine for a third of it, and the night was the same.

A Warning About the Next Three Trumpets: Three Woes

¹³Then I looked, and I heard one eagle flying directly overhead in the sky crying with a loud voice, "Woe, woe, woe to those who dwell on the earth because of the trumpet blasts that remain, for the three angels are about to sound them."

Sounding the Fifth Trumpet: The First Woe

Chapter Nine

¹The fifth angel sounded his trumpet, and I saw a star that had fallen from heaven to the earth, and the key to the entrance shaft of the Abyss was given to him. ²He opened the entrance shaft of the Abyss, and smoke rose from the shaft like the smoke of a great furnace; and the sun and the air were made dark from the smoke of the entrance shaft. ³Then locusts came out from the smoke to the earth, and authority was given to them, like the scorpions of the earth have authority. ⁴They were told that they could not harm the grass of the earth, nor anything green, nor any tree, but only the men who do not have the seal of God on their foreheads. ⁵But they were not given authority to kill them, only to torture them for five months, and their torture was like the pain of a scorpion when it strikes a man. ⁶In those days, men will seek death, but will not find it. They will crave death, but death will escape them.

⁷The locusts were similar to horses prepared for war. Upon their heads were something like crowns of gold, and their faces

---

[i] "Wormwood" is also the name of a bitter herb known as Artemisia Absinthium.

were like the faces of men. ⁸They also had hair like the hair of women, and their teeth were like the teeth of lions. ⁹They had breastplates like breastplates of iron, and the sound of their wings were like the sound of chariots with many horses running into battle. ¹⁰They had tails and stingers like scorpions, and they carry in their tails their authority to harm men for five months. ¹¹They have a king over them, the angel of the Abyss. In the Hebrew dialect his name is Abaddon, but in the Greek his name is Apollyon.

¹²The one woe is past, but see, there are still two woes coming after these things.

Sounding the Sixth Trumpet: The Second Woe

¹³Then the sixth angel sounded his trumpet, and I heard one voice from the four corners of the golden altar that is before God. ¹⁴The voice was saying to the sixth angel, the one who had the trumpet, "Free the four angels who are bound at the great river Euphrates." ¹⁵Then the four angels who had been prepared for this hour, day, month, and year were freed so that they might kill the third of men. ¹⁶The number of the cavalry soldiers was twice ten thousand ten thousands.[ii] I heard their number.

¹⁷In this same way, in the vision, I also saw the horses and those who sat on them. They had breastplates that were as red as fire, as blue as hyacinth, and as yellow as sulfur. The heads of the horses were like the heads of lions, and from their mouths fire, smoke, and sulfur burst forth. ¹⁸The third of men were killed by these three horses, by the fire, the smoke, and the sulfur that burst forth from their mouths. ¹⁹For the authority of the horses is carried in their mouths and in their tails; for their tails are like snakes that have heads, and they do harm with them.

²⁰Then the rest of men, those who were not killed by these plagues, did not repent of the works of their hands, so that they would no longer worship demons, idols of gold, silver, bronze, stone, and wood; things that are not able to see, hear, or walk.

[ii] Or, "Two myriads of myriads."

²¹They also did not repent for their murders, their drug-fueled witchcraft,ⁱ their illicit sexual relationships, or their acts of theft.

The Powerful Angel and the Little Scroll

Chapter Ten

¹Then I saw another powerful angel descending from heaven. He was clothed with a cloud, a rainbow was over his head, his face was like the sun, and his feet were like pillars of fire. ²In his hand he held a little scroll that had been opened. He put his right foot on the sea, and his left foot on the land; ³and he roared with a loud voice (like a lion roaring), and when he roared, the seven thunders spoke with their own voices. ⁴When the seven thunders spoke, I began to write, but I heard a voice from heaven saying, "Seal the things which the seven thunders have spoken, and do not write them."

⁵Then the angel, the one I saw taking his stand on the sea and upon the land, lifted his right hand to heaven, ⁶and vowed by the one who lives forever and ever, who created the sky and the things in it, the land and the things on it, and the sea and the things in it, "Time is up. ⁷In the days of the sound of the seventh angel, when he is about to sound his trumpet, the mystery of God will be complete, just as he proclaimed as good news to his servants the prophets."

⁸Then the voice which I heard from heaven spoke to me again and said, "Go, take the scroll, the one that has been opened in the hand of the angel who has taken a stand upon the sea and upon the land."

⁹So, I went to the angel and told him to give the little scroll to me. He said to me, "Take it and eat it. It will make your stomach bitter, but it will be sweet as honey in your mouth."

ⁱ Attempting to access the spiritual realm or achieve spiritual insight using drugs or potions.

¹⁰I took the little scroll from the angel's hand and ate it. It was sweet as honey in my mouth, but when I ate it, my stomach became bitter. ¹¹Then they said to me, "You must again prophesy against many peoples, nations, languages, and kings."

The Two Witnesses

Chapter Eleven

¹Then a measuring reed the length of a staff was given to me, and I was told, "Rise up and measure the sanctuary of God, the altar, and those who are worshiping in the sanctuary. ²Set aside the outer court outside of the temple, and do not measure it, for it has been given to the Gentiles. They will trample the holy city for forty-two months. ³I will also appoint my two witnesses, and they will prophesy one thousand two hundred sixty days, clothed with sackcloth."

⁴These are the two olive trees and the two lampstands which have taken their stand in front of the Lord of the earth. ⁵If anyone wants to harm them, fire goes out from their mouths and devours their enemies. If anyone desires to harm them, it is fitting that he be put to death in this way. ⁶The witnesses have the authority to shut up the skies so that rain will not fall during the days of their prophecy; they have the authority over the waters to turn them to blood, and to strike the earth with every kind of plague whenever they desire.

⁷Then, when they have completed their testimony, the beast that comes up out of the Abyss will make war against them, prevail over them, and kill them. ⁸Their dead bodies will remain on the streets of the great city, which is spiritually called Sodom and Egypt, where also their Lord was crucified. ⁹Then those from among the people, tribes, languages, and nations will look at their dead bodies for three and a half days, and they will not allow them to be put in a tomb. ¹⁰Those who dwell on the earth will be glad and rejoice over them, and they will send gifts to

each other, because these two prophets tormented those who dwell upon the earth.

¹¹But after three and a half days, the Spirit of Life from God came into them, and they stood up on their feet. Great fear fell upon those who were watching, ¹²and they heard a loud voice from heaven saying to them, "Come up here!" Then they went up into the sky in a cloud, even while their enemies were watching them. ¹³There was a great earthquake at that very hour, and the tenth of the city fell, and seven thousand notable men[i] were killed in the earthquake, but those who remained were frightened and gave glory to the God of heaven.

¹⁴The second woe has gone forth, but see, the third woe is coming swiftly.

Sounding the Seventh Trumpet: The Third Woe

¹⁵Then the seventh angel sounded his trumpet, and there were loud voices in heaven saying,

> "The kingdom of the world has become the kingdom of our Lord and of his Christ, and he will reign forever and ever."

¹⁶And the twenty-four elders who sit on their thrones before God fell upon their faces and worshiped God ¹⁷saying,

> "We give thanks to you, Lord God, Ruler of all things, who is and who was, for you have taken up your great power and have begun to reign. ¹⁸The nations were furious, but your vengeance has come. It is the time to judge the dead, and to give your servants the prophets their reward, as well as your saints and those who fear your name, the youngest

---

[i] Literally, "names of men." In Greek culture, "name" often referred to "reputation."

and the oldest;[ii] and to destroy those who are destroying the earth."

¹⁹Then the temple of God in heaven was opened, and the ark of his covenant was revealed in his temple, and there were flashes of lightning, voices, crashes of thunder, an earthquake, and a severe hail.

The Sign in the Heavens: The Woman and the Male Child
Chapter Twelve

¹Then a great sign[iii] was revealed in the sky, a woman who was clothed with the sun, and the moon was beneath her feet, and a crown of twelve stars was on her head. ²She had a child in her womb, and because she was in labor and experiencing birth pains, she cried out. ³Then another sign was revealed in the sky, and remarkably, it was a great fiery red dragon which had seven heads and ten horns, and on his heads were seven diadems. ⁴His tail dragged the third of the stars from the sky and tossed them to the earth. The dragon took his stand in front of the woman who was about to give birth, so that when she gave birth he might devour the child. ⁵She gave birth to a son, a male child, who is destined to shepherd all the nations with an iron shepherd's staff. Then the child was caught away to God and to his throne. ⁶The woman escaped into the desert, where she had a place that was prepared by God, so that there they would care for her one thousand two hundred and sixty days.

Michael and His Angels Expel the Dragon

⁷Now a battle began in heaven. Michael and his angels fought against the dragon, and the dragon and his angels fought back. ⁸But the dragon was not powerful enough to win, and

---

[ii] "Youngest and oldest" could also be translated "the small and the great," or (less likely) "the least important and the most important."

[iii] Or, "a great portent." See Genesis 1:14 for this purpose of the constellations.

their position in heaven was lost. ⁹The great dragon was thrown out of heaven. The ancient serpent, who is called the Accuser and Satan, who deceives the entire inhabited world, was thrown down to the earth, and his angels were thrown down with him.

¹⁰Then I heard a loud voice in heaven saying,

> "Now the salvation, the power, the kingdom of our God and the authority of his Christ have come. For the accuser of our brothers was thrown down. He accused them before our God day and night."
>
> ¹¹"They overcame him through the blood of the Lamb, through the word of their testimony, and they did not love their lives when threatened with death.
>
> ¹²"For this reason, rejoice, O heavens and you who reside in them. Woe to the earth and the sea, because the Accuser has come down to you. He is filled with great anger, because he knows he has little time.

¹³Then, when the dragon saw that he was thrown down to the earth, he persecuted the woman who gave birth to the male child. ¹⁴Two wings of a great eagle were given to the woman, so that she could fly into the desert to her place there where she would be sustained for time, times, and half a time, away from the presence of the snake. ¹⁵Then the snake sent water like a river from his mouth after the woman, so that she would be swept away in it. ¹⁶But the earth came to the aid of the woman, and the earth opened its mouth and swallowed the river which the dragon sent from his mouth. ¹⁷The dragon was furious with the woman, and went away to make war against the rest of her offspring, those who keep the commands of God and hold tightly to the testimony of Jesus.

Chapter Thirteen

¹The dragon took his stand upon the sand by the sea.

The Beast Rises from the Sea

Then I saw a beast rising up out of the sea. He had ten horns and seven heads, and on its horns were ten diadems, and on its heads were slanderous names. ²The beast that I saw was like a leopard, but its feet were like a bear and its mouth was like the mouth of a lion. The dragon gave his power, his throne, and great authority to the beast. ³One of its heads had been slain and was dead, but its mortal wound had been healed. The whole earth was filled with wonder and followed behind the beast. ⁴They worshiped the dragon because he had given authority to the beast, and they worshiped the beast saying, "Who is like the beast, and who can fight against him?"

⁵A mouth was given it so that it might speak strange words and slanderous things; it was also given authority to be active for forty-two months. ⁶Then it opened its mouth for slanderous accusations against God, to slander his name, his tabernacle, and those who reside in heaven. ⁷It was given authority to make war against the saints and to overcome them. Authority was also given to it over every tribe, people, language, and nation. ⁸Everyone who dwells upon the earth will worship it, that is, anyone whose name has not been written in the scroll of the Lamb's book of life—the one who was slaughtered as a sacrifice from the founding of the world.

⁹If anyone has ears, let him understand.
¹⁰If anyone leads others into captivity, he will go into captivity.
If anyone kills with the sword, he will be killed with the sword.
Let the endurance and the trust of the saints be on display here.

The Beast Rising from the Land

¹¹Then I saw another beast rising up from the land. It had two horns like Lamb, but it spoke like Dragon. ¹²It uses all the authority of the first beast in its presence, and made the earth and those who dwell in it worship the first beast—the one whose mortal wound had been healed. ¹³It also performed great miracles, so that it even made fire fall from the sky to the earth in the presence of the people. ¹⁴Because of the miracles which it was given authority to perform in the presence of the beast, it deceived those who dwell on the earth, and it told those who dwell on the earth to make an image to the beast who had the fatal sword wound but lived. ¹⁵Then it was given authority to give breath to the image of the beast, so that the image of the beast could also speak, and to sentence all those who did not worship the image of the beast to death. ¹⁶It also made everyone, from the youngest to the oldest, whether rich or poor, free or slave, receive an imprint that its followers would give them upon their right hand or upon their forehead, ¹⁷so that nobody was able to buy or sell unless they had the imprint—the name of the beast or the number of its name.

¹⁸Here is wisdom, the one who has understanding must calculate the number of the beast, for it is the number of a man, and his number is six hundred sixty-six.

The Lamb and the One Hundred Forty-Four Thousand

Chapter Fourteen

¹Then I looked, and suddenly, the Lamb took his stand on Mount Zion, and with him were one hundred forty-four thousand who had his name and the name of his Father written on their foreheads. ²I heard a sound from heaven, like the sound of many waters and like the sound of loud crashes of thunder. The sound which I had heard was like the sound of harpists singing while they played. They were playing their harps ³and singing a new song before the throne, and before the four living

beings and the elders. No one was able to learn the song except the hundred forty-four thousand, those who had been redeemed from the earth. ⁴These are those who were not morally compromised by women, for they are virgins. These are those who follow the Lamb wherever he may go. These were bought from among men as firstfruits to God and the Lamb. ⁵No falsehood was found in their mouths. They are spotless.

The Announcements of the Three Angels

⁶Then I saw another angel flying directly overhead who had the eternal gospel to proclaim as good news to those who remain upon the earth, to every nation, tribe, language, and people. ⁷He said in a loud voice, "Fear God and give him glory, for the hour of his judgment has come. Worship him who made the heaven and the earth, the sea, and the springs of water."

⁸Then another angel, a second one, followed calling, "Babylon the Great has fallen! It has fallen! She who made all nations drink from the wine of the overheated passions of her sexual lewdness."

⁹Then another angel, a third one, followed them calling in a loud voice, "If anyone worships the beast and its image, and receives its imprint upon his forehead or on his hand, ¹⁰he will also drink from the undiluted wine of God's anger, which has been poured out into the cup of his vengeance. He will be tormented in fire and sulfur in the presence of the holy angels and the Lamb. ¹¹The smoke of their torment will ascend forever and ever, and those who worship the beast and its image will have no respite day or night, as well as anyone who receives the imprint of its name."

¹²Let the endurance of the saints be on display in this way: they keep God's command and are faithful to Jesus.

¹³Then I heard a voice from heaven saying, "Write this:

> " 'Blessed are the dead who die in the Lord from this time forward.'"

Revelation 14:14

"Yes," says the Spirit, "So that they may rest from their labors, for their works will follow after them."

The Harvest of the Earth

[14] Then I looked, and remarkably, there was a white cloud, and one like the Son of Man was seated on the cloud. He had a golden crown upon his head, and a sharp sickle in his hand. [15] Then another angel came out from the temple shouting in a loud voice to him who was seated on the cloud, "Swing your sickle and reap, for the hour to harvest has come, since the fruit of the earth has withered."[i] [16] He who was seated on the cloud swung his sickle over the earth, and the earth was reaped.

[17] Then another angel came out from the temple, the one in heaven. He also held a sharp sickle. [18] Another angel also went out from the altar who had authority over the fire. He called out with a loud voice to the angel who held the sharp sickle and said, "Swing your sharp sickle and gather the clusters of grapes from the vineyard of the earth, for its grapes are at their prime."

[19] The angel swung his sickle on the earth and gathered the fruit from the vineyard of the earth. Then he threw it into the winepress of the great anger of God. [20] The winepress was pressed[ii] outside the city, and blood of the grapes[iii] from the winepress flowed out to the height of the bridles of the horses for a distance of two thousand stadia.[iv]

---

[i] The Greek word means withered. The contrast is between the fact that there is very little good fruit on the earth, and verse 18 where the fruit of evil is flourishing. See the parable of the wheat and the tares (Mt. 13:24ff.)

[ii] The word translated "pressed" is a word that means "trodden underfoot," the normal way that grapes were pressed in that day.

[iii] See Genesis 49:11 and Deuteronomy 32:14 for the fact that "the blood of grapes" is what came from a winepress.

[iv] About 200 miles.

The Seven Last Plagues

Chapter Fifteen

¹Then I saw another great and astonishing sign in heaven, seven angels who held the seven last plagues. They are last because with them the anger of God is spent. ²Then I saw something like a sea of glass mixed with fire, and those who had overcome the beast, its image, and the number of its name, taking their stand on the sea of glass. They were holding harps from God, ³and they sang the song of Moses, the servant of God, and the song of the Lamb, singing,

> "Great and astonishing are your works, O Lord God,
>   Ruler of all things; Righteous and true are your ways,
>   King of the nations.
> ⁴"Who will not fear you, O Lord, and praise your name?
>   For only you are holy. For all the nations will come
>   and worship before you, because your righteous deeds
>   have been made known."

⁵Then, after these things, I looked, and the temple, specifically the tabernacle of testimony, was opened in heaven, ⁶and the seven angels who held the seven plagues came out from the temple. They were dressed in bright clean linen with golden sashes around their chests. ⁷One of the four living beings gave seven golden bowls to the seven angels. They were full of the anger of the God who lives forever and ever. ⁸Then the temple was filled with smoke from the glory of God and from his power; and no one was able to enter into the temple until the seven plagues of the seven angels were carried out.

Pouring Out the Seven Bowls of God's Judgment

Chapter Sixteen

¹Then I heard a loud voice from the temple saying to the seven angels, "Go and pour out the seven bowls of God's anger on the earth."

²The first went out and poured his bowl on the earth, and what he poured became a harmful and evil sore upon the men who had the imprint of the beast and worshiped its image.

³The second poured out his bowl on the sea, and what he poured became blood like the blood of a dead man, and every living thing in the sea died.

⁴The third poured out his bowl on the rivers and the springs of water, and what he poured became blood. ⁵Then I heard the angel of the waters saying,

> "You are righteous, you who are and who were, the Holy One, because you have judged these things, ⁶for they poured out the blood of your saints and prophets, and you have given them blood to drink. The judgments are fitting."

⁷Then I heard the altar saying,

> "Yes, Lord God, Ruler of all things, your judgments are true and righteous."

⁸The fourth angel poured out his bowl upon the sun, and it was given authority to burn men with its fire. ⁹Men were burned by severe heat, and they slandered[i] the name of the God who has the authority over these plagues, but they did not repent so that they could give glory to him.

¹⁰Then the fifth poured out his bowl upon the throne of the beast, and its kingdom fell into darkness, and they chewed their tongues from their anguish. ¹¹They also slandered the God of heaven because of their afflictions and their sores, but they did not repent from their actions.

¹²The sixth poured out his bowl upon the great river, the Euphrates, and its water dried up, so that the way was prepared for the kings who come from the east.[ii] ¹³Then I saw three unclean spirits like frogs from the mouth of the dragon, from

---

[i] Or, "blasphemed." Also in verses 11 and 21.

[ii] More literally, "the kings who came from the direction of the rising sun."

the mouth of the beast, and from the mouth of the false prophet, ¹⁴for they are the spirits of demons that are going out to the kings of the entire inhabited world. They perform miracles to gather them together for the war on the great day of God, the Ruler of all things.

> ¹⁵"Look, I am coming like a thief. Blessed are those who are alert and hold tightly to their garments, that they do not walk about naked so people will see their shame."

¹⁶They gathered them together to the place which is called in the Hebrew dialect, Harmageddon.ⁱⁱⁱ

¹⁷The seventh poured out his bowl into the air, and a loud voice came out from the temple, out from the throne saying, "It is over." ¹⁸Then there were flashes of lightning, voices, crashes of thunder. There was also a great earthquake. It was so great an earthquake that nothing like it had happened since the time man was created on the earth. ¹⁹The great city tumbled into three parts, and the cities of the nations fell. Babylon the Great was brought to mind in the presence of God, so that he gave her the cup of the wine which is the fury of his vengeance. ²⁰Then every island fled, and the mountains were not found, ²¹and large hailstones, as heavy as a talent,ⁱᵛ fell down from the sky upon the men; and the men slandered God for the plague of hail stones, because the plague of hail stones was very intense.

The Judgment on the Great Prostitute

Chapter Seventeen

¹One from among the seven angels who had the seven bowls came and spoke with me saying, "Come! I will show you the judgment of the great prostitute who is sitting on many waters. ²The kings of the earth indulged in sexual encounters with her,

---

ⁱⁱⁱ Harmageddon means "Mount Megiddo."

ⁱᵛ About 100 pounds.

and those who dwell on the earth were intoxicated by the wine of her sexual misconduct."

³Then he took me in spirit to a desert. I saw a woman sitting on a scarlet beast. It was full of slanderous names and had seven heads and ten horns. ⁴The woman was clothed in purple and scarlet, and she was covered with gold ornaments, valuable gems, and pearls. She held a golden cup in her hand filled with detestable things and impurities from her sexual promiscuity.

⁵A name was written on her forehead:

Mystery, Babylon the Great, The Mother of Prostitutes and the Detestable Things of the Earth.

⁶Then I saw the woman was drinking freely from the blood of the saints and the blood of the martyrs of Jesus. When I saw her, I was overwhelmed with wonder.

⁷The angel said to me, "Why are you amazed? I will tell you the mystery of the woman and the beast with seven heads and ten horns that is bearing her. ⁸The beast which you saw was, and is not, and is about to come up out of the Abyss, and will go into destruction. Those who dwell on the earth, whose name has not been written in the scroll of life from the founding of the world, when they see the beast will be bewildered by it because it was, and is not, and will come.

⁹"Let the mind having wisdom show itself. The seven heads are seven high hills where the woman is sitting. There are also seven kings, ¹⁰five have fallen, one is, another has not yet come. When he has come, he must remain for a little while. ¹¹The beast who was, but is not, is an eighth king and is from among the seven, and is going to destruction. ¹²The ten horns that you saw are ten kings. They have not yet received a kingdom, but they will receive authority as kings for one hour along with the beast. ¹³These kings have one purpose, that they give their power and authority to the beast. ¹⁴These kings will wage war against the Lamb, but the Lamb will overcome them, because he is

Lord of lords and King of kings, and his called, elect, and faithful ones are with him."

¹⁵Then he said to me, "The waters that you saw, where the prostitute sits, are peoples, crowds, nations, and languages. ¹⁶The ten horns and the beast you saw, they will hate the prostitute and will leave her stripped and naked. They will eat her flesh and burn her with fire. ¹⁷For God put it in their heart to do his purpose and to have one intent, to give their kingdom to the beast until the words of God are fulfilled. ¹⁸And the woman you saw is the great city that has dominion over the kings of the earth."

The Fall of Babylon the Great

Chapter Eighteen

¹After these things, I saw another angel coming down from heaven. He had great authority, and the earth was given light by his glory. ²He cried out with a powerful voice, "Babylon the Great has fallen! It has fallen! She has become a house for demons and a prison for every unclean spirit, a prison for every unclean bird, and a prison for every unclean and despised animal. ³For all the nations and kings of the earth have drunk of the wine of the overheated passions of her sexual lewdness. and have indulged in sexual misconduct with her, and the merchants of the earth have become rich from her overwhelming sensual indulgence."

⁴Then I heard another voice from heaven saying, "Come out from her my people, so that you do not participate in her sins, and so that you do not receive punishment from her plagues; ⁵for her sins have bunched together and reached heaven, and God has remembered her unrighteous acts. ⁶Repay her as also she has repaid, and double and redouble that payment appropriately for her deeds. In the cup which she has mixed, mix double for her. ⁷As much as she has honored herself and lived in sensual indulgence, to that same degree give her torment and

grief, because in her heart she says, 'I am seated as a queen. I am not a widow. I will never see grief.' ⁸For this reason, her plagues, death, grief, and famine, will occur in one day; and she will be burned with fire, for the Lord God who judges her is powerful.

⁹"Then the kings of the earth who committed sexual immorality with her and lived in sensual indulgence, will weep and mourn over her when they see the smoke of her immolation. ¹⁰They will take their stand at a distance for fear of her torment, and they will say,

> " 'Woe! Woe! The great city, Babylon, the mighty city, for your judgment has come in one hour.'

¹¹"The merchants of the earth will weep and mourn over her, because no one is buying their shipments any longer—¹²shipments of gold, silver, valuable gems, pearls, fine linen, purple, silk, scarlet, all kinds of wood from the citron tree, every type of ivory container, all types of containers made from precious wood, bronze, iron, and marble; ¹³and shipments of cinnamon, spice, incense, fragrant oil, frankincense, wine, olive oil, fine flour, grain, herd animals and sheep, horses, carriages, and the bodies and souls of men.

¹⁴"The fruit that your soul desired has fled from you, and all the costly things, and the splendid things are lost to you, and they will not find them anymore. ¹⁵The merchants who sold these things, who became rich from them, will take their stand at a distance for fear of her torment, and they will weep and mourn ¹⁶saying,

> " 'Woe! Woe to the great city, she who was clothed with fine linen, purple, and scarlet, and covered with gold, valuable gems, and pearls, ¹⁷for such wealth as this has been stripped away in one hour.'

"Then every ship's captain, everyone who sails as a passenger, every sailor, and as many as work on the sea, took their stand at a distance, ¹⁸and when they saw the smoke of her immolation, they cried out saying, 'What city is like this great city?'

¹⁹"Then they threw dust on their heads and began crying, weeping, and mourning saying,

> " 'Woe! Woe to the great city. In her all those who have ships on the sea were made rich from her wealth; now it has been stripped away in one hour.'

²⁰"Rejoice over her, O heaven, and you saints, apostles, and prophets, because God has passed judgment on your behalf against her."

²¹Then a powerful angel lifted a stone as large as a millstone, and threw it into the sea saying,

> "In this way, Babylon, the great city, will be thrown down with great violence, and after this it will never be found.
>
> ²²"After this, the sound of the harpists playing and singing, the musicians, the flute players, and trumpeters will never be heard in you; and after this, no craftsman of any trade will ever be found in you, and after this, the sound of the mill will never be heard in you, ²³and after this, the light of a lamp will never shine in you, and after this, the voice of the bridegroom and bride will never be heard in you, because your merchants were the nobility of the earth, because all the nations were deceived by your drug-fueled witchcraft;[i] ²⁴and the blood of the prophets and saints was found in her, and everyone who was slaughtered on the earth."

The Lord Reigns

Chapter Nineteen

¹After these things, I heard something like the loud noise of a great multitude in heaven saying,

---

[i] Attempting to achieve spiritual insight etc. using drugs or potions.

> "Hallelujah! The salvation, the glory, and the power belong to our God; ²for true and righteous are his judgments; because he has judged the great prostitute who was corrupting the earth with her sexual misconduct, and he has avenged the blood of his servants shed by her hand."

³Then they said next, "Hallelujah! Her smoke rises up forever and ever!"

⁴The twenty-four elders and the four living beings fell down and worshiped God who was seated on the throne saying, "Amen! Hallelujah!"

⁵A voice came out from the throne and said, "Praise our God all you his servants and those who fear him, the young and the old."

⁶Then I heard something like a noise of a great multitude, like the sound of many waters, and like the sound of powerful crashes of thunder that said,

> "Hallelujah! For our Lord God, Ruler of all things, reigns! ⁷Let us rejoice and celebrate, let us give glory to him, because the marriage of the Lamb has come, and his bride has prepared herself."

⁸Fine linen clothing, radiant and clean, was given to her that she might put it on; for the fine linen clothing is the right actions of the saints.

⁹Then he said to me, "Write, 'Blessed are those who are invited to the marriage feast of the Lamb.'" He also said to me, "These are the true words of God."

¹⁰Then I fell in at his feet to show respect to him. But he said to me, "Take care not to do that! I am a fellow servant of you and your brothers who hold tightly to the testimony of Jesus. Show respect to God, for the testimony of Jesus is the spirit of prophecy."

The Word of God Rides Forth

¹¹Then I saw that heaven had been opened, and suddenly a white horse appeared, and he who was sitting on it was called Faithful and True, and in righteousness he judges and wages war. ¹²His eyes were like a flame of fire, and upon his head were many diadems. He has a name written on him which no one knows except he himself. ¹³He is clothed in a garment that was dipped in blood, and his name is called The Word of God. ¹⁴The armies that are in heaven followed him upon white horses. They were clothed in fine linen, white and clean. ¹⁵From his mouth a sharp sword goes out, so that he might strike the nations with it. He will shepherd them with a rod of iron, and he treads the winepress of the fury of the vengeance of God, the Ruler of all things. ¹⁶He has a name written on his cloak and on his thigh, "King of kings, and Lord of lords."

¹⁷Then I saw one angel taking his stand in the sun, and he cried out in a loud voice speaking to all the birds flying in the sky directly overhead,

> "Come! Gather together for the great feast of God, ¹⁸so that you may eat the flesh of kings, the flesh of high ranking military officers, the flesh of powerful men, the flesh of horses and those who are sitting on them, the flesh of all men, both free and slave, young and old."

¹⁹Then I saw the beast, and the kings of the earth and their armies gathering to make war against the one seated upon the horse, and against his army. ²⁰But the beast was captured, and with it the false prophet who performed miracles before it, by which he deceived those who had received the imprint of the beast and worshiped its image. The two of them were thrown alive into the lake of fire that is burning with sulfur. ²¹Then the rest of them were killed by the sword of him who was seated on the horse, by the sword that came out of his mouth; and all the birds were filled with their flesh.

The Thousand Years

Chapter Twenty

¹Then I saw an angel coming down from heaven. He held the keys of the Abyss and a great chain in his hand. ²He captured the dragon, the ancient snake, who is the Accuser and Satan, and he bound him for a thousand years; ³and he threw him into the Abyss and locked it and sealed it over him, so that he would no longer deceive the nations after this until the thousand years has ended. After these things, he must be freed for a short time.

⁴Then I saw thrones, and those who had been given matters for judgment sat upon them. The souls of those who had been beheaded because of the testimony of Jesus and the word of God, and who had not worshiped the beast or its image and had not received the imprint upon their forehead or upon their hand, came to life and reigned with Christ a thousand years. ⁵The rest of the dead did not come to life until the thousand years had ended. This is the first resurrection. ⁶Blessed and holy is the one who has a part in the first resurrection. The second death has no authority over these people. Instead, they will be priests of God and of Christ, and they will reign with him a thousand years.

⁷When the thousand years is finished, Satan will be set free from his prison ⁸and will go out to deceive the nations, Gog and Magog, that are in the four corners of the earth, to gather them together for the war. The number of them is like the sand of the sea. ⁹They came up over the breadth of the earth, and they surrounded the camp of the saints and the cherished city. But fire came down from the sky and devoured them. ¹⁰Then the Accuser who had deceived them was thrown into the lake of fire and sulfur where the beast and the false prophet also are. They will be tormented day and night forever and ever.

¹¹Then I saw a great white throne and the one who sat upon it. The earth and the sky fled from before him, and no place was found for them. ¹²Then I saw the dead, both the old and the young. They took their stand before the throne, and scrolls were opened, and another scroll was opened, which is the scroll of life.

The dead were judged by what is written in the scrolls according to their works. ¹³The sea handed over the dead which were in it, and death and Hades handed over the dead which were in them, and each one was judged according to their works. ¹⁴Then death and Hades were thrown into the lake of fire. This is the second death, the lake of fire. ¹⁵If anyone was not found enrolled in the scroll of life, he was thrown into the lake of fire.

The New Jerusalem Descending

Chapter Twenty-One

¹Then I saw a new heaven and a new earth. For the first heaven and the first earth disappeared, and the sea no longer existed. ²I saw the Holy City, the new Jerusalem, coming down out of heaven from God. She was prepared as a bride made attractive for her husband. ³Then I heard a loud voice from the throne saying,

> "Look! The tabernacle of God is with men, and he will dwell with them, and they will be his people, and God himself will be with them, and he will be their God, ⁴and he will wipe every tear from their eyes. Death will no longer exist, and grief, cries of fear, and pain will no longer exist, for the first things have disappeared."

⁵He who is sitting on the throne said, "See, I am making all things new," and he said, "Write! For these words are faithful and true."

⁶Then he said to me,

> "It has happened. I am the Alpha and the Omega, the Beginning and the End. I will freely give him who thirsts water from the spring of the water of life. ⁷He who overcomes will inherit these things, and I will be his God, and he will be my son. ⁸Now for those who are cowardly, not trustworthy, loathsome, murderers, sexually immoral, practitioners of drug-fueled

Revelation 21:9

witchcraft,[i] idolaters, and all those who lie, their portion will be in the lake of burning fire and sulfur, which is the second death."

[9] Then one from among the seven angels who held the seven bowls filled with the seven last plagues also spoke with me, and said, "Come! I will show you the bride, the wife of the Lamb."

[10] Then he took me in spirit to a great and high mountain, and he showed me the holy city, Jerusalem, descending out of heaven from God. [11] It bore the glory of God. Her radiance was like a precious stone, like a jasper stone shining like crystal. [12] It had a great and high wall that had twelve gates, and twelve angels were at the gates, and names were written on them, the names of the twelve tribes of the sons of Israel. [13] There were three gates for those coming from the east,[ii] three gates for those coming from the north, three gates for those coming from the south, and three gates for those coming from the west. [14] The wall of the city had twelve foundations, and on them were the twelve names of the apostles of the Lamb.

[15] The one who was speaking with me held a gold measuring reed so that he might measure the city, its twelve gates, and its wall. [16] The city was arranged with four corners, and its length was as great as its width. Then he measured the city with the measuring reed at twelve thousand stadia;[iii] its length, width, and height were equal. [17] He measured its wall at one hundred forty-four cubits,[iv] a measurement of a man done by an angel.

[18] The foundation of its wall was made of jasper, and the city was pure gold like spotless glass. [19] The foundations of the walls of the city were decorated with every kind of valuable gem. The

---

[i] Attempting to access the spiritual realm or achieve spiritual insight using drugs or potions.

[ii] More literally, "from the direction of the rising sun."

[iii] About 1400 miles.

[iv] Ancient cities usually measured their walls by how thick they were. In this instance, the wall would be one hundred forty-four cubits thick, or about 216 feet.

first foundation was jasper, the second sapphire, the third onyx, the fourth emerald, ²⁰the fifth sardonyx, the sixth carnelian, the seventh chrysolite, the eighth beryl, the ninth topaz, the tenth chrysoprase, the eleventh hyacinth, and the twelfth was amethyst. ²¹The twelve gates were twelve pearls, each one of the gates was one pearl. The streets of the city were pure gold, like transparent glass.

²²I did not see a temple in it, for the Lord God, the Ruler of all things, and the Lamb are its temple. ²³The city does not have any need for the sun or the moon to shine on it, for the glory of God will give it light, and the Lamb is its lamp. ²⁴Then the nations who are among the saved will walk in its light, and the kings of the earth will bring their glory into it. ²⁵Its gates will never be closed during the day, and there is no night there. ²⁶They will bring the glory and the honor of the nations into it, ²⁷but nothing profane will ever come into it; neither will the one who does detestable things or lies, only those who have been written in the Lamb's scroll of life.

The Tree of Life

Chapter Twenty-Two

¹Then he showed me a river of the water of life, shining like crystal, coming out from the throne of God and the Lamb. ²In the middle of its street, and on both sides of the river was the tree of life, producing twelve crops, giving its fruit each month; and the leaves of the tree were for the healing of the nations. ³Then there will no longer be anything that is cursed. The throne of God and the Lamb will be in it, and his servants will serve him, ⁴and they will see his face and his name will be on their foreheads. ⁵Darkness will no longer exist, and they will not have need of the light of a lamp or the light of the sun, for the Lord God will shine upon them, and they will reign forever and ever.

⁶Then he said to me,

"These words are faithful and true, and the Lord God of the spirits of the prophets has sent his angel to show to his servant what must happen soon."

Jesus is Coming Soon

7"Look, I am coming soon. Blessed is he who keeps the words of the prophecy of this scroll."

8I, John, am the one who heard and saw these things, and when I had heard and saw them, I fell at the feet of the angel who showed these things to me to show respect to him; 9but he said to me, "Take care not to do that! I am a fellow servant of you and your brothers the prophets, and of those who keep the words of this scroll. Show respect to God."

10Then he said to me, "Do not seal the words of the prophecy of this scroll, for the time is near at hand. 11Let those who bring harm continue to bring harm, let the impure continue to be impure, and the righteous continue to do righteous activities, and let the holy continue to be holy."

12"Look, I am coming soon, and my reward is with me, to repay each one as he has worked. 13I am the Alpha and Omega, the First and the Last, the Beginning and the End."

The Alpha and Omega and His Reward

14Blessed are those who wash their robes, so that they may have authority to partake of the tree of life, and that they may enter into the city by its gates. 15Outside are the dogs, those who practice drug-fueled witchcraft,[i] the sexually immoral, the murderers, the idolaters, and those who love falsehood and make a habit of it.

16"I, Jesus, have sent my angel to testify these things to you for the churches. I am the root and the direct descendant of David. I am the bright morning star."

---

[i] Attempting to access the spiritual realm or achieve spiritual insight using drugs or potions.

¹⁷Now the Spirit and the Bride say, "Come!" Let the one who hears say, "Come!" Let the one who is thirsty come. Let the one who wants it, take freely of the waters of life.

¹⁸I testify to everyone who hears the teachings of the prophecy in this scroll: If anyone adds to it, God will add to him the plagues that are written in this scroll. ¹⁹If anyone takes away from the teachings of this prophecy in the scroll, God will take away his portion from the tree of life and from the holy city that are written about in this scroll.

²⁰He who is testifying to these things says, "Yes, I am coming soon."

Amen. Come Lord Jesus.

²¹The grace of our Lord Jesus be with you all. Amen.

www.ingramcontent.com/pod-product-compliance
Lightning Source LLC
Chambersburg PA
CBHW052055230426
43662CB00037B/1768